Bali
& Lombok
a travel survival kit

Tony Wheeler
James Lyon

Bali & Lombok – a travel survival kit

5th edition

Published by
Lonely Planet Publications
Head Office: PO Box 617, Hawthorn, Vic 3122, Australia
Branches: 155 Filbert St, Suite 251, Oakland, CA 94607, USA
               10 Barley Mow Passage, Chiswick, London W4 4PH, UK
               71 bis rue du Cardinal Lemoine, 75005 Paris, France

Printed by
SNP Printing Pte Ltd

Photographs by

Gregory Adams (GA)	Margaret Jung (MJ)	Phil Weymouth (PW)
Glenn Beanland (GB)	James Lyon (JL)	Tony Wheeler (TW)
Greg Elms (GE)	Pauline Lyon (PL)	Tamsin Wilson (Tass)
Sue Graefe (SG)	Tom Smallman (TS)	

Bali & Lombok title pages (GA)
Front cover: Legong dancers, Legong Kraton dance, Jeff Hunter, The Image Bank

First Published
January 1984

This Edition
September 1994

National Library of Australia Cataloguing in Publication Data

Lyon, James.
     Bali & Lombok.

     5th ed.
     Includes index.
     ISBN 0 86442 215 6.

     1. Bali Island (Indonesia) – Guidebooks. 2. Lombok
     (Indonesia) – Guidebooks. I. Wheeler, Tony, 1946-. II. Title.
     III. Title: Bali and Lombok. (Series : Lonely Planet travel survival kit).

915.986

text & maps © Lonely Planet 1994
photos © photographers as indicated 1994
climate charts compiled from information supplied by Patrick J Tyson, © Patrick J Tyson, 1994

Tony Wheeler

Tony Wheeler was born in England but spent most of his youth overseas. He returned to England to do a university degree in engineering, worked as an automotive engineer, returned to university to complete an MBA then dropped out on the Asian overland trail with his wife Maureen. They've been travelling, writing and publishing guidebooks ever since, having set up Lonely Planet Publications in the mid-70s. Travel for the Wheelers is now considerably enlivened by their daughter Tashi and their son Kieran.

James Lyon

James is by nature a sceptic and by training a social scientist. He worked for five years as an editor at Lonely Planet's Melbourne office, imposing unreasonable demands on its authors, until he decided to 'jump the fence' and try for himself the life of a travel writer. He has travelled on Bali both by himself and also with his wife, Pauline, and their two young children. A keen gardener, he finds the flowers and landscapes of Bali a special delight. He also enjoys walking, which is another attraction of Bali and Lombok, and skiing, which isn't.

From the Author

Thanks to Richard, Tini and Nancy at Lovina; Asri and Raka in Ubud; Hadji Radiah on Lombok; Yarnt and Simon on the Gili Islands; Debbie Cullen (send your *address)*; and to the many other people who helped me and smiled at me. The tourist offices in Kuta, Ubud, Singaraja and Mataram were also very helpful. At home, thanks to Ansett airlines; the editors and artists who did such a good job on this book; and to Pauline, my research assistant, administrator, wife and muse.

This Book

Bali & Lombok – a travel survival kit is the result of the work of several authors over a number of years. Tony Wheeler first covered Bali and Lombok in his pioneering *South-East Asia on a shoestring*, then expanded and improved the coverage to create the first

edition of this title, for which Mary Covernton researched Lombok. Alan Samagalski updated both Bali and Lombok for the second edition, Tony returned for the third edition, and James Lyon helped him with the fourth. James Lyon covered all of Bali and Lombok for this edition.

Additional material for this book was contributed by: Michael Sklovsky who provided extra information for the Arts & Crafts section and allowed us to photograph items from his Ishka Handcrafts stores in Melbourne; and Kirk Willcox, who wrote the original Bali surfing section. The cycling information is based on Hunt Kooiker's now out of print *Bali by Bicycle*. Thanks to Peter Morris and Benny Tantra for their distinctive and humorous cartoons.

From the Publisher

Mapping, design, illustration and layout of this 5th edition of *Bali & Lombok – a travel survival kit* were coordinated by Michelle Stamp. Tamsin Wilson designed the cover, and along with Michelle drew the illustrations. Katie Cody, Michelle Coxall and Jenny Missen edited this book; Tom Smallman took it through layout.

Thanks to the following LP staff in our international offices for their help in updating the Getting There & Away chapter: Andrea Webster & Charlotte Hindle (UK); Ann Neet (USA) and Caroline Guilleminot (France).

Thanks also to Sharon Wertheim for compiling the index.

Thanks to all those readers who wrote to Lonely Planet; a list of their names is at the back of this book.

Warning & Request

Things change – prices go up, schedules change, good places go bad and bad places go bankrupt – nothing stays the same. So if you find things better or worse, recently opened or long since closed, please write and tell us and help make the next edition better. Your letters will be used to help update future editions and, where possible, important changes will be included in a Stop Press section in reprints.

We greatly appreciate all information that is sent to us by travellers. Back at Lonely Planet we employ a hard-working readers' letters team to sort through the many letters we receive. The best ones will be rewarded with a free copy of the next edition or another Lonely Planet guide if you prefer. We give away lots of books, but, unfortunately, not every letter or postcard receives one.

Contents

LOMBOK

Map Legend

BOUNDARIES

───────────── ....International Boundary

───────────── ....Internal Boundary

ROUTES

═══════════ ....Freeway

──────────── ....Highway

──────────── ....Major Road

─ ─ ─ ─ ─ ─ ─ ....Unsealed Road or Track

════════════ ....City Road

──────────── ....City Street

┼┼┼┼┼┼┼┼┼┼ ....Railway

──────────── ....Underground Railway

▬▬▬▬▬▬▬ ....Tram

─ ─ ─ ─ ─ ─ ─ ....Walking Track

•••••••••••••• ....Walking Tour

─ ─ ─ ─ ─ ─ ─ ....Ferry Route

┼┼┼┼┼┼┼┼┼┼ ....Cable Car or Chairlift

AREA FEATURES

.....................Park, Gardens

..........................National Park

..........................Built-Up Area

..........................Pedestrian Mall

.................................Market

+ + + + + + + ...Cemetery

.................................Reef

..........................Beach or Desert

.................................Rocks

HYDROGRAPHIC FEATURES

..........................Coastline

..........................River, Creek

.........Intermittent River or Creek

................Lake, Intermittent Lake

..........................Canal

..........................Swamp

SYMBOLS

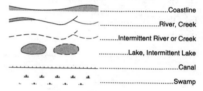

○ CAPITAL ....National Capital

◉ Capital ....District Capital

🐗 CITY ....Major City

● City ....City

● Town ....Town

● Village ....Village

■ ....Hotel, Pension (Place to Stay)

▼ ....Restaurant (Place to Eat)

▼ ....Pub, Bar (Place to Drink)

✉ ☎ ....Post Office, Telephone

ⓘ ⑨ ....Tourist Information, Bank

◗ ℗ ....Transport, Parking

🏛 ⛺ ....Museum, Youth Hostel

⚏ ⚑ Caravan Park, Camping Ground

† ⬛ † ....Church, Cathedral

☪ ✡ ....Mosque, Synagogue

🌲 ⚖ ..Balinese Temple, Other Temple

○ ★ ....Hospital, Police Station

✈ ✛ ....Airport, Airfield

⚐ ✿ ....Golf Course, Gardens

❖ 🐘 ....Shopping Centre, Zoo

🍇 ⛱ ...Winery or Vineyard, Picnic Site

← ⛽ ...One Way Street, Petrol Station

∴ ....Archaeological Site or Ruins

🏛 ⚱ ....Stately Home, Monument

🏰 ◼ ....Castle, Tomb

⌒ ⌂ ....Cave, Hut or Chalet

▲ ☀ ....Mountain or Hill, Lookout

🏄 ⚓ ....Surf Beach, Shipwreck

)(⚲ ....Pass, Spring

...................Ancient or City Wall

.........................Rapids, Waterfalls

⟶ ....Cliff or Escarpment, Tunnel

....................................Railway Station

Note: not all symbols displayed above appear in this book

Introduction

Say Bali, and most people in the West think of paradise, and tourism. The image of Bali as a tropical paradise dates back to Western visitors in the '20s, and it has been cultivated by the tourist industry rather than the Balinese, who do not have a word for paradise in their language. But Bali is a good candidate for paradise – so picturesque and immaculate it could almost be a painted backdrop, with rice paddies tripping down hillsides like giant steps, volcanoes soaring up through the clouds, lush tropical jungle, long sandy beaches and warm blue water. However, the landscape is more than a backdrop; it is imbued with spiritual significance, and forms a part of the rich cultural life of the Balinese, whose natural grace fits the image of how people should live in paradise.

Perhaps the image has done Bali a disservice, because it denies the reality of Bali as a real place in the real world, and many visitors are disappointed when they find that Balinese drive cars, watch TV and like making money. Many visitors are also appalled that Bali has so many tourists, but this is only a problem if they allow their experience of Bali to be packaged and sanitised by the tourist industry. It's amazing how many visitors only stay in tourist areas and complain about the number of tourists, while a few km away there are villages which rarely see a tourist at all.

The Balinese seem to handle tourism better than the tourists, and Bali has a long history of absorbing, and profiting from, foreign influences. Six centuries ago, when Islam swept across the islands of south-east Asia, the last great Hindu dynasty on Java retreated to Bali with their entire entourage of scholars, artists and intelligentsia. Bali's fertility and the extraordinary productivity of its agriculture permitted the further development of this cultural heritage, with distinctive movements in art, architecture, music and dance; a culture with a vitality which has hardly faltered to this day.

Although Bali is, for many of its Western visitors, simply a place with cheap living and

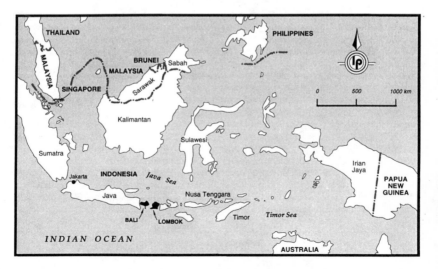

pleasant beaches, it's much, much more than that. Festivals, ceremonies, dances, temple processions and other activities take place almost continuously on Bali and they're fun to watch, easy to understand and instantly accessible. It's the great strength of Bali's culture that makes the island so interesting.

The island of Lombok, just to the east, has as much natural beauty as Bali, but far fewer tourists. Its beaches are better, its great volcano is larger and more spectacular, and it has a greater variety of landscapes – parts of Lombok drip with water while pockets are chronically dry, parched and cracked like a crocodile skin. The culture is rich, but not as colourful or as accessible as on Bali. Its indigenous people, the Sasaks, are predomi-

nantly Muslim, though elements of ancient animist beliefs survive, and there is a Balinese community which contributes variety to the cultural landscape.

There are fewer facilities for tourists, and tourism seems largely peripheral to daily life on Lombok, whereas on Bali it's a challenge to escape from it. In economic terms, Lombok is less developed in almost every way, and this is part of the appeal it holds for travellers. Daily life is simple and unembellished, while on Bali the constant round of offerings, prayers, processions and festivals can seem almost artificial.

The two islands provide a great variety and contrast, and a combination of the two makes for a great travel experience.

BALI

Facts about Bali

HISTORY

There is no trace of the Stone Age on Bali although it's certain that the island was already populated before the Bronze Age commenced there about 300 BC. Nor is much known of Bali during the period when Indian traders brought Hinduism to the Indonesian archipelago. The earliest records found on Bali, stone inscriptions, date from around the 9th century AD and by that time Bali had already developed many similarities to the island you find today. Rice was grown with the help of a complex irrigation system, probably very like that employed now. The Balinese had also already begun to develop the cultural and artistic activities which have made the island so interesting to visitors right down to the present day.

Hindu Influence

Hindu Java began to spread its influence into Bali during the reign of King Airlangga from 1019 to 1042. At the age of 16, when his uncle lost the throne, Airlangga fled into the forests of western Java. He gradually gained support, won back the kingdom once ruled by his uncle and went on to become one of Java's greatest kings. Airlangga's mother had moved to Bali and remarried shortly after his birth, so when he gained the throne there was an immediate link between Java and Bali. At this time the courtly Javanese language known as Kawi came into use amongst the royalty of Bali, and the rock-cut memorials seen at Gunung Kawi near Tampaksiring are a clear architectural link between Bali and 11th-century Java.

After Airlangga's death Bali retained its semi-independent state until Kertanagara became king of the Singasari dynasty in Java two centuries later. Kertanagara conquered Bali in 1284 but the period of his greatest power lasted only eight years until he was murdered and his kingdom collapsed. However, the great Majapahit dynasty was founded by his son. With Java in turmoil Bali

regained its autonomy and the Pejeng dynasty, centred near modern day Ubud, rose to great power. Later Gajah Mada, the legendary chief Majapahit minister, defeated the Pejeng king Dalem Bedaulu in 1343 and brought Bali back under Javanese influence.

Although Gajah Mada brought much of the Indonesian archipelago under Majapahit control this was the furthest extent of their power. In Bali the 'capital' moved to Gelgel, near modern Klungkung, around the late 14th century and for the next two centuries this was the base for the 'king of Bali', the *dewa Agung*. As Islam spread into Java the Majapahit kingdom collapsed into disputing sultanates. However, the Gelgel dynasty on Bali, under Dalem Batur Enggong, extended its power eastwards to the neighbouring island of Lombok and even across the strait to Java.

As the Majapahit kingdom fell apart many of its intelligentsia, including the priest Nirartha, moved to Bali (see the Ulu Watu section in the South Bali chapter and Tanah Lot in the South-West Bali chapter). Nirartha is credited with introducing many of the complexities of Balinese religion to the island. Artists, dancers, musicians and actors also fled to Bali at this time and the island experienced an explosion of cultural activity. The final great exodus to Bali took place in 1478.

European Contact

Marco Polo, the great explorer, was the first recorded European visitor to Indonesia back in 1292 but the first Europeans to set foot on Bali were Dutch seamen in 1597. Setting a tradition that has prevailed right down to the present day, they fell in love with the island and when Cornelius Houtman, the ship's captain, prepared to set sail, half of his crew refused to come with him. At that time Balinese prosperity and artistic activity, at least among the royalty, were at a peak and the king who befriended Houtman had 200 wives and a chariot pulled by two white buffaloes, not to mention a retinue of 50 dwarves whose bodies had been bent to resemble kris (traditional dagger) handles! Although the Dutch returned to Indonesia in later years they were interested in profit, not culture, and barely gave Bali a second glance.

Dutch Conquest

In 1710 the capital of the Gelgel kingdom was shifted to nearby Klungkung but local discontent was growing, lesser rulers were breaking away from Gelgel rule and the Dutch began to move in using the old policy of divide and conquer. In 1846 the Dutch used Balinese salvage claims over ship-wrecks as the pretext to land military forces in northern Bali. In 1894 the Dutch chose to support the Sasaks of Lombok in a rebellion against their Balinese rajah. The rajah capitulated to Dutch demands, only to be overruled by his younger princes who defeated the Dutch forces in a surprise attack. Dutch anger was roused, a larger and more heavily armed force was dispatched and the Balinese overrun. Balinese power on Lombok finally came to an end with the loss of their stronghold at Cakranegara – the crown prince was killed and the old rajah was sent into exile.

With the north of Bali long under Dutch control and Lombok now gone, the south was not going to last long. Once again it was disputes over the ransacking of wrecked ships that gave the Dutch the excuse they needed to move in. In 1904, after a Chinese ship was wrecked off Sanur, Dutch demands that the rajah of Badung pay 3000 silver dollars in damages were rejected, and in 1906 Dutch warships appeared at Sanur. The Dutch forces landed against Balinese opposition and four days later had marched the five km to the outskirts of Denpasar.

On 20 September 1906 the Dutch mounted a naval bombardment on Denpasar and then commenced their final assault. The three princes of Badung realised that they were outnumbered and outgunned and that defeat was inevitable. Surrender and exile,

however, was the worst imaginable outcome so they decided to take the honourable path of a suicidal *puputan* – a fight to the death. First the palaces were burnt then, dressed in their finest jewellery and waving golden krises, the rajah led the royalty and priests out to face the Dutch with their modern weapons.

The Dutch begged the Balinese to surrender rather than make their hopeless stand but their pleas went unheard and wave after wave of the Balinese nobility marched forward to their death. In all, nearly 4000 Balinese died in defence of the two Denpasar palaces. Later, the Dutch marched east towards Tabanan, taking the rajah of Tabanan prisoner, but he committed suicide rather than face the disgrace of exile.

The kingdoms of Karangasem and Gianyar had already capitulated to the Dutch and were allowed to retain some of their powers but other kingdoms were defeated and their rulers exiled. Finally, the rajah of Klungkung followed the lead of Badung and once more the Dutch faced a puputan. With this last obstacle disposed of, all of Bali was now under Dutch control and became part of the Dutch East Indies. Fortunately, the Dutch government was not totally onerous and the common people noticed little difference between rule by the Dutch and rule by the rajahs. Some far-sighted Dutch officials encouraged Balinese artistic aspirations which, together with a new found international interest, sparked off an artistic revival. Dutch rule over Bali was short-lived, however, for Indonesia quickly fell to the Japanese after the bombing of Pearl Harbor in WW II.

Independence

On 17 August 1945, just after the end of WW II, the Indonesian leader Sukarno proclaimed the nation's independence but it took four years to convince the Dutch that they were not going to get their great colony back. In a virtual repeat of the puputan nearly half a century earlier a Balinese resistance group was wiped out in the battle of Marga on 20 November 1946 and it was not until

1949 that the Dutch finally recognised Indonesia's independence. The Denpasar airport, Ngurah Rai, was named after the leader of the Balinese forces at Marga.

Independence was not an easy path for Indonesia to follow at first and Sukarno, an inspirational leader during the conflict with the Dutch, proved less adept at governing the nation in peacetime. The ill-advised 'confrontation' with Malaysia was just one event that sapped the country's energy.

To Sukarno, British involvement in Malaysian federation meant the consolidation of British military power on its own doorstep and the threat of Western imperialism. In 1963 his decision to embark on a 'confrontation' led to military action between Indonesian forces and 50,000 British, Australian and New Zealand soldiers along the border between Kalimantan and Malaysia. Though the confrontation was never a serious threat to the survival of Malaysia, the military expense caused severe economic problems for Indonesia.

The 1965 Coup & Backlash

On 30 September 1965 an attempted communist coup led to Sukarno's downfall. General Suharto emerged as the leading figure in the armed forces, displaying great military and political skill in suppressing the coup. The communist party was outlawed, and a wave of anti-communist reprisals followed, which escalated into a wholesale massacre of suspected communists throughout the archipelago.

In Bali, the events had an added local significance as the main national political organisations, the Nationalist Party (PNI) and the Communist Party (PKI), crystallised existing differences – between traditionalists who wanted to maintain the old caste system, and radicals who saw the caste system as repressive and who were urging land reform. After the failed coup, religious traditionalists on Bali led the witch-hunt for the godless communists who were seen as threatening all the old values. Some of the killings were particularly brutal, with numerous suspect people, not all of them communists, being rounded up and clubbed to death by fanatical mobs. The Chinese community was particularly victimised. Eventually the military stepped in to control the anti-communist purge, but no-one on Bali was untouched by the killings, estimated at between 25,000 and 50,000, from a population of about 2.5 million.

The Suharto Government

Following the failed coup and its aftermath, Suharto established himself as president and took control of the government, while Sukarno disappeared from the limelight. Though the Suharto government has been criticised for limiting Western-style political freedoms and failing to end corruption, it has provided a long period of stable growth, with improving standards of health, education, housing and transport. Bali in particular has seen dramatic improvements in infrastructure, especially roads, telecommunications, electricity and water supply, much of it a result of the strategy to develop tourism. Nevertheless, some feel that the tourist industry is too much dominated by Javanese business interests, and the Balinese have had little control over its development.

GEOGRAPHY

Bali is a small fertile island midway along the string of islands which makes up the Indonesian archipelago, stretching from Sumatra in the north-west to Irian Jaya, on the border of Papua New Guinea, in the south-east. It's adjacent to Java, the most heavily populated island, and is the first in the chain of smaller islands comprising Nusa Tenggara. Bali has an area of 5620 sq km, measures approximately 140 km by 80 km and is only 8° south of the equator. It's dramatically mountainous: the central mountain chain which runs the whole length of the island includes several peaks approaching or over 2000 metres and Gunung Agung, known as the 'mother mountain', is over 3000 metres.

Bali is volcanically active and extremely fertile. The two go hand in hand because eruptions contribute to the land's exceptional fertility and the high mountains provide the dependable rainfall which irrigates Bali's complex and amazingly beautiful patchwork of rice terraces. Of course, the volcanic element is a two-edged sword – Bali has often had disastrous eruptions and no doubt will again in the future. The huge eruption of Gunung Agung in 1963 killed thousands, devastated vast areas of the island and forced many Balinese to accept resettlement in other parts of Indonesia.

The central mountain chain reaches its highest point in the east. Balinese mythology relates that the Hindu holy mountain, Mahameru, was set down on Bali but split into two parts – Gunung Agung and Gunung Batur. These two holy mountains, both active volcanoes, are respectively 3140 metres and 1717 metres high – at least Gunung Agung was 3140 metres prior to its eruption in 1963. The other major mountains are Batukau, the 'stone coconut shell', at 2278 metres, and Abang, at 2152 metres. Apart from the great central range, there are other, lesser, highlands in the lower plateau region of the Bukit Peninsula in the extreme south of Bali, and in hilly Nusa Penida.

South and north of the central mountains are Bali's fertile agricultural lands. The southern region is a wide, gently sloping area where most of Bali's abundant rice crop is grown. The south-central area is the true rice basket of the island. The northern coastal strip is narrower, rising more rapidly into the foothills of the central range, and has less rain, but coffee, copra and rice are grown here and cattle are also raised in this area.

Despite the fertility of these zones Bali also has arid and lightly populated regions. These include the western mountain region and its northern slopes down to the sea – an area virtually unpopulated and reputed to be the last home of the Balinese tiger. The eastern and north-eastern slopes of Gunung Agung are also dry and barren while in the south the Bukit Peninsula and the adjacent island of Nusa Penida also have a low rainfall and cannot support intensive wet-rice agriculture.

CLIMATE

Just 8° south of the equator, Bali has a tropical climate which is hot all year. The average temperature hovers around 30°C (mid-80s°F) year round, but the humidity can make the heat feel very oppressive. Direct sun feels incredibly hot, especially in the middle of the day when you'd be crazy if you didn't stay in the shade. There are dry and wet seasons – dry from April to September and wet from October to March – but it can rain at any time of year and even during the wet season rain is likely to pass quickly. In general, April to September are the best

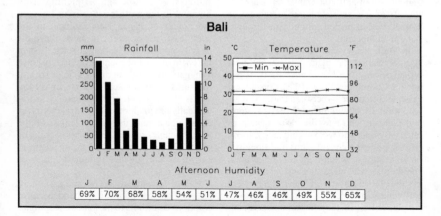

months on Bali. At that time of year the humidity is lower and the rains light and infrequent.

Overall the climate is gently tropical, but there are marked variations across the island: around the coast, sea breezes temper the heat and as you move inland you also move up so the altitude works to keep things cool. In fact, at times it can get very chilly up in the highlands and a warm sweater or light jacket can be a good idea in mountain villages like Kintamani or Penelokan. The northern slopes of Gunung Batur always seem to be wet and misty, while a few km away the east coast is nearly always dry and sunny. Air-conditioning is not really a necessity on Bali – a cool breeze always seems to spring up in the evenings and the architecture can make the most of the breeze with open bamboo windows to encourage air circulation.

FLORA & FAUNA

Bali has an interesting collection of animal and plant life. Nearly all of the island is cultivated and only in west Bali, in the Bali Barat National Park, are there traces of Bali's earliest plant life. The island is geologically young and virtually all its living things have migrated from elsewhere, so there's really no such thing as 'native' plants and animals. This is not hard to imagine in the heavily populated and extravagantly fertile south of Bali, where the orderly rice terraces are so intensively cultivated as to look more like a work of sculpture than a natural landscape.

Though the rice fields are an everyday sight and the common image of Bali, in fact they cover only about 20% of the island's surface area, and there is a great variety of other landscapes to be seen – the dry scrub of the north-west, the extreme north-east and the southern peninsula; patches of dense jungle; forests of bamboo; and harsh volcanic regions which are barren rock and volcanic tuff at higher altitudes.

Flora

Trees Like most things on Bali, trees have a spiritual and religious significance, and you will often see them decorated with scarves and black-and-white check cloths. The *waringin* (banyan) is the holiest Balinese tree and no important temple is complete without a stately one growing within its precincts. The banyan is an extensive shady tree with an exotic feature: creepers which drop from its branches take root to propagate a new tree. Thus the banyan is said to be 'never-dying' since new offshoots can always take root. The shady frangipani trees with their beautiful and sweet-smelling white flowers are almost as common a tree in temples as the banyan.

Bali has monsoonal rather than tropical rainforest, so it lacks the valuable rainforest hardwoods that require rain all year. The Forestry Department is experimenting with new varieties in plantations round the national park, but at the moment nearly all the wood used for carving is imported from Sumatra and Kalimantan. The boom in building, and limits on the availability of timber have contributed to enormous price rises in timber over the last couple of years.

A number of plants have great practical and economic significance. Bamboo *(tiing)* is grown in several varieties, and is used for everything from *sate* sticks and string to rafters and *gamelan* resonators (see under Music, Dance & Drama). The various types of palm provide coconuts, sugar, fuel and fibre. Rice is the most important plant, with spiritual and social importance as well as being an economic mainstay (see the Economy section for more comments on rice cultivation).

Flowers & Gardens Balinese gardens are a delight. The soil and climate can support a huge range of plants, and the Balinese love of beauty, and the abundance of cheap labour, mean that every space can be landscaped. The style is generally informal, with curved paths, a rich variety of plants and usually a water feature.

You can find almost every type of flower on Bali, but some are seasonal and others are restricted to the cooler mountain areas. Many of the flowers will be familiar to visitors – hibiscus, bougainvillaea, poinsettia, oleander, jasmine, water lily and aster are commonly seen in the southern tourist areas. Roses, begonias and hydrangeas occur mainly in the mountains. Less familiar flowers include: Javanese ixora (called *soka* or *angsoka*), with round clusters of bright red-orange flowers; champak, or *cempaka*, (*Michelia champaca*), a very fragrant member of the magnolia family; flamboyant, flower of the royal poinciana flame tree (*Delonix regia*); *manori* (or *maduri*, *Calotropis giganta*), which has a number of traditional uses, and water convolvulus (*Ipomoea aquatica*), or *kangkung*, the leaves of which are commonly used as a green vegetable. There are literally thousands of types of orchid.

Flowers can be seen everywhere – those in this book were photographed in easily accessible gardens, or just by the roadside. Nevertheless, any flower fancier should make a trip to the Bedugul area where the botanical gardens, the Candikuning flower market, and flower nurseries are particular attractions. (See the Lake Bratan section in the Central Mountains chapter for details.) A visit to the plant nurseries along the road between Denpasar and Sanur is also interesting.

Fauna

Domestic Animals Bali is thick with domestic animals, including ones that wake you up in the morning and others that bark all night. Chickens and roosters are kept both for food purposes and as pets. Cockfighting is a popular male activity and a man's fighting bird is a prize possession. Balinese pigs are related to wild boar, and look gross with their sway backs and sagging stomachs. They inhabit the family compound, cleaning up all the garbage and eventually end up spit-roasted at a feast – they taste a lot better than they look.

Balinese cattle, by contrast, are delicate and graceful animals which seem more akin to deer than cows. Although the Balinese are Hindus they do not generally treat cattle as holy animals, yet cows are rarely eaten or milked. They are, however, used to plough rice paddies and fields and there is a major export market for Balinese cattle to Hong Kong and other parts of Asia.

Ducks are another everyday Balinese domestic animal and a regular dish at feasts. Many families keep a flock of ducks which are brought out of the family compound and led to a convenient pond or flooded rice paddy to feed during the day. They're led using a stick with a small flag tied to the top which is left planted in the pond. As sunset approaches the ducks gather around the stick and wait to be led home again. The morning and evening parade of ducks is a familiar sight throughout the island and is always one of Bali's small delights.

To some people the mangy, horrible mongrels which roam every village on the island are the one thing on Bali which isn't perfect. In fact, some have even said that the dogs are there simply to provide a contrast and to point out how beautiful everything else is!

Bali has plenty of lizards and the small ones *(cecak)* that hang around light fittings in the evening, waiting for an unwary insect to venture too near, are a familiar sight. Geckos, on the other hand, though fairly large lizards, are often heard but rarely seen. The loud and regularly repeated two-part cry 'geck-oh' is a nightly background noise, and it is considered lucky if you hear the lizard call seven times.

Bats are quite common and not only in well-known haunts like the Bat Cave (Goa Lawah) near Kusamba. They materialise at sunset to start their nocturnal hunt. The little chipmunk-like Balinese squirrels are occasionally seen in the wild, though more often in cages. The Balinese keep a variety of caged birds as pets. Cats are common domestic animals but are nowhere near as familiar a sight as the miserable dogs.

Marine Life There is a rich variety of coral, seaweed, fish and other marine life in the coastal waters. Much of it can be appreciated by snorkellers, but the larger marine animals are only likely to be seen while diving (see the Facts for the Visitor chapter). Turtles are endangered, but can still be seen wild in the waters around Nusa Penida. Cavorting dolphins are an attraction at sunrise off Lovina, on the north coast.

Birds There are over 300 species of bird, though only one is unique to Bali. The diversity is partly due to Bali's position between the northern and southern hemispheres, close to both the Asian and Australian regions. Most of the birds are adapted to Bali's intensively cultivated landscape, and can be seen in many of the tourist areas or not far away. Bali's most famous bird, and the only endemic bird on the island, is the Bali starling, or Rothschild's mynah *(Leucopsar rothschildi)*, an endangered species with a wild population estimated to be as small as 40 birds. There is a project to re-establish the starling in the Bali Barat National Park, using birds reclaimed from collectors' cages. Keen birders should get a copy of *Birds of Bali* by Victor Mason (Periplus Editions), and then join him at the Beggar's Bush pub in Ubud for a guided walk.

Wildlife The only wilderness area, the Bali Barat National Park, has a number of wild species, including grey and black monkeys, deer, *muncak* (or mouse deer), squirrel and

---

Sea Turtles
Sea turtles are marine reptiles. They are found in the waters around Bali and throughout Indonesia and are a popular delicacy, particularly for feasts. In several places they are herded before being slaughtered. In fact, Bali is the site of the most intensive slaughter of green sea turtles in the world. Green sea turtles are killed mainly for their meat, and the shells of the hawksbill turtle are used

to make jewellery, haircombs and other trinkets, which are sold to tourists. It's estimated that more than 20,000 turtles are killed in Bali each year.

The environmental group Greenpeace has long campaigned to protect Indonesia's sea turtles. It appeals to travellers to Indonesia not to eat turtle meat or buy any sea-turtle products, including tortoiseshell items, stuffed turtles or turtle-leather goods. In any case, it's illegal to export any products made from green sea turtles from Indonesia (see the Customs section in the Facts for the Visitor chapter). And in many countries including Australia, the USA, the UK and other EC countries it's illegal to import turtle products without a permit. ■

iguana. Bali certainly used to have tigers and although there are periodic rumours of sightings in the remote north-west of the island, nobody has proof of seeing one for a long time. Hickman Powell in *The Last Paradise*, his tale of Bali in the 1920s, tells of an unsuccessful tiger hunt.

Bali Barat National Park

The Bali Barat (West Bali) National Park covers a large area which includes most of the western end of Bali. The management of the area is to be integrated with a conservation and environment plan for the whole island. For more information on this park, see the North Bali and South-West Bali chapters.

GOVERNMENT

Indonesian government is centralised and hierarchical and the important strategic decisions regarding Bali's development are made by the national government in Jakarta. Executive power rests with the president of the republic. Under the national government are 27 *propinsi* (provinces) of which Bali is one.

The propinsi government does not have the same sort of autonomy as a state does in a federal system, such as the USA, Australia or Germany. It acts more as a delegate of the central government, responsible for implementing national policy in the province. The governor of a province is appointed by the president for a five-year term, from a short list of candidates nominated by the provincial house of representatives, the Dewan Perwakilan Rakyat Daerah. The provincial house of representatives is elected by popular vote every five years. The current governor of Bali is Professor Dr Ida Bagus Oka.

Within Bali there are eight *kabupaten* or districts, which under the Dutch were known as regencies. They are, with their district capitals:

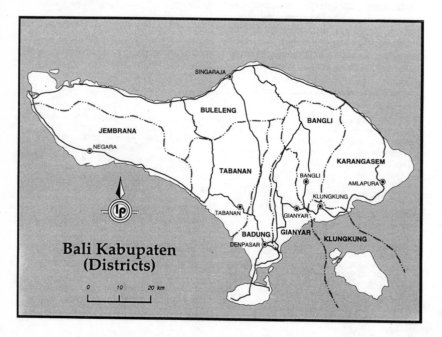

Bali Kabupaten (Districts)

District	Capital
Badung	Denpasar
Bangli	Bangli
Buleleng	Singaraja
Gianyar	Gianyar
Jembrana	Negara
Karangasem	Amlapura
Klungkung	Klungkung
Tabanan	Tabanan

Badung in the south is the most populous district. Each district is headed by a government official known as a *bupati*. The districts are further subdivided into the subdistricts headed by a *camat*, then come the *perbekels*, headmen in charge of a *desa* (village) and, finally, an enormous number of *banjars*, the local divisions of a village.

ECONOMY

Bali's economy is basically agrarian: the vast majority of the Balinese are peasants who work in the fields, and agriculture contributes about 40% of Bali's total economic output, but a much smaller proportion of its export income. Coffee, copra and cattle are major agricultural exports – most of the rice goes to feed Bali's own population. Economically Bali as a whole is a poor island, with an annual per capita income of around US$400, but it is growing at the fast rate of 8% per year. Much of the economic activity is in the non-cash sector (subsistence farming and barter), so the figures probably understate the value of Balinese output.

Tourism amounts to about one third of the economy – not only in providing accommodation, meals and services to the many visitors but also in providing a market for all those arts and crafts. The clothing industry has had a spectacular growth from making beachwear for tourists – it now makes up around half the value of Balinese exports. Handcrafts are also exported directly as well as being sold to tourists, and Balinese woodcarvings are sold as souvenirs from the Cook Islands to the Caribbean.

Although the Balinese are an island people, their unusual tendency to focus on the mountains rather than the sea is reflected in the relatively small output of the fishing

---

Pancasila

The five principles of Pancasila were expounded by Sukarno in 1945 as the philosophical basis of the Indonesian republic. The principles are a common theme in roadside statues and are expressed symbolically on the national coat of arms.

- Belief in the divine omnipotence and oneness of God, symbolised by the star which shines over everything. Whether it is Allah, Vishnu or Buddha, all Indonesians are expected to believe in God.
- Just and civilised humanity, symbolised by the circle of chain which represents the interdependence of people and nations.
- The unity of Indonesia, symbolised by the banyan tree, under which all can take shelter together.
- Democracy, led by wise conduct in consultation and representation, symbolised by the head of the bull, which represents strength.
- Social justice, symbolised by stalks of rice which represent food, and cotton which represents clothing. ■

Pancasila crest

industry. Most of the exported fish are sardines, but there is some export of tuna and processed fish products.

Rice

Although the Balinese grow various crops, rice is by far the most important. It's not just that rice is such a staple crop, the whole landscape has been moulded to rice growing. There are at least three words for rice in Indonesian – *padi* is the growing rice plant (hence padi or paddy fields), *beras* is the uncooked grain, and *nasi* is cooked rice, as in *nasi goreng* and *nasi puti*. There can be few places where people have played such a large part in changing the natural landscape, yet at the same time making it so beautiful. The terraces trip down hillsides like steps for a giant, in shades of gold, brown and green as delicately selected as an artist's palette.

The intricate organisation necessary for growing rice is a large factor in the strength of Balinese community life. The *subak*, the rice growers association, has to carefully plan the use of irrigation water. The Balinese use irrigation so successfully that they are reputed to be some of the best rice growers in the world. They manage two harvests a year although there are no distinct times for planting and harvesting the rice.

The process of rice growing starts with the bare, dry and harvested fields. The remaining rice stalks are burnt off and the field is then liberally soaked and repeatedly ploughed. Nowadays this may be done with a mechanical, petrol- powered cultivator, but often they will still use two bullocks or cattle pulling a wooden plough. Once the field is reduced to the required muddy consistency, a small corner of the field is walled off and the seedling rice is planted there. The rice is grown to a reasonable size then lifted and replanted, shoot by shoot, in the larger field. After that it's easy street for a while as the rice steadily matures. The walls of the fields have to be kept in working order and the fields have to be weeded but generally this is a time to practise the gamelan, watch the dancers, do a little woodcarving or painting or just pass the time. Finally, harvest time

The Continuing Harvest

A legend relates how a group of Balinese farmers promised to sacrifice a pig if their harvest was good. As the bountiful harvest time approached no pig could be found and it was reluctantly decided to sacrifice a child. Then one of the farmers had an idea: they had promised the sacrifice *after* the harvest. If there was always new rice growing, then the harvest would always be about to take place and no sacrifice would be necessary. Since then the Balinese have always planted one field of rice before harvesting another. ■

rolls around and the whole village turns out for a period of solid hard work. Planting the rice is strictly a male occupation but everybody takes part in harvesting it.

The rice paddies are a complete ecological system, home for much more than just rice. In the early morning you'll often see the duck herders leading their flocks out for a day's paddle around a flooded paddy and, at night, young boys heading out with lights to trap tasty frogs and eels. Other crops are often grown on the levees between the fields, or planted as a rotation crop after several rice harvests.

Rice production on Bali has increased substantially with the widespread adoption of new high-yield varieties of rice in place of the traditional rice, *padi Bali*. The best known of these is called IR36, developed in Java, and first introduced in 1969. The new rice varieties can be harvested sooner (four months after planting instead of five for the traditional variety) and are resistant to many diseases. New strains now account for over 90% of the rice planted on Bali, but there have been problems. IR36 required the use of more pesticides, and over-use of these chemicals resulted in ecological changes such as the depletion of frog and eel populations, which depend on the insects. These problems are being tackled by more selective use of insecticides using 'integrated pest management' techniques, and by breeding varieties which are more insect-resistant.

The new varieties also lead to changes in traditional practices and customs. Because the new rice falls easily from the stalk, it cannot be carried to the village after harvesting and it must be threshed in the fields. The husking is now done by small mechanical mills, rather than by women pounding it in wooden troughs. A number of songs, rituals and festivals associated with old ways of harvesting and milling rice are dying out, and everyone agrees that the new rice doesn't taste as good as padi Bali. Small areas of padi Bali are still planted and harvested in traditional ways to placate the rice goddess Dewi Sri, and there are still temples and offerings to her in every rice field.

PEOPLE & POPULATION

Bali is a very densely populated island, with 2.7 million people, according to the 1990 census. The population is almost all Indonesian; 95% are of Balinese Hindu religion and could be described as ethnic Balinese. Most of the other residents are from other parts of Indonesia, particularly Java, but also Sumatra and Nusa Tenggara – the tourist industry is a magnet to people seeking jobs and business opportunities. It is said that Bali is being Indonesianised, and some population movement between the islands is an inevitable part of that process. Quite a few Balinese have moved to less populated islands as part of the transmigration program.

The Balinese people are predominantly of the 'Malay' race, descendants of those groups who moved south-east from China in the migrations of around 3000 BC. Before that Bali may have been populated by people related to Australian Aborigines, who appear to have mixed at least a little with the group which displaced them. Other ethnic strands may have come from India, Polynesia and Melanesia, and a diverse range of physical features from all those groups can be seen in Bali's current population. What defines the Balinese people is cultural rather than racial, and the Balinese culture embraces both the minority Bali Aga groups, whose Hindu traditions predate the arrival of the Majapahit court from Java in the 15th century, and the vast majority of Balinese whose culture is a legacy of that influx.

Caste Divisions

There is a strong sense of Balinese cultural identity, based on a unique religion, elaborate ritual, language and caste. These elements are interrelated, as the castes derive from religious traditions, have prescribed roles in religious ritual, and determine the form of language to be used in every social situation. Most aspects of Balinese culture have proved to be adaptable, as Bali becomes more and more a part of Indonesia and the rest of the world, but the question of caste is most problematic. There were pressures on and within the caste system even before the Dutch arrived, and the colonial period entrenched a caste structure which suited the Dutch interests rather than the Balinese. The 1960s communists opposed the caste system as a feudal relic, a view shared by many liberals and intellectuals until the anti-communist massacres of 1965-66.

There is still much ambivalence on the question of caste, which on the one hand is seen as good because it is Balinese and traditional and bound up with religious belief and ritual, and on the other hand is seen as inconsistent with modern, national values. Over 90% of the population belongs to the common Sudra caste. Despite the persistence of honorific titles (Ida, Dewa, Gusti etc), the practical importance of caste is diminishing as status becomes more a matter of education, economic success and community influence. The importance of caste differences in language are mitigated by the use of 'polite' forms of Balinese language, or by using the national Indonesian language (Bahasa Indonesia), itself a sign of some status. In a traditional village, however, caste is still very much a part of life, and caste concepts are still essential to religious practices.

Minority Groups

Ethnic minorities on Bali include some communities of the indigenous Bali Aga people, a small Chinese contingent in the larger towns, a few thousand Indian and Arab merchants in Denpasar, plus a number of more-or-less permanent Western visitors, many of them women married to Balinese men. The island is a model of religious tolerance, with minority communities of Muslims on the north coast and elsewhere, two Christian villages (one Catholic, one protestant), some Chinese temples, and even a Buddhist monastery.

Population Growth

Population control is a priority of the Indonesian government, and the family planning slogan *dua anak cukup* ('two children enough') is a recurring theme in roadside posters and statuary on Bali. It seems to have been quite successful, as many young families are limiting themselves to two children, or sometimes maybe three, but certainly not the seven or nine children common two or three generations ago. Yet, there are still many families where women continue bearing children until they have a boy. Nevertheless, the success of the programme can be measured in the decline of the birth rate, to around 1.5%, one of the lowest in the country.

ARTS
Music, Dance & Drama

Music, dance and drama are all closely related on Bali – in fact drama and dance are synonymous. Some dances are more drama and less dance, others more dance and less drama but basically they can all be lumped together. The most important thing about Balinese dances, however, is that they're fun and accessible. Balinese dance is definitely not some sterile art form requiring an arts degree to appreciate – it can be exciting and enjoyable for almost anyone with just the slightest effort.

Balinese dances are not hard to find: there are dances virtually every night at all the tourist centres – admission is generally around 5000 rp for foreigners. Dances are put on regularly at the tourist centres to raise money but are also a regular part of almost

every temple festival and Bali has no shortage of these. Many of the dances put on for tourists offer a smorgasbord of Balinese dances – a little Topeng, a taste of Legong, some Baris to round it all off. A nice introduction perhaps, but for some dances you really need the whole thing. It will be a shame if the 'instant Asia' mentality takes too strong a grip on Balinese dance.

The dances take various forms but with a few notable exceptions, in particular the Kecak and the Sanghyang trance dance, they are all accompanied by music from the gamelan orchestra. Some are dances almost purely for the sake of dancing – in this category you could include the technically precise Legong, its male equivalent the Baris, or various solo dances like the Kebyar. Mask dances like the Topeng or the Jauk also place a high premium on dancing ability.

Then there are dances like the Kecak, where the story is as important as the dancing. Or dances which move into that important area of Balinese life where the forces of magic, of good and evil, clash. In the Barong & Rangda dance, powerful forces are at work and elaborate preparations must be made to ensure that the balance is maintained. All masked dances require great care as, in donning a mask, you take on another personality and it is wise to ensure that the mask's personality does not take over. Masks used in the Barong & Rangda dance are treated with particular caution. Only an expert can carve them and between performances the masks must be carefully put away. A rangda mask must even be kept covered until the instant before the performance starts. These masks can have powerful *sakti* (spirits) and the unwary must be careful of their magical, often dangerous, spiritual vibrations.

As the Mexican artist, Miguel Covarrubias pointed out, the Balinese like a blend of seriousness and slapstick and this also shows in their dances. Some have a decidedly comic element, with clowns who serve both to counterpoint the staid, noble characters and to convey the story. The noble characters may use the high Balinese language or classical Kawi while the clowns, usually servants of the noble characters, converse in everyday Balinese. There are always two clowns – the leader, or *punta*, and his follower, the *kartala*, who never quite manages to carry off his mimicry.

Dancers on Bali are almost always ordinary folk who dance in the evening or their spare time, just like painters or sculptors who may indulge their artistry in their spare time. Dance is learnt by performing, and long hours may be spent in practice, usually by carefully following the movements of an expert. There's little of the soaring leaps of Western ballet or the smooth flowing movements often found in Western dance. Balinese dance tends to be precise, jerky, shifting and jumpy. In fact it's remarkably like Balinese music with its abrupt changes of tempo and dramatic contrasts between silence and crashing noise. There's also virtually no contact in Balinese dancing, each dancer moves completely independently.

To the expert, every movement of wrist, hand and fingers is important; even facial expressions are carefully choreographed to convey the character of the dance. Don't let these technicalities bother you though, they're just icing on the cake; basically, most Balinese dances are straightforward 'ripping yarns'. Don't give the dancers your complete attention either – the audience can be just as interesting, especially the children. Even at the most tourist-oriented of dances there will be hordes of local children clustered around the stage. Watch how they cheer the good characters and cringe back from the stage when the demons appear – how can TV ever win against the real thing?

The Gamelan Balinese music is based around an instrument known as the gamelan – in fact the gamelan is such a central part of Balinese music that the whole 'orchestra' is also referred to as a gamelan. Gamelan music is almost completely percussion – apart from the simple *suling* flute and the two-stringed *rebab*, there are virtually no wind or string instruments. Unlike many forms of Asian music the Balinese gamelan is accessible to

ears attuned to Western music. Though it sounds strange at first with its noisy, jangly percussion (there are none of the soothing passages found in some Western music) it's exciting and enjoyable.

The main instruments of the gamelan are the xylophone-like *gangsa*, which have bronze bars above bamboo resonators. The player hits the keys with his hammer in one hand while his other hand moves close behind to dampen the sound from each key just after it is struck. Although the gangsa make up the majority of the instruments and it is their sound which is most prevalent, the actual tempo and nature of the music is controlled by the two *kendang* drums – one male and one female.

Other instruments are the deep *trompong* drums, the small *kempli* gong and the small *cengceng* cymbals used in faster pieces. The whole gamelan orchestra is known as a *gong*. A *gong gede* is the traditional form – *gede* means large or big, and the gong gede comprised the complete traditional orchestra, with between 35 and 40 musicians. The *gong kebyar* is the modern, popular form of gong, and usually has up to 25 types of instrument. There are even more ancient forms of the gamelan such as the *gamelan selunding* still occasionally played in Bali Aga villages like Tenganan.

A village's gamelan is usually organised through a banjar, which owns the instruments and stores them in the *bale gong*. The musician's club is known as a *seksa*, and the members meet to practise in the bale banjar. Traditionally, gamelan playing is a male occupation, but a women's gamelan has been established in Ubud. The pieces are learnt by heart and passed down from father to son; there is little musical notation or recording of individual pieces.

The gamelan is also played in Java and Javanese gamelan music is held to be more 'formal' and 'classical' than Balinese. A perhaps more telling point is that Javanese gamelan music is rarely heard, apart from at special performances, whereas on Bali you seem to hear gamelans playing everywhere you go! In *The Last Paradise* Hickman

Powell tells of the cremation of a rajah of Ubud where no fewer than 126 gamelans from the area turned up!

Gamelan music, in both Balinese and Javanese styles, is available on cassette tapes, and the occasional CD. Look in the music shops in the Kuta area (try Mahogany Music, on Jalan Legian in Seminyak) and the bigger department stores.

Kecak Probably the best known of the many Balinese dances, the Kecak is unusual in that it does not have a gamelan accompaniment. Instead the background is provided by a chanting 'choir' of men who provide the 'chak-a-chak-a-chak' noise. Originally this chanting group was known as the kecak and was part of a Sanghyang trance dance. Then, in the 1930s, the modern Kecak developed in Bona, a village near Gianyar, where the dance is still held regularly.

The Kecak tells a tale from the *Ramayana*, one of the great Hindu holy books, about Prince Rama and his Princess Sita. With Rama's brother, Laksamana, they have been exiled from the kingdom of Ayodya and are wandering in the forest. The evil Rawana, King of Lanka, lures Rama away with a golden deer (which is really Lanka's equally evil prime minister who has magically changed himself into a deer). When Rama fails to return, Sita persuades Laksamana to search for him. When Sita is alone, Rawana pounces and carries her off to his hideaway.

Hanuman, the white monkey god, appears before Sita and tells her that Rama is trying to rescue her. He brings her Rama's ring to show that he is indeed the prince's envoy and Sita gives him a hairpin to take back to Rama. When Rama finally arrives in Lanka he is met by the evil king's evil son Megananda, who shoots an arrow at him, but the arrow magically turns into a snake which ties Rama up. Fortunately Rama is able to call upon a *garuda*, a mythical creature, part man and part bird, for assistance and thus escapes. Finally, Sugriwa, the king of the monkeys, comes to Rama's assistance with his monkey army and after a great battle good wins out over bad and Rama and Sita return home.

Throughout the dance the surrounding circle of men, all bare-chested and wearing checked cloth around their waists, provide a nonstop accompaniment that rises to a crescendo as they play the monkey army and fight it out with Rawana and his cronies. The chanting is superbly synchronised; members of the 'monkey army' sway back and forth, raise their hands in unison, flutter their fingers and lean left and right, all with an eerily exciting coordination.

Barong & Rangda The Barong & Rangda dance rivals the Kecak as Bali's most popular dance for tourists. Again it's a straightforward battle between good, the *barong*, and bad, the *rangda*. The barong is a strange creature, half shaggy dog, half lion, propelled by two men like a circus clown-horse. It's definitely on the side of good but is a mischievous and fun-loving creature. The widow-witch rangda is bad through and

Barong dancer

through and certainly not the sort of thing you'd like to meet on a midnight stroll through the rice paddies.

Barongs can take various forms but in the Barong & Rangda dance it will be as the *barong keket*, the most holy of the barongs. The barong flounces in, snaps its jaws at the gamelan, dances around a bit and enjoys the acclaim of its supporters – a group of men with krises. Then rangda makes her appearance, her long tongue lolling, human entrails draped around her neck and her terrible fangs protruding from her mouth.

The barong and rangda duel, using their magical powers, but when things look bad for the barong its supporters draw their krises and rush in to attack the rangda. Using her magical powers the rangda throws them into a trance and the men try to stab themselves with their krises. But the barong also has great magical powers and casts a spell which stops the krises from harming the men. This is the most dramatic part of the dance. As the gamelan rings crazily the men rush back and forth, waving their krises around, all but foaming at the mouth, sometimes even rolling on the ground in a desperate attempt to stab themselves. There often seems to be a conspiracy to terrify tourists in the front row!

Finally, the rangda retires, defeated, and good has won again. This still leaves, however, a large group of entranced barong supporters to bring back to the real world. This is usually done by sprinkling them with holy water, sanctified by dipping the barong's beard in it. Performing the Barong & Rangda dance is a touchy operation – playing around with all that powerful magic, good and bad, is not to be taken lightly. Extensive ceremonies have to be performed, a *pemangku* (priest) must be on hand to end the dancers' trance and at the end a chicken must be sacrificed to propitiate the evil spirits.

Legong The Legong is the most graceful of Balinese dances and, to sophisticated Balinese connoisseurs of dancing, the one arousing most interest and discussion. A

Legong dancer

legong, as a Legong dancer is known, is a young girl – often as young as eight or nine years, rarely older than her early teens. Such importance is attached to the dance that even in old age a classic dancer will be remembered as a 'great legong' even though her brief period of fame may have been 50 years ago.

There are various forms of the Legong but the Legong Keraton (Legong of the Palace) is the one most often performed. Peliatan's famous dance troupe, which visitors to Ubud often get a chance to see, is particularly noted for its Legong. The story behind the Legong is very stylised and symbolic – if you didn't know the story it would be impossible to tell what was going on.

The Legong involves just three dancers – the two legongs and their 'attendant', the *condong*. The legongs are identically dressed in gold brocade, so tightly bound that it is something of a mystery how they manage to move so rapidly and agitatedly. Their faces are elaborately made up, their eyebrows plucked and repainted, their hair decorated with frangipanis. The dance relates how a king takes a maiden, Rangkesari, captive. When Rangkesari's brother comes to release her, Rangkesari begs the king to free her rather than go to war. The king refuses and on his way to the battle meets a bird bringing ill omens. He ignores the bird and continues on to meet Rangkesari's brother and gets killed.

That's the whole story but the dance only tells of the king's preparations for battle and it ends with the bird's appearance – when the king leaves the stage it is to join the battle where he will meet his death. The dance starts with the condong dancing an introduc-

Ramayana ballet dancer

tion and then departing as the legongs come on. The two legongs dance solo, in close identical formation and in mirror image, as when they dance a nose-to-nose 'love scene'. The dance tells of the king's sad departure from his queen, Rangkesari's bitter request that he release her and then the king's departure for the battle. The condong reappears with tiny golden wings as the bird of ill fortune, and the dance ends.

Baris The warrior dance, known as the Baris, is traditionally a male equivalent of the Legong – femininity and grace give way to energetic and warlike martial spirit. The Baris dancer has to convey the thoughts and emotions of a warrior preparing for action and then meeting an enemy in battle. It's a solo dance requiring great energy and skill. The dancer has to show his changing moods through facial expression as well as movement – chivalry, pride, anger, prowess and finally a little regret all have to be there. It's said that the Baris is one of the most complex of the Balinese dances.

Ramayana Ballet The *Ramayana* is, of course, a familiar tale on Bali but the dance is a relatively recent addition to the Balinese repertoire. Basically, it tells the same story of Rama and Sita as told in the Kecak but without the monkey ensemble and with a normal gamelan gong accompaniment. Fur-

thermore, the *Ramayana* provides plenty of opportunity for improvisation and comic additions. Rawana may be played as a classic bad guy, Hanuman can be a comic clown, and camera-clicking tourists among the spectators may come in for a little imitative ribbing.

Kebyar The Kebyar is a male solo dance like the Baris but with greater emphasis on the performer's individual abilities. Development of the modern Kebyar is credited in large part to the famous prewar dancer Mario. There are various forms of Kebyar including the Kebyar Duduk, where the 'dance' is done from the seated position and facial expressions, as well as movements of the hands, arms and torso, are all important. In the Kebyar Trompong the dancer actually joins the gamelan and plays the trompong drum while dancing.

Barong Landung The giant puppet dances known as Barong Landung are not an every-day occurrence – they take place annually on the island of Pulau Serangan and a few other places in southern Bali. The legend of their creation relates how a demon, Jero Gede Macaling, popped over from Nusa Penida disguised as a standing barong to cause havoc on Bali. To scare him away the people had to make a big barong just like him. The Barong Landung dances, a reminder of that ancient legend, feature two gigantic puppet figures – a horrific male image of black Jero Gede and his female sidekick, white Jero Luh. Barong Landung performances are often highly comic.

Janger The Janger is a relatively new dance which suddenly popped up in the '20s and '30s. Both Covarrubias and Powell commented on this strange, almost un-Balinese, courtship dance. Today it has become part of the standard repertoire and no longer looks so unusual. It has similarities to several other dances including the Sanghyang, where the relaxed chanting of the women is contrasted to the violent chak-a-chak-a-chak of the men. In the Janger, formations of 12 young women and 12 young men do a sitting dance, and the gentle swaying and chanting of the women contrasts with the violently choreo-graphed movements and loud shouts of the men.

Topeng This is a mask dance where the dancers have to imitate the character repre-sented by the mask. *(Topeng* means 'pressed against the face', as with a mask.) The Topeng Tua is a classic solo dance where the mask is that of an old man and the dancer has to dance like a creaky old gentleman. In other dances there may be a small troupe who dance various characters and types. A full collection of Topeng masks may number 30 or 40.

Jauk The Jauk is also a mask dance but strictly a solo performance – the dancer plays an evil demon, his mask an eerie face with bulging eyes and fixed smile, while long

Topeng mask, Bali Museum, Denpasar

wavering fingernails complete the demonic look. Mask dances are considered to require great expertise because the dancer is not able to convey the character's thoughts and meanings through his facial expressions – the dance has to tell all. Demons are unpleas-ant, frenetic and fast-moving creatures so a Jauk dancer has to imitate all these things.

Pendet The Pendet is normally neither a major performance nor something that requires arduous training and practice. It's an everyday dance of the temples, a small pro-cedure to go through before making temple offerings. You may often see the Pendet being danced by women bringing offerings to a temple for a festival but it is also some-times danced as an introduction and a closing for other dance performances.

Sanghyang The Sanghyang trance dances originally developed to drive out evil spirits from a village. The Sanghyang is a divine spirit which temporarily inhabits an entranced dancer. The Sanghyang Dedari dance is performed by two young girls who dance a dream-like version of the Legong but with their eyes closed. The dancers are said to be untrained in the intricate pattern of the Legong but dance in perfect harmony, with their eyes firmly shut. Male and female choirs, the male choir being a Kecak, provide a background chant but when the chant stops the dancers slump to the ground in a faint. Two women bring them round and at the finish a pemangku blesses them with holy water and brings them out of the trance. The modern Kecak dance developed from the Sanghyang.

In the Sanghyang Jaran a boy in a trance dances round and through a fire of coconut husks, riding a coconut palm 'hobby horse'. It's labelled the 'fire dance' for the benefit of tourists. Like other trance dances (such as the Barong & Rangda dance) great care must be taken to control the magical forces at play. Experts must always be on hand to take care of the entranced dancers and to bring them out of the trance at the close.

Other Dances There are numerous other dances on Bali, some of them only performed occasionally, some quite regularly but not often seen by tourists. Of course, old dances still fade out and new dances or new developments of old dances still appear. Dance on Bali is not a static activity. The Oleg Tambulilingan was developed in the 1950s, originally as a solo female dance. Later, a male part was added and the dance now mimics the flirtations of two *tambulilingan* (bumblebees).

One of the most popular comic dances is the Cupak, which tells a tale of a greedy coward (Cupak) and his brave but hard-done-by younger brother Grantang, and their adventures while rescuing a beautiful princess.

The Arja is a sort of Balinese soap opera, long and full of high drama. Since it requires much translation of the noble's actions by the clowns it's hard for Westerners to understand and appreciate. Drama Gong is in some ways a more modern version of the same romantic themes.

Wayang Kulit
The shadow puppet plays known as wayang

Wayang kulit puppet

kulit are popular not only on Bali but throughout Indonesia. The plays are far more than mere entertainment, however, for the puppets are believed to have great spiritual power and the *dalang*, the puppet master and storyteller, is an almost mystical figure. He has to be a man of considerable skill and even more considerable endurance. Not only does he have to manipulate the puppets and tell the story, he must also conduct the small gamelan orchestra, the *gender wayang*, and beat time with his chanting – having long run out of hands to do things with, he performs the latter task with a horn held with his toes!

His mystical powers come into play because the wayang kulit, like so much of Balinese drama, is another phase of the eternal struggle between good and evil. The endurance factor comes in because a wayang kulit performance can last six or more hours and the performances always seem to start so late that the drama is only finally resolved as the sun peeps up over the horizon.

Shadow puppets are made of pierced buffalo hide – they're completely traditional in their characters and their poses, so there's absolutely no mistaking who is who. The dalang sits behind a screen on which the shadows of the puppets are cast, usually by an oil lamp which gives a far more romantic flickering light than modern electric lighting would do. Traditionally, women and children sit in front of the screen while men sit behind the screen with the dalang and his assistants.

The characters are arrayed to the right and left of the puppet master – goodies to the right, baddies to the left. The characters include nobles, who speak in the high Javanese language Kawi, and common clowns, who speak in everyday Balinese. (The dalang also has to be a linguist!) When the four clowns (Delem and Sangut are the bad ones, Twalen and his son Merdah are the good ones) are on screen the performance becomes something of a Punch and Judy show with much rushing back and forth, clouts on the head and comic insults. The noble characters are altogether more refined – they include the terrible Durga and the noble Bima. Wayang kulit stories are chiefly derived from the great Hindu epics, the *Mahabharata* and the *Ramayana*.

Kamasan Paintings

The village of Kamasan, a few km from Klungkung, has long been a bastion of traditional painting, the origins of which can be traced back at least 500 years. Highly conventionalised, the symbolism of equating right and left with good and evil, as in wayang kulit performances, is evident in the compositions and placement of figures in Kamasan paintings. Subject matter derives largely from Balinese variations of the ancient Hindu epics, the *Ramayana* and the *Mahabharata*. *Kakawins*, poems written in the archaic Javanese language of Kawi, provide another important source, as does indigenous Balinese folklore with its pre-Hindu/Buddhist beliefs in demonic spirit forces. The style has also been adapted to create large versions of the zodiacal and lunar calendar, especially the 210-day wuku calendar which still regulates the timing of Balinese festivals.

The earliest paintings were done on bark cloth, said to have been imported from Sulawesi, although a coarse handspun cloth and later machine-made cloth were used as backing for the bark cloth. Kamasan art is essentially linear – the skill of the artist is apparent in its composition and in the sensitivity of its lines. The colouring was of secondary importance and was left to apprentices, usually the artist's children. Members of the family would assist in preparing the colours, stiffening the cloth with rice paste and polishing the surface smooth enough to receive the fine ink drawing.

Paintings were hung as ceremonial backdrops in temples and houses and were also sufficiently prized by the local rulers to be acceptable gifts between rival royal households. Although they were traditionally patronised by the ruling class, paintings also helped fulfil the important function of imparting ethical values and customs *(adat)* to the ordinary people, in much the same way as traditional dance and wayang puppetry. In fact, it is from the wayang tradition that Kamasan painting takes its essential characteristics – the stylisation of human figures, their symbolic gestures, the depiction of divine and heroic characters as refined, and of evil ones as vulgar and crude, as well as the primary function of narrating a moral tale.

It's worth noting that there are striking similarities between Kamasan paintings and a now almost totally abandoned form of wayang theatre, the *wayang beber*. The slender horizontal format of Balinese paintings almost certainly derives from the *wayang bebe*, which is a large hand scroll, held vertically and unrolled and expounded upon by the puppet-master, accompanied by the gamelan orchestra. The wayang beber was still being performed during the Dutch occupation, but a performance now is very rare, although artisans in eastern Java still produce scenes from such scrolls for the tourist trade.

The wayang style can be traced back to 9th-century Javanese sculpture, and its most mature form can be seen at the 14th-century temple complex at Panataran in eastern Java. The relief sculptures at Panataran display the characteristic wayang figures, the rich floral designs, the flame-and-mountain motifs – all vital elements of Balinese painting.

In Kamasan, at Banjar Siku, there's a gallery where you can buy good quality Kamasan paintings. (See also Klungkung in the East Bali chapter). ■

Painting & Carving

Traditionally painting, carving and other decorative arts were employed only for the adornment of temples and the making of ritual offerings and festival trappings. It was not until the arrival of Western artists in the 1930s that paintings and sculptures were seen as artistic creations in their own right, and the range of themes, techniques and styles expanded enormously. Tourism has created a huge market for arts and crafts, and there are many excellent examples showing the Balinese flair for decoration, colour and creativity. For more information, look at the Arts & Crafts section.

Architecture

Traditional Balinese architecture is employed for the structures referred to below in the sections on Culture and Religion – family compounds, community meeting halls and the many types of temple. Modern structures, for hotels, banks and government offices, have used elements from traditional architecture, and adapted them for new materials and new requirements.

A basic element of Balinese architecture is the *bale*, a rectangular, open-sided pavilion with a steeply pitched hip roof of palm thatch. A family compound will have a number of bale for eating, sleeping and working. The focus of a community *(banjar)* is a large pavilion, the *bale banjar*, for meeting, debate, gamelan practice etc. Large, modern buildings like restaurants and the lobby areas of new hotels are often modelled on the bale, and they can be airy, spacious and handsomely proportioned. Beyond a certain size traditional materials cannot be used; concrete is substituted for timber, and sometimes the roof is tiled rather than thatched. These structures are not traditional, but they do represent a genuine, modern style of Balinese architecture.

Other elements of Balinese architecture are derived from traditional temple design. A temple compound contains a number of *gedongs* (shrines) of solid brick and stone, of varying sizes but always heavily decorated with carving. The entrance to larger temples is through a sculptured tower split down the middle (a *candi bentar),* and the entrance to the inner courtyard is through a carved door in another tower, also heavily carved. This style of decorative carving is frequently seen in fancier modern buildings like banks and hotels.

Visitors may be disappointed by Balinese palaces *(puri)*, which are neither large nor imposing. These are the traditional residences of the Balinese aristocracy, though now they may be used as hotels, or as a regular family compound. A Balinese palace would never be built more than one storey high – a Balinese noble could not possibly use a ground-floor room if the feet of people on an upper floor were walking above.

CULTURE & CUSTOMS

For the average Balinese, the working day is not a long one for most of the year. Their expertise at growing rice means that large crops are produced without an enormous labour input, and this leaves time for elaborate cultural events. Each stage of Balinese life, from conception to cremation, is marked by a series of ceremonies and rituals known as Manusa Yadnya. They are the basis of the rich, varied and active cultural life of the Balinese.

Birth

The first ceremony of Balinese life takes place even before birth – when women reach the third month of pregnancy they take part in ceremonies at home and at the village river or spring. A series of offerings are made to ensure the wellbeing of the baby. Another ceremony takes place soon after the birth, during which the afterbirth is buried with appropriate offerings. Women are considered to be 'unclean' after giving birth and 12 days later they are 'purified' through another ceremony. The father is also *sebel* (unclean), but only for three days. At 42 days another ceremony and more offerings are made for the baby's future.

The first major ceremony takes place at 105 days, halfway through the baby's first Balinese year. Then, for the first time, the

Top Left: Oleg Tambulilingan (Bumblebee) dancer, Teges, Bali (GA)
Top Right: Muslim girl, Klungkung, Bali (GA)
Bottom Left: Roadside seller in Tampaksiring, Bali (GA)
Bottom Right: Comedian at Barong dance, Batubulan, Bali (GA)

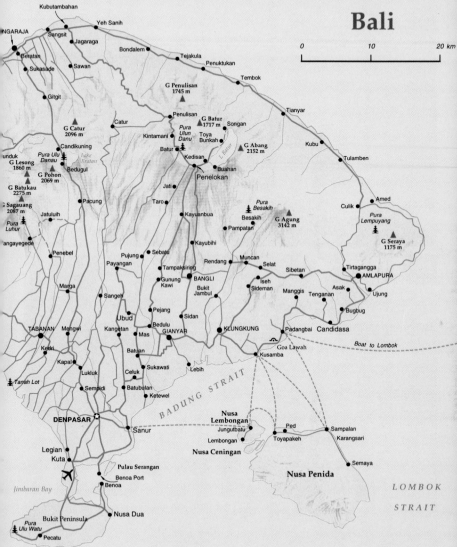

Bali

0   10   20 km

Kubutambahan
NGARAJA
Yeh Sanih
Sangsit
Jagaraga
Beratan
Bondalem
Sukasade
Sawan
Tejakula
Gitgit
Penuktukan

G Penulisan
1745 m
Tembok

G Catur
2096 m
Catur
Penulisan
G Batur
1717 m
Songan
Tianyar

Pura
Ulun
Danau
Kintamani
Toya
Bunkah

unduk
G Lesong
1860 m
Candikuning
Pura Ulu
Danau
Batur
Kedisan
G Abang
2152 m
Kubu

Bedugul
Buahan
Tulamben

G Pohon
2069 m
Pacung
Penelokan

G Batukau
2275 m
Jati

G Sagauang
2087 m
Taro
Kayuanbua
Pura
Besakih
Culik
Amed

Pura
Luhur
Jatuluih
Pampatan
Besakih
G Agung
3142 m
Pura
Lempuyang

angayegede
Penebel
Kayubihi
Rendang
Muncan
G Seraya
1175 m

Marga
Pujung
Sebatu
Tampaksiring
Selat
Sibetan
Tirtagangga

Payangan
BANGLI
Iseh
AMLAPURA

Sangeh
Gunung
Kawi
Bukit
Jambul
Sideman
Manggis
Tenganan
Asak
Ujung

Ubud
Pejang
Sidan
Bugbug

TABANAN
Mengwi
Kangetan
Bedulu
GIANYAR
KLUNGKUNG
Padangbai
Candidasa

Kedri
Mas
Goa Lawah
Boat to Lombok

Kapal
Lukluk
Batuan
Sukawati
Lebih
Kusamba

Tanah Lot
Celuk
Sempidi
Batubulan
Ketewel

DENPASAR
BADUNG STRAIT

Sanur
**Nusa
Lembongan**
Ped
Sampalan
Karangsari

Legian
Jungutbatu
Toyapakeh

Kuta
Lembongan
Nusa Ceningan
Semaya

Pulau Serangan
Nusa Penida
LOMBOK

Benoa Port
Benoa
STRAIT

Jimbaran Bay
Nusa Dua

Bukit Peninsula
Pura
Ulu Watu
Pecatu

Top: Barong dance, Bali (TW)
Bottom: Cidomo (horse and cart), Lombok (JL)

baby's feet are allowed to touch the ground. Prior to that babies are carried continuously because the ground is believed to be impure, and babies, so close to heaven, should not be allowed to come into contact with it. The baby is also ceremonially welcomed to the family at this time. Another ceremony follows at 210 days, at the end of the first Balinese year, when the baby is welcomed to the ancestral temple.

It's said that the Balinese still regard boy-girl twins as a major calamity, although according to Covarrubias it has only ever really applied to ordinary people, not the nobility. The reasoning is that boy-girl twins are said to have committed a sort of spiritual incest while in the womb and that this is dangerous for the whole village. Extensive and expensive rituals and ceremonies must be performed in order to purify the children, the parents and the whole village. Same-sex twins, however, are quite OK.

Names

The Balinese basically only have four first names. The first child is Wayan, the second child is Made, the third is Nyoman and the fourth is Ketut. And the fifth, sixth, seventh, eighth and ninth? Well, they're Wayan, Made, Nyoman, Ketut and Wayan again. It's very simple and surprisingly unconfusing although it actually doesn't make their names any easier for Westerners to remember. (Now was he another Made, or a Ketut? Which Nyoman was that?) The only variation from this straightforward policy seems to be that first-born boys are sometimes also known as Gede and first-born girls as Putu.

The Balinese have a series of titles which depend on caste: the Brahmanas have the prefix Ida Bagus; the Wesia, the main caste of the nobility, are Gusti; the Satria caste are Cokodor; but the poor Sudra, the general mass of the Balinese people, have no prefix at all.

Childhood

If ever there were a people who love children it must be the Balinese – anybody who visits Bali with their children can attest to that.

In Bali, coping with a large family is made much easier by the policy of putting younger children in the care of older ones. One child always seems to be carrying another one around on his or her hip. Despite the fact that Balinese children are almost immediately part of a separate society of children they always seem remarkably well behaved. Of course you hear kids crying occasionally but tantrums, fights, screams and shouts all seem to happen far less frequently than we're used to in the West. It's been said that parents achieve this by treating children with respect and teaching them good behaviour by example.

After the ceremonies of babyhood come the ceremonies marking the stages of childhood and puberty, including the important tooth-filing ceremony. The Balinese prize even, straight teeth. Crooked fangs are, after all, one of the chief distinguishing marks of evil spirits, just have a look at a rangda mask! A priest files the upper front teeth to produce an aesthetically pleasing straight line. Today the filing is often only symbolic – one pass of the file.

Marriage

Every Balinese expects to marry and raise a family, and marriage takes place at a comparatively young age. Marriages are not, in general, arranged as they are in many other Asian communities, although strict rules apply to marriages between the castes. There are two basic forms of marriage on Bali – *mapadik* and *ngorod*. The respectable form, in which the family of the man visit the family of the woman and politely propose that the marriage take place, is mapadik. The Balinese, however, like their fun and often prefer marriage by elopement (ngorod) as the more exciting option.

Of course, the Balinese are also a practical people so nobody is too surprised when the young man spirits away his bride-to-be, even if she loudly protests about being kidnapped. The couple go into hiding and somehow the girl's parents, no matter how assiduously they search, never manage to find her. Eventually the couple re-emerge, announce that it is too late to stop them now, the marriage is officially recognised and everybody has had a lot of fun and games. Marriage by elopement has another advantage, apart from being exciting and mildly heroic – it's cheaper.

The Household

Although many modern Balinese houses, particularly in Denpasar or the larger towns, are arranged much like houses in the West, there are still a great number of traditional Balinese homes. Wander the streets of Ubud sometime: nearly every house will follow the same traditional walled design. Like houses in ancient Rome the Balinese house looks inward; the outside is simply a high wall. Inside there will be a garden and a separate small building or bale for each function. There will be one building for cooking, one building for washing and the toilet, and separate buildings for each 'bedroom'. What there won't be is a 'living room' because in Bali's mild tropical climate you live outside – the 'living room' and 'dining room' will be open verandah areas, looking out into the garden.

Covarrubias compared traditional Balinese house design to the human body: there's a head – the ancestral shrine; arms – the sleeping and living areas; legs and feet – the kitchen and rice storage building; and even an anus – the garbage pit. There may also be an area outside the house compound where fruit trees are grown or a pig may be kept. Usually the house is entered through a gateway backed by a small wall known as the *aling aling*. It serves a practical and a spiritual purpose, both preventing passersby from seeing in and stopping evil spirits from entering. Evil spirits cannot easily turn corners so the aling aling stops them from simply scooting straight in through the gate!

Men & Women

Social life on Bali is relatively free and easy and, although Balinese women are not kept cloistered away, the roles of the sexes are strictly delineated. There are certain tasks clearly to be handled by women, and others reserved for men. Thus running the household is very much the women's task. In the morning women sweep and clean and put out the offerings for the gods. Every household has a shrine or god-throne where offerings must be placed, and areas on the ground,

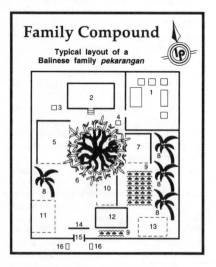

Family Compound

Typical layout of a Balinese family *pekarangan*

1   Sanggah Kemulan (Family temple)
2   Uma Meten (Sleeping pavilion for the family head)
3   Tugu (Shrine)
4   Pengidjeng (Shrine)
5   Bale Tiang Sanga (Guest pavilion)
6   Natar (Courtyard, with frangipani or hibiscus shade tree)
7   Bale Sikepat (Sleeping pavilion for other relatives)
8   Fruit trees & coconut palms
9   Vegetable garden
10 Bale Sekenam (Working & sleeping pavilion)
11 Paon (Kitchen)
12 Lumbung (Rice barn)
13 Rice-threshing area
14 Aling Aling (Screen wall)
15 Lawang (Gate)
16 Apit Lawang (Gate shrines)

such as at the compound entrance, where offerings for the demons are derisively cast. While the women are busy attending to these tasks the men of the household are likely to be looking after the fighting cocks and any other pets.

Marketing is also a female job, although at large markets cattle selling is definitely a male job. The traditional position of women as preparers of food, and as the buyers and sellers, placed them in a good position to take part in the tourist industry. A successful Balinese restaurant or shop is much more likely to have been established by a local woman than a man. In agriculture there's also a division of labour based on sex roles: although everybody turns out in the fields at harvest time, planting the rice is purely a male activity.

In Balinese leisure activities the roles are also sex differentiated. Both men and women dance but usually only men play the gamelan. The artistic skills are almost totally left to men although today you do see some women painters, sculptors and woodcarvers.

Community Life

The Balinese have an amazingly active and organised village life – you simply cannot be a faceless nonentity on Bali. You can't help but get to know your neighbours as your life is so entwined and interrelated with theirs. Or at least it still is in the small villages that comprise so much of Bali. Even in the big towns, however, the banjar ensures that a strong community spirit continues.

The village is known as the desa and village plans generally follow a similar pattern. In the centre, usually at the crossroads of the two major streets, there will be the open meeting space known as the *alun alun*. It's actually more than just a meeting space because you will also find temples, the town market, or even the former prince's home. The *kulkul* (warning drum) tower will be here and quite likely a big banyan tree. In Ubud the palace, the banyan tree with its kulkul drums, and the temple are all in the centre of town near the bemo stop and the market. In Bangli see how the Artha Sastra

Inn, in the family compound of the local prince, looks right out on the main square.

Although village control by the desa authorities is no longer as strict as it once was, there is still detailed and careful organisation of land ownership because of the necessary interrelation of water supply to the rice fields. Each individual rice field is known as a *sawah* and each farmer who owns even one sawah must be a member of his local subak (rice growers association). The rice paddies must have a steady supply of water and it is the subak's job to ensure that the water supply gets to everybody. It's said that the head of the local subak will often be the farmer whose rice paddies are at the bottom of the hill, for he will make quite certain that the water gets all the way down to his fields, passing through everybody else's on the way!

Of course, Bali being Bali, the subak has far more to do than share out the water and ensure that the water channels, dykes and so forth are in good order. Each subak will have its small temple out amongst the rice fields where offerings to the spirits of agriculture are made and regular meetings held for the subak members. Like every temple on Bali there are regular festivals and ceremonies to observe. Even individual sawahs may have small altars.

The subak is not the only organisation controlling village life. Each desa is further subdivided into banjars, which each male adult joins when he marries. It is the banjar which organises village festivals, marriage ceremonies and even cremations.

Throughout the island you'll see the open-sided bale banjars – they're nearly as common a sight as temples. They serve a multitude of purposes, from a local meeting place to a storage room for the banjar's musical equipment and dance costumes. Gamelan orchestras are organised at the banjar level and a glance in a bale banjar at any time might reveal a gamelan practice, a meeting going on, food being prepared for a feast, even a group of men getting their roosters together to raise their anger a little in preparation for the next round of cockfights.

Death & Cremation

There are ceremonies for every stage of Balinese life but often the last ceremony – cremation – is the biggest. A Balinese cremation can be an amazing, spectacular, colourful, noisy and exciting event. In fact it often takes so long to organise a cremation that years have passed since the death. During that time the body is temporarily buried. Of course an auspicious day must be chosen for the cremation and since a big cremation can be a very expensive business many less wealthy people may take the opportunity of joining in at a larger cremation and sending their own dead on their way at the same time. Brahmanas, however, must be cremated immediately.

A cremation ceremony is a fine opportunity to observe the incredible energy the Balinese put into creating real works of art which are totally ephemeral. A lot more than a body gets burnt at the cremation. The body is carried from the burial ground (or from the deceased's home if it's an 'immediate' cremation) to the cremation ground in a high, multi-tiered tower made of bamboo, paper, string, tinsel, silk, cloth, mirrors, flowers and anything else bright and colourful you can think of. The tower is carried on the shoulders of a group of men, the size of the group depending on the importance of the deceased and hence the size of the tower. The funeral of a former rajah or high priest may require hundreds of men to tote the tower.

Along the way to the cremation ground certain precautions must be taken to ensure that the deceased's spirit does not find its way back home. To ensure this doesn't happen requires getting the spirits confused as to their whereabouts, which you do by shaking the tower, running it around in circles, spinning it around, throwing water at it, generally making the trip to the cremation ground anything but a stately and funereal crawl. Meanwhile, there's likely to be a priest halfway up the tower, hanging on grimly as it sways back and forth, and doing his best to soak bystanders with holy water. A gamelan sprints along behind, providing a suitably exciting musical accompaniment. Camera-toting tourists get all but run down and once again the Balinese prove that ceremonies and religion are there to be enjoyed.

At the cremation ground the body is transferred to a funeral sarcophagus – this should be in the shape of a bull for a Brahmana, a winged lion for a Satria and a sort of elephant-fish for a Sudra. These days, however, almost anybody from the higher castes will use a bull. Finally up it all goes in flames – funeral tower, sarcophagus, body, the lot. The eldest son does his duty by poking through the ashes to ensure that there are no bits of body left unburnt.

And where does your soul go after cremation? Why, to a heaven which is just like Bali!

RELIGION

The Balinese are nominally Hindus but Balinese Hinduism is a world away from that of India. At one time Hinduism was the predominant religion in Indonesia (witness the many great Hindu monuments in Java) but it died out with the spread of Islam through the archipelago. The final great Hindu kingdom, that of the Majapahits, virtually evacuated to Bali, taking not only their religion and its rituals but also their art, literature, music and culture. It's a mistake, however, to think that this was purely an exotic seed being implanted on virgin soil. The Balinese probably already had strong religious beliefs and an active cultural life. The new influences were simply overlaid on the existing practices – hence the peculiar Balinese interpretation of Hinduism. Of course there are small enclaves of other religions on Bali, particularly Muslims, whose mosques are often seen at ports and fishing villages around the coast.

Religion on Bali has two overwhelming features – it's absolutely everywhere and it's good fun! You can't get away from religion on Bali: there are temples in every village, shrines in every field, offerings being made at every corner. The fun element comes in because the Balinese seem to feel that religion should be an enjoyable thing – something the mortals can enjoy as well as the gods. It's summed up well in their attitude to offerings – you make up a lot of fancy food for offerings, but once the gods have eaten the 'essence' of the food, you've got enough 'substance' left over for a fine feast.

Basically, the Balinese worship the same gods as the Hindus of India – the trinity of Brahma, Shiva and Vishnu – although the Balinese have a supreme god, Sanghyang Widi. This basic threesome is always alluded to, never seen, on Bali – a vacant shrine or empty throne tells all. Others of the secondary Hindu gods may occasionally appear, such as Ganesh, Shiva's elephant-headed son, but a great many other purely Balinese gods, spirits and entities have far more everyday reality. The rangda may bear a close relation to Durga, the terrible side of Shiva's wife Parvati, but it's certain that nobody in India has seen a barong! The interpretation of the Hindu pantheon as being many manifestations of a single god makes the religion consistent with the first of the five national principles of Pancasila, a belief in one God.

To the Balinese, spirits are everywhere; it's a reminder that animism is the basis of much of Balinese religion. The offerings put out every morning are there to pay homage to the good spirits and to placate the bad ones – the Balinese take no chances! And if the offerings thrown on the ground are immediately consumed by dogs? Well, so it goes, everybody is suspicious of dogs anyway.

Temples

The number of temples on Bali is simply astonishing – they're everywhere. In fact, since every village has several and every home has at least a simple house-temple there are actually more temples than homes. The word for temple on Bali is *pura*, which is a Sanskrit word literally meaning 'a space surrounded by a wall'. Like a traditional Balinese home a temple is walled in, so the shrines you see in rice fields or at magical spots such as by old trees are not real temples. You'll find simple shrines or thrones at all sorts of unusual places. They often overlook crossroads, intersections or even just dangerous curves in the road. They protect passers-by, or give the gods a ringside view of the accidents!

Like so much else of Balinese religion the temples, although nominally Hindu, actually owe much to the pre-Majapahit era. Throughout most of the year the temples are quiet and empty but at festival times they are colourful and active, with offerings being made, dances performed, gamelan music ringing out and all manner of activities from cockfights to gambling going on.

All temples are oriented not north-south but mountains-sea. *Kaja*, the direction towards the mountains, is the most important direction so at this end of the temple the holiest shrines are found. The direction towards the sea is *kelod*. The sunrise or *kangin* direction is the second most important direction so on this side you find the secondary shrines. Kaja may be towards a particular mountain – Pura Besakih is pointed directly towards Gunung Agung – or it may just be the mountains in general, which run east-west along the length of Bali.

Temple Types There are three basic temple types which almost every village will have. The most important is the *pura puseh* (temple of origin) which is dedicated to the village founders and is located at the kaja end of the village. In the middle of the village is the *pura desa* for the spirits which protect the village community in its day-to-day life. At the kelod end of the village is the *pura dalem* (temple of the dead). The graveyard is also located here and the temple will often include representations of Durga, the terrible side of Shiva's wife Parvati. Both Shiva and Parvati have a creative and destructive side and it's their destructive powers which are honoured in the pura dalem.

Other temples include those dedicated to the spirits of irrigated agriculture. Rice growing is so important on Bali and the division of water for irrigation purposes is handled with such care that these *pura subak* or *pura ulun suwi* can be of considerable importance. Other temples may also honour dry-field agriculture as well as the flooded rice paddies.

In addition to these 'local' temples, Bali also has a lesser number of great temples. Each family worships its ancestors in the family temple, the clan in its clan temple and the village in the pura puseh. Above these come the temples of royalty or state temples and in many cases a kingdom would have three of these – a main state temple in the heartland of the state (like Pura Taman Ayun in Mengwi), then a mountain temple (like Pura Besakih or Pura Luhur at Batukau) and a sea temple (like Pura Luhur Ulu Watu or Pura Luhur Rambut Siwi).

Every house on Bali has its house temple which is at the kaja-kangin corner of the courtyard. There will be shrines to the Hindu 'trinity' of Brahma, Shiva and Vishnu, to *taksu*, the divine intermediary, and to *tugu*, the lord of the ground.

Directional Temples & World Sanctuaries
Certain special temples on Bali are of such importance that they are deemed to be owned by the whole island rather than by individual villages or local community organisations.

There are nine *kahyangan jagat* or 'directional temples' and six *sad-kahyangan* or 'world sanctuaries'. The directional temples are:

Temple	Place	Region
Pura Besakih	Besakih	centre
Pura Ulun Danu (Batur)	Kintamani	north
Sambu	Gunung Agung	north-east
Pura Lempuyang Luhur	near Tirtagangga	east
Pura Goa Lawah	near Padangbai	south-east
Pura Masceti	near Gianyar	south
Pura Ulu Watu	Ulu Watu	south-west
Pura Luhur	Batukau	west
Pura Ulu Danu (Candikuning)	Lake Bratan	north-west

Most of these temples are well known, easily accessible and familiar objectives for many tourist groups. Pura Besakih is the holiest of Balinese temples and encompasses separate shrines and temples for all the clans and former kingdoms. Pura Besakih is said to be a male temple; its female counterpart is Pura Ulun Danu. Overlooking the outer crater of Gunung Batur, Pura Ulun Danu was built in 1927 after its predecessor, actually within the crater, was destroyed by an eruption.

Goa Lawah is the famous bat cave temple, while Pura Ulu Watu is at the extreme southern end of Bali, at the end of the Bukit Peninsula. Pura Luhur on the slopes of Gunung Batukau is a rather remote temple with a reclusive feel while Pura Ulu Danau at Candikuning perches right on the edge of Lake Bratan.

Some of the temples are rarely seen by visitors to Bali. Pura Masceti, on the coast south of Gianyar, is easily reached but infrequently visited. It takes a stiff walk to reach remote Pura Lempuyang at the eastern end of the island.

It's not so easy to list the six 'world sanctuaries' as there is considerable dispute as to which ones make the grade. Usually the six are drawn from the list of nine directional temples but other important temples like Pura Pusering Jagat with its enormous bronze drum at Pejeng, near Ubud, or Pura

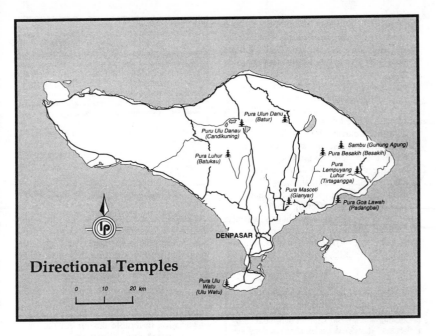

Directional Temples

Pura Ulun Danu (Batur)
Puru Ulu Danau (Candikuning)
Pura Luhur (Batukau)
Sambu (Gunung Agung)
Pura Besakih (Besakih)
Pura Lempuyang Luhur (Tirtagangga)
Pura Masceti (Gianyar)
Pura Goa Lawah (Padangbai)
DENPASAR
Pura Ulu Watu (Ulu Watu)

0   10   20 km

Kehen in Bangli may also creep on to some lists.

Other Important Temples There are numerous other important temples around the island apart from the world sanctuaries and directional temples. They include:

Pura Maduwe Karang – an agricultural temple on the north coast famous for its spirited bas reliefs, including one of a bicycle rider.
Pura Taman Ayun – the large and imposing state temple at Mengwi, north-west of Denpasar.
Pura Luhur Rambut Siwi – a beautiful coastal temple towards the western end of the island.
Pura Tirta Empul – the beautiful temple at Tampaksiring with springs and bathing pools at the source of the Pakerisan River, north of Ubud.
Tanah Lot – the enormously popular sunset temple perched on a rock just off the coast west of Denpasar.

Temple Festivals For much of the year Balinese temples are deserted, just an empty space. But every now and then they come alive with days of frenetic activity and nights of drama and dance. Temple festivals occur at least once each Balinese year of 210 days. The annual 'temple birthday' is known as an *odalan*. Since most villages have at least three temples that means you're assured of at least five or six annual festivals in every village. But that's only the start – there can be special festival days common throughout the islands, festivals for certain temples, festivals for certain gods, and festivals because it just seemed like a good idea to have one.

While the men slaughter their prized fighting birds the women bring beautifully arranged offerings of prepared food, fruit and flowers to the temple, artistically piled in huge pyramids which they carry on their heads. Outside the temple, food stalls *(warungs)* and other stalls selling toys and trinkets are set up. In the outer courtyard a gamelan provides further amusement.

While all this activity is going on in and around the temple, the pemangkus suggest to the gods that they should come down for a visit and enjoy the goings-on. That's what those little thrones are for in the temple shrines – they're symbolic seats for the gods to occupy during festivals. Sometimes small images known as *pratimas* are placed on the thrones, to represent the gods.

At some festivals the images and thrones of the deities are taken out of the temple and ceremonially carried down to the sea (or just to a suitable expanse of water if the sea is too distant) for a ceremonial bath. Gamelans follow the merry procession and provide a suitable musical accompaniment.

Back in the temple women dance the stately Pendet, an offering dance for the gods, and all night long there's activity, music and dancing. It's just like a country fair, complete with food stands, amusements, games, stalls, gambling, noise, colour and confusion.

Cockfights

Cockfights are a regular part of temple ceremonies – they're a convenient combination of excitement, sport, gambling and a blood sacrifice all rolled into one. Men keep fighting cocks as prized pets: carefully groomed and cared for, they are lovingly prepared for their brief moment of glory or defeat. On quiet afternoons the men will often meet in the banjars to compare their roosters, spar them against one another and line up the odds for the next big bout.

You'll often see the roosters by the roadside in their bell-shaped cane baskets – they're placed there to be entertained by passing activity. When the festivals take place the cocks are matched one against another, a lethally sharp metal spur tied to one leg and then, after being pushed against each other a few times to stir up the blood, they're released and the feathers fly. It's usually over in a flash – a slash of the spur and one rooster is down and dying. Occasionally a cowardly rooster turns and flees but in that case both roosters are put in a covered basket where they can't avoid fighting. After the bout the successful betters collect their pay-offs and the winning owner takes home the dead rooster for his cooking pot. ■

Trances

Trances are an everyday feature of Balinese life, particularly at festivals. People seem to be able to go into a trance state in a flash and at that time they're supposed to be a medium of communication for the gods who temporarily possess their bodies. You may see a pemangku go into trance while offering his prayers, a young girl's eye's glaze over as she carries offerings into the temple, or the trance dancers, particularly in the Barong & Rangda dance. It's regarded as a holy state, so people in trance are carefully tended to and sprinkled with holy water to break the trance afterwards. ■

Finally, as dawn approaches, the entertainment fades away, the women perform the last Pendet, the pemangkus suggest to the gods that maybe it's time they made their weary way back to heaven, and the people wend their weary way back to their homes.

Typical Temple Design There is a great deal of variation in temple design but the small two-courtyard temple illustrated includes all the basic elements. Larger temples may have more courtyards and more shrines and even a similar small temple may have the less important buildings and shrines arranged in a different pattern.

1. Candi Bentar

    The *candi bentar* is the temple gateway; it's an intricately sculptured tower which looks as if it has been split down the centre and then moved apart.
2. Kulkul Tower

    This is the warning drum tower from which a wooden split drum (known as a 'kulkul') is sounded to announce events at the temple or warn of danger.
3. Bales

    These are pavilions, generally open-sided, for temporary use or for storage. They may include a bale gong (3A), where the gamelan orchestra plays during festivals, or a *paon* (3B), used as a temporary kitchen to prepare offerings for temple ceremonies. A particularly large bale used as a stage for dances or cockfights is known as a *wantilan* (3C).

Temple Plan

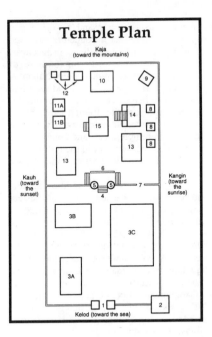

Kaja
(toward the mountains)

Kauh
(toward
the
sunset)

Kangin
(toward
the
sunrise)

Kelod (toward the sea)

1 Candi Bentar
2 Kulkul Tower
3A Bale Gong
3B Paon
3C Wantilan
4 Kori Agung or Paduraksa
5 Raksa or Dwarapala
6 Aling Aling
7 Side gate
8 Small shrines or Gedongs
9 Padmasana
10 Meru
11A 11-roofed Meru to Sanghyang Widi
11B Three-roofed Meru to Gunung
 Agung
12 Small shrines or Gedongs
13 Bale Piasan
14 Gedong Pesimpangan
15 Paruman or Pepelik

4. Kori Agung or Paduraksa

The gateway to the inner courtyard is an intricately sculptured stone tower (like the candi bentar), but you gain entry through a doorway reached by steps in the middle of the tower. The door is normally kept closed except during festivals.

5. Raksa or Dwarapala

The Raksa or Dwarapala are the statues of fierce guardian figures who protect the doorway and keep out evil spirits. Above the doorway there will be the equally fierce face of a *bhoma*, with hands outstretched to keep back unwanted spirits.

6. Aling Aling

If Raksa and the bhoma slip up and an evil spirit does manage to slither through the entrance, the aling aling, a low wall directly behind the entrance, should keep them at bay since evil spirits find it notoriously difficult to make right-angle turns.

7. Side Gate

For most of the year, when no ceremony is in process, entry to the inner courtyard is made through this side gate which is always open. Presumably, evil spirits don't think of getting in this way.

8. Small Shrines or Gedongs

These usually include shrines to Ngrurah Alit and Ngrurah Gede who organise things and ensure that the correct offerings are made.

9. Padmasana

This is the stone throne for the sun god Surya, and is situated at the most auspicious kaja-kangin corner. The throne rests on the 'world turtle' or *badawang* which is held by two snake-like *nagas* (mythological serpents).

10. Meru

These are multi-roofed Balinese shrines. Usually there will be an 11-roofed *meru* (11A) to Sanghyang Widi, the supreme Balinese deity, and a three-roofed meru (11B) to the holy mountain Gunung Agung.

12. Small Shrines or Gedongs

More small shrines will be found at the kaja (mountain) end of the courtyard. Typically these could include a shrine like a single-roofed meru to Gunung Batur, another of Bali's sacred mountains; a shrine known as the Maospait dedicated to the original Majapahit settlers who brought the Hindu religion to Bali; and a shrine to the taksu who acts as an interpreter for the gods. Trance dancers are said to be mouthpieces for the taksu or it may use a medium to convey the gods' wishes.

13. Bale Piasan

These are open pavilions used for the display of temple offerings. There may be several of these bales.

14. Gedong Pesimpangan

This is a stone building dedicated to the village founder or a local deity.

15. Paruman or Pepelik
    This open pavilion in the centre of the inner
    courtyard is where the gods are supposed to
    assemble to watch the ceremonies of a temple
    festival.

Temple Behaviour There are a number of
ground rules for visiting Balinese temples.
Except on rare occasions, anybody can enter
a temple any time they feel like it. The
attitude is nothing like that found in parts of
India where non-Hindus are firmly barred
from temples. You don't have to go barefoot
as in many Buddhist shrines, but you are
expected to be appropriately dressed. You
should always wear a temple scarf as a sash
around your waist – see the What to Bring
section in the Facts for the Visitor chapter.

Priests should be shown respect, particularly at festivals. They are the most important
people at the temple and should, therefore,
be on the highest plane. Don't put yourself
higher than them by, for example, climbing
up on a wall to take photographs.

There will usually be a sign outside temple
entrances warning you to be well dressed and
respectful and also requesting that women do
not enter the temple during their periods. The
pleasant little lakeside temple at Bedugul
once had a 'no entry' sign announcing that
'It is forbidden to enter women during
menstruation'. Unfortunately the sign was
later changed to eliminate the double
entendre.

LANGUAGE

The indigenous language, Bahasa Bali (see
below), is a spoken language with various
forms based on traditional caste distinctions.
Bahasa Indonesia is the national language,
used in the education system and for all legal
and administrative purposes. It is becoming
more and more widely used, partly because
of its importance in official use, partly
because of the number of non-Balinese now
living and working on Bali, and also because
it is a polite form of language which avoids
the intricacies of the caste system.

English is spoken very widely in the
tourist areas, and usually very well (despite

a tendency to confuse 'p' and 'f' – one diving
operation offered an introductory dive and
'fool training'!). Many Balinese in the tourist
industry also have a smattering (or more) of
German, Japanese, French and/or Italian. A
few old people speak Dutch, and are often
keen to practice it. The Balinese facility for
learning and speaking foreign languages is
very impressive. Nevertheless, if you want
to travel in remote areas, and communicate
with people who are not in the tourist business, it is a good idea to learn some Bahasa
Indonesia.

Written Indonesian can be idiosyncratic,
however, and there are often inconsistent
spellings of place names. Compound names
are written as one word or two – Airsanih or
Air Sanih; Padangbai or Padang Bai, etc.
Words starting with 'Ker' sometimes lose the
'e', as in Kerobokan/Krobokan. Some Dutch
spellings remain, mainly in business names,
with 'tj' instead of the modern 'j'
(Tjampuhan/Campuan), and 'oe' instead of
'u' (Soekano/Sukarno). In this book I have
tried to use the spelling you will see on road
signs, or the sign outside a business. Even
this is not always consistent, but it's not
really a problem (except for editors).

Bahasa Bali

Bahasa Indonesia, the national language of
Indonesia, is widely used on Bali but it is not
Balinese. Balinese, or Bahasa Bali, is
another language entirely, with a completely
different vocabulary and grammar and much
more complex rules for its use. It is an
extremely difficult language for a foreigner
to come to grips with and, because it is not a
written language, there is no definitive guide
to its grammar or vocabulary, and there is
considerable variation in usage from one part
of the island to another. Bahasa Bali is not
taught in schools, and the dictionaries and
grammars that do exist are attempts to docu-
ment current or historical usage, rather than
rules for correct syntax or pronunciation.

Balinese is greatly complicated by its
caste influences. In effect, different vocabularies and grammatical structures are used,
depending on the relative social position of

the speaker, the person being spoken to, and the person being spoken about. Even traditional usage has been somewhat arbitrary because of the intricacies of the caste system. The forms of the language (or languages) have been categorised as follows:

Basa Lumrah, also called *Biasa* or Ketah, is used when talking to people of the same caste or level, and between friends and family. It is an old language of mixed origin, with words from Malayan, Polynesian and Australasian sources.

Basa Sor, or *Rendah*, is used when talking to people of a lower caste, or to people who are non-caste.

Basa Alus is used among educated people, and is derived from the Hindu-Javanese court languages of the 10th century.

Basa Madia, or *Midah*, a mixture of Basa Lumrah and Basa Alus, is used as a polite language which is used for speaking to or about strangers or people to whom one wishes to show respect.

Basa Singgih, virtually a separate language, is used to address persons of high caste, particularly in formal and religious contexts. Even Balinese are not always fluent in this language. It is based on the ancient Hindu Kawi language, and can be written using a script that resembles Sanskrit, as seen in the *lontar* books where it is inscribed on strips of palm leaf. Written Basa Singga is also seen on the signs that welcome you to, and farewell you from, almost every village on Bali.

The different vocabularies only exist for about 1000 basic words, mostly words concerned with people and their actions. Other words, an increasing proportion of the modern vocabulary, are the same regardless of relative caste levels. Also, usage is changing with the decline of the traditional caste system and modern tendencies towards democratisation and social equality. It is now common to describe the language in terms of only three forms:

Low Balinese, or *Ia*, which is equivalent to Basa Lumrah, is used between friends and family, and also when speaking to persons of equal or lower caste, or about oneself.

Polite Balinese, or *Ipun*, is equivalent to Basa Madia, used for talking to superiors or strangers, and is becoming more widespread as a sort of common language which is not so related to caste.

High Balinese, or *Ida*, is a mixture of Basa Alus and Basa Singgih, used to indicate respect for the person being addressed, or the person being spoken about.

The polite and high forms of the language often use the same word, while the low form frequently uses the same word as Bahasa Indonesia. The polite form, Basa Madia or Midah, is being used as a more egalitarian language, often combined with Bahasa Indonesia to avoid the risk of embarrassment if one does not make the correct caste distinctions. How does one Balinese know at which level to address another? Well, initially, a conversation between two strangers would commence in the high language. At some point the question of caste would be asked and then the level adjusted accordingly. But among friends a conversation is likely to be carried on in low Balinese no matter what the caste of the conversationalists.

Bahasa Bali uses very few civilities and greetings on an everyday basis. There are no equivalents for 'please' and 'thank you'. There is no usage that translates as 'Good morning' or 'Good evening', though the low Balinese *kenken kebara?* ('how are are you?'; 'how's it going?') is sometimes used. More common is *lunga kija?*, which literally means 'where are you going?' (in low, polite, and high Balinese). This is a standard greeting, as are equivalent expressions in Indonesian or English, and should be answered politely – people are not really being nosey.

Some other Balinese expressions which a visitor might encounter are listed at the top of the next page, in Low, Polite and High forms. Some of them may occur in place names. Try to pronounce them as you would a Bahasa Indonesia word of the same spelling; they are Romanised here on the same basis. Indonesian words are also given for comparison.

Numbers illustrate some further complexities (see the table at the bottom of the next page). Though only the numbers one, two and three have different words in high and low Balinese, there are different forms of

English	Indonesian	Low Balinese	Polite Balinese	High Balinese
yes	ya	nggih, saja	inggih, patut	patut
no	tidak	sing, tuara	tan	nenten, tan wenten
good, well	bagus, baik	melah	becik	becik
bad	jelek	jele, corah	corah	kaon, durmaga
sleep	tidur	pules	sirep sare	makolem
eat	makan	madaar, neda	ngajeng, nunas	ngrayunang

Note: Balinese has different words for eating by animals.

this/these	ini	ne	niki, puniki	puniki
that/those	itu	ento	punika	punika
big	besar	gede	ageng	agung
small	kecil	cenik, cerik	alit	alit
water	air	yeh	toya	tirta
stone	batu	watu	watu	batu
north	utara	kaja	kaler	lor
south	selatan	kelod	kelod	kidul
east	timur	kangin	kangin	wetan
west	barat	kauh	kulon	kulon

numbers for different contexts. The simple form is just for counting, in cardinal or ordinal numbers. The independent form is used when answering a simple 'how many?' question. The dependent form is used in conjunction with a unit of measurement – six metres, as opposed to six of something.

If you're really interested in Bahasa Bali, get a copy of *Bali – pocket dictionary* by N Shadeg (see Books, in the Facts for the Visitor chapter). It won't teach you how to speak the language, but it will give you an appreciation of its complexities. The average traveller need not worry about Balinese though. It's interesting to consider and fun to pick up a few words, but for practical travel-

ling purposes, and to communicate with Balinese, it's wiser to put your efforts into learning Indonesian.

Bahasa Indonesia

There are a vast number of local languages and dialects in Indonesia but Bahasa Indonesia (literally, 'Indonesia language') is all but identical with Malay, and is actively promoted as the one national language. Almost anywhere you go in Indonesia, including Bali, people will speak Bahasa Indonesia as well as their own local language. A good number of them will also speak English as a third language.

Number	Simple	Independent	Dependent
1	besik (L), siki (P), asiki (H)	abesik	a
2	dua (L & P), kalih (H)	dadua (L), kakalih (H)	duang (L), kalih (H)
3	telu, tiga (L), tiga (H)	tetelu (L), tetiga (H)	telung (L), tigang (H)
4	pat	patpat	petang
5	lima	lelima	limang
6	nem	nemnen	nem
7	pitu	pepitu	pitung
8	kutus	akutus	kutus (L), ulung (H)
9	sia	asia	sia (L), sangang (H)
10	dasa	adasa	dasa

Low Balinese = L, Polite Balinese = P, High Balinese = H

Like any language, Indonesian has its simplified colloquial form and its more developed literate language. For the visitor who wants to pick up enough to get by in the common language, *pasar* or 'market' Indonesian is very easy to learn. In fact it is rated as one of the simplest languages in the world as there are no tenses, no genders and often one word can convey the meaning of a whole sentence. Furthermore, it's an easy language to pronounce, with no obscure rules and none of the tonal complications that make some Asian languages very difficult. It can also be a delightfully poetic language – *hari*, for example, is day and *mata* is eye, therefore *mata hari* is the 'eye of the day', the sun!

Apart from the ease of learning a little Indonesian there's another very good reason for trying to pick up at least a handful of words and phrases – few people are as delighted with foreigners learning their language as the Indonesians. They don't criticise you if you mangle your pronunciation or tangle your grammar. They make you feel like you're an expert if you know only a dozen or so words. And bargaining seems to be a whole lot easier when you do it in their language. For a handy introduction to Indonesian, specially designed for the needs of travellers, see Lonely Planet's *Indonesia Phrasebook*. Formal courses in Indonesian for foreigners are offered at some Indonesian universities, but admission is difficult – you really need to access them through an institution in your home country. Some private tutors are available.

Pronunciation Most sounds are the same as in English although a few vowels and consonants differ. The sounds are nearly the same every time.

There is no strong stress in Indonesian, and nearly all syllables have equal emphasis, but a good approximation is to stress the second to last syllable. The main exception to the rule is the unstressed 'e' in words such as *besar* (big), pronounced be-SARRR.

Pronunciation of the vowels is as follows:

a   as in 'father'

e   as in 'bet' when unstressed, although sometimes it is hardly pronounced at all, as in the greeting *Selamat*, which sounds like 'slamat' when spoken quickly. When stressed it is like the 'a' in 'may', as in *becak* (rickshaw), pronounced 'baycha'. There is no general rule as to when the 'e' is stressed or unstressed.

i   as the 'i' sound in 'unique'

o   as in 'hot'

u   as in 'put'

There are also three vowel combinations: *ai, au* and *ua*. The sounds of the individual vowels do not change, but are simply run on by sliding from one to the other:

ai   is pronounced like 'i' as in 'line'

au   is pronounced like a drawn out 'ow' as in 'cow'

ua   at the start of a word is rather like a 'w' sound, such as *uang* which means 'money'.

The pronunciation of consonants is very straightforward. Each is pronounced consistently and most sound like English consonants, with the following exceptions:

c   is always pronounced 'ch' as in 'chair'

g   is always pronounced hard, as the 'g' in garden

ng   is pronounced like 'ng' in 'singer'

ngg   is pronounced like 'ng' in 'anger'

j   is pronounced like the 'j' in 'join'

r   is pronounced clearly and distinctly, and is slightly trilled – achieved by rolling your tongue

h   is always pronounced, except at the end of a word. It is stressed a bit more strongly than in English, as if you were sighing.

k   is pronounced like the English 'k' except when it appears at the end of the word – in which case you just stop short of actually saying the 'k'

ny   is a single sound like the beginning of 'new', before the 'oo' part of that word

General Rules Articles are not used in Indonesian – there's no 'the' or 'a' – nor is the intransitive verb 'to be' used. Thus where we would say 'the room is dirty', in Indonesian it is simply *kamar kotor* – 'room dirty'. To make a word plural, in some cases you double it – thus 'child' is *anak*, 'children' *anak anak*, but in many other cases you simply use the same singular form and the context or words such as 'many' *(banyak)* to indicate the plurality.

Probably the greatest simplification in Indonesian is that verbs are not conjugated and nor are there different forms for past, present and future tenses. Words like 'already' *(sudah)*, 'yesterday' *(kemarin)*, 'will' *(akan)* or 'tomorrow' *(besok)* indicate the tense. Sudah, 'already', is the all purpose past tense indicator. 'I eat' is *saya makan*, while 'I have already eaten' is simply *saya sudah makan*.

Except for the adjectives 'all' *(semua)*, 'many' *(banyak)* and 'a little' *(sedikit)*, adjectives follow the noun. Thus a 'big bus' is *bis besar*.

People & Pronouns Pronouns, particularly 'you', are rarely used in Indonesian. Speaking to an older man (or anyone old enough to be a father) it's common to call them *bapak* (father) or simply *pak*. Similarly, an older woman is *ibu* (mother) or simply *bu*. *Tuan* is a respectful term, like 'sir'. *Nyonya* is the equivalent for a married woman, and *nona* for an unmarried woman. *Anda* is the egalitarian form designed to overcome the plethora of words for the second person.

Greetings & Civilities
welcome
selamat datang
good morning
selamat pagi
good day
selamat siang
good afternoon
selamat sore
good night
selamat malam

good night (to someone going to bed)
selamat tidur
goodbye (to person staying)
selamat tinggal
goodbye (to person going)
selamat jalan

Early morning is *pagi-pagi*. Morning *(pagi)* extends from about 7 to 11 am. *Siang* is the middle of the day, around 11 am to 3 pm. *Sore* is from around 3 to 7 pm and *malam* really starts when it gets dark.

thank you
terima kasih
please
silakan
sorry
ma'af
excuse me
permisi
How are you?
Apa kabar?
I'm fine.
Kabar baik.
What is your name?
Siapa nama saudara?
My name is....
Nama saya....
another, one more
satu lagi
no/not/negative
tidak/bukan
good
bagus
good, fine, OK
baik

To indicate negation, *tidak* is used with verbs, adjectives and adverbs, *bukan* with nouns and pronouns.

Accommodation
one night
satu malam
one person
satu orang
sleep
tidur

bed
  tempat tidur
room
  kamar
bathroom
  kamar mandi
toilet (WC)
  way say
soap
  sabun

Useful Words & Phrases
What is this?
  Apa ini?
How much? (money)
  Berapa? (harga)
expensive
  mahal
I don't understand.
  Saya tidak mengerti.
He/she is not English.
  Dia bukkan orang Inggeris.
this/that
  ini/itu
big/small
  besar/kecil
finished
  habis
open/closed
  buka/tutup
very
  sekali

Getting Around
ticket
  karcis
bus
  bis
train
  kereta-api
ship
  kapal
bicycle
  sepeda
motorcycle
  sepeda motor
station
  setasiun

here
  disini
stop
  berhenti
north
  utara
south
  selatan
east
  timor
west
  barat
entry
  masuk
How many km?
  Berapa kilometre?
Where is...?
  Dimana ada...?
Which way?
  Kemana?
I want to go to....
  Saya mau ke....

street	*jalan*
village	*desa*
town	*kota*
bank	*bank*
post office	*kantor pos*
immigration	*imigrasi*
police station	*kantor polisi*

Emergencies
Help!
  Tolong!
Call a doctor!
  Panggil dokter!
Call an ambulance!
  Panggil ambulin!

Time
when?
  kapan?
tomorrow/yesterday
  besok/kemarin
hour
  jam
day
  hari
week
  minggu

month
bulan
year
tahun
What time?
Jam berapa?
How many hours?
Berapa jam?
7 o'clock
jam tujuh
five hours
lima jam

If you ask what time the bus is coming and you're told *jam karet* don't panic, it means 'rubber time', in other words it will come when it comes!

Monday
Hari senen
Tuesday
Hari selasa
Wednesday
Hari rabu
Thursday
Hari kamis
Friday
Hari jum'at
Saturday
Hari sabtu
Sunday
Hari minggu

Numbers

1	*satu*
2	*dua*
3	*tiga*
4	*empat*
5	*lima*
6	*enam*
7	*tujuh*
8	*delapan*
9	*sembilan*
10	*sepuluh*

A half is *setengah* which is pronounced 'stenger', ie half a kg is 'stenger kilo'. 'Approximately' is *kira-kira*. After the numbers one to 10 the 'teens' are *belas*, the 'tens' are *puluh*, the hundreds are *ratus* and the thousands *ribu*. Thus:

11	*sebelas*
12	*duabelas*
13	*tigabelas*
20	*dua puluh*
21	*dua puluh satu*
25	*dua puluh lima*
30	*tiga puluh*
99	*sembilan puluh sembilan*
100	*seratus*
150	*seratus limapuluh*
200	*dua ratus*
888	*delapan ratus delapan puluh delapan*
1000	*seribu*

Western Visitors in the '30s

Modern tourism started in Bali in the late '60s but the island had an earlier, and in many ways much more intriguing tourist boom in the 1930s. There was no international airport in those days and visitors came either by ship to Singaraja or overland through Java and across the narrow strait from Banyuwangi to Gilimanuk. A prime source of inspiration for these between-the-wars visitors was Gregor Krause's book *The Island of Bali*, published in 1920. Krause had worked in Bangli as a doctor between 1912 and 1914 and his photographs of an uninhibited lifestyle in a lush, tropical environment aroused Western interest in Bali.

By the early '30s about 100 tourists a month were visiting the island and the first concerns were already being raised about whether Balinese culture could withstand such a massive onslaught! Visitors included some talented and very interesting individuals who not only played a great part in creating the image of Bali which still persists today but also aided the rejuvenation of many dormant or stultified Balinese arts. Furthermore, they ensured their own immortality with the numerous books they wrote about their experiences on the island. Nothing has emerged from the current Bali tourist boom to match the great books of the '30s, many of which are still in print. (See the Books & Maps section in the Facts for the Visitor chapter for details.) Some of the Western visitors included:

Miguel Covarrubias (1904-1957) A Mexican artist, Miguel Covarrubias' book *Island of Bali* is still the classic introduction to the island and its culture. Born in 1904, Covarrubias visited Bali twice in the early '30s and, like many visitors at that time, Walter Spies was his introduction to the island and its people. First published in 1937 his book concisely and readably tells of Bali's history, people, community structure and culture. The book contains many illustrations and paintings by Miguel Covarrubias and photographs by his wife Rose. His later books included *Mexico South* (1950) about the Tehuantepec region of his country and *The Eagle, the Gajuar and the Serpent* (1954) about the Indians of North America. He was also involved in theatre design and printmaking.

Walter Spies (1895-1942) Walter Spies was the father figure for the cast of '30s visitors and in many ways played the largest part in interpreting Bali to them and in establishing the image of Bali which still prevails today. The son of a wealthy diplomat, Spies was born in Moscow in 1895 and raised there during the final years of Czarist rule. At the age of 15 he was sent away to school in Dresden but returned to his family just as WW I broke out. Twice in his life Spies was imprisoned due to his nationality - on the first occasion he was interned as an enemy national, first near Moscow and then in a small town in the Ural mountains.

As the upheavals of the revolution swept Russia, Spies returned to his family in Moscow, then escaped from the country in disguise. In 1919 he was in Dresden, then moved to Berlin where he joined a circle of artists, musicians and film makers. In 1923 Spies abruptly left Europe for Java in what was then the Dutch East Indies. In Bandung (Java) he played the piano in a cinema and taught music to Dutch children in Yogyakarta. He then managed the Sultan of Yogyakarta's European orchestra, learning the gamelan along the way. He first visited Bali in 1925 and two years later moved there permanently.

Befriended by the important Sukawati family he built a house at the confluence of two rivers at Campuan, west of Ubud. Today the house is part of the Campuan Hotel, overlooking Murni'sWarung. His home soon became the prime gathering point for the most famous visitors of the '30s and Spies, who involved himself in every aspect of Balinese art and culture, was an important influence on its great renaissance. His visitors included Barbara Hutton, Charlie Chaplin, Noel Coward and Margaret Mead as well as many of the Western writers and artists whose names are now firmly linked with Bali in that era. Spies also attracted a talented and growing circle of Balinese artists.

In 1932 he became curator of the Bali Museum in Denpasar and with Rudolf Bonnet and Cokorda Gede Agung Sukawati, their Balinese patron, he founded the Pita Maha artists' co-operative in 1936. He co-authored *Dance & Drama in Bali*, which was published in 1938 and he created that most Balinese of dances, the Kechak, for a visiting German film crew. Despite his comfortable life in Ubud, he moved to the remote village of Iseh in eastern Bali in 1937.

In 1938 things suddenly went very wrong for poor Spies when a puritan clampdown in Holland spread to the Dutch colony and he was arrested for homosexual activities with minors. Spies was imprisoned in Denpasar, then moved to Java where he was held in jail in Surabaya for eight months. He was no sooner released than WW II commenced and, when the Germans invaded Holland in 1940, he was arrested again, this time as an enemy alien. Spies was held in Sumatra until the Pacific war began and on 18 January 1942 Spies, with other prisoners of war, was shipped out of Sumatra on the *Van Imhoff*, bound for Ceylon (Sri Lanka). The next day the ship was bombed by Japanese aircraft and sank near the island of Nias. Walter Spies was drowned.

Spies' paintings were a curious mixture of Rousseau and surrealism, the Rousseau influence mirrored in many Balinese paintings today. Attentive visitors will catch glimpses of what he saw all over the island. However, if Spies was only a talented artist his memory would be a much fainter one today. To his ability as a painter must be added his consuming interest in all aspects of Balinese art, culture and life, as well as his role as a window to Bali for other Western visitors and as a vital force in the encouragement and growth of Balinese art. Last, but far from least, he was also a colourful and fascinating character, clearly in love with life and in headlong pursuit of all it could offer.

Colin McPhee (1900-1965) A chance hearing of a record of gamelan music compelled American musician Colin McPhee to join the stream of talented '30s visitors. Artists, writers and anthropologists all recorded their impressions of the island but as a musician McPhee's outlook was unique. *A House in Bali* was not published until 1944, long after his departure from the island, but it remains one of the best written of the Bali accounts and his tales of music and house building are often highly amusing. The house in question was in Sayan, just west of Campuan and Ubud. More recent short-term residents in Sayan have included Mick Jagger and David Bowie. The beautiful Ayung River Gorge through Sayan and Kedewatan is now the site for some of Ubud's most luxurious small hotels.

After the war, McPhee taught music at UCLA and played an important role in introducing Balinese music to the West, encouraging gamelan orchestras to visit the USA.

Rudolf Bonnet (1895-1978) Rudolf Bonnet was a Dutch artist who, along with Walter Spies, played a major role in the development of Balinese art in the mid-30s. Bonnet arrived in Bali in 1929, two years after Spies, and immediately contacted him. In 1936 he was one of the principal forces behind the foundation of the Pita Maha artist's co-operative, and his influence on Balinese art to this day is very clear. Where Spies' work was often mystical, Bonnet's work concentrated on the human form and everyday Balinese life. To this day the numerous classical Balinese paintings with their themes of markets, cockfights and other aspects of day-to-day existence are all indebted to Bonnet.

Bonnet was imprisoned in Sulawesi by the Japanese during WW II and returned to Bali in the '50s to plan the Puri Lukisan Museum in Ubud. Foreigners, even one as in love with Bali as Bonnet, were not always welcome in Indonesia at this time and he left the island, but returned in 1973 to help establish the museum's permanent collection. He died in 1978, on a brief return visit to Holland. That same year brought the deaths of Cokorda Gede Agung Sukawati, the Ubud patron of both Bonnet and Spies, and Gusti Nyoman Lempad, the Balinese artist who had also played a prime role in the establishment of the Pita Maha. Bonnet's ashes were returned to his beloved Bali to be scattered at the 1979 cremation of Cokorda Gede Agung.

K'tut Tantri A woman of many aliases K'tut Tantri was still Vannine Walker, or perhaps it was Muriel Pearson, when she breezed in from Hollywood in 1932. She was born on the Isle of Man and grew up there and in Scotland before working as a journalist in Hollywood. The film *Bali, The Last Paradise* had served as the inspiration to send her to Bali, where she dyed her red hair black (only demons have red hair) and was befriended by the prince of the kingdom of Bangli.

She teamed up with Robert Koke to open the Kuta Beach Hotel in 1936, the first hotel at Kuta Beach. Later she fell out with the Kokes and established her own hotel, the Sound of the Sea. She stayed on when war swept into the archipelago, was imprisoned by the Japanese, survived long periods of solitary confinement during the war and then worked for the Indonesian Republicans in their postwar struggle against the Dutch. As Surabaya Sue she broadcast from Surabaya in support of their cause. Her book *Revolt in Paradise* (written as K'tut Tantri) was published in 1960 but those searching for more insights into Bali and its characters should note that the names not only of the people but also the villages have been changed. She was also known as Meng or Manx, from her childhood on the Isle of Man.

Robert & Louise Koke In 1936 Americans Robert Koke and Louise Garret arrived in Bali as part of a long trip through South-East Asia. They fell in love with the island and Kuta Beach and soon established the Kuta Beach Hotel, at first in partnership with K'tut Tantri although their accounts of the hotel differ widely!

Although the Dutch insisted that the hotel was nothing more than a few 'dirty native huts' it was an instant hit and Bali's '30s tourist boom ensured that it was always full. The rooms were a series of individual thatched-roof cottages, remarkably like the cottage-style hotels which are still popular in Bali today. Robert Koke, who learnt to surf in Hawaii, can also claim the honour of introducing surfing to Bali (the hotel logo includes a surfer). Boards were provided for use by hotel guests.

The Koke's success continued until the Japanese entry into the war. The pair made a last-minute escape from Bali, and when Robert Koke visited Bali just after the war, only traces of the hotel's foundations remained. In 1955 a new Kuta Beach Hotel was opened, the first postwar hotel at Kuta and close to the site of its original namesake. Robert Koke retired from a long career with the CIA in the '70s and in 1987 Louise Koke's long-forgotten story of their hotel was published as *Our Hotel in Bali*, illustrated with her incisive sketches and her husband's excellent photographs.

Other Western Visitors Numerous other Western personages made pilgrimages to Bali in the '30s. Charlie Chaplin and Noel Coward were the equivalents of today's rock star visitors, adding a touch of glamour to Bali as a destination.

Others played their part in chronicling the period - writers like Hickman Powell, whose book *The Last Paradise* was published in 1930 (the current paperback edition carries a publisher's note that the copyright owner is untraceable), and German author Vicki Baum, whose book *A Tale from Bali*, a fictionalised account of the puputan of 1906, is still in print.

Colin McPhee's wife Jane Belo does not even make a fleeting appearance in her husband's book *A House in Bali*, but in fact she was a talented anthropologist who also played a key role in interpreting Bali in the '30s. Margaret Mead also visited and wrote about Bali at this time. Another visitor from the '30s was the American dancer Katherine Mershon.

Artists in Postwar Bali

Bali's postwar visitors have never matched that brilliant period of the '30s when the island seemed to be packed with talented Western residents, all busy painting, composing or scribbling down their unique experiences. The war brought the artistic renaissance of the '30s to a juddering halt and it was not until the '50s that a new artistic impetus arrived, an impetus which has to some extent been waylaid by the spawning of 'mass-art' by mass tourism since the '70s.

While the visitors of the '30s ranged from artists and anthropologists to musicians and writers, more recent noted visitors have almost all been artists. Plenty of rock stars have been short-term visitors and *A House in Bali* has been recreated thousands of times with Australian or European vacation homes but there have been no writers to hold the faintest candle to the earlier chroniclers.

Arie Smit (1916-) Dutch painter Arie Smit was born in 1916 and was working as an artist in the colonial topographical service in Batavia, modern day Jakarta, when the Pacific war commenced. Captured by the Japanese he was taken first to Singapore and then to Thailand where he survived the infamous labour camps building the railway up to the Burmese border crossing - the 'Bridge on the River Kwai'.

Smit returned to Indonesia after the war and taught art in Bandung before moving to Bali to live as an artist from 1956. Smit's paintings have been exhibited in Bali and elsewhere in South-East Asia but his name will go down in the history books as the inspiration for the Young Artists movement. Arie Smit still lives in Ubud in Bali.

Theo Meier (1908-1982) A Swiss artist, Meier first visited Bali in 1936 and lived in Sanur before the war. Much of his prewar work was lost when the Japanese destroyed his Sanur studio but he returned to Bali after the war and lived for some time in Iseh in the house that Spies had established just before the war. In 1957 he moved to Chiang Mai in Thailand, where he lived until his death in 1982, although he was a frequent visitor to Bali.

Le Meyeur Belgian-born Le Mayeur moved to Bali in 1932 and lived there until his death in 1958.

Le Mayeur succeeded in living the complete Balinese fantasy: marrying Ni Polok, a beautiful *legong* dancer. His fine house at Sanur is now preserved as a museum, in the shadow of the Hotel Bali Beach.

Donald Friend (1915-1990) Peripatetic Australian artist Donald Friend travelled to Bali in 1966 and, with occasional interruptions, spent most of his time there until he returned to Australia in 1977. He produced some of his finest work in Bali.

Antonio Blanco (1926-) Manila-born Spanish artist Antonio Blanco married a Balinese woman and moved to Bali in the late '50s. His house, near the river confluence in Campuan, is where he paints and where he lives the life of a colourful (and comfortable) artist. Visitors who pay the small admission price to enter his fine home often get a chance to hear his views on life, the universe and everything.

Han Snel (1925-) Dutch artist Han Snel was a conscript soldier sent to recapture the Dutch East Indies after the war. He deserted, took Indonesian citizenship and has lived in Bali since the 1950s, running one of Ubud's finest hotels with his Balinese wife. ■

Arts & Crafts

Arts & Crafts

Craft shop in Bali (JL)

Paintings outside art gallery, Ubud (TW)

An offering to the gods on the beach at
Rambut Siwi (GA)

The richness of Bali's arts & crafts has its origins in the fertility of the land and the extraordinary productivity of its agriculture. An abundance of food can be produced with a small input of labour, leaving plenty of time for cultural activities. Appropriately, the purest forms of Balinese art are the depictions of Dewi Sri, the rice goddess, made from dried and folded strips of palm leaf. These are used as offerings to ensure the fertility of the rice fields. Many of the more highly developed art forms actually have their origins in Java, India and elsewhere.

On Lombok, where periodic droughts and famine beset the countryside, there are relatively few objects made for purely decorative purposes, though functional objects show a high degree of skill and artisanship. Fine examples of Lombok's weaving, basketware and pottery are highly valued by collectors.

Bali

Every Balinese is an artist and craftsperson and, until the tourist invasion, painting or carving was simply an everyday part of life. Bali had no art galleries or craft shops in those days – what was produced went into temples or was used for festivals. It's a different story now with hundreds, even thousands, of galleries and craft shops in every possible place a tourist might pass. The real problem with Balinese art and craft today is that there is simply too much of it. You can't turn around without tripping over more carved *garudas* (legendary gigantic birds), and in the galleries there are so many paintings that they're stacked up in piles on the floor.

Unfortunately, much of this work is rubbish, churned out quickly for people who want a cheap souvenir. There is still much beautiful work produced, but you have to sort through a lot of junk to find it. Part of the problem is that Balinese art has always been something that is produced today, deteriorates tomorrow, is worn out the next day and thrown away the day after. As a result, very little you see will be old, and even less antique.

Indeed, it's the everyday, disposable crafts which are probably the most surprising on Bali. Even the simplest activities are carried out with care, precision and the Balinese artistic flair. Just glance at those little offering trays placed on the ground for the spirits every morning – each one a throwaway work of art. Look at the temple offerings, the artistically stacked pyramids of fruit or other beautifully decorated foods. Look for the *lamaks*, long woven palm leaf strips used as decorations in festivals and celebrations or the stylised female figures known as *cili*, which are representations of Dewi Sri. See the intricately carved coconut-shell wall hangings or, at funerals, simply marvel at the care and energy that goes into constructing huge funeral towers and exotic sarcophagi, all of which will soon go up in flames. The Balinese were always creators rather than preservers and this has never really been a problem because there is no shortage of time to be spent simply creating more works of art.

Temple offerings, Sempidi (GA)

The repetition that is so characteristic of Balinese arts and crafts is partly motivated by respect and admiration for traditional values and a need to feel a part of society, and partly by the economic benefits of mass-production. Yet, whatever the object – be it a frog with a leaf, a barong mask, or a cartoon figure – the end product will always be distinctly Balinese.

To understand the crafts of Bali it's important to know the crafts of Java, as the cultural and trading relationship between the two islands has always been strong. The ceremonial dagger (kris), so important in a Balinese family, will often have been made in Java. Most of the sarongs that are worn for important ceremonies are made in central Java, except for the ikat sarongs from Gianyar. Similarly, Java is the main supplier of puppets and metalwork items, including sacred images.

In many ways, Bali is a showroom for all the crafts of Indonesia. A typical tourist shop will sell puppets and batiks from Java, *ikat* garments from Sumba, Sawa and Flores, and textiles and woodcarvings from Bali, Lombok and Kalimantan. ■

Stylised depiction of Dewi Sri, rice goddess

Preparing cremation bulls, Peliatan (GA)

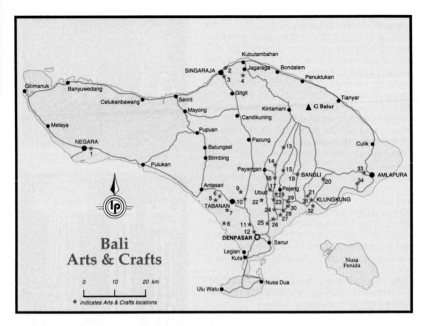

Bali Arts & Crafts

★ indicates Arts & Crafts locations

1 Jembrana – Bamboo Gamelan
2 Banyuning – Pottery
3 Beratan – Silver Work & Weaving
4 Sawan – Gamelan Instruments
5 Penarukun – Carving
6 Krambitan – Painting
7 Pejaten – Pottery
8 Pataen – Pottery
9 Belayu – Songket Weaving
10 Mengwi – Weaving
11 Sempidi – Ceramics & Tiles
12 Ubung – Pottery
13 Jati – Woodcarving
14 Pujung – Woodcarving
15 Tampaksiring – Coconut & Bone Carving, Fashion Jewellery
16 Tegallalang – Woodcarving
17 Ubud – Painting & Woodcarving
18 Bedulu – Painting (Classical Calendars)

19 Bangli – Coconut & Bone Carving, Silver Work
20 Sideman – Weaving
21 Tihingan – Gongs
22 Tohpati – Painting
23 Mas – Wood & Mask Carving
24 Batuan – Basketware & Painting
25 Batubulan – Stone Carving
26 Celuk – Silver & Gold Work
27 Puaya – Mask Carving & Puppet Making
28 Blahbatuh – Gongs & Gamelan
29 Gianyar – Weaving
30 Bona – Basketware
31 Klungkung – Painting (Classical Calendars)
32 Kamasan – Painting, Silver & Gold Work
33 Budakaling – Silver & Gold Work
34 Tenganan – Double Ikat Weaving (Gringsing)

ARCHITECTURE & SCULPTURE
Of all the Balinese arts it's said that architecture and sculpture have been the least affected by Western influence and the tourist boom – nobody's taking temples home and your average stone statue can't be rolled up and stuffed in your bag too easily. Architecture and sculpture are inextricably bound together – a temple gateway is not just put up, every square cm of it is intricately carved and a diminishing series of demon faces is placed above it as protection. Even then it's not finished without a couple of stone statues to act as guardians. Thus architecture becomes sculpture and sculpture becomes architecture.

Architecture
Although Balinese houses are often attractive places – due in large part to their beautiful gardens – they've never been lavished with the architectural attention reserved for *puras* (temples) and *puris* (palaces). Household layout is more or less standardised (see The Household section in the Facts about Bali chapter) and palaces are not exactly regular constructions these days, although some of the flashy new hotels are making considerable use of traditional architectural and sculptural features – the Nusa Dua Beach Hotel at Nusa Dua is a good example. Basically, however, it's in the temples where you'll find traditional Balinese architecture and sculpture.

Temples are designed to set rules and formulae (for details see the Temples section in the Facts about Bali chapter). Sculpture serves as an adjunct, a finishing touch, to these design guidelines and in small or less important temples the sculpture may be limited or even nonexistent. In other temples, particularly some of the exuberantly detailed temples of northern Bali, the sculpture may be almost overwhelming in its intricacy and interest.

Sculpture
Sculpture often appears in a number of set places in temples. Door guardians – representations of legendary figures like Arjuna or other protective personalities – flank the steps to the gateway. Similar figures are also often seen at both ends of bridges. Above the main entrance to a temple Kala's monstrous face often peers out, sometimes a number of times – his hands reaching out beside his head to catch any evil spirits foolish enough to try to sneak in. Else-

Pura Dalem, Sidan (JL)

Kala, Pura Luhur, Rambut Siwi (TW)

Stone carvings, Batubulan (TW)

Top Left: Stone-carved Singa (winged lion) (JL)
Top Right: Stone Ganesh (GB)
Bottom: Stone carver, Batubulan (JL)

where other sculptures make regular appearances – the front of a *pura dalem* (temple of the dead) will often feature prominently placed images of the *rangda* (witch) while sculptured panels may show the horrors that await evildoers in the afterlife. Fine stonework, often on a monumental scale, is also evident in the construction of new five-star hotels.

Batubulan, on the main highway from Denpasar to Gianyar, is a major stone-carving centre. Stone figures, varying in height from 25 cm to two metres, line both sides of the street. Stone craftsmen can be seen in action in the many workshops here as well as in an area north of the main road, around Karang.

Stone carving is the most durable art form. Most of the local work is made from a soft sandstone that, when newly worked, can be mistaken for cast cement. It can be scratched with a finger nail and is not particularly strong or dense. With age and exposure to the elements, the outer surface becomes tougher and darker.

Sculpture on Bali is still very much for local consumption rather than, as with painting or woodcarving, for visitors to take home. Yet, although it's less affected by foreign influence than other art forms, many modern trends can still be seen and sculptors are happy to work on new and non-traditional themes. Japanese-style stone lanterns are currently popular.

Young sculptors, Batubulan (TW)

Buying Sculpture

Balinese stone is surprisingly light and it's not at all out of the realms of possibility to bring a friendly stone demon back with you in your airline baggage. A typical temple door guardian weighs around 10 kg. The stone, however, is very fragile so packing must be done carefully if you're going to get it home without damage. Some of the Batubulan workshops will pack figures quickly and expertly, usually with shredded paper. There are also many capable packing and forwarding agents, although bear in mind that shipping costs will almost certainly be more than the cost of the article. A typical Balinese stone door guardian, however, can be bought for around US$20 (including packaging) with a little negotiation. It'll scare the hell out of your neighbour's garden gnomes! ■

Contemporary stone carving (JL)

Ceiling of the Kertha Gosa, Klungkung
(TW)

PAINTING

Of the various art forms popular on Bali, painting is probably the one most influenced by Western ideas and Western demand. Prior to the arrival of Western artists after WW I, painting was, like other Balinese art, primarily for temple and palace decoration. The influence of Western artists not only expanded it beyond these limited horizons, it also showed the way to whole new subject areas and, possibly most important of all, gave the artists new materials to work with.

Before the '30s

Until the arrival of the Western artists, Balinese painting was strictly limited to three basic kinds – *langse*, *iders-iders* and calendars. Langse are large rectangular decorative hangings used in palaces or temples. Iders-iders are scroll paintings hung along the eaves of temples. The calendars pictorially represent the days of the month, showing the auspicious days.

Paintings were almost always executed in *wayang* style – that is, they were imitative of *wayang kulit* (leather shadow puppets) with the figures almost always shown either in profile or three-quarters view.

'Wrongdoers get their just deserts', ceiling detail, Kertha Gosa, Klungkung (TW)

Figures in classical paintings were also like the wayang figures. The *alus* or 'refined' heroes were narrow and elongated and richly dressed while their *kasar* or 'rough' opponents were short, squat and ugly. The paintings were generally in a narrative style, rather like a comic strip, with a series of panels telling a story. Even the colours artists could use were strictly limited to a set list of shades.

At one time, classical paintings were all made on cotton cloth hand woven only on the island of Nusa Penida. Today, modern cloth is used although it is still coated with a rice-flour paste and burnished with a shell. Traditional natural colours (made from soot, clay, pig's bones and other such ingredients) are no longer employed either; today the paint is all modern oil and acrylic. Nevertheless, the final burnishing gives an aged look even to the new paints and these pictures are known as *lukisan antik* or 'antique paintings'.

Paintings are still done in these traditional styles – Klungkung is a centre for the wayang style of painting and you can see a fine original example of the style in the painted ceiling of the Kertha Gosa (Hall of Justice) in Klungkung. The village of Kamasan, a few km south of Klungkung, is the place where many of these paintings are actually produced. Krambitan, near Tabanan, to the north-west of Denpasar, is another centre for classical painting.

Classical paintings today may depict scenes from Balinese mythology or the Hindu epics and may still show action in comic-strip style. Balinese calendars are still used to set dates and predict the future, although today most of them are painted for tourists. There are two types – the simpler yellow-coloured calendars from Bedulu, near Ubud, and the more complex classical calendars from Klungkung.

The Pita Maha

Walter Spies and Rudolf Bonnet were the Western artists who turned Balinese artists around in the '30s. (See the Western Visitors in the '30s section in the Facts about Bali chapter for more information.) At that time painting was in a serious decline: painting styles had become stagnant and since few commissions were forthcoming from palaces and temples, painting was virtually dying out as an art form.

Bonnet and Spies, with their patron Cokorda Gede Agung Sukawati, formed the Pita Maha

Cartoon-style painting with narrative panels (GB)

Young Artist painting by I Nyoman Dana (TW)

Rural scene by I Dab Alit, Taman, Ubud (GB)

Classical three-quarter view figure (GB)

Young Artist painting by M D Raju,
Penestanan (GB)

Rural scene by DW MD Dharmadi,
Batuan (GB)

(literally 'great vitality'), to encourage painting as an art form and to find a market for the best paintings. The group had more than 100 members at its peak in the 1930s.

The changes Bonnet and Spies inspired were revolutionary – suddenly Balinese artists started painting single scenes instead of narrative tales and using everyday life rather than romantic legends as their themes. Paintings influenced by the Pita Maha association are typically scenes of everyday life – harvesting rice, bartering in the market, watching a cockfight, presenting offerings at a temple or preparing a cremation.

Batuan is a noted painting centre which came under the influence of the Pita Maha at an early stage. Batuan painters produced dynamic black-ink drawings, good examples of which can be seen at Ubud's Puri Lukisan Museum. The style is noted for its inclusion of some very modern elements, such as sea scenes with the odd windsurfer.

Not only the themes changed, the actual way of painting also altered. More modern paint and materials were used and the stiff formal poses of old gave way to realistic three-dimensional representations. Even more importantly, pictures were painted for their own sake – not as something to cover a space in a palace or temple. The idea of a painting being something you could do by itself (and for which there might be a market!) was wholly new.

In one way, however, the style remained unchanged – Balinese paintings were packed with detail, every spare corner of the picture was filled in. A painted Balinese forest has branches and leaves reaching out to fill every tiny space and is inhabited by a whole zoo of creatures. For many of the new artists, idyllic rural scenes from some Balinese Arcadia or energetic festival scenes were the order of the day. Others painted engagingly stylised animals and fish. You can see fine examples of these new styles at the Puri Lukisan Museum in Ubud and, of course, find them in all the galleries and art shops.

The new artistic enthusiasm was short-lived, however, for WW II interrupted and then in the '50s and '60s Indonesia was wracked by internal turmoil and confusion. The new styles degenerated into stale copies of the few original spirits, with one exception: the development of the Young Artists style.

The Young Artists

Dutch painter Arie Smit survived imprisonment by the Japanese during WW II and arrived on Bali in 1956. One day while painting in Penestanan, just outside Ubud, he noticed a young boy drawing in the dirt and wondered what he would produce if he had proper equipment to paint with. The story is regularly told of how the lad's father would not allow him to take up painting until Smit offered to fund somebody else to watch the family's flock of ducks.

Painter in Ubud (TW)

Other 'young artists' from Penestanan soon joined that first pupil, I Nyoman Cakra, but Arie Smit did not actively teach them. He simply provided the equipment and the encouragement and unleashed what was clearly a strong natural talent. An engaging new naive style quickly developed, as typically Balinese rural scenes were painted in brilliant technicolour.

The style quickly caught on and is today one of the staples of Balinese tourist art. Of course not all the artists are young boys any more, and the style is also known as work by 'peasant painters'. I Nyoman Cakra, the original Young Artist, still lives in Penestanan, still paints and cheerfully admits that he owes it all to Smit.

Painter in Ubud (PW)

Modern Painting

There are a relatively small number of creative original painters on Bali today, and an enormous number of imitators who produce copies, or near copies, in well-established styles. Many of these imitative works are nevertheless very well executed and attractive pieces. Originality is not considered as important in Balinese art as it is in the West. A painting is esteemed not for being new and unique but for taking a well-worn and popular idea and making a good reproduction of it.

One constant factor in Balinese painting is that it is almost always 'planned' – ie, drawn out and refined before any paint is applied. When the actual painting does take place it can often be done in an almost 'colour by number' manner. Indeed, some name artists will simply draw out the design, decide the colours and then employ apprentices to actually apply the paint. This once again leads to the mass production of remarkably similar themes which is so characteristic of Balinese art.

Unfortunately, much of the painting today is churned out for the tourist market and much of that market is extremely undiscriminating about

Festival scene by A A Rai, Ubud (TW)

Batuan painting by I Made Nyana (TW)

Gallery in Ubud (TW)

Barong dancer (GB)

what it buys. Thus the shops are packed full of paintings in the various popular styles – some of them quite good, a few of them really excellent, many of them uniformly alike and uniformly poor in quality. Even worse, many artists have turned to producing paintings purely attuned to tourist tastes and with nothing Balinese about them. It's rare to see anything really new – most painters aim for safety and that means painting what tourists will buy.

Buying Paintings

If you want to buy wisely then try to learn a little about Balinese painting before making a purchase. Visit the galleries and the Neka and Puri Lukisan museums in Ubud to see some of the best of Balinese art as well as some of the European influences that have shaped it. Look at some books on Balinese art. An excellent short introduction to the subject is *Balinese Paintings* by A A M Djelantik (Images in Asia series, Oxford University Press, Singapore, 1986). *The Development of Painting in Bali* is a handy little booklet published by the Museum Neka which describes the various styles, and illustrates them with paintings from the Neka collection.

Finally, and most importantly, simply look at paintings. Once you've visited the two Ubud museums and seen some of the best work and examples of paintings that set the styles, visit other galleries. The Neka Gallery in Padangtegal near Ubud (not to be confused with the Museum Neka where the art is not for sale), the Agung Rai Gallery in Peliatan and the Sanggraha Kriya Asta Arts Centre in Tohpati, on the Ubud side of Denpasar, are excellent places to view high-quality work and get an idea of prices. There are many other galleries and you'll soon start to appreciate what's good and what isn't. If it looks good and you like it, then buy it.

Paintings can be transported in the cardboard tubes from rolls of fabric, as supplied to drapers. Otherwise you can buy plastic tubes from hardware stores. If you do buy a painting, and can handle the additional weight, consider taking a frame back as well. These are often elaborately carved and works of art in themselves, and are very cheap, especially compared to framing costs in the West. ■

WOODCARVING

Like painting, woodcarving has undergone a major transformation over the past 50 years, from being a decorative craft to something done for its own sake. Prior to this change in attitude, woodcarving was chiefly architectural decoration – on carved doors or columns for example – or of figures such as garudas or demons with a protective or symbolic nature. There were also decorative carvings on minor functional objects, such as bottle stoppers, and the carved wooden masks used in Balinese dance and theatre. Yet, as with painting, it was the same demand from outside which inspired new carving subjects and styles. It was also some of the same Western artists who served as the inspiration.

As with the new painting styles, Ubud was a centre for the revolution in woodcarving. Some carvers started producing highly stylised and elongated figures, and the wood was sometimes left with its natural finish rather than being painted. Others carved delightful animal figures, some totally realistic, others complete caricatures. Other styles and trends developed: whole tree trunks carved into ghostly, intertwined 'totem poles'; and curiously exaggerated and distorted figures.

Any visitor to Bali is likely to be exposed to woodcarving in all its forms, whether it be the traditional ornate carved double doors seen in houses and losmen, the carved figures of gods carried in processions and seen in temples, or the myriad carved items in craft shops.

Almost all carving is of local woods, including *belalu*, a quick-growing light wood, and the stronger fruit timbers such as jackfruit wood. Ebony from Sulawesi has been used for the last 30 years or so.

Woodcarving is a craft practised throughout Bali. Tegallalang and Jati, on the road from Ubud to Batur, are noted woodcarving centres. Many workshops line the road east of Peliatan, near Ubud, to Goa Gajah. The route from Mas, through Peliatan, Petulu and up the scenic slope to Pujung, is also a centre for family-based workshops; listen for the tapping sound of the carvers' mallets. Carvers hold the timber steady with their feet while they work and groups of children are often given the task of painting the finished articles. Despite the gentle pace of this work, the volume and repetition can be daunting. You may pass a whole village producing nothing but fruit

Detail from carved temple doors, Sanur
(TS)

Woodcarver, Celuk (SG)

Wooden dragon (GB)

Carved banana leaves & fruit (JL)

replicas, while another family may only carve garuda images.

An attempt to separate traditional and foreign influences is difficult. Like any craftspeople, the Balinese are keen observers of the outside world and have, it seems, always incorporated and adapted foreign themes in their work. Balinese carvings of religious figures may be based on Hindu mythology, but are very different from the same figures made in India. An Indian Ganesh is mostly a well-rounded, gentle elephant man, while the Balinese version bristles with intense emotion.

Carving, however, suffers from similar problems to painting in that there's an overwhelming emphasis on what sells, with the successful subjects mimicked by every carver on the block. 'Not another technicolour garuda' could easily be the tourist's lament. Still, there's always something interesting to see, the technical skill is high and the Balinese sense of humour often shines through – a frog clutches a large leaf as an umbrella, or a weird demon on the side of a wooden bell clasps his hands over his ears. You'll even find perfect replicas of every tropical fruit under the Balinese sun, including a complete, life-size banana tree!

1: Painted carvings (GB)
2: Woodcarving painter (TW)
3: Carved wooden naga (dragon); wheeled toys with an Indian influence(GB)
4: Wooden figure 'praying for prosperity', Celuk (TS)
5: Painting woodcarvings, Ubud (JL)

Wooden masks for sale (JL)

Detail of wall frieze (Tass)

Unpainted woodcarvings (GB)

Mask Carving

Mask making is a specialised form of woodcarving, and only experts carve the masks used in so many of Bali's theatre and dance performances. A particularly high level of skill is needed to create the 30 or 40 masks used in the Topeng dance. The mask maker must know the movements that each topeng performer makes so that the character can be shown by the mask.

Other Balinese masks, such as the barong and rangda, are brightly painted and decorated with real hair, enormous teeth and bulging eyes.

Mas is recognised as the mask-carving centre of Bali. The small village of Puaya, near Sukawati, also specialises in mask making. The Bali Museum in Denpasar has a good mask collection and is a good place to visit to get an idea of styles before buying anything from the craft shops.

Buying Woodcarvings

There are few fixed prices for carved wooden items. Many factors determine costs, including the type of wood used, the novelty of the item and your powers of negotiation. If your idea is to send items home, packing and shipping costs can easily be more than the cost of the article. The simplest small carving can be found for 1000 rp or even less, while many good pieces can be bought for 30,000 rp, and there's no upper limit. If you're shopping around, you may see the same article vary in price by anything from 10% to 1000%!

Note that items made from harder woods may have an excess of moisture from Bali's tropical climate and in drier environments, the wood may shrink and crack. ■

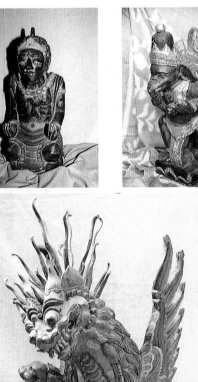

1	4	5
2		6
3		

1: Hindu-influenced
   carving (GB)
2: Balinese monkey
   god (GB)

3: Devil woman from
   Borneo (GB)
4: Balinese god (GB)
5: Ganesh (GB)

6: Singa (GB)

1: Lambada, Lambretta, rooster etc (GB)
2: Traditional frog mask, fruit, duck & bike (GB)
3: Wooden lilies (GB)
4: Woodcarver's shop (TW)
5: Carved banana tree (GB)

1	5
2	6
3	7
4	

1: Topeng masks (GB)
2: Lombok masks (GB)
3: Topeng mask (GB)
4: Rangda mask (TW)

5: Topeng mask (GB)
6: Rangda mask (GB)
7: Barong mask (TW)

1: Flying dragon mobile (GB)
2: Bat mobile (Tass)
3: Flying frog mobiles (GB)
4: Balinese fisherman statue (GB)

JEWELLERY

Bali, along with Thailand and Mexico, is a major producer of world fashion jewellery and variations on the same designs are common to all three centres. The Balinese work is nearly always hand-constructed, rarely involving casting techniques, and uses imported silver. Balinese silver, mined near Singaraja, is also used for filigree and other traditional silver work.

Celuk has always been the village associated with silversmithing. The large shops that line the road into Celuk have imposing, bus-sized driveways and slick credit-card facilities. If you want to see the 'real' Celuk, walk about a km east of the main road to visit the family workshops. Other silver-work centres include Kamasan, near Klungkung in eastern Bali and Beratan, south of Singaraja, in northern Bali.

Jewellery can be purchased ready-made, or made-to-order – there's a wide range of earrings, bracelets and rings available, some using gemstones imported from all over the world. Different design influences can be detected from African patterning to the New Age preoccupation with dolphins and healing crystals. Patriot-missile pendants are also available! Prices start at around 1000 rp for silver stud earrings.

You'll find many jewellery workshops in other areas around Ubud. Tampaksiring, north-east of Ubud, has long been a centre for cheaper styles of fashion jewellery. Brightly painted, carved wooden earrings are popular and cheap, at around 800 rp. One of the more expensive jewellers producing modern European designs is Purpa, on Monkey Forest Rd, Ubud. Stop when you see the marble mansion and a prominent display of new cars. Many of the large exporters, including Mirah and Jonathon Jewellers, have outlets on the Legian and Kuta Beach roads. ■

Rings, bracelets and a Bali suntan (GB)

Balinese bracelet (Tass)

Silver worker (JL)

Balinese ikat from Gianyar (GB)

FABRICS & WEAVING

Weaving is a popular craft and the standard woven Balinese sarong is an attractive workaday item. The sarong is not only a comfortable article of clothing but can serve as a sheet, a towel and a multitude of other uses. The more elegant fabrics, like *endek* and *songket* are necessary for special occasions – it is a religious obligation to look one's best at a temple ceremony. Dress for these occasions is a simple shirt or blouse, a sarong, and a *kain*, a separate length of cloth wound tightly around the hips over the sarong. For more formal occasions, the blouse is replaced by a length of songket wrapped around a woman's chest. These chest cloths are called *kamben*. The styles of wearing the sarong are different for men and women.

Gianyar, in eastern Bali, is a major textile centre with a number of factories where you can watch sarongs being woven; a complete sarong takes about six hours to make. You can buy direct from the factories, although prices can be inflated in the tourist season. Any market will have a good range of textiles, if you know how to bargain.

Batik sold in Bali (PW)

Left and right: Sarongs (GB)
Bottom: Weaving stall in Tenganan, Bali (PW)

Balinese cloth bags (GB)

Bags made from cloth, leather and
rattan (GB)

Batik

Traditional batik sarongs are handmade in central Java. The dyeing process has been adapted by the Balinese to produce brightly coloured and patterned fabrics for clothing, etc, although batik is not an indigenous Balinese technique. Watch out for 'batik' fabric which has actually been screen-printed in factories. The colours in this are washed out compared to the rich colour of real batik cloth, and the pattern is often only on one side (in true batik cloth, the dye penetrates to colour both sides).

Ikat

In various places in Indonesia you'll find material woven by the complex *ikat* process where the pattern is dyed into the threads *before* the material is woven. Ikat usually involves pre-dyeing either the warp threads, those stretched on the loom, or the weft threads, those which are woven across the warp. The usual Balinese technique, in which the weft threads are pre-dyed is known as *endek*. The resulting pattern is geometric and slightly wavy, like a badly tuned TV. Its beauty depends on the complexity of the pattern and the

Ikat & batik cloth camera bags, passport wallets & cap (GB)

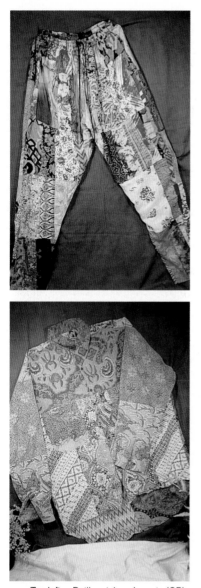

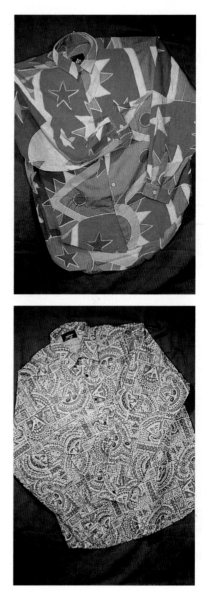

Top left: Batik patchwork pants (GB)
Top right: Screen-printed shirt (GB)
Bottom left: 'Antique' batik shirt (GB)
Bottom right: Batik shirt (GB)

Weaving Songket, Beratan (JL)

Woven fabrics worn in a procession,
Tegalalang (GA)

harmonious blending of colours. Typically the pattern is made in colours of similar tone – blues and greens; reds and browns; yellows, reds and orange. Ikat sarongs and kain are not everyday wear, but they are not for strictly formal occasions either.

Gringsing

In the Bali Aga village of Tenganan, in eastern Bali, a double-ikat process is used in which both the warp *and* weft are pre-dyed. Called *gringsing* (or geringsing), this complex and extremely time-consuming process is practised nowhere else in Indonesia. Typical colours are red, brown, yellow and deep purple. The dyes used are obtained from natural sources, and some of the colours can take years of mixing and ageing. The dyes also weaken the cotton fabric, so old examples of gringsing are extremely rare.

Songket

A more elaborate material, for ceremonial and other important uses, songket cloth has gold or silver threads woven into the tapestry-like material and motifs include birds, butterflies, leaves and flowers. Songket material is used for kamben, kain, and sarongs worn exclusively for ceremonial occasions. Belayu, a small village in south-western Bali between Mengwi and Marga, is a centre for songket weaving. Songket is also woven near Singaraja.

Prada

Another technique for producing very decorative fabrics for special occasions, *prada* involves the application of gold leaf, or gold or silver paint or thread to the surface of a finished material. Motifs are similar to those used in songket. The result is not washable, so prada is reserved for kain, which are worn over the top of a sarong. ■

KRIS

Often with an ornate, jewel-studded handle and sinister-looking wavy blade, the kris is the traditional and ceremonial dagger of Bali and Indonesia. Although a Balinese-made kris is slightly larger and more elaborate than one from Java, they are almost exactly the same shape. A kris can be the most important of family heirlooms, a symbol of prestige and honour. It is supposed to have great spiritual power and an important kris is thought to send out magical energy waves requiring great care in its handling and use. Even making a kris requires careful preparation, as does anything on Bali which involves working with the forces of magic. ■

Balinese kris & scabbard (Tass)

WAYANG KULIT

Like krises, wayang kulit figures are also magical items since the shadow plays are again part of the eternal battle between good and evil. The intricate lace figures are carefully cut from buffalo hide with a sharp, chisel-like stylus and then painted. Although wayang kulit performances usually take place at night there are sometimes daytime temple performances, where the figures are manipulated without a screen. The figures are completely traditional: no variation is made from the standard list of characters and their standardised appearance. (For more details, see the Wayang Kulit section in the Facts about Bali chapter.)

Puppets are made in the village of Puaya, near Sukawati, south of Ubud, and in Peliatan, near Ubud. ■

CERAMICS

Nearly all local pottery is made from low-fired terracotta. If you wish to see potters at work, visit the village of Pataen near Tanah Lot. Kapal and Ubung, north of Denpasar, are also pottery centres.

Most styles are very ornate, even for functional items such as vases, flasks, ash trays and lamp bases. Pejaten, near Tabanan, also has a number of pottery workshops producing small ceramic figures and glazed ornamental roof tiles. ■

Ceramic lantern (GB)

Playing gamelan, Ubud (TS)

Ceramic lanterns (GB)

GAMELAN INSTRUMENTS

The Balinese and Javanese gamelan look similar but are tuned to different scales (see the Gamelan section in the Facts about Bali chapter for more details about Balinese gamelan). If you are interested in seeing them being made visit the village of Blahbatuh on the main road between Denpasar and Gianyar and ask for Gablar Gamelan. In northern Bali, Sawan, a small village east of Singaraja, is also a centre for the manufacture of gamelan instruments. Jembrana, near Negara, makes giant gamelan instruments with deep resonating tones. ■

Lombok

On Lombok there is more craft than art. There are few of the purely decorative objects which characterise both modern and traditional Balinese work. The main crafts of Lombok are practical items made for everyday use, but showing great skill and finish, traditional techniques and natural, local materials. Perhaps the best place to get an idea of Lombok's arts & crafts is the vast, covered market in Sweta. This is the largest market on Lombok, and you'll find a number of stalls specialising in local crafts like woodcarving, weaving and pottery.

Villages specialise in certain crafts, and it's interesting to travel to a number of them, seeing handweaving in one village, basketware in another and pottery in a third. ■

Lombok basket (GB)

CARVING

Most carving on Lombok is to decorate functional items; typical applications are containers for tobacco and spices, and the handles of betel-nut crushers and knives. Materials include wood, horn and bone. Sindu and Senanti are centres for carving. ■

Wedding musicians, East Lombok (JL)

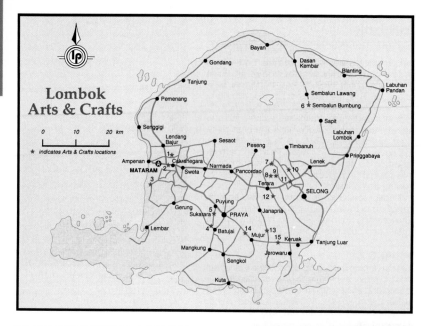

1   Sayang – Palm Leaf Boxes
2   Mataram & Cakranegara – Ikat Weaving
3   Banyumulek – Pottery
4   Penujak – Pottery
5   Sukarara – Ikat & Songket Weaving
6   Sembalun Bumbung – Hand Weaving
7   Kotaraja – Blacksmithing & Basketware
8   Loyok – Basketware
9   Rungkang – Pottery & Basketware
10 Pringgasela – Ikat & Songket Weaving
11 Masbagik – Pottery
12 Suradadi – Palm Leaf Boxes & Basketware
13 Beleka – Basketware & Pottery
14 Penjanggik – Weaving
15 Sukaraja – Woodcarving

Baskets, Central Lombok (JL)

Left: Terracotta pots, Lombok (JL)
Top: Splitting bamboo, East Lombok (JL)
Bottom: Weaver at work, Lombok (JL)

Wooden surveying tool (plumb line), Lombok (GB)

Beaded basket, Lombok (GB)

WEAVING

A number of classic Indonesian weaving techniques are used. Weaving factories around Cakranegara and Mataram produce ikat on old hand-and-foot-operated looms. You can visit them, see the dyeing and weaving processes and buy fabrics by the metre or made up as shirts, blouses etc.

Sukarara and Pringgasela are villages which specialise in traditional ikat and songket weaving. Sarongs, Sasak belts, and clothing edged with brightly coloured embroidery are sold. ■

BASKETWARE

Lombok is noted for its spiral woven rattan basketware, bags made of lontar or split bamboo, small boxes made of woven grass, and plaited rattan mats. Decorative boxes of palm leaves made in the shape of rice barns and decorated with small shells are another Lombok exclusive. Much of the work is sold directly for export, and may be easier to find on Bali than Lombok.

Beleka, Suradadi, Kotaraja and Loyok are noted for fine basketware, while Rungkang, a few km east of Loyok, combines pottery and basketware, as pots are often finished with a covering of woven cane for decoration and extra strength. Sayang is known for palm-leaf boxes. ■

POTTERY

Lombok pots have become quite widely known. The small village of Penujak, six km south of Praya, is well known for its *gerabah* pottery, made from a local red clay. You can watch the pots being hand-built and fired in traditional kilns in the roadside workshops along the main street. Some of the larger pots would be difficult to carry, but there are also small animal-shaped figurines. Banyumulek and Masbagik are also centres for the production of traditional pottery. ■

Potter, Penujak (JL)

Facts for the Visitor

VISAS & EMBASSIES

Visitors from Australia, New Zealand, Japan, Malaysia, the UK, Canada, the USA and most of Western Europe don't need a visa to enter Indonesia. Provided you have a ticket out of the country and your passport has at least six months' validity at the time of your arrival, you'll be issued with a tourist card which is valid for a 60-day stay. They rarely ask to see an onward/return ticket when you arrive on Bali but they may ask to see one, or evidence of sufficient funds, if you look like you're broke. Keep the tourist card with your passport as you'll have to hand it back when you leave the country. Remember it's good for 60 days, not two months – some travellers have been fined for overstaying by only a day or so.

It's not possible to get an extension on a tourist pass, unless there's a medical emergency or you have to answer legal charges. If you want to spend more time in Indonesia you have to leave the country and re-enter. Some long-term foreign residents have been doing this for years.

If you have a good reason for staying longer, eg for a course of study, or for family reasons, you can apply for a 'social visa'. You will need an application form from an Indonesian embassy or consulate, and a letter from an Indonesian who will sponsor your visit. There's an application fee too (A$50 in Australia). In the first instance it's only good for one month, but it can be extended at an immigration office within Indonesia up to a maximum of six months, though this is not automatic. There is also a business visitor's visa, for which you will need evidence that you are performing a necessary task in Indonesia. In all cases you must register with an immigration office after being in Indonesia for three months.

In Denpasar the immigration office *(kantor imigrasi)* is in the Renon area, in south Denpasar, just around the corner from the main post office. If you have to visit this office, make sure you wear your most respectable clothes.

Indonesian Embassies & Consulates

Embassies and consulates outside Indonesia include:

Australia
  Embassy, 8 Darwin Ave, Yarralumla, Canberra ACT 2600 (☎ 273 3222)
  Consular offices in Sydney, Darwin, Melbourne and Perth
Canada
  Embassy, 287 Maclaren St, Ottawa, Ontario K2P OL9 (☎ 236 7403/4/5)
  Consular offices in Toronto and Vancouver
Denmark
  Embassy, Orejoj Alle I 2900, Hellerup, Copenhagen (☎ 624422, 625439)
Germany
  Embassy, Bernkasteler Strasse 2, 5300 Bonn 2 (☎ 382990)
  Consular offices in Berlin, Bremen, Dusseldorf, Frankfurt, Hamburg, Hannover, Kiel, Munich and Stuttgart
Hong Kong
  Consulate General, 127-129 Leighton Rd, Causeway Bay, Hong Kong (☎ 5 890 4421/2/3/4)
Malaysia
  Embassy, Jalan Tun Razak 233, Kuala Lumpur (☎ 984 2011, 984 1354, 984 1228)
  Consular offices in Kota Kinabalu and Penang
Netherlands
  Embassy, 8 Tobias Asserlaan, 2517 KC Den Haag (☎ 070 310 8100)
New Zealand
  Embassy, 70 Glen Rd, Kelburn, Wellington (☎ 475 8697/8/9)
Norway
  Embassy, Inkonitogata 8, 0258 Oslo 2 (☎ 441121)
Papua New Guinea
  Embassy, Sir John Guisa Drive, Waigani, Port Moresby (☎ 253544, 253116/7/8)
Philippines
  Embassy, 185/187 Salcedo St, Legaspi Village, Makati, Manila (☎ 855061/2/3/4)
  Consular office in Davao
Singapore
  Embassy, 7 Chatsworth Rd, Singapore 1024 (☎ 737 7422)

Sweden
> Embassy, Strandvagen 47/V, 11456 Stockholm (☎ 663 5470/1/2/3/4)

Switzerland
> Embassy, 51 Elfenauweg, 3006 Bern (☎ 440983/4/5)

UK
> Embassy, 38 Grosvenor Square, London W1X 9AD (☎ 499 7661)

USA
> Embassy, 2020 Massachusetts Ave NW, Washington DC 20036 (☎ 775 5207)
>
> Consular offices in Chicago, Honolulu, Houston, Los Angeles, New York and San Francisco

Foreign Embassies & Consulates

With the growing number of foreign visitors to Bali, the extent of diplomatic representation is increasing. However, most of the foreign representatives on Bali are consular agents (or honorary consuls) who can't offer the same services as a full consulate. The embassies are all in Jakarta, the national capital, and for many nationalities this means a long trek there if your passport is stolen. For emergency passports, US citizens will have to go to the US Consulate General in Surabaya.

In Bali Fortunately for the great number of Australian visitors there is an Australian consulate in the Renon district of Denpasar. The Australian consul will also help citizens of other Commonwealth countries while they're on Bali, including those from Canada, New Zealand, Papua New Guinea and the UK. (Commonwealth citizens, including Aussies, make up around 50% of visitors to Bali, so the office can be overworked at times.) Japan also has a full consulate in Denpasar, but all the others listed below are consular agents. Both the Australian consulate and the US consular agent emphasise the importance of visitors to Bali taking out adequate travel insurance, preferably with a cover for emergency medical evacuation.

Australia
> Jalan Mochammad Yamin 51, Renon, Denpasar; PO Box 243 (☎ 235092/3, fax 231990)

France
> Jalan Raya Sesetan 46D, Banjar Pesanggaran, Denpasar; (☎ & fax 233555)

Germany
> Jalan Pantai Karang 17, Sanur; PO Box 3100 Denpasar (☎ 288535, fax 288826)

Italy
> Jalan Cemara, Banjar Semawang, Sanur Kauh; PO Box 158 Denpasar (☎ 288996, fax 287642)

Japan
> Jalan Mochammad Yamin 9, Renon, Denpasar; (☎ 234808, fax 231308)

Netherlands
> Jalan Iman Bonjol 599, Kuta; PO Box 337 (☎ 751517, fax 752777)

Norway & Denmark
> Jalan Jaya Giri VIII/10, Renon, Denpasar; Box 188 Denpasar (☎ 235098, fax 234834)

Sweden & Finland
> Segara Village Hotel, Jalan Segara Ayu, Sanur (☎ 288407/8)

Switzerland
> Swiss Restaurant, Jalan Pura Bagus Taruna, Legian (☎ 751735, fax 754457)

USA
> Jalan Segara Ayu 5, Sanur (☎ 288478, fax 287760)

In Jakarta Indonesia is a big country, and important in the Asian region. Most nations have an embassy in Jakarta, including:

Australia
> Jalan M H Thamrin 15, Jakarta (☎ 323109)

Canada
> Wisma Metropolitan, 5th floor, Jalan Jen Sudirman, Kav 29, Jakarta (☎ 510709)

Denmark
> Bina Mulia Building, 4th floor, Jalan H R Rasuna Said, Kav 10, Jakarta (☎ 5204350)

Germany
> Jalan M H Thamrin 1, Jakarta (☎ 323908)

India
> Jalan H R Rasuna Said S-1, Kuningan, Jakarta (☎ 5204150)

Japan
> Jalan M H Thamrin 24, Jakarta (☎ 324308, 324948, 325396, 325140, 325268)

Malaysia
> Jalan Imam Bonjol 17, Jakarta (☎ 336438, 332864)

Netherlands
> Jalan H R Rasuna Said, Kav S3, Kuningan, Jakarta (☎ 511515)

New Zealand
> Jalan Diponegoro 41, Jakarta (☎ 330680)

Norway
> Bina Mulia Building I, 4th floor, Jalan H R Rasuna Said, Kav 10, Jakarta (☎ 511990)

Papua New Guinea
> Panin Bank Centre, 6th floor, Jalan Jen Sudirman, Jakarta (☎ 711218, 711225/6)

Philippines
> Jalan Imam Bonjol 6-8, Jakarta (☎ 3848917)

Singapore
> Blok X14, Jalan H R Rasuna Said, Kav S3, Kuningan, Jakarta (☎ 5201491)

Sri Lanka
> Jalan Diponegoro 70, Jakarta (☎ 321018, 321896)

Sweden
> Bina Mulia Building I, 7th floor, Jalan H R Rasuna Said, Kav 10, Jakarta (☎ 5201551/2/3)

Thailand
> Jalan Imam Bonjol 74, Jakarta (☎ 3904225)

UK
> Jalan M H Thamrin 75, Jakarta (☎ 330904)

USA
> Jalan Medan Merdeka Selatan 5, Jakarta (☎ 360360)

DOCUMENTS

Apart from your passport and visa, there is no particular documentation required to visit Bali and Lombok. Although a health certificate isn't necessary, you should get any vaccinations you need (see the Health section in this chapter). If you plan to drive yourself, or ride a motorbike, you should bring an International Driving Permit, endorsed for motorbikes if necessary. If you have a driving licence at home, an international permit is easy to obtain from your national motoring organisation. You should take out travel insurance, and it's a good idea to bring a copy of the policy and/or evidence that you're covered. Also, photocopy the relevant pages of your passport, driving permit and any other essential papers, and keep the copies separate from the originals.

CUSTOMS

Indonesia has the usual list of prohibited imports including drugs, weapons and anything remotely pornographic. In addition, any printed matter in Indonesian, any books containing Chinese characters, Chinese medicines, cassette players, and Indonesian currency in excess of 50,000 rp are prohib-

ited. You can bring in two litres of alcohol, 200 cigarettes, and cameras and film without restriction. If you have nothing to declare, customs clearance is quick and painless.

Indonesia is a signatory to the Convention on International Trade in Endangered Species (CITES) and as such bans the import and export of products made from endangered species. In particular, it is forbidden to export any product made from green sea turtles or turtle shells (see the Sea Turtles aside in the Facts about Bali chapter). In the interests of conservation, as well as conformity to customs laws, please don't buy turtle shell products. There are also some ivory artefacts for sale on Bali, and the import and export of these is also banned in some countries.

It's also forbidden to export antiquities, ancient artefacts or other cultural treasures, so if someone tries to sell you an 'ancient' bronze statue, remind them of this law and they may decide it's not so old after all!

MONEY

Currency

The unit of currency in Indonesia is the rupiah (rp) – there is no smaller unit. You get coins of 5, 10, 25, 50 and 100 rp, but 5s and 10s are really only found in banks – nothing costs less than 25 rp. Notes come in 100, 500, 1000, 5000, 10,000, 20,000 and 50,000 rp denominations. There is a new series of notes for the higher denominations – 50,000 rp notes are not common. A new series of coins is coming into circulation – gold-coloured 50 and 100 rp coins, and a 1000 rp coin in silver with a gold-coloured centre.

Exchange Rates

The exchange rate is not artificially set – it's a more-or-less free market rate which is reasonably stable as the rate of inflation is quite low. There's no black market.

Australia	A$1	=	1542 rp
Canada	C$1	=	1566 rp
France	FF1	=	382 rp
Germany	DM1	=	1305 rp
Japan	¥100	=	2122 rp

New Zealand	NZ$1	=	1248 rp
UK	UK£1	=	3274 rp
USA	US$1	=	2157 rp
Australia	1000 rp	=	A$0.65
Canada	1000 rp	=	C$0.64
France	1000 rp	=	FF2.62
Germany	1000 rp	=	DM0.77
Japan	1000 rp	=	¥47
New Zealand	1000 rp	=	NZ$0.80
UK	1000 rp	=	UK£0.31
USA	1000 rp	=	US$0.46

Carrying Money

Bring most of your money in travellers' cheques, for security and convenience, and some cash for those times when changing a cheque is difficult. It's wise to bring a couple of different brands of travellers' cheques, or have a credit card for back-up. There are periodic thefts or frauds involving travellers' cheques, and many moneychangers and businesses just won't accept that brand until they get the all-clear, perhaps months later. Banks will usually change them as they have more up-to-date lists of dodgy cheque numbers, but changing at banks is slower and less convenient.

US dollars are the most negotiable currency, particularly in more remote areas. British, Canadian, German, Dutch, French, Japanese, Malaysian, Singapore, Australian, New Zealand and other currencies are negotiable at competitive rates in tourist areas, but the rate may be significantly lower in towns where only one bank will cash a travellers' cheque.

The major credit cards (Visa, MasterCard, American Express) are accepted by most of the bigger businesses that cater to tourists. You sign for the amount in local currency (rupiah) and the bill is converted into your domestic currency – the rate of exchange is usually quite good. You can also get cash advances on major credit cards at banks and some tourist businesses.

Dutch national giro cards can be used at Indonesian post offices with giro facilities – look for the sign that says *kantor pos dan giro*.

Changing Money

Changing money is quite easy on Bali. The exchange rate for travellers' cheques may be slightly better than for cash, but is generally about the same. In the main tourist centres – Kuta, Sanur, Ubud etc – there are lots of moneychangers, as well as the occasional bank. The exchange rates offered by moneychangers are very similar to the banks, often better, and their service is quicker. The exchange counters at the airport may give slightly lower rates than places in town.

Banking hours are from 8 am to noon, Monday to Friday and from 8 to 11 am on Saturday with some banks closing an hour earlier. Moneychangers have longer opening hours but usually open later in the morning.

Away from the main centres, the story is a little more complicated, though it's by no means difficult. Smaller tourist towns may not have banks, and even if they do, you might not be able to exchange foreign currency, but there are always moneychangers with competitive rates. The larger non-tourist towns have banks, but few moneychangers. Not all of the banks will change travellers' cheques, and those that do will may give a low rate on some currencies, including Australian and New Zealand dollars.

If you're out in the sticks, it's difficult to change big notes – breaking a 10,000 rp note in an out-of-the-way location can be a major hassle. Secondly, away from the major centres notes tend to stay in circulation much longer and can get very tatty – when they get too dog-eared and worn looking, people won't accept them.

Receiving Money

Having money sent to you in Bali can take time, so don't wait until you're desperate. The Bank Ekspor-Impor is supposedly the best for inward money transfers from abroad. It takes about a week, and is paid in rupiah. Some overseas banks can transfer funds via the 'Swift' system to Bank Ekspor-Impor branches on Bali and Lombok, which takes around 24 hours. American Express also has a money transfer service called MoneyGram, which is expensive but quick and reliable. A cash advance on your credit card might be easier and cheaper than having money sent.

Costs

On Bali you can spend as much as you want to – there are hotels where a double can be US$500 or more a night, where lunch can cost more than US$75 per person and a helicopter can be arranged for you if you're desperate to see Bali *fast*. At the other extreme you can find rooms for US$3 and get a filling meal from a warung (food stall) for 1000 rp – say 50c.

In general, travellers who don't need air-con and 24-hour service will discover they can get good rooms almost anywhere on Bali for under US$10; sometimes as little as US$5 will get you a fine room. US$8 will get you an excellent meal for two, with a big cold bottle of beer, at most tourist restaurants, while even at relatively flashy places like Poppies in Kuta it's hard to spend more than US$20 for two (unless you want wine which is, alas, expensive). A good meal for two for US$6 is no problem and you don't even have to get into the really rock-bottom warungs to eat for under US$2.

Transport is equally affordable – remember that Bali and Lombok are small islands. Public minibuses, or *bemos*, are the local form of public transport and they're pretty cheap – a 60-km (35 mile) trip will cost you about 2000 rp, say US$1. If you want your own wheels you can hire a motorbike for around US$6 a day, a Suzuki jeep for US$16 a day, or charter your own bemo, complete with driver, from about US$20 a day.

Entry Charges Nearly every temple or site of tourist interest will levy an entry charge or ask for a donation from foreigners – which means a Javanese just as much as a German, as any non-Balinese is a foreigner. Usually the charge will be 500 rp, occasionally less, very occasionally more. If there is no fixed charge, and a donation is requested, 500 rp is also a good figure. Ignore the donation book showing somebody has just 'donated'

over 2500 rp – figures are easy to add. Car or motorbike parking is extra.

Government-run tourist attractions, such as the Bali Barat National Park, sometimes charge an insurance premium of 50 rp or so on top of the admission price. This supposedly covers you against accident or injury while you're there, or maybe it just covers the management against you suing them. It won't add greatly to your peace of mind, but it's only a few cents and you have to pay it anyway.

Tipping

Tipping is not a normal practice on Bali or Lombok so please don't try to make it one. The expensive hotels slap a 17.5% service charge and government tax on top of their bills but there are no additional charges at lower-priced establishments.

Begging

You may be approached by the occasional beggar on the streets of Kuta – typically a woman with a young child. Begging has no place in traditional Balinese society, so it's likely that most of these beggars come from elsewhere. Children often ask for sweets, pens, cigarettes etc, and this should not be encouraged.

Bargaining

Many everyday purchases on Bali require bargaining. This particularly applies to clothing and arts and crafts. Meals in restaurants are generally fixed price, as is any transport where you buy a ticket. Accommodation has a set price, but it's often negotiable; when supply of rooms exceeds demand you may often find hotels willing to bend their prices, rather than see you go next door. This particularly applies in places like Kuta, Lovina and Candidasa where there are lots of 'next doors' to go to! On the other hand, many *losmen* (small hotels) will charge more than their usual price if they have to pay a commission to a taxi driver, or if they think you look so tired or disoriented that you won't make it to the place next door. Bemo drivers have a well-earned reputation for taking visitors for as much as possible – see the Getting Around Bali chapter.

In an everyday bargaining situation the first step is to establish a starting price. It's usually easier to ask the sellers their price rather than make an initial offer. You will have to make an offer sooner or later, but ask straight away if that is the 'best price', and you may get an immediate reduction.

Your 'first price' should be a worthwhile notch below what you're willing to pay, but not so low as to be ludicrous. A silly offer suggests that the customer hasn't any idea of what the price should be, and is therefore a target for some serious overcharging. Of course lots of people have ended up buying things they didn't want because their silly offer was accepted!

As a rule of thumb your first price could be anything from one-third to two-thirds of the asking price – assuming that the asking price is not completely crazy. Then, with offer and counter offer, you move closer to an acceptable price – the seller asks 25,000 rp for the painting, you offer 15,000 rp and so on until eventually you compromise at 20,000 rp – 22,000 rp if they're a better bargainer, 18,000 rp if you are! Along the way you can plead end-of-trip poverty or claim that Ketut down the road is likely to be even cheaper. The seller is likely to point out the exceptional quality of the item and plead poverty too. An aura of only mild interest helps – if you don't get to an acceptable price you're quite entitled to walk away. On the other hand, if you're obviously desperate or pressed for time, vendors will not be in a hurry to drop their price.

Remember it's not a matter of life or death. Bargaining should be an enjoyable part of shopping on Bali so maintain your sense of humour and keep things in perspective – remember, 1000 rp is about US$0.50. When you name a price, you're committed – you have to buy if your offer is accepted. The best buy is said to be at the 'morning price'. The seller feels that making a sale to the first customer will ensure good sales for the rest of the day, so is more likely to lower the price for an early-morning customer.

To bargain effectively you should know, before you start, approximately how much the 'right' price is, ie the lowest price which the vendor will accept. At the very least you should have an idea of what you consider is a fair price for the article, and not just try to get it for less than the first asking price.

There's always going to be someone who will boast about how they got something cheaper than you did. Don't go around feeling that you're being ripped off all the time. At times you will be, and in most instances the locals will pay less than foreigners. The Balinese consider this to be eminently fair, as in their eyes, all Westerners are wealthy, as are any Javanese who can afford to travel; and as for Japanese visitors... With handcrafts and clothes, remember that quality is more important than price – when you get that treasure home, you won't be worried that you might have got it for a few thousand rupiah less, but you will be disappointed if it falls apart.

If you are accompanied by a local (driver, guide, friend or whatever) on a shopping spree, you may find it harder to bargain the price down. Even if your companion is not on a commission for taking you to the place, he/she will tend to feel very uncomfortable seeing a fellow Balinese being 'beaten down' by a foreigner. It reflects on both the guide and the shopkeeper, and each loses face. The advantages of finding things more easily and quickly is often outweighed by this local loyalty.

WHEN TO GO

Just considering the weather, the cooler dry season, from April to October, is the best time to visit Bali or Lombok, but there are also distinct tourist seasons which alter the picture. The European summer holidays bring the biggest crowds – July, August and early September are busy. Accommodation can be tight in these months and prices are higher. From Christmas till the end of January, airfares to/from Australia are higher and flights can be booked solid. The school holidays in early April, late June-early July, and late September also see more Australians, but most of them stay in Kuta, or are on package tours to resort areas in south Bali. Many Indonesians ('domestic tourists') visit Bali around Christmas, and during some Indonesian holidays. Outside these times Bali has surprisingly few tourists and there are empty rooms and restaurants everywhere.

Balinese festivals, holidays and special celebrations occur all the time, and most of them are not scheduled according to Western calendars, so don't worry about timing your visit to coincide with local events. Just make some enquiries when you arrive, and be prepared to travel round the island.

WHAT TO BRING

'Bring as little as possible' is the golden rule of good travelling. It's usually better to leave something behind and have to get a replacement when you're there than to bring too much and have to lug unwanted items around.

You need little more than lightweight clothes – short-sleeved shirts or blouses, T-shirts and light pants. A light sweater is a good idea for cool evenings and particularly if you're going up into the mountains. Kintamani, Penelokan and the other towns in the central mountains can actually get bloody cold, so a light jacket may also be necessary. You'll also need more protective clothes if you're going to be travelling by motorbike. A hat and sunglasses are useful protection from tropical sun.

Remember that in much of Asia, including Bali and particularly Lombok, shorts are not considered polite attire for men or women. Similarly, sleeveless singlet tops are not considered respectable – you're supposed to cover your shoulders and armpits. At Kuta and the other beach resorts, shorts and singlets have become a part of everyday life, and in any case tourists are considered a little strange and their clothing habits are expected to be somewhat eccentric. Bikini tops are a rare sight on Bali's tourist beaches, but bring one for less touristy beaches, and definitely if you're going to Lombok.

In temples and government offices, you're expected to be 'properly' dressed, and shorts and singlets don't fulfil that expectation. Thongs are acceptable in temples if you're otherwise well dressed, but not for government offices. The 'how to dress' posters you see on Bali may be amusing but there's a message behind them. If you want to renew a visa, or even get a local driving licence, ask yourself how you'd dress in a similar situation back home.

To be properly dressed in a temple you should be generally respectable, and also wear a temple scarf – a simple sash loosely tied around your waist. Many of the larger temples rent them out for about 200 rp, but you can buy one yourself for 1000 rp or so. You'll soon recoup the cost if you visit many temples, and you're certain of being politely dressed even at temples where there are no scarves for rent.

TOURIST OFFICES

Indonesia does not have a national tourist office pumping out useful brochures. Garuda, the Indonesian airline, has better information brochures than you're likely to find from the government offices. In Denpasar there is both the Badung district tourist office (for southern Bali) and a Bali government tourist office. In Kuta, the tourist office on Jalan Benesari is pretty good, and the local offices in Ubud and Singaraja are very helpful. They can often answer specific questions, but are at a loss if you ask for general information.

Overseas Representatives

There are a number of Indonesian Tourist Promotion Offices (ITPO) abroad where you can get some brochures and information about Indonesia. The ITPO headquarters is at the Directorate General of Tourism (☎ 3101146), Jalan Kramat Raya 81, PO Box 409, Jakarta. Overseas, try Garuda Airlines or the following ITPO offices:

Australia
    Level 10, 5 Elizabeth St, Sydney, NSW 2000 (☎ (02) 233 3630)
Germany
    Wiessenhuttenstrasse 17 D.6000, Frankfurt am Main 1 (☎ (069) 233677)
Japan
    2nd Floor, Sankaido Building, 1-9-13 Akasaka, Minatoku, Tokyo 107 (☎ (03) 3585-3588
Singapore
    10 Collyer Quay, Ocean Building, Singapore 0104 (☎ 534 2837)
USA
    3457 Wilshire Blvd, Los Angeles, CA 90010 (☎ (213) 387 2078)

BUSINESS HOURS

Most government offices are open from 8 am daily except Sunday and close at 3 pm Monday to Thursday, 11.30 am on Friday and 2 pm on Saturday. Usual business office hours are from 8 am to 4 pm, Monday to Friday. Some also open on Saturday morning. Banks are open from 8 am to noon, Monday to Friday and from 8 to 11 am on Saturday. Some shops and businesses close

in the middle of the day, from about 12.30 to 2 pm.

HOLIDAYS & FESTIVALS

Apart from the usual Western calendar, the Balinese also use two local calendars, the *saka* and the *wuku* calendar. The wuku calendar is used to determine festival dates. The calendar uses 10 different types of weeks between one and 10 days long, and all running simultaneously! The intersection of the various weeks determines auspicious days. The seven-day and five-day weeks are of particular importance. A full year is made up of 30 individually named seven-day weeks.

The Galungan Festival, Bali's major feast, is held throughout the island and is an annual event in the wuku year. During this 10-day period all the gods, including the supreme deity, Sanghyang Widi, come down to earth for the festivities. Barongs prance from temple to temple and village to village. The last and most important day of the festival is Kuningan. There are numerous festivals around the time of Galungan and Kuningan or shortly afterwards. Forthcoming dates are:

	Galungan	*Kuningan*
1994	6 April	16 April
	2 November	12 November
1995	31 May	10 June
	27 December	6 January '96
1996	24 July	3 August
1997	19 February	1 March

The Hindu saka calendar is a lunar cycle that more closely follows the Western calendar in terms of the length of the year. Nyepi is the major festival of the saka year – it's the last day of the year, the day after the new moon on the ninth month. It usually falls in March. Nyepi also marks the end of the rainy season and the day before is set aside as a day of purification across the island; absolutely nothing goes on – like a sort of super-Sabbath. That night evil spirits are noisily chased away with cymbals, gongs, drums and flaming torches and on Nyepi everyone stays quietly at home. Nyepi generally falls towards the end of March or the beginning of April.

Certain major temples celebrate their festivals by the saka rather than the wuku calendar. This makes the actual date difficult to determine from our calendar since the lunar saka does not follow a fixed number of days like the wuku calendar. The full moons which fall around the end of September to the beginning of October or from early to mid-April are often times for important temple festivals.

The Balinese also have a major annual festival by the Western calendar – Indonesian Independence Day falls on 17 August, celebrating Sukarno's proclamation of independence on that day in 1945. New Year's Day, Good Friday and Christmas Day are also public holidays. Muslims on Bali observe the Islamic holidays – see Lombok's Facts for the Visitor chapter for dates.

When you arrive on Bali, go to a tourist office and ask what festivals and celebrations will occur during your stay, and whereabouts. Try to get to at least one.

POST & TELECOMMUNICATIONS
Post Offices
Every substantial town has a post office (*kantor pos*), open from 8 am to 2 pm most days, 8 am to noon on Friday, closed Sunday. Smaller postal agencies serve small towns, or supplement the official post office in a big town. Agencies often give better service and may be open longer hours.

Postal Rates Airmail for postcards is 600 rp to all foreign destinations. Aerogrammes and airmail letters up to 20 grams cost 1000 rp to Australia, 1400 rp to Europe, and 1600 rp to the USA and Canada. Sending large parcels (maximum size, 10 kg) is quite expensive, but at least you can get them properly wrapped and sealed at low cost from nearly every post office or postal agency.

Receiving Mail There are poste restante services at the various post offices around Bali. The Denpasar post office is inconveniently situated, so you're better off having mail sent to you at Kuta, Ubud, Singaraja or other more convenient locations. Mail should be addressed to you with your surname underlined and in capital letters, then 'Kantor Pos', the town name, then Bali, Indonesia.

Telephone
The telecommunications service in Indonesia is provided by Telkom, a government monopoly. The system is being modernised to the latest international standards, and all of Indonesia is covered by a domestic satellite telecommunications network. It's usually possible to get on to the international operator or get an international connection within a couple of minutes, but it can take longer from areas with old-style exchanges that route international calls through Jakarta.

Telephone Area Codes The country code for Indonesia is 62. Bali has five telephone zones. Southern Bali (the districts of Tabanan, Badung, Gianyar and Bangli) is in the 0361 zone which covers all the main tourist areas, and most of Karangasem (including Candidasa). Telephone zones are shown on the map.

Telephone Numbers Many phone numbers changed during 1993, especially in southern Bali. New numbers in Denpasar, Kuta, Sanur and Ubud have six digits, usually an extra digit added to the old number. In Denpasar, add a 2 to the front of an old five-digit number (which usually starts with a 2, 3 or 6); for Kuta, add a 7 to the front of old five-digit numbers (which start with a 5); for Sanur, add a 2 to the front of old five-digit numbers (which usually starts with an 8); for Ubud, insert a 7 between the first two digits of an old five-digit number (which usually starts with 95; numbers starting with 96 are unchanged). If you dial an old number you should get a recorded message telling you how to convert it to a new number – don't hang up too quickly because the message is repeated in English after the Indonesian version.

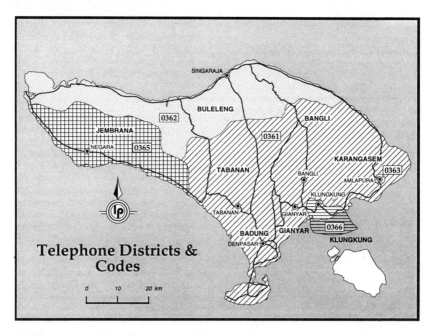

Telephone Districts & Codes

0   10   20 km

Phone books can be hard to come by, but the directory assistance operators (☎ 108) are very helpful and some of them do speak English. If you call directory assistance, and have to spell out a name you want, try to use the Alpha, Bravo, Charlie system of saying the letters. It's widely understood, whereas the usual English letter pronunciation (ay, bee, see etc) can get hopelessly confused with the way letters are pronounced in Indonesian. If you don't know the Alpha, Bravo, Charlie system, just use simple, common English words to help the operators identify the letters.

Telephone Offices *Kantor telekomunikasi* (telecommunications offices), usually called *wartels (warung telekomunikasi)*, are operated by both Telkom, and private businesses. From them you can make local, international and long-distance calls. Sample costs for a one-minute call from a Telkom wartel are 4550 rp to Australia, New Zealand and the USA, 5200 rp to Canada and the UK, and 6180 rp to Europe, plus 10% tax on all calls. Person-to-person calls cost more.

The official charge for international calls is the same from anywhere on Bali, but the conditions vary. In areas without a computerised, automatic exchange there is a three-minute minimum, and increments of one minute thereafter. When you book the call, they may ask you how long you want to talk for, and cut you off as soon as the time you requested is up. In areas with modern exchanges you dial the call yourself, and the cost increases in *pulsa* – a unit of time which varies with the destination. The number of pulsa is shown on a display on the front of the phone. This display also shows the price, sometimes including the 10% tax, sometimes not. You pay at the desk when you've finished the call. Make sure you are not charged twice for the tax, and check the clerk's arithmetic. You're supposed to get discounts (25%) for calls on Sunday, but in practice this is unlikely, and many wartels close on Sunday anyway. You can make reverse-charge (collect) calls from Telkom wartels.

Private wartels are found in Kuta, Sanur, Lovina and other places, often in a hotel or with a moneychanging business. They provide a pretty good service but charge higher prices than Telkom offices. Many private wartels do not let you make reverse-charge calls, and those that do will charge a fee for the privilege, typically equal to the cost of one minute of your call.

Public Telephones There are several types of public phones, some of which can be used for international calls. You can call overseas from most of them if you have a foreign telephone credit card (see below). There are also some Home Country Direct phones, where one button gets you through to your home country operator and you pay with a credit card or reverse the charges. These phones can be found outside the international terminal at the airport, in the Grand Bali Beach Hotel in Sanur, the Kuta Beach Hotel in Kuta and at the Galleria shopping centre in Nusa Dua. The phones which take locally purchased Telkom phone cards are called *telepon kartu*, and are becoming more common.

Indonesian Telephone Cards You can buy Telkom telephone cards *(kartu telepon)* with a face value of 60, 100, 140, 280, 400 or 680 units. The standard cost is 82.5 rp per unit, so a 60-unit card is 4950 rp, a 100-unit card is 8250 rp, and so on, but some places charge a lot more than the standard rate for the cards. If you pay the standard price for a card, an international call from a card phone costs about the same per minute as a call from a wartel; it may even be cheaper if you call on Sunday or an off-peak time and can't get a discount from the wartel.

Foreign Telephone Cards Some phone companies issue a card that enables you to call your home country from overseas and have the cost billed to your home phone account. You arrange this before you leave home. You can use the facility from most public and private phones (fancy hotels will charge a fee) by ringing a special number to access your home country operator, and quoting your card number and a PIN number. Your phone company will give you a list of the access codes for foreign countries, and a schedule of prices. This facility is convenient, but not necessarily cheap.

Reverse-Charge Calls Some travellers believe it is cheaper to call reverse-charges (collect) from Indonesia than to pay on the spot, but this isn't always true. There's probably not much difference these days, and it depends on your home telephone company and the rate of exchange.

Fax, Telex & Telegram
Telegram, telex and fax services are available at most wartels. At some of them you can arrange to receive a fax from elsewhere, and they may even deliver faxes to a specified address for an extra fee.

TIME
Bali and Lombok and the islands of Nusa Tenggara to the east are on Central Indonesian Standard Time, which is eight hours ahead of GMT or two hours behind Australian Eastern Standard Time. There is a one-hour time difference between Bali and Java.

Thus, not allowing for variations due to daylight-saving time, when it's noon in London it's 8 pm on Bali and Lombok, 8 pm in Perth, 10 pm in Sydney and Melbourne, 7 am in New York and 4 am in San Francisco and Los Angeles.

As Bali is close to the equator, days and nights are approximately equal in length. The sun pops up over the horizon at 6 am and drops down in the west at 6 pm. The sunsets are often orange-fire spectaculars, but don't expect to enjoy a pleasant twilight – it gets dark almost immediately.

'Bali time' is an expression which refers to the Balinese reluctance to be obsessed by punctuality. It is equivalent to *jam karet*, the 'rubber time' found in other parts of Indonesia, but more elastic. Actually, many Balinese in the tourist industry and other 'modern' sectors of the economy are having to learn about deadlines, and punch-card clocks are a depressing sight near staff entrances.

ELECTRICITY

Electricity is usually 220-240 volts AC on Bali. In some smaller villages it's still 110 volts (if they have electricity at all), so check first. Wall plugs are round with two pins four mm in diameter, 19 mm apart (centre to centre; ie from the centre of each pin) and 18 mm long. Electricity is usually fairly reliable, and blackouts are not an everyday occurrence, though the electricity grid is running at its maximum capacity. In many small towns, and even in parts of larger towns, electricity is a recent innovation – if you travel around very much you're likely to stay in the odd losmen where lighting is provided with oil lamps.

Even where there is electricity, the lighting can be very dim. Lots of losmen seem to have light bulbs of such low wattage that you can almost see the electricity crawling around the filaments. If 25 watts isn't enough to light your room it might be worth carrying a more powerful light bulb with you.

Street lighting can also be a problem – there often isn't any. If stumbling back to your losmen down dark alleys in Kuta or through the rice paddies in Ubud doesn't appeal, a torch (flashlight) can be very useful.

LAUNDRY

All the fancier hotels advertise laundry services, and charge quite steeply for them. The cheaper places don't advertise the fact, but generally will wash clothes for you at a pretty reasonable price. Allow 24 hours, or a bit longer if it's been raining. Laundry charges are directly proportional to the cost of staying at the hotel, starting at about 500 rp for a shirt to be washed, dried and folded.

WEIGHTS & MEASURES

All of Indonesia, including Bali and Lombok, uses the metric system. For those accustomed to the imperial system, there is a conversion table at the back of this book.

BOOKS

It is striking how much has been published about Bali in the Western world, and how little of it has been written by Balinese. It says a lot about the Western fascination with Bali. The few articles in English by Balinese are quite recent, and are academic rather than popular titles. Various Indonesian academic journals regularly have articles about aspects of Bali – its geography, economy, history and so on, but they are not very accessible to a general audience. Oxford University Press publishes a number of good titles on Bali, in paperback, as part of the Oxford in Asia series. Another publisher of interest is KITLV in Leiden, the Netherlands. Their *Bibliography of Bali* (1992) lists over 70,000 publications on Bali.

Early Descriptions

The Western descriptions of Bali start with the observations of colonial officials and the letters of the first tourists and visiting artists. Credit for launching today's image of Bali as an island paradise can be given to Gregor Krause, a German doctor who worked for the Dutch government in the southern Bali town of Bangli in 1912. Krause was a talented photographer as well as a doctor and his images of Bali, published in Germany in 1920 in two volumes under the title *Bali*, was an instant success. It was later republished in a single volume and in a number of other languages.

Krause's images of Bali as an exotic paradise with colourful ceremonies and handsome people played a large part in the Western fascination with Bali in the late '20s and '30s. Krause can also claim credit for bringing the bare Balinese breast to Western attention, an aspect of Bali to which he paid great attention in both photographs and prose. A selection of his pioneering photographs and text have recently been published as *Bali 1912* (January Books, Wellington, 1988), a book of great interest but such stunningly bad design that it's almost painful to look at.

Art & Culture There are many interesting books on Bali's art and culture but the best is still *Island of Bali* by the Mexican artist Miguel Covarrubias. First published in 1937 by Alfred A Knopf and widely available today as an Oxford University Press Paperback, this book is a very worthwhile investment for anybody with a real interest in Bali; few people since have come to grips with Bali as well as Covarrubias. It's readable yet learned, incredibly detailed yet always interesting. Every subsequent guide to Bali owes this book a great debt. The closing speculation (remember, this was written in the 1930s) that tourism may spoil Bali is thought-provoking but it's also a real pleasure to discover, through reading the book, how some aspects of Bali are still exactly the way Covarrubias describes them.

The Oxford Paperback series also includes *Dance & Drama in Bali* by Beryl de Zoete & Walter Spies. Originally published in 1938 this excellent book draws from Walter Spies' deep appreciation and understanding of Bali's arts and culture.

The '30s Visitors Western visitors to Bali in the '30s were a cultured and varied lot, many of whom had an irresistible urge to put their experiences down on paper. Fortunately many of those classic early accounts have been republished. Oxford University Press' Asian-based Oxford Paperback series is doing great work in this area. Hickman Powell's very readable *The Last Paradise* (Oxford Paperback) was first published in 1930 and was one of the first signs of the explosion of Western accounts which followed. At times, however, it gets quite cloyingly over-romantic – everything is just too beautiful and too noble.

Colin McPhee's *A House in Bali* (Oxford Paperback) is a wonderful account of a musician's lengthy stays on Bali to study gamelan music. He's an amazingly incisive and delightfully humorous author and the book itself is superbly written. Like so many other Western 'discoverers' of Bali his stay was in the 1930s but his book was not published till much later – 1944 in this case.

Vicki Baum's *A Tale from Bali* (Oxford Paperback) is again from that magical time in the 1930s. She was another visitor who came under the spell of Walter Spies and her historical novel is based around the events of the 1906 puputan which brought the island under Dutch control.

K'tut Tantri's *Revolt in Paradise* (Harper & Row, New York, 1960) tells, through the eyes of a Western woman, of life on the island during the 1930s and in the midst of the post WW II Indonesian revolution. Besides her Balinese name she has also been known as Vannine Walker, Muriel Pearson or a number of other pseudonyms. She lived for some time at Kuta Beach in the 1930s, stayed in Indonesia when the war broke out and suffered at the hands of the Japanese, and then worked on the Indonesian side during its struggle for independence from the Netherlands.

Our Hotel in Bali by Louise G Koke (January Books, New Zealand, 1987) is interesting because K'tut Tantri may have been in partnership with the Kokes in their hotel at some point, though perhaps not; it's very hard to tell from either book! Louise and Robert Koke established the original Kuta Beach Hotel in the mid-30s and ran it until WW II spread to the Pacific. Louise Koke's fascinating account of running their hotel was written during the war but not published until 1987. It's a long way from the prewar Kuta to the Kuta of today.

Walter Spies was the keystone of the prewar Bali set and his colourful, multidimensional and ultimately tragic life make him a fascinating character, quite apart from his undeniable role in the development of Balinese art. *Walter Spies & Balinese Art* by Hans Rhodius & John Darling (Terra, Zutphen, 1980) is an intriguing account of his life, his work and his influence on Balinese art.

Modern Descriptions

The modern history, and contemporary economics and politics of Bali are inseparable from those of the country as a whole, and there are a number of good books about modern Indonesia which will fill in the background. Bali often features in travel and other magazines, including *National Geographic* which has had a number of articles on Bali over the years, including one (September 1963) on the disastrous eruption of Gunung Agung earlier that year. Some of the modern books on Bali include the following:

Hugh Mabbett's *The Balinese* (January Books, New Zealand, 1985) is a readable collection of anecdotes, observations and impressions of Bali and its people. Although it doesn't pretend to be a new version of Covarrubias' classic account it does, in many respects, bring that book up to date. *In Praise of Kuta* is another fascinating book from the same author.

Adrian Vickers' *Bali – A Paradise Created* (Penguin Books, Ringwood, 1989 in Australia; Periplus in the USA and Indonesia) traces Balinese history and development by concentrating on the island's image in the West. Vickers' thesis is that the impression is a manufactured one, the result of a conscious decision to create an image of an ideal island paradise. There's some fascinating material on the Western visitors of the '30s, energetic image creators every one of them.

Bali – Sekala & Niskala; Vol I: Essays on Religion, Ritual & Art and *Bali – Sekala & Niskala; Vol II: Essays on Society Tradition & Craft* (Periplus Editions, Singapore, 1989 & 1990), by Fred B Eiseman, are attractive anthologies of essays covering many aspects of Balinese life.

Bali, The Ultimate Island by Leonard Leuras & R Ian Lloyd (Times Editions, Singapore, 1987) is the ultimate coffee-table book on Bali. It's a heavyweight volume with superb photographs, both old and new, together with an interesting text which manages to take some new angles on this heavily written about and photographed island.

Leonard Leuras, this time in partnership with Rio Helmi, takes another look at the island in *Bali High – Paradise from the Air* (Times Editions, Singapore, 1990). It's a collection of photographs of Bali taken from a helicopter and provides some surprising new perspectives and angles. Some of the most interesting shots are actually not of Bali at all, but of neighbouring Lombok.

Archaeology For descriptions of the ancient sites of Bali, with text which puts them in historical and cultural context, look at *Monumental Bali* by A J Bernet Kempers (Periplus, 1991). It's interestingly written and well illustrated and could turn a casual tourist into a Balinese temple buff. It has a serious bibliography.

History Most material on Balinese history is included in books on Indonesia, or as it relates to art, culture or religion which is uniquely Balinese. *Bali in the 19th Century* (Yayasan Obor Indonesia, 1991) covers the early colonial period and the ritual capitulation of the Balinese nobility, and is interesting because the author, Ide Anak Agung Gede, is himself of the Balinese nobility.

Anthropology Margaret Mead and Gregory Bateson were two of the many prominent anthropologists who have worked on Bali. Their *Balinese Character – a photographic analysis* (New York Academy of Sciences) was first published in 1942, and has been heavily discussed and criticised. For example, a passivity which they observed in children, and explained in cultural terms, was more probably attributable to malnutrition. *The Balinese people – a reinvestigation of character* (Oxford, Singapore, 1992) by G D Jensen & L K Suryani (a Balinese) is a critique of the Mead-Bateson book. The noted American anthropologist Clifford Geertz has written extensively on Bali, but often in the context of broader anthropological theory; his book *The Interpretation of Cultures* (Basic Books, New York, 1973) includes three essays on Bali.

Art & Culture For information on Bali's complex and colourful artistic and cultural heritage look for the huge and expensive *The Art & Culture of Bali* (Oxford University Press) by Urs Ramseyer.

Balinese Paintings by Anak Agung Made Djelantik (Oxford University Press, 1986) is a concise and handy overview of the field written by a Balinese. *Perceptions of Paradise: images of Bali in the arts* is a substantial, well-produced and beautifully illustrated book on Balinese art, published by the Neka Museum in Ubud. An economical and useful introduction to Balinese painting can also be found in *The Development of Painting in Bali* published by the Neka Museum. It covers the various schools of painting and also has short biographies of well-known artists, including many of the Western artists who have worked on Bali.

For a study of traditional Balinese myth and painting, see *The Epic of Life – a Balinese journey of the soul* (Bullfinch Press) which tells the story of the Bhima Swarga as illustrated in the paintings on the ceiling of Kerta Ghosa in Klungkung.

Balinese Textiles, by Brigitta Hauser, Marie-Louise Nabholz-Kartaschoff & Urs Ramseyer (Periplus Editions, 1991), is a large and lavishly illustrated guide to various styles of weaving and their significance. Another special interest guide is *Masks of Bali*, by Judy Slattim (Chronicle Books). Woodcarving is refined to the stage of an artform on Bali, as explained in *Woodcarvings of Bali*, by Fred Eiseman, another nice little book from Periplus Editions.

Colin McPhee's *Music in Bali* (Da Capo Press, New York, 1976 edition) is the most thorough and scholarly study of the subject. *Balinese Music*, by Michael Tenzer (Periplus Editions, 1991), is a more up-to-date and very readable treatment.

Other Subjects Periplus Editions produces a number of small, attractive and informative books which will appeal to those with specific interests. Titles are widely available on Bali. Everyone will enjoy the beauty of Bali's plant life, and *Flowers of Bali* and *Fruits of Bali*, both by Fred & Margaret Eiseman, are nicely illustrated books which will tell what you're admiring or eating. *Birds of Bali* is written by Victor Mason, who conducts guided bird walks from the Beggar's Bush pub in Ubud, with lovely water-colour illustrations by Frank Jarvis. A truly mouth-watering book is *The Food of Bali*, by Heinz von Holzen, Lothar Arsana & Wendy Hutton, which not only explains the cultural context of Balinese food, but also describes ingredients and techniques, and has over 70 recipes for delicious-looking dishes so you can recreate the taste of Bali at home.

Guidebooks
For travel further afield in Indonesia look for Lonely Planet's *Indonesia – a travel survival kit* or to continue beyond Indonesia there's *South-East Asia on a shoestring*. There are a number of travel guides to Bali, but many of them are long on background reading and colour photos but short on up-to-date travel information and useful maps. *Insight Bali* (APA Productions, Singapore) is a guidebook-cum-photographic souvenir with some excellent photographs. Periplus Editions produces a number of beautifully illustrated, useful and detailed books about Indonesia, including a guide to Bali, and some more specialised publications, several of which are already listed here. Their *Underwater Indonesia* is a beautiful and detailed guide for scuba divers pursuing their interest in Indonesian waters.

Another specialist guidebook is *Indo Surf & Lingo*, by Peter Neely, which tells surfers where and when to find good waves on Bali. It also has some tips on surfing around other islands, and a language guide with Indonesian translations of useful words like 'big', 'wave' and 'tube'. It's not a totally professional publication, but it has good information and a good attitude. Order from the publisher at PO Box 950 Noosa Heads 4567, Queensland, Australia (fax 074 475937); A$20 including postage.

Phrasebooks

The most useful language for travellers to know on Bali is Bahasa Indonesia, and a good phrasebook is a wise investment. *Indonesia Phrasebook* is a concise and handy introduction to Bahasa Indonesia from the Lonely Planet Language Survival Kit series.

There's little need to use the Balinese language (rather than Bahasa Indonesia) on Bali, and it's far too complicated to pick up without serious study, but a few words can be interesting and fun. A handy little booklet entitled *Bali Pocket Dictionary* by N Shadeg (Yayasan Dharma Bhakti Pertwiwi, 1992) is available on Bali. It's an unassuming book with a little background information on Bali, some interesting observations on caste and language, and a list of 1000 words in English with translations into Bahasa Indonesia and three of the forms of Balinese which are used in conversation with persons of various caste.

Bookshops

There are bookshops in Kuta, Sanur and Ubud, with limited selections of new books. Elsewhere, bookshops have mostly second-hand books. Interesting books can also be found at the Bali Foto Centre at Kuta, at Murni's Warung in Ubud, and at the Neka Gallery in Ubud. None of them has a lot of books but they all have interesting selections, including some books you won't find elsewhere. You will often find Asian-based Oxford Paperback books and Periplus titles at these places. Prices of the same book will vary widely so it may be worth shopping around. In some (but not all) of the big hotels the mark-up on books is particularly severe.

If you just want something easy to read on the beach then your best bet will be the numerous second-hand bookshops and book exchanges – many budget hotels sell used books too. You might find the odd interesting book on Bali as well, but they're mostly paperback fiction. Used copies of Lonely Planet guides are also available, often for more than than the original cover price – don't complain if they're out of date.

MAPS

Nelles Verlag's 1:180,000 full-colour sheet map of Bali is excellent for topography and roads, though the maps of built-up areas are not as helpful. It's easily obtained on Bali. *Explorer's Bali* is a very colourful 1:165,000 map of Bali, with good detail of many of the smaller rural roads. The larger scale inset maps have even more detail, and show many of the one-way traffic restrictions and the location of petrol stations – very useful if you're driving. The tropical fish which decorate the maps are an interesting cartographic feature. The *Bali Pathfinder* map is a bit cluttered, but it has the best depiction of the area round Ubud and good maps of some non-tourist towns. The *Travel Treasure* publication has a colourful annotated map of Bali on one side, and sketch maps of main tourist areas on the back. The maps aren't brilliantly clear, detailed or accurate, but they have lots of handy snippets of information around the edges.

Because Bali is so humid, paper gets damp and soggy and maps start coming to pieces after a few days' use. One reader suggested bringing some adhesive plastic film and covering the whole map with it.

MEDIA

In the past, many foreigners have regarded Indonesian media as vehicles for government propaganda, and have been suspicious of government censorship, and self-censorship by the press. Generally the government does regard the mass media as an instrument of policy, and has managed the distribution of information in the interests of what it sees as national unity and development. But the increasing availability of news and information from international sources (including satellite TV), and the improving standard and extent of education, enable Balinese to be increasingly well informed.

Critical discussions, views and ideas are heard more frequently than a few years ago, but their acceptability depends greatly on how those ideas are expressed. One can discuss the impact of a government policy, but it is unwise to attack the government itself, and particularly to criticise officials and leaders, who should be shown appropriate respect. Even in the international media, most stories about Indonesia depend on local sources, which could be sanctioned if they were to disseminate material regarded as contrary to the national interest.

Newspapers & Magazines

The English-language *Bali Post* comes out twice a month, and has quite good information on what's happening on Bali. There are Indonesian-language papers too, both national and local, but nothing in the Balinese language. Other English-language papers available on Bali include the *Jakarta Post*, the *Indonesian Observer* and the *Indonesian Times*.

Time, *Newsweek* and the *International Herald Tribune* are on sale in tourist areas. Recent Australian, American and European papers are available only a day or so after publication date – some are sold on the streets in Kuta.

Bali Tourist Guide is a free monthly tabloid for tourists and the tourism industry, full of advertisements for restaurants, shops and tourist services. It also has a lot of very useful information – addresses, phone numbers, sketch maps, temple festival dates etc. The coverage extends to Lombok, east Java and even Yogyakarta.

TV

The government operates a national TV network, Televisi Republik Indonesia (TVRI), which reaches the whole country via satellite and microwave links. It broadcasts every afternoon and evening. As well as pro-government news and information services in Indonesian, there are also Indonesian music, dance and drama programmes, subtitled reruns of imported entertainment programmes (usually from the USA) and pro-government news programmes in English. There's an English-language news service and weather report for tourists on Bali at about 6.30 pm every evening.

Another government station, TPI, is an educational station which broadcasts every morning. Every village is supposed to have at least one TV set, as part of the government's information and education policies.

Places with the necessary satellite dish (*parabola* is the local term) and decoder can pick up a number of commercial stations, and also international networks like CNN, ESPN and TV Australia. This facility is a popular feature in mid-range, upwardly mobile tourist hotels.

TV may pose a much greater threat to Balinese culture than mass tourism. It's not so much that the content of the TV programming threatens to undermine traditional beliefs – but when you see a whole warung-full of people watching a sit-com (even a Balinese sit-com; there is such a thing) with obvious enjoyment, you wonder if there will ever be enough time for practising traditional dances, playing the gamelan or attending to the business of the banjar.

Radio

The government radio station, Radio Republic Indonesia (RRI) has information and entertainment, and an English-language news service twice a day. There's also a commercial radio station in Denpasar which broadcasts contemporary Indonesian music, amongst other things. Other commercial radio is from Java, via repeater stations on Bali. Some of the disk jockeys have very cool Western-style presentation.

Short-wave broadcasts, including Radio Australia, Voice of America and the BBC World Service, can be picked up, though the Indonesian government might not like what is said at times. Officially you need a permit to bring a radio/cassette player into the country.

PHOTOGRAPHY
Film & Processing

Bali is very photogenic – you can go through lots of film. Fortunately, a good variety of film is widely available at reasonable prices. For print film, 100 ASA Fujicolor or Kodacolor Gold costs about 6000 rp for a 24-exposure roll, 9000 rp for a 36-exposure roll. A 36-exposure roll of 100 ASA Fuji-chrome slide film costs around 10,000 rp, processing not included. For serious photographers, Fujichrome RHP and Ektachrome are available at 13,000 to 15,000 rp for 36 exposures. It pays to shop around for film if you want to buy a lot or if you have special requirements.

Developing and printing is widely available, very cheap and of quite good quality. You can get colour print film done in a few hours in the innumerable photographic shops in Kuta, Sanur, Ubud and elsewhere, while slide film takes two or three days. The processing cost for a roll of 24 colour prints is about 9000 rp and for a roll of 36, about 12,000 rp. There are all sorts of deals for larger prints, double prints and enlargements.

Taking Photos

Shoot early in the day – from 9 am until 3 pm the sun is intense and straight overhead, so you're likely to get a bluish washed-out look to your pictures. In the late afternoon the sky is often overcast or hazy, and it's hard to get really clear sharp images. If you do shoot in the middle of the day, a skylight filter may cut the haze. When the sun is low in the sky, a lens hood can help reduce problems with reflection or direct sunlight on the lens.

Those picturesque, green rice fields come up best if backlit by the sun. For those oh-so-popular sunset shots at Kuta or Lovina, set your exposure on the sky without the sun making an appearance – then shoot at the sun. It's surprisingly dark in the shade of the trees, particularly in the understorey of a forest, so you can find it difficult to take photos of lush gorges or monkeys without a flash. Faster film (400 ASA) can be useful.

Photographic Etiquette

Photograph with discretion and manners. It's always polite to ask first, and if they say no then don't. A gesture, a smile and a nod are all that is usually necessary. Often people will ask you to take their photo, and you more-or-less have to – the problem is getting

them in a natural pose. If you promise to send them a copy, get their address and do so.

Military installations are not widespread on Bali, but you should be aware that these are sensitive subjects – if in doubt, ask before you shoot.

There's one place not to take photographs at all – public bathing places. Just because the Balinese bathe in streams, rivers, lakes or other open places doesn't mean they don't think of them as private places. Balinese simply do not 'see' one another when they're bathing, and to intrude with a camera is like sneaking up to someone's bathroom window and pointing your camera through.

HEALTH

Travel health depends on your predeparture preparations, your day-to-day health care while travelling and how you handle any medical problem or emergency that does develop. Few travellers experience more than upset stomachs on Bali. The greatest risk is that of accidental injury, particularly traffic accidents. That's when it pays to have travel insurance.

Travel Health Guides

There are a number of books on travel health:

Staying Healthy in Asia, Africa & Latin America, Volunteers in Asia. Probably the best all-round guide to carry, as it's compact but very detailed and well organised.

Travellers' Health, Dr Richard Dawood, Oxford University Press. Comprehensive, easy to read, authoritative and also highly recommended, although it's rather large to lug around.

Where There is No Doctor, David Werner, Hesperian Foundation. A very detailed guide intended for someone going to work in an undeveloped country, like a Peace Corps worker, rather than for the average traveller.

Predeparture Preparations

Travel & Health Insurance You should regard travel insurance as essential, mainly to ensure your access to the best treatment in the event of illness or injury, but also to protect you against cancellation penalties on advance-purchase flights, and against theft or other loss of your possessions. Travel insurance policies offered by travel agents are becoming more expensive, but they are usually good value for the range of risks they cover, and the peace of mind. Medical costs, and therefore medical insurance, are not outrageously expensive in Indonesia, so premiums are not high and you can afford not to skimp on your cover.

If you plan to engage in an activity which an insurer might consider high risk, like trekking, surfing, scuba diving or motorcycling, make sure it is covered. Read the small print carefully as it's easy to be caught out by exclusions.

Personal liability cover is a good idea, particularly if you plan to rent a car or motorbike ('third party' insurance is not usually included in the rental deal), but some policies specifically exclude liability arising from use of a motor vehicle.

Some travel insurance policies include access to a medical evacuation service if first-class medical care is unavailable when and where you need it. Medical evacuation firms serving Bali include Asian Emergency Assistance (AEA), World Access International (WAI), and International SOS Assistance. Evacuation cover is recommended for all visitors to Bali. While there are hospitals, clinics and doctors, the standards of casualty and intensive care are not what you might expect at home. (See the end of this Health section.)

Medical Kit A small, straightforward medical kit is a wise thing to carry. Check the use-by dates on the stuff left over from your last trip. A possible kit list includes:

Aspirin or Panadol – for pain or fever

antihistamine (such as Benadryl) – useful as a decongestant for colds, allergies, to ease the itch from insect bites or stings or to help prevent motion sickness. Some capsules which relieve flu symptoms, such as Vicks HeadClear or Drixora, contain antihistamines.

antibiotics – useful if you're travelling well off the beaten track, but they must be prescribed and you should carry the prescription with you.

kaolin preparation (Pepto-Bismol), Imodium or Lomotil – if really necessary, for reducing the severity of diarrhoea

rehydration mixture – for treatment of severe diarrhoea; this is particularly important if you're travelling with children.

antiseptic, Betadine, and antibiotic powder or similar 'dry' spray – for cuts and grazes

antifungal powder or cream – for tinea or other fungal infections of the feet or crotch

calamine lotion or Caladryl cream – to ease irritation from bites, stings, rashes and sunburn

bandages and Band-aids – for minor injuries

scissors, tweezers, needle and a thermometer (note that mercury thermometers are prohibited by airlines)

insect repellent – a tropical strength one with di-ethyl toluamide (DEET), like *Off* or *Rid*

sunblock – take a full strength 15+ sunblock for maximum protection, as well as a product which will enable you to get a suntan if you want one. Take a chapstick for lip protection.

water purification tablets or iodine – if you plan to stay in remote areas

Health Preparations Make sure you're healthy before you start travelling. Ensure your teeth are OK; it's not hard to find a dentist *(doktor gigi)* on Bali, but it's probably not how you want to spend your holiday.

If you wear glasses take a spare pair and your prescription. You can get new spectacles made up quickly, cheaply and competently in Kuta, Sanur and Denpasar.

If you need to take some particular drug or medication, it's wise to bring it with you, along with the prescription to allay suspicions of police and customs officers. If the pharmaceutical you need is available at all it's more than likely to be available without prescription.

Immunisation There are no health entry requirements for most visitors to Indonesia but it's wise to be vaccinated against typhoid and tetanus and have them recorded in a yellow International Health Certificate booklet. You can arrange these vaccinations through your doctor or at your local health centre.

Plan ahead for getting your vaccinations as some of them require an initial shot followed by a booster, while others should not be given together. Most travellers from Western countries will have been immunised against various diseases during childhood but your doctor may still recommend booster shots against measles or polio, diseases still prevalent in many developing countries. The period of protection offered by vaccinations differs widely and some are contraindicated if you are pregnant.

Cholera – Protection is not required, not very effective, lasts only three to six months and is contraindicated for pregnancy.

Hepatitis A – Gammaglobulin, as a single dose, offers limited protection against hepatitis A for three to six months only. It's a blood product, so don't get it in countries where you're not 100% sure the blood supply is free of HIV. A course of Havrix injections over several months is more effective, and will provide 10 years' protection against hepatitis A. It's quite expensive.

Polio – Top up your protection every 10 years.

Tetanus & Diptheria – Boosters are necessary every 10 years and protection is highly recommended.

Typhoid – Protection lasts for three years and is useful if you are travelling for long in rural, tropical areas. You may get some side effects such as pain at the injection site, fever, headache and a general unwell feeling.

Malaria Prophylaxis There is very little risk of malaria on Bali (see below), but if you're going to Lombok you should start a course of anti-malarial drugs at least a week before you get there. See the Lombok Facts for the Visitor chapter for more information.

Medical Problems & Treatment
Stomach Upsets The infamous 'Bali Belly', or travellers' diarrhoea, affects many visitors but it's usually not a serious health risk, it doesn't last long and with a little care you can generally avoid it completely. Most Bali Bellies are usually just stomachs rebelling against something new and different.

Be a little careful in what and where you eat – avoid small local warungs until your digestive system has built up a little resistance. Water, uncooked food, and cooked food that has been left to cool for too long are all big risks. Most ice is made with purified water, but it can be risky. Well-cooked food is always safest. Never drink unboiled tap water. Mineral water, in sealed plastic bottles, is available almost everywhere. Major brands of packaged ice cream are usually OK, but don't touch the locally made ice cream sold on the street.

Bali is not an inherently unhygienic place and most of the time you can eat and drink pretty much anything you please with little risk. High standards of cleanliness are required in all tourist restaurants, and even food carts are licensed and always look reasonably clean.

If you do come down with something, it's better if you can fight it off without medication, so you build up some resistance against a repeat performance. Dehydration is the main danger with any diarrhoea, particularly for children, so fluid replenishment is the number one treatment. Weak black tea with a little sugar, soda water, or soft drinks allowed to go flat and diluted 50% with water are all good. With severe diarrhoea a rehydrating solution is necessary to replace minerals and salts. Stick to a bland diet as you recover and avoid fruit and fruit juice which can aggravate diarrhoea.

If you have to resort to medication, Lomotil or Imodium can bring relief from the symptoms, although they do not actually cure the problem. Only use these drugs if absolutely necessary, eg, if you *must* travel. For children Imodium is preferable, but do not use these drugs if the patient has a high fever or is severely dehydrated. Don't use these drugs for more than 48 hours, and never if there is blood or pus in the stools.

Antibiotics can be very useful in treating severe diarrhoea especially if it is accompanied by nausea, vomiting, stomach cramps or mild fever. Three days of treatment should be sufficient and an improvement should occur within 24 hours.

Dysentery Although it's unlikely that you would get dysentery on Bali or Lombok, it's worth pointing out the symptoms to avoid confusion with Bali Belly. Dysentery is a serious illness caused by contaminated food or water and is characterised by severe diarrhoea, often with blood or mucus in the stool. While you will recover from a simple case of the runs in a couple of days, dysentery will continue for a week or more depending on the type.

There are two kinds of dysentery. Bacillary dysentery is characterised by a high fever and rapid development; headache, vomiting and stomach pains are also symptoms. It generally does not last longer than a week, but it is highly contagious. Amoebic dysentery is more gradual in developing, has no fever or vomiting but is a more serious illness. It is not a self-limiting disease: it will persist until treated and can recur and cause long-term damage. A'stool test is necessary to diagnose which kind of dysentery you have, so you should seek medical help urgently.

Giardiasis The intestinal parasite which causes this is present in contaminated water. The symptoms are stomach cramps, nausea, a bloated stomach, watery, foul-smelling, grey/khaki diarrhoea and frequent gas. Giardia can appear several weeks after you have been exposed to the parasite. The symptoms may disappear for a few days and then return; this can go on for several weeks. Fasigyn (Tinidazole) is the recommended drug, but it should only be taken under medical supervision. Antibiotics are of no use.

Viral Gastroenteritis This is caused not by bacteria but, as the name suggests, by a virus. It is characterised by stomach cramps, diarrhoea, and sometimes by vomiting and/or a slight fever. All you can do is rest and drink lots of fluids.

Hepatitis A The more common form of this disease, hepatitis A is spread by contaminated food or water. The first symptoms are fever, chills, headache, fatigue, weakness, aches and pains. This is followed by loss of appetite, nausea, vomiting, abdominal pain, dark urine, light-coloured faeces and jaundiced skin; the whites of the eyes may also turn yellow. In some cases there may just be a feeling of being unwell or tired, accompanied by loss of appetite, aches and pains and the jaundiced effect. You should seek

medical advice, but in general there is not much you can do apart from resting, drinking lots of fluids, eating lightly and avoiding fatty foods. People who have had hepatitis must forego alcohol for six months after the illness, as hepatitis attacks the liver and it needs that amount of time to recover. There are some effective prophylactic drugs.

Hepatitis B Formerly called serum hepatitis, hepatitis B is spread through sexual contact or through skin penetration – for instance, it could be transmitted via dirty needles or via blood transfusions. Avoid having your ears pierced, tattoos done or injections where you have doubts about the sanitary conditions. The symptoms and treatment of type B are much the same as for type A. There is a vaccine available, but is probably not necessary for travellers on Bali who refrain from high risk activities.

Worms These parasites are most common in rural, tropical areas. They can be present on unwashed vegetables or in undercooked meat and you can pick them up through your skin by walking in bare feet, especially in areas with animal droppings. Some of the symptoms to watch for include distended stomach and an itchy anus. Infestations may not show up for some time, and although they are generally not serious, if left untreated they can cause severe health problems. A stool test is necessary to pinpoint the problem and medication is often available over the counter.

Malaria Bali and Lombok are officially within the malarial zones, but the risk of contracting malaria in the tourist areas of southern Bali is almost nonexistent. In northern Bali there is a very low risk of malaria after the rainy season when there is open water in puddles where mosquitoes can breed. There is no indication of drug resistant strains of malaria on Bali. It's not necessary to take antimalarial drugs for travel on Bali during the dry season, providing you are careful to avoid mosquito bites (confirm this with your own doctor to be sure). Lombok is a high-risk area for malaria, and you should start a course of prophylactic drugs before you go there – see Lombok's Facts for the Visitor chapter for details.

In any case, the first line of defence is to protect yourself against mosquitoes. In the evening, when mosquitoes are most active, cover bare skin, particularly your ankles. Use an insect repellent on exposed skin. Burn mosquito coils to discourage them – light one in your room an hour before you go to bed. Sleep under a cover, and use a mosquito net if your room is not well screened and mosquitoes are prevalent. Don't wait till you hear them buzzing – the anopheles mosquito which carries malaria doesn't make a sound: the stealth mozzie. Actually, mosquitoes are not a real nuisance on Bali – at certain times of the year you don't even see them. The risk of infection is higher in rural areas and during the wet season.

Dengue Fever There is no prophylactic available for this mosquito-spread disease; the main preventative measure is to avoid mosquito bites. A sudden onset of fever, headaches and severe joint and muscle pains are the first signs before a rash starts on the trunk of the body and spreads to the limbs and face. After a further few days, the fever will subside and recovery will begin. Serious complications are not common.

Tetanus This potentially fatal disease is found in undeveloped tropical areas. It is difficult to treat but is preventable with immunisation. Tetanus occurs when a wound becomes infected by a germ which lives in the faeces of animals or people, so clean all cuts, punctures or animal bites. Tetanus is known as lockjaw, and the first symptom may be discomfort in swallowing, or stiffening of the jaw and neck; this is followed by painful convulsions of the jaw and whole body.

Rabies There are no current indications of rabies on Bali, but obviously one should avoid being bitten or scratched by animals.

Any bite, scratch or even lick from a mammal should be cleaned immediately and thoroughly, and treated with Betadine.

Sunburn In Bali you can get sunburnt very quickly, even through cloud and while swimming. Use a 15+ sunblock and take extra care with areas which don't normally see sun, like your feet. A broad-brimmed hat provides good protection, but you should also put sunblock on nose and lips. Even good sunblocks wash off with heavy sweating or swimming, so reapply every two or three hours. People get badly burned on the shoulders while snorkelling. For surfers, a helmet protects your head against the sun as well as the coral. Calamine lotion or Caladryl cream provides some relief from mild sunburn.

Prickly Heat Prickly heat is an itchy rash caused by excessive perspiration trapped under the skin. It usually strikes people who have just arrived in a hot climate and whose pores have not yet opened sufficiently to cope with greater sweating. Keeping cool, bathing often, using talcum powder, or even resorting to air-conditioning may help until you acclimatise.

Heat Exhaustion Dehydration or salt deficiency can cause heat exhaustion. Take time to acclimatise to high temperatures and make sure you get sufficient liquids (*not* alcohol). Salt deficiency is characterised by fatigue, lethargy, headaches, giddiness and muscle cramps, and salt tablets may help relieve these symptoms. Vomiting or diarrhoea can deplete your liquid and salt levels. Anhydrotic heat exhaustion, caused by an inability to sweat, is quite rare. Unlike the other forms of heat exhaustion it is likely to strike people who have been in a hot climate for some time, rather than newcomers.

Heat Stroke This serious, sometimes fatal, condition can occur if the body's heat-regulating mechanism breaks down and the body temperature rises to dangerous levels. Long, continuous periods of exposure to high temperatures can leave you vulnerable to heat stroke. You should avoid excessive alcohol or strenuous activity when you first arrive in a hot climate.

The symptoms are feeling unwell, not sweating very much or at all, and a high body temperature (39°C to 41°C). Where sweating has ceased the skin becomes flushed and red. Severe, throbbing headaches and lack of coordination will also occur, and the sufferer may be confused or aggressive. Eventually the victim will become delirious or convulse. Hospitalisation is essential, but meanwhile get the patient out of the sun, remove their clothing, cover them with a wet sheet or towel and fan them continually.

Fungal Infections Hot weather fungal infections are most likely to occur on the scalp, between the toes or fingers (tinea, or athlete's foot), in the groin (jock itch or crotch rot) and on the body (ringworm). You get ringworm (which is a fungal infection, not a worm) from infected animals or by walking on damp areas, like shower floors.

To prevent fungal infections wear loose, comfortable clothes, avoid artificial fibres, wash frequently and dry carefully. If you do get an infection, wash the infected area daily with a disinfectant or medicated soap and water, and rinse and dry well. Apply an antifungal powder like the widely available Tinaderm. Try to expose the infected area to air or sunlight as much as possible and wash all towels and underwear in hot water as well as changing them often.

Motion Sickness Eating lightly before and during a trip will reduce the chances of motion sickness. If you are prone to motion sickness try to find a place that minimises disturbance – near the wing on aircraft, close to midships on boats, near the centre on buses. Fresh air usually helps; reading or cigarette smoke doesn't. Commercial anti-motion-sickness preparations, which can cause drowsiness, have to be taken before the trip commences; when you're feeling sick it's too late. Ginger is a natural preventative and is available in capsule form.

Sexually Transmitted Diseases Sexual contact with an infected sexual partner spreads these diseases. While abstinence is the only 100% preventative, using condoms is also effective. Sores, blisters or rashes around the genitals, and discharges or pain when urinating are common symptoms of gonorrhoea and syphilis. Symptoms may be less marked or not observed at all in women. Syphilis symptoms eventually disappear completely but the disease continues and can cause severe problems in later years. The treatment of gonorrhoea and syphilis is by antibiotics. Other sexually transmitted diseases include hepatitis B (see above), AIDS and genital herpes.

AIDS/HIV Quite widespread in Thailand, AIDS is also prevalent in other South-East Asian countries. The risk of sexual transmission of the HIV virus can be dramatically reduced by the use of a condom *(kondom)*. These are available from supermarkets and drugstores in tourist areas, and from the pharmacy *(apotik)* in almost any town; about 500 rp each.

AIDS can also be spread through infected blood transfusions; most developing countries cannot afford to screen blood for transfusions. It can also be spread by the use of dirty needles for acupuncture, tattooing, vaccinations or intravenous drug use. If you do need an injection, buy a new syringe and ask the doctor to use it. If you need a transfusion, a travelling companion you know may be safer than a blood donor you don't know, if you have the same blood group. It helps to know what your blood group is.

Cuts, Bites & Stings Skin punctures can easily become infected in hot climates and may be difficult to heal. Any cuts should be washed carefully and treated with Betadine. Where possible avoid bandages and Band-aids, which can keep wounds wet. Cuts on your feet and ankles are particularly troublesome – a new pair of sandals can quickly give you a nasty abrasion that can be difficult to heal.

Coral cuts are notoriously slow to heal, as

the coral injects a weak venom into the wound. Avoid coral cuts by wearing shoes when walking on reefs, and clean any cut thoroughly.

Avoid contact with jellyfish – there are none of the deadly ones around Bali, but stings from many types of jellyfish can be painful. Dousing in vinegar will de-activate any stingers which have not 'fired'. Calamine lotion, antihistamines and analgesics may reduce the reaction and relieve the pain. Seek local advice if you think jellyfish are around.

Women's Health

Gynaecological Problems Poor diet, lowered resistance due to the use of antibiotics, and even contraceptive pills can lead to vaginal infections when travelling in hot climates. Keeping the genital area clean, and wearing skirts or loose-fitting trousers and cotton underwear will help to prevent infections. Have showers rather than baths.

Yeast infections like thrush, characterised by a rash, itch and discharge, can be treated with a douche of diluted vinegar (one tablespoon to a litre of water), or even a lemon-juice douche or yoghurt. Nystatin suppositories are the usual medical prescription, with the external use of Canestan cream.

Trichomonas is a more serious vaginal infection; symptoms are a discharge and a burning sensation when urinating. Male sexual partners must also be treated, and if a vinegar-water douche is not effective, medical attention should be sought. Flagyl is the prescribed drug.

Pregnancy Most miscarriages occur during the first three months of pregnancy, so this is the most risky time to travel. The last three months should also be spent within reasonable distance of good medical care, as quite serious problems can develop at this time. Pregnant women should avoid all unnecessary medication, but vaccinations and malarial prophylactics should still be taken where possible. Additional care should be taken to prevent illness and particular attention should be paid to diet and nutrition.

Medical Facilities on Bali

Despite the appearance of modernity in tourist areas, Bali is part of a developing country, and most medical facilities are basic. Specialist facilities for neurosurgery and cardiac surgery are nonexistent, and the range of available drugs (including painkillers) is very limited. For emergencies, about the best place to go is the main hospital in Denpasar, RSUP Sanglah, on the south side of town (☎ 227911, 235456). It's open 24 hours a day, and has a relatively modern casualty section and English-speaking doctors. The medical centre in Nusa Dua (☎ 71118) is modern and well equipped, and can arrange an evacuation to a first-class hospital in Singapore or Darwin.

There are also private clinics and medical practices. The Surya Husadha Clinic (☎ 225249 or 223786), Jalan Pulau Serangan 1-3, Denpasar, is used to treating tourists and is open 24 hours. Another private medical practice which deals with visitors is the Iamat Center (☎ 288466), Jalan Sanur 101 Bunderan, Renon. Your hotel should be able to recommend a local English-speaking doctor, or call one of the expensive hotels in a resort area and ask them. Travel insurance policies often have an emergency assistance phone number, which might be able to recommend a doctor or clinic, or use its contacts to find one in a remote area.

Away from the main southern tourist areas you will have to cope at the local hospital or clinic. Health care is not free anywhere on Bali, and you will get more prompt attention if you can pay cash up front for treatment, drugs, surgical equipment, food, drinking water and so on. Offer to pay in advance for anything you need, including a private doctor to visit you. Try to get receipts and paperwork so you can claim it all later on your travel insurance. A lot of the basic hospital services on Bali, like meals, washing, and clean clothing, are normally provided by the patient's family. If you are unfortunate enough to be on your own in a Bali hospital, contact your consulate – you need help.

Try to keep calm – anger is counterproductive. Be grateful that you have the resources to get the best medical care available on Bali, and that you were wise enough to take out travel insurance.

WOMEN TRAVELLERS

Women travelling solo on Bali will get a lot of attention from Balinese guys, which could be a hassle, but generally the guys are unlikely to get aggressive or violent. Sometimes young boys will touch up Western women, which can be infuriating.

Many Balinese guys are very charming, and there is a gigolo scene at Kuta, Sanur and Lovina. It's usually pretty harmless, though some guys are con-artists who practise elaborate deceits, or downright theft, to get a woman's money.

Many guys will try their luck with female tourists, and it's fair to say that some of them get enough encouragement to keep a lot of others trying. Never respond to come-ons or rude comments. Completely ignoring them is always best. A haughty attitude can work wonders. In India you might call it a hint of the *memsahib*!

A husband (which equals any male partner) and/or children confer respectability. Even an imaginary husband can be used as a deterrent – he may arrive at any moment.

Some precautions are simply the same for any traveller, male or female, but women should take extra care not to find themselves alone on empty beaches, down dark streets or in other situations where help might not be available.

On the whole, Bali and Lombok are safer for women than most areas of the world and, with the usual care and caution, women can feel secure travelling alone there.

DANGERS & ANNOYANCES
Theft

Violent crime is relatively uncommon, but there is some bag snatching, pickpocketing and thieving from losmen rooms.

Snatchers often work in pairs from a motorbike – they pull up next to someone in a busy area, the guy on the back grabs the bag and slashes the strap, the guy on the front hits the throttle, and they're gone within half

a second. The bulky money belts which many travellers now wear *outside* their clothes are particularly vulnerable.

Pickpockets on bemos are also prevalent. The usual routine is for somebody to start a conversation to distract you while an accomplice steals your wallet, purse or whatever. Bemos tend to be pretty tightly packed, and a painting, large parcel, basket or the like can serve as a cover.

Losmen rooms are often not at all secure. Don't leave valuables in your room and beware of people who wander in and out of losmen; keep your room locked if you're not actually in it. Keep valuables at more than an arm's length from any unsecured window. Thefts from unlocked cars have also been reported. Many foolish people lose things by simply leaving them on the beach while they go swimming. You can leave airline tickets or other valuables in the safe deposit boxes which are found at many moneychangers, banks and hotels.

Some years ago there were mugging incidents down some of Kuta's less frequented *gangs* (alleys) at night, but that activity rapidly diminished when Kuta banjars organised vigilante groups to patrol at night.

Rip-Offs & Cons

Bali has such a relaxed atmosphere, and the people are so friendly that you may not be on the lookout for some scam. They're not all that common, but they do happen. Petrol stations have become notorious for getting 10 or 20 litres on the gauge before any petrol has hit the tank. It's hard to say when an accepted practice like overcharging becomes an unacceptable rip-off, but be warned that there are some people on Bali (not always Balinese) who will engage in a practised deceit in order to get money from a visitor.

One such con involves a friendly local discovering a serious problem with your car or motorbike – it's blowing smoke, leaking oil, or a wheel is wobbling badly. Fortunately, he has a brother/cousin/friend nearby who can help, and before you know it they've put some oil in the sump, or changed the wheel, and are demanding an outrageous sum for their trouble. At that stage you have to pay – you can't return the oil, or the work that has been done. The con relies on creating a sense of urgency, so beware of anyone who tries to rush you into something without mentioning a price.

Another con involves exploiting the sympathy which a relatively affluent visitor might have for a poorer Balinese. The routine often involves a Balinese guy taking a foreign friend to see 'his' village – usually it's not the guy's own village but the friend doesn't know that. The visitor may be shocked by the poor circumstances of the Balinese friend, who might also concoct a hard-luck story about a sick mother who can't pay for an operation, a brother who needs money for his education or an important religious ceremony that they can't afford. Visitors have often been persuaded to hand over quite large sums of money on such a pretext. A healthy scepticism is your best defence.

Most Balinese would never perpetrate a rip-off, but it seems that very few would warn a Westerner when one is happening. Not many people would pick your pocket on a bemo, but neither would they expose a pickpocket if they saw his fingers in your bag. Bystanders will watch someone put oil in your car unnecessarily for a rip-off price, and they may look uncomfortable and embarrassed about it, but they won't tell you what the right price is. Be suspicious if you notice that bystanders are uncommunicative and perhaps uneasy, and one guy is doing all the talking.

Hawkers, Pedlars & Touts

Many visitors regard the persistent attentions of people trying to sell things as *the* major annoyance on Bali. These activities are officially restricted in certain areas, like the waterside at Kuta Beach, or the environs of just about any decent hotel or restaurant, but elsewhere visitors are frequently, even constantly, hassled to buy things. Hawkers often display a superb grasp of sales techniques, in several different languages, and have a patience and persistence that's as impressive

as it is infuriating. Some of Bali's most successful tourist businesses are run by people who started by selling postcards to tourists.

The best way to deal with hawkers is to ignore them from the first instance. Eye contact is crucial – don't make any! Even a polite 'no thank you' seems to encourage them ('You don't want a watch, then perhaps you'd like a ring...'). Never ask the price or comment on the quality unless you're interested in buying, or you want to spend half an hour haggling. It may seem very rude to ignore people who smile and greet you so cheerfully, but you might have to be a lot ruder to get rid of a hawker after you have spent a few minutes politely discussing his/her watches, rings and prices. In Asian terms, it is impolite to say 'no' anyway – it's better form to firmly change the subject to anything other than what is for sale.

Many hawkers can be genuinely friendly and helpful people. Don't let their commercial imperatives get to you. They are just trying to make a living.

Traffic

Apart from the dangers of actually driving on Bali (see the Getting Around chapter), the traffic in most tourist areas is often annoying, and frequently dangerous to pedestrians. Footpaths can be rough, even unusable, so you often have to walk on the roadway. Those zebra stripes across the road are mainly decorative – don't expect traffic to stop because you think you're on a pedestrian crossing.

Swimming

The beaches at Kuta and Legian are subject to heavy surf and strong currents – swim between the flags. Other beaches are protected by coral reefs, but be careful when walking or swimming over coral. It can be very sharp and coral cuts can easily become infected. Swimming whilst under the influence of any intoxicant is dangerous.

Drugs

The old image of floating sky-high over Bali has faded considerably. There are some government posters around suggesting that 'you don't need drugs to experience the magic of Bali', and even the posters have faded. The marijuana and mushrooms of the Bali drug scene were imported tastes, and were never a part of traditional Balinese culture. You may well be offered dope on the street, particularly in Kuta, but you're unlikely to get a good deal, and you may even be turned in to the police by the dealers themselves. The authorities take a dim view of recreational drug use, and losmen owners can be quick to turn you in. It is an offence not to report someone whom you know to be using drugs, and there are not many places on Bali where you could light up a joint without someone getting a whiff of it.

Bali's famed magic mushrooms (*oong*) come out during the rainy season, but their effect is very variable. The mushrooms contain psilocybin, which is a powerful hallucinogen, though the dosage in a mushroom omelette is pretty inexact. Psilocybin may give you a stratospheric high, but it may also result in paranoid or psychotic reactions which can be extremely unpleasant. The likely response of the authorities to this form of tourism is also unpredictable, so it really can't be recommended.

When you come back home remember that, though drugs are scarcely available on Bali, your local customs department may still think that it's a hippie dope scene.

One drug that is very popular amongst Bali visitors is alcohol. There are lots of bars and pubs around, and an awful lot of beer bottles being recycled. The local firewater, *arak*, is distilled from rice wine and can be very strong. Overdosing on this stuff has probably caused more foreigners to freak out than all the other drugs on Bali combined.

Fortunately, the number of Westerners in jail for drug offences on Bali is now quite small. It's not that the authorities are becoming lenient – they're not. It's just that the whole scene is way out of fashion.

TAKING THE CHILDREN

Travelling with children anywhere requires energy and organisation (see Lonely Planet's *Travel with Children* by Maureen Wheeler), but on Bali the problems are somewhat lessened by the Balinese affection for children. They believe that children come straight from God, and the younger they are, the closer they are to God. To the Balinese, children are considered part of the community and everyone has a responsibility towards them, not just the parents. If a young child cries the Balinese get most upset and insist on finding the mother and handing the child over with a reproachful look. The expression is *tidak boleh* ('no crying'). Sometimes they despair of uncaring Western parents, and the child will be whisked off to a place where it can be cuddled, cosseted and fed. In tourist areas this is less likely, but it is still common in a more traditional environment. A toddler may even get too much attention!

Children are a social asset when you travel on Bali, and people will display great interest in any Western child they meet. You will have to learn to give their ages in Bahasa Indonesia (*bulan* means month, *tahun* means year), say what sex they are (*laki* is a boy, *perempuan* is a girl). You should also make polite enquiries about *their* children, present or absent.

Accommodation

You can choose between a package tour where everything is booked in advance, or travelling independently. Hotels with pools, air-con and a beachfront location are fun for kids, very convenient and provide a good holiday from domestic work, but you won't see much of Bali unless you make a real effort to get out. A beachfront place in Sanur or Candidasa, or a place with a pool in Ubud, would be the best choices for a package holiday with kids. The Kuta-Legian area has very heavy traffic and the surf can be rough. At most mid-range hotels it's pretty likely that there will be other kids to play with.

If you travel independently you can stay in losmen or small hotels, in smaller, quieter areas with minimal traffic and few tourists. The facilities aren't as good, but you can get perfectly acceptable accommodation and good clean food for a lot less than the cost of a package-tour hotel. You will have much closer contact with the Balinese, and your children will be pretty secure with the losmen owner's family watching over them. Most places, at whatever price level, have a 'family plan' which means that children up to about 12 can share a room with their parents free of charge. The catch is that hotels charge for extra beds – from a couple of thousand rupiah in a losmen up to US$30 in a really expensive hotel. If you need more space, just rent a separate room for the kids. You can usually negotiate a cheaper price for the second room (single room rate is a common deal). Very few hotels offer special programmes or supervised activities for kids, though most of them can arrange a baby-sitter. The Segara Village Hotel in Sanur has a children's play group from 9 am to 2 pm, set up like a kindergarten with lots of activities. Club Med in Nusa Dua will entertain them from breakfast till bedtime, and the cost is included, but it's an expensive place to stay.

Food

The same rules apply as for adults – kids should drink only clean water, eat only well-cooked food, or fruit that you have peeled yourself. If you're travelling with a young baby, it's much easier if it's breast-fed. For older babies, mashed bananas, eggs, peelable fruit and *bubur* (rice cooked to a mush in chicken stock – also known as chicken porridge) are all generally available. In tourist areas, restaurants serve yoghurt, pancakes, bread, fruit juices, ice cream and milk shakes, and supermarkets sell jars of baby food and packaged UHT milk and fruit juice. Bottled drinking water is available everywhere. Bring plastic bowls, plates, cups and spoons, for do-it-yourself meals.

Health

If your child develops stomach trouble, it may be no more than 'tourist trots'. If there is no pain or stomach cramps, put the child on a light, bland diet, and make sure the fluid intake is kept high. The major danger is dehydration and it is a good idea to carry an electrolyte mixture with you for such cases. Ask your doctor to recommend a kaolin mixture for your child; Pepto Bismal is very good. If the child has a fever, the stools contain blood or mucus, or the diarrhoea persists for more than two days, you should continue the fluid replacement treatment and find a doctor quickly.

Bali is officially in a malaria zone, but the risk is so slight that it is probably not worth a child taking antimalarial drugs (confirm this with your own doctor before you go). In any case, the first defence against malaria is to protect your child from mosquito bites. If you're going to Lombok then a course of antimalarials is definitely required – see Lombok's Facts for the Visitor chapter.

Never let your child run around in bare feet as worms and other parasites can enter through the feet. Any cut or scratch should be washed immediately and treated with Betadine. Head lice are common on Bali; lice shampoo will get rid of them. Tropical sun is a very real hazard. Use a total sunblock (SPF 15+) on all exposed skin, whenever they are out, and reapply it every few hours, especially if they have been swimming. Hats, shirts and shorts should always be worn in the sun. The lightweight lycra T-shirts which kids can wear while swimming are excellent. If your child does get sunburnt, apply Caladryl.

Dangers

The main danger is traffic, so try to stay in less busy areas. If your children can't look after themselves in the water then they must be supervised at all times – don't expect local people to act as lifesavers. Steep stairways and unfenced drops are other common hazards.

Other Problems

In Bali things are not always set up for children with the sorts of facilities, safeguards and services which Western parents regard as basic. In Bali children are part of a small community and they share the same furniture, food, transport and entertainment as everyone else. Not many restaurants provide a high-chair, and hardly any hotels have supervised activities for children. Many places with great views have nothing to stop your kids falling over the edge, and shops often have breakable things at kiddie height. Violent videos are sometimes shown in circumstances and at volumes where they can't be ignored.

Hotel and restaurant staff are usually very willing to help and to improvise, so always ask if you need something for your children. The situation is improving as more young kids come to Bali and more parents make their wishes known.

What to Bring
Apart from those items already mentioned in the Health section, bring some infant analgesic (like Panadol for kids), anti-lice shampoo, a medicine measure, and a thermometer.

You can bring disposable nappies with you, but they're widely available on Bali. Cloth nappies are more environmentally friendly, and not too much trouble – just rinse them in the bath with the hand-held shower head, soak them in a plastic bucket (always available) and wash them in the bucket or basin when you can.

For small children, bring a folding stroller or pusher, or you will be condemned to having them on your knee constantly, at meals and everywhere else. However, it won't be much use for strolling as there are very few paved footpaths which are wide and smooth enough to use the things. A papoose (for babies) or a backpack carrier is a much more useful way to move around with children. Take a stroller *and* a backpack if you can, and leave something else at home.

Give your children their own bag and have them choose what they want to take. Bring a few books for older children, and a scrap book for their cuttings and drawings.

If they will be spending some time snorkelling, it's a good idea to bring a well-fitting mask, snorkel and fins from home. Other water toys, like a boogie board, can keep kids entertained for hours. A simple camera, or a couple of the throwaway ones, will help your child look and feel like a real tourist. A pair of binoculars can make looking at things more fun.

Baby-Sitting & Child Care
Most expensive hotels advertise a baby-sitter service (often written as a 'baby sister'). The price is proportional to the cost of the hotel and can be quite expensive by local standards – several thousand rupiah per hour, most of which goes to the hotel. It's fine for a few hours in the evening, but the baby-sitter may not be so good at entertaining and supervising active kids for a whole afternoon. In small, family-style losmen, you'll always find someone to look after your children – often the owners' daughters, sisters or nieces. They will be much more comfortable looking after your child in their own family compound or village. Generally speaking, most Balinese over the age of 14 will be responsible child minders.

For more regular child care, what you need is a *pembantu*, which roughly translates as a nanny. Ask around to find a good one. They generally prefer to look after kids at their own place rather than yours – 6000 rp for two children for one day seems to be about the going rate at the moment.

Activities
Many of the things which adults want to do on Bali will not interest their children. Have days when you do what they want, to offset the times you drag them to shops or temples. Encourage them to learn about Bali so they can understand and enjoy more of what they see.

Water play is always fun – for 5000 rp or so you can often use a hotel's pool, even if you're not staying there. Or try the new Waterbom in Kuta, with a water slide and other watery entertainments. If your kids can swim a little, they can have a lot of fun with a mask and snorkel. Chartering a boat for a few hours sailing and snorkelling is good value. Hiring paddle boards, pedal boats etc is OK for a while, but can get pretty expensive. You can buy a model *prahu* (small boat) and try sailing it on a quiet beach. Colourful kites are sold in many shops and market stalls; get some string at a supermarket and the sky's the limit.

If you want to take kids shopping in Denpasar, bribe them with a promise of some rides in the amusement park at Tiara Dewata shopping centre, or a session on the video games there. A ride in a horse-drawn *dokar* is another Denpasar attraction.

In Ubud there are a number of craft courses like woodcarving and batik. Balinese dances can be entertaining for children – go for the ones with monkeys and frogs. Some restaurants have video movies for kids in the early evening. At least one TV station shows cartoons in the afternoon, in English with Indonesian sub-titles.

Things to Buy

Kuta and Ubud both have shops specialising in kids clothing and hand-made toys. Two colouring books with a Bali flavour are *Ketut Kodok the Frog* and *Color Bali in Color*. *Ayu & the Perfect Moon* is a children's book with a Balinese setting, published in Australia by Angus & Robinson. Western-style toys are available too, often quite cheaply, but check the quality.

SURFING

Thanks to Kirk Willcox, former editor of the Australian surfing magazine *Tracks*, who compiled much of the following surfing information in this book.

In recent years, the number of surfers on Bali has increased enormously, and good breaks can get very crowded. Many Balinese have taken to surfing *(main ski)*, and the grace of traditional dancing is said to influence their style. The surfing competitions on Bali are a major local event. Facilities for surfers have improved, and surf shops in Kuta will sell just about everything you need.

There are charter yachts which take groups of surfers for day trips around various local reefs, or for two-week 'surfaris' to great breaks on east Java (Grajagan), Nusa Lembongan, Lombok and Sumbawa, some of which just can't be reached by land. You'll see them advertised in the surfing press, and at numerous agents in Kuta. Yacht charter prices start at around US$75 per person per day. Even surfing on Bali has gone upmarket.

Indo Surf & Lingo, by Peter Neely, tells surfers where and when to find good waves around Bali and other islands, and how to avoid the crowds (see the Books section for details). The tide table from Tubes Bar, Poppies Gang II in Kuta, is an essential adjunct.

Equipment

A small board is usually adequate for the smaller breaks, but a few extra inches on your usual board length won't go astray. For the bigger waves, eight foot and upwards, you will need a gun. For a surfer of average height and build a board around the seven foot mark is perfect.

To get your boards to Bali in reasonable condition, you need a good board cover. Bali-bound airlines are used to carrying boards, but fins still get broken off. Bring a soft roof rack to secure your boards to a car, taxi or bemo. Long hikes with your board are difficult unless you have a boardstrap – add some foam padding to the shoulder. Take a good pair of running shoes for walking down steep, rocky paths on cliff faces.

Wax is available locally, but take your own anyway if you use it – in the tepid water and the hot sun a sticky wax is best. Board repairs are done in Kuta, and materials are available, but it is always advisable to have your own, especially if you're going to more remote spots. You can carry resin in a well-sealed container, but don't carry hardener or acetone on a plane.

To protect your feet take a pair of wetsuit booties or reef boots. A wetsuit vest is also very handy for chilly, windy overcast days, and it also protects your back and chest from sunburn, and being ground into the reefs. If you are a real tube maniac and will drive into anything no matter what the consequences, you are advised to take a short-sleeved springsuit. A lycra swimshirt (a 'rashie' to

Australians) is good protection against chills and sunburn.

Bring Betadine or surgical spirit, and cotton buds to put it on your cuts each night. Also bring a needle and pointy tweezers to remove sea urchin spines. Adhesive bandages that won't come off in the water are also necessary – Elastoplast is excellent. There are fairly well stocked chemists on Bali but it is easier to take your own.

A surfing helmet is a good idea, not just for protection from the reefs, but also to keep the sun off while you wait in the lineup. And it will probably give you better protection in a motorbike accident than the helmets which come with rented bikes.

Surviving Surfing

Wear a shirt when surfing and take ample supplies of a good sunblock, or you will miss out on good surf because you're too burnt to move. Riding a motorbike with a surfboard is deadly – hiring a car between a few surfers is just as cheap, and a lot safer. Brush up on basic mouth-to-mouth resuscitation – you might be called upon to use it, especially around the beach breaks of Kuta where foreigners often get into trouble.

If you write yourself off severely while surfing, or on the way to surf, head to the top hotels where there are good doctors. The medical centre at Nusa Dua is pretty good, and handy to the surfing areas of the Bukit Peninsula. Go for the more expensive private surgeries, be prepared to pay cash up front, and be glad you took out travel insurance. If you feel really bad, get the next plane home.

Where to Surf

The swells come from the Indian Ocean, so the surf is on the south side of the island, and strangely, on the north-west coast of Nusa Lembongan where the swell funnels into the strait between there and the Bali coast. In the dry season, from around May to September, the west coast has the best breaks, with the trade winds coming in from the south-east; this is also when Nusa Lembongan works best. In the wet season, October to March, surf the east side of the island, from Nusa

Dua round to Padangbai. If there's a north wind, or no wind at all, there are also a couple of breaks on the south coast of the Bukit Peninsula. There's lots of places to stay around Kuta, but nothing affordable near the breaks on the Bukit peninsula, so you'll need some transport. (Some of the main surf breaks are shown on the map of South Bali, at the start of that chapter.)

The most well known breaks are listed below, but there are other places which you can find. As you learn more about the weather and the ocean conditions you'll know where to look. No-one is giving away any 'secret spots'.

Kuta & Legian For your first plunge into the warm Indian Ocean, try the beach breaks at **Kuta Beach**; on full tide go out near the lifesaving club at the south end of the beach road. At low tide try the tubes around **Halfway Kuta**, probably the best place on Bali for beginners to practise. Start at the beach breaks if you are a bit rusty. The sand here is fine and packed hard, so it can be hard when you hit it. Treat even these breaks with respect. They provide zippering left and right barrels over shallow banks and can be quite a lot of fun. Some days you will not feel like travelling anywhere on the island looking for surf and you will be content with little sessions out here.

Further north, **Legian Beach** breaks can be pretty powerful, with lefts and rights on the sand bars off Jalan Melasti and Jalan Padma.

At Kuta and Legian you will encounter most of the local Balinese surfers. Over the years their surfing standard has improved enormously and because of this, and also because it is their island, treat them with respect. By and large they're usually quite amenable in the water, although some surfers have found their holidays cut short by a falling out with the locals. Give them the benefit of the doubt on a wave, and avoid getting into fights.

Further north again, there are more beach breaks off Seminyak and around the **Bali Oberoi** hotel. This is the trendy end of Kuta-

Legian and the beach scene can be fun, but the sea is fickle and can have dangerous rip tides – take a friend, and take care.

For more serious stuff, go to the reefs south of the beach breaks, about a km out to sea. **Kuta Reef**, a vast stretch of coral, provides a variety of waves. You can paddle out in around 20 minutes, but the easiest way there is by outrigger. You will be dropped out there and brought back in for a fee. The main break is a classic left-hander, best at mid to high tide with a five to six-foot swell, when it peels across the reef and has a beautiful inside tube section; the first part is a good workable wave. Over seven feet it tends to double up and section. The reef is well-suited for backhand surfing. It's not surfable at dead low tide but you can get out there not long after the tide turns. The boys on the boats can advise you if necessary. It gets very crowded here, but if conditions are good there's another, shorter left, 50 metres further south along the reef which usually has fewer surfers. This wave is more of a peak and provides a short, intense ride. On bigger days, check out breaks on the outer part of the reef, 150 metres further out.

South of Kuta Reef there are some good breaks around the end of the airport runway. Offshore from Pertamina Cottages is a reef break called **Airport Lefts**, with a workable wave at mid to high tide. Further south, **Airport Rights** has three right handers that can be a bit fickle, and are shallow and dangerous at low tide – best for good surfers at mid to high tide with a strong swell. Get there by outrigger from Kuta.

Ulu Watu When Kuta Reef is five to six feet, Ulu Watu, the most famous surfing break on Bali, will be six to eight feet with bigger sets. Kuta and Legian sit on a huge bay. Ulu is way out on the southern extremity of the bay, and it consequently picks up more swell than Kuta. It's about a half-hour journey. Just before the temple, a sign points to Suluban surf beach. You can't drive right in by car – get a ride on a motorbike from the road, or walk about three km; in any case you have

to walk the last few hundred metres – a boardstrap and a small backpack are useful.

A concrete stairway leads into the Ulu Gorge and in front of you is a sight you will never forget, especially if a decent swell is running. The thatched warungs (food stalls) are set on one side of the gorge, above the cave; one warung is right on the edge of the cliff. The Ulu Watu bay stretches out in front of you. In the shade you can eat, drink, rest, even stay overnight. It is one of the best set ups for surfers in the world and everything is carried in by the Balinese. Local boys will wax your board, get drinks for you and carry the board down into the cave, one of the only ways out to the waves.

Ulu Watu has about seven different breaks. If it is your first trip here, sit for a while in the shade and survey the situation. See where other surfers are sitting in the line up and watch where they flick off. **The Corner** is straight in front of you to the right. It's a fast-breaking, hollow left that holds about six foot. The reef shelf under this break is extremely shallow so try to avoid falling head first. At high tide, **The Peak** starts to work. This is good from five to eight feet with bigger waves occasionally right on the Peak itself. You can take off from this inside part or further down the line. A great wave. At low tide, if the swell isn't huge, go further south to **The Racetrack**, a whole series of bowls.

At low tide when the swell is bigger, **Outside Corner** starts operating, further out from The Racetrack. This is a tremendous break and on a good day you can surf one wave for hundreds of metres. The wall here on a 10-foot wave jacks up with a big drop and bottom turn, then the bowl section. After this it becomes a big workable face. You can usually only get tubed in the first section. When surfing this break you need a board with length, otherwise you won't be getting down the face of any of the amazing waves.

Another left runs off the cliff which forms the southern flank of the bay. It breaks outside this in bigger swells and once it's seven foot a left-hander pitches right out in front of a temple on the southern extremity.

Out behind the Peak, when it's big, is a bombora appropriately called **The Bommie**. This is another big left-hander and it doesn't start operating till the swell is about 10 foot. On a normal five to eight-foot day there are also breaks south of the Peak. One is a very fast left, and also very hollow, usually only ridden by goofy-footers because of its speed.

Observe where other surfers paddle out and follow them. If you are in doubt, ask someone. It is better having some knowledge than none at all. Climb down into the cave and paddle out from there. When it's bigger you will be swept to your right. Don't panic, it is an easy matter to paddle around the whitewater from down along the cliff. Coming back in you have to aim for the cave. When it's bigger, come from the south side of the cave as the current runs to the north. If you miss the cave, paddle out again and repeat the procedure. If you get into trouble ask for help from a fellow surfer.

Padang Padang Just Padang for short, this super-shallow, left-hand reef break is just north of Ulu towards Kuta. There are a number of ways to get there. If you are at Ulu you can simply walk along a narrow cliff track and climb down to the beach. Again, check this place carefully before venturing out. A driveable road goes to a carpark with a warung, a short walk from the beach. It's a very demanding break that only works over about six feet from mid to high tide – a great place to watch from the cliff top.

If you can't surf tubes, backhand or forehand, don't go out. Padang is a tube. After a ledgey take-off, you power along the bottom before pulling up into the barrel. So far so good, now for the tricky part. The last section turns inside out like a washing machine on fast forward. You have to drive high through this section, all the time while in the tube. Don't worry if you fail to negotiate this trap, plenty of other surfers have been caught too. After this the wave fills up and you flick off. Not a wave for the faint-hearted and definitely not a wave to surf when there's a crowd.

Bingin North of Padang and accessible by road, this once secret spot can now get crowded. It's best at mid tide with a six-foot swell. The outside reef, **Impossibles**, has fast tube sections, but don't stay on too long.

Balangan At the end of a rough road north of Bingin, Balangan is an alternative when the tide is too high or the crowds are too big. It's a fast left over a shallow reef, unsurfable at low tide. It can work on swells less than four feet, and doesn't get deadly until the swell hits about 10 feet.

Canggu North of Kuta/Legian/Seminyak, on the northern extremity of the bay, Canggu has a nice white beach, a warung, one losmen, and sometimes a lot of surfers. There are right and left breaks over a 'soft' rock ledge – well, it's softer than coral. Five to six foot is an optimum size for Canggu. There's a good right-hander that you can really hook into, which works on full tide, and what Peter Neely calls 'a sucky left ledge that tubes like Ulu but without the coral cuts', which works from mid tide. A driveable track goes to the beach – get there early, before the crowds and the wind.

Medewi Further up the island is a softer left called Medewi. This wave has a big drop, which fills up then runs into a workable inside section. It's worth surfing if you feel like something different, but to catch it you need to get up early in the morning because it gets blown out as the wind picks up. It works best at mid to high tide with a six-foot swell, but depends on the direction.

Nusa Lembongan In the Nusa Penida group, this island is separated from the south-east coast of Bali by the Selat Badung (Badung Strait). You get there by boat from Sanur – see the Nusa Penida chapter for details. The strait is very deep, and generates huge swells which break over the reefs off the north-west coast of Lembongan. There's cheap accommodation and great views. **Shipwreck**, clearly visible from the beach, is the most popular break, a classic right which works well at low tide and even better at high tide. A bit to the south, **Lacerations** is a very fast right breaking over a very shallow reef – hence the name. Further south is a smaller, more user-friendly left-hander called **Playgrounds**. There's also a break off **Nusa Ceningan**, the middle island of the group, but it's very exposed and only surfable when it's too small for the other breaks. Remember that Lembongan is best with an easterly wind, like Kuta and Ulu Watu, so it's dry-season surfing.

Nusa Dua During the wet season, roughly October/November to March/April, you surf on the east side of the island, where there are some very fine reef breaks. The reef off the expensive resort area of Nusa Dua has very consistent swells. There's nowhere cheap to stay, but access is easy on the big road from the airport. The main break is a km off the beach to the south of the resort area – go past the golf course and look for the small hand-written sign that tells you where to park. There's a warung here, and some boats to take you out. There are lefts and rights which work well on a small swell at low to mid tide. On bigger days take a longer board and go further out, where powerful peaking waves offer long rides, fat tubes and lots of variety. Further north, in front of the Club Med, is a tubing, fast right break called **Sri Lanka**, which works best at mid tide and can handle swells from six to 10 feet.

Sanur Sanur reef has a hollow, right-hand wave with excellent barrels. It's fickle, and doesn't even start till you get a six-foot swell, but anything over eight feet will be world-class, and anything over 10 feet will be brown-boardshorts material. There are other reefs further offshore and most of them are surfable. **Hyatt Reef**, over two km from shore, has a shifty right peak which can give a great ride at full tide. Closer in, in front of the Sanur Beach market, **Tanjung Sari** gives long rides at low tide with a big swell. A couple of km north, **Padang Galak** is a beach break at high tide on a small to medium swell, but it can be very dirty.

Ketewel & Lebih These two beaches are north-east of Sanur, but access is from the main Gianyar road. They're both right-hand beach breaks which are dodgy at low tide and close out over six feet. There are probably other breaks along this coast all the way to Padangbai, but there needs to be a big swell to make them work.

South Coast The extreme south coast, round the end of the Bukit Peninsula, can be surfed any time of the year providing there is a northerly wind, or no wind at all – get there very early to avoid onshore winds. The peninsula is fringed with reefs and gets big swells, but access is a problem. There are a few roads, but the shoreline is all cliffs. If you want to explore it, charter a boat on a day with no wind and a small swell. **Nyang Nyang** is a right-hand reef break, reached by a steep track down the cliff. **Green Ball** is another right, which works well on a small to medium swell, ie when it's almost flat everywhere else. Get there on the road to the Bali Cliffs Hotel, and take the steps down the cliff. The south coast has no facilities and tricky currents, and it would be a bad place to get into trouble – be very careful on the cliff tracks and in the water.

DIVING

With its warm water, extensive coral reefs and abundant marine life, Bali offers some superb diving possibilities. If you just want to do a little snorkelling, there's pretty good coral reef off Nusa Dua, Sanur and along the Lovina Beach strip on the north coast. There's also good snorkelling at Padangbai, off the beach or from boats which can take you out to the fine reefs offshore. Most places that have coral will have a place that rents masks, snorkels and fins for a few thousand rupiah per day, but check the quality of the equipment before you take it away.

Scuba diving offers more demanding possibilities, though obviously it is more expensive and often requires transport, by land or water, to get to the best sites. There are a number of operations conducting diving trips for visitors, and there are also package tours specifically for scuba divers. Diving may not be as good during the wet season, from about October to April, as storms tend to reduce visibility – Menjangan and Nusa Penida can still be good.

Diving Tours

If you want to do a package diving tour, find a reputable operator near where you live, through a Garuda office, your local dive club, or one of the scuba diving magazines. Failing that, contact one of the Bali-based dive operations listed below, and ask them to recommend a package-tour operator in your area.

If you're a keen diver travelling independently, it might still be a good idea to book your diving trips in advance, to ensure you get a good guide who speaks your language, and to allow them to make up a group with a similar level of experience. Let them know what areas interest you most, and what your level of experience is. Make sure you bring your scuba certification, even if you just want to do the occasional dive. The international safety code does not enable operators to let you dive without a recognised certification. Most of the main qualifications are recognised, including those of PADI, NAUI, BSAC, FAUI and SSI.

Equipment

All the equipment you need is available on Bali, but you may not be able to get exactly what you want in the size you need, and the quality is variable – some operators use equipment right to the end of its service life. The basic equipment to bring is a mask, snorkel and fins – you know they'll fit and they're not too hard to carry. You'll save around US$2.50 a day in rent, and you can use them when you just want to snorkel off the beach as well.

Your next priority is a thin, full-length wetsuit, which is important for protection against stinging animals and coral abrasions, and a thicker one (three mm) would be preferable if you plan frequent diving, deep dives or a night dive – the water can be cold,

especially deeper down. Wetsuits rent from US$3 to US$5 per day. Some small, easy-to-carry things include protective gloves, spare straps, silicone lubricant and extra globes for your flashlight. Most operators have good quality regulators and BC vests, but if you bring your own you'll save maybe US$10 per dive, and it's a good idea if you're planning to dive in more remote locations than Bali, where the rental equipment may not be as good.

A set of all the above equipment will cost around US$15 per day on top of the basic cost of a dive. Tanks and weight belt are included in the deal. You're not allowed to take sealed tanks on a plane anyway, and you'd be crazy to carry lead weights.

Diving Courses

There are many operators who are licensed to take out certified divers (ie those with recognised open-water qualifications), but only a few of them have qualified instructors who can train a beginner to this level. If you're not a qualified diver, and you want to try some scuba diving on Bali, you have three options.

Nearly all the operators offer an 'introductory', 'orientation' or 'initial' dive for beginners, usually after some classroom training and shallow-water practice. These 'courses' are cheap (from around US$40 for one dive) and can be nasty. Some of the less professional outfits conduct these 'introductory' dives with unqualified, inexperienced dive-masters and minimal backup, in sometimes difficult conditions, to depths as low as 20 metres. Many experienced divers are horrified by this practice, and warn that a serious accident is inevitable – certainly there are a quite a few scary stories. Experienced divers can make their own judgements about the professionalism of an operation, the competence of its staff, the quality of the equipment and the suitability of the conditions. Novices would be well advised to stick with well-known and reputable operators, and ensure that the people actually conducting the dive (not the ones who sign you up, or the owners of the company) are properly qualified instructors.

Some of the larger hotels offer four or five-day 'resort courses' which certify you for basic dives in the location where you do the course. A resort course will give you a better standard of training than just an introductory dive, but it doesn't make you a qualified diver. These courses cost from US$250 upwards, which is not much cheaper than a full course on Bali, and you have to be a guest at a pretty expensive hotel to start with.

If you are at all serious about diving, the best option is to enrol in a full open-water diving course which will give you an internationally recognised qualification. A four-day open-water course, to CAMS or PADI standards, with a qualified instructor, manual, dive table and certificate, will cost from about US$300, which is a lot cheaper than an equivalent course in many other countries. Experienced divers can upgrade their skills with advanced open-water courses in night diving, wreck diving, deep diving and so on, from around US$150 depending on the course and the operator.

Diving Operations

Dive operators in the southern tourist area can arrange trips to the main dive sites around the island. The cost depends on the number of people in the group and the distance to the dive site. For a group of six divers on a local trip, count on about US$45 for two dives. A trip to Pulau Menjangan from Sanur will cost about US$70 or US$80.

Another option is to get yourself to an area near where you want to dive, and contact a local dive operation. This gives you a chance to do some sightseeing on the way, and might be a bit cheaper as you're not paying the dive operator to arrange transport for you or your equipment. It also permits a much more comfortable schedule – going from Sanur to Menjangan Island, doing two dives and driving back can be a long day, and require a very early start.

There are quite a few dive operations on Bali and the number is growing. The following is a partial list of established, reputable operators. There are others who are just as good, but satisfy yourself as to the reliability of any operation you plan to dive with.

Bali Marine Sports
  Jalan Bypass Ngurah Rai, Blanjong, Sanur (☎ 288776, fax 287872)
Baruna Water Sports
  Jalan Bypass Ngurah Rai 300B, Kuta; PO Box 3419 Denpasar (☎ 753820, fax 752779)
  Baruna also has sales and information counters in hotels in Kuta, Sanur, Nusa Dua, Candidasa and at Senggigi Beach on Lombok.
  This is the biggest dive operation on Bali; it's very well regarded by divers, and the only place with a decompression facility. Full courses are available with PADI-qualified instructors.
Barrakuda
  Candidasa Beach Bungalows II in Candidasa; PO Box 252 Denpasar (☎ 235536, fax 235537)
  Barrakuda is also at Sanur (☎ 288619) and Lovina, and has all levels of dive courses with PADI-qualified instructors.
Oceana Dive Centre
  Jalan Bypass Ngurah Rai 78XX, Sanur (☎ 288652, fax 288652)
  Equipment is available for sale, and the dive school has CAMS and PADI-qualified instructors.
Spice Dive
  Lovina Beach, Buleleng (☎ 0362 23305)
  This is a small, friendly and very efficient operation with CMAS, POSSI and PADI-qualified staff.

Dive Sites

Some of Bali's main dive sites are listed below, roughly in order of their accessibility from southern Bali. For more details on accommodation, food and getting to these places, see the entries in the chapters on Bali.

Nusa Dua The beach is nice, white and gently sloping, but for the best diving, take a boat trip to the reef. There's a drop-off, and colourful corals are seen between three and 20 metres.

Sanur Very accessible by boat from the main tourist beach, Sanur's reef is colourful and has lots of tropical fish which can be seen at depths of less than 12 metres.

Padangbai This beautiful bay is not overrun with tourists, but has diving facilities, food and accommodation. You can dive from the beach, or get an outrigger canoe – it's not far to the dives, which feature the **Blue Lagoon**, lots of fish and colder water than south Bali.

Candidasa There are quite a few dive sites on the reefs and islands round Candidasa, and it's a comfortable base for diving trips to the east coast. The fish life here is particularly rich and varied, and is said to include sharks. The currents on this coast are strong and unpredictable – it's recommended for experienced divers only. The **Canyon** at Tepekong is a particularly challenging dive.

Tulamben The big diving attraction is the wreck of the **USS Liberty**, which is spectacular but eerie, encrusted with marine flora and inhabited by thousands of tropical fish. It's close to the shore and can easily be appreciated by snorkellers, but divers will find it even more interesting – depths are less than 30 metres. There's also the **Tulamben Wall**, a 60-metre drop-off into Lombok Strait. The wreck is a hugely popular dive, and to avoid other groups you can stay at Tulamben, where there is a dive operation, and dive early or late in the day.

Amed Also on the east coast, not far south of Tulamben, Amed has a very isolated black sand beach. You dive from the beach (actually at Cemeluk, near Amed), which slopes gently then drops off to about 35 metres, with a spectacular wall. There are lots of fish of many types, and a great variety of coral.

Lovina Beach Area The strip of beaches west of Singaraja has an extensive coral reef, with pools of very calm water. You can dive or snorkel from a boat, but you don't have to go deep to enjoy the area – it's a good spot for beginners.

Pulau Menjangan 'Deer Island' is in the Bali Barat (West Bali) National Park, accessible by boat from Teluk Terima. It has superb, unspoilt coral (partly because of the absence of human development in the area), lots of sponges and fish, great visibility and a spectacular drop-off. It's regarded as the best diving on Bali. The remote location and the park entrance fees make this a more expensive dive, but it's worth it. Spice Dive, in Lovina, is the nearest diving operation.

Nusa Penida There are dive sites all round Nusa Penida and Nusa Lembongan. At Lembongan you enter from the white sand beach which slopes gently out to the reef, where diving is from five to 20 metres down. Dives around Penida are more demanding, with big swells, strong and fickle currents, and cold water. There are some impressive underwater grottoes in the area, and the amount of large marine life, including sharks, manta rays and turtles, is impressive. There are no dive operators on Penida or Lembongan, so you'll need to organise the trip from mainland Bali (Candidasa or Sanur), an hour or so away by boat. Choose a good operator who knows the area well.

OTHER ACTIVITIES
Windsurfing
Most windsurfing is done in the tourist areas of southern Bali, though there are certainly lots of other possible locations. Equipment can be hired on the beach at Sanur, and near Benoa Point where the Nusa Dua watersports enthusiasts are catered for. You'll also find windsurfers at Kuta, Candidasa, Bedugul and Lovina. Advertised prices are around US$10 per hour. Often you'll have to wait for high tide, when the lagoons inside the coral reefs are deep enough. Windsurfing has caused damage to coral formations in some areas, so be aware of where you're going.

Whitewater Rafting
Rafting is a newcomer to Bali's range of outdoor activities, and is easy to enjoy as a day trip from Kuta, Sanur, Nusa Dua or Ubud. Operators will pick you up from your hotel, take you to the put-in point (usually on the Ayung River), provide all the equipment

and guides, and return you to your hotel afterwards. Lunch is also included.

There are at least two operators. Sobek Expeditions (☎ 287059) runs rafting trips all over the world and is associated with Bali Maharani Tours & Travel in Sanur. Its trips cost US$57 all-inclusive. Bali Adventure Tours (☎ 751292) is a local operation which runs slightly shorter trips for US$45. Bookings can be made at Yanies Restaurant in Legian.

Trekking

Bali is not usually thought of as a trekking destination, but so many people climb Gunung Batur to see the sunrise that it can get crowded up there some mornings. In fact there are numerous other possibilities for treks in the Batur area, and also around the volcanoes near Bedugul and in the Bali Barat National Park. Perhaps the biggest challenge is a climb of Gunung Agung (3142 metres).

Bali does not offer remote wilderness treks – it's too densely populated. For the most part, you make day trips from the closest village, often leaving before dawn to avoid the clouds which usually blanket the peaks by mid-morning, so you won't need a tent, sleeping bag or stove. However, waterproof clothing and a sweater at least are essential for trekking in the central mountains. Treks in the national park must be accompanied by a guide, which is best arranged the day before at the park offices at Cekik or Labuhan Lalang.

There are many guides, with varying degrees of competence, who will show you the way up Gunung Batur or Gunung Agung. Jero Wijaya, in Toya Bungkah, can give you information about treks in other parts of Bali as well as the Batur area where he is based, but unfortunately he's not on the phone. Sobek Expeditions (☎ 287059) runs one-day treks to mountain rainforest areas for US$42 per person, and Bali Adventure Tours (☎ 751292) organises shorter treks from US$36.

Walking is a good way to explore the backblocks. You can walk from village to village on small tracks and between the rice paddies, eating in warungs and staying in losmen in the larger villages – there's usually somewhere to stay, or someone to put you up. You can flag down a bemo if you do find yourself stuck and it's not too late in the day (not many bemos operate after 4 or 5 pm). Despite the enormous number of tourists on Bali, it's relatively easy to find places where tourists are a rarity. Of course you have to be content with a pretty basic standard of food and accommodation. If you're considering a walking trip, look carefully at a map, note the places near your planned route and look them up in this book.

Bird Watching

The best places to see bird life are the forested areas of the central mountains and foothills, and the Bali Barat National Park. Some of the guides who take walks in the park are quite knowledgeable, so mention that you have a special interest in birds when you book your guide. On Sunday, Tuesday and Friday morning, Victor Mason (author of the Periplus Editions *Birds of Bali*) conducts guided bird walks in the area around Ubud for US$28. Other guided field trips can be arranged – phone ☎ 975009 or visit him at the Beggar's Bush pub near the Campuan bridge in Ubud.

Cycling

For information on cycling, see the Getting Around chapters for both Bali and Lombok. Bali Adventure Tours (☎ 751292) and Sobek Expeditions (☎ 287059) will organise a day trip, for US$45 or US$49 per person respectively.

Pony Treks

An all-inclusive guided pony-trekking day trip is available, traversing rice fields, beaches and river valleys in Tabanan district, west of Tanah Lot temple. It costs US$55 per person – phone ☎ 751572 or 751672 for more information and bookings. Mesari stables (☎ 751401) in Seminyak also arranges pony rides, from 20,000 rp per person per hour.

Cruises & Water Sports

The best known day cruise is with the *Bali Hai*, a big luxury catamaran which does a trip to the islands of Nusa Penida and Nusa Lembongan, with a buffet lunch, snorkelling, glass-bottom boats for viewing the reefs, morning and afternoon tea, and a shore excursion to Lembongan village. It leaves from Benoa Harbour at 9.30 am and costs US$68 per person. The *Bali Hai* also does surfing and scuba-diving trips, and brochures are available everywhere.

Beluga Water Sports (☎ 71969, fax 71976), at Benoa village north of Nusa Dua, also offers day cruises to Nusa Penida, at US$85 per head. Features include viewing coral reefs from a semi-submersible boat. Beluga also offers sunset dinner cruises (US$40) and a variety of water sports including fishing trips from US$50 and banana boat rides at US$10 for 15 minutes (a banana boat is a large inflated rubber sausage which you sit on while it's dragged through the water by a powerful boat).

A number of other boats operate from Benoa, offering day cruises and fishing trips. Prices vary, but typically start around US$75 for a day. For fishing trips you probably need a power boat to get you to the best spots as quickly as possible. For a cruise, the big sailing boats look much more fun – a variety of vessels do sailing cruises, from a refitted and restored island trading ship to a converted ocean-racing 'pocket maxi'.

Helicopter Tours

About the fastest way to spend money on Bali, prices start at around US$95, plus 15% tax and service, for a half-hour flight, with four passengers. That's enough to go round the Bukit Peninsula taking in the Ulu Watu cliff temple, the Bali Cliffs Hotel and Nusa Dua. Contact Bali Avia (☎ 752282, 751257) or Motive Bali (☎ 289435).

ACCOMMODATION

Finding a place to stay on Bali is no problem. In fact, at the bottom end of the market, accommodation on Bali is probably the best in the world for the price. Four or five dollars can get you a fine room in many places, and US$10 can get you something terrific. The various places to stay listed in this book are intended to give you a feel for the various types of accommodation available, and the going price for a room of a certain standard, so you can make an informed choice which meets your own needs. In areas with lots of accommodation, it's impossible to list every place, but there's always a good cross section, including the cheapest, the most expensive, and anything that is unusual, special or interesting. In particular, we try to include out-of-the-way places that might otherwise be missed.

The tourist business on Bali is so competitive that places of a similar standard usually cost about the same price, give or take a couple of thousand rupiah. Places which are highly recommended in guidebooks tend to be full when you arrive, and raise their prices if their business booms. Also, when there is lots of accommodation at a similar standard and price, it's not fair to 'recommend' one place when others down the street are just as good. If a place listed in this book seems overpriced for what it offers, discuss the price with them or go elsewhere. If you find a great place that's not listed, write and tell us and we'll check it out for the next edition.

Bottom End

Cheap hotels on Bali are usually known as losmen, and most of them are simple, but clean and comfortable. The best of them are in interesting locations with friendly, helpful staff who can really make your stay a pleasure. A losmen is a small hotel, often family-run, which rarely has more than 10 or 12 rooms; names usually include the word 'losmen', 'homestay' or 'inn'. (The word losmen is a corruption of the Dutch 'logement'.) In theory a 'wisma' is a smaller place, more like a guesthouse, but in practice just about any cheap place is called a losmen.

Losmen are often built in the style of a Balinese home – that is, a compound with an outer wall and separate buildings around an inner garden. In Bali you usually live outside – the 'living room' is an open verandah. It's pleasant sitting out in the garden, and you're out there with all the other travellers, not locked away inside a room.

There are losmen all over Bali and they vary widely in standards but not so widely in price. In a few places you'll find a room for as low as 6000 rp, but generally they're in the 8000 to 12,000 rp range. Bigger and better rooms in popular locations go up to 20,000 or 25,000 rp, and can still be very good value. Some of the cheap rooms are definitely on the dull and dismal side, but others are attractive, well kept and excellent value for money. A nice garden can be one of the most attractive features, even in very cheap places. The price usually includes a light breakfast (sometimes just tea), and these days there is usually an attached bathroom with a shower, basin, toilet and cold water only. All but the cheapest rooms have a fan, usually a small table-top one called a 'box fan'. A ceiling fan is considered classier, and always costs more.

Bottom-end places are identified by a small sign on the street, often hand written. They don't have brochures, but they often have a business card.

Middle

In Kuta, Legian, Denpasar, Lovina, Ubud and Sanur you can also find a good selection of middle-range hotels. At the beaches they're often constructed in Balinese bungalow style. They're often called something or someone's bungalows or cottages – *Made's Beach Bungalows* or *Sunset Cottages*. There's a pretty clear distinction between the lower mid-range places, which are nice losmen which have gone upmarket, and the upper mid-range places, which were built as cheap package-tour hotels but will take all the walk-in trade they can get.

The cheaper mid-range places are priced at about 25,000/30,000 to 35,000/40,000 rp per night for a single/double room, and perhaps 5000 rp more for an extra bed or two to accommodate a family. This price should include a light breakfast (pineapple, banana and mango fruit salad, toast and tea/coffee), tea or coffee on request throughout the day,

a fan (preferably a ceiling fan) and your own bathroom with shower and toilet. There's often a pool, though it can be pretty tiny.

Upper mid-range hotels always give their price in US dollars – a sure sign that they are aspiring to the package-tour market. The dollar figure is the 'publish rate', on which the package-tour prices are based, and is always negotiable if you walk in during the off season. These places start at about US$20 to US$50, and cost more if they have facilities like a sunken bar in the swimming pool (often unattended, but it looks good on the brochure), air-con (especially in coastal areas), hot water (especially in the hills), colour TV, colour satellite TV, and a fridge and phone in your room. At this price level, they start charging extra for breakfast and adding 17.5% for tax and service. Mid-range hotels often have a variety of rooms and prices, with the main difference being air-con versus a fan. Their 'superior' rooms are usually the cheapest, with 'de luxe' or 'executive' rooms costing more.

Upper mid-range places have a larger and more professional sign out the front. From around the US$35 level, they usually have a colour brochure (with bad printing, amusing English and over-the-top descriptions of their luxuries), and a separate sheet with their prices in US dollars. Always look at the room first, otherwise you may be paying for a lot of 'luxury features' you don't want, and missing out on the friendly informality of a cheap losmen.

Top End

The top of the top end on Bali is world class. The biggest concentration of super-luxury five-star hotels is at Nusa Dua, but various hotels at Sanur, Kuta, Legian and Ubud are not far behind, while some of the very best ones are at secluded, isolated points around the coast or in the countryside. (See the aside on The Best Hotels in Bali.) For this book, top-end means any place where the cheapest room is over about US$55 a double – about two or three stars and up. They usually have more expensive rooms, villas, bungalows, suites or whatever. If you want a luxurious room, with lots of space and fancy extras, get

The Best Hotel on Bali

The 'best' hotel is obviously a matter of opinion, but if the best means the most expensive, then the best place to stay in Bali is the Presidential Suite at the Grand Bali Beach Hotel in Sanur, at US$3000 per night (plus 17½% tax and service, which adds another US$525). If the best is the most luxurious, then it's impossible to differentiate at the top end – they all have large, luxurious air-conditioned rooms and neither an extra metre of marble nor an extra channel on the in-house video system will make them any more comfortable.

How do the top hotels differentiate among themselves? To judge by their brochures, the most important things are the swimming pool and the view. On the first score we can be reasonably objective – the best swimming pool in Bali is at the Sheraton Lagoon Resort at Nusa Dua. It's so large they call it a lagoon, and it's complete with sandy beaches, islands, waterfalls, bridges, and bars. For a few extra dollars you can get a room with a balcony overhanging the lagoon, so you can drop in anytime.

As for the best view in Bali – do you look towards the mountains or the sea? The best mountain view may well be from a five-dollar flea-pit in Penelokan, while the best ocean view is a matter of how much water you can look at – looking south from the Bali Cliffs Hotel you will see nothing else. But if you want a view that is uniquely Balinese it must be of sculpted rice terraces stepping down a steep hillside in 50 shades of green, and for that you can do no better than looking at the Ayung river gorge from a room at Kupu Kupu Barong, a few km west of Ubud.

If you think the best hotel is the one with the richest history and the strongest links with a place and its past, then Ubud has two top contenders. The Hotel Tjampuhan was originally the home of the artist Walter Spies, and his house guests included Noel Coward, Charlie Chaplin, Margaret Mead and a constellation of the celebrated artists, writers and musicians of the era. The hotel now has little resemblance to the guesthouse of the '30s, but the site on the lush ravine of the Campuan River is still special, as are the many paintings which are a legacy of the revolution in Balinese art which commenced on this very spot.

Another hotel (of sorts) with a history, the Puri Saren Agung is actually a part of Ubud's royal family palace – though it's not as old as it looks. The late Tjokorde Sukawati was one of Spies' patrons, and he saw the potential of 'cultural tourism' before the term was coined. After a fire in the '50s, the palace was rebuilt with a number of bale for guests, in classic Balinese style but with modern Western facilities. The rooms are almost casually decorated with the sort of antiques and artworks you would expect in the home of a Balinese prince and patron of the arts. There's no swimming pool and no air-conditioning, and the rooms are appropriately dusty, but the ambience is so thick you can chew on it.

You could judge a hotel by how it feels and how it makes you feel – as a sort of walk-in work of art which should leave an impression long after check-out time. By this standard, any one of the three Aman hotels is a masterpiece. They all have sensational views, superb decor, sublime architecture and swimming pools so perfect it seems a shame to swim in them. The Amankila, east of Padangbai, for example, combines its spectacular view over the Badung Strait with three swimming pools, which step down towards the sea in matching shades of blue. While every other top-end hotel in Nusa Dua has a huge and imposing lobby with a formidable front desk, the Amanusa has a simple, open sided pavilion with two low tables and a view of half of Bali. Many hotels put on Balinese dances as a special attraction, but the Amandari, near Ubud, sponsors a local Legong troupe, and they practise in a pavilion a few metres from the front desk. Instead of in-house video movies the Aman resorts offer a sound system in every room. Instead of a disco, they have a library. Instead of a big building with hundreds of rooms, they have a few dozen free-standing suites.

Are they expensive enough to be the best? With US$100 price differences between almost identical suites, you can pay as much as you want, starting at US$300. Do they offer five-star luxury? They do not have a star rating at all, apparently because they refuse to provide a TV in their rooms – now that's class! ■

the best room in a cheaper hotel. If you want a big pool and garden, or access to special sporting facilities, get the cheapest room in a more expensive hotel. At a five-star hotel, the rooms start at around US$140 a double, suites at around US$300, and most have something over US$1000 a night (often called the 'Presidential Suite'), plus 17.5%

tax and service, plus a US$25 high-season supplement, plus US$12 per head for breakfast, plus...

The most tasteful of these hotels feature contemporary architecture in a modern but genuine Balinese style which is both distinctive and attractive. A luxury resort hotel on Bali does not look like a clone of one on Majorca or Maui or Mazatlán. Typically the rooms face inwards, to a lush landscaped garden, in a layout that has its origins in a traditional family compound (pekarangan). The hotel lobby is often styled on a bale banjar, the meeting hall of a community or village. The rooms and public areas are decorated with Balinese paintings, woodcarvings and stonework of the highest quality, and commissions for these works can keep a whole village gainfully employed for months.

From the outside, they are usually surrounded by a wall, with a large illuminated sign and a sweeping driveway leading to a huge and lavishly decorated reception area. Their brochures are beautiful glossy productions with superb colour photos – above about US$80 per night they don't have spelling mistakes.

Accommodation in Remote Areas

Visitors who only go to the tourist areas don't believe this, but there are lots of areas on Bali with no losmen, restaurants or tourist facilities at all. In remote villages, you can often find a place to stay by asking the village chief or headman, the kepala desa. It will usually be a case of dossing down in a pavilion in a family compound – don't expect privacy. The price is negotiable, maybe around 4000 rp. Your hosts may not even ask for payment, and in these cases you should definitely offer some gifts, like cigarettes, bottled water, sweets or fruit. If they give you a meal, it is even more important to make an offer of payment or gifts – maybe bring a bag of rice. The opportunity to stay in untouristed villages should not be exploited as a cheap accommodation option by impecunious freeloaders. If you want to stay in such places, make local enquiries about appropriate gifts and protocol, and be very sensitive to the social environment.

Camping

There are no organised campgrounds, and few suitable empty sites. Even trekking in the mountains or the national park you will rarely need to use a tent – there are usually shelters of some sort.

Package Holidays

Many of the two and three-star standard hotels are very cheap – cheap that is, for the people on package holidays who have bought a return ticket and a week's accommodation in one of these palaces for not much more than the cost of a standard excursion airfare. It works because the fare which is built into the package is substantially lower than the excursion airfare, or any other cheap airfare available. The catch is that to qualify for the cheap airfare, you have to book and pay for every night of your accommodation in advance, at a relatively expensive hotel to make sure that the travel agent makes a profit from the land content of the package.

If you want to stay for longer than a couple of weeks, and you're quite happy to stay in cheaper hotels, the cost advantage of a package tour diminishes – the extra cost of the normal airfare is offset by the saving in accommodation. If you're only going to Bali for a short holiday, and you really want to stay in a hotel with air-conditioning and a swimming pool, then a package tour can be a good deal. An awful lot of package tourists think so.

There are two big catches with this type of holiday. One is that you get stung savagely for drinks, tours, meals and other extras at the hotel, and this can add a lot to the cost of a trip you thought you had already paid for. Everything from a Legong dance to your laundry will cost more if you get it through the hotel.

The other catch is that you might see very little of Bali. Your prepaid accommodation, the high cost of tours, and a lack of information about alternatives, can keep you at your hotel, within the comfortable boundaries of the restaurant, the pool, the bar, the beach and your air-conditioned room. It's holiday inertia.

Those who buy their own milk, fruit and bread for breakfast in their room, then sneak out for a day's independent sightseeing with lunch at a street stall and dinner in the night market, can see a bit of the real Bali, and have a touch of decadence, at a budget price. Just make sure you book into a place that isn't too isolated. If you're in a hotel in the golden ghetto of Nusa Dua, or somewhere by itself on the coast, it's very difficult to get out of its expensive clutches. If you stay in Sanur, Candidasa, Ubud or especially Kuta, there are dozens of restaurants, tour agents, craft shops and bars that will give you much better value for money than the equivalent services in a package-tour hotel.

The Mandi

Nearly all the places to stay in tourist areas of Bali have Western-style showers, but in remote areas you will still encounter the traditional *mandi*. The word 'mandi' simply means to bathe or to wash. Instead of taps and a sink or bath, the mandi is a large water tank beside which you'll find what looks like a plastic saucepan (it used to be half a coconut shell on a stick). What you do is scoop water out of the mandi tank and pour it over yourself, then soap yourself down and repeat the scooping and showering procedure. You *do not* climb in the tank. In cheaper losmen there is often a hybrid bathroom, with a mandi-style tank of water *and* a shower head. Many people prefer the splash method, and it's a good back-up when the water pressure fails. The mandi scoop is also used for flushing the toilet, and for washing one's bottom afterwards. The bathroom is meant to have water splashed around in it, and a mandi can be a lot of fun for kids or couples.

A warning: mandi water is often icy cold – it usually comes from wells way down deep. You will have to get used to cold water because losmen have nothing else. Anyway you're in the tropics and you will soon forget what hot water feels like.

In rural areas, many villages don't even have mandis, and bathing in a pool, lake, stream or irrigation channel is a regular and social practice.

The Toilet

Just as mandis are disappearing in favour of Western-style showers, the old Asian-style toilets are also being replaced by Western-style, sit-down toilets. You'll still encounter the Asian toilets though, and they're like those you find everywhere east of Europe – two footrests and a hole in the ground. You squat down and aim. You soon get used to them.

Apart from places which definitely cater to the tourist trade, you won't find toilet paper in restaurant toilets – so bring your own, or learn to wash yourself with water (left hand only, if you're a purist). To locate a toilet ask for the *kamar mandi, kamar kecil* (little room) or the WC (pronounced 'way-say').

FOOD

There's no question that you'll eat well on Bali; the dining possibilities are endless, the prices often pleasantly low and the taste treats terrific. For the most part, however, real Balinese food is not on the menu.

Balinese Food

Though Bali does have its own cuisine, it is not readily adaptable to a restaurant menu. The everyday Balinese diet at home is a couple of meals and a few snacks of cold steamed rice, with some vegetables, some crunchy stuff like nuts or *krupuk* (prawn crackers), and a little chicken, pork or fish. The food is prepared in the morning and people help themselves individually throughout the day. Balinese *haute cuisine* is reserved for the elaborate food offerings made to the gods, and sumptuous feasts to celebrate important occasions.

The dishes for a traditional Balinese feast require some time to cook, and the elaborate preparations and ritual are a major community exercise. Two of the great feast dishes, *babi guling* (spit-roasted suckling pig) and *betutu bebek* (duck roasted in banana leaves), are the only truly Balinese dishes you'll see with any regularity in restaurants, and they usually have to be ordered a day in advance. The best places to look for Balinese specialities are around Denpasar and in Ubud – see the aside about Ketu Suartana's Balinese feasts in the Ubud section. Upmarket tourist hotels also do elaborate re-creations of a Balinese feast, but the ambience can be more like a suburban barbecue.

Snacks, Food Stalls & Tourist Restaurants

Balinese like to eat snacks throughout the day, and when they're away from home, they go to food stalls *(warungs)* or street-carts serving food which is likely to be Javanese, Chinese or even Sumatran in style. The most common is *bakso*, a soup with noodles and meatballs. *Nasi campur* is the most Balinese-style dish served in warungs.

Most of the budget tourist restaurants do Chinese-Indonesian style food, with the standard dishes being *nasi goreng, nasi campur, cap cai* and *gado gado*. In many of Bali's tourist areas you'll be lucky to find even Indonesian food – apart from a token nasi goreng – amongst all the Western dishes. Some of these have been so well assimilated in to the Balinese menu you'd be forgiven for thinking they originated there. Take pancakes and jaffles for example! Spaghetti, potato chips, pizza and guacamole are common offerings, and usually pretty well cooked with fresh ingredients. The less touristy the place, the shorter the menu, which is very often the same standard range of Indonesian dishes.

The great paradox of eating on Bali is that the cheaper the place, the tastier the food. The really cheap places are for the locals, and they serve the genuine article. At a street stall, for under 1000 rp you can get a nasi goreng that's out of this world – hot and spicy, with fresh ingredients that are cooked while you wait. Of course you might have to sit on the curb to eat it, and the plate may not be as carefully washed as you would like. At

the tourist restaurant around the corner, a nasi goreng could cost 2500 rp, but it mightn't be freshly cooked and it won't have the same spicy taste (dishes tend to be wimped down for what the Balinese see as 'tourist tastes'). Fried noodles *(mie goreng)*, satay *(sate)* and soup *(soto)* are other street-stall staples which cost more and taste less when you get them in a restaurant.

International Food

There are a growing number of very good restaurants with what can only be described as international menus. They serve excellent meals for a fraction of what you'd pay in Europe, the USA or Australia, and they are usually spacious open-air places with friendly and efficient service. The best ones are in Ubud and the Kuta-Legian-Seminyak strip. Many of the upmarket hotels will also have first-class kitchens, but the cost will not be much less than back home.

Local Dishes

Food in Indonesia is Chinese influenced, although there are a number of purely Indonesian dishes. The following is a list of some of the dishes you're most likely to find:

apam – delicious pancake filled with nuts and sprinkled with sugar

bakmi goreng – fried noodles

bakso ayam – chicken soup with noodles and meatballs; a street-stall standard

cap cai – usually pronounced 'chop chai', this is a mix of fried vegetables sometimes with meat as well.

es campur – ice with fruit salad; a warung standard

fu yung hai – a sort of sweet-and-sour omelette

gado gado – another very popular Indonesian dish, steamed bean sprouts, various vegetables and a spicy peanut sauce

lontong – rice steamed in a banana leaf

mie goreng – fried noodles, sometimes with vegetables, sometimes with meat; much the same story as nasi goreng

mie kuah – noodle soup

nasi campur – steamed rice topped with a little bit of everything (some vegetables, some meat, a bit of fish, a krupuk or two). It's a good, simple, usually tasty and filling meal.

nasi goreng – this is the most everyday of Indonesian dishes, almost like hamburgers are to Americans, meat pies to Australians, fish & chips to the British. Nasi goreng simply means fried *(goreng)* rice *(nasi)* and a basic nasi goreng may be little more than fried rice with a few scraps of vegetable to spice it up a little. Fancier nasi gorengs may include meat, while a 'special' (or *istemiwa*) nasi goreng usually means with a fried egg on top. Nasi goreng can range from the blandly dull to the very good.

nasi Padang – Padang food, from the Padang region of Sumatra, is popular all over Indonesia. It's usually served cold and consists of rice (once again) with a whole variety of side dishes. A whole selection of dishes are laid out before you and your final bill is calculated by the number of empty dishes. Nasi Padang is traditionally eaten with your fingers and it's also traditionally very hot *(pedas* not *panas)*. It's hot enough to burn your fingers, let alone your tongue.

nasi putih – white rice, usually plain, and either boiled or steamed

opor ayam – chicken cooked in coconut milk

pisang goreng – fried banana fritters, a popular streetside snack

pisang molen – deep-fried bananas

rijstaffel – Dutch for 'rice table'; Indonesian food with a Dutch interpretation, it consists of lots of individual dishes with rice. It's rather like a glorified nasi campur or a less heated nasi Padang. Bring a big appetite.

sambal – a hot spicy chilli sauce served as an accompaniment with most meals

sate – one of the best known Indonesian dishes, sate are tiny kebabs of various types of meat served with a spicy peanut sauce. Street sate sellers carry their charcoal grills around with them and cook the sate on the spot.

The following is a list of food words which may be useful:

asam manis – sweet and sour; for example, ikan asam manis (sweet and sour fish)

ayam – chicken; for example, ayam goreng (fried chicken)

babi – pork; since most Indonesians are Muslim, pork is rarely found elsewhere in the archipelago but on Bali it's a popular delicacy.

daging – beef

dingin – cold

enak – delicious

garam – salt

gula – sugar

ikan – fish; there's a wide variety available on Bali.

ikan belut – eels; another Balinese delicacy, kids catch them in the rice paddies at night.

kare – curry, as in kare udang (curried prawns)

kentang – potatoes; *kentang goreng* are fried potatoes, also known as potato chips or French fries, and served in all tourist restaurants.

kepiting – crab

kodok – frog; frogs' legs are very popular on Bali and frogs are caught in the rice paddies at night.

krupuk – prawn crackers; they often accompany meals.

makan – the verb 'to eat' or food in general, *makan pagi* is breakfast, *makan siang* is the midday meal.

manis – sweet

mentega – butter

pahat – no sugar

panas – hot (temperature)

pasar malam – night market, often a great source of interesting and economical food stalls

pedas – hot (spicy)

rumah makan – restaurant, literally 'house to eat' or 'house for food'

sayur – vegetables

soto – soup, usually fairly spicy

telor – egg

udang – prawns

udang karang – lobster; very popular on Bali and comparatively economical.

warung – food stall combined with a sort of Indonesian small general store

The locally produced brands of ice cream are safe to eat. Peters (the locally licensed version of the well-known Australian brand) is quite good though Campina is generally the best. Indonesians are keen snackers so you'll find lots of street-stall snacks such as peanuts in palm sugar, shredded coconut cookies, pisang goreng, or even roasted dragonflies!

Fruit

It's almost worth making a trip to Bali or Lombok just to sample the tropical fruit. If you've never gone beyond apples, oranges and bananas you've got some rare treats in store when you discover rambutans, mangosteens, salaks or zurzat. Some of the favourites include:

avocat – avocado enthusiasts may suffer from overkill on Bali, they're plentiful and cheap; Balinese regard them as a sweet fruit, and drink avocado juice mixed with sweetened condensed milk.

blimbing – the 'starfruit' is a cool, crispy, watery tasting fruit – if you cut a slice you'll immediately see where the name comes from.

Blimbing (Starfruit)

durian – the most infamous tropical fruit, the durian is a large green fruit with a hard,

spiky exterior. Cracking it open reveals a truly horrific stench. Hotels and airlines in Asia often ban durians so it's not surprising that becoming a durian aficionado takes some time! One description of the durian compared it to eating a superb raspberry blancmange inside a revolting public toilet but true believers even learn to savour the smell.

Durian

jambu – guava; the crispy, pink, pear-shaped ones are particularly popular.

jeruk – jeruk is the all-purpose term for citrus fruit and there is a wide variety available on Bali. Jeruk are chiefly grown in the central mountains. The main varieties include the huge *jeruk muntis* or *jerunga*, known in the West as the pomelo. It's larger than a grapefruit but with a very thick skin, a sweeter, more orange-like taste and segments that break apart very easily. Regular oranges are known as *jeruk manis*, sweet jeruk. The small tangerine-like oranges which are often quite green are *jeruk baras*. Lemons are *jeruk nipis*.

makiza – like a big yellow passionfruit

manggu – mango; cheap and delicious in season.

mangosteen – one of the most famous tropical fruits the mangosteen is a small purple-brown fruit. The outer covering cracks open to reveal tasty pure-white segments with an indescribably fine flavour. Queen Victoria once offered a reward to anyone able to transport a mangosteen back to England which would still be edible on arrival.

nanas – pineapples

Nana (Pineapple)

nangka – also known as jackfruit, this is an enormous yellow-green fruit that can weigh over 20 kg. Inside there are hundreds of individual bright-yellow segments with a distinctive taste and a slightly rubbery texture. As they ripen on the tree each nangka may be separately protected in a bag.

Nangka (Jackfruit)

papaya or *paw paw* – these fruits are not that unusual in the West

pisang – these are bananas, and the variety of pisang found on Bali is quite surprising.

rambutan – a bright red fruit covered in soft, hairy spines; the name means hairy. Break it open to reveal a delicious white fruit closely related to the lychee.

salak – found chiefly in Indonesia, the salak is immediately recognisable by its perfect brown 'snakeskin' covering. Peel it off to reveal segments that in texture are like a cross between an apple and a walnut but in taste are quite unique. Bali salaks are much nicer than any others.

sawo – they look like a potato and taste like a pear.

zurzat – also spelt sirsat, and known in the West as soursop. The warty green skin of the zurzat covers a thirst-quenching interior with a slightly lemonish, tart taste. You can peel it off or slice it into segments. Zurzats are ripe when the skin has begun to lose its fresh green colouring and become darker and spotty. It should then feel slightly squishy rather than firm.

DRINKS

Bottled drinking water is available everywhere on Bali. A 500-ml bottle costs about 500 rp; a 1.5-litre bottle is around 1000 to 1200 rp. It's cheapest in supermarkets and local shops, and some brands, like Aqua, are more popular and a little dearer.

A variety of the popular Western soft-drink brands are available on Bali and Lombok – usually in small bottles rather than cans. Coca-Cola, 7-Up, Sprite and Fanta are all there. Prices are typically from around 700 rp in warungs and can be more than 1500 rp in expensive restaurants.

Fruit juice and UHT milk are available in sealed cartons from supermarkets and most small shops.

Beer is expensive compared to other things on Bali, but served cold in a bar or restaurant it's still cheaper than in most Western countries. The three popular brands are San Miguel, Anchor and Bintang. Bintang is the most common. The usual prices are around 3000 to 3500 rp for a large bottle (620 ml) or 2000 to 2500 rp for a small

(320 ml), but you can pay much more in pricier restaurants. In a five-star hotel at Nusa Dua a large beer will set you back 10,000 rp or more.

Wine is expensive on Bali; ordinary Australian red or white is around 3000 rp a glass. You can bring two litres per person from home, duty free, and restaurants are happy to serve it for you – ice bucket and all.

Some other popular Indonesian and Balinese drinks, both alcoholic and non-alcoholic, include:

air jeruk – lemon or orange juice

air minum – drinking water *(air* is water)

arak – distilled rice brandy, one stage on from brem; it can have a real kick. It's usually homemade although even the locally bottled brands look home produced. It makes quite a good mixed drink with 7-Up or Sprite. Mixed with orange juice it's called an *arak attack*.

brem – rice wine, either home produced or the commercially bottled brand Bali Brem. It tastes a bit like sherry – an acquired taste but not bad after a few bottles!

es buah – more a dessert than a drink, es buah is a curious combination of crushed ice, condensed milk, shaved coconut, syrup, jelly and fruit. It can be delicious.

es juice – although you should be a little careful about ice and water, the Balinese make delicious fruit drinks which are generally safe to try. In particular the ice-juice drinks are a real taste treat – just take one or two varieties of tropical fruit, add crushed ice and pass through a blender. You can make mind-blowing combinations of orange, banana, pineapple, mango, jackfruit, zurzat or whatever else is available.

kopi – fresh coffee, grown on Bali. *Kopi Bali* is strong, black and thick; the bottom third is textured, like Turkish coffee in a big cup. *Kopi susu* is milk coffee. Instant coffee is also available in places.

lassi – a refreshing yoghurt-based drink

stroop – cordial

susu – milk; not a very common drink in Indonesia although you can get long-life milk in cartons; ask for 'ultra'.

teh – tea; some people are not enthusiastic about Indonesian tea but if you don't need a strong, bend-the-teaspoon-style brew you'll probably find it's quite OK.

tuak – palm beer, usually homemade; it's a white or pinkish colour, and almost slimy.

ENTERTAINMENT
Cinemas

You'll find a *bioskop* (cinema) in every large town on Bali, and quite a few on Lombok as well. Lurid posters advertising the latest offering are highly visible – often they'll be mounted on a truck which cruises through town with a loudspeaker blasting out rave reviews and bites from the soundtrack. Balinese tastes in movies are varied in that they like blood-and-guts epics from anywhere in the world – Hong Kong or Hollywood, India or Java. They don't mind a bit of romance or some humour either, but mainly it's action, excitement, suspense and passion.

Films are usually played with the original soundtrack, subtitled in Indonesian, so if it's something from the USA, in theory you'll be able to understand it. In practice, there can be a high level of audience participation as they don't need to hear the words, and you probably don't either in most of the films. Films seem to be losing audiences to TV and video, and bioskop are closing in many towns. It's a pity, because the bioskop is a big social scene for young Balinese and there's usually a good atmosphere.

In the tourist areas you can see a fair selection of recent popular films, but they're most commonly shown on a video in a bar or restaurant. Bali's not a great place for film buffs to indulge their hobby.

Other Entertainment

Balinese dance performances and shadow puppet plays are popular entertainments for tourists, but of course they're much more than that. For more information see the section on Music, Dance & Drama in the Facts about Bali chapter.

Cockfights are the most popular entertainment among Balinese men, although technically they're illegal except as part of a temple festival. For more details, see the section on Temples in the Facts about Bali chapter.

Bull racing is an annual event in Negara, and is also held occasionally in the Buleleng district on the north coast.

THINGS TO BUY

The most popular purchases are Balinese and Indonesian arts and crafts, which are discussed in the colour Arts & Crafts section, and also clothes.

All sorts of clothing is made locally, and sold in hundreds of small shops in all the main tourist areas, but especially Kuta. It's mostly pretty casual, but it's not just beach-wear – you can get a tailor-made purple leather battle jacket, or just about anything else you want.

There are a growing number of Western-style department stores and shopping centres in Denpasar, Kuta and Nusa Dua which sell a large variety of clothing, shoes, leather goods, sports gear and toys. There's a huge range, the service is very good, and prices are slightly cheaper than in Australia, and competitive with US prices. If you're into shopping, you won't need any more advice. They take plastic!

Getting There & Away

Most international visitors to Bali will arrive by air, either directly or via Jakarta. For island hoppers, there are frequent ferries and local flights between eastern Java and Bali, and from Bali to Lombok, Sulawesi and other islands. Lombok is usually visited as a side trip from Bali, by plane, ferry or fast boat – see the Getting There & Away chapter for Lombok.

Note that the usual 60-day tourist pass for travel to Indonesia requires an onward or return ticket out of the country. If you want to leave by land or sea (eg to Malaysia from Sumatra), get an air ticket out of the country which is refundable or transferable.

AIR

Though Jakarta, the national capital, is the gateway airport to Indonesia, there is an increasing number of international flights to Denpasar, Bali. Nevertheless, you can fly to Jakarta first and travel overland through Java to Bali, or transfer to a domestic flight to Denpasar, which may give you more choices of when you fly. International airlines flying to Bali include Garuda (the Indonesian airline), Air France, Air New Zealand, Ansett Australia, Cathay Pacific, China Air, Continental, KLM, Korean Airlines, Lufthansa, Malaysian Airlines, Qantas, Singapore Airlines and Thai International. Merpati, Sempati and Bouraq are domestic carriers which link Bali to other Indonesian islands.

Arriving in Bali

The airport arrival procedures are fairly typical. The hotel booking counter in the luggage arrival hall has only the more expensive places on its list, with nothing much under US$20. Once through customs you're out with the touts, tour operators and taxi drivers. There's a tourist information counter inside the arrival area while outside there are two money change offices which are usually open for international arrivals. Both are quick and efficient, though one sometimes gives a better rate of exchange, almost as good as the moneychangers in the main towns. The touts will be working hard to convince you to come and stay at their place in Kuta and if you're not sure where you intend to stay they may be worth considering, but you will pay more for accommodation if you get taken there by a tout or a taxi driver – see the Kuta section for more details.

Transport from the airport is quite simple. To stop tourists being fleeced by taxi drivers there's an official taxi counter where you pay for a taxi in advance. Prices from the airport are:

Kuta Beach (to Jalan Bakung Sari)	4500 rp
Kuta-Legian (to Jalan Padma)	6500 rp
Legian (beyond Jalan Padma)	9000 rp
Oberoi Hotel (beyond Legian)	10,000 rp
Denpasar	9000 rp
Sanur	12,000 rp
Nusa Dua	12,000 rp
Ubud	34,000 rp

If you walk out across the airport carpark, north-east to Jalan Raya Tuban, taxi drivers may stop, and will take you to your destination for the metered rate, but this is unlikely to be much cheaper. Another option is to get a taxi at the standard rate to Bemo Corner in Kuta, and then get a taxi at metered rates, or a chartered minibus (at whatever you can bargain) to a more distant destination – this should save a few thousand rupiah if you're heading to Legian, Sanur or Denpasar.

The truly impecunious should keep walking on Raya Tuban, which is on the route for the S1 bemos (minibuses) which loop back to Kuta (500 rp) then continue to Denpasar (1000 rp). The bemos don't run late at night, and there can be other complications – see under Public Bus & Bemo in the Getting Around chapter. The even more impecunious (and lightly laden) can walk straight up the road to Kuta (about 2½ km), although it's a more pleasant stroll along the beach.

To/From Australia

There are direct flights to Denpasar from Sydney, Melbourne, Brisbane, Perth, Darwin and, believe it or not, Port Hedland. Only Garuda operates the Darwin service and only Qantas flies from Brisbane. Both airlines operate flights on the other sectors. Ansett Australia, the well-established domestic airline, is making its first international flights to Bali, from Melbourne, Sydney, Darwin and Perth. Connections from Adelaide and Brisbane are available, at the same prices as the Sydney and Melbourne flights. If you're flying between Bali and the south-eastern capitals, Ansett can give you a stopover in Darwin, which could be an attractive option.

Australia-wide telephone numbers for these airlines are:

Ansett International – ☎ 131767
Garuda – ☎ 008-800873
Qantas – ☎ 131313

Some Garuda flights go from Melbourne to Denpasar via Sydney while others go from Sydney via Melbourne. Flight time from Melbourne to Denpasar is about 5½ to 6½ hours; Sydney to Denpasar is slightly shorter. For West Australians Bali is almost a local resort. Perth to Denpasar flying time is just 3½ hours, less time than it takes to go from Perth to the east coast of Australia.

There are two types of discount fares available between Australia and Bali – inclusive-tour (IT) fares which are only available when purchased as part of a holiday package, and excursion fares (for 45 or 90 days maximum stay). IT fares have a high and a low season – the high season is the Christmas holiday period, from 22 November to 31 January. The fare you pay is based on the date of your departure from Australia. The 90-day excursion fare is the same year round, but for the cheaper 45-day excursion fare, travel must commence in the low season, between 1 February and 21 November. At certain times during the peak season, flights to or from Australia are very heavily booked and you must plan well ahead if you want to visit Bali then. In particular getting back to Australia at the end of January, just before Australian schools start after the summer break, can be difficult.

Fares to Denpasar in Australian dollars are:

From	Season	One-Way	Return	IT
Melbourne, Sydney or Brisbane	high	753	–	–
	low	637	–	–
	90-day	–	1084	959
	45-day	–	915	827
Perth or Darwin	high	434	–	–
	low	367	–	–
	90-day	–	756	688
	45-day	–	671	581
Port Hedland	high	457	–	–
	low	390	–	–
	90-day	–	791	722
	45-day	–	705	616

Package Tours To get the IT fare you must purchase the airfare as part of a package which includes accommodation for each night of your trip, and has a prepaid land content which must be more than a specified dollar value. There are a variety of tour types available. Straightforward tours include

Air Travel Glossary

Apex Apex, or 'advance purchase excursion' is a discounted ticket which must be paid for in advance. There are penalties if you wish to change it.

Bucket Shop An unbonded travel agency specialising in discounted airline tickets.

Bumped Just because you have a confirmed seat doesn't mean you're going to get on the plane – see Overbooking.

Cancellation Penalties If you have to cancel or change an Apex ticket there are often heavy penalties involved; insurance can sometimes be taken out against these penalties. Some airlines impose penalties on regular tickets as well, particularly against 'no show' passengers.

Check In Airlines ask you to check in a certain time ahead of the flight departure (usually 1½ hours on international flights). If you fail to check in on time and the flight is overbooked the airline can cancel your booking and give your seat to somebody else.

Confirmation Having a ticket written out with the flight and date you want doesn't mean you have a seat until the agent has checked with the airline that your status is 'OK' or confirmed. Meanwhile you could just be 'on request'.

Cross-Border Tickets Sometimes it is cheaper to fly to countries A, B and C rather than just B to C, usually because country A's airline is desperate to sell tickets or because the currency in A is very weak. Authorities in B can get very unhappy if you turn up for the flight from B to C without having first flown from A to B. Be cautious about discounted tickets which have been issued in another city, particularly in Eastern European cities.

Discounted Tickets There are two types of discounted fares – officially discounted (see Promotional Fares) and unofficially discounted. With unofficially discounted tickets you usually get what you pay for and the lowest prices often impose drawbacks like flying with unpopular airlines (Eastern European or Middle Eastern airlines for example), inconvenient schedules (only one flight a week and it leaves at 1 am) or unpleasant routes and connections (you get from A to B by a roundabout route and have to change airlines halfway with a long wait at the airport). A discounted ticket doesn't necessarily have to save you money – an agent may be able to sell you a ticket at Apex prices without the associated Apex advance booking and other requirements. Discounted tickets only exist where there is fierce competition; they are rarely available on domestic routes if the country only has one or two domestic airlines or in similarly tightly controlled regions.

Freedoms An airline's right to take passengers between various cities is defined by six 'freedoms'. Unofficially discounted tickets are often associated with fifth freedom flights – where an airline from country A has the right to fly passengers between country B and country C – or sixth freedom flights – where the airline in country B can fly passengers from A to C as long as the flight goes through B.

Full Fares Airlines traditionally offer first class (coded F), business class (coded J) and economy class (coded Y) tickets. These days there are so many promotional and discounted fares available that few passengers pay full economy fare.

Inclusive Tour An Inclusive Tour (or IT) fare is applicable when an airfare is booked as part of a complete package, with accommodation for each night of the trip booked and paid for in advance. IT fares can be much cheaper than regular excursion fares.

Lost Tickets If you lose your airline ticket an airline will usually treat it like a travellers' cheque and, after enquiries, issue you with another one. Legally, however, an airline is entitled to treat it like cash and if you lose it then it's gone forever. Take good care of your tickets.

Maximum Permitted Mileage (MPM) Between city A and city Z there is an officially defined MPM and so long as you do not exceed that distance you can fly via B, C, X, Y and points in between

your airfare, airport transfers, hotel accommodation and perhaps some meals and the odd sightseeing tour. Some tour operators and travel agencies can arrange packages that cost about the same as the cheapest return airfare, with IT fares, no meals, and accommodation at cheaper hotels, but you cannot combine these with a period of independent travel. Packages are particularly good value for a short trip as the saving on airfares can cover the cost of the accommodation in the cheaper mid-range hotels. In an IT package, children between two and 12 are charged 67% of the adult airfare, and their if you have a full fare, unlimited stopover ticket. These days, however, full-fare tickets are rather rare.

No Shows No shows are passengers who fail to show up for their flight, sometimes due to unexpected delays or disasters, sometimes due to simply forgetting, sometimes because they made more than one booking and didn't bother to cancel the one they didn't want.

On Request An unconfirmed booking for a flight; see Confirmation.

Open Jaws A return ticket where you fly out to one place but return from another. If available this can save you backtracking to your arrival point.

Overbooking Airlines hate to fly with empty seats and since every flight has some passengers who fail to show up (see No Shows) airlines often book more passengers than they have seats. Usually the excess passengers balance those who fail to show up but occasionally somebody gets bumped. If this happens guess who it is most likely to be? The passengers who check in late of course.

Promotional Fares Officially discounted fares like Apex fares which are available from any travel agent or direct from the airline.

Reconfirmation At least 72 hours prior to departure time of an onward or return flight you must contact the airline and 'reconfirm' that you intend to be on the flight. If you don't do this the airline can delete your name from the passenger list and you could lose your seat. You don't have to reconfirm the first flight on your itinerary or if your stopover is less than 72 hours. It doesn't hurt to reconfirm more than once.

Restrictions Discounted tickets often have various restrictions on them – advance purchase is the most usual one (see Apex). Others are restrictions on the minimum and maximum period you must be away, such as a minimum of 14 days or a maximum of one year. See Cancellation Penalties.

Standby A discounted ticket where you only fly if there is a seat free at the last moment. Standby fares are usually only available on domestic routes.

Tickets Out An entry requirement for many countries is that you have an onward or return ticket, in other words, a ticket out of the country. If you're not sure what you intend to do next, the easiest solution is to buy the cheapest onward ticket to a neighbouring country or a ticket from a reliable airline which can later be refunded if you do not use it.

Transferred Tickets Airline tickets cannot be transferred from one person to another. Travellers sometimes try to sell the return half of their ticket, but officials can ask you to prove that you are the person named on the ticket. This is unlikely to happen on domestic flights but can easily happen on an international flight where tickets may be compared with passports.

Travel Agencies Travel agencies vary widely and you should ensure you use one that suits your needs. Some simply handle tours while full-service agencies handle everything from tours and tickets to car rental and hotel bookings. A good one will do all these things and can save you a lot of money but if all you want is a ticket at the lowest possible price, then you really need an agency specialising in discounted tickets. A discounted ticket agency, however, may not be useful for other things, like hotel bookings.

Travel Periods Some officially discounted fares, Apex fares in particular, vary with the time of year. There is often a low (off-peak) season and a high (peak) season. Sometimes there's an intermediate or shoulder season as well. At peak times, when everyone wants to fly, not only will the officially discounted fares be higher but so will unofficially discounted fares or there may simply be no discounted tickets available. Usually the fare depends on your outward flight – if you depart in the high season and return in the low season, you pay the high-season fare. ■

accommodation is usually charged as an addition to the adult price, although sometimes one or two kids are included in the adult package fare.

The price of a package varies depending on when you go, how long you stay and what class of hotel you stay in. The hotels will generally be in Kuta, Sanur, Ubud or Nusa Dua, though some packages offer accommodation in Jimbaran, Candidasa, Lovina and elsewhere, and side trips to Lombok, Java or Sulawesi. Some typical costs, per person, from Sydney or Melbourne on a twin-share basis are from around A$900 for eight days (six nights) and from A$1040 for 15 days. (The last night is usually spent on the plane coming home, not in a hotel.) Extra nights can cost from as little as A$20 per person.

See the Accommodation section of Bali's Facts for the Visitor chapter for more discussion on the advantages and disadvantages of package tours. Travel agencies and airline offices will have plenty of colourful brochures to whet your appetite. Check a few brochures because costs vary quite a bit from one operator to another – even on packages using the same hotels. Sightseeing tours and extensions can be made, but a lot of the tours offered can be obtained far more cheaply in Bali.

Via Timor & Nusa Tenggara An interesting alternative to the direct flights is to take Merpati from Darwin to Kupang on the island of Timor. From there you can get one of the regular flights to Bali, or island-hop through the Nusa Tenggara archipelago to Bali. The Merpati agent in Darwin is Natrabu (☎ 81 3695) at 10 Westlane Arcade off Smith St Mall. The Darwin to Kupang fare in low season is A$198 one-way or A$330 return (high season, December and January, it's A$248 and A$407). In Kupang you can buy a ticket to Bali for 199,000 rp, plus 10% tax, which makes a total of about A$163. So the total low-season cost is A$361, compared to the low-season one-way fare from Darwin to Bali of A$367. In the high season the Kupang connection totals A$411 compared with a direct flight at A$434. Look on it as a free stopover, rather than a big money-saver, but island hopping from Kupang would be cheaper and a more interesting trip.

To/From New Zealand

Both Garuda (reservations in Auckland: ☎ 09-366-1855/1862) and Air New Zealand (reservations in Auckland: ☎ 09-357 3000) operate direct flights between Auckland and Denpasar. In the low season (18 January to 14 December) return fares with both airlines are NZ$1358; in the high season (15 December to 17 January), the return fare is NZ$1518. There is a 14-day advance-purchase requirement, a minimum stay of five days, and a maximum stay of 35 days. Other fares are available on application.

To/From the UK

Ticket discounting is a long-established business in the UK and it's wide open – the various agencies advertise their fares and there's nothing under the counter about it at all. To find out what is available and where to get it, pick up a copy of the giveaway newspapers *TNT, Southern Cross,* or *Trailfinder* or the weekly 'what's on' guide *Time Out.* These days discounted tickets are available all over the UK, they're not just a London exclusive. The magazine *Business Traveller* also covers cheap fare possibilities.

A couple of excellent places to look are Trailfinders and STA. Trailfinders is at 194 Kensington High St, London W8 (☎ 938 3939) and at 46 Earls Court Rd (☎ 938 3366). It also has offices in Manchester (☎ 061-839 6969) and Glasgow (☎ 041-353 2224). STA is at 74 Old Brompton Rd, London W7 (☎ 581 1022) and at Clifton House, 117 Euston Rd (☎ 388 2261).

Garuda is one of the enthusiastic fare discounters in London so it's relatively easy to find cheap fares to Australia with stopovers in Indonesia. It's not, however, such a bargain to travel one-way or return to Bali. With Garuda in the low season (around June) a return flight from London to Denpasar (via Jakarta) is £528 (£592 with Qantas). In the high season (December), it's £670 with Garuda and £700 with Qantas.

A one-way London to Australia flight in the low season is £387 with Qantas (£516 after 15 June) and £368 with Garuda. In the high season (December), it's £607 with Qantas (£656 after 16 December) and £676 with Garuda (£479 for a November flight). There is no extra charge for a stopover in Bali on a one-way flight.

Airline reservation telephone numbers in London are:

Garuda – ☎ 486 2644
Qantas – ☎ 0345-747 767

Round-the-World (RTW) tickets vary according to the itinerary, but the usual route includes London-Singapore-Bali-Australia-New Zealand-Los Angeles-London. It's £849 in the low season. In the high season (December) expect to pay around £1100.

Another alternative is to fly from London to Singapore for around £225/395 one-way/return, and then make your own way down to Bali by sea or land.

To/From Europe

Fares from European destinations are substantially higher than those quoted ex London. It may in fact be cheaper to fly to the UK and travel from there, rather than fly direct from other European cities. A sample of low/high-season fares quoted at the time of writing follows.

To/From Germany With Lufthansa (reservations in Frankfurt: ☎ 069-255255), return fares to Denpasar from Frankfurt start at DM1899 in the low season (April to the end of June) to DM2618 in the high season (16 to 26 December).

To/From France With Air France (reservations in Paris: ☎ 44 08 22 22), the return fare to Denpasar from Paris starts at FFr6000 in the low season (September to December) and FFr7500 in the high season (July and August).

To/From the Netherlands With KLM (reservations in Amsterdam: ☎ 20-4 747 747), return fares to Denpasar start from f2160 in the low season (September to October) to f2850 in the high season (16 to 26 December).

To/From the USA

You can pick up interesting tickets from the USA to South-East Asia, particularly from the US West Coast or from Vancouver. In fact the intense competition between Asian airlines has resulted in ticket-discounting operations very similar to the London bucket shops. To find cheap tickets simply scan the travel sections of the Sunday papers for agencies – the *New York Times, San Francisco Chronicle-Examiner* and the *Los Angeles Times* are particularly good. Try the network of student travel offices known as Council Travel or the Student Travel Network offices which are associated with STA travel.

There are plenty of competitive fares offered to Indonesia from the USA. Fares from Los Angeles to Denpasar cost around US$650/1080 one-way/return in the low season (6 January to 31 May and 1 September to 14 December), and US$775/1300 in the high season (1 June to 31 August and 13 December to 5 January). These prices don't include tax (about an additional US$35).

Garuda (reservations in Los Angeles: ☎ 213-387 0149) has a Los Angeles-Honolulu-Biak-Denpasar route which is an extremely interesting back-door route into Indonesia. Tickets are valid for six months and are good value at US$599/1099 one-way/return in the low season and US$719/1179 in the high season. Biak, an island north of Irian Jaya (the Indonesian part of New Guinea), is a no-visa entry point for most nationalities – check your country's status with an Indonesian embassy.

To/From Asia

You are certain to find cheap fares to Bali from Asia (Bangkok, Singapore and Hong Kong for example) and an increasing number of these will be direct flights to Denpasar. For some flights, however, you will have to enter Indonesia at Jakarta and then fly to Bali.

Discount tickets for a Hong Kong to Denpasar flight can be bought for around HK$3000 (roughly US$400) and return tickets for around HK$4500 (about US$600). You can also find interesting fares from Hong Kong via Bali to Australia. Singapore to Denpasar costs around S$300 one-way and S$550 return. Garuda is the main carrier, but recently Air France has been offering competitive fares.

To/From Java

Garuda fares to/from Denpasar include Surabaya for 78,000 rp, Yogyakarta for 104,000 rp and Jakarta for 195,000 rp. Merpati, Sempati and Bouraq also fly from Denpasar to various centres in Java, and their fares will always be equal to or lower than Garuda's.

To/From Other Indonesian Islands

In some instances it is cheaper to fly to other parts of Indonesia from Bali than from Java. For example, from Denpasar to Ujung Pandang (Sulawesi) the fare is cheaper (136,000 rp) than from Surabaya (Java; 183,000 rp). There are flights from Denpasar to other parts of Nusa Tenggara including Mataram (Lombok; 43,000 rp), Maumere (Flores; 181,000 rp), Kupang (Timor; 199,000 rp) and Dili (Timor).

SEA
To/From Java

The standard travellers' route from Java to Bali is by bus from Surabaya to Denpasar, crossing the Bali Strait by ferry. There are numerous bus companies operating on this route, and many of them travel overnight. The fare includes the ferry crossing and often a meal at a rest stop along the way. There are also direct bus services between Denpasar and Yogyakarta, and even Jakarta.

In Bali you can get tickets from numerous agencies in and around Kuta, Ubud and other tourist areas. You'll also find a collection of bus company offices in Denpasar, which will be a bit cheaper but perhaps less convenient. Fares depend on the bus and cost more with air-con. Buses to Surabaya range in price from 18,000 to 22,000 rp for the 10 to 12-hour trip, and to Yogyakarta (a 16-hour trip) they vary from 25,000 to 36,000 rp. Air-con buses to Jakarta, a 30-hour marathon, cost around 56,000 rp. Mostly the buses will actually leave from Denpasar's Ubung bus terminal, so you'll have to get there from Kuta. Ubung is the cheapest place to buy a ticket – agencies add on their percentage.

Buses also go to/from Java from Singaraja and Lovina on the north coast. Prices are similar to the fares from Denpasar. You may have to change buses at Gilimanuk.

When you book you're assigned a seat number; check the seating chart and try to avoid the front rows – the night-bus drivers rush along like maniacs, and who wants to be first to find out about the accident? In fact the night buses make the Denpasar to Surabaya trip so rapidly that early evening departures are liable to arrive at an uncomfortably early hour in the morning.

The ferry that shuttles back and forth across the narrow strait between Bali and Java takes only 15 minutes to cross one-way. Costs are 650 rp for an adult, 450 rp for a child. You can take a car across for about 7400 rp (the cost depends on the size of the car), a motorbike for 1800 rp and a bicycle for 950 rp. On the Java side the bus terminus is not actually in the Java ferry port of Banyuwangi. It's right out of the town at Ketapang but there is regular transport into Banyuwangi. Buses to other parts of Java depart straight from the ferry terminal.

To/From Other Indonesian Islands

The national shipping line, Pelni, has passenger ships doing regular loops through the islands of Indonesia, typically calling at Benoa once a fortnight. The exact dates and routes can change, so enquire well in advance. The Pelni office (☎ & fax 238962) in Bali is at Jalan Pelabuhan, Benoa.

On the current schedule, *Kelimutu* makes a loop every two weeks through the islands of Sumbawa, Sumba, Flores, Lombok, Alor and Timor.

The *Awu* has two different 14-day routes through various ports on Kalimantan, Sulawesi, Java and Bali.

To/From Australia

For those with plenty of time up their sleeves, the *Golden Star*, a modified 35-metre Indonesian sailing vessel, departs monthly from Hudson Creek, in Darwin, to Benoa Harbour (Bali). The journey takes from 10 to 13 days. The one-way fare is A$270/320/340 in basic eight/four/two berth cabins. In Australia, contact All Points Travel (☎ 089-410066; fax 089-411602), Unit 7, Anthony Plaza, Smith St Mall, PO

Box 2561, Darwin NT 0801. The agent in Bali is Tall Ship Cruises (☎ & fax 287431).

LEAVING BALI

Don't forget to reconfirm your flight between 24 and 72 hours before departure. Reconfirming is very important in the peak holiday periods when there always seem to be people waiting at the airport hoping for a spare seat. Most airlines have offices at the airport, and at the Natour Grand Bali Beach hotel in Sanur (see Sanur for details). Garuda also has offices in Denpasar (☎ 225245), Nusa Dua (☎ 71444, 71864) and at the Natour Kuta Beach in Kuta (☎ 751179). Air New Zealand (☎ 751067) is at the Kartika Plaza Hotel on the south side of Kuta. Travel agencies will offer to reconfirm for you, for a fee, but some have been lax about actually making the reconfirmation – they should give you a small computer printout with all the details on it, in cryptic airline-speak.

Come departure time Denpasar airport holds no surprises. Alcohol drinkers can try the airport snack bar or wait until they've passed through immigration and try the cafeteria bar. The duty-free shop and souvenir shops here are expensive, and only accept foreign currency. The departure lounge cafeteria is also pricey, but takes rupiah. You can change excess rupiah back into hard currency at a bank counter by the check-in desks.

Departure Tax

There's a departure tax on domestic (5500 rp) and international (14,000 rp) flights. Only children under two years of age are exempt.

Getting Around

The main forms of public transport on Bali are the cheap buses and *bemos* that run on more or less set routes within or between towns. If you want your own transport, you can charter a whole bemo or rent a car, motorbike or bicycle. Tourist shuttle buses, running between the major tourist centres, are more expensive than public transport, but are more comfortable and convenient. Transport on Lombok is similar, but see the Getting Around Lombok chapter for more information.

PUBLIC BUS & BEMO

Bemos are *the* Balinese form of public transport. These days most bemos are minibuses with a row of seats down each side, although the old basic version, a small pick-up truck with two rows of seats, is still around. The tiny three-wheeled type, like a motor scooter with a van on the back, is still used in Denpasar. The word 'bemo' is a contraction of *becak* (a bicycle rickshaw) and *motor*, but these days only the three-wheelers resemble a motorised rickshaw. A bemo may be called a 'colt', from the Mitsubishi Colt minibuses made under licence in Indonesia, though the term is no longer widespread. As well as the driver, a bemo usually has a young guy who acts as a salesman, luggage handler and fare collector – let's call him the jockey. He hangs out the door when the vehicle is going, and hustles on the road or the bemo terminal when it stops.

Most bemos operate on a standard route for a set fare. They leave when they're full, and pick up and drop off people and goods anywhere along the way. Unless you get on at a regular starting point, and get off at a regular finishing point, the fares are likely to be fuzzy. The cost per km is pretty variable, but it's cheaper on longer trips. The minimum fare is about 300 rp. On short trips, all bemos operate the same way and charge the same fares, regardless of whether they are old-style bemos, colts, or any other type

of minibus. On longer routes there are larger minibuses or regular buses operating from the same terminals as the bemos, though they don't cruise around looking for passengers. They are less regular than bemos, but cheaper and faster, as they do not stop as often on the way.

Bemos are famous for overcharging tourists, and finding out the 'correct' fare requires local knowledge, subtlety and cool. The Catch 22 is that if you ask what the fare is, you obviously don't know, and are therefore a candidate for overcharging. The best procedure is to hand over the correct fare as you get off, as the locals do. To find out the correct fare, consult a trusted local before you get on – if you're staying at a cheap losmen, the owner will usually be helpful; at an expensive hotel they'll discourage you from using bemos and offer to call you a taxi.

Bemo fares are often given in this book, but they won't always be exactly right. For short trips you can make a good estimate based on a proportion of the fare between the main towns at the start and end of the route, rounded upwards. Note what other passengers pay when they get off, bearing in mind that school children and the driver's friends pay less. If you speak Indonesian, you can ask your fellow passengers what the *harga biasa* (standard price) should be, though in a dispute they will probably support the bemo jockey. If the bemo jockey asks 500 rp, and you know damn well it should only be 300 rp, they'll take the correct fare with a grin. If you hand over 300 rp, and the jockey puts up a big protest that the correct fare is 500 rp, he's probably right. If you offer 1000 rp you might even get change, but don't count on it – it's best to have the right money.

The *harga turis* (tourist price) for bemos is increasingly prevalent on Bali, and the whole business is a bit of a game. Bemo drivers and jockeys are usually good-humoured about it, but some tourists take it very seriously and have unpleasant arguments over a few hundred rupiah – often less than 25 US cents. Sometimes they'll charge extra (double the passenger price) if you have a big bag, which seems pretty fair as two Balinese might fit in the space taken up by some travellers' backpacks. Make sure you know where you're going, and accept that the bemo won't go till it's full and will take a roundabout route to collect/deliver as many passengers as possible. Don't make it a hassle for bemos to carry tourists as the drivers will become even more reluctant to do so, and may feel justified in overcharging them.

Around Kuta and Sanur, beware of getting on an empty bemo. There are some unscrupulous drivers who will inform you, at the end of the ride, that they weren't really plying the route, and you've just chartered the whole bemo!

Every large town has at least one terminal for long-distance buses, a *terminal bis*, which is also a stop for bemos running around town. Even a small town will have a place where the buses and bemos to/from other towns depart and arrive. Larger towns may have several bus/bemo terminals. Denpasar is the hub of Bali's transport system, and it has five terminals as well as

stops for local bemos. These places can be confusing, but there are usually areas where bemos for a specific destination assemble, with lots of jockeys hustling for passengers. There is usually an office in the terminal with a notice board showing fares to various destinations – this is helpful though the fares can be out of date.

To go from one part of Bali to another it is often necessary to go via one or more of the Denpasar terminals, or via a terminal in one of the other larger towns. For example, to go by public bemo from Sanur to Ubud, you would go first to the Kereneng bus station in Denpasar (600 rp), then transfer to the Batubulan bus station (600 rp), then take a third bemo to Ubud (1000 rp).

Chartering a Bemo
An excellent way for a group to get around is to charter a whole minibus, because for many trips it's much more convenient than using public bemos. As an alternative to the Sanur-Ubud trip described above, you can, with a little bargaining, charter a vehicle to take you straight there for around 16,000 rp. Between eight people that works out about the same as the roundabout route through Denpasar, but it's much faster, and you can

'Leaving on the bemo' (cartoon by Benny Tantra)

be dropped at the door of your final destination. If you want to make stops on the way this will add a little to the cost.

Bemos are licensed to work only on particular routes, and they cannot legally be chartered for trips away from their standard route. This is enforced in tourist areas, and only vehicles with yellow plates are allowed to carry tourists anywhere on the island. The charter minibuses have conventional seats, rather than benches down each side, and are often air conditioned. It's easy to arrange a charter – just listen for one of the frequent offers of 'transport, transport' in the street, or approach a driver yourself, and start negotiating. In Kuta they congregate at Bemo Corner and at certain points up Jalan Legian. In other tourist areas you'll find them in the main street or around the bemo terminal. Try to deal directly with the driver because any intermediaries or touts will expect a cut somewhere.

To charter a minibus for a day, work on about 40,000 to 60,000 rp, although the cost depends on where you want to go. If you're planning to start early, finish late, and cover an awful lot of territory, then you will have to pay more. Sometimes you will be given a lower rate if you agree to pay for petrol, but this can be difficult to arrange on a fair basis, so it's better to negotiate a fixed price. The cost is comparable to hiring a car for a single day, so you get the driver virtually for nothing. You don't have to worry about a licence or insurance, and a driver who speaks English and knows the way round can be a real asset, particularly if you're in Denpasar or one of the larger towns. A good driver will act as a personal guide, interpreter, and source of information for just about everything. You can stop when you like, to take photos, shop or whatever, but if you're shopping, you might finish up going where your driver wants you to go and not where you thought you wanted to go.

Outside the tourist areas, people do charter regular bemos, but the negotiations are more complicated and the driver probably won't speak English. Prices start at around 25,000 rp for a day, but you have to pay extra for petrol, and also for petrol for the return trip if you're only going one-way. You're expected to buy meals for the driver (nasi campur and water is the standard), especially if you stop to eat yourself.

Warning

Beware of pickpockets on bemos. You'll find them mainly on the Denpasar to Kuta and Denpasar to Ubud routes, where they tend to prey on unwary travellers. Their mode of operation seems to be for one operator to engage you in friendly conversation while his accomplice cleans you out, often using a painting, parcel or similar cover to hide the activity. Sometimes half the people on the bemo will be in on the game, and the odds will really be stacked against you.

TOURIST SHUTTLE BUS

In the main tourist areas you'll see signs advertising tourist shuttle buses direct to other destinations on Bali, and they are usually comfortable and reliable. Although considerably more expensive than public transport, these minibuses are much cheaper and more convenient than chartering a bemo.

Tourist shuttle buses have been organised into a virtual network by the Perama company. Perama operates regular, scheduled minibuses, and full-sized buses, to and from all the main tourist areas on Bali, with connections to Java, Lombok and Sumbawa. There are other tourist bus companies which also provide a good service, but Perama seems to be the most established and is widely recommended. Perama's head office in Kuta is at Jalan Legian 20 (☎ 0361-751551, 751875, fax 751170), and there are also offices in Candidasa, Lovina and Ubud. In Sanur, Perama buses stop outside the Si Pino Restaurant, near the Grand Bali Beach Hotel, and you can phone the Kuta office to book. Always try to book the day before with Perama; a bigger bus will be put on if needed.

Occasionally people complain that shuttle buses take a roundabout route to their destination. For example, one reader took a bus from Ubud to Lovina which went via Kuta and the airport. On other occasions people expected to be taken to a specific hotel, but finished up at the usual stop. It's a good idea to clarify these things when you get your ticket, and if the driver offers to take you to a certain hotel, have him write it on the ticket. If he won't undertake to give you a reasonably direct service, go to another bus company.

Perama's prices are fixed, and you can get a list of fares at any of its offices. Fares with the other shuttle bus companies are very similar to Perama's; for example: Kuta to Ubud via Sanur, 7500 rp; to Lovina 12,500 rp; to Padangbai and Candidasa 10,000 rp. The fare from Kuta to Mataram and Senggigi on Lombok is 20,000 rp including the regular ferry from Padangbai to Lembar; Perama can do connections with the faster boats to Lombok by arrangement.

Perama also acts as an agent selling tickets for long-distance buses operated by other companies, but they are no cheaper than other agencies, and will be more expensive than going directly to the bus company at the terminal. They now also offer tours, like the seven-day 'Land-Sea Adventures' between Lombok and Flores, which include boat and bus travel, meals, accommodation and sightseeing, including the Komodo dragons. At 525,000 rp, these are more expensive than some other similar tours, and much more expensive than doing the trip by yourself.

TAXI

Taxis are becoming more common in Denpasar and some tourist areas, notably Kuta. They're blue and yellow with meters and air-con. The fare is 800 rp flagfall, 800 rp for the first km or two, dropping to about 500 rp a km. They're good, and a lot less hassle than haggling with bemo jockeys and charter minibus drivers. You can always find them at the airport, but taxis can be unpopular in areas where charter operators are trying to hustle tourist business at rip-off rates. Taxis probably won't stop on Jalan Legian or near Bemo Corner in Kuta. Don't get in a taxi if the driver says the meter isn't working – it may suddenly 'fix' itself but if not, get another taxi.

CAR & MOTORBIKE
Car Rental

Car rental is easy on Bali. The big international rental operators have a token presence, but they're very expensive and you'll do far better with the local operators. The most popular vehicles for rent are the small Suzuki Jimnys, but you can also find open VW safari vehicles, regular cars, minibuses and virtually anything else. Automatic transmission is uncommon on rental cars. Suzukis, with their compact size, good ground clearance and low gear ratio are well suited to exploring Bali's back roads, though the bench seats at the back are uncomfortable on a long trip. With a larger group, it may be better to rent a Toyota Kijang, which seats six, but is still economical and lightweight. Soft-top vehicles, like the VW safari, can't be locked up, so your things are not as secure. Typical costs are around 35,000 to 40,000 rp a day including insurance and unlimited km. If you rent for a week you can expect a discount, to as little as 30,000 rp per day. A Kijang costs from about 55,000 rp per day. Agencies at Kuta, Sanur, Ubud, Lovina and other tourist areas will have signs out advertising cars for rent. Generally, Kuta is the cheapest place to rent a car.

It's a good idea to check a rental car carefully before you drive off. Don't wait until you really need the horn, wipers, lights, spare tyre, or registration papers before you find they're not there. It's unusual to find a car on which everything works.

All rental vehicles should have registration plates starting with 'RC' (for rental car), otherwise they are not legally allowed to be rented. If you drive a vehicle without RC plates and the police stop you, it will be inconvenient at best. You also need an International Driving Permit, which you should get from a motoring organisation at home. Driving without a licence could incur a fine of 2,000,000 rp.

There are some drawbacks to renting cars though. Being in a car makes removes you from the people and the countryside; you won't hear the birds and you won't smell the flowers, and you'll miss out on a lot of personal contact. You might feel very conspicuous too – there's no way you can merge with the scenery when you're in a private car. You won't want to stop too long in one place, however appealing, if you're paying 30,000 rp or more a day for a car (rental cars have to be returned to the place from which they were rented – you can't do a one-way rental). Car rental is expensive compared with public transport, and can cost as much, or more than, chartering a vehicle and driver. Also, you may be charged higher prices at hotels and shops if you arrive by car – the staff know you can afford it. (This goes both ways of course – they know you can easily go somewhere else.)

A major drawback is that driving in Bali is potentially very hazardous, and the consequences of an accident can be very serious. You should be experienced at driving on narrow, rough roads, able to cope with some chaotic traffic, and confident about dealing with local officials. Read the comments that follow about road rules, risks and insurance before you decide to rent a car.

The final drawback is the impact on Bali's road system, parking facilities and environment generally – what would happen if every tourist wanted to drive around Bali in their own car? For a group or a family wanting to have a quick trip around the whole island, a rental car is a good option, if the driver is capable. If you want to travel more slowly, stopping for a day or so in a number of places, then you'd be better off on tourist shuttle buses (for convenience) or public bemos and buses (for value and lots of local contact). If you want the convenience of a car, without the risks, consider chartering a vehicle with a driver.

Motorbike Rental

Motorbikes are a popular way of getting around Bali, with similar advantages and disadvantages to rental cars. Motorcycling is just as convenient and flexible as driving but potentially even more dangerous. The environmental impact and the cost are much less, and though motorcycling does distance

you from the people and the countryside, you won't be nearly as cut off as in a car.

There is no denying the dangers of a motorbike on Bali: combined with all the normal terrors of riding are narrow roads, unexpected potholes, crazy drivers, children darting out in front of you, dogs and chickens running around in circles, unmarked road works, unlit traffic at night, and 1001 other opportunities for you to do serious harm to yourself. Every year a number of visitors to Bali come home in a box. Bali is no place to learn to ride a motorbike.

You don't meet people the way you do on a bemo, and many things can be missed because you are concentrating on the road. Furthermore, motorbikes are a noisy, unpleasant intrusion in many places on Bali. On the other hand, there are now so many Balinese riding motorbikes that the addition of a few hundred more for tourists will hardly add to the problem.

The major advantage is the enormous flexibility that a motorbike gives you. Bali may have various not-to-be-missed sights but the best things it has to offer are completely unplanned. You come round a corner and there it is – a procession, a mouthwateringly beautiful piece of scenery, or a temple decked out for a festival. If you're travelling around on a bike you can stop if you want to, and recommence your journey whenever you choose. If you're travelling in a bemo you may just shoot straight by. Even in a car you'll find that it's harder to stop, more difficult to park, a hassle to get out, and just too hot outside to venture out of the air-conditioned interior. Robert Pirsig in *Zen & the Art of Motorcycle Maintenance* relates driving a car to watching TV and compares riding a bike to being *in* the picture. Riding in a bemo can be like watching TV with a dozen people between you and the screen!

Finding a Motorbike Motorbikes for rent in Bali are almost all between 90 and 125 cc with 100 cc as the usual size. You really don't need anything bigger as the distances are short and the roads are rarely suitable for travelling fast. Anyway what's the hurry?

Rental charges vary with the bike and the period of rental. The longer the rental period the lower the rate, the bigger or newer the bike the higher the rate. Typically you can expect to pay around 9000 to 12,000 rp a day. A newish 125 cc in good condition might cost 12,000 rp a day. If you want a bike for only one day you might have to pay more.

The majority of the bikes are rented out by individual owners. There are a few places around Kuta which seem to specialise in motorbike rent but generally it's travel agencies, restaurants, losmen or shops with a sign out saying 'motorcycle for rent'. You can ask around, or if you have an 'I need a motorbike' look, somebody is certain to approach you. Kuta is the main bike rental place, but you'll have no trouble finding a motorbike to rent in Ubud, Sanur or Lovina. Check the bike over before riding off – there are some poorly maintained pieces of junk around.

Motorbike Licence If you have an International Driving Permit endorsed for motorbikes you have no problems. If not, you have to obtain a local licence, good for one month in Bali only. This is straightforward and easy, but time-consuming and moderately expensive at 50,000 rp. It's not worth getting a bike licence for a day or two – rent or charter a car or minibus instead.

The bike owner will take you into Denpasar where you'll probably find 50 or so other would-be bike renters lined up for their licence. You stop on the way to be photographed (four photos required), and you're given a written test when you arrive (20 multiple-choice questions; the bike owner will ensure you know the answers). Then comes the hard part. After a friendly sendoff from the police riding tester, who wishes you luck, you ride a short slalom and do a couple of figure eights round some cones. So long as you don't put your feet down, fall off or run into the police officer's car you'll pass. If you don't pass, you can try again – eventually everyone passes and then it's fingerprints, paperwork, and you're unleashed onto Bali's roads. The whole process takes about four hours.

Don't be tempted to ride without a licence. Your insurance company will disown you if you have an accident, and in any case, enforcement is becoming stricter. The fine for riding without a licence is 2,000,000 rp. Some police may let you off with an 'on-the-spot fine' of 50,000 to 60,000 rp, but don't count on it. They can impound the motorbike and put you in jail till you pay up.

Other Motorcycling Essentials You must carry the bike's registration paper with you on the bike. Make sure the owner gives it to you before you ride off.

Helmets are compulsory, and the requirement is enforced in tourist areas, if not in the countryside. The standard helmets you get with rental bikes are pretty lightweight – probably better than nothing, but not much.

Despite the tropical climate, it's still wise to dress properly for biking. Thongs, shorts and a T-shirt are not going to protect your skin from being ground off as you slide along the pavement. As well as protection against a spill, be prepared for the weather. It can get pretty cold on a cloudy day in the mountains. Coming over the top of Batur you might wish you were wearing gloves. And when it rains in Bali, it really rains, so be ready for that as well. If you're riding on a hot day, your hands, arms and face can get sunburned very quickly, so cover up and use a sunblock.

Insurance
These days insurance seems to be a fixed requirement in Bali, for both cars and motorbikes. It's quite expensive – for a motorbike it can cost nearly as much as the rental charge. For a car the cost reduces greatly as the period increases, but for a single day it can run to 16,000 rp or more. Whether it actually does you much good if worst comes to worst is not entirely clear.

A typical policy would cover the vehicle for a fixed amount, usually the amount shown in a table for a vehicle of the same type and age, plus a fixed amount for damage to other people or their property, ie 'Third Party' cover. The main concern seems to be insuring the vehicle – a policy might cover the car for 10,000,000 rp, but provide for only 2,000,000 rp Third Party cover, with the renter liable for the first 40,000 rp of any claim and any amount above the sum insured. Your travel insurance may provide some additional protection, though liability for motor accidents is specifically excluded from many policies.

Make sure that your personal travel insurance covers you for injuries incurred while driving or motorcycling. Some travel insurance policies specifically exclude coverage for motorbike riding.

Fuel

Petrol *(Bensin)* is sold by the government-owned Pertamina company and is still reasonably cheap – around 700 rp a litre from a petrol station, 750 rp from a roadside vendor.

Bali has quite a few petrol (gas) stations but they often seem to be out of petrol, out of electricity or simply on holiday. In that case look for the little roadside fuel shops where they fill your tank with a plastic container and a funnel. They usually have a handwritten sign that reads 'premium' ('solar' is diesel fuel). I was once told to avoid these places because the petrol they sold was 'second hand'! In fact, it does sit round in open containers and is quite likely to be contaminated with water or dirt, though I've never had any trouble with it.

James Lyon

Petrol pumps usually have a meter, and a table which shows how much to pay for various amounts, but cheating is still prevalent. Make sure the pump is reset to zero before the attendant starts to put petrol in your vehicle, and check the total amount that goes in before the pump is reset for the next customer. Ensure the amount you are charged is consistent with the capacity of your tank, and that the arithmetic is accurate.

Around the Island

Once you've cleared the southern Bali traffic tangle the roads are remarkably uncrowded. The traffic is heavy from Denpasar south to Kuta and Sanur; to the east about as far as Klungkung; and to the west about as far as Tabanan. Over the rest of the island the traffic is no problem at all.

Finding your way around is not difficult.

Roads are well signposted and maps are easily available. Off the main routes, roads often become very potholed, but are usually surfaced – there are few dirt roads in Bali.

Don't plan on any island tour in Bali running to schedule – festivals, ceremonies, cremations, processions or almost anything could be there to distract you from your intended itinerary. Given a minimum of a week a possible round-trip route could be:

Day 1	Kuta to Candidasa	79 km
Day 2	Candidasa to Penelokan via Amlapura	86 km
Day 3	around Lake Batur	
Day 4	Penelokan to Lovina	71 km
Day 5	at the beach	
Day 6	Lovina to Kuta via Bedugul	98 km

Of course that's a fairly high-speed trip and your starting and finishing point doesn't have to be Kuta, it could just as easily be Ubud, Singaraja or anywhere else you choose. Some of the most interesting detours include a trip round the south-eastern tip of Bali; the east-coast road between Tulamben and Yeh Sanih; the north-coast road from Lovina to Gilimanuk; and the roads across the island between Seririt and the south coast.

Road Rules & Risks

It's very common to hear visitors complaining about crazy Balinese drivers, but often it's because they don't understand the local conventions of road use. Most of the drivers on Bali's roads are professionals, and usually they're pretty good. The main thing to remember is the 'watch your front' rule – it's your responsibility to avoid anything that gets in front of your vehicle. A car or motorbike pulling out in front of you, in effect, has the right of way. Often drivers won't even look up the road to see what's coming, though they usually listen for the horn. So that's the second rule – use your horn to warn anything in front that you're there, especially if you're about to overtake. The third rule is to drive on the left side of the road, though it's often a case of driving on whatever side of the road is left, after avoiding the road works, livestock and other vehicles.

Avoid driving at night, or even at dusk. Many bicycles, carts and other horse-drawn vehicles don't have proper lights, and street lighting is limited to the main towns. It's terrifying to discover that you're about to run up the back of a mobile sate stand when there are at least three invisible bicycles which you'll hit if you try to avoid it, and the bemo behind you is blaring its horn and about to overtake. Motorcycling at dusk offers the unique sensation of numerous insects, large and small, hitting your face at 60 km per hour – at least you won't fall asleep.

Accidents

The best advice is: don't have an accident, but remember if you do that it will be considered your fault. The logic behind this is Asian and impeccable: 'I was involved in an accident with you. I belong here, you don't. If you hadn't been here there wouldn't have been an accident. Therefore it was your fault'.

It is not unusual for the driver of an offending vehicle to be roughed up by aggrieved locals after an accident, or for them to demand immediate promises of compensation. The incident may be seen as a once-in-a-lifetime chance to get some quick and easy money. In these circumstances it is essential to keep a cool head and avoid being pressured into an admission or commitment.

If you are involved in a serious accident (one involving death or injury), insist that the police come as soon as possible, and have someone you trust contact your consulate. If your vehicle is still going, it may be advisable to drive straight to the nearest police station, rather than stopping at the scene and risking a violent confrontation. The police are unlikely to take your side, but at least they will ensure that formalities are complied with and excessive reactions are moderated. It is likely that they will impound your vehicle, and may even detain you in jail until the matter is sorted out. At least you will be safe there, and any settlement should be offi-

cial enough to satisfy your insurance company. If you admit liability, it could invalidate both your travel insurance policy and the policy you took out when you rented the vehicle.

If it's a minor accident (property damage only), it may be better to negotiate a settlement directly, rather than spend days hassling with police, lawyers, insurance companies and so on. Try to delay matters a little, so you can recover from the shock, get someone with local knowledge whom you trust to advise you, and perhaps contact your consulate and/or a lawyer *(adpokat)*.

BICYCLE

Seeing Bali by pushbike has become much more popular in recent years, and the quality of rental bikes has really improved. More places are renting bikes and more visitors are bringing bikes with them. Mountain bikes are the most common type, and with their low gear ratios and softer tyres they are much better suited to Bali than 10-speed touring bikes.

You can usually bring your pushbike with you in your baggage – some airlines, including Garuda and Qantas, will carry it free of charge. (Most of the following information is from Hunt Kooiker, whose handy little booklet *Bali by Bicycle* is now, unfortunately, out of print.)

Cycling in Bali

With its high mountains, tropical heat, heavy traffic and frequent rain showers, Bali may not seem like a place for a bicycle tour. However, with the use of two short bemo trips to scale the central mountains you can accomplish a beautiful, 200-km circle trip of Bali. The breeze as you ride on the level or downhill really moderates the heat, and once you're out of the congested southern region the traffic is relatively light. The roads are pretty good and frequent roadside food stalls make it easy to duck out of a passing rain shower.

The main advantage of seeing Bali by bicycle is the quality of the experience. By bicycle you can be totally immersed in the environment – you can hear the wind rustling in the rice paddies and the sound of a gamelan orchestra practising, and catch the scent of the flowers. Even in the highly touristed Bali of the 1990s, cycle tourers on the backroads still experience the unhassled friendliness which seems all but lost on the tourist circuit.

Buying or Renting a Bicycle

There are plenty of bicycles for rent in Bali. If you want to buy a bicycle, 15-speed mountain bikes are becoming quite common and Denpasar has a number of shops selling spare parts and complete bicycles. There are numerous bike rental places in Kuta, Legian, Sanur and Ubud. The challenge, though, is finding a bike on which everything works! Common problems include worn tyres, chains which break, ineffective brakes, stiff gear changes, terrible seats, no reflectors and no bell. It's unusual to find a rental bike with lights. Some bike rental places are open to making special arrangements; for example, selling you a bike and then buying it back at the end of your trip.

If you are planning a short trip, you can rent a bicycle – asking prices start at around 8,000 rp a day (or even more if the vendor is feeling lucky), but you should get it down to about half this figure if you take it for a week or longer. Before you even start negotiating, look at the bike and make sure it suits your needs and is in good condition. Buy a new padded seat in Denpasar, take it to the rental shop and offer to replace the old, distorted, hard-as-tacks seat with the new seat if you are given a good discount.

For touring it is absolutely essential that your bike is in good repair.

Brakes Both the front and rear brakes must be able to stop your bike individually in case one should malfunction on a steep downhill stretch. Check the brake blocks to see that they are symmetrically positioned and show even wear with plenty of rubber left. They should not rub any part of the rim when you spin the wheel. The real test is whether or not they can hold the bike still when clamped

while you push forward with all your strength. If in doubt, buy new brake blocks – they're very cheap. Do not go into the central mountains without good brakes.

Wheels & Tyres Turn the bike upside down and spin the wheels. Check the rims carefully for deep rust spots which could cause the wheel to buckle under stress. Look at the rim as it moves by the brake blocks. If the wheel wobbles you will have shimmering problems. Also squeeze the spokes to check for loose or broken ones. Avoid bikes with bald or soft tyres. The shop will pump them up once, but you'll have to do it every day after that.

Bell, Light & Back Reflector A bell and light are both very useful things to have in working order. The bell should be positioned so it can be used with your hand still gripping the brake. A new back reflector is a good investment if there isn't one on the bike.

Seat Consider buying a new, soft, padded one or at least a tie-on foam seat cover. You can purchase either of these at a Denpasar bike shop. Have the seat adjusted so that when you are sitting on it you can straighten your leg fully to touch the lower pedal with your heel. If you are very tall, buy an extra long pipe to raise the seat.

Other Accessories A carrier rack over the rear mudguard is ideal for carrying a small bag. One or two elastic shock cords with hooks at each end will secure it. A sturdy steel cable lock is worthwhile.

Final Checks & Repairs Lightly oil all moving parts including the crankshaft and chain. Check to see if all the nuts are securely tightened, especially those to the seat, the brake linkage cables and the brake rims, which tend to vibrate loose.

Even the smallest village has some semblance of a bike shop. Some will allow you to borrow tools to work on your own bike (give the owner a small gift if payment isn't requested). If you're not used to working on bicycles ask someone from the shop to repair it for you. Labour charges are very low – a flat tyre should cost less than 1000 rp. The best shops for any extensive repairs are in Denpasar.

Packing for Touring

It is quite possible to tour Bali by bicycle with nothing but the clothes on your back, and this book. The distance between losmen is always within a day's ride, food stalls are numerous and there is no need for camping equipment. A shady hat or bicycle helmet, riding shorts, a T-shirt and shoes are all you need to ride in. Long trousers, a shirt, and a skirt or a good sarong are required for visiting temples, as well as a temple sash. Bring a sweater for cool mountain evenings and some walking shoes. Other essentials include a swimsuit, torch, mosquito coils, matches, soap, towel, toothbrush and sunblock.

Bring as little as possible. Besides having to carry the baggage on your bicycle, if you want to explore an area on foot you'll have to carry your bag or find a secure place to stash it.

The 200-km Circle Tour

This route is designed to take in the greatest number of points of interest with the minimum use of motorised transport and the maximum amount of level or downhill roads. The tour involves six days of riding in a clockwise direction. Evening stops have been planned where there are convenient losmen. The minimum daily distance is about 24 km; the maximum is 60 km, but 20 to 30 km of this distance will probably be covered by bemo. The total distance is not exactly 200 km – it varies depending on the length of the detours and the bemo legs. There are other places to stop, and lots of possible detours, so it can easily evolve into a two-week trip. The trip can also be done in an anticlockwise direction.

Day 1 – Kuta to Candi Kuning 60 km (37 km by bicycle), riding time seven hours.

The first day is a long one so it's best to get an early start. Leave the tourists and Westernised Balinese of Kuta and ride north along Jalan Legian. Soon the traffic will disappear and you'll be riding along exquisitely terraced rice fields interspersed with small villages. Continue north to Sempidi where numerous roadside food stalls offer tea, bananas and peanuts to boost your energy reserves.

If you begin your trip at low tide you can do the first seven km north along the beach's firm, moist sand. Turn inland around the Bali Oberoi Hotel as further on the sand becomes soft and you'll get bogged down. The hotel's long driveway connects with the main road and you can continue north to Sempidi, the junction with the Denpasar to Gilimanuk road.

Ride west towards Gilimanuk from Sempidi until you reach the turn-off north to Mengwi. Pura Taman Ayun is only half a km east of the main road in Mengwi. Continuing north 15 km from Mengwi to Luwus you will notice by your breathing that the gentle 1% to 5% gradient is gradually increasing. From Luwus to Bedugul is a 700-metre vertical rise spread over 16 km so this is the place to throw your bicycle into the back of a bemo. Bemos come along every 10 to 30 minutes until about 4 pm. The fare for one bicycle usually equals the fare for one person.

Bedugul has several places to stay, but there are better places around Candi Kuning, a bit further north. The next km is uphill, followed by a breezy downhill sprint past the Bukit Mungsu market which sells vegetables and wild orchids. The road skirts around the lake, where there are good places to stay.

Day 2 – Candi Kuning to Singaraja 30 km, riding time three hours.

Before continuing north, have a look at Pura Ulu Danau, the famous temple in the lake. From there the road goes up and downhill for several km, then there is a steep 1½-km ascent to a 1400-metre pass – stop frequently to catch your breath and look back at the view of the lake. From the pass there is a steep 15-km descent to the coastal town of Singaraja. This is where good brakes are most needed. You may want to stop periodically to cool the brake rims and unmould your hands from the brake levers. An interesting stop is at Gitgit, where a 15-minute walk through souvenir stalls brings you to a pretty waterfall.

Singaraja can be rather hot and dusty after the cool of the mountains, but it's a pleasant town with reminders of the Dutch administration, some bicycle repair shops, and hotels. You can stay in Singaraja, or detour west to the beach strip around Lovina (seven to 13 km from Singaraja) – you'll have to backtrack the next day, but at least it's flat.

Day 3 – Singaraja to Penelokan 60 km (12 km to Kubutambahan, 36 km up to Penulisan by bemo, then the final 10 km by bike).

Ride 12 km east of Singaraja to Kubutambahan where there are some interesting temples. You can also make a detour to the pools at Air Sanih, a little to the east on a pretty tree-lined stretch of road. At Kubutambahan you'll find the turn-off heading south to Kintamani and Gunung Batur. It's 36 steep km uphill from there to Penulisan so once again it's wise to load your bicycle aboard a bemo, although there aren't many going this way.

Penulisan is the highest point on the ride and it's an easy descent from there to Kintamani (four km) or Penelokan (10 km). At 1745 metres, Penulisan's Pura Tegeh Koripan is Bali's highest temple and on a clear day, which is rare, it offers a superb panorama of half the island.

Kintamani (1504 metres) has several losmen, and a large and colourful market every three days. Penelokan (1371 metres) has a couple of losmen perched on the rim of the volcano looking down to Lake Batur and Gunung Batur. Frequent stops by tour buses encourage swarms of vendors. You can take the windy road from Penelokan down to the village of Kedisan on Lake Batur, and around the lake's north shore to the hot springs at Toyah Bungkah. You can also

climb to the top of the volcano, or hike around the southern shore to the Bali Aga village of Trunyan.

From Penelokan there are at least five routes down the slopes of Gunung Batur back to Denpasar. Listed here is the route via Klungkung with a side trip to the temple at Besakih. Two alternate routes are listed in the following section – they lead either to the Ubud area or Bangli.

Day 4 – Penelokan to Klungkung 31 km (excluding Besakih), riding time four hours.

Half a km east of the road down to Lake Batur, turn left. A small sign reads 'Bandjar Abang' and the narrow road leads uphill. If you reach a fork in the main road with a sign for Denpasar and Bangli you've gone too far – retreat. The road goes up and down small hills as it heads east along the southern rim of the crater with lovely views of Gunung Batur and the lake. Approximately four km along the road is a dip with a sign 'Menanga'. Turn right and continue downhill to Rendang with fine views of Gunung Agung all the way. Rendang is the turn-off for Besakih.

From Rendang to Besakih is six km, mostly uphill. There's a 500-metre rise in eight km. Consider leaving your bike at the crossroads and taking a bemo both ways or putting the bike in a bemo going up and having a nice ride down. Pura Besakih, at 1000 metres, on the misty slopes of Gunung Agung, is the 'mother temple' of Bali.

The stretch from Rendang to Klungkung, a gradual downhill ride of 12 km, is one of the most pleasant bike trips in Bali. The road passes through some of Bali's richest rice land. Klungkung has several restaurants and places to stay. The main attraction is the Kertha Gosa (Hall of Justice) at the town's main intersection. Two km south is the village of Kamasan, known for the wayang style of painting and for its gold and silver work.

Day 5 – Klungkung to Denpasar 40 km, riding time six hours.

The entire road is well surfaced but traffic is quite heavy. Although there is a total descent of 70 metres, the road crosses several lush river gorges, causing some uphill walking and downhill gliding. Main places of interest along the way are Gianyar (local weaving industry), Batuan (painting and weaving), Celuk (woodcarving and silversmithing) and Batubulan (stone sculpture). A bike is ideal for stopping at any of the workshops which catch your eye – you can buy things without any commissions for guides or drivers, or not buy anything with the excuse that it's too hard to carry.

Day 6 – Denpasar to Kuta (via Sanur & Benoa) 24 km, riding time five hours.

Take your life in your hands and head east on Jalan Gajah Mada, the main street of Denpasar, and continue the six km to Sanur. From Sanur the 'super highway' runs about eight km to the turn-off south to the Benoa Port causeway – a possible detour. You can diverge to the old and now virtually deserted Sanur to Kuta road which runs parallel to the new highway, just to its north. You eventually emerge on the main Kuta to Denpasar road next to a petrol station. You have completed the 200-km round trip and are back where you started. Congratulations!

Alternative Routes from Penelokan to Denpasar

On the fourth day of the circle tour, you have a choice of routes from Penelokan back to Denpasar. As alternatives to Klungkung, you can go via either Ubud or Bangli.

Penelokan to Ubud The route from Penelokan to Ubud via Tampaksiring is 35 km long and riding time is about five hours.

About half a km east of Penelokan the road forks. Take the right fork marked 'Denpasar' and nine km later you're in the small junction town of Kayuambua. The left fork leads to Bangli, the right fork takes you to Tampaksiring eight km further on. The road runs down verdant volcano slopes past fields of banana, sweet potato and corn, all partially obscured by roadside groves of bamboo.

As you approach Tampaksiring, the temple and holy spring of Tirta Empul are on the right. Another km down from Tirta Empul is the turn-off to the 11th-century rock-face memorials at Gunung Kawi, about a km east of the main road. Back on the road it's an easy 10 km downhill ride to Bedulu, via the small village of Pejeng with its 'Moon of Pejeng' bronze drum. Turn right at the Bedulu junction and half a km along the road is the Goa Gajah (Elephant Cave). Then it's on to Peliatan and Ubud.

Ubud to Denpasar & Kuta The route from Ubud to Denpasar is 26 km and riding time is about four hours.

There are several ways down to Kuta from the Ubud area. Heading straight south for four km the road passes through the woodcarving village of Mas, another six km is the weaving village of Batuan and then you'll pass through Celuk, known for its woodcarvings as well as fine gold and silversmiths. From Batuan to Denpasar (16 km) there are many trucks, bemos and cars competing for road space, which makes that part of the trip mentally exhausting.

An interesting alternative is the quieter backroad via Sibang. Except for the first few km, which require some uphill walking, it's an easy descent with little traffic until you are in Denpasar proper. From Denpasar to Kuta you can take the route via Sanur described earlier, or a direct route down Jalan Iman Bonjol.

Penelokan to Bangli The 20-km route from Penelokan to Bangli takes about three hours. At the fork in the road half a km south of Penelokan take the left fork marked 'Bangli' and head south. Bangli has an important temple, Pura Kehen, and a couple of places to stay. Continue south from Bangli and you join the Klungkung to Denpasar route about 26 km from Denpasar.

Several people have written to us about

cycling in Bali. Nigel Daniel provides this account:

I had no problems in transporting my bike on Garuda, on both international and domestic flights. All I did was remove the pedals from each arm. I did not even have to play around with the handle bars.

I followed the around Bali itinerary which was in the book and did not resort to bemos on the climb to Bedugul and Kintamani. The Bedugul climb is not too steep and I feel that anyone who has an OK bike (10-speed) and is fit can make this climb without a bemo. The Penulisan climb is a completely different story. It's very, very tough going, especially in the tropical heat. Also you cannot get any drinking water until you reach Penelokan so if you intend to ride that stretch carry lots of water – at least four cyclist bottles. I had about 15 warm Sprites that day because I ran out of water!

The ride from Rendang to Amlapura has great scenery and no traffic. Except for a few easy hills between Muncan and Selat it's pretty well downhill all the way. From Amlapura it's not far to Candidasa and dead flat on to Klungkung.

Nigel Daniel, Australia

HITCHING

Yes, you can even hitchhike around Bali. Two Dutch travellers have reported that while hitching you meet a lot of nice people, enjoy the scenery and 'it's a good experience to ride around Bali, standing in the back of a truck!'. Bear in mind, however, that hitching is never entirely safe in any country in the world, and we don't recommend it. Travellers who decide to hitch should understand that they are taking a small but potentially serious risk. People who do choose to hitch will be safer if they travel in pairs and let someone know where they are planning to go.

Denpasar

The capital of Bali, with a population of around 300,000, Denpasar has been the focus of a lot of the island's growth and wealth over the last 15 or 20 years. It now has all the bustle, noise and confusion which one associates with the fast-growing cities of Asia. It also has an interesting museum, an arts centre and lots of shops. Denpasar means 'next to the market', and the main market (called Pasar Badung) is said to be the biggest and busiest in Bali. The city, sometimes referred to as Badung, is the capital of the Badung district which incorporates most of the tourist areas of southern Bali and the Bukit Peninsula.

Those who have visited Bali over a number of years will tell you that Denpasar was a quiet little town 15 years ago. It still has the tree-lined streets and some pleasant gardens, but today the traffic, noise and pollution make it a difficult place to enjoy. Most tourists and travellers find it more comfortable and convenient to stay at Kuta, Legian, Sanur or Ubud, and venture into Denpasar only for the few bits of bureaucratic business which cannot be done elsewhere, and increasingly for shopping. As the local population, or sections of it, have become more affluent, the variety and quality of goods has increased, and there are now a number of Western-style department stores and shopping centres.

Many of Denpasar's residents are descended from immigrant groups such as Bugis mercenaries and Chinese, Arab and Indian traders. More recent immigrants have been attracted by the wealth in Denpasar, including Javanese civil servants, tradespeople and workers, and Balinese from all over the island. They give the city a cosmopolitan air, and it is increasingly a Java-oriented modern Indonesian city rather than a parochial Balinese capital. As the city grows it is engulfing the surrounding villages, but their banjars and village life continue amid the urbanisation. The recent immigrants tend to occupy detached houses outside the family compounds, which may eventually supplant the traditional communal way of life.

Denpasar is a centre from which nationalism and modernisation is transmitted to the rest of Bali. The Balinese offices of the Jakarta government are here, as are the headquarters of the Java-based banks and businesses. Bahasa Indonesia is becoming the common language of Denpasar, rather than Balinese, and it is here that the Hindu religious council has interpreted the Hindu pantheon as comprising many manifestations of one God, in conformity with the first principle of Pancasila.

If you're one of those who feel that Bali is overcrowded with tourists, you'll find that tourists are vastly outnumbered in Denpasar – it mightn't be a tropical paradise, but it's as much a part of 'the real Bali' as the rice paddies and temples.

Orientation & Information

The main street of Denpasar, Jalan Gajah Mada, is called Jalan Gunung Agung where it enters the west side of town. It then changes to Jalan Wahidin, then Gajah Mada in the middle of town, then Jalan Surapati, then Jalan Hayam Wuruk on the east side of town, and finally Jalan Sanur before turning south then east and heading towards Sanur. This name-changing is common for Denpasar streets, and is one source of confusion. Another problem is the proliferation of one-way traffic restrictions, sometimes for only part of a street's length, which often change and are rarely marked on any maps. For example, sections of Gajah Mada and Surapati are one-way only, from west to east, but there's a short section near the Jalan Veteran intersection where it's two-way. Despite, or perhaps because of, these control measures, the traffic jams can be intense. Parking can also be difficult, so avoid driving – take taxis, bemos or walk. It's

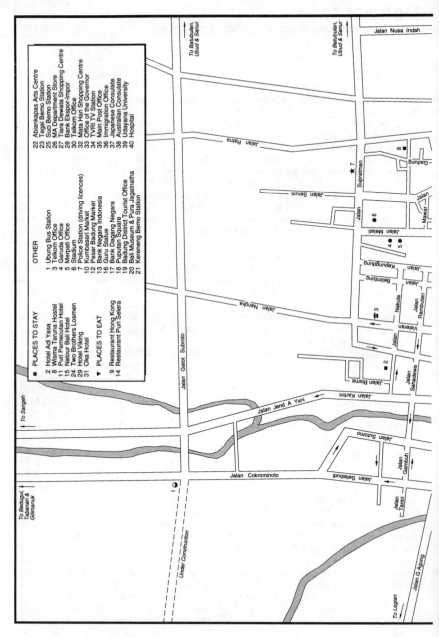

PLACES TO STAY

2 Hotel Adi Yasa
8 Wisma Taruna Hostel
11 Puri Pemecutan Hotel
15 Natour Bali Hotel
24 Two Brothers Losmen
29 Hotel Viking
31 Oka Hotel

▼ PLACES TO EAT

9 Restaurant Hong Kong
14 Restaurant Puri Selera

OTHER

1 Ubung Bus Station
3 Telkom Office
4 Garuda Office
5 Merpati Office
6 Stadium
7 Police Station (driving licences)
10 Kumbasari Market
12 Pasar Badung Market
13 Bank Negara Indonesia
16 Guru Statue
17 Bank Dagang Negara
18 Puputan Square
19 Badung District Tourist Office
20 Bali Museum & Pura Jagatnatha
21 Kereneng Bemo Station
22 Abiankapas Arts Centre
23 Tegal Bemo Station
25 Suci Bemo Station
26 MA Department Store
27 Tiara Dewata Shopping Centre
28 Bank Ekspor-Impor
30 Telkom Office
32 Mata Hari Shopping Centre
33 Office of the Governor
34 TVRI TV Station
35 Main Post Office
36 Immigration Office
37 Japanese Consulate
38 Australian Consulate
39 Udayana University
40 Hospital

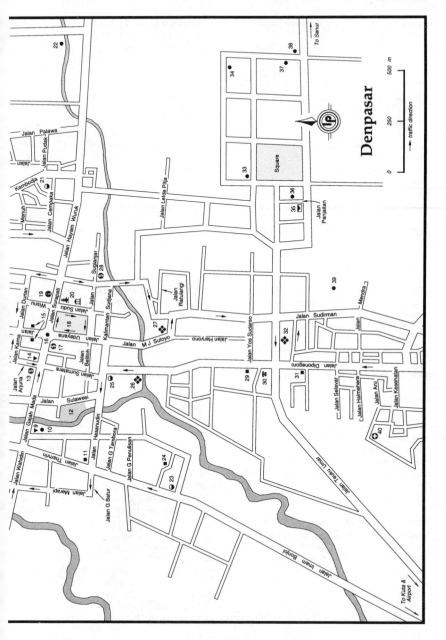

Denpasar

pretty flat, so a bicycle would be good if you could survive the traffic.

Both Kumbasari market and the main Pasar Badung are just south of Gajah Mada, on the west side of town. The main shopping centres are between Jalan Diponegoro (which is one-way, going north towards Gajah Mada) and Jalan Sudirman (which is one-way going south).

In contrast to the rest of Denpasar, the Renon area, south-east of the town centre, is laid out on a grand scale with wide streets, large carparks and big landscaped blocks of land. This is the area of government offices, many of which are impressive structures, built with lavish budgets in modern Balinese style. If you come here to collect mail or visit the immigration office you can have a look around. It's reminiscent of Canberra or Brasilia or the embassy district of New Delhi – a place to visit in a chauffeured limousine.

Tourist Office The Badung district tourist office (☎ 223602) is on Jalan Surapati 7, just north of the Bali Museum. A useful calendar of festivals and events in Bali, and a pretty good map, are available. It also has information on using Bali's bemo system. The office is open Monday to Thursday from 7 am to 2 pm, Friday from 7 to 11 am and Saturday from 7 am to 12.30 pm. The Bali government tourist office (☎ 222387) is in the Renon area, but doesn't provide much information.

Money All the major Indonesian banks have their main Bali offices in Denpasar, principally along Jalan Gajah Mada. The Bank Ekspor-Impor Indonesia, which is a block to the south, is probably the best for transfers from overseas.

Post The main Denpasar post office, with a poste restante service, is in the Renon area. It's a quite a long way from the nearest bemo terminal, which is a real nuisance if you have only come into town to pick up your mail. The offices in Kuta or Ubud are much more convenient.

Telecommunications Telkom, the telecom-

munications authority, has an office at Jalan Teuku Umar 6, near the intersection with Diponegoro. You can make international phone calls and send telegrams and faxes. Direct dial international calls cost 5000 rp per minute to Australia and New Zealand, 5720 rp to Canada, the USA and UK, and 6800 rp to continental Europe, including the 10% tax.

The telephone code for Denpasar (and most of southern Bali) is 0361. The new phone numbers have six digits – old, five-digit numbers starting with 2, 3 or 6 need an extra 2 added to the front.

Foreign Consulates See the Facts for the Visitor chapter for information about foreign diplomatic representation on Bali, including addresses of the consulates and consular agents in Denpasar.

Immigration The immigration office, or kantor imigrasi (☎ 227828), is at Jalan Panjaitan 4, in the Renon area, just around the corner from the main post office. It's open Monday to Thursday from 7 am to 2 pm, Fridays from 7 to 11 am and Saturdays from 7 am to 12.30 pm. If you have to apply for changes to your visa, get there on a Sanglah-bound bemo and make sure you're neatly dressed.

Medical Services Denpasar's main hospital (☎ 235456), Rumah Sakit Umum Propinsi (RSUP) is in the southern part of town in Sanglah, a couple of blocks west of Jalan Diponegoro. It has a relatively modern casualty department and intensive care unit, supported by a Japanese aid project, and is probably the best place to go on Bali if you have a serious injury or urgent medical problem.

Walking Tour
Starting from the tourist office on Surapati, the museum and adjacent state temple, Pura Jagatnatha, are round the corner and just to the south on Sudu Wisnu. Opposite the museum is the large Puputan Square, commemorating the heroic but suicidal stand the

rajahs of Badung made against the invading Dutch in 1906.

Heading west on Surapati, you come to the towering statue of Batara Guru at the intersection with Jalan Veteran. The four-faced, eight-armed statue is of the god Guru, Lord of the Four Directions. He keeps a close eye (or is it eight eyes?) on the traffic swirling around him. West of the statue the street becomes Gajah Mada, and you can keep going, past banks, shops and restaurants, to the bridge over the unattractive Badung River. On the left, just before the bridge, is the multi-storey Pasar Badung, the main market. On the left, just after the bridge, is Pasar Kumbasari, a handcraft and textiles market, also in a multi-storey building.

Turn left at Jalan Thamrin and head south past the Thamrin Wisita Cineplex cinema and Lokitsari shopping centre. A block further south, at the junction of Jalan Hasanudin, is the Puri Pemecutan, a palace destroyed during the 1906 invasion, now rebuilt and operating as a hotel. Here Thamrin changes names to Jalan Imam Bonjol, which is the road to Kuta, a 500 rp bemo ride from Tegal bus/bemo terminal, about 200 metres further south.

Bali Museum

The museum consists of an attractive series of separate buildings and pavilions, including examples of the architecture of both the palace (puri) and temple (pura). There is a split gateway (candi bentar), a warning drum (kulkul) tower, and an elevated lookout. The large building in the second courtyard, with its wide verandah, is like the palace pavilions of the Karangasem kingdom where rajahs held audiences. Various other palace building styles from Tabanan and Singaraja can also be seen in this courtyard.

Exhibits are not always well presented, but include both modern and older paintings, arts and crafts, tools and various items of everyday use. Note the fine wood and cane carrying cases for transporting fighting cocks, and the tiny ones for fighting crickets. There are superb stone sculptures, krises, wayang kulit figures and an excellent exhibit of dance costumes and masks, including a sinister rangda, a healthy looking barong and a towering barong landung figure. It's a good place to see authentic, traditional paintings, masks, woodcarving and weaving before you consider buying something from the craft and antique shops. There are some excellent examples of double *ikat* weaving.

The museum was originally founded by the Dutch in 1932. Admission is 200 rp for adults, 100 rp for children. It's open daily (except Monday) from 8 am to 5 pm and closes 1½ hours earlier on Friday.

Pura Jagatnatha

Adjacent to the museum is the state temple Pura Jagatnatha. This relatively new temple is dedicated to the supreme god, Sanghyang Widi; his shrine, the *padmasana*, is made of white coral. The padmasana (throne, symbolic of heaven) tops the cosmic turtle and the naga (mythological serpent) which symbolise the foundation of the world.

Arts Centres

The Abiankapas arts centre, quite a large complex on Jalan Nusa Indah, has an exhibit of modern painting and woodcarving together with a dancing stage, craft shop, restaurant and other facilities. Dances are held regularly and temporary exhibits are held along with the permanent one. It's open from 8 am to 5 pm Tuesday to Sunday; 250 rp entry and 200 rp car parking.

Further out of town is the Conservatory of Performing Arts (SMKI), which was established in 1960 as the Konservatori Kerawitan (KOKAR). This is a training institution for high-school-age students, and in the mornings you can watch dance practices and hear a variety of gamelan orchestras. Sekolah Tinggi Seni Indonesia (STSI), formerly called the Academy of Indonesian Dance (ASTI), is near the arts centre and runs more advanced courses. Here you may also see dance practices. Both groups hold public performances at the Abiankapas centre, particularly during the summer arts festival in June and July.

Places to Stay

Most people who stay in Denpasar are Indonesian visitors, mostly business travellers. There are also domestic tourists, especially in July-August and around Christmas, and hotels can fill up. The noise, confusion and pollution are too much for most foreigners. Once upon a time Denpasar was the *only* place to stay, and people made day trips to the beaches at Sanur or Kuta. Now Sanur and Kuta are far more comfortable environments, and people who want to visit more than just beaches in Bali head up to Ubud. There are plenty of places to stay in Denpasar, however, and you won't be bothered by a surfeit of foreign tourists.

Even quite small hotels catering to Indonesians often have a wide range of rooms, facilities and prices. If the first room you're offered is too expensive, or too grotty, it's always worth asking for something else.

Places to Stay – bottom end

Adi Yasa (☎ 222679), at Jalan Nakula 23B, was once one of the most popular travellers' hotels in Bali. The rooms are arranged around a garden, and it's a pleasant, well-kept and friendly place, and quite a few people still stay here, even if it's no longer a travellers' mecca. Rooms are 8000/10,000 rp for singles/doubles with shared mandi, 10,000/12,000 rp with private bathroom, breakfast included. *Two Brothers*, near the Tegal bus/bemo terminal, is another old-style losmen, and there are several other cheap places around. *Bali Yuai Mansion* (☎ 228850), at Jalan Satelit 22, in Sanglah, has been recommended by some readers. Rooms are from 10,000/15,000 rp and the owner is very helpful. It's about 500 metres south of the hospital; call first for directions, or they may pick you up from Tegal terminal.

Recently opened is the *Bali International Youth Hostel* at Jalan Mertesari, Desar Sidakarya, Denpasar, with 120 beds in two and four-bed Bali-style rooms, some with air-con. It's south of Denpasar and west of Sanur, and is signposted from the Airport-Sanur Bypass road.

Places to Stay – middle

There are a number of mid-range places on or near Jalan Diponegoro, the main road on the south side of town. The *Hotel Viking* (☎ 223992), at No 120, has economy rooms from 15,000 rp for singles and air-con rooms up to 50,000 rp.

Further south on the eastern side of Diponegoro is the *Hotel Rai*, a middling to expensive place catering mainly to business travellers. Other hotels in the southern part of Diponegoro include the *Dirgapura* (☎ 226924), the *Artha* and the *Oka*.

The *Puri Pemecutan Hotel* (☎ 223491) is in the rebuilt palace at the junction of Jalan Hasanudin and Jalan Imam Bonjol (the road to Kuta), handy to the Tegal terminal. Singles/doubles with air-con, phone, TV and private bathroom cost 40,000/50,000 rp, 12,000 rp for an extra bed.

Places to Stay – top end

There are no real luxury hotels in Denpasar, but the once-popular *Hotel Denpasar* at Diponegoro 103 is being rebuilt, and will be the first new top-end hotel in quite a while. The former Bali Hotel is now the government-owned *Natour Bali* (☎ 225681/5), at Jalan Veteran 3, and is a notch down from luxury standard. A pleasantly old-fashioned place dating from the Dutch days, it was never a masterpiece of colonial architecture but now seems destined to lose all its sense of history. There are still some nice Art Deco details (look at the light fittings in the dining room) but incongruous Balinese decorations are being added, like the carved panels next to the leadlight windows in the lobby. Standard singles/doubles start at about US$60/65 including breakfast and air-con; 'superior rooms' cost an extra US$5 and a suite is US$90. Some of the rooms are actually on the other side of Jalan Veteran, so you'll have to walk across the road to use the dining room, bar and swimming pool. If you want to sample the atmosphere without paying for a room, just come for the rijstaffel dinner (10,000 rp).

Places to Eat

The eating places in Denpasar cater for local people, recent immigrants and Indonesian visitors rather than for Western tourists, so they offer a good selection of authentic food from Indonesia's various cuisines. A number of restaurants along and near Jalan Gajah Mada are operated by and for the Chinese community, and many of them serve very good Chinese food.

The *Restaurant Atoom Baru*, at Gajah Mada 98, is a typical Asian (as opposed to Western) Chinese restaurant. Its interesting menu has lots of seafood, and dishes such as beef balls soup and pig's bladder with mushrooms. Other main courses are from 3000 to 7000 rp. Across the road is the *Restaurant Hong Kong* with Chinese and Indonesian food and cafeteria-style self-service or a menu. It's a bit classier, with tablecloths, and a bit pricier. The *Ha Ha Restaurant*, 20 metres to the west, has good food at reasonable prices. The *Restaurant Hawaii*, around the corner in the Kumbasari market, has Asian and European set menus, and there are food stalls in this market, especially in the evening. Further down Gajah Mada is the relatively expensive *Restaurant Puri Selera*, which does excellent Chinese food. There are also several Padang food restaurants along Gajah Mada.

You'll find excellent and cheap food at the market stalls by the Suci bus terminal and at the other markets, especially in the evenings. South of there, Jalan Diponegoro has more eating possibilities, like the *Melati Indah*, next to the MA department store, and the *Minang Indah*, further south, with good Padang food. A number of rumah makans down Jalan Teuku Umar, like *Kak Man*, serve real Balinese food, as well as the standard Indonesian fare. *Ayam Bakar Taliwag*, in the same street, does Lombok-style food – very pedas (hot-spicy). To try street-stall type food in a very clean, hygienic setting, try the food hall at *Tiara Dewata Shopping Centre*.

The *Natour Bali Hotel*, on Jalan Veteran, still has some features in the Dutch East Indies colonial style, and you can get a rijstaffel in the old-fashioned dining room for 10,000 rp.

Entertainment

Dances in and around Denpasar are mainly for tourists – there are regular Kejak performances at the Abiankapas arts centre, and a Barong & Rangda dance every morning at the SMKI or STSI schools. Wayang kulit performances can be seen a couple of times a week at the Puri Pemecutan.

There are a number of cinemas (bioskop) in Denpasar, though they are losing ground to TV and videos. US movies are popular, particularly 'action movies', along with kung fu titles from Hong Kong, the occasional Indian epic and some Indonesian productions. Movies are usually in the original language, subtitled in Bahasa Indonesia. They are advertised in the papers, and also with garish posters on which your favourite actor may be unrecognisable. The Thamrin Wisita Cineplex, on Jalan Thamrin, has a number of cinemas so you'll have a choice.

For Western-style bars, discos and nightclubs you'll have to go to Kuta or Sanur. You'll find the younger, more affluent denizens of Denpasar congregating around the shopping centres in the evening, and later around their local bioskop. There are always students keen to practise their English, and you might meet some around the Udayana University campus near the southern end of Jalan Sudirman.

Things to Buy

Denpasar has no particular crafts of its own, but there are numerous 'factories' around town churning out mass-produced handcrafts. There are also many shops selling crafts from Bali and from other Indonesian islands. You'll find some craft shops on Jalan Gajah Mada, and some more round the corner in Jalan Thamrin. Shops often close around 12.30 pm and reopen around 5 or 6 pm.

The main market, the three-storeyed building of the Pasar Badung, is near the east bank of the river. Fruit and vegetables are on the ground floor; household goods, foods, spices etc can be found on the 2nd floor; and clothing, sarongs, baskets, ceremonial accessories and other handcrafts are on the top floor. It's very busy in the morning and evening, and would be a great place to browse and bargain if it were not for the women who attach themselves to you as unsolicited guides-cum-commission takers; even so, it's pretty interesting, colourful and pungent. Jalan Sulawesi, near the market, has many shops with batik, ikat, and other fabrics. Gold jewellery is also a speciality in this area, which is known as Kampung Arab for the many people there of Middle Eastern or Indian descent. Kumbasari is another market/shopping centre on the opposite side of the river from Pasar Badung, with handcrafts, fabrics and gold work.

Other places that have been recommended include Bali Nusa, at Jalan Diponegoro 98 and also Jalan Sumbawa 24, for batik; Emi, at Jalan Hasanudin 53 for woodcarving; and Arts of Asia, just west of Jalan Thamrin, for antiques.

At Tohpati, about six km north-east of town just beyond the Sanur to Batubulan road intersection, is the government handcraft and arts centre, Sanggraha Kriya Asta (☎ 222942). This large shop has a collection of most types of Balinese arts and crafts. Prices are fixed (a bit high) and most of the items are of good quality so it's a good place to look around to get an idea of what's available, what sort of quality to expect and at what prices. It's open Monday to Friday from 8.30 am to 5 pm, and on Saturday from 8.30 am to 4.30 pm, closed Sunday. If you telephone they'll send a minibus to collect you from Denpasar, Kuta, Legian or Sanur.

There are now Western-style shopping centres in Denpasar – quite a recent innovation. As the number of affluent citizens in Denpasar has increased, so have the number and quality of retail outlets, and the variety of goods on offer. Increasingly, visitors are attracted to the large, fixed-price shopping centres, not so much for Balinese handcrafts, but for clothing, shoes, toys and electronic goods.

The MA department store in Jalan Diponegoro was one of the first, but has been eclipsed by the bigger, newer places and now feels like a general store in a large country town. The Tiara Dewata shopping centre on Jalan MJ Sutoyo has a much better range, and incorporates a miniature fun fair with amusements which will entertain very young children, and a video arcade and swimming pool (500 rp) for older kids. Mata Hari, on Jalan Dewi Sartika between Jalan Surdiman and Jalan Diponegoro, is one of the newest and biggest department stores with a big range of clothes, cosmetics, leather goods, sportswear, toys and baby things. Genuine name brands like Calvin Klein, Reebok and Elizabeth Arden are around 20% cheaper than in Australia (perhaps not so competitive with US or European prices, depending on the level of consumer taxes you pay at home). Of course if you're just buying the name, you can get credible fakes in Kuta for a fraction of the price!

Getting There & Away

Denpasar is the hub of road transport in Bali – here you'll find buses and minibuses bound for all corners of the island. There are also buses for Java, boat tickets, train tickets and the Garuda, Merpati, Bouraq and Sempati airline offices.

See the Getting There & Away chapter for details of transport between Bali, Lombok, Java and the other Indonesian islands.

Air It's not necessary to come into Denpasar to arrange booking, ticketing or reconfirmation of flights. Most of the travel agencies in Kuta, Sanur, Ubud or other tourist areas can provide these services.

The Garuda office (☎ 225245), at Jalan Melati 61, is open Monday to Friday from 7.30 am to noon and 1 to 4.45 pm, Saturday from 9 am to 1 pm. Merpati (☎ 235358) is just down the road at Jalan Melati 51, and is open from 7.30 am to 9 pm every day. Merpati has flights to Lombok and the other islands of Nusa Tenggara. Bouraq (☎ 223564), at Jalan Sudirman 19A, has similar fares to Merpati and flies to destinations in Java and Nusa Tenggara. Sempati

Air (☎ 288823, 288824), a good choice for domestic flights, is on Jalan Hang Tuah, the Denpasar-Sanur road.

Bus The usual route for land travel between Bali and Java is the Denpasar to Surabaya day or night bus. There are a number of bus companies for this run, mainly with offices along Jalan Hasanudin. Buses leave from Ubung terminal, which is the best place to buy a ticket. Prices include the short ferry trip between Bali and Java. See the Getting There & Away chapter for more details.

Surabaya	10-12 hours; 18,000 rp
Yogyakarta	16 hours; 29,000 rp, air-con 36,000 rp
Jakarta	30 hours; 56,000 rp with air-con

Bemo For travel within Bali, Denpasar has five terminals for bemos and buses, so in many cases you'll have to transfer from one terminal to another if you're making a trip through Denpasar. Bemos and buses for northern and eastern Bali operate from the terminal at Batubulan, about six km north-east of town. If, for example, you were travelling from Kuta to Ubud you'd get a bemo from Kuta to the Tegal bemo terminal in Denpasar (500 rp), transfer to Batubulan (700 rp), then take a bemo from there to Ubud (1000 rp).

The cute little three-wheeled mini-bemos are only used within the congested city itself – 500 rp between the terminals, less for shorter trips in the city. More conventional looking four- wheeled minibuses do the routes between towns, while full-size buses are also used on many of the longer, more heavily travelled routes. Buses tend to be cheaper than smaller vehicles on the same route, but they are less frequent and do not usually stop at intermediate points. Anyone who uses the bemos will know how difficult it is to get a precise figure for the harga biasa (standard price) on any bemo trip. The following prices should be accurate to within a couple of hundred rupiah, but try to confirm them with a local before you get on.

Tegal – south of the centre on the road to Kuta, this is the terminal for the southern peninsula.

Kuta	500 rp
Legian	600 rp
Airport	800 rp
Nusa Dua	1000 rp
Sanur (blue bemo)	600 rp
Ulu Watu	1500 rp
Ubung	500 rp
Suci terminal	300 rp
Kereneng terminal	500 rp
Batubulan terminal	700 rp

Ubung – north of the centre on the Gilimanuk road, this is the terminal for the north and west of Bali. To get to Tanah Lot take a bemo to Kediri, and another one from there. To get to the Lovina beaches, take a bemo to Singaraja, and another one from there.

Kediri	1000 rp
Mengwi	900 rp
Negara	3500 rp
Gilimanuk	4500 rp
Bedugul	1800 rp
Singaraja	2000 rp
Tegal terminal	500 rp
Kereneng terminal	500 rp
Batubulan terminal	500 rp

Kereneng – east of the centre, off the Ubud road, this is mainly an urban transfer terminal, but it does have direct bemos to Sanur (500 rp), Tegal terminal (500 rp), Ubung terminal (500 rp), Suci terminal (500 rp) and Batubulan terminal (600 rp).

Batubulan – this is the terminal for the east and central area of Bali.

Ubud	1000 rp
Gianyar	1000 rp
Tampaksiring	1200 rp
Klungkung	1200 rp
Bangli	1200 rp
Padangbai	2000 rp
Candidasa	2200 rp
Amlapura	3000 rp
Kintamani	2000 rp
Tegal terminal	700 rp

Suci – south of the centre, this terminal is mainly just the bemo stop for Benoa (500 rp) but the offices of many of the Surabaya bus lines and shipping line agencies are also around here. Benoa bemos also leave from the Sanglah market.

Train There are no railways in Bali but there is a railway office where you can get tickets to Surabaya or other centres in Java. This includes a bus ride to Gilimanuk and the ferry across to Banyuwangi in Java from where you take the train.

Boat The usual boat route out of Bali (not counting the short Bali to Java ferry which is included in bus-ticket prices) is the ferry from Padangbai to Lombok. Usually you get tickets for one of the daily ferries at Padangbai, but some agencies now sell inclusive bus-ferry-bus tickets through to destinations on Lombok. See the Getting to Lombok chapter for details.

Bali is not a great place to look for boat connections to other Indonesian islands. Pelni ships only stop in Bali once a month, on an irregular schedule, and their Bali office, Jalan Pelabuhan, Benoa (☎ 238962) is hard to contact. Other shipping agencies are around the Suci bus terminal if you wish to enquire about boat transport.

Getting Around

Squadrons of three-wheeled mini-bemos (tiga rodas) shuttle around the city centre – all the bigger minibus bemos have to skirt the central area when going between the various Denpasar bus/bemo terminals and to other points around town. You'll find transfer bemos lined up for various destinations at each of the terminals; they are marked with a letter on the back which indicates which route they take. You can get a list of these routes from the tourist office. The set fares between terminals are around 500 rp. You can also charter bemos (from 4000 rp) or little three-wheelers (cheaper) from the various terminals for short trips. Agree about all prices before getting on board because there are no meters.

Blue and yellow taxis are also available, for 800 rp plus around 500 rp per km, but there are far fewer of them than the bemos. They should have meters – if the driver says it's not working, get another taxi.

Despite the traffic, dokars (horse-drawn carts) are still very popular around Denpasar. They should cost the same as a bemo, but tourists are always charged more because of the novelty value; agree on prices before departing. Note that dokars are not permitted on Jalan Gajah Mada and may also be barred from some other streets with heavy vehicle traffic.

South Bali

The southern part of Bali, south of the capital, Denpasar, is the tourist end of the island. The overwhelming mass of visitors to Bali is concentrated down here. Nearly all the package-tour hotels are found in this area and many tourists only get out on day trips. Some never get out at all.

The Balinese have always looked towards the mountains and away from the sea – even their temples are aligned in the kaja direction (towards the mountains) and away from the inauspicious kelod direction (towards the sea). So Sanur and Kuta, being fishing villages, were not notable places until the arrival of the Dutch, and the development of mass tourism.

The Dutch takeover of south Bali started at Sanur in 1906, after a dispute over salvaging rights (or plundering shipwrecks, if you take the Dutch point of view). The Balinese retreated from Sanur to Denpasar and there, under the threat of Dutch artillery, three princes of the kingdom of Badung made a suicidal last stand, a puputan which wiped out the old kingdoms of the south. After these massacres, the Dutch administration was relatively benign, and the south of Bali was little affected until the first Western tourists and artists started to arrive, via Singaraja. An airfield near Denpasar made southern Bali more directly accessible, but also became a strategic asset for invading Japanese, who landed at Sanur in 1942. The airfield made Bali a good base for the invasion of Java. After WW II, the Dutch again returned to Bali at Sanur, and moved the Balinese capital to Denpasar during their short-lived postwar administration of the islands east of Java.

As tourism has grown, local residents have made the most of the opportunities, particularly in Kuta where an enormous number of small, locally run losmen and restaurants have sprung up (though many of the workers in Kuta and Sanur are from other parts of the island, and even from other parts of Indonesia).

The Indonesian government, which makes all the strategic decisions regarding tourism on Bali, plans to confine future large-scale tourist development to this southern region. The strategy is very much to encourage upmarket tourism – three, four and five-star hotels. The budget, backpacker end of the market is seen as generating too little revenue from too many visitors. The most conspicuous growth in the last couple of years has been around the expensive resort enclave of Nusa Dua, but new luxury hotels have also been developed in Jimbaran Bay, south of the airport, and along the coast north of Legian.

The most obvious environmental impact of the building explosion in the south has been the spread of built-up areas into surrounding agricultural land, but there are other effects. Tourist resorts are very thirsty, and water is now piped down to southern Bali from dams in the hills. If rapid growth continues, water may have to be piped in from Java. Around Nusa Dua, village wells dried up because the big hotels dug theirs much deeper, lowering the water table. The loss of palm trees has detracted from the appearance of many areas, and there is a lot of unsightly litter, particularly plastic bottles and bags. Of course similar problems have occurred with development everywhere, but the speed and the scale of change in south Bali makes it particularly alarming.

Coral reefs have been mined for building material, both ground down to make lime and cut as whole building blocks. But as the coral is removed, it destroys the marine environment, and the unprotected beaches can quickly disappear, as has happened at Candidasa. Coral is an attractive material and, since it grows a little after it has been removed from the water, the blocks actually lock themselves together. You can see whole stretches of coral reef turned into walls at the Bali Hyatt at Sanur, the Bali Oberoi in Seminyak, and Poppies Cottages at Kuta.

KUTA

Kuta is Bali's biggest tourist beach area. Counting the areas of Tuban, Kuta, Legian and Seminyak, the *kelurahan* (local government area) of Kuta extends for nearly eight km along the beach and foreshore. Most visitors come to Kuta sooner or later, because

165

South Bali

	Surf Breaks
1	Canggu
2	Oberoi
3	Balangan
4	Bingin
5	Padang Padang
6	Ulu Watu (Suluban)
7	Nyang Nyang
8	Green Ball
9	Nusa Dua
10	Sri Lanka
11	Hyatt Reef
12	Tanjung Sari
13	Sanur Reef
14	Padang Galak

it's close to the airport, has the biggest range of cheap tour and travel agents, and the biggest concentration of shops – it's all some tourists see of Bali. Some people will find Kuta overdeveloped and seedy, but if you have a taste for a busy beach scene, shopping and nightlife, you can have a great time here. Just don't expect a quiet, unspoilt, tropical hideaway.

It is fashionable to disparage Kuta for its rampant development, low-brow nightlife and crass commercialism, but the cosmopolitan mixture of beach-party hedonism and entrepreneurial energy can be exciting – it feels a bit like southern California, though it's also been compared to Tijuana. It's a tourist gold-rush town with a get-rich-quick mentality and a planning horizon to match. It's not pretty, but it's not dull either, and the amazing growth is evidence that a lot of people find something to like in Kuta.

It's still the best beach on Bali, especially since the activities of the hawkers have been restricted, and watching the spectacular sunset is almost an evening ritual. Kuta has the only surf on the island which breaks over sand instead of coral, and beginning surfers can wipe out without being cut to pieces on the reefs. Lots of cheap accommodation is available, as well as good-value mid-range places and luxury hotels. The drunken excesses of young Australians have been moderated somewhat, and there is much more sophisticated nightlife as well. There's a huge choice of places to eat, and a growing number of shops with everything from genuine antiques to fake fashion items. The tourists themselves have become a tourist attraction, and visitors come from Java to ogle the topless bathers, and from the other resorts to tut-tut at the tackiness of it all.

History

Mads Lange, a Danish copra trader and adventurer, set up at Kuta in about 1839, after an earlier trading venture on Lombok fell victim to local conflicts. Lange established a successful trading enterprise near modern Kuta, and had some success in mediating between local rajahs and the Dutch, who were encroaching from the north. His business soured in the 1850s, and he died suddenly, perhaps poisoned, as he was about to return to Denmark. His grave, and a monument erected later, is near Kuta's night market.

The original Kuta Beach Hotel was started by a Californian couple in the 1930s, but closed with the Japanese occupation of Bali in 1942. (Its modern incarnation was opened in 1959, rebuilt in 1991, and is now run by the government's hotel chain as the Natour Kuta Beach.) Kuta really began to change in the late '60s, when it became known as a stop on the hippie trail between Australia and Europe. At first, most visitors stayed in Denpasar and made day trips to Kuta, but more accommodation opened and, by the early '70s, Kuta had relaxed losmen, pretty gardens, friendly places to eat and a delightfully laid-back atmosphere. Surfers also arrived, enjoying the waves at Kuta and using it as a base to explore the rest of Bali's coastline. Enterprising Indonesians seized opportunities to profit from the tourist trade, often in partnership with foreigners who wanted a pretext for staying longer.

Legian, the village to the north, sprang up as an alternative to Kuta in the mid-70s. At first it was a totally separate development but Kuta sprawled north towards Legian and Legian spread back towards Kuta until today you can't tell where one ends and the other begins. Legian has now merged with Seminyak, the next village north. To the south, new developments are filling in the area between Kuta and the airport.

All this rampant development, totally unplanned, has taken its toll. One of the few planning decisions was the construction of a beach road, which resulted in the loss of all the beachfront coconut palms and a steady stream of traffic between the beach and most of the hotels in Kuta itself. Most of the drainage and sewerage problems have been dealt with, and electricity and telephone services are now quite reliable, but the area still presents a chaotic mixture of shops, bars,

Kuta Banjars

Despite all the excesses Kuta is still a village, a place where little offerings are put out in front of house entrances and at tricky gang junctions. It's this part of Kuta which makes it so much more interesting than the antiseptic Nusa Dua.

The banjar is visible evidence of Kuta's thriving village life. A banjar is rather like a small town council and the bale banjar is a meeting place: a place for discussions, ceremonies, dancing or gamelan practice. If you hear a gamelan ringing out over Kuta some quiet evening it's probably a banjar practise session and nobody will mind if you wander in to watch and listen.

Most banjars are little more than an open pavilion or courtyard but they're easy to spot by the warning drum (kulkul) tower; Kuta banjars, with lots of tourist-generated rupiah, can afford some pretty fancy towers. Check out the one at Banjar Pande Mas next to Made's Warung on Kuta Beach Rd, or the one at Banjar Buni Kuta next to The Pub. Best of all is the superb multi-storey tower at Banjar Tegal Kuta, further down the lane from Banjar Buni Kuta. ■

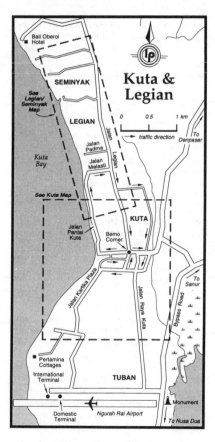

Bali Oberoi Hotel

SEMINYAK

See Legian/ Seminyak Map

LEGIAN

Jalan Legian

Kuta Bay

Jalan Padma

Jalan Melasti

See Kuta Map

Jalan Pantai Kuta

KUTA

Bemo Corner

Jalan Kartika Plaza

Jalan Raya Kuta

Bypass Road

To Denpasar

To Sanur

Pertamina Cottages

International Terminal

TUBAN

Monument

Domestic Terminal

Ngurah Rai Airport

To Nusa Dua

Kuta & Legian

0   0.5   1 km

traffic direction

restaurants and hotels on a confusing maze of streets and alleys, often congested with heavy traffic, thick with fumes and painfully noisy.

Kuta has transformed itself from a fishing village to a hippie hideaway to a low-budget beach-resort boom town, and the changes continue as more and more hotels try to attract mid-range package tourists – Kuta is moving upmarket, and shopping is the big growth area. Nearly all the clothing sold in Kuta is locally made, and a growing Balinese garment industry is exporting world-wide. Some of Kuta's many visitors have stayed

on, and have helped make Kuta what it is; lending their cuisines, their style and their money to restaurants, boutiques, losmen and other enterprises. Lots of them rent houses or bungalows round Seminyak; many are married to Balinese and are permanent residents. Others have business visas or are staying on whatever basis they can arrange with *imigrasi*. Modern Kuta is an international scene – a place in which you can get guacamole from an Italian restaurant where the Balinese staff speak English and most of the diners speak German.

Despite the influx of people and influences from all over the world, a traditional Balinese community survives in Kuta. The religious practices are observed, and the banjars are still active in governing the local community. Temples are impressive and well kept, processions and festivals are elaborate and offerings are made every day. The observance of Nyepi, the day of stillness when no work is done, has left many tourists perplexed at the closure of their favourite bar or restaurant.

Orientation

Kuta can be a disorienting place – it's flat, with few landmarks or signs other than a riot of advertising; the streets and alleys are crooked and often walled on one or both sides so it feels like a maze; and it's impossible to get a good map of the place. The main road is Jalan Legian, which runs roughly parallel to the beach from Seminyak in the north, through Legian, to Kuta. The south end of Jalan Legian is 'Bemo Corner', its junction with Jalan Pantai Kuta (Kuta Beach Rd). This one-way street runs west from Bemo Corner then north along the beach to Jalan Melasti, which goes back to Jalan Legian. From Melasti down to Bemo Corner, Jalan Legian is one-way, going south.

Between Jalan Legian and the beach is a tangle of narrow streets, tracks and alleys. A small lane or alley is known as a gang, and many of them are too small for cars, although this doesn't stop some drivers trying. The best known is Poppies Gang, an almost invisible lane leading off Jalan Legian to Poppies

Restaurant. (Streets are often known by the first or most conspicuous business on them, and may have a proper name as well. Poppies Cottages II are on Poppies Gang II, which is rarely called by its 'correct' name, Jalan Segara Batu Bolong.)

Lining the gangs is an amazing hodge-podge of big hotels, little hotels, losmen, small shops, restaurants, building construction sites and even a few remaining stands of coconut palms. Most of the bigger shops, restaurants and bars are along several km of Jalan Legian (which is wheel-to-wheel traffic most of the day and night) and a few of the side streets which head towards the beach.

The grounds of the big, expensive hotels are dotted along the beach north to Seminyak and south along Jalan Kartika Plaza towards Tuban. The beach is public, though, and you can walk along it for the length of the tourist area, stopping for swimming, refreshments and to deal with the vendors of watches, sunglasses, sarongs etc.

There are hotels, restaurants, bars, travel agencies, banks, moneychangers, post offices, doctors, markets, motorbike and car rental places; you name it and Kuta has it. It's a totally self-contained scene and, with so many places to work through, it's hardly surprising that so many people get stuck here semipermanently.

What's Wrong with Kuta?

What's gone wrong with Kuta? There are many good restaurants, the beach and surf can be terrific, the quiet losmen down remote gangs can be relaxed and pleasant but at some time or other you have to venture back on to Jalan Legian and the traffic down this main street is horrific. The constant stream of sellers importuning you to buy, buy, buy can be a little wearing too, but the main problem is planning and people. There's too little of one and too many of the other.

Too little doesn't describe Kuta's planning – there's none at all. Anybody seems to have been able to build almost anything anywhere. The result is that many hotels are only accessible down narrow gangs – which is not a problem except that people insist on using these footpaths for motorbike races and even try to squeeze cars and trucks down them. Jalan Legian is a typical narrow island road, wide enough for one vehicle or perhaps one and a half at a squeeze, yet it carries a near continuous flow of buses, bemos, taxis, cars, trucks and motorbikes. Even a complicated one-way traffic system has not saved the road; it remains a noisy, confused, evil-smelling, frustrating cacophony.

As for the people – well, 25 years ago Kuta was one of the great overland travel stops, one of 'the three Ks' – Kabul in Afghanistan, Kathmandu in Nepal and Kuta. But travellers don't come to Kuta anymore. It's strictly a beach resort for people who want surf and sand, cheap food and cold beer. Where you used to get peacefully stoned freaks gazing at the sunset you now have numerous bars where loud-mouthed drunks get plastered every afternoon, clamber clumsily on to their motorbikes and, mercifully, fall off at the first corner. ■

Information

Tourist Office The Bali government tourist information service (☎ 753540) is in the foyer of a new building on the north side of Jalan Benesari; they have some printed information and can answer most questions. They should know where temple festivals and special events are being held.

Money There are now several banks around Kuta but for most people the numerous moneychangers are faster, more efficient, open longer hours and offer equally good rates of exchange. The only reason to use a real bank is for a money transfer or a credit card advance.

A number of moneychangers have safety deposit boxes where you can leave airline tickets or other valuables and not have to worry about them during your stay on Bali.

Post There's a post office near the night market, on a small dirt road east of Jalan Raya Kuta, the airport road. It's small, efficient and has a sort-it-yourself poste restante service. The post office is open Monday to Saturday from 8 am and closes at 11 am on Friday and at 2 pm on other days. There's also a postal agency on Jalan Legian, about half a km along from Bemo Corner. If you want mail sent there have it addressed to 'Kuta Postal Agent, Jalan Legian, Kuta'. There's another postal agent on Jalan Melasti in Legian, and another in Seminyak on the main road.

Telephone There are several wartels (telephone offices) on Jalan Legian and on Jalan Bakung Sari in Kuta (see map). Hours are generally from 7 am to 9 pm. In most of them you can dial international calls yourself and send faxes, paying in cash. There are some card phones around, and Home Country Direct phones in the Natour Kuta Beach Hotel and outside the airport's international terminal.

The whole South Bali tourist area is in the 0361 telephone zone. Phone numbers were changed in October 1993; the new Kuta numbers have six digits starting with 75. If you have an old five-digit number, just add 7 to the front of it.

Books & Bookshops If you develop a real interest in Kuta read Hugh Mabbett's *In Praise of Kuta* (January Books, Wellington, New Zealand, 1987). It's widely available on Bali and recounts Kuta's early history and its frenetic modern development. There are fascinating accounts of Kuta's local entrepreneurs, the development of surfing and what happens to visitors who get caught with drugs. There are lots of places to buy new and second-hand books.

Dangers & Annoyances Theft is not an enormous problem, but visitors do lose things from unlocked hotel rooms or from the beach. Always lock your room, even at night. Valuable items should be checked with reception or, if not needed, left in a security box. Going into the water and leaving valuables on the beach is simply asking for trouble. There are also some snatch thefts, so hang on to your bag and keep your money belt under your shirt.

Some years ago Kuta had a number of muggings but the problem was handled with quite amazing efficiency and in a very traditional fashion. The local banjars organised vigilante patrols and anybody they came across who wasn't a tourist or a local Balinese had to have a damn good reason for being there. Thefts in the dark gangs stopped dead and there has been no repeat performance.

Water Safety The surf can be tricky, with a strong current on some tides, especially in Legian. There are drownings every year, many of them visitors from other Asian countries who are not good swimmers. The number of deaths has diminished greatly since the formation of the efficient Kuta Lifesaving Club, modelled on the Australian system. Lifeguards patrol areas at Kuta and Legian, indicated by red-and-yellow flags on the beach. If they say the water is to rough or unsafe to swim in, they mean it.

Hawkers & Hasslers The activities of hawkers, touts, and would-be guides are a major annoyance in Kuta. Beach selling is now restricted to the upper part of the beach, where professionals with licence numbers on their conical hats will importune you to buy anything from a cold drink to a massage or a hair-beading job. Closer to the water, you can lie on the sand in peace – you'll soon find out where the invisible line is. On the street, guys try hard to sell fake fashion watches from boxes which open like jaws as you approach. The best way to deal with unwanted sales pitches is to ignore them completely – if you just say 'no' it seems to encourage them.

Places to Stay

Kuta and Legian have hundreds of places to stay with more still being built. The most expensive hotels are along the beachfront. Mid-range places are mostly on the bigger roads between Jalan Legian and the beach, interspersed with cheaper hotels and restaurants. More cheap losmen are found on the smaller lanes in between these roads. Standards have risen over the years and although you can still find a few of the old rock-bottom places, even cheaper losmen have bathrooms these days, and the squat toilet is a rarity.

Beware of throwaway words like 'beach', 'seaview', 'cottage' and 'inn' when it comes to Kuta hotel names. Places with 'beach' in their name may not be anywhere near the beach and a featureless three-storey hotel block may rejoice in the name 'cottage'. The honourable line about building nothing taller than a palm tree also seems to be going out the window, unless there are plans to grow some awfully tall palm trees. Note that any hotel north of Jalan Pantai Kuta and south of Jalan Melasti is going to be separated from the beach by the coast road, even if the hotel is described as being on the beachfront.

Places to Stay – bottom end

The best type of Kuta losmen, even at the bottom end, is an attractive and relaxed place built around a lush and well-kept garden. Unfortunately there are lots of other places which have been thrown together as quickly

and cheaply as possible to try and turn over maximum rupiah with minimum effort.

Look for a losmen which is far enough off the main roads to be quiet but close enough so that getting to the beach, shops and restaurants is no problem. The real Balinese-style losmen is fairly small and enclosed by an outer wall and built around a central courtyard and garden – an attractive and peaceful place to sit around and read or talk. Many cheaper losmen still offer breakfast, even if it's only a couple of bananas and a cup of tea. It's a pleasant little extra that disappears as you move up the price scale. Tea used to be included throughout the day on request, but this is becoming less common.

If you are taken to a place by a taxi driver or a tout, you will be charged extra for your accommodation to cover their commission. It's common to be overcharged on your first night in Kuta, so remember that there are lots more losmen. If you don't like your first choice, or it's too expensive, it's very easy to move somewhere else.

Outside busy seasons you can find a good basic losmen for around 10,000 rp a double with your own bathroom, a table fan, a light breakfast and a pleasant relaxed atmosphere. As you move up the price scale you get bigger rooms, a ceiling fan, better furnishings and a generally less spartan appearance. Bottom-end places usually quote their prices in rupiah, up to about 30,000 rp per night for a double (US$15); above that is middle range.

With so many losmen to choose from it's impossible to list them all, and many of them are very similar in what they offer. The following ones are grouped by location, from the south of Kuta to the areas north of Legian. There will be other places of similar standard and price in the same areas as the ones listed here, so if your first choice is full there will be others within walking distance.

South Kuta There are mostly mid-range to expensive places down Jalan Kartika Plaza, but some cheapies are appearing in the back streets. The location is not great, but it's close

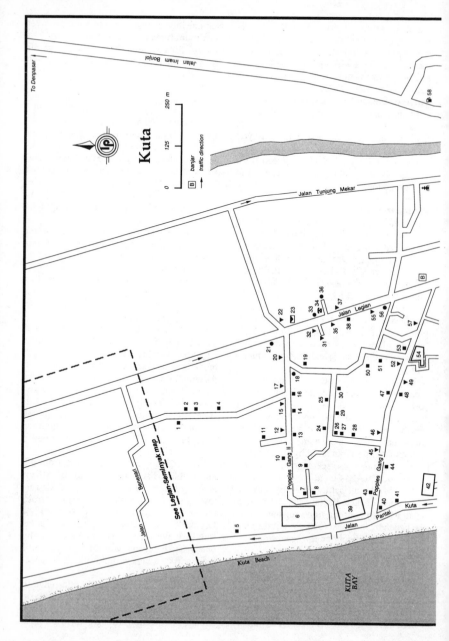

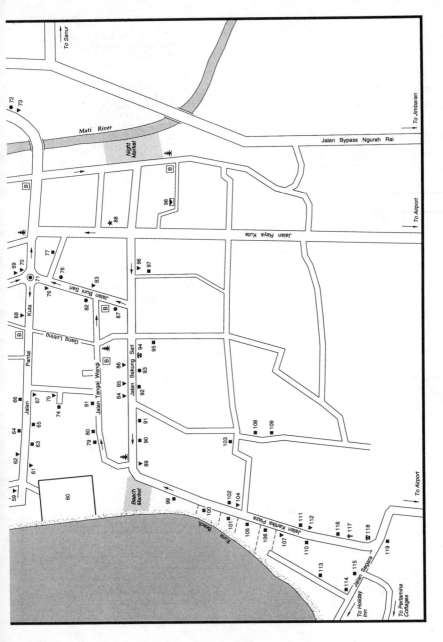

■ PLACES TO STAY

1 Meka Jaya
2 Bendesa I
3 Bendesa II
4 Bali Dwipa, Bali Indah & Losmen Cempaka
5 Bali Anggrek Hotel
6 Sahid Bali Seaside Hotel
7 Puri Beach Inn
8 Indah Beach Hotel
9 Bali Sandy Cottages
10 The Bounty Hotel
11 Kuta Suci Bungalows
13 Poppies Cottages II
14 Palm Gardens Homestay
16 Barong Cottages
19 Jus Edith
24 Sorga Cottages
25 Sari Bali Bungalows
26 Arena Bungalows & Hotel
27 Mimpi Bungalows
28 Berlian Inn
29 Suji Bungalows
30 Puri Ayodia Inn
38 Viking Beach Inn
39 Kuta Seaview Cottages
40 Sari Yasa Samudra Bungalows
41 Aneka Beach Bungalows
42 Yasa Samudra Bungalows
43 Kuta Puri Bungalows
44 Cempeka
47 Mutiara Cottages
48 La Walon Bungalows
50 Kempu Taman Ayu
51 Lima Satu (51) Cottages
53 Komala Indah I
54 Poppies Cottages I
60 Natour Kuta Beach
63 Yulia Beach Inn
64 Kodja Beach Inn
65 Suci Bungalows
66 Budi Beach Inn
74 Ida Beach Inn
77 Anom Dewi Youth Hostel
79 Kuta Cottages
80 Asana Santhi Homestay (Willy II)
81 Asana Santhi Homestay (Willy I)
90 Ramayana Seaside Cottages
91 Kuta Beach Club
92 Agung Beach Bungalows
95 Flora Beach Hotel
97 Bamboo Inn, Zet Inn & Jesen's Inn II
99 Melasti Hotel & Karthi Inn
100 Bali Garden Hotel
101 Kartika Plaza Hotel

102 Adhi Jaya Cottages
103 Pendawa Bungalows
105 Bali Dynasty Resort
106 Santika Beach Hotel
108 Mustika Inn
109 Flamboyan Inn
110 Bintang Bali Hotel
111 Bali Rani Hotel
113 Palm Beach Hotel
114 Rama Beach Cottages
115 Risata Bali Resort
116 Bali Bagus Cottages
119 Mandara Cottages

▼ PLACES TO EAT

12 Nana's Swedish Restaurant
15 The Corner Restaurant
17 Twice Pub
20 Batu Bulong Restaurant
22 Gandhi's
31 KFC
32 Sari Club Restaurant
35 Mini Restaurant
37 Indah Sari Seafood
45 Tree House Restaurant
46 Warung Transformer
49 Fat Yogi's Restaurant
52 TJs
55 Aleang's
57 Poppies
59 Made's Juice Shop
61 Green House Restaurant
62 Tony's Restaurant
67 Lenny's Restaurant
68 Made's Warung
69 Sushi Bar
70 Quick Snack Bar
73 KFC
75 Iki Japanese Restaurant
76 Wayan's Tavern
83 Serrina Japanese Restaurant
84 Dayu I
85 Nagasari Restaurant
86 Bali Bagus Restaurant
89 Rama Bridge Restaurant
96 Kuta Plaza Restaurant
104 Lily Restaurant
107 Kaiser Restaurant
112 Mandarin & Café Français

OTHER

18 Tubes Bar
21 SC (Sari Club)
23 Kuta Postal Agency
33 Hard Rock Cafe

34	Wartel	82	Bagus Pub
36	Peanuts Disco, Koala Blu Pub, Warehouse & Crazy Horse	87	The Pub
		88	Police Station
56	Perama	93	Supermarket
58	Petrol Station	94	Wartel
71	Bemo Corner	98	Post Office
72	Supermarket	117	Catholic Church
78	Casablanca Bar	118	Telkom Wartel

to the airport and the beach is good. Closer to central Kuta, the streets south of Jalan Pantai Kuta have some of the area's longest running low-budget places.

Mandara Cottages (☎ 751775) – this is a friendly and spacious place with a large garden and a small pool. The fan-cooled cottages are from 20,000/25,000 rp; more with air-con. There's some noise from the airport, and cheap rooms get road noise as well.

Flamboyan Inn (☎ 752610) – south of Kuta in one of the lanes east of Jalan Kartika Plaza, this is one of several newer places in the area which have good rooms but an uninteresting location. Others are the *Mustika Inn* and *Pendawa Bungalows*. They may ask more, but should come down to about 25,000 rp a double in the low season.

Bamboo Inn (☎ 751935) – this traditional little losmen in central Kuta is some distance from the beach but close to the restaurants and bars. It's in a gang south of Jalan Bakung Sari, but far enough away to be quiet. Good rooms cost from 12,000/17,000 rp including breakfast.

Jesen's Inn II (☎ 752647) & *Zet Inn* (☎ 753135) – these are pleasant little places near the Bamboo Inn, at around 17,500/20,000 rp.

Anom Dewi Youth Hostel (☎ 752292) – close to Bemo Corner, this is a cheap but well-run youth hostel-associated losmen with standard rooms at 10,000 and 12,000 rp, superior rooms at 12,000/15,000 rp, 3000 rp high season supplement.

Jalan Pantai Kuta A number of cheap places are on this street between Bemo Corner and the beach. Rooms away from the road aren't too noisy.

Budi Beach Inn (☎ 751610) – an old-style losmen with a garden and rooms from 10,000/15,000 rp up to 20,000/25,000 rp.

Kodja Beach Inn (☎ 752430) – some of the rooms here are set well away from the road; fan-cooled rooms are 10,000/12,500 rp, rooms with air-con and hot water are up to 45,000 rp.

Suci Bungalows (☎ 753761) – well established with a good restaurant, not too noisy, and not far from the beach, with singles/doubles from 12,000/15,000 to 17,500/25,000 rp.

Yulia Beach Inn (☎ 751893) – this standard small hotel has been going for years and offers a very central location with bungalows from US$10/12 to US$22/25. Tax, service and breakfast are extra.

Around Poppies Gang I The gangs between the beach and Jalan Legian are a maze, and a hassle to drive a car through. But many of the cheapest and best-value places to stay are in these blocks, only a short walk from the shops and the surf, but still nice and quiet.

Komala Indah I – in Poppies Gang right opposite Poppies Cottages I but much more basic. It's clean, and great value for the location at 10,000 rp for a room. There are a few other cheap places in Poppies Gang – *Rita's* has been recommended.

Kempu Taman Ayu – in a back lane off Poppies Gang, just round the corner from TJ's restaurant, this long-running and friendly little place has fairly standard cheap rooms from 9000 to 12,000 rp.

Berlian Inn – just off Poppies Gang, with good rooms from 16,000/20,000 rp including breakfast, this place is good value in a good location.

Arena Bungalows & Hotel – a new place, with a pool, a bit of style and rooms from 15,000/25,000 rp upwards.

Sorga Cottages (☎ 751897) – there's a pool, the location is quiet and the rooms are from 17,500 to 25,000 rp with fan or from 25,000 to 35,000 rp with air-con. The open meals area upstairs is a pleasant bonus.

Bali Sandy Cottages – these cottages still manage to be in a coconut plantation close to the beach and Poppies Gang II; this place is small, nice and inexpensive at 15,000/20,000 rp.

Puri Ayodia Inn – this small and very standard losmen is in a quiet but convenient location and has rooms for just 10,000 rp.

Jus Edith – a basic place, but quiet and central, with rooms at 7000/10,000 rp to 12,000/15,000 rp.

Around Poppies Gang II There are lots of cheap places here, and on the gangs running north from it, which are also called Poppies Gang II, or sometimes Poppies Gang II Utara (north). It's about the best place to look for cheap accommodation.

Palm Gardens Homestay (☎ 752198) – a neat and clean place, good value from 15,000 to 20,000 rp including breakfast; the location is convenient but reasonably quiet.

Arthawan Losmen – on Poppies Gang II about 30 metres west of Tubes Bar, with clean rooms from 8000 rp including breakfast.

Bali Dwipa, Bali Indah & Losmen Cempaka – these places are on the gang going north of Poppies Gang II. They don't have a lot of character or comfort, but they're well located and cheap at around 12,000 rp a double, including breakfast.

Meka Jaya, Bendesa I & II & Beneyasa Beach Inn – these places are on the same gang, and also have cheap rooms from 12,000/15,000 rp including breakfast and tax.

Kuta Suci Bungalows – on a cul-de-sac off Poppies Gang II, this is a plain two-storey place with rooms from 12,500/15,000 rp.

Legian Cheap accommodation in Legian tends to be north of Jalan Padma. There's no road along the beach up here, so there are places fronting the beach which you reach on side streets from Jalan Legian, or back lanes from the side streets. If you really want a beachfront place, walk along the beach and look from that angle.

Sayang Beach Lodging (☎ 751249) – although it's tucked away on a windy lane south of Jalan Melasti, this place is handy to the beach and not too far from the action. It has a pool, and a variety of rooms from basic ones at 7000/10,000 rp to larger air-con ones at 30,000/40,000 rp.

Legian Mas Beach Inn – it's a basic place in a quiet location, and it has clean rooms from 10,000/12,000 rp.

Legian Beach Bungalows – in the centre of Legian on busy Jalan Padma, with singles from US$10 to US$15 and doubles from US$12 to US$18. It's friendly and the rooms are OK, set back from the street in a nice garden.

Puspasari Beach Cottages (☎ 751088) – also well located on Jalan Padma, this place is a bit cramped but has a pool and special low-season prices from 15,000/24,000 rp for its standard single/double rooms, including tax and breakfast.

Puri Damai Cottages (☎ 751965) – also on Jalan Padma, this budget place has singles/doubles from 15,000/20,000 rp.

North Legian & Seminyak The development up here is quite spread out, and there's not much public transport so getting around can be difficult. But there are places within an easy walk of both the beach and the facilities on Jalan Legian.

Sinar Indah – on Jalan Padma Utara, the rough lane between Jalan Padma, in central Legian, and Jalan Pura Bagus Taruna, in north Legian, this standard-style losmen has singles/doubles from 12,000/15,000 rp (without breakfast), plus bigger rooms with kitchen facilities.

Sinar Beach Cottages – east of Jalan Padma Utara at the north end of Legian, this pleasant little place has a thriving garden and rooms at 15,000 rp.

Sari Yasai Beach Inn – on Jalan Pura Bagus Taruna, this is a small losmen with rooms at 7000/12,000 rp.

LG Beach Club Hotel (☎ 751060) – well located behind the beachfront restaurant, this is budget accommodation near Legian Beach, at 25,000 rp for a room. There are other places to stay behind the beachfront bars/restaurants around here.

Mesari Beach Inn (☎ 751401) – one of the few budget places up in Seminyak, off Jalan Dhyana Pura behind the stables, with single/double rooms for 12,000/15,000 rp, and bungalows at around 140,000 rp per week.

Surya Dharma Cottages (☎ 753028) – at Jalan Dhyana Pura 9A, this is another cheapie by Seminyak standards, at 40,000/50,000 rp plus 15% tax and service.

Places to Stay – middle

There are a great many mid-range hotels, which at Kuta means something like US$15 to US$60. Prices quoted in US dollars on a printed sheet are the 'publish rates' for the package-tour market – this rate is always negotiable, up to 50% off in low season, especially when a lot of rooms are empty. All but the cheapest places add 17.5% for tax and service, but this is an element in the negotiations – before you agree on the price make sure the tax is not extra. New hotels can have trouble filling their rooms, and often give big discounts.

Many of the package-tour hotels are utterly featureless and dull. They seem to have a checklist of amenities which must be supplied and so long as these 'essentials' (like air-conditioning and a swimming pool) are in place, nothing else matters. Balinese style is unlikely to make an appearance and monotonous rectangular blocks or places with the maximum number of rooms crammed into the minimum space are all too familiar.

The best of the mid-range hotels are former budget places which have proved popular and have improved their facilities. The following list includes places which are either good value or offer some style; all have air-con and swimming pools unless otherwise noted. Again, places are listed by location, going from south to north.

South of Kuta New places are going up around Jalan Segara, at the south end of Jalan Kartika Plaza. It's quiet and near the beach, but otherwise the area is not very interesting. The north end of Jalan Kartika Plaza is closer to central Kuta, and the beach market is an attraction.

Risata Bali Resort (☎ 753340) – on Jalan Segara at the south end of Jalan Kartika Plaza, this is a new place with nice rooms, pool and garden. It's a short walk to the beach but a long way from most of Kuta's shops and nightlife. Prices start at US$60/65 but they give big discounts at quiet times.

Palm Beach Hotel (☎ 751661) – off Jalan Segara and close to the beach, this is a motel-style place with rooms stacked three storeys high, from US$50/55.

Adhi Jaya Cottages (☎ 753607) – on Jalan Kartika Plaza, this place is nothing special to look at, but it has a pool, and fan-cooled rooms from US$15/20, air-con suites up to US$42.

Karthi Inn (☎ 754810) – at the north end of Jalan Kartika Plaza, and surrounded on three sides by the more expensive Melasti Hotel, Karthi has a pool and offers all the mod cons in the rooms packed around it. Standard rooms are US$35/40, but with the 40% low-season discount it's only US$21/24.

Around Jalan Bakung Sari This area was at the centre of Kuta, but with all the growth further north it now feels like it's on the edge of things. Nevertheless, it's close to the beach, has all the facilities you'll need, and it's only a few hundred metres to Bemo Corner. There is some redevelopment at the beach end of these streets.

Ramayana Seaside Cottages (☎ 751864) – on Jalan Bakung Sari, a short walk to the beach, this is a long-established place. Lots of rooms are fitted in a limited space, with the cheapest ones around US$35/45.

Kuta Cottages (☎ 751101) – close to the beach, on Jalan Tengal Wangi, this old hotel has been relocated, but is still central and reasonably priced from US$15/20 for fan-cooled rooms up to US$35/50 with air-con.

Asana Santhi Homestay (Willy I) (☎ 751281) – near the heart of Kuta on Jalan Tengal Wangi, not far from the beach, this attractive small hotel is surprisingly quiet and relaxed for its location. The well-kept rooms have interesting furnishings and art and there's a good central swimming pool. Air-con rooms are US$30 to US$35. *Asana Santhi Homestay (Willy II)*, a little further west, is not as attractive but cheaper at US$20/25.

Ida Beach Inn (☎ 751205) – this place is in a secluded location south of Jalan Pantai Kuta; there are a lot of rooms on a small site but the place has some style and a nice garden. Air-con rooms are US$20/25, or US$15/20 with fan.

Central Kuta The back lanes between Jalan Legian and the beachfront road have a mixture of cheap to mid-range places which are handy both to the beach and to shops and restaurants. They don't have much traffic so it's a relatively quiet area.

La Walon Bungalows (☎ 752463) – on Poppies Gang, handy to the beach and the Kuta 'scene', La Walon is an established budget hotel which has acquired a pool and some air-con units, but it still has pleasant little rooms with verandahs, open-air bathrooms and ceiling fans for US$19/25.

Mutiara Cottages (☎ 752091) – conveniently located on Poppies Gang, the Mutiara is excellent value with a pool, spacious lush garden and plain, slightly tatty, fan-cooled rooms with verandah at US$12/15 including breakfast.

Poppies Cottages I (☎ 751059) – still setting the standard for what a good Bali hotel should be, Poppies has an exotically lush garden with cleverly designed and beautifully built rooms. It's in the centre of things on Poppies Gang and has a swimming pool every bit as stunning as the overall design. At US$58/63 for singles/doubles it's right at the top of the mid-range category. Make a reservation – it's very popular.

Mimpi Bungalows – on a back lane north of Poppies Gang, this small hotel is good value in a pleasant location with a nice little pool. Rooms cost US$17 to US$35.

Kuta Seaview Cottages (☎ 751961) – on Jalan Pantai Kuta at the end of Poppies Gang, it's opposite the beach but separated from it by the busy beach road. Most of the rooms are in a three-storey block, definitely not cottages, and don't have any view of the sea. The site is a bit cramped, but it's still a good, central location, with rooms from US$40/45 for singles/doubles.

Poppies Cottages II – the original Poppies (despite the name) is not as fancy nor as central as newer Poppies I, and there are only four cottages, but they are nice and spacious, at US$23/28. Guests can use the pool at Poppies I.

Legian Around Jalan Benesari you're in Legian, and there are plenty of mid-range places, some near the beach, others on the lanes behind.

Kuta Bungalows – well located on Jalan Benesari, the bungalows are a bit stark but OK. Normal price is US$35/40, but during renovations they were asking as little as US$15.

Bruna Beach Hotel (☎ 751565) – this simple place has a good central location on the beach road. The rooms are nothing special but they're cheap with prices from US$15/18 up to US$30/35 with aircon.

Ocean Blue Club – once the Hotel Camplung Mas, this is quite a nice place, pitched at the young Aussie package tourists – it's the only one that quotes prices in Australian dollars: A$60/120 for singles/doubles (about US$40/80).

Legian Beach Hotel (☎ 751711), PO Box 308, Denpasar – on the beach at Jalan Melasti in the heart of Legian this large, popular hotel has a wide variety of rooms, most of them in three-storey blocks, with singles/doubles from US$50/60 to US$80/90.

Garden View Cottages (☎ 751559) – just north of Jalan Padma in Legian, this place is well located and the rooms have hot water, phone and fridge, but look a little like concrete boxes. Singles/doubles are US$34/38.

Bali Sani Hotel (☎ 752314) – on Jalan Padma Utara (the lane going north of Jalan Padma), this smaller hotel is a short walk from the beach and has attractively designed rooms, some of them with a touch of eccentricity. Rooms are US$50/55 for singles/doubles.

Maharta Beach Inn (☎ 751654) – on a lane off Jalan Padma Utara, this is a pretty place with cottages around a pool in a lush garden which extends to the beach; US$60 for singles or doubles.

Bali Niksoma Inn (☎ 751946) – right on the beach towards the northern end of Legian this smaller hotel has two-storey units in relatively spacious grounds with rooms from US$21/25 to US$65/80.

Baleka Beach Inn – at the north end of Legian on Jalan Pura Bagus Taruna, this place has a pool and asks from US$15/20 to US$30/35, but it's worth discussing the price.

Seminyak This area starts around Jalan Pura Bagus Taruna (also called Rum Jungle Rd). Some of the best restaurants and most popular nightspots are up here. The development is pretty spread out, and mostly upmarket – you don't want to walk round here looking for a cheap place – but there is some good mid-range accommodation. Phone first, and they may even pick you up. There are also houses and bungalows to rent by the week or month.

Legian Garden Cottages (☎ 751876) – on Legian Cottages Rd (also called Double Six St and Jalan Legian Kaja), off Jalan Legian but close to the beach, this attractive place is well located with pool, gardens, and standard rooms from US$38/45.

Prince of Legian Cottages – further along Legian Cottages Rd, this place has serviced bungalows with kitchen facilities and room for at least four people. It's 60,000 rp per night, but would really suit a longer stay.

Sing Ken Ken (☎ 752980) – also on Legian Cottages Rd, this new, nice-looking place charges US$35/40 in high season, but only US$20 at other times.

Ramah Village (☎ 753793) – for longer stayers, this place has 15 comfortable bungalows, sleeping up to six people, from US$450 to US$1050 per week. They're on Gang Keraton, off Jalan Legian near the Alas Arum supermarket.

Bali Holiday Resort (☎ 753547) – in a beachfront location south of Jalan Dhyana Pura, and close to popular restaurants and nightclubs, this place is good value with rooms from US$55/60.

Dhyana Pura Hotel (☎ 751422) – on Jalan Dhyana Pura in Seminyak, with a beach frontage, this is a YMCA-affiliated hotel run by Bali's Protestant Christian Church. The profits are used to support the church's community projects on Bali. Air-con rooms and bungalows are set in an attractive garden and have all the usual facilities at very reasonable prices – from US$35/45 including tax and breakfast. There's no proselytising, but occasionally large groups of visitors dominate the place.

Bali Agung Village (☎ 754267, fax 754269) – this small place is off Jalan Dhyana Pura, on the northern edge of the tourist area next to the rice fields. It's in a nice Balinese style, and is quite good value at US$55/60.

Nusa di Nusa (☎ 751414) – right on the beach, but some distance from the Jalan Legian restaurants and shops, it's still in a trendy area close to popular nightspots like Chez Gado Gado. Very pleasant rooms start at US$30/35 for singles/doubles, but check the room first – some readers say this place is not as well kept as it should be.

Places to Stay – top end

It's not Nusa Dua or Sanur, but Kuta has quite a few places in the top-end category, and more are going up. All of the hotels in this bracket will have air-conditioning, swimming pools and, as the price goes up, facilities like TV (with access to satellite stations and/or in-house video movies), hot and cold water, and telephones (with International Direct Dialling to really augment your room bill). Other luxuries include room service, a hair dryer, and a private safe for your cash and jewellery. There will be at least 17.5% tax and service charge on top of the quoted prices. They nearly all have beach frontage, so they're easy to locate on a map.

Going from south (the airport end) to north, some of the more popular or interesting top-end places include:

Pertamina Cottages (☎ 751161), PO Box 3121, Denpasar – on the beach at Tuban, the airport end of Kuta (see the Kuta & Legian map), this large deluxe hotel has rooms from US$120. It's one of

the first luxury hotels in Kuta and has lovely beachfront gardens and an excellent Japanese restaurant.

Holiday Inn Bali Hai (☎ 753035) – this place has excellent Balinese architecture, despite being part of an international chain, and a beautiful pool and gardens. Rooms cost from US$120, bungalows from US$180.

Bintang Bali Hotel (☎ 753810) – this is one of a number of new top-end places south of Kuta. It's big (400 rooms), with sports facilities (gym, pool, tennis), disco and karaoke. Rooms start at US$95/105.

Santika Beach Hotel (☎ 751267), PO Box 1008 Tuban – on Jalan Kartika Plaza, this place has swimming pools, tennis courts, all the usual facilities, and a variety of rooms from US$80.

Bali Dynasty Resort (☎ 752403), PO Box 20047 Kuta – a large new place on Jalan Kartika Plaza, with rooms from US$95.

Kartika Plaza Hotel (☎ 751067), PO Box 3084, Denpasar – right on the beach, just south of central Kuta, this large hotel has rooms from US$100/110.

Natour Kuta Beach (☎ 751361), PO Box 3393, Denpasar – this hotel is a successor to the original Kuta Beach Hotel, which was close by. It was called by that name until 1991 when it was taken over by the Natour group and virtually rebuilt. Unfortunately there's no sense of history at all, but there are nice views and the location is very central, at the beach end of Jalan Pantai Kuta. Singles/doubles are from US$65/75, up to US$300 for the executive suite.

The Bounty Hotel (☎ 753030) – away from the beach and not quite as well appointed as the most expensive hotels, this hotel is still central on Poppies Gang II, and is a nice looking place. Free passes to well-known nightspots are given to guests, which might suggest something about the clientele. The published rates start at US$80 (including tax and service), but 50% off-season discounts were being offered at the time of writing.

Kul Kul Resort (☎ 752520), PO Box 3097, Denpasar – separated from the beach by the road just south of Jalan Melasti in Legian, this big and popular hotel has two and three-storey blocks plus bungalows in relatively spacious grounds. Rooms cost from US$83.

Bali Intan Cottages (☎ 51770, fax 751891) – on Jalan Melasti, close to the beach in Legian, this very standard large hotel has rooms in two-storey blocks plus cottages with rooms from US$80/85 to US$90/95.

Bali Padma Hotel (☎ 752111), PO Box 1107 TBB, Legian – this is a big 400-room hotel by the beach on Jalan Padma in the middle of Legian, with some of the lushest gardens on Bali. Rooms are in two or three-storey blocks or in six-room units and cost from US$100/110 to US$120/130 for singles/doubles, with a US$20 high-season supplement; suites are from US$165 to US$1500.

Kuta Palace Hotel (☎ 751433), PO Box 3244, Denpasar – at the northern end of Legian, this big hotel is right on the beach at the end of Jalan Pura Bagus Taruna, and has pleasant swimming pools and gardens. Rooms cost from US$85/100 to US$95/110.

Bali Imperial Hotel (☎ 754545, fax 751545) – at the beach end of Jalan Dhyana Pura in Seminyak, this hotel is not central but it offers a shuttle service to Kuta. The architecture is very imposing, and the prices are substantial, with rooms from US$140, villas from US$400, and the Imperial Villa at US$1600.

Tjendana Paradise Hotel (☎ 753573) – on the south side of Jalan Dhyana Pura, the impressive Balinese foyer hides a very standard layout of three storey motel-style rooms which cost from US$75/85 upwards.

Bali Oberoi Hotel (☎ 751061), PO Box 3351, Denpasar – situated right on the beach at Seminyak, at the end of its own road way up beyond Legian (see the Kuta & Legian map), the Bali Oberoi is isolated and decidedly deluxe with beautiful individual bungalows and even some villa rooms with their own private swimming pools. The regular rooms are US$175 to US$240, while the villa rooms start at around US$400.

Further North Expensive hotels are appearing along the coast even further north than the Oberoi. They should offer a full range of services because there's not much else up this way.

Persona Bali (☎ 753914, fax 753915) – just north of the Oberoi, this is a new, nice-looking beachfront place with friendly staff and all the usual mod cons; rooms from US$70 to US$110.

Puri Ratih Bali (☎ 751146, fax 751549) – in Petitenget, the area north of Seminyak, this place has a swimming pool, gym, tennis court, and two-bed bungalows from US$80 to US$250.

Intan Bali Village (☎ 752191, fax 752193) – billing itself as a spa and club, but with most of the rooms in a four-storey block, this place is pretty isolated but has a full range of recreational facilities. Rooms are from US$80/85 to US$90/95.

Places to Eat

There are countless places to eat around Kuta and Legian, from tiny hawker's carts to fancy restaurants, cheap warungs to bars and

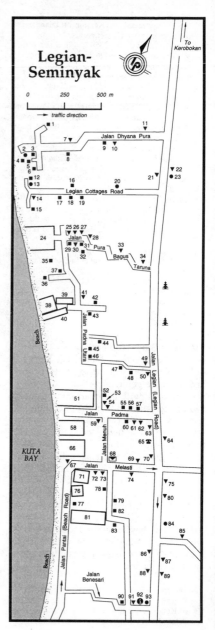

■ PLACES TO STAY	▼ PLACES TO EAT
1 Bali Agung Village	7 Pino Lotus Restaurant
3 Dhyana Pura Hotel	10 Jimbaro Cafe
4 Nusa di Nusa Hotel	11 Benny's Cafe II
5 Mesari Beach Inn	14 Puri Naga
6 Bali Holiday Resort	22 Goa 2001 Pub Restaurant
8 Tjendana Paradise Hotel	25 Topi Koki Restaurant
9 Surya Dharma Cottages	26 Swiss Restaurant
12 Sheraton Hotel	27 Twice Cafe
15 LG Beach Club Hotel	28 Rum Jungle Road Bar & Restaurant
16 Legian Garden Cottages	30 Sawasdee Thai Restaurant
17 Sing Ken Ken	33 Bamboo Palace Restaurant
18 Bali Subak	34 Benny's Café
19 Suri Bunga Bungalows	41 Poco Loco Mexican Restaurant
24 Kuta Palace Hotel	49 Restaurant Glory
29 Orchid Garden Cottages	50 Warung Kopi
31 Sari Yasai Beach Inn	53 Legian Snacks
32 Baleka Beach Inn	54 Joni Sunken Bar & Restaurant
35 Mabisa Beach Inn	59 Padma Club Restaurant
36 Puri Tantra Beach Bungalows	61 Rama Garden Restaurant
37 Mabisa Hotel	62 Norman Garden Restaurant
38 Bali Niksoma Inn	63 MS Restaurant
39 Bali Coconut Hotel	64 Ned's Place
40 Maharta Beach Inn	67 Karang Mas Restaurant
42 Sinar Beach Cottages	69 Gosha Restaurant
43 Adika Sari Bungalows	70 Do Drop Inn
44 Surya Dewata Beach Cottages	72 Restaurant Puri Bali Indah
45 Sinar Indah	73 Legian Garden Restaurant
46 Bali Sani Hotel	74 Orchid Garden Restaurant
47 Sri Ratu Cottages	75 Manhattan Restaurant & Bar
48 Three Brothers	80 Made's Restaurant
51 Bali Padma Hotel	85 Il Pirata
52 Garden View Cottages	86 The Bounty
55 Legian Village Hotel	87 Depot Viva
56 Puspasari Hotel	88 Za's Bakery & Restaurant
57 Puri Damai Cottages	89 Mama's German Restaurant
58 Bali Mandira Cottages	91 Midnight Oil Restaurant
60 Legian Beach Bungalows	
66 Legian Beach Hotel	OTHER
71 Bali Intan Cottages	
76 Kul Kul Resort	2 Chez Gado Gado
77 Bruna Beach Hotel	13 66 Club
78 Ocean Blue Club	20 Strand Bar
79 Legian Mas Beach Inn	21 Luna Cafe
81 Kuta Jaya Cottage	23 Jaya Pub
82 Puri Tanah Lot	65 Wartel (Telephone Office)
83 Sayang Beach Lodging	68 Postal Agent
90 Kuta Bungalows	84 Peanuts II
	92 Government Tourist Information
	93 Krishna Bookshop

pubs, steakhouses to juice bars. Like so much else about Kuta there's not much which is truly Indonesian or Balinese – you could stay in Kuta for a month, eat in a different place for every meal and never have to confront so much as a humble nasi goreng. In Kuta the cuisine is international and multicultural. The restaurant business is very competitive, and they're quick to pick up on new trends, whether it's a spate of Mexican restaurants or the discovery of pizzas. Japanese dishes (perhaps not authentic, but very tasty) are appearing on many menus, and Thai dishes are starting to become popular.

If you want to eat cheaply, try the places which cater to local workers. Food carts appear in the afternoon near Legian Beach, and there are warungs at the night market near the post office, and also at the beach market at the end of Bakung Sari. To supplement losmen breakfasts, buy bread, jam, cheese, drinks etc from the bakeries and supermarkets in Jalan Legian, and fruit from the public market.

For middle-budget eating, most tourist restaurants have the standard Indonesian dishes (nasi goreng, nasi campur etc), depending on the restaurant, but hamburgers, jaffles, spaghetti and salads are common offerings for a light meal (between 2000 and 4500 rp at most places), while a pizza, seafood or steak dish will cost between 6000 and 10,000 rp. The quality varies from indifferent to excellent, and seems to depend as much on when you go and what you order as on the establishment and the price. You can check the menu and the prices before you sit down, and check the other customers too.

It makes sense to eat at a place which is reasonably busy – high turnover means fresher ingredients, and some of those other customers must know something. On the other hand, service at those very big, barn-like places, often seafood specialists, can be inconsistent – an unexpectedly busy night can mean 100 extra meals, slow service, and fish from the freezer instead of from the tanks out the front.

For fancier food, you'll find French, German, Italian, Japanese, Korean, Mexican, Swiss and Swedish restaurants – the more expensive places really specialise, but the cheaper ones have a variety of dishes regardless of their name. One 'Mexican' restaurant also advertises European, Chinese, Japanese and Indonesian food! Wine is expensive, but some places have Australian wine by the glass for around 4000 rp. Beer

goes well with most meals, and is a fair index of prices – in cheap places a large beer is around 3000 rp; in expensive places it costs from 4000 rp upwards.

South Kuta Jalan Kartika Plaza is not a low-budget strip, but there are a couple of interesting places to eat. The *Café Français* is a good patisserie for a croissants (1300 rp), coffee and fruit juice breakfast. *Bali Seafood*, opposite the Bintang Bali Hotel, is a big place where you can select your main course while it's still swimming. It's not cheap, but the fish is fresh. The Cantonese restaurant at the *Dynasty Hotel* has a good reputation.

Around Kuta The beach market, where Jalan Kartika Plaza meets Jalan Bakung Sari, has some cheap Indonesian food stalls doing sate, noodles, soup etc. The *Rama Bridge Restaurant*, on the corner, seems expensive, but going east on Bakung Sari there are several reliable restaurants including *Dayu I* and *Nagasari*, and a supermarket which has many Western supermarket-style goods.

Jalan Buni Sari, which connects Jalan Pantai Kuta with Jalan Bakung Sari, has some more long-term survivors including the *Bali Indah, Wayan's Tavern* and *Dayu II*. Further along this short street are some popular pubs including *The Pub* itself, the original Kuta pub. You'll also find *Restaurant d'Este*, which has great Italian food.

Along Jalan Pantai Kuta, between Bemo Corner and the beach, is popular *Made's Warung*, a simple open-front place which is good for people-watching – the food is very good though a touch expensive. *The Suci Restaurant*, in the Suci Bungalows, on the south side of the road, is good value with delicious fruit drinks.

Poppies Gang, the tiny lane between Jalan Legian and the beach, is named for *Poppies Restaurant* (☎ 751059), one of the oldest and most popular in Kuta. The prices are quite high, from 7000 to 10,000 rp for main courses, but the food is well prepared and presented, though not spectacularly innovative, and the garden setting and the atmosphere are delightful. It's been amazingly consistent for years – make a reservation. A few steps west of Poppies is *TJ's* (☎ 751093), a deservedly popular Mexican restaurant, with a good ambience and main courses from 8000 to 12,000 rp.

Further down Poppies Gang, towards the beach, there are several popular places for light meals – try *Warung Transformer* or the pleasant *Tree House Restaurant*. The Tree House is a good place for an excellent and economical breakfast.

Along Jalan Legian There are lots of possibilities along Jalan Legian. Most of the time the road is an almost continuous traffic jam and a table near the road can mean you have to shout to be heard. Right on Bemo Corner is the *Quick Snack Bar*, a good place for a snack or breakfast; the yoghurt is particularly good. A little further up is a *Sushi Bar*, with excellent sushi for 1200 to 3000 rp, and sashimi from 7000 to 10,000 rp. Continue north towards Legian, and you reach the *Twice Bar & Bakery*, which might be good for a breakfast but is noisy and a little overpriced for dinner, and *Mini Restaurant*, a huge place despite the name, but busy, serving good straightforward food at low prices. The *Sari Club Restaurant* is similar in style, price and quality. There's a new *KFC* on a side alley here, and a new *McDonalds* just up the road. On the east side of the road, the quite expensive *Indah Sari* is another big seafood place, though the service and the food are of variable standard.

Around the corner, Poppies Gang II has a lot of cheap eateries, like the popular *Batu Bulong*, *Nana's Swedish Restaurant*, *Twice Pub* and *The Corner Restaurant*.

Continue north to *Mama's German Restaurant* (see the Legian map), which has pretty authentic German food with sauerbraten, bratwurst, pork knuckles, weiner schnitzel (7200 rp) and other main courses for around 8000 rp. The *Depot Viva* is an open-roofed place with surprisingly good Indonesian and Chinese food despite its bare and basic appearance. The prices are pleasantly basic too, which accounts for its steady

popularity. Across the road is *Za's Bakery & Restaurant*, a good spot for breakfast which also has a menu featuring everything from pasta dishes to curries.

A little further along Jalan Legian is *Il Pirata*, noted both for its very good pizzas at 5000 to 7000 rp, and for its late opening hours. Continuing north to the heart of Legian, you'll come to the ever-popular *Do Drop Inn*, the well-regarded *Warung Kopi*, and the long-standing *Restaurant Glory*.

Around Legian The streets west of Jalan Legian have numerous restaurants and bars. On Jalan Melasti is the big *Orchid Garden Restaurant*, the *Legian Garden Restaurant* and the *Restaurant Puri Bali Indah* with excellent Chinese food. Jalan Padma has a number of tourist restaurants, and *Legian Snacks*, just north of Padma, is good for lighter meals. At the *Joni Sunken Bar & Restaurant*, on Padma, you can eat and drink while semi-immersed in a swimming pool – if your hotel doesn't run to this indulgence, here's your chance to try it (you don't get bruised if you fall off your stool).

Further north, things get more expensive but the standards are higher – this is the trendy end of town. Some of the most interesting places are on Jalan Pura Bagus Taruna (also known as Rum Jungle Rd), the twisting road leading from Jalan Legian to the big Kuta Palace Hotel. Right by the hotel entrance is the *Topi Koki Restaurant* which has a pretty good go at la cuisine Français, and is about the most expensive place around, with main courses at 7000 to 11,000 rp, wine by the glass at 7000 rp – a full meal for two with drinks will cost over 50,000 rp, which is not bad for good French food. A little further back from the beach is the *Swiss Restaurant*, which is adjacent to the Swiss consul so should have some credibility. Other restaurants along this street include the *Sawasdee Thai Restaurant*, *Yudi Pizza* and, nearer to Jalan Legian, the distinctive and very popular *Bamboo Palace Restaurant*, and the smaller, but also popular, *Benny's Café*, with delicious pastries and coffee for a splurge breakfast.

Seminyak Good, though not cheap, places to eat up here include the *Ibiza* Italian restaurant and the *Goa 2001 Pub Restaurant*, both on Jalan Legian. On Jalan Dhyana Pura you'll find *Benny's Cafe II* and *Jimbaro Cafe*, which are mid-range places. On a beach track past the Oberoi, near the Petitenget temple, *La Lucciato* is an Italian place with food that people rave about, and prices which are expensive but not excessive – main courses are around 9000 rp.

Entertainment

Nightspots are scattered around Kuta, Legian and Seminyak, many along Jalan Legian. The wild, drunken excesses of Kuta are mostly a scene for young Australians on cheap package holidays. The scene centres around a short side alley off Jalan Legian, with *Peanuts Disco* at the far end, and bars like *Crazy Horse*, the *Warehouse* and *Koala Blu Club* on either side. Peanuts gets going around 11 pm, and charges 6000 rp admission, which includes one drink. The bars start earlier and finish later, and entry is free. Later on, lines of bemos and dokars wait to haul the semiconscious back to their hotels. The whole Peanuts complex is due to be closed and redeveloped as a shopping centre (a sign of the times!), and the owners have established *Peanuts II*, up in Legian, to continue the reputation (or notoriety) of the original. Other nearby drinking places include the *Sari Club* (or 'SC' for short), just up the road, *Norm's Life Be In It* bar, further up, and *Tubes Bar*, around the corner in Poppies Gang II, which is a surfers' hangout. The glossy *Hard Rock Cafe*, just north of the Peanuts alley, is a new landmark in Kuta, and will doubtless prove popular with those who go for this sort of thing.

Up in Legian you'll find a few more Aussie drinking places on Jalan Padma, like the *Bali Aussie*. There are also a few bars/pubs in the south of Kuta, like *Un's Pub* near Bemo Corner and, on Jalan Buni Sari, in order of noisiness, *The Pub*, one of Kuta's original bars, the *Bagus Pub* and *Casablanca*.

There is somewhat classier nightlife further north in Seminyak, with trendy expatriates setting the style, and well-connected visitors providing new faces and fashions. The scene kicks off on Jalan Legian, where the sophisticates start with drinks and/or dinner at the *Goa 2001 Pub Restaurant*. They then move on (but not before 10 pm) to the *Jaya Pub* for relaxed music and conversation, or do some cafe society at *Luna Cafe*, where you can see the comings and goings at the Jaya Pub across the road, and be seen yourself. Later on, but *never* before 1 am, the action shifts to the beachside *66 Club* (pronounced 'double six'), or the chic *Chez Gado Gado*, at the beach end of Jalan Dyana Pura; if you don't like one, you can stroll along the beach to the other. After some hours of this, you could do breakfast at *Benny's Café*, if you haven't found a better option.

Large-screen video (or laser disk) movies are featured at some of the restaurants/pubs, including the *Batu Bulong*, the *Twice Bar* and the *Bounty*. They're pretty loud and easy to find, but only go if you want to see the movie – they're impossible to ignore and the service slows down as the staff get involved in the interesting bits.

Things to Buy

Parts of Kuta are now almost door-to-door shops and over the years these have become steadily more sophisticated. Of course there are still many simple stalls as well, and many of these cheaper shops are now crowded together in 'art markets' like the one at the beach end of Jalan Bakung Sari. For everyday purchases, like food, toiletries and stationery, there are supermarkets on Jalan Legian, Jalan Bakung Sari and Jalan Raya Kuta. The biggest is the Galael supermarket on the road to Denpasar. The big duty-free shop is nearby, though it seems expensive. The department store at Plaza Bali, on the airport road, has a good selection of clothing and leather at reasonable prices.

With so many things to buy around Kuta it's very easy to be stampeded into buying things you don't really want during the first few days of your stay. You'll need real sales resistance not to succumb to something, as there are so many people who are so good at selling things. Unless you want to end up with lots of things you can definitely do without, get an overall impression before you consider buying anything and shop around before you buy.

Crafts If it's made anywhere on Bali then 10 to one you can find it on sale at Kuta. Of course, Kuta isn't really the centre for any of Bali's notable crafts but the Kuta shops have arts and crafts from almost every part of the island, from woodcarvings to paintings to textiles and just about everything else in between. There are also many interesting pieces from other parts of Indonesia, and it can be difficult to assess their authenticity and value – many of the 'Irian Jaya antiques' are made locally and recently.

Clothing Clothes, on the other hand, are a Kuta speciality and Kuta has become the centre for Bali's energetic garment industry, which is exporting world-wide. Countless boutiques for men and women display Balinese interpretations of the latest styles which now find their way all over the world. You may never need to wear a sports coat or leather boots on Bali but you can certainly find plenty of them on sale and at competitive prices. You'll probably see the same items later on in shops from Berkeley to Double Bay at 10 times the cost.

Silver Work Many shops sell silver and jewellery, but the quality is often suspect. Well-established places like Jonathon's and Mirah, are probably best – have a look in these places before you buy anywhere else.

Other Items The cassette business is 100% legal, with a huge variety of tapes, from golden oldies to the latest hits, from about 8000 rp. Reggae music is enormously popular; classical music less so. CDs are also available, but the range is not as good and the prices – at around 26,000 rp – are not as competitive. There are lots of tape shops around Kuta with a wide range. Mahogany,

on the main road in Legian, has an excellent range, including gamelan music on tape and CD.

One thing there is no harm in paying for as soon as you arrive is a massage. Kuta has countless masseurs who operate along the beach or call around to the hotels. For just a few thousand rp (don't pay more than 5000 rp), they'll quickly prove you have dozens of muscles you never knew existed.

Getting There & Away

Air See the Getting There & Away chapter for details of flying to or from Bali. Kuta has lots of travel agencies but if you're looking for onward tickets, Bali is no place for air-travel bargains.

If you already have tickets you can reconfirm your booking at the small Garuda office (☎ 751179) in the Natour Kuta Beach Hotel at the beach end of Jalan Pantai Kuta. The office sometimes gets hopelessly crowded so it's a good idea to arrive before opening time or during the lunch break (noon to 1 pm) to be at the head of the queue. It's open from 7.30 am to 4 pm Monday to Friday, 9 am to 1 pm on weekends.

Most airlines, including Garuda, Qantas, Continental, Lufthansa and KLM, have offices at the Natour Grand Bali Beach hotel in Sanur. It's a local call from Kuta, and their numbers are listed in the Sanur entry. The Air New Zealand office is at the Kartika Plaza Hotel (☎ 751067). The myriad Kuta travel agencies will offer to make reconfirmations for you but there's a charge and some agencies are said to be less than scrupulous about actually reconfirming. Big hotels will also reconfirm for their guests.

Bus Lots of agents in Kuta sell bus tickets to Java, although they're cheaper at the Ubung bus station from where the buses depart. Fares include Surabaya from 19,000 rp, Yogyakarta from around 29,000 rp and Jakarta for 56,000 rp.

There are regular tourist shuttle buses to other places on Bali. Services include Ubud for 7500 rp, Padangbai and Candidasa for 10,000 rp and Lovina for 12,500 rp. Perama

(☎ 751551), on Jalan Legian, is the best-known operator, but other shuttle bus companies have similar fares. Perama also operates bus-ferry-bus services to Lombok. You can travel directly to Mataram or Senggigi Beach for 20,000 rp or to Bangsal, from where the boats cross to the Gili Islands, for 25,000 rp. To Nusa Lembongan is 22,500 rp.

Bemo Public bemos go to/from the Tegal terminal in Denpasar (600 rp). Most 'S' bemos go only to the terminal area in Kuta, just beyond Bemo Corner, but the S1 does a loop round the beach road. In practice you will probably have to go to the terminal near Bemo Corner to get a bemo out of town (see below). For virtually any destination on Bali you'll have to go to one (or more) of the Denpasar terminals first.

Motorbike Groups of motorbikes for rent are assembled at various points along Jalan Legian. They cost about 10,000 rp per day; less by the week, perhaps more for one day only. You'll need a valid motorbike licence.

Car There are lots of car rental places, large and small, and it's cheaper here than in Sanur, Ubud or other tourist centres. The moneychanger just up from Bemo Corner (☎ 751738) advertises the cheapest rates around, and you don't even have to haggle – a Suzuki hardtop jeep with air-con is 33,000 rp per day including insurance, with a 10% discount if you take it for a week. A larger Kijang is 55,000 rp per day. There are lots of other car rental places – try to bargain them down to these levels.

Tours There are countless tours organised from Kuta which can be booked through the many travel agencies. Day and half-day trips are offered to tourist attractions on Bali, though some make lots of stops where you're encouraged to buy things. Full day trips start at around 15,000 to 20,000 rp. There are also specialist operators, with tours for scuba diving, whitewater rafting, pony treks, cycling and surfing. See the Facts for the Visitor chapter for details, or just walk up Jalan Legian and look at the offers from the various agents.

Some tours go further afield. Trips to Mt Bromo in East Java are popular. Others take in the main sights in west Lombok, but it's much better value to get to Lombok first and organise a tour from there. Tours to Komodo or Sulawesi are also offered.

Agencies also rent cars, motorbikes and bicycles, sell bus and train tickets to Java and perform other travel agency services.

Getting Around

Kuta is a pain to get around because it's so spread out, and the guys with charter minibuses try to preclude any cheaper transport alternatives.

To/From the Airport The official taxi fare is 4500 rp from the airport to any place south of Jalan Bakung Sari (the southern part of Kuta), 6500 rp for anywhere north of Bakung Sari but south of Jalan Padma (central Kuta right up to the centre of Legian), 10,000 rp north of Jalan Padma (the northern part of Legian) and 12,000 rp to the Oberoi Hotel (way north of Legian in Seminyak).

From Kuta to the airport you should be able to charter a minibus for about the same fares (haggle like hell), or get a metered taxi. The Perama bus service to the airport costs about 5000 rp. Theoretically, you could get to the airport from Kuta by regular public bemo for just a few hundred rp, but you'd have to walk to the S1 bemo route (near the corner of Jalan Bakung Sari and Jalan Raya Kuta would be a good place to try) and it's also a fair walk from the closest stop on the bemo route to the airport terminal.

Taxi & Charter There are plenty of taxis around Kuta Beach. They're blue and yellow, with meters and air-con, and they charge 800 rp flag fall and 800 rp per km. They seem reluctant to stop for passengers on Jalan Legian or round Bemo Corner, where the transport touts hustle for business.

Minibuses available for charter are easy to

find – listen for the offers of 'transport' which follow any pedestrian. Vehicles which can legally be chartered by tourists have yellow licence plates. They don't have meters so you have to negotiate the fare before you get on board. You should be able to get from the middle of Kuta to the middle of Legian for around 3000 rp. If you reckon that a full-day charter should run to about 45,000 or 50,000 rp, then you can estimate a price for shorter trips on a proportional basis, but you'll have to bargain hard. They shouldn't cost more than an equivalent trip in a metered taxi, which is another way to estimate a reasonable fare. The 'first price' for transport can be truly outrageous.

Public Bemo In theory, S1 bemos do a loop through Kuta and Legian on their route from Tegal terminal in Denpasar to Kuta, the airport and back to Tegal. In practice it's almost impossible for tourists to use the system for local transport within Kuta, at the public price. They only do a limited route – from Bemo Corner, west then north on Jalan Pantai Kuta, south on Jalan Legian back to Bemo Corner – then continue their route to the airport or Denpasar. They don't seem to go down Jalan Legian very often during the day, and even less in the evening. For many short trips you're almost certainly going to have to charter transport.

Bicycle There are lots of places to rent bikes, for around 5000 rp per day. It's a good way to get around because Kuta is pretty flat, you can go up the narrowest gangs, park anywhere and even push it the wrong way up a one-way street. Lock it when you leave it and beware of thieves who might snatch things from the basket or luggage rack.

BEREWA

This beach is a few km up the coast from the north end of the Kuta strip, but to reach it you have to take the small roads west of Kerobokan – there's no coast road north of Petitenget. Signs point to *Bolare Beach Hotel* (☎ 0361 262358), with a great beachfront location, pool, restaurant etc.

Standard rates are US$50/55 plus 15% tax and service, but there's a US$10 high-season supplement, and you should be able to negotiate a discount in the low season. *Legong Keraton Beach Cottages* (☎ 0361 238049, fax 238050) is just next door and not quite as fancy, but it has very nice individual cottages and a pool, set in a pretty garden right by the beach. Standard cottages are good value at US$45; deluxe ones are US$55 and super deluxe US$75. A low-season discount would make this a very attractive option for a quiet stay by the beach.

The top-end option at Berewa is the *Dewata Beach Hotel* (☎ 0361 237663, fax 234990), a member of the Best Western chain. It has a handsome lobby area, restaurants, disco, pool, tennis courts and conference facilities. The 168 rooms are comfortable, but nothing special – a bit like a US motel – and cost from US$65/80 and up. There's no traffic here and they have a children's playground, so it could be a good place for those with young children. The hotel offers a free shuttle service to Kuta, which should reduce the isolation. Otherwise there is no public transport.

CANGGU

A well-known surf spot with right and left-hand breaks, Canggu has a nice beach, though there is sometimes polluted water at the river mouth. There's a warung, and you can stay at the *Canggu Beach Club* for 20,000/25,000 rp; less if you stay longer. To get there, go east at Kerobokan and follow the signs to Pererenan. There's no public transport.

SANUR

Sanur is an upmarket alternative to Kuta for those coming to Bali for sea, sand and sun, and a down-market alternative to Nusa Dua for those who want a package-tour holiday in an air-conditioned hotel with a swimming pool. There are some cheap places to stay, as well as some good restaurants (prices similar to equivalent places at Kuta), so you don't have to swallow the high prices at hotel restaurants. Other tourist services are here,

with some interesting craft, clothing, art and
'antique' shops.

An early home for visiting Western artists,
Sanur is still an artistic centre, famed for its
gamelan orchestras; the courtly Arja opera
and wayang kulit (shadow puppets) are also
popular.

The beach is pleasant, and sheltered by a
reef. At low tide it's very shallow, and you
have to pick your way out over rocks and
coral through knee-deep water. The
Indonesians, both locals and 'domestic
tourists', think it's ideal and you'll find many
of them paddling here on Sunday and holidays, particularly at the northern end of the
beach. At high tide the swimming is fine, and
there is an array of water sports on offer –
windsurfing, snorkelling, water-skiing,
parasailing, paddle boards etc – all for a
price, and a classic but fickle surf break.

What Sanur doesn't have, thankfully, is
the noise, confusion and pollution of Kuta.
You're not in constant danger of being mown
down by motorbike maniacs, the traffic isn't
horrendous and you're not constantly badgered to buy things – badgered yes, but not
constantly. The nightlife is sedate by comparison, but you can always go over to Kuta
for a wild night.

Orientation

Sanur stretches for about three km along an
east-facing coastline, with the landscaped
grounds and restaurants of expensive hotels
fronting right onto the beach. The conspicuous, '60s style Hotel Bali Beach (now
officially the Natour Grand Bali Beach, but
still commonly called by the original name)
is at the northern end of the strip, and the
newer Surya Beach Hotel, invisible behind
its walls and gardens, is at the southern end.

West of the beachfront hotels is the main
drag, called Jalan Danau Toba in the north,
but changing to Jalan Danau Tamblingan
(formerly Jalan Tanjung Sari) in the middle.
It has a few bends, but basically runs parallel
to the beach, with the hotel entrances on one
side and wall-to-wall tourist shops and restaurants down the other side. To the west of
this road are some small streets and lanes,

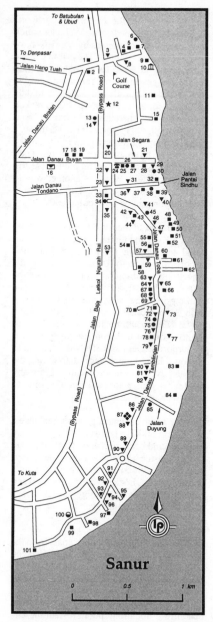

Sanur

■ PLACES TO STAY

1 Bali Sanur Bungalows Sanur
  VillageClub
2 Hotel Bali Continental
4 Watering Hole Homestay &
  Restaurant
5 Alit's Beach Bungalows &
  Restaurant
7 Ananda Hotel & Restaurant
9 Diwangkara Beach Hotel
11 Natour Grand Bali Beach
15 Natour Grand Bali Beach -
  Cottage Section
17 Hotel Sanur-Indah
18 Hotel Taman Sari
19 Hotel Rani
25 Puri Kelapa Cottages
27 Tourist Beach Inn
28 Segara Village Hotel
32 Baruna Beach Inn
33 Abian Srama
37 Queen Bali Hotel
39 Natour Sindhu Beach
43 Homestays Yulia, Luisa & Coca
48 La Taverna Bali Hotel
49 Respati Beach Village
50 Gazebo Beach Hotel
51 Bali Sanur Bungalows Irama
52 Tandjung Sari Hotel
54 Bumi Ayu Bungalows
55 Made Homestay & Pub
56 Kalpataharu Homestay & Restaurant
58 Prima Cottages
60 Besakih Beach Hotel
61 Santrian Beach Cottages
62 Werdha Pura
66 Laghawa Beach Inn
67 Swastika Bungalows
70 Bali Wirasana Hotel
71 Hotel Ramayana
78 Hotel Satai
83 Bali Sanur Bungalows
  Peneeda View
84 Bali Hyatt Hotel
97 Santrian Beach Resort
98 Semawang Beach Inn
99 Hotel Sanur Beach
101 Surya Beach Hotel

▼ PLACES TO EAT

3 Si Pino Restaurant
8 Bali 16 Pizza
14 Kentucky Fried Chicken &
  Swensens Ice Cream
20 Lenny's Restaurant
21 Rana's Coffee Shop

22 The Corner Restaurant
23 Merry Bar & Restaurant
29 Warungs
31 Borneo Restaurant
35 Aga Restaurant
36 Queen Bali Restaurant
40 Mango Bar & Restaurant
41 Bali Moon Restaurant
42 Lotus Pond Restaurant
44 Swastika I Restaurant
46 Sindhu Corner Restaurant
47 Kuri Putih Restaurant
53 Sita Restaurant
57 Ratu's Pizza
59 Arena Restaurant
63 Bayu Garden Restaurant
64 Warung Aditya
65 Laghawa Grill
69 Swastika II Restaurant
72 Jineng Restaurant
73 Nam Ban Kan Japanese Restaurant
76 Penjor Restaurant
77 New Seoul Korean Restaurant
79 Karya Seafood & Taiwanese
  Restaurant
80 Kulkul Restaurant
81 Melanie Restaurant
82 Restaurant Telaga Naga
86 Paon Restaurant
88 Legong Restaurant
89 Oka's Bar Restaurant
90 Cafe Jepun
91 Kesumasari
92 Norman's Bar
93 Donald's Cafe & Bakery
94 Alita Garden Restaurant
95 Trattoria da Marco
96 Pualam Restaurant

OTHER

6 Boats to Nusa Lembongan
10 Museum Le Mayeur
12 Police Station
13 Supermarket
16 Post Office
24 Wartel
26 US Consular Agency
30 Sanur Beach Market
34 Night Market
38 Rumours Nightclub
45 Subec Disco
68 Temptation
74 Handcraft Market
75 Number One Club
85 Supermarket
87 Double U Shopping Centre
100 Bemo Stop

then Jalan Baja Letkol Ngurah Rai, the main Sanur bypass road, which runs south, then west to Kuta and the airport, and north towards Ubud. It's usually just called the Bypass road, or Jalan Bypass. For some reason, most of the streets in Sanur are now named after Indonesian lakes – Jalan Danau Toba, Jalan Danau Bratan etc.

Information

Sanur has travel agencies, moneychangers, film processing, supermarkets and other facilities, mostly along Jalan Danau Tamblingan.

Post & Telecommunications Sanur's post office is on the southern side of Jalan Danau Buyan (the part of Jalan Segara west of the Bypass road). If you're an American Express customer you can have your mail sent to their office, c/o PT Pacto Ltd, PO Box 52, Sanur (☎ 288449), which is in the Natour Grand Bali Beach. Of course, you can also have mail addressed to the large hotels.

There's a Telkom wartel at the top end of Jalan Danau Toba, on the corner of Jalan Segara, where you can make international calls, send faxes and buy telephone cards at the right price. Near the south end of Jalan Tamblingan there's a private wartel, also with international phone and fax facilities. A Home Country Direct phone is next to the Malaysian Airlines office in the Natour Grand Bali Beach. You can make reverse-charge (collect) calls or pay with your credit card; it's very easy to use.

Sanur is in the 0361 telephone district.

Foreign Embassies The US consular agency (☎ 288478) is on Jalan Segara, 80 metres west of the Segara Village Hotel, open from 8 am to 4.30 pm, Monday to Friday. A number of other consulates and consular agencies are in Sanur, or not far away in the Renon area of Denpasar. See under Visas & Embassies in the Facts for the Visitor chapter for the addresses of other embassies.

Museum Le Mayeur

Sanur was one of the places on Bali favoured by Western artists during their prewar discovery of the island. It was a quiet fishing village at that time but few traces of the Sanur of 50 years ago remain. The exception is the former home of the Belgian artist Le Mayeur who lived here from 1932 to 1958. It must have been a delightful place then, a peaceful and elegant home right by the beach. Today it's squeezed between the Natour Grand Bali Beach and the Diwangkara Beach Hotel. It's still maintained by his widow, Ni Polok, once a renowned and beautiful Legong dancer.

The home displays paintings and drawings by Le Mayeur but unfortunately many of them are yellowed, dirty and badly lit. They are nevertheless interesting, impressionist-style paintings from his travels in Africa, India, Italy, France and the South Pacific. The more recent works, from the 1950s, are in much better condition, with the vibrant colours of Bali and the scenes of daily life which later became popular with Balinese artists. All the works have titles, descriptions, dates, etc in both Indonesian and English. The museum is also an interesting example of architecture in its own right. Notice the beautifully carved window shutters which recount the story of Rama and Sita from the *Ramayana*.

Admission is 200 rp (children 100 rp) and it's open from 8 am to 2 pm Sunday, Tuesday, Wednesday and Thursday, from 8 to 11 am Friday and from 8 am to noon on Saturday. It's closed on Monday.

Water Sports

The diving off Sanur is not great, but there is a good variety of fish on the reef, and at low tide they are in water shallow enough to be enjoyed by snorkellers. There are a number of dive operations with their headquarters on the Bypass road, and some with offices in a few of the big hotels (see the Facts for the Visitor chapter). Sanur is not a bad place for divers to base themselves, and it's a good departure point for dive trips to the islands

Kites

Asian children don't enjoy the same variety and quantity of toys that children in the West commonly have but they certainly do fly kites: almost anywhere in Asia the sky is likely to be full of kites of all sizes and types. Bali is no exception – you'll see children flying kites in towns and villages and even in the middle of the rice paddies. At Sanur, however, kite flying is not just child's play. Here the local banjars compete in kite- flying competitions, where size seems to be a major factor. July, August and September are the months for competitive kite flying.

The kites are enormous – traffic is halted when they're carried down the road and it takes half a dozen men to launch them, two men to carry the drum of heavy nylon cord, and a sturdy tree to tie the kite to once it's up and flying. Kites can be up to 10 metres long, and the cord tensioning the main cross-piece (itself a hefty length of bamboo) makes a low 'whoop-whoop-whoop' noise during flight. Not unexpectedly, such big kites are a danger to aircraft – one of these monsters could bring down a 747 – and kite flying has been restricted on the airport approaches, particularly across Pulau Serangan.

Many of the craft shops sell kites in the shape of birds, bats or butterflies. They come in a variety of sizes and fold up ingeniously so you can get them home. Look for ones with feathers and other details carefully painted – there's a lot of junk around. ■

of the Nusa Penida group, prominent on the horizon if the weather is clear.

For surfers there is a classic right-hand break on the reef, but it needs a big swell to make it work, and it's only good in the wet season, from November to April. Boats to Nusa Lembongan, another great surf spot, leave from the northern end of Sanur Beach.

Other water sports and activities are expensive, especially if arranged through a beachfront hotel. A paddle board (usually called a canoe, though you definitely sit on it rather than in it) costs about US$10 per hour from a hotel, but guys on the beach rent them for half that if you negotiate. The hotel price for a windsurfer is also US$10 per hour, and snorkelling gear is around US$5 an hour. Some package tours include non-motorised water sports, and this would be quite a valuable extra if you enjoy these activities – make sure you get vouchers or some written confirmation that these activities are included or, when you get to Sanur, you may find that there has been a 'misunderstanding'.

Other Attractions

Just wandering around Sanur, along the beach or through the rice paddies, is an interesting activity in itself. The rice farmers of Sanur are said to grow some of the finest rice on Bali. The beach at Sanur is always full of interesting sights such as the colourful out-

riggers known as *jukungs* ready to take you for a quick trip out to the reef. At low tide you can walk across the sand and coral to this sheltering reef.

Beyond the Hotel Sanur Beach, at Belanjong, there's a stone pillar with an inscription recounting military victories of over 1000 years ago. Tanjung Sari, with its coral pyramid, was once a lonely temple by the beach.

Places to Stay

There are no rock-bottom Kuta-style places in Sanur although there are a few cheapies. There's also a handful of mid-range places, a few of which are as good value as equivalent places at Kuta. Principally, however, Sanur is a medium to high-price resort, a place of 'international standard' hotels for package tours. The prices quoted in the following sections don't include the 17.5% additional charge for tax and service.

Note, also, that the prices given in the top-end section are the quoted walk-in rates, but hardly anyone just walks in to these places. It may actually be cheaper to book ahead through a travel agency, especially as part of a package.

Places to Stay – bottom end

The cheapest places are away from the beach, and at the northern end of town. On

Jalan Danau Buyan (Jalan Segara east of the main road) there are three lower-priced places side by side. The *Hotel Sanur-Indah*, closest to Denpasar, is the most basic and the cheapest at about 15,000 rp for a room. The *Hotel Taman Sari* and the *Hotel Rani* (☎ 288578) have singles/doubles for around 12,500/17,000 rp, up to 45,000 rp with aircon and hot water.

There are three basic homestays at the north end of Jalan Danau Toba, the *Yulia,* the *Luisa* and the *Coca*, where clean, simple rooms with private mandi go for around 20,000 rp per night. They're inconspicuously located behind shops at Nos 38, 40 and 42. Further south, on a side street west of the main road, the *Bali Wirasana* (☎ 288632) is cheap at 20,000/40,000 rp; it doesn't have a pool but guests can use the one at Swastika Bungalows.

Places to Stay – middle

At the northern end of Sanur Beach the *Ananda Hotel* (☎ 288327) is behind the restaurant of the same name, right by the beach. It's neat and clean and rooms with fan and cold water cost 25,000/30,000 rp for singles/doubles.

The *Watering Hole Homestay*, (☎ 288289) on Jalan Hang Tuah (the Sanur to Denpasar road) opposite the Natour Grand Bali Beach entrance, has clean, pleasant rooms from 25,000 rp for a single. It's a friendly, well-run place, recently remodelled, with good food and a bar. On Hang Tuah, on the other side of the Bypass road, the *Hotel Bali Continental* (☎ 288250) is mainly for Indonesian guests, with singles and doubles with air-con, TV and hot water from 50,000 rp.

The *Kalpataru Homestay & Restaurant* (☎ 288457), on the west side of Jalan Danau Toba, is a pleasant place with a garden and swimming pool. It's clean, and not bad value at US$25/30 for budget rooms, US$30/35 for better rooms with air-con.

A little further south, on a side road which runs towards the beach between some government buildings, is the *Werdha Pura*. It's a government-run 'beach cottage prototype',

the service is OK, and it's cheap enough at 25,000/50,000 rp for singles/doubles and 60,000 rp for family rooms.

The more expensive mid-range places tend to quote their prices in US dollars and add on about 15% for tax and service. Starting again from the northern end of town, the *Sanur Village Club* (one of the Bali Sanur Bungalows group), on Jalan Hang Tuah, costs US$40/45 with air-con but is not in a good location. *Alit's Beach Bungalows* are also on Hang Tuah, a bit closer to the beach, costing US$37/40 with air-con and hot water.

On Jalan Segara, the *Tourist Beach Inn* (☎ 288418) is new, clean and well located, but expensive at US$45/50. On Jalan Pantai Sindhu, a block further south and right on the beach, is the *Baruna Beach Inn* (☎ 288546) with a great location and only nine rooms from US$30/45 including breakfast, tax and air-con. Rooms cost a few dollars extra in the high season. On the south side of Jalan Pantai Sindhu, a bit further from the beach, the *Queen Bali Hotel* (☎ 288054) has standard rooms at US$25/30 and bungalows at US$30/35; extra beds are US$7.50. The price includes tax, breakfast, air-con and hot water.

Next to the night market, and running through to the Bypass road, *Abian Srama* has a little swimming pool and over 50 rooms on a small site, but some of them are pretty cheap at US$12/16, while better air-con rooms are US$25/30. It caters mostly to Indonesian guests.

Going down the main drag, you find the small *Respati Beach Village* (☎ 288046) which asks US$45 to US$55 for ordinary motel-style double rooms, but should give a discount in the off season. Next door is the *Gazebo Beach Hotel*, a popular beachfront place with a lush garden and singles/doubles from US$35/40 to US$47/55, US$15 extra in the high season. A small side track west of Jalan Danau Tamblingan leads to a T-junction, north of which you'll find *Bumi Ayu Bungalows* (☎ 289101), which cost from US$45/50. They're nice but pricey for a place this far from the beach. Going south on

Top: Street vendor, Kuta Beach, Bali (GE)
Bottom: Poppies, Kuta, Bali (TW)

Top: Dressed in his best for the festival, Sanur, Bali (JL)
Bottom: Cremation Mask, Ubud, Bali (GE)

the same back lane brings you to *Prima Cottages* (☎ 289153), a clean place with a pool and a friendly atmosphere, at about US$22/25.

Continuing along Jalan Danau Tamblingan you'll find the *Laghawa Beach Inn* (☎ 288494, 287919) on the beach side of the road, with air-con singles/doubles for US$35/40; fan-cooled rooms are US$10 less and all prices include continental breakfast. An extra bed costs US$7. The inn has an attractive garden setting, restaurant and bar and looks like quite good value for Sanur. On the other side of the road, *Swastika Bungalows* (☎ 288693, fax 287526) has pretty gardens, two swimming pools, and comfortable rooms for US$27.50/35, or US$37.50/45 with air-con. A few metres further south is the *Hotel Ramayana* (☎ 288429) with air-con rooms at US$23 for singles or doubles, excluding tax and breakfast. South again is the *Hotel Satai* (☎ 287314), a two-storey place with rooms facing inwards to the pool – nothing special, but clean and comfortable, and only US$23/25 including breakfast.

At the southern end of town, on a small road between the big hotels, the *Semawang Beach Inn* (☎ 288619) is close to the beach and offers good facilities and breakfast at US$22 to US$30 for air-con singles or doubles.

Places to Stay – top end

The Hotel Bali Beach was Bali's first 'big' hotel and is still one of the biggest hotels on Bali. Dating from the Sukarno era of the mid-60s, it was built as a Miami Beach-style rectangular block facing the beach. Damaged by fire in 1992, it has been substantially remodelled with a Balinese-style lobby, and renamed the *Natour Grand Bali Beach* (☎ 288511, fax 287917; PO Box 3275, Denpasar), though as a landmark it is more commonly known by its old name. Managed by the government Natour group, it has all the usual facilities from bars, restaurants and a nightclub to swimming pools and tennis courts, as well as an adjacent golf course and bowling alley. Air-con rooms in the main block cost from US$115/135 to US$150/170, and there are suites from US$190 to US$400, some with kitchenettes. Adjoining the hotel to the south is the cottage section, in a more Balinese style, from US$110/130. The Presidential Suite is about the most expensive accommodation on Bali, at US$3000 per night.

Almost all the more expensive hotels are on the beachfront. Immediately north of the Bali Beach and adjacent to the Museum Le Mayeur is the partially secluded *Diwangkara Beach Hotel* (☎ 288577, fax 288894; PO Box 3120, Denpasar). Air-con rooms with breakfast cost from US$45 to US$55 a double.

On Jalan Segara, the new *Puri Kelapa Cottages* is a smaller place, away from the beach, and not great value at US$50/60. At the beach end of Jalan Segara, the *Segara Village Hotel* (☎ 288407/8, fax 287242) has motel-style rooms and two-storey cottages from US$66 to US$200. The hotel is in a pleasant landscaped area with swimming pools and a children's playground, and it's one of the few places with an organised programme of kids' activities; only US$5 for a 9 am to 2 pm session. Unfortunately it costs US$20 for an extra bed, which makes it pretty expensive if you have a couple of kids, but it's a nice place with a good atmosphere.

The *Natour Sindhu Beach* (☎ 288351/2, fax 289268), right on the beach, has 50 air-con rooms from US$55/66 to US$77/88, but seems to specialise in conferences and package groups. The *La Taverna Bali Hotel* (☎ 288497; PO Box 40, Denpasar), also right on the beach, is an attractive place with air-con rooms from US$80/90 and suites from US$160; there's a US$15 high-season supplement.

The main street has several places to stay in the Bali Sanur Bungalows (BSB) group (☎ 288421, fax 288426). Heading south you come first to the *Irama* then to the *Respati*, both priced from US$50 a double. Further south you come to the *Peneeda View* bungalows, which are more expensive at US$60/70. Breakfast, tax and service are extra. The *Besakih Beach Hotel* is no longer a member of the BSB group, but it's a nice beachfront place with rooms from US$60/70.

In between the Irama and the Besakih is the *Tandjung Sari Hotel* (☎ 288441, fax 287930), one of the original Balinese beach bungalow places, which started as an extension of a family home in 1962. Individual bungalows are in traditional style and beautifully decorated with crafts and antiques. There's a swimming pool and the restaurant has an excellent reputation, but it's an expensive place, with the bungalows starting at US$200.

The *Santrian Beach Cottages* (☎ 288181, fax 288185; PO Box 3055, Denpasar) have private cottages set in a lush garden with a pool and a beach frontage. It's a very attractive place, well located and quite good value at US$60/65 to US$70/75.

Going south on Jalan Danau Tamblingan, the next top-end place is the *Bali Hyatt* (☎ 288271/7; PO Box 392, Denpasar), one of the biggest hotels in Sanur with 36 acres of grounds between the main road and the beach. It's an interesting contrast with the Hotel Bali Beach built 10 years earlier. The lesson had been learnt in the '60s and a regulation was passed that no hotel could be 'taller than a palm tree'. The Hyatt, with its sloping balconies overflowing with tropical vegetation, blends in remarkably well. Look for the interesting pottery tiles used as decorations on various walls. Air-con rooms start at around US$160.

The *Santrian Beach Resort* (☎ 288184, fax 288185), on the beachfront, has air-con double rooms from around US$70, plus two swimming pools and tennis courts. The newer *Sativa Sanur Cottages* (☎ 287881), also near the beach, are attractively arranged around a swimming pool and gardens, with air-con rooms from US$62/72 to US$85/95; US$15 extra in high season.

Further south is the huge *Hotel Sanur Beach* (☎ 288011, fax 287566), with hundreds of air-con rooms from US$110/120 to US$175/200, and suites and bungalows from US$350 to US$900. The *Surya Beach Hotel* (☎ 288833, fax 287303) is the southernmost place in the Sanur strip, so it's pretty tranquil with a frontage to an uncrowded beach – rooms and suites cost from US$90 to US$350.

Places to Eat

All the top-end hotels have their own restaurants, snack bars, coffee bars and bars of course – generally with top-end prices too! The restaurants at Sanur are basically for tourists, and most of them are along the main street so it's easy to compare a few – many have similar menus and prices. Most tourist places have the standard Indonesian dishes, but for cheaper and more authentic Indonesian food, try the rumah makans on the Bypass road, the warungs at the night market, and the food carts and stalls at the northern end of the beach, close to where boats leave for Nusa Lembongan.

The *Jineng Restaurant* does Balinese feasts, and quite a few hotels offer Balinese buffet dinners with Balinese dancing, from about US$15 up to US$75 per head, though you couldn't vouch for the authenticity of either the food or the dancing at some of these functions.

There are lots of places with European food, even a place for homesick pasta lovers – *Trattoria da Marco*, down at the southern end of the beach road – which boasts the best Italian food on Bali. *Ratu's Pizza* is recommended for pizza, as is the *Pualam Restaurant*, at the south end of the main street. The large and conspicuous tourist restaurants on the main street are useful landmarks (that's why they're on the map), but the service can be slow and the food is often disappointing.

For Asian food, there's the *New Seoul Korean Restaurant* halfway down Jalan Danau Tamblingan on the beach side, and the *Nam Ban Kan* Japanese restaurant, a bit further north. *Karya* does Taiwanese and seafood. *Telaga Naga*, opposite the Bali Hyatt which owns it, is about the most expensive place to eat in Sanur, but it offers excellent Szechuan-style Chinese food.

For breakfast, *Donald's Cafe & Bakery* and the *Merry Restaurant* both have excellent coffee, pastries and fruit drinks. The

Borneo Restaurant is one of several places which advertise 'the coldest beer in town', but it is also recommended for breakfast. If you want to eat on the beach, by all means try the food at one of the expensive beachfront hotels, but the restaurants at the *Sanur Beach market* are quite OK. The *Swastika I* and *Swastika II* restaurants get mixed reports, but they're not expensive, and some people say they're great, so they might be worth a try. Agung and Sue's *Watering Hole*, opposite the Natour Grand Bali Beach entrance, has good food at affordable prices. Fast-food addicts can get a fix at the *Kentucky Ayam Goreng* (KFC) or *Swensen's Ice Cream*, both next to the supermarket, on the Bypass road opposite the golf course.

Entertainment
Nightlife is not great in Sanur, but there are a few places to go. Most of the big hotels have bars, but there are not usually enough resident ragers to make them interesting. The fanciest nightspot is the *Matahari* disco at the Hyatt, but drinks are expensive and it's not usually a very energetic scene. The *No 1 Club* has been pretty popular, while *Rumours Nightclub* is a new place that promises more action (if you phone 288054, extension 71, they'll pick you up from your hotel). The slick *Subec* disco is supposed to be popular with locals, but tourists also come here, along with some of the local beachboys and some bar girls who like expensive drinks and Marlboro cigarettes.

Things to Buy
Like Kuta, Sanur has many shops, selling everything from T-shirts to fluoro-print beachwear, as well as a whole range of handcrafts from Bali and other Indonesian islands. The Sanur Beach market, just south of the Natour Grand Bali Beach, has a variety of stalls, so you can shop around. There are plenty of other shops down the main street, as well as two small market areas, each with a cluster of shops. Temptation, near the Hotel Ramayana, has a curious collection of 'artyfacts', including their popular range of fibreglass antiquities from ancient Egypt.

There are a few other art and antique shops, some with very interesting stock – browse on the Bypass road as well as the main tourist road. The sellers are not afraid to ask for an astronomical 'first price', so shop around for some idea of quality and price before you consider parting with your money.

For serious spending sprees, it's easy to commute to shopping centres in Denpasar, Kuta and Nusa Dua. If you're really interested in handcrafts, Sanur is also close to many of the villages which produce stone and woodcarving, jewellery, weavings, basketware and so on. (See the Denpasar to Ubud section at the start of the Ubud chapter.)

The supermarket on the Bypass road is a good place for those small odds and ends that you might need. There's another supermarket at the southern end of town near the Bali Hyatt. The night market, between the Bypass road and Jalan Danau Toba near the northern end of the main street, is open most of the day. It caters a bit for tourists, but still sells fresh vegetables, dried fish, pungent spices, plastic buckets and other household goods.

Getting There & Away
Air See the Getting There & Away chapter for information about flying to or from Bali.

To enable passengers to reconfirm onward flights or buy tickets, most airlines serving Bali have offices in the Natour Grand Bali Beach. Most of them are open Monday to Friday from 8.30 am to 4.30 pm (usually closing for an hour at lunch time), and also on Saturday morning.

Telephone numbers for major airlines are:

Air France – ☎ 287734
Ansett Australia – ☎ 289635
Cathay Pacific – ☎ 288576
China Air – ☎ 287840
Continental – ☎ 287774
Garuda – ☎ 288243, 287920
KLM – ☎ 287576/7
Korean Air – ☎ 289402
Lufthansa – ☎ 287069
Malaysian Airlines – ☎ 288716
Qantas – ☎ 288331
Singapore Airlines – ☎ 288124, 287940
Thai International – ☎ 288063, 288141

Sempati (☎ 281117, 288824), the efficient domestic airline, is open 24 hours a day, every day.

Bemo There is a bemo stop at the southern end of town near where the main street rejoins the Bypass road, and another stop at the northern end of town outside the entrance to the Natour Grand Bali Beach. There are two different bemos operating between Sanur and Denpasar. Coming from Sanur the blue ones go past Kereneng station, across town to Tegal station (the Kuta station), and then back to Kereneng. The green bemos *sometimes* take this route around town but usually just go straight to the Kereneng station. The fare is about 600 rp.

To get from Kuta to Sanur you have to go into Denpasar and then out again. You get one bemo from Kuta into the Tegal bemo station, then get a blue bemo to Sanur via Kereneng. If you get a green bemo at Tegal, it will stop at Kereneng and you'll have to get a third one out to Sanur.

Charter Vehicle You can charter a car or minibus for short trips – it's much faster and more convenient than a public bemo, and between a few people it's not that much more expensive. They congregate at certain points on the main street, and offer their services to any tourist who's on foot. They should take 4000 rp for a trip to Denpasar, 8000 rp to Kuta and 15,000 rp to Ubud, but you'll have to haggle to get them down to these prices.

Boat Boats to Nusa Lembongan leave from the northern end of the beach, in front of the Ananda Hotel & Restaurant. There's a ticket office there, and the fixed price is 15,000 rp (including your surfboard) to get to the island.

Getting Around
To/From the Airport The taxi fare from the airport to Sanur is 12,000 rp, while in the other direction (from Sanur to the airport) the fare is between 8000 and 10,000 rp. Bali's 'super highway', Jalan Baja Letkol Ngurah Rai (the Bypass road), runs from Nusa Dua

in the south, past the airport and Kuta to Sanur and Denpasar. It makes transport along this route quite fast.

Bemo Small bemos shuttle up and down the beach road in Sanur at a cost of 200 rp. Make it clear that you want to take a public bemo, not charter it. Know where you want to go and accept that the driver may take a circuitous route to put down or pick up other passengers.

Rental There are numerous places around Sanur renting cars, motorbikes and bicycles, for about 50,000 rp, 12,000 rp and 5000 rp a day respectively. Vehicle hire is more expensive in Sanur than elsewhere, and some heavy bargaining may be called for.

PULAU SERANGAN
Very close to the shore, south of Sanur and close to the mouth of Benoa Harbour, is Pulau Serangan (Turtle Island). At low tide you can actually walk across to the island. Turtles are captured and fattened here in pens before being sold for village feasts. Eggs are also obtained and hatched, but this is not really a breeding programme – most of the animals (or their eggs) have been taken from the wild, and no contribution is made to the maintenance of natural turtle populations; in fact, this practice may even be depleting them further. (See the Turtles aside in the Facts about Bali chapter for more information on the plight of turtles in Bali.) The island has an important temple, Pura Sakenan, noted for its unusual shrines *(candi)*. Twice a year major temple festivals are held here, attracting great crowds of devotees. The giant puppet figures used in the Barong Landung dance are brought across to the island for these festivals.

Day trips to Serangan have become popular with the travel agencies at Kuta and Sanur, but Serangan has a very strong tourist-trap air and is not terribly popular with visitors. You can see large turtles in their holding lagoon, and baby ones in smaller tanks; you may even see them being fed some seaweed for a bit of action, but no background information is provided on the breeding, farming or traditional importance of turtles. You may be hassled to buy things, even followed and cajoled, but bored indifference is not uncommon treatment.

One traveller who actually enjoyed Serangan said that the southern end of the island was less 'developed' and had nice beaches. The problem is to negotiate a return trip which gives you enough time to walk the length of the island, enjoy the beach, and then walk back. If you want to try this, a boat from Benoa village to the south of Serangan may be a better option, though still quite expensive (see the following section).

Getting There & Away

You can get to Serangan on an organised tour or charter a prahu yourself. The starting price to charter a boat may be around 30,000 rp for a boat big enough for about six people, but you should be able to negotiate the price down to around 12,000 rp. Allow about 20 minutes each way for the trip, and an hour to look around the island. Charters are available from Suwang, a small mangrove inlet near a rubbish dump. Alternatively you can get a prahu from Sanur Beach and back for about 50,000 rp.

JIMBARAN BAY

Just beyond the airport, south of Kuta, Jimbaran Bay is a superb crescent of white sand and blue sea. Jimbaran is a fishing village which has acquired some luxury hotels over the last few years, and seems destined to get more. It doesn't look like any budget hotels, shops or eating places will be allowed to sully the first-class ambience, but if you just want to see the beach, it's accessible from Kuta, only a short distance away. Fishing boats still come in here, and there's a daily fish market at the northern end of the beach.

Places to Stay

The only place resembling budget accommodation, *Puri Indra Prasta*, is away from the beach, on the other side of Jalan Ulu Watu at No 28A. Unfortunately it's not a well-run

place – the rooms are grimy and unattractive, the service is reluctant and the swimming pool is murky. They charge 25,000 rp for singles or doubles, and breakfast is extra.

Puri Bambu Bungalows (☎ 753377, fax 753440) are on the western side of Jalan Ulu Watu, a short walk from the beach. It's a new place, with air-con rooms in three-storey blocks round the pool, but they do have some character and the staff are friendly. Prices range from US$55/65 to US$75/90 which is cheap for Jimbaran, but because it's a new place they may give a good discount.

The first of the 1st-class hotels here, the *Pansea Puri Bali* (☎ 752605, fax 752220), has a full range of facilities and services, including a big swimming pool, two bars, two restaurants (one on the beach) and about 40 air-con bungalows and rooms. They cost US$115/130/160 for singles/doubles/triples (US$30 more in high season), dinner, breakfast and water sports facilities included. To sample the facilities and the location, try a

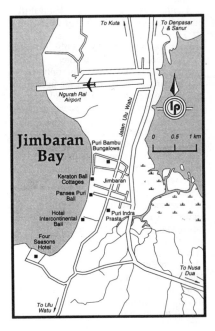

lunch at the beachfront restaurant. A bit to the north, the *Keraton Bali Cottages* (☎ 753991, fax 753881), opened in 1991, are a really fine example of Balinese hotel architecture, with spacious rooms in two-storey cottages surrounded by tastefully landscaped gardens which extend to the beach. They cost from US$100/110 to US$120/140, plus US$10 in the high season.

Further south you'll find the massive *Hotel Intercontinental Bali* (☎ 755055, fax 755056), opened in 1993. The architecture has some Balinese elements, but the scale is so huge that it resembles a fortress from the front. Behind the big front buildings, multistorey wings run towards the beach, with hundreds of rooms in long corridors in a very standard layout, but the whole complex is beautifully decorated with very interesting Balinese arts and handcrafts. Published room rates are from US$165 to US$220 plus US$20 in the high season. Substantial discounts were available soon after the hotel opened.

Another new place, in a completely different style, is the *Four Seasons Hotel* (☎ 71288, fax 71280), with over 100 individual villas spreading down a hillside on the southern edge of Jimbaran Bay – it's like Bali-style tract housing. Not only is the whole complex isolated, but the accommodation is so spread out that little golf buggies are provided to transport guests between their villas and the reception area, restaurants, tennis courts etc – if the service is slow, you'll have to trudge up and down the hillside or you won't be going anywhere. The villas are delightful however, beautifully finished with great views, and yours from just US$275 per night.

If you really like Jimbaran, you can buy a recurring slice of it at the timeshare resort just beyond the Four Seasons.

Places to Eat

The big hotels all have their own restaurants. You can eat in them even if you're not staying there, but expect to pay at least US$10 for lunch or dinner. There are some warungs in the main street, and you'll find cheap food in the market on market days.

BENOA PORT

The wide but shallow bay east of the airport runway, Labuhan Benoa (Benoa Harbour), is one of Bali's main ports. It's also the main harbour for visiting yachts and there are nearly always a few overseas vessels moored here. Pelni ships stop here on their two-week circuits through the islands (☎ 238962; see the Getting There & Away chapter for details). It's also a base for luxury cruises, and for fishing, diving and surfing trips, which are all well publicised in the tourist areas.

Benoa is actually in two parts. Benoa Port is on the northern side, with a two-km-long causeway connecting it to the main Kuta to Sanur road. It consists of little more than a wharf and a variety of port offices. Benoa village is on Tanjung Benoa, the point on the southern side of the bay.

Mabua Express

The *Mabua Express* (☎ 72370, 72521), a luxury jet-powered catamaran providing a fast boat service to Lombok, arrives and departs from Benoa Port. If you've booked your ticket through an agent such as Perama, the deal should include transport to and from Benoa Port. The more expensive 'Diamond Class' tickets include transfer on arrival from Benoa to Kuta, Sanur or Nusa Dua, but you still have to find your own way to Benoa for departures. The *Mabua Express* leaves Benoa Port at 8.30 am and 2.30 pm, takes about two hours to reach Lombok's Lembar Harbour, and costs US$17.50 for 'Emerald Class' and US$25 for 'Diamond Class'; the latter includes transfer from the port of arrival, and drinks and a snack on the boat. Children between two and 12 are charged half price, but may be subjected to two hours of violent video entertainment. Initial demand for the service was low, with only a few of the 248 seats being filled, so prices may eventually be lowered. Telephone for the latest details.

Bali Hai

The *Bali Hai* (☎ 234331) is a luxury tourist excursion boat that operates from Benoa Port. Its sightseeing, diving and surfing trips to various locations around Bali and the offshore islands are well promoted in the main tourist areas. One popular trip is for well-heeled surfers, who pay 115,000 rp to anchor offshore and paddle *in* to the reef breaks off Nusa Lembongan.

Getting There & Away

A public bemo from Denpasar will cost around 600 rp from Suci bemo station, or 1000 rp from Tegal station. A chartered bemo to/from Kuta or Sanur should cost around 5000 rp.

TANJUNG BENOA

On the southern side of Benoa Harbour, the peninsula of Tanjung Benoa extends north from the resort of Nusa Dua. To get to Benoa village, at the northern tip of the peninsula, take the highway to Nusa Dua and then the smaller road along the coast from there. Boats also shuttle back and forth between Benoa Harbour and Benoa village. Benoa is one of Bali's multi-denominational corners, with an interesting Chinese temple, a mosque and a Hindu temple within 100 metres of each other.

The village of Benoa has become much cleaner and more affluent in recent years and the area is something of an activities centre for Nusa Dua. If you want to go windsurfing, parasailing, scuba diving or indulge in various other water sports, there are quite a few water sports centres along the beach. Typical prices are US$10 for an hour of windsurfing, half an hour of snorkelling for two people, one round of parasailing, or a 15-minute ride on a water banana. Waterskiing is US$15 for 15 minutes and a jet ski is US$18 for 15 minutes. The Beluga water sports complex (☎ 71969), at the northern end of the beach, offers most of these, plus a swimming pool in the shape of a beluga whale, scuba courses, cruises and a submarine tour.

The beach is actually nicer at Benoa than in front of the luxury resort hotels, and as you go south, groins and breakwaters are an ominous sign that beach erosion may be under way. Benoa also provides some much cheaper accommodation options than Nusa Dua.

Places to Stay

The places to stay are near the beachfront on the eastern side of the peninsula, and there are many new ones proliferating along the road which heads south to Nusa Dua. They're mostly upper mid-range places, but not nearly as opulent or expensive as the top-end ones in the enclave of Nusa Dua itself.

The *Sorga Nusa Dua* (☎ 71604, fax 71394) is the northernmost hotel, an attractive place with a pool, gardens and a tennis court. Prices for singles/doubles are US$60/65 for standard rooms with air-con and hot water, and US$70/75 for deluxe rooms. *Chez Agung Pension/Homestay* is managed by the Sorga Nusa Dua, and is quite a bit cheaper, around US$40. The *Tanjung Mekar* has nice upstairs rooms for 35,000 rp and downstairs rooms for 25,000 rp, and it's handy to restaurants and the beach. The cheapest place is the simple *Homestay Hasam*, behind the Tanjung Mekar on a lane just west of the main road, which has clean, comfortable singles and doubles from 17,000 rp – good value for this area.

Heading south towards Nusa Dua, the hotels are nearly all upper middle to top-end places with pools and a beach frontage. The *Bali Resort Palace Hotel* (☎ 72026) looks nice, with its cheapest rooms at US$80 a double. *Matahari Terbit Bungalows* have just seven apartments for US$40/50 for singles/ doubles. Just down from there, on the cheap side of the road but only a short walk to the beach, *Rasa Sayang Beach Inn* (☎ 71643) is a cheapie, at 20,000/25,000 rp for fan-cooled rooms, 32,000/40,000 rp with air-con.

Further south, on the beachfront, the *Grand Mirage* (☎ 72147, fax 72148) is a big, brand-new hotel with everything including a four-storey interior waterfall and a price tag

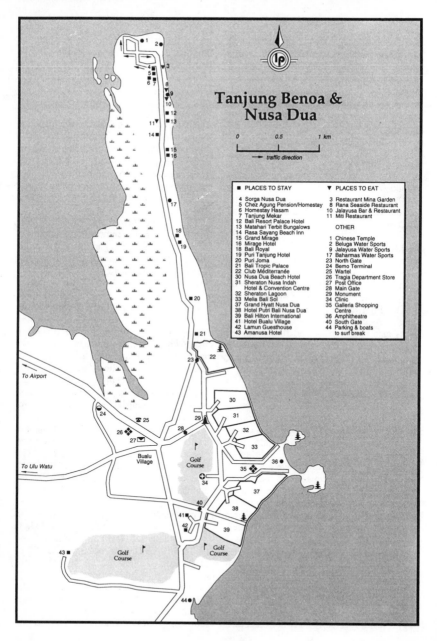

Tanjung Benoa & Nusa Dua

0   0.5   1 km

→ traffic direction

■ PLACES TO STAY

4 Sorga Nusa Dua
5 Chez Agung Pension/Homestay
6 Homestay Hasam
7 Tanjung Mekar
12 Bali Resort Palace Hotel
13 Matahari Terbit Bungalows
14 Rasa Sayang Beach Inn
15 Grand Mirage
16 Mirage Hotel
18 Bali Royal
19 Puri Tanjung Hotel
20 Puri Joma
21 Bali Tropic Palace
22 Club Méditerranée
30 Nusa Dua Beach Hotel
31 Sheraton Nusa Indah
   Hotel & Convention Centre
32 Sheraton Lagoon
33 Melia Bali Sol
37 Grand Hyatt Nusa Dua
38 Hotel Putri Bali Nusa Dua
39 Bali Hilton International
41 Hotel Bualu Village
42 Lamun Guesthouse
43 Amanusa Hotel

▼ PLACES TO EAT

3 Restaurant Mina Garden
8 Rana Seaside Restaurant
10 Jalayusa Bar & Restaurant
11 Miti Restaurant

OTHER

1 Chinese Temple
2 Beluga Water Sports
9 Jalayusa Water Sports
17 Baharmas Water Sports
23 North Gate
25 Bemo Terminal
26 Tragia Department Store
27 Post Office
28 Main Gate
29 Monument
34 Clinic
35 Galleria Shopping
   Centre
36 Amphitheatre
40 South Gate
44 Parking & boats
   to surf break

To Airport

To Ulu Watu

Bualu Village

Golf Course

Golf Course

Golf Course

from US$145 a double (and that may be a cheap introductory offer). Prices at the *Mirage Hotel*, next door, are not quite so grand, from US$115; it's the older of these comfortable siblings, which are currently sharing a phone number.

After some construction sites (more hotels!) you reach the *Bali Royal* (☎ 71039), a small place with a pretty garden and just 14 air-con suites from US$95/140 for singles/doubles. The *Puri Tanjung* (☎ 72121, fax 72424) is a little bigger, with 64 rooms, and a lot cheaper at US$60 to US$90 for doubles. Continuing south, the last place before the entrance gate to the Nusa Dua enclave is another small one, the *Puri Joma* (☎ 71526), with only 10 rooms and a very quiet atmosphere. It's good value for this area at US$45/55, and US$10 more in high season.

Places to Eat

There are several restaurants in Benoa village, like the *Barakuda Bar & Restaurant*, the *Miti Restaurant*, the *Jalayusa Restaurant* and the *Rana Seaside Restaurant*. They're mostly on the beachfront opposite the hotels, and they're a little expensive by Bali's usual standards, but bargains compared with Nusa Dua prices. You should be able to find a warung in the village for even cheaper food. Down towards the Bali Resort entrance, the *Bambu Indah* is popular with hotel staff, and some tourist restaurants are starting to emerge along this road.

Getting There & Away

Public bemos go up and down the Tanjung Benoa road. First get to the Bualu terminal just outside the Nusa Dua enclave (1000 rp from Tegal), then get another one from there going north.

NUSA DUA

Nusa Dua is Bali's top-end beach resort – a luxury tourist enclave, planned to ensure that the mistakes of Kuta would not be repeated! In a major departure from the development at Kuta, Nusa Dua was planned from the early 1970s, with advice from the World Bank. The site was chosen not just for its fine

weather and white beaches, but also because the area was dry, relatively barren, sparsely populated, and isolated from most of Bali's population centres. The objective was an isolated luxury resort, which would bring in the tourist dollars whilst having minimal impact on the rest of Bali.

The underlying philosophy reflects a change in tourism strategy. The idea of 'cultural tourism', which emerged in Ubud in response to the hedonism and 'cultural pollution' of Kuta, was to protect Bali's culture by selectively promoting and presenting aspects of it to tourists. There was an attempt to restrict tourism development to the Kuta-Sanur-Ubud area, but as mass-tourism boomed, the sheer number of visitors was seen as a problem. The solution was a strategy of 'elite tourism', which would derive more revenue from fewer visitors. The authorities were probably not so naive as to think that rich tourists would be more culturally sensitive, but at least their impact could be largely confined to resort enclaves, where the cultural tourist attractions could be recreated with visiting dance troupes, gamelan muzak and Balinese decor.

The strategy has succeeded in that Nusa Dua has sprouted a crop of suitably sumptuous five-star hotels, with international connections to market their attractions and prices high enough to generate the desired revenue. It has also succeeded in creating a resort which is totally isolated from the realities of everyday life on Bali. Within the resort compound there are no schools, no banjars and no independent developments – you have a km or so to walk if you want to get even so much as a Coke at less than international hotel prices, or if you want to get a bemo to the rest of Bali.

Nusa Dua literally means 'two islands', which are actually small raised headlands, connected to the mainland by sand spits. The beach itself is very pleasant, but the water is shallow at low tide, there is a lot of seaweed, and some signs of erosion on the beaches just north of the resort. Other environmental impacts include the huge demand for electricity and water, both of which may have to be imported from Java in the future if development continues.

Information

Telephone Nusa Dua is in the 0361 telephone zone.

Activities

The best surfing at Nusa Dua is on the reef to the north and south of the two 'islands'. 'Sri Lanka' is a right hander in front of Club Med. The other breaks are reached by boat from the beach south of the Hilton. They work best with a big swell during the wet season.

Even if you're not staying in Nusa Dua, you could probably get a game of golf at the country club, hire a bicycle to explore the resort on the many cycle paths, or try some horse riding, from the stables behind the Bali Tourist Development Corporation (BTDC) office. For water sports, go to the centres on Tanjung Benoa (see the previous section).

Shopping is a very popular activity in Nusa Dua (see under Things to Buy).

Places to Stay

The Nusa Dua hotels all have swimming pools, a variety of restaurants and bars, entertainment and sports facilities and various other international hotel mod cons. All these places add 17.5% tax and service, and many charge an extra US$25 or so as a high-season supplement.

Starting at the northern end of the resort enclave, there is *Club Méditerranée Bali*, which is strictly a package-tour operation. It differs from other hotels in that all meals, activities and water sports facilities are included in the price, and the place is so self-contained that it's an enclave within an enclave. Rates start at around US$90 per person per night in the low season, or US$45 for children. A complete range of children's activities is a feature of Club Med holidays.

A Westin Resort is under construction next to Club Med, and south of that is the five-star *Nusa Dua Beach Hotel* (☎ 71210, fax 71229) which is huge (400 rooms), with all the luxuries you could expect and prices from around US$140 to US$150 for standard rooms, plus service and tax. It's attractively designed using Balinese architecture and statuary, but then how seriously can you take a hotel that promotes itself as being the place where Ronald Reagan stayed when he came to Bali?

The *Sheraton Nusa Indah Hotel* (☎ 71906, fax 71908) hasn't as many Balinese decorative touches, but it has all the luxuries, and it pitches for the conference market with the adjacent Bali International Convention Centre, which has a large auditorium and exhibition facilities. The *Sheraton Lagoon* (☎ 71327, fax 72326) unashamedly caters for those who want a luxury holiday, with all sorts of recreational facilities and a huge swimming pool (they call it a swimmable lagoon) which features sandy beaches, landscaped islands and cascading waterfalls. Rooms start at US$165, but for US$205 you can get one with a balcony from which you can flop straight into the pool.

The 500-room *Hotel Melia Bali Sol* (☎ 71510) is run by a Spanish hotel group, and does offer some Mediterranean touches in the food and entertainment, as well as rooms from US$150, and suites from US$325 to US$1000. It's just north of Nusa Dua's 'amenity core', which has the large Galleria shopping centre, restaurants, bank, phones, an amphitheatre and an emergency clinic.

South of the amenity core is the new, 750-room *Grand Hyatt Nusa Dua* (☎ 71234, fax 71084), where Ronald Reagan probably would have stayed but it wasn't finished in time. Built on a massive budget, it is pressing for the title as one of the best hotels on Bali, and charges US$150/170 for its cheapest rooms, but has suites and villas from US$450 to US$2000. Two of the Grand Hyatt's chefs wrote the Periplus book on the food of Bali, which is a good reason to stay here. Another reason might be the Camp Nusa kids programme, which offers a whole day of supervised activities for US$30.

South again is the *Hotel Putri Bali Nusa Dua* (☎ 71020, fax 71139) which has 384 rooms, plus suites, cottages and so on. It's cheaper than some Nusa Dua palaces, from US$110/125 to US$165, but has a comprehensive list of extra charges for tennis courts (US$5 to US$7 per hour), racket (US$2 per hour), shoes (US$2 per hour), a ball boy (US$1.50 per hour) and just about every other recreational facility – even chess is an extra US$1 per hour.

The *Bali Hilton* (☎ 71102, fax 71199) is the most southerly hotel on the Nusa Dua beach. It's a massive place with a full range of convention and leisure facilities, and rooms from US$110 to US$170, suites from US$395 to US$895, and the Ayodya Palace suite at US$1850.

Just inland from the Hilton is the smaller *Hotel Bualu Village* (☎ 71310, fax 71313). Formerly Hotel Club Bualu, it was the first hotel at Nusa Dua, and was used as a training facility by the BPLP (the Hotel & Tourism Training Institute) to prepare staff for employment in the luxury hotels which were then in the planning stages. It's away from the beach, and not as elegant as its newer neighbours, but it's smaller with just 50 rooms, and it has a more friendly, informal atmosphere. Most sporting facilities are included, and the prices are quite modest at US$69/79 for single/double rooms, and US$112 for a suite.

Adjacent to the Hotel Bualu Village is the closest you will come to budget accommodation in Nusa Dua. The *Lamun Guesthouse* (☎ 71983, fax 71985) is the current training ground of the Hotel & Tourism Training Institute, and has air-con rooms for US$22/25 including tax. Unfortunately the rooms are very ordinary, the location is nowhere and the service could be anything from overattentive to nonexistent.

On a hill overlooking the golf course to the south of the resort area, the *Amanusa* (☎ 72333, fax 72335) is one of Bali's three new Aman resorts. Small, understated, with sublime architecture, superb decorations and brilliant views, it is setting new standards in taste and elegance, from US$300 to US$700.

Places to Eat

The Nusa Dua hotels offer a large number of restaurants, usually several in each hotel. There are also a few eating possibilities in the Galleria shopping centre, but they're just as expensive, and still a fair hike from most hotels. For cheaper eating, it's a long walk to get out of the resort area – you can't just stroll

outside to other restaurants, as you can at Sanur. If you can make it to Bualu village, just to the west, you can find the places where the hotel staff eat, which offer better value for money.

Things to Buy

Shopping facilities are becoming a major attraction at Nusa Dua. The large Galleria complex (☎ 71662, 71663) in the middle of the resort enclave has an excellent range of clothing, footwear and leather goods, from local manufacturers and major international brand names. There's also imported sporting gear, and handcrafts from Bali and all over Indonesia – not the cheapest, but some of the most interesting examples. It's fully air-conditioned, credit cards are accepted, and the service is attentive but not pushy. The general price levels are competitive by international standards, and there are occasional sales with some real bargains. The Galleria also features smaller shops, stalls and boutiques, services like photo processing, and an outdoor amphitheatre for cultural shows. Unexpected delights like a Rangda undulating through the complex, or a playful Hanuman monkey making mischief, add a touch of fun and remind you that it's not really a mall in California, even if it looks like one.

Just outside the Nusa Dua enclave, along the Denpasar road near the Bualu village area, are a number of Kuta-Sanur style tourist shops, and the Tragia supermarket and department store (☎ 72170, 72172). They're probably a bit cheaper than the Galleria, but not as flashy. There's actually a bit of Kuta bustle out here, and it's a refreshing change from the orderly, uncrowded enclave inside the gates. If you want to shop for quality goods, you'll probably enjoy a day trip to Nusa Dua.

Getting There & Away

The taxi fare from the airport is 12,000 rp. A bemo from Denpasar costs around 700 rp from Suci bemo station (1000 rp from Tegal station) to the bemo terminal in Bualu village, just outside the Nusa Dua compound. It is about a km from there to the hotels. The bemo service operates on demand but there's usually one every hour, and more when the hotel staff are finishing their shifts – many people commute from Denpasar to Nusa Dua. You can easily charter a whole bemo between Kuta and Nusa Dua for around 8000 rp, but avoid being pressured into chartering a bemo by yourself if you're happy to wait for the public one. If you want to shop, call the Galleria or Tragia and they may provide transport.

BUKIT PENINSULA
The southern peninsula is known as Bukit (*bukit* means 'hill' in Indonesian), but was known to the Dutch as Tafelhoek (Table Point). This is a dry, sparsely inhabited area – a contrast to the lush, rice-growing country which seems to begin immediately north of the airport. The road south from Kuta goes around the end of the airport runway, and the main route goes south then east to Nusa Dua. A couple of turn-offs to the west will take you to Jimbaran village, where the main road, Jalan Ulu Watu, continues right down to the end of the peninsula at Ulu Watu. The road is now sealed for the whole distance. At times the road climbs quite high, reaching 200 metres, and there are fine views back over the airport, Kuta and southern Bali. When you see the Ugly Boys 'restaurant' on the left side near the top of a rise, you'll know you're getting close to the surf.

Along the road you'll notice numerous limestone quarries where large blocks of stone are cut by hand. Many of the buildings in southern Bali are constructed from such blocks. Further inland there are some industrial developments, making pre-formed concrete products from the local limestone cement.

Pura Luhur Ulu Watu
The temple of Ulu Watu perches at the south-western tip of the peninsula, where sheer cliffs drop precipitously into the clear blue sea – the temple hangs right over the edge! You enter it through an unusual arched gateway flanked by statues of Ganesh;

there's a resident horde of monkeys in the compound. Ulu Watu is one of several important temples to the spirits of the sea to be found along the southern coast of Bali. Others include Tanah Lot and Rambut Siwi.

Ulu Watu, along with the other well-known temples of the south – Pura Sakenan on Pulau Serangan, Pura Petitenget at Kerobokan and the temple at Tanah Lot – is associated with Nirartha, the Javanese priest credited with introducing many of the elements of the Balinese religion to the island. Nirartha retreated to Ulu Watu for his final days.

Surfing
Ulu Watu has another claim to fame. It's Bali's surfing mecca, made famous through several classic surfing films. It's a popular locale for surfers who flock to Bali from all over the world, but particularly from Australia. At a dip in the road, just before the Ulu Watu carpark, a sign indicates the way to the Suluban Surf Beach (Pantai Suluban). There will be a crowd of guys on motorbikes here, waiting to taxi you down towards the beach. It's two or three km down a narrow footpath – OK for motorbikes but nothing more. Take care on a motorbike – the path is narrow, some of the corners are blind and there have been some nasty accidents. From a motorbike park at the end of the track you continue on foot another 250 metres, down to the small gorge which gives access to the surf. There are half a dozen warungs on the northern side of the gorge, perched on a cliff with great views of the various surf breaks. All the serious surfers bring their own boards, but you can hire one here for about 5000 rp an hour. You can also get wax, ding repair stuff, food, beer and a massage, depending on what you need most.

There are other great surf breaks around the south-west tip of the Bukit Peninsula, notably Padang Padang, Bingin, and Balangan. All of them are now well known to surfers – for details, see under Surfing in the Facts for the Visitor chapter. Most of them are accessible by somewhat rough roads, and a short walk. Typically there is a carpark at the end of the road (parking costs a few hundred rupiah), and a warung or two with snacks and beer. There's usually a well-maintained track down the cliffs to a sandy cove between high bluffs, and these are some of the prettiest beaches on Bali, practically deserted when the surf isn't working.

On the south coast of the Bukit Peninsula are two quite dangerous breaks. They are much more exposed, and not as suitable for a casual visit. Nyang Nyang is reached by a difficult track down the cliffs, but Green Ball is more accessible since the opening of the Bali Cliffs Resort Hotel.

Places to Stay & Eat

The surf spots have warungs around the cliff tops which offer basic Indonesian food (nasi and mie), Western fare (jaffles and pancakes) and expensive beer. These warungs are not really places to stay, but surfers are sometimes able to crash in them to get an early start on the morning waves. Apart from these, there are virtually no places offering cheap accommodation – the few cheap losmen look like pretty makeshift arrangements and are possibly not legal.

The *Bali Cliffs Resort Hotel* is a luxury hotel perched on the cliff top, with rooms offering great ocean views. A scenic elevator goes down the cliff to the restaurant and the beach. It's expensive of course, from around US$110, but you might be able to negotiate a good rate in the off season until it's well established on the package-tour market – they won't get any passing trade here.

There are a few places to eat along the road into Ulu Watu. The *Pub Batu Karung* has food and beer at near Kuta prices, and is planning to provide some bungalows. The *Restaurant Puncak Pesona* is expensive, probably a stop for tour groups. *Ugly Boys* is mainly for beer, while the *Warung Indra*, opposite, looks more like a restaurant and has good, cheap food and a shop selling a few basics like sunblock and film. Further on is the *Corner Pub* and a place to buy petrol.

Ubud & Around

Perched on the gentle slopes leading up towards the central mountains, Ubud is the cultural centre of Bali and has attracted visitors interested in Bali's arts and crafts ever since Walter Spies established it as the centre for the cultured visitors of the '30s. Apart from the many places of interest in Ubud itself, there are also numerous temples, ancient sites and interesting craft centres around the town, while the road up to Ubud from the southern tourist centres (Denpasar, Nusa Dua, Sanur and Kuta) leads through a dense corridor of craft shops and galleries.

Denpasar to Ubud

The road from Denpasar via Batubulan, Celuk, Sukawati, Batuan and Mas is lined with places making and selling handcrafts. Many tourists stop and shop along this route, but there are also alternative, quieter routes between the two towns, where much of the craftwork is done in small workshops and family compounds.

BATUBULAN

Soon after leaving Denpasar the road is lined with outlets for stone sculpture, the main craft of Batubulan, which means 'moon stone'. Stone carvers continue along the road to Tegaltamu, where the main road to Ubud does a sharp right turn while the back-road route continues straight on. Batubulan is where the temple gate guardians – seen all over Bali – come from. The sculpting is often done by quite young boys and you're welcome to watch them chipping away at big blocks of stone. The stone they use is surprisingly soft and light, so if you've travelled to Bali fairly light it's quite feasible to fly home with a stone demon in your baggage!

Not surprisingly the temples around Batubulan are noted for their fine stone sculptures. Pura Puseh, just a couple of hundred metres to the east of the busy main road, is worth a visit.

Batubulan is also a centre for a variety of antique crafts, textiles and woodwork, and has some well-regarded dance troupes. A Barong & Rangda dance is held in Batubulan every morning. It's touristy and there's a stampede of souvenir sellers afterwards but if you don't get a chance to see a performance elsewhere then it's worth catching. Starting time is 10 am and the cost is about 6000 rp.

CELUK

Travelling from Batubulan to Celuk you move from stone to filigree, for Celuk is the silver and goldsmithing centre of Bali. There are numerous jewellery specialists, with a wide variety of pieces on sale, or you can order your own design. All are generally very busy after the morning dance in Batubulan finishes.

SUKAWATI

Before the turn-off to Mas and Ubud, Sukawati is a centre for the manufacture of those noisy wind chimes you hear all over the island, and also specialises in temple umbrellas and lontar (palm) baskets, dyed

with intricate patterns. Sukawati, a bustling town with a morning produce market, also has a busy art and craft market, the Pasar Seni. It's just across from the produce market and sells semifinished artwork to craft shops who add the final touches themselves. The old palace is behind the produce market.

The town has a long tradition of dance and wayang kulit shadow puppet performance. The small village of Puaya, about a km west from the main road, specialises in making high-quality leather shadow puppets and masks.

There's an alternative little-used route via the coast, bypassing Batubulan and Celuk and rejoining the main road to Ubud just before Sukawati. It passes through the coastal village of Gumicik (which has a good beach) and, just back from the coast, the village of Ketewel, a surf spot. A road branches off from Ketewel to the beach at Pabean, a site for religious purification ceremonies. Just north of Ketewel, before the main road, is Guang, another small wood-carving centre.

BATUAN

Batuan is a noted painting centre which came under the influence of Bonnet, Spies and the Pita Maha artists' co-operative at an early stage. Batuan painters produced dynamic black-ink drawings, good examples of which can be seen in Ubud's Puri Lukisan Museum. The big Batuan galleries have the usual range of work on display but some original work still comes from this village.

Today, the distinct Batuan style of painting is noted for its inclusion of some very modern elements. Sea scenes are likely to include the odd windsurfer while tourists with video cameras or riding motorbikes pop up in the otherwise traditional Balinese scenery. Batuan is also noted for its traditional dance classes and is a centre for carved wooden relief panels and screens.

MAS

Mas means 'gold' but it's woodcarving, particularly mask carving, which is the craft here. The great Majapahit priest Nirartha

once lived here and Pura Taman Pule is said to be built on the site of his home. During the three-day Kuningan Festival, a Wayang Wong performance (an older version of the Ramayana ballet) is put on in the temple's courtyard.

The road through Mas is almost solidly lined with craft shops which do most business by the tour bus-load, but there are plenty of smaller carving operations in the lanes off the busy main road. Many of these places produce carvings in bulk, which are then sold to the numerous craft shops. The bigger and more successful outlets are often lavishly

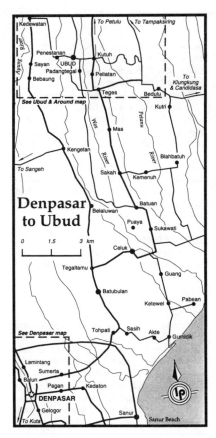

Topeng masks

decorated with fine woodcarvings. The renowned artist Ida Bagus Tilem, whose father was also a noted woodcarver, has a particularly fine gallery.

If you want to stay in Mas, *Taman Harum Cottages* has elegant individual bungalows, some of them two-storeyed with balconies overlooking the rice paddies, and there's a swimming pool – prices are from about US$40.

From Mas you can follow the main road the last few km into Ubud or take back-road routes and approach the town through Pengosekan, Padangtegal or even the Monkey Forest.

BLAHBATUH

Although the most direct route to Ubud is to turn off the main road at Sakah and head north through Mas, you can continue on a few km to the turn-off to Blahbatuh and go via Kutri and Bedulu before turning off again for Ubud. In Blahbatuh the Pura Gaduh has a metre-high stone head said to be a portrait of Kebo Iwa, the legendary strongman and minister to the last king of the Bedulu kingdom (see under Bedulu and Gunung Kawi in the Around Ubud section of this chapter). Gajah Mada, the Majapahit strongman, realised that he could not conquer Bedulu, Bali's strongest kingdom, while Kebo Iwa was there so he lured him away to

Java (with promises of women and song) and had him killed.

The stone head is thought to be very old, possibly predating Javanese influence on Bali, but the temple is a reconstruction of an earlier temple destroyed in the great earthquake of 1917.

About a km west of Blahbatuh on the Petanu River is the Tegenungan Waterfall (also known as Srog Srogan) at Belang Singa village. There's a signpost to 'Air Terjun Tegenungan' (*terjun* means waterfall) from the village of Kemenuh on the main road.

KUTRI

Just north of Blahbatuh on the western side of the road is Pura Kedarman (also known as Pura Bukit Dharma). If you climb Bukit Dharma nearby (*bukit* means hill), you'll find a panoramic view, and a hilltop shrine with a stone statue of the eight-armed goddess Durga killing a demon-possessed water buffalo. The statue is thought to date from the 11th century and shows strong Indian influences.

Another theory is that the image is of Airlangga's mother Mahendradatta, who married King Udayana, Bali's 10th-century ruler. When her son succeeded to the throne she hatched a bitter plot against him and unleashed *leyaks* (evil spirits) upon his kingdom. She was eventually defeated but this incident eventually led to the legend of the rangda, a widow-witch and ruler of evil spirits. The temple at the base of the hill has images of Durga and the body of a barong can be seen in the *bale barong*; the sacred head is kept elsewhere.

Ubud

In the hills north of Denpasar, Ubud is the centre of 'cultural tourism' on Bali. It has undergone tremendous development in the past few years, and now has problems of traffic congestion in the centre and urban sprawl on the edges. On the whole though, Ubud has managed to stay relaxed and beautiful, a place where the evenings are quiet and you can really tell you're on Bali. Electricity only arrived in Ubud in the mid-70s (and is still not completely reliable), and telephones in the late-80s. There's an amazing amount to do in and around Ubud so don't plan to do it in a day. You need at least a few days to appreciate it properly and Ubud is one of those places where days can quickly become weeks and weeks become months.

Orientation
The once small village of Ubud has expanded to encompass its neighbours – Campuan, Penestanan, Padangtegal, Peliatan and Pengosekan are all part of what we see as Ubud today. The crossroads, where the bemos stop, marks the centre of town. On the north (kaja) side is the Ubud Palace, on the south (kelod) side is the market. Monkey Forest Rd, beside the market, runs south to, of course, the Monkey Forest and Ubud's pura dalem (temple of the dead). The main east-west road is Jalan Raya Ubud.

There's a one-way traffic system in the centre of town. The top of Monkey Forest Rd, north of the football field, is north-bound only to the main road; the main road is one-way going east from there to Jalan Hanoman; Jalan Hanoman is south-bound to Jalan Bima, which goes west to Monkey Forest Rd, completing the clockwise-only circuit. It means a substantial detour if you want to drive through town on the main road from east to west.

Continuing west of Ubud, the road drops steeply down to the ravine at Campuan where you find Murni's Warung on one side of the suspension bridge, artist Antonio Blanco's house on the other and the Campuan Hotel on the site of Walter Spies' prewar home. From there the road bends north past many craft shops and galleries. Penestanan, famous for its painters, is just west of Campuan. Further west again is Sayan, where musician Colin McPhee lived in the '30s.

Entering Ubud from Denpasar the road passes through Peliatan before reaching the junction on Ubud's east side.

Information
Ubud is just high enough to be noticeably cooler than the coast. It's also noticeably wetter. For getting around Ubud, and especially the surrounding villages, the best map is *Bali Pathfinder*, obtainable in the main street just west of the tourist office – look for their logo, a figure with a pointing hand instead of a head.

Tourist Office Ubud has a very friendly and helpful tourist office *(bina wisata)* on the main street. The Ubud tourist office is a local venture, set up in an effort to defend the village from the tourist onslaught – not by opposing tourism but by providing a service aimed at informing and generating a respect amongst visitors for Balinese culture and customs.

The sheer number of tourists, and the insensitivity of a few, can still be intrusive, but to some extent these problems have been alleviated by increasing commercialisation of the tourist industry. Most visitors who witness traditional ceremonies do so through a tour agency or guide. Part of the guide's job is to ensure that his or her charges go only where they are welcome and behave with appropriate decorum. If they don't the community hold the guides responsible, and will perhaps deny them access in the future. Also, the Balinese have made some decisions as to which ceremonies can be open and public, and which must be conducted with discretion; visitors will not learn of the latter ones through the normal sources of information.

Post The pleasant little post office, with a poste restante service, is towards the east end of Jalan Raya. Have mail addressed to Kantor Pos, Ubud, Bali, Indonesia. You can also get stamps at a few places around town, identified by a 'postal services' sign.

Telephone Many hotels and losmen have telephones, but it can be expensive to use them with the hotel taking a large cut. You can make international direct-dial calls and send faxes from the telephone offices in Ubud. There's a private one upstairs on the main street near the Nomad Restaurant, between the market and the post office turnoff. A Telkom wartel is at the east end of town, on the road going north towards Penelokan. All of Ubud and the surrounding villages are in the 0361 telephone district. Old five-digit phone numbers starting with 95 need an extra digit; they should now start with 975.

Bookshops The Ubud Bookshop is excellent; it's on the main road right next to Ary's Warung in central Ubud. The Ganesha Bookshop, on the main street almost opposite the post office, has sections on travel, women's issues, arts etc.

Other Information There's the usual varied selection of bicycle and motorbike hire places and a number of shops selling most items you might require. The supermarket is in the main street west of the tourist office. Ubud has a couple of banks in the main street, but they're not as fast as the numerous moneychangers and they do not offer as good an exchange rate.

Ubud's colourful produce market operates every third day. It starts early in the morning but pretty much winds up by lunch time. The craft market in the building on the corner of Monkey Forest Rd and Jalan Raya Ubud operates every day, as does the *pasar malam* (night market).

Museums

Ubud has two interesting museums, numerous galleries with art for sale and there are a number of artists' homes which you can visit to view their work.

Puri Lukisan Museum On the main street of Ubud the Puri Lukisan (Palace of Fine Arts) was established in the mid-50s and displays fine examples of all schools of Balinese art. It was in Ubud that the modern Balinese art movement started, where artists first began to abandon purely religious and court subjects for scenes of everyday life. Rudolf Bonnet, who played such an important role in this change, helped establish the museum's permanent collection in 1973. It's a relatively small museum and has some excellent art.

You enter the museum by crossing a river gully beside the road and wander from building to building through beautiful gardens with pools, statues and fountains.

The museum is open from 8 am to 4 pm daily and admission is 500 rp. There are exhibitions of art for sale in other buildings in the gardens and in a separate display just outside the main garden.

Museum Neka If you continue beyond the suspension bridge at Campuan for another km or so, you'll find the Museum Neka. The museum, opened in 1982, is housed in a number of separate buildings and has a diverse and interesting collection, principally of modern Balinese art. Also on display is some of the work of other important Indonesian artists and Western artists who have resided or worked on Bali.

Balinese paintings have been defined as falling into four groups or styles, all of which are represented in the Museum Neka. First, there are the classical or Kamasan paintings from the village of Kamasan near Klungkung. Then there are the Ubud paintings which basically fall into two subgroups: the older or traditional Ubud paintings are still heavily influenced by the prewar Pita Maha artists' circle while the postwar

Young Artists' styles were influenced by Dutch artist Arie Smit, still an Ubud resident. The third group is the Batuan paintings which, in some respects, look like a blend of the old and new Ubud styles but are also notable for the modern elements which often sneak into their designs. Finally, there are the modern or 'academic' paintings, which can be loosely defined as anything which doesn't fall into the main Balinese categories – they show influences of everything from the Post-Impressionists to Rothko.

The Balinese collection includes numerous works by I Gusti Nyoman Lempad, the Balinese artist who played a key role in the establishment of the Pita Maha group. Some of these works were from the collection of Walter Spies. Other works read like a roll call of the best Balinese artists including Gusti Made Deblog, Gusti Ketut Kobot, Ida Bagus Made, Anak Agung Gede Sobrat, Made Sukada and many others. Works by artists from other parts of Indonesia include those of Abdul Aziz, Dullah, Affandi and Srihadi Sudarsono.

The museum's collection of work by Western artists is superb and covers almost every well-known name. Current residents like Arie Smit, Han Snel and Antonio Blanco are represented but there are also works by Theo Meier, Willem Hofker, Le Mayeur de Merpres, Walter Spies and Rudolf Bonnet. Miguel Covarrubias, whose book *Island of Bali* remains the best introduction to the island's art and culture, is represented, as is Australian artist Donald Friend with, among others, his delightful painting of Batu Jimbar village. The collection includes works by Louise Koke who, with her husband Robert Koke, founded the original hotel at Kuta Beach in the 1930s.

Admission to the museum is 500 rp.

Galleries

Ubud is dotted with galleries – every street and alley seems to have a place exhibiting artwork for sale. They're enormously variable in the choice and quality of items on display. There are two 'must see' Ubud art galleries where a huge variety of work is displayed, generally of a very high quality, at prices which are often similarly elevated. Suteja Neka not only operates the Museum

---

Dogs

If there's one thing wrong with Bali it has to be those horrible, mangy, flea-bitten, grovelling, dirty, noisy, disgusting *anjing* (that's the Indonesian word for dog) or, in high Balinese, *asu* or in low Balinese *cicing*. If you prefer, use asu when you're referring to dogs in a good way, cicing in a bad. Dogs are rarely referred to as asu!

Just why does Bali have so many dogs? Well, they're scavengers, garbage clearers, and they're simply accepted as part of the picture. It's widely, and probably correctly, thought that demons inhabit them, which is why you often see them gobbling down the offerings put out for the bad spirits. A popular theory is that they were created simply to keep things in balance – with

everything in Bali so beautiful and picturesque the dogs were put there to provide a contrast. Ubud is particularly well endowed with anjing – terrible, apocalyptic dogs that howl all night long like it's the end of the world.

There may have been some decline in the dog population over the last few years, though there has been no mass extermination campaign. Wherever the subject was raised, locals made knowing comments about people, always from another part of Bali, who allegedly caught the dogs to eat them. Balinese dogs certainly don't look appetising, but if it's helping to get rid of them, *selamat makan* (bon apetit). ∎

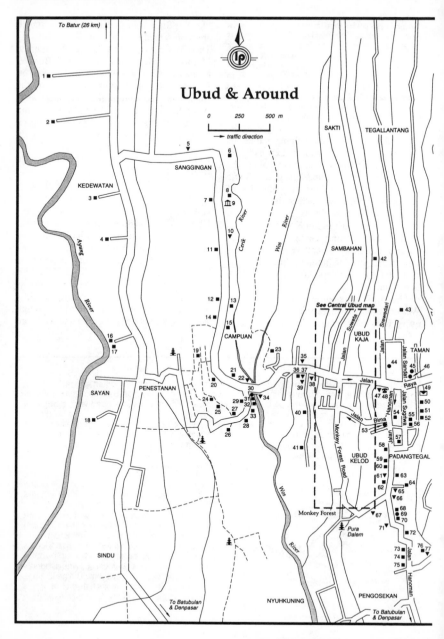

To Batur (26 km)

Ubud & Around

0   250   500 m

→ traffic direction

SAKTI   TEGALLANTANG

SANGGINGAN

KEDEWATAN

Cerik River

Wos River

SAMBAHAN

See Central Ubud map

CAMPUAN

UBUD KAJA

Jalan Suweta

Jalan Srewedari

Jalan Sandat

Jalan

TAMAN

PENESTANAN

Jalan Raya

SAYAN

Jalan Hanoman

Jalan Bima

Jalan Suqriwa

PADANGTEGAL

Monkey Forest Road

Jalan

UBUD KELOD

Wos River

Monkey Forest

Pura Dalem

Jalan Hanoman

SINDU

To Batubulan & Denpasar

NYUHKUNING

PENGOSEKAN

To Batubulan & Denpasar

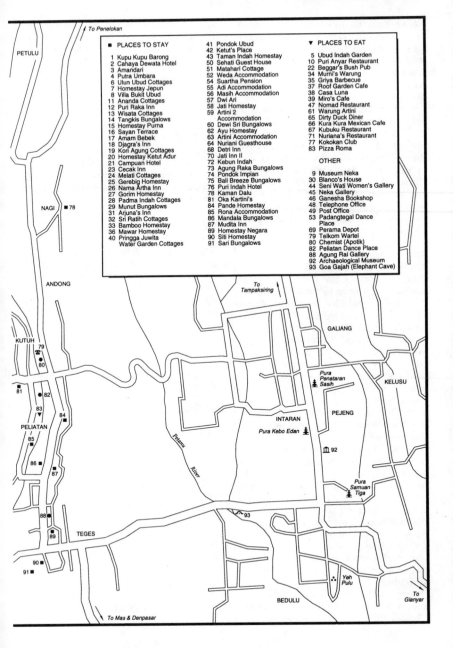

■ PLACES TO STAY

1 Kupu Kupu Barong
2 Cahaya Dewata Hotel
3 Amandari
4 Putra Umbara
6 Ulun Ubud Cottages
7 Homestay Jepun
8 Villa Bukit Ubud
11 Ananda Cottages
12 Puri Raka Inn
13 Wisata Cottages
14 Tangkis Bungalows
15 Homestay Purna
16 Sayan Terrace
17 Amam Bebek
18 Djagra's Inn
19 Kori Agung Cottages
20 Homestay Ketut Adur
21 Campuan Hotel
23 Cecak Inn
24 Melati Cottages
25 Gerebig Homestay
26 Nama Artha Inn
27 Gorim Homestay
28 Padma Indah Cottages
29 Munut Bungalows
31 Arjuna's Inn
32 Sri Ratih Cottages
33 Bamboo Homestay
36 Mawar Homestay
40 Pringga Juwita
   Water Garden Cottages

41 Pondok Ubud
42 Ketut's Place
43 Taman Indah Homestay
50 Sehati Guest House
51 Matahari Cottage
52 Weda Accommodation
54 Suartha Pension
55 Adi Accommodation
56 Masih Accommodation
57 Dwi Ari
58 Jati Homestay
59 Artini 2
   Accommodation
60 Dewi Sri Bungalows
62 Ayu Homestay
63 Artini Accommodation
64 Nuriani Guesthouse
68 Detri Inn
70 Jati Inn II
72 Kebun Indah
73 Agung Raka Bungalows
74 Pondok Impian
75 Bali Breeze Bungalows
76 Puri Indah Hotel
78 Kaman Dalu
81 Oka Kartini's
84 Pande Homestay
85 Rona Accommodation
86 Mandala Bungalows
87 Mudita Inn
89 Homestay Negara
90 Siti Homestay
91 Sari Bungalows

▼ PLACES TO EAT

5 Ubud Indah Garden
10 Puri Anyar Restaurant
22 Beggar's Bush Pub
34 Murni's Warung
35 Griya Barbecue
37 Roof Garden Cafe
38 Casa Luna
39 Miro's Cafe
47 Nomad Restaurant
61 Warung Artini
65 Dirty Duck Diner
66 Kura Kura Mexican Cafe
67 Kubuku Restaurant
71 Nuriana's Restaurant
77 Kokokan Club
83 Pizza Roma

OTHER

9 Museum Neka
30 Blanco's House
44 Seni Wati Women's Gallery
45 Neka Gallery
46 Ganesha Bookshop
48 Telephone Office
49 Post Office
53 Padangtegal Dance
   Place
69 Perama Depot
79 Telkom Wartel
80 Chemist (Apotik)
82 Peliatan Dance Place
88 Agung Rai Gallery
92 Archaeological Museum
93 Goa Gajah (Elephant Cave)

Neka but also the Neka Gallery where most of the work is for sale. Across the road from the post office at the eastern end of the main road, the extensive Neka Gallery displays fine pieces from all the schools of Balinese art as well as work by European residents like Han Snel and Arie Smit.

Ubud's other important commercial gallery is the Agung Rai Gallery at Peliatan, south east of central Ubud. Again the collection extends for room after room and covers the full range of Balinese styles plus works by Western and Javanese artists like Antonio Blanco, Arie Smit, Han Snel, Theo Meier and Affandi. The gallery also has some important works which are not for sale, including paintings by I Gusti Nyoman Lempad and Walter Spies.

Artists' Homes

The home of I Gusti Nyoman Lempad is on the main street of Ubud, just across from the market, and is open to the public although there are no works by the artist on display. He is well represented at the Puri Lukisan Museum and the Museum Neka.

Walter Spies and Rudolf Bonnet, the two Western artists who played a key role in changing the course of Balinese art from a purely decorative skill, both lived for some time at Campuan, near the suspension bridge. Spies' home is now one of the rooms at the Campuan Hotel and can be inspected if it is not in use; you can even stay there if you book well ahead.

These original visiting artists have been followed by a steady stream of Western dreamers, right down to the present day. Just beside the Campuan suspension bridge, across the river from Murni's Warung, a driveway leads up to Filipino-born artist Antonio Blanco's superbly theatrical house. Entry to the beautiful house and gallery is 500 rp. Blanco's speciality is erotic art and illustrated poetry, though for him playing the part of the artist is probably just as important as painting.

Arie Smit and Han Snel are other well-known Western artists currently residing in Ubud. In the 1960s Smit sparked the Young Artists' school of painting in Penestanan, just west of Campuan. Han Snel's work is exhibited in a private collection at his restaurant and hotel, just off the main road through Ubud.

Walks Around Ubud

The growth of Ubud has engulfed a number of nearby villages, though these have still managed to retain their distinct identities. There are lots of interesting walks in the area, to surrounding villages, or through the rice paddies. You'll frequently see artists at work in open rooms and verandahs on the quieter streets.

Monkey Forest Monkey Forest Rd is lined with hotels, restaurants and shops for its whole length, but at the far end, at the bottom of the hill, you'll arrive in a small but dense forest. It's inhabited by a handsome band of monkeys, ever ready for passing tourists who just might have peanuts available for a handout. Peanut vendors usually wait to provide monkey sustenance, but be warned, the monkeys have become far too used to visitors and can put on ferocious displays of temperament if you don't come through with the goods, and quick. If they think you've got something interesting in your pocket or bag they may try to snatch it from you. Tickets to enter the forest cost 500 rp.

Ubud's interesting old **pura dalem** (temple of the dead) is in the forest, for this is the inauspicious, kelod side of town. Look for the rangda figures devouring children at the entrance to the inner temple. The road swings east at the Monkey Forest, and you can follow it around to the villages of Padangtegal or Pengosekan.

If you turn right down the track immediately after the Monkey Forest Hideaway (see Places to Stay), there's a pool down in the gorge on the left.

Nyuhkuning This small village, south of the Monkey Forest, is noted for its woodcarving, and there's a small woodcarving museum here.

Campuan At the confluence of the Wos and Cerik rivers, Campuan actually means 'where two rivers meet'. Far below the bridges is the **Pura Gunung Labuh**, a temple thought to date back as far as 1000 years. From the temple a walking track leads north along the ridge between the rivers.

Penestanan The road bends sharply as it crosses the river at Campuan and then runs north, parallel to the river. Take the steep uphill road which bends away to the left of the main road to reach Penestanan. There are galleries, many of them specialising in paintings of the Young Artists' style, and some losmen and houses to rent.

Sayan & Kedewatan West of Penestanan is Sayan, site of Colin McPhee's home in the '30s, so amusingly described in his book, *A House in Bali*. North of Sayan is Kedewatan, another small village where a road turns east and swings back towards Ubud via Campuan. Just west of the villages and the main road is the Ayung River (Yeh Ayung). The deep gorge of the swift-flowing river offers magnificent panoramas, and several very expensive hotels, and the homes of a number of modern-day McPhees, are perched on the edge. Whitewater rafting trips offer another perspective on the river.

Petulu In the late afternoon each day you can enjoy the spectacular sight of thousands of herons arriving home in Petulu. They nest in the trees along the road through the village and make a spectacular sight as they fly in and commence squabbling over the prime perching places.

The road north of Ubud's bemo stop continues through the village of **Junjungan**, which is heavily into the carving of garudas. Half a dozen shops by the roadside offer them in all sizes from a few cm high to giant two-metre garudas which probably weigh a tonne. A little further, on the right, there's a well-marked turn-off to Petulu.

Walk quickly under the trees if the herons are already roosting – the copious droppings on the road will indicate if it's wise not to

hang around. Donations are requested at the other end of the village. About a km past the village you reach the Tegal Lalang to Ubud road, from where it's a couple of km back to the centre of Ubud.

Places to Stay
Ubud itself has many small homestays, where a simple, clean room in a pretty garden will cost around 10,000 to 12,000 rp for a single/double, with private bathroom and a light breakfast. In the surrounding villages (or on the outskirts of growing Ubud, depending on how you look at it) there are also cheap places, often in a much quieter, greener environment.

For a little more, up to 25,000 or 35,000 rp, you can get a very nice room or bungalow, often well decorated with local arts and crafts, perhaps with a view of rice fields, jungle or garden. Upper mid-range tourist hotels, ie those with swimming pools, hot water and US-dollar prices, are mostly on Monkey Forest Rd and near Jalan Raya. The really expensive hotels are perched on the edges of the deep, steep valleys of nearby rivers, with super views and decorative art and craft works that rival many galleries.

Many small losmen are run by people involved with the arts, who are interesting to talk to and often have useful information about what's happening. At most cheaper and mid-price places, breakfast is included in the price. Some of the accommodation is geared to longer stayers (several weeks at least) and usually offers cooking facilities rather than meals.

Just about everyone who stays in Ubud says they had a wonderful place run by lovely, helpful people, and they will recommend it highly.

Places to Stay – bottom end
Many cheap places are very small, just two, three or four rooms. What follows is just a sample; there are many other excellent places apart from those mentioned.

Central Ubud In central Ubud, the *Mumbul Inn* (☎ 975364) is near the Puri Lukisan

Museum on Jalan Raya, and has simple, spartan rooms from 12,000/20,000 rp. *Rojas II* (☎ 975107) bungalows are right by the Puri Lukisan Museum, with a jungle setting close to the middle of town.

Close to the top of Monkey Forest Rd, near the market, is one of Ubud's really long runners – *Canderi's* (also Candri's or Tjanderi's depending on which sign or spelling style you choose). It's a typical, straightforward losmen-style place with singles from 8000 to 10,000 rp and doubles at 15,000 rp. On Jalan Arjuna, the small street off the other side of Monkey Forest Rd, *Anom Bungalows* and *Suarsena House* cost about the same. Going down Monkey Forest Rd, other cheap places include *Pandawa Homestay* at 10,000/15,000 rp, *Igna Accommodation* at 6000/8000 rp, *Karyawan Accommodation* with nice, traditional-style rooms from 12,000/15,000 rp, and the very clean and well-kept *Frog Pond Inn* with a welcoming atmosphere and breakfast for 10,000/15,000 rp a single/double. Nearby *Mandia Bungalows* are well kept and friendly, at 20,000/25,000 rp for singles/doubles. Further down is *Ibunda Inn*, a pleasant place with rooms from 12,000/15,000 rp, or 25,000 rp with hot water. At the south end of Monkey Forest Rd is the secluded *Monkey Forest Hideaway* (☎ 975354), with rooms at 15,000/20,000 rp, some romantically overlooking the forest, and others far too close to the road.

The small streets to the east of Monkey Forest Rd, including Jalan Karna and Jalan Goutama, have heaps of small homestays – just look for the small signs near the gates. They are mostly family compounds with three or four bungalows at around 10,000/15,000 rp including breakfast and tax, though prices depend somewhat on demand. There's nothing to choose between these numerous losmen, just wander down the narrow lanes, have a look in a few, compare the prices and facilities and make your choice.

North of Ubud A few roads run north of Jalan Raya, towards the fringe of town. Jalan

Kajang has a number of more expensive places with great views over the river gorge to the west, and a few budget places like *Roja's Homestay*, with rooms at 8000/10,000 rp and 12,000/15,000 rp. Jalan Suweta has the *Suci Inn*, across from the banyan tree, a very straightforward losmen-style place with simple rooms with bath from 9000 rp in front and 12,000 rp in the back. The rooms look out on to the central garden, and it's a friendly, relaxed place that's quiet yet very central. Continue up Jalan Suweta for about 10 minutes to Sambahan, where there's a small group of places, best known of which is *Ketut's Place* (☎ 975304), with rooms in a family compound from 10,000/15,000 rp for singles/doubles in the front rooms to 25,000 rp for cottages at the back, or 35,000 rp with hot water. *Sambahan Village Guest House* has also been recommended. A really secluded place is *Taman Indah Homestay*, a walk into the rice fields at the north end of Jalan Sandat, with three rooms at 8000/10,000 rp.

South-East of Ubud More accommodation can be found in Padangtegal, in the streets east of central Ubud which run south of Jalan Raya; Jalan Hanoman, Jalan Sugriwa and Jalan Jembawan. *Puri Asri*, on Hanoman, has six rooms at 20,000/25,000 rp, while *Nuriani Guesthouse* (☎ 975346), just off to the east side on the rice fields, costs 25,000 to 30,000 rp a double.

Hanoman continues south to Pengosekan, past the pleasant *Jati Inn II* which has two-storey rooms for only 8000/10,000 rp, and the *Bali Breeze* with bungalows at 30,000 rp.

Further east is Peliatan, where Jalan Tebesaya has some possibilities, including the very popular *Rona Accommodation* (☎ 976229), a very nice place with rooms at 10,000/12,000 rp and 17,000/20,000 rp, and a book exchange with a good selection. They have lots of useful information and can organise tours, car and bike rental, and baby-sitting.

On the main road south, *Mudita Inn* has two rooms in its shady garden for 8000/12,000 rp for singles/doubles, and there are other places nearby. At the junction where the road bends sharp left to Denpasar, you'll see a sign for the *Sari Bungalows*, just 100 metres or so off the road. It's a pleasantly quiet location and good value with singles from 5000 to 6000 rp and doubles from 8000 rp, all including a 'big breakfast'. Nearby is the pleasant *Siti Homestay*, with a garden and rooms at 8000/12,000 rp, and also *Nyoman Astana Bungalows* and *Mandra Cottages*.

West of Ubud Heading west on Jalan Raya brings you to Campuan, where the rivers meet. Cross the suspension bridge by Murni's Warung, and take the steep road uphill by Blanco's house to Penestanan, a quiet but arty area. Along this road you'll find a little group of pretty homestays including the attractive *Arjuna's Inn*, run by the artist's daughter, with rooms at 15,000 to 20,000 rp. Also along here are *Sri Ratih Cottages* and *Bamboo Homestay*.

There are more places further back into the rice fields – you have to walk to get to them. Ones near this road include *Gerebig*, *Gorim*, *Reka* and *Made Jagi*. Others are in the rice paddies further north, more easily reached by climbing the stairs west of the Campuan road, and following the sign boards. Places to look for include *Siddharta*, *Danau* and *Pugur*. Asking price is from around 15,000/ 20,000 rp for singles/doubles, up to around 40,000 rp per night for a larger bungalow, but many people stay much longer and negotiate a much lower rate.

Further west is Sayan, where there are a few small places with great views over the Ayung River; one of cheapest is *Putra Umbara*, at 20,000/25,000 rp.

Places to Stay – middle

Many good mid-range places cost from 25,000 to 35,000 rp, with hot running water being the most touted feature. There are a growing number of new or renovated hotels with prices up to US$50, almost always equipped with a swimming pool. For lower mid-range hotels, service, tax and breakfast are usually included, but the more expensive ones, with US-dollar prices, often add 10% to 15%.

Central Ubud The Monkey Forest Rd has a number of newer mid-range places, although some of them are very dull and featureless. Near the top of the Monkey Forest Rd and off to the right you'll find *Oka Wati's Sunset Bungalows* (☎ 975063), still with a rice paddy in view but being built out. It's still pretty quiet, and very handy to the centre of town. The rooms range from US$25/30 to US$45/55. There's a swimming pool and a restaurant presided over by Oka Wati herself, a familiar face to Ubud visitors since the early '70s.

A little further down, the *Ubud Village Hotel* (☎ 975069) is one of the few new places built with some imagination and taste. The pleasantly decorated rooms, each with a separate garden entrance, cost from US$35. There's a swimming pool with swim-up bar and other luxuries.

Also on Monkey Forest Rd and almost at the forest, the *Ubud Inn* (☎ 975188) is a well-established place with a variety of bungalows and rooms dotted around a spacious garden area with a swimming pool. Rates are US$25/35 with fan, US$30/40 with air-con, and two-storey family rooms at US$45. The brick rooms have carved wood and thatched roofs and they're quite cool, each with a private bathroom. The upstairs verandah on the two-storeyed rooms is ideal for gazing out over the fast-disappearing rice paddies. Next door, the *Fibra Inn* (☎ 975451) has a pool, and bungalows from US$30.

The newer Monkey Forest Rd hotels are not always so interesting. *Pertiwi Bungalows* (☎ 975236) has comfortable rooms, plenty of outdoor space for kids, and a swimming pool, but there's nothing very special about it. Nightly costs are from US$32/38 to US$65/75 but service, tax and breakfast are all extra.

There are a number of places along the main road through Ubud but one of the nicest has to be artist Han Snel's *Siti Bungalows* (☎ 975699), hidden away behind the Lotus Cafe. Some of the very pleasant individual cottages are perched right on the edge of the river gorge, looking across to the Puri Lukisan Museum on the other side. There are seven rooms, the nightly cost is US$40/50 for singles/doubles and it's pleasantly quiet, back off the main road, yet close to the town centre. Further west, another good place is *Abangan Bungalows* (☎ 975082), up a steep driveway off the main road; you'll see the sign on the south side. They have a pool, and 12 rooms from US$20/30 to US$35.

Several places to stay along the main road are associated with the old palaces of Ubud. The pleasant and well-kept *Puri Saraswati Cottages* (☎ 975164), near the Saraswati palace, has rooms at US$17/22 and US$32/37. The *Hotel Puri Saren Agung* (☎ 975957), near the bemo stop in the centre of Ubud, is part of the home of the late head of Ubud's royal family. It's not signposted as a hotel, but walk into the courtyard and enquire – it costs US$30/40. Balinese dances are held regularly in the outer courtyard, and the bungalows have displays of Balinese antiques.

Some small streets climb the slope south of the main road, with a few places to stay – *Pringga Juwita Water Garden Cottages* (☎ 975734) is family-run, with pretty gardens, ponds and a swimming pool, from US$37/45. *Pringga Juwita Inn*, not unrelated, is also a very nice, friendly place, and a bit cheaper at US$23.

East & South of Ubud Most of the places to stay in Padangtegal are budget accommodation, but *Dewi Sri Bungalows* are an attractive mid-range option, with a pool and a good restaurant, and nicely decorated rooms from US$25 to US$50.

Further east in Peliatan, on the main road, is *Oka Kartini's* (☎ 975135), another long-term survivor now with a swimming pool and other mod cons, but retaining a family atmosphere; from US$25/30 to US$35/45. On the main road south, *Mandala Bungalows* (☎ 975191) are another long-standing Ubud establishment, with rooms from about 35,000 rp.

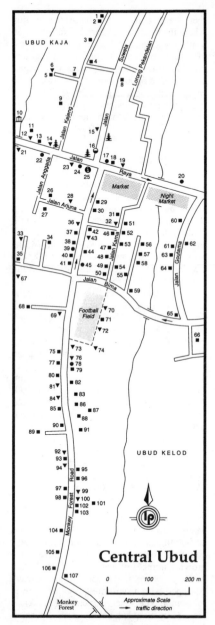

Central Ubud

■ PLACES TO STAY

1   Kajeng Home Stay
2   Gusti's Garden Bungalow
3   Lecuk Inn
4   Arjana Accommodation
5   Siti Bungalows
7   Shanti's Homestay
8   Suci Inn
9   Roja's Homestay
11 Mumbul Inn
13 Puri Saraswati Cottages
18 Sudharsana Bungalows
26 Anom Bungalows
27 Suarsena House
29 Happy Inn
30 Canderi's Losmen & Warung
31 Yuni's House
34 Oka Wati's Sunset Bungalows
35 Igna 2 Accommodation
37 Alit's House
38 Puri Muwa Bungalows
40 Dewa House
41 Igna Accommodation
42 Pandawa Homestay
44 Badra Accommodation
46 Gandra House
47 Sudartha House
48 Seroni Bungalows
49 Mertha House
50 Surawan House
51 Widiana's House Bungalows
52 Sania's House
53 Wija House
54 Ning's House
55 Devi House
56 Sayong's House
57 Dewi Putra House
58 Raka House
59 Esty's House
60 Wayan Karya Homestay
61 Wena Homestay
62 Shana Homestay
63 Nirvana Pension
64 Agung's Cottages
65 Sidya Homestay
66 Ramasita Pension
68 Bendi's Accommodation
71 Wahyu Bungalows
75 Accommodation Kerta
77 Karyawan Accommodation
79 Frog Pond Inn
80 Ubud Village Hotel
82 Mandia Bungalows
83 Puri Garden Bungalow
85 Pertiwi Bungalows
86 Adi Cottages
87 Rice Paddy Bungalows
88 Sri Bungalows
89 Jati 3 Bungalows &
     Putih Accommodation
90 Villa Rasa Sayang
91 Nani House (Karsi Homestay)
93 Jaya Accommodation
95 Ibunda Inn
96 Ubud Bungalows
97 Dewi Ayu Accommodation
98 Ubud Tenau Bungalows
101 Sagitarius Inn
102 Fibra Inn
103 Ubud Inn
104 Lempung Accommodation
105 Pande Permai Bungalows
106 Monkey Forest Hideaway
107 Hotel Champlung Sari

▼ PLACES TO EAT

6   Han Snel's Garden Restaurant
12 Mumbul's Cafe
14 Lotus Cafe
15 Coconut's Cafe
19 Restaurant Puri Pusaka
21 Menara Restaurant
23 Ary's Warung
28 Satri's Warung
32 Seroni's Warung
33 Oka Wati's Warung
36 Ayu's Kitchen
43 Gayatri Restaurant
67 Beji's Cafe
69 Bendi's Restaurant
70 Legian Cafe & Video
72 Ubud Dancer Restaurant
73 Ibu Rai Restaurant
74 Cafe Bali
76 Dian Restaurant
81 Coco Restaurant
84 Cafe Wayan
92 Jaya Cafe
94 Yudit Restaurant & Bakery
99 Warsa's Cafe
100 Ubud Restaurant

OTHER

10 Puri Lukisan Museum
16 Bemo Stop
17 Palace & Hotel Puri Saren Agung
20 I Gusti Nyoman Lempad's home
22 Supermarket
24 Ubud Bookshop
25 Tourist Office (Bina Wisata)
39 Bookshop
45 Ibu Rai Gallery
78 Batik Workshop & Crackpot Cafe

West of Ubud Close to the river junction in Campuan, the *Cecak Inn* (☎ 975238) is good value with attractive, well-located bungalows from around 25,000/32,000 rp and up. *Murni's House*, run from Murni's Warung, has apartments with verandahs for US$40 and also complete six-roomed houses for US$80. Right across the river from the warung, squeezed between the river and Blanco's house behind the Bridge Café, is the *Pondok Tjampuhan Guest House* (☎ 975085) with doubles at US$25. Further out on the main road, opposite and a little before the Museum Neka, the relaxed and pretty *Ananda Cottages* (☎ 975376) has rooms at US$35/45 or two-storeyed family rooms for US$95; prices include breakfast.

In the rice fields of Penestanan, up the stairs west of the road through Campuan, some of the cottages have mid-range facilities and prices, including the charming *Kori Agung* at 35,000/40,000 rp for singles/doubles, and *Penestanan Bungalows* (☎ 975604), with a pool and tranquillity, which probably cost a bit more, but you won't even think about money after a few days here. For even more rice-field luxury, *Melati Cottages* (☎ 975088) also has a pool, restaurant and quiet location, for US$25/35. Remember that to get here, you have to walk. Imagine a place with no traffic!

Further west in Sayan, overlooking the Ayung River, *Sayan Terrace* (☎ 975384) has a brilliant view and attractive rooms for US$20, bungalows at US$25, and family-size accommodation for US$60. Also overlooking the river, *Djagra's Inn* is a bit hard to get to and impossible to phone, but delightfully secluded, with good-sized rooms from US$30.

Places to Stay – top end

Top-end hotels in Ubud feature some combination of artistic connections, traditional decor, lush landscaping, rice-field views and modern luxuries. They all charge about 17.5% for tax and service, on top of the advertised prices.

Just up beyond the suspension bridge, the long-established *Hotel Tjampuhan* (☎ 975368, fax 975137) is beautifully situated overlooking the river confluence and Pura Gunung Labuh. The hotel is built on the site of artist Walter Spies' 1930s' home and his small house is now one of the rooms. He was also responsible for the hillside swimming pool although it, like the rest of the hotel, has had a major renovation since then. The rooms are individual bungalows in a wonderful garden and cost from US$45/52 to US$65/80. Up the steep road opposite the Tjampuhan, the *Padma Indah Cottages* (☎ 975719, fax 975091) were established by a collector of Balinese art, which is displayed in all the cottages and an on-site gallery. Rooms with a garden view cost US$90; US$10 more for a rice-field view.

From the Campuan bridge, the road out of Ubud passes the Neka Gallery, about a km further on, and just beyond the gallery is the turn-off to the *Ulun Ubud Cottages* (☎ 975024, fax 975524). The bungalows are beautifully draped down the hillside overlooking the Cerik River, and there are some wonderful carvings, paintings and antiques. Double rooms cost US$55, US$65 or US$90, and there are also larger, two-bedroom family units at US$110. Rates include breakfast, taxes and service and there's a restaurant, bar and swimming pool.

Beyond Ulun Ubud Cottages, near the Kedewatan junction, is Ubud's most beautifully designed hotel, the *Amandari* (☎ 975333, fax 975335). Accommodation is in private pavilions, simply priced at US$300, US$400, US$500, US$600 and US$700 (plus 17.5% service and tax). They're spacious, exquisitely decorated and have superb views over the rice paddies or down to the Ayung River. The most expensive rooms have their own private swimming pool. The hotel's main swimming pool seems to drop over the edge right down to the river. The Amandari is close to where Colin McPhee built his home.

If you head north from the Kedewatan junction you soon come to *Cahaya Dewata* (☎ 975495, fax 975495) which overlooks the same magnificent river gorge. The rooms are US$55/60 for singles/doubles or US$80 for suites, plus 15.5% service and tax. It has great views and some really interesting artworks and decorations. A little further north is *Kupu Kupu Barong* (☎ 975478/9, fax 975079). Clinging precariously to the steep sides of the Ayung River Gorge, each of the beautiful two-storeyed bungalows has a bedroom and living room; they cost from US$305 to US$635 a night, plus 17.5% tax and service. Six of the 17 bungalows have two bedrooms, some of them have open-air spa baths. The views from the rooms, the pool and the restaurant are unbelievable. Children under 12 years are not welcome (they might fall out of the restaurant).

Other expensive hotels are found around the very edges of the Ubud area – nowhere is a view of wet-rice cultivation more bankable than here. The *Hotel Champlung Sari* (☎ 975418, fax 975473), at the bottom end of Monkey Forest Rd, has nice views but very ordinary rooms for US$50/60 to US$70/90 for singles/doubles. The new *Puri Kamandalu* (☎ 975825, fax 975851), four km north-east of Ubud, seems to be aiming more for the convention market, with convention facilities and a business centre. Nevertheless, it has a wonderful outlook, and attractive, well-decorated, thatched bungalows from US$175 to US$300. Down in Pengosekan, *Puri Indah* (☎ 975742, fax 975332) is owned by Agung Rai, proprietor of the well-respected gallery, and has nice views, interesting architecture and fine decor. There's a range of rooms from US$65 to US$120, or US$200 for a complete house.

Places to Eat

Ubud's numerous restaurants probably offer the best and most interesting food on the island. You can get excellent Western food, all the Indonesian standards, and Balinese dishes will often be on the menu as well. The very best places might cost 20,000 to 30,000 rp per hungry person (US$10 to US$15), but they are well worth it for the quality, service and atmosphere, and many good places will cost less than half that price range. A bottle of wine will cost from 50,000 to 100,000 rp, or 4500 rp by the glass.

Jalan Raya The main east-west road offers plenty of interesting dining possibilities. The pasar malam (night market) sets up at dusk right beside the main market area, and probably attracts more foreigners than any other market on Bali. It's the only one where visitors seem to outnumber locals. There are the usual range of market warung dishes, and you can really fill yourself up going from one stall to another trying them all out. It looks healthier at night than in the light of day, but most people survive and come back for more. Dishes start at about 500 rp.

Just east of the pasar malam is the *Nomad Restaurant*, which does serve meals but is mainly a spot for a sociable drink, as it stays open later than most places in Ubud.

West of the Tourist Office along Jalan Raya are some of Ubud's trendiest restaurants – it's a really excellent area to go out for dinner. *Ary's Warung* is not quite as expensive or as trendy as some places, but it's getting close on both counts. It's very central and does good Indonesian and Western food from an extensive menu. Further along, on the other side, the *Lotus Cafe* was for a long time *the* place to eat, and it is still very fashionable, the lotus pond outlook is delightful, and the food is good but pricey – main courses are 6000 to 8000 rp. Try it at least for a light lunch or a snack, just for the atmosphere (closed on Mondays). A little further on is *Mumbul's Cafe* – small, friendly with good service and excellent food, and even a children's menu. The *Menara Restaurant*, opposite the Lotus, does good Balinese banquet dishes and has laser disk video entertainment, but don't attempt to enjoy both at the same time.

Further down is *Casa Luna*, with a superb international menu including *tiropitakia*, Vietnamese salad, tandoori chicken, Balinese paella and Tex-Mex pizza. They also have bread and pastry from their own bakery, great desserts, and half serves for kids. The service is efficient and the atmosphere is pleasant and friendly; they even run courses in Balinese cooking. It's not too expensive, with main courses from around 7500 rp, but the food is worth blowing your budget on.

The *Roof Garden Cafe*, a little further west, is well established and serves excellent dessert. Up the slope south of the road is *Miro's Cafe*, another top place to eat, with a varied menu and a cool garden setting. The prices are upper mid-range but worth it, with well-prepared Indonesian dishes at 3500 rp, and other main courses at around 8000 rp. On the other side of Jalan Raya, the *Griya Barbeque* does very good pork, chicken, steak and fish in outdoor and indoor settings.

Continuing to Campuan, *Murni's Warung*, right beside the suspension bridge, offers excellent Indonesian and Western-style food in a beautiful setting. It's been amazingly consistent for years and is still a place to see and be seen – like Ubud's answer to Poppies in Kuta. The sate, hamburgers, lasagne, nasi campur and deserts are all first class, and the staff are charming. Again, it's not cheap, but good value. It's closed on Wednesday. Above the bridge and across the river from Murni's Warung, *Beggar's Bush* is a British-style pub but with better food.

North of Jalan Raya One of Ubud's real dining pleasures is *Han Snel's Garden Restaurant*, north of the main road and more or less directly behind the Lotus Cafe. The setting is beautiful, with frogs croaking in the background. It's a bit expensive, but the food is OK with generous serves – their rijstaffel is famous – but it's mainly the atmosphere and the hospitable owners which make this place attractive. It's closed on Sundays.

For a Balinese feast, book into *Ketut's Place*, up beyond the palace on the north side of the town centre, and for 12,500 rp per person you get a great Balinese meal, and an excellent introduction to Balinese life and customs.

Monkey Forest Rd Going south of Jalan Raya are some more budget-priced possibilities, and some really excellent places. Near the northern end, *Satri's Warung* is an inexpensive place with good food. *Canderi's Warung* is an old Ubud institution, with standard Indonesian and Western dishes. *Gayatri Restaurant* is recommended for families, with inexpensive meals and a play area for kids. Just off the Monkey Forest Rd, *Oka Wati's*, is another Ubud institution, and still a pleasant, friendly and economical place to eat. *Ibu Rai Restaurant*, near the football field, also has some good dishes.

Further south, *Cafe Wayan* is more expensive but has some of the best food in town,

---

A Balinese Feast

Finding real Balinese food in Bali is often far from easy but Ketut Suartana, who can be contacted at the Suci Inn (near the bemo stop on Jalan Suweta) or at Ketut's Place (further up the same road), puts on regular Balinese feasts at 12,500 rp per person. They're held in a pavilion in his parents' family compound where Ketut's Place is also located.

This is an opportunity to sample real Balinese food at its best. Typical meals include duck or Balinese sate, which is minced and spiced meat wrapped around a wide stick and quite different from the usual Indonesian sate. A variety of vegetables will include several that we normally think of as fruits – like papaya, jackfruit (nangka) and starfruit (blimbing). *Paku* is a form of fern and *ketela potton* is tapioca leaves, both prepared as tasty vegetables. Red onions known as *anyang* and cucumber known as *ketimun* will also feature. Then there might be gado gado and mie goreng, both prepared in Balinese style, and a special Balinese dish of duck livers cooked in banana leaves and coconut. Of course there will be prawn crackers (krupuk) and rice. To drink there will be Balinese rice wine (brem) and you'll finish up with Balinese coffee, peanuts and bananas or Balinese desserts like *sumping*, a leaf-wrapped sticky rice concoction with coconut and palm sugar or banana and jackfruit.

The dining area is hung with palm-leaf decorations, again as for a Balinese feast, and a gamelan can be heard away in the background. It's fun, delicious and a rare chance to sample real Balinese food. It's also a great opportunity to learn more about Bali and its customs as Ketut talks about his house, his family and answers all sorts of questions about life in Bali. ■

with a small room in the front and delightful tables in the open air at the back. The nasi campur at 5500 rp is terrific, the curry ayam (curried chicken) at 7500 rp is superb. Western dishes like spaghetti at 6500 rp also feature. Desserts include the famed coconut pie or you could even risk 'death by chocolate', a definite case of chocolate cake overkill.

Continue on to *Yudit Restaurant & Bakery*, which makes pretty good pizzas for around 6500 rp, as well as good bread, rolls and other baked goods. The long-running *Ubud Restaurant* is towards the bottom end of the road, but worth the walk.

Around Ubud In the surrounding areas, anywhere with tourist accommodation will usually have a selection of places to eat. On Jalan Karna, east of Monkey Forest Rd, for instance, you'll find quite a few traditional losmen, and also top food at the budget-priced *Seroni's Warung*. Further east in Peliatan, on Jalan Tebesaya, are a couple of good, inexpensive places, including *Pizza Roma*, where the Italian food will not disappoint you.

South of Ubud, Padangtegal has some really interesting places. The *Dirty Duck Diner* does delectable deep-fried duck dishes, and has a menu full of good food and bad puns. Going south you pass the *Kura Kura Mexican Cafe* and, near Perama, *Ubud Raya*, which has a selection of well-prepared Japanese and international dishes. Around the corner in Pengosekan is a great splurge possibility, the *Kokokan Club* (☎ 975742), at the Puri Indah Villas. It serves delicious Thai, seafood and other dishes in opulent surroundings, and the prices are not excessive – soups at 4000 rp, main courses around 7000 rp and desserts at 4000 rp. It's in a beautiful, open-sided bale with a bar downstairs and a dining area upstairs, with marble floors, potted palms, linen tablecloths, and a general air of understated elegance. If you phone them they may help with transport.

There are fewer restaurants west of Ubud – long-term stayers in Penestanan eat at their losmen or walk to Murni's Warung. You can eat in the restaurants of the expensive hotels overlooking the Ayung River even if you're not staying there. Try the *Amandari* for excellent food in a sophisticated atmosphere, or *Kupu Kupu Barong* for a brilliant view.

Entertainment
Music & Dance The main entertainment in Ubud is Balinese dancing. If you're in the right place at the right time you can still catch dances put on for temple ceremonies and an essentially local audience, but even the tourist dances are conducted with a high degree of skill and commitment, and usually have appreciative locals in the audience. The competition between the various Ubud dance troupes is intense, and local connoisseurs speculate endlessly about whether the Peliatan troupe is still the best, or if standards have slipped at Bona.

The tourist office has information on current performances, and sells tickets, which are also widely available in town. The usual entry price for the dances is 5000 rp – sometimes with transport to performances away from central Ubud. They start at about 7 to 7.30 pm – for out-of-town performances, transport leaves at 6 pm. The programme has several performances every day, including Kecak, Sanghyang, Legong, Mahabharata, Barong & Rangda dances, a women's gamelan and dance, wayang kulit, Ramayana and so on. For descriptions of these dances, see the Music, Dance & Drama section in the Facts about Bali chapter.

Other Entertainment A number of restaurants run laser-disk video movies, which are becoming popular. Casa Luna sometimes has a kids' session at 4 pm. Some restaurants also have Balinese dances, but it's much better to attend one of the performances listed above.

Activities
Bird enthusiasts should enquire about the three-hour guided walks conducted by Victor Mason. They cost US$28, including a guidebook and lunch, and depart from the Beggar's Bush pub (☎ 975009) at 9.15 am on Sunday, Tuesday and Friday.

Courses

There are quite a few courses on offer; for more information, start by asking at the tourist office.

Courses in Balinese music are offered at Ganesha Bookshop in Jalan Raya. Anom's Samara Ratih dance school has courses in Balinese dancing, as well as some music classes. Children's dance classes are also available. Also try the dance centre in Peliatan.

In the artists' community of Penestanan various teachers conduct painting classes. Enquire about a woodcarving course in Nyuhkuning, near the woodcarving museum. Some of the classes are suitable for children, and mask-making classes are also available. Also popular with kids is the batik workshop conducted behind the Crackpot Cafe in Monkey Forest Rd.

For lessons in Balinese and Indonesian cooking, enquire at the Casa Luna Restaurant. The Meditation Shop on Monkey Forest Rd has courses on meditation, and sells publications on Yoga and New Age subjects.

Courses in Balinese language and Bahasa Indonesia are also available – see Oka Wati, at Oka Wati's restaurant. Language courses can also be arranged in Kemenuh, seven km south of Ubud. If you really want to learn one of these languages, you would probably do better staying in a less touristed area than Ubud – you will hear too much English here.

Things to Buy

Ubud has a wide variety of shops and galleries, or you can use Ubud as a base to explore and plunder craft and antique shops all the way down to Batubulan (see the Denpasar to Ubud section). The art and craft market at Sukawati is a great place to look, but you should get there early – between 6 and 8 am.

Murni's, down by the river, always seems to have something unusual, and has two other shops, not far away up the main road. They have interesting pieces and fixed prices. Nearby, Kunang Kunang has a wide selection, and Sakti, opposite the football field, is another shop with a variety of quality goods.

Paintings You'll find paintings for sale everywhere. The main galleries have excellent selections, but prices are often well over the US$100 mark. You should be able to get better prices direct from the artist or an artist's workshop. If your budget is limited, look for a smaller picture of high quality, rather than something that resembles wallpaper in size and originality.

Woodcarvings Small shops by the market and along the Monkey Forest Rd often have good woodcarvings, particularly masks. There are some other good woodcarving places along the road from Peliatan to Goa Gajah and south to Mas, and also north from Tegal Lalang to Pujung.

Other Things to Buy The market in the centre of Ubud sells clothing, sarongs, footwear, and souvenirs of variable quality at negotiable prices. At Goa Gajah there is a host of stalls selling leather work. Shops selling antiques in Ubud tend to be overpriced – bargain hard or go back to Batubulan, Denpasar or even Kuta. Silver work is not a local speciality, but have a look in Patra's, on Jalan Hanoman. The Kubuku Restaurant, east of the Monkey Forest, has a shop specialising in wind chimes. For childrenswear and toys try Kumara Kids, next to the Ganesha Bookshop, or Gayatri Kids, at the Gayatri Restaurant. Satu Satu, in the main street, and Babylon, near the Neka Museum, sell interesting clothing and accessories, as do a few other boutiques.

For everyday needs, the Toko Tino Supermarket (opposite the Lotus Cafe) has most things, including a good range of film. Next door, Ubud Music has a fair selection of cassettes. Photo processing is available at a couple of places nearby.

Getting There & Away

In Ubud bemos leave from the stop in Jalan Suweta, in the middle of town. To get to Denpasar or the southern tourist centres you first take a bemo to Denpasar's Batubulan

Top: Time for a snack, Tampaksiring, Bali (GA)
Left: Harvest worker after threshing rice, Tampaksiring, Bali (GA)
Right: Air Terjun, Gianyar, Bali (GA)

Top: Early morning in Ubud, Bali (JL)
Left: A gamelan in procession, Ubud, Bali (TW)
Right: Drive-through Banyan tree, Cupuan, Bali (JL)

bus/bemo terminal for about 1000 rp. From there bemos run to places all over eastern Bali. There are direct bemos between Batubulan and Sanur but for Kuta you have to take a bemo from the Batubulan terminal to the Tegal terminal on the Kuta side of Denpasar for 700 rp and another bemo from there.

A typical charter fare to Sanur or Denpasar is about 15,000 rp; Kuta or the airport is about 23,000 rp while the official taxi fare from the airport to Ubud is 34,000 rp.

Tourist shuttle buses operate to a fixed schedule directly between Ubud and other tourist centres. The Perama office is inconveniently located down in Padangtegal, but there are lots of signs around Ubud announcing departure times and ticket sales with other companies. Fares to Sanur, Kuta, Padangbai, Candidasa or the airport are 7500 rp; and to Singaraja and Lovina Beach 12,500 rp.

Getting Around

To get to the places around Ubud you can generally count on about 300 rp a km with a 200 rp minimum. There are numerous places in Ubud which rent mountain bikes at 5000 rp a day or 4000 rp a day for a longer term rental. Places hiring out cars and motorbikes are equally plentiful, but it pays to shop around and to haggle. It's hard to get them for Kuta prices, and the range of vehicles is not as good.

Numerous tours (day trips or longer) are also operated from Ubud. Ones offered by the tourist office are good value – between 15,000 and 30,000 rp for a full day tour, with full itineraries which don't include shopping (except the ones to craft centres).

Around Ubud

The Pejeng region around Ubud encompasses many of the most ancient monuments and relics on Bali. Many of them predate the Majapahit era, and raise as yet unanswered questions about Bali's history. Some sites are

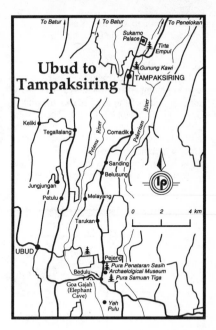

more recent, and in other instances newer structures have been built on and around the ancient remains.

The majority of sites are found along the route round Goa Gajah (south-east of Ubud) and Bedulu, and near the road from there to Tampaksiring. This route follows the Pakerisan River, descending from the holy spring at Tirta Empul near Tampaksiring. Some of the temples and ancient sites in this area are heavily overrun by tourist groups, others are just far enough off the beaten track to leave the crowds behind; some lesser sites are overgrown and so difficult to access that you'd probably need a guide.

Getting Around

You can reach most of the places around Ubud by bemo and on foot. If you're planning to see a lot of them it's a good idea to start at Tirta Empul (about 15 km from Ubud), then any walking you have to do is back downhill. It's only two km from Tirta

Empul down to Gunung Kawi – you can follow the path beside the river.

GOA GAJAH

Only a short distance beyond Peliatan, on the road to Pejeng and Gianyar, a carpark on the northern side of the road marks the site of Goa Gajah (Elephant Cave). There were never any elephants on Bali; the cave probably takes its name from the nearby Petanu River which at one time was known as Elephant River. The cave is reached by a flight of steps down from the other side of the road.

The cave is carved into a rock face and you enter through the cavernous mouth of a demon. The gigantic fingertips pressed beside the face of the demon push back a riotous jungle of surrounding stone carvings. Inside the T-shaped cave you can see fragmentary remains of lingam, the phallic symbols of the Hindu god Shiva, and their female counterpart the yoni, plus a statue of the elephant-headed god Ganesh. In front of the cave are two square bathing pools with water gushing into them from waterspouts held by six female figures.

Goa Gajah was certainly in existence at the time of the Majapahit takeover of Bali. One tale relates that it was another example of the handiwork of the legendary Kebo Iwa, but it probably dates back to the 11th century and shows elements of both Hindu and

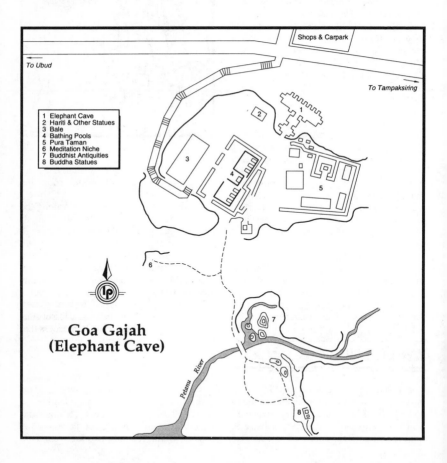

Shops & Carpark

To Ubud

To Tampaksiring

1 Elephant Cave
2 Hariti & Other Statues
3 Bale
4 Bathing Pools
5 Pura Taman
6 Meditation Niche
7 Buddhist Antiquities
8 Buddha Statues

**Goa Gajah
(Elephant Cave)**

Petanu River

Buddhist use. The cave was discovered in 1923 but it was not until 1954 that the fountains and pool were unearthed.

From Goa Gajah you can clamber down through the rice paddies to the Petanu River where there are crumbling rock carvings of stupas (domes for housing Buddhist relics) on a cliff face and a small cave.

Admission to Goa Gajah is 550 rp, and you'll have to pay if you use the carpark, and run the gauntlet of souvenir shops. There are places to buy food near the cave.

YEH PULU

Although it's only a km or so from Goa Gajah to Yeh Pulu, it attracts fewer visitors. The path there is well marked and easy to find, just follow the signs off the road beyond Goa Gajah. Eventually, a small gateway leads to the ancient rock carvings at Yeh Pulu (compulsory 'donation' of 550 rp).

Only excavated in 1925 these are some of the oldest relics on Bali. The carved cliff face is about 25 metres long and is believed to be a hermitage dating from the late-14th century. Apart from the figure of elephant-headed Ganesh, the son of Shiva, there are no religious scenes here. The energetic frieze includes various scenes of everyday life – two men carrying an animal slung from a pole, a man slaying a beast with a dagger (and a frog imitating him by disposing of a snake in like manner – clearly the Balinese sense of humour is not new!), and a man on horseback either pulling a captive woman along behind him or with a woman holding the horse's tail.

On the way through the rice paddies to Yeh Pulu you pass a bathing place with female fountain figures remarkably similar to those at Goa Gajah. The Ganesh figures of Yeh Pulu and Goa Gajah are also quite similar, indicating a close relationship between the two sites. *Yeh* is the Balinese word for water and, as at Goa Gajah, water and fountains play an important part at Yeh Pulu.

BEDULU

Just beyond Goa Gajah is the road junction where you can turn south to Gianyar or north to Pejeng and Tampaksiring. It's hard to imagine Bedulu, the small village at the junction, as the former capital of a great kingdom. The legendary Dalem Bedaulu ruled the

---

The Legend of Bedaulu
A legend relates how Bedaulu possessed magical powers which allowed him to have his head chopped off and then replaced. Performing this unique party trick one day the servant entrusted with lopping off his head and then replacing it unfortunately dropped it in a river and, to his horror, watched it float away. Looking around in panic for a replacement he grabbed a pig, cut off its head and popped it upon the king's shoulders. Thereafter the king was forced to sit on a high throne and forbade his subjects to look up at him; Bedaulu means 'he who changed heads'. ∎

Pejeng dynasty from here and was the last Balinese king to withstand the onslaught of the powerful Majapahits from Java. He was eventually defeated by Gajah Mada in 1343. The capital shifted several times after this, ending up at Gelgel and then later at Klungkung.

AROUND BEDULU

There are several interesting sites around Bedulu and up the road towards Pejeng.

Pura Samuan Tiga

The Pura Samuan Tiga (Temple of the Meeting of the Three, probably a reference to the Hindu trinity) is about 100 metres east of the Bedulu junction. This important 11th-century temple is packed with Balinese during the Odalan Festival.

Bedulu Arkeologi Gedong Arca

The Bedulu Archaeological Museum is about two km north of Bedulu and includes a collection of pre-Hindu artefacts including stone sarcophagi from the time before cremations were practised on Bali.

PEJENG

Continuing up the road to Tampaksiring you soon come to Pejeng and its famous temples. Like Bedulu this was once an important seat of power, the capital of the Pejeng kingdom which fell to the Majapahit invaders in 1343.

Pura Kebo Edan

The Crazy Buffalo Temple (Pura Kebo Edan) with its nearly four-metre-high statue of Bima, also known as the Giant of Pejeng, is on the western side of the road as you come in to Pejeng (entry is 500 rp).

There's considerable conjecture over what this fearsome image is all about. The dead body which the image tramples upon appears to relate to the Hindu Shiva cult but it may also have Tantric Buddhist overtones. Other figures flank the main one and male and female buffaloes lie before it. There is also conjecture about the giant's genitalia – it has either six small penises or one large one, and if that large thing is a penis, what are the interesting lumps and the big hole in the side?

Pura Pusering Jagat

The large Navel of the World Temple (Pura Pusering Jagat) is said to be the centre of the old Pejeng kingdom. Dating from 1329, this temple is visited by young couples who pray at the stone lingam and yoni.

Pura Penataran Sasih

In the centre of Pejeng, Pura Penataran Sasih was once the state temple of the Pejeng kingdom. In the inner courtyard, high up in a pavilion where you really cannot see it very well, is the huge bronze drum known as the Moon of Pejeng.

The hourglass-shaped drum is more than three metres long, the largest single-piece cast drum in the world. Estimates of its age vary from 1000 to 2000 years, and it is not certain whether it was made locally or imported. The intricate geometric designs are said to resemble patterns from as far apart as Irian Jaya and Vietnam.

A Balinese legend relates how the drum came to earth as a fallen moon, landing in a tree and shining so brightly that it prevented a band of thieves from going about their unlawful purpose. One of the thieves decided to put the light out by urinating on it but the moon exploded, killed the foolhardy thief, and fell to earth as a drum – with a crack across its base as a result of the fall.

TAMPAKSIRING

Tampaksiring is a small town with a large and important temple and the most impressive ancient monument on Bali.

Gunung Kawi

On the southern outskirts of Tampaksiring a sign points off the road to the right to Gunung Kawi. From the end of the access road a steep stone stairway leads down to the river, at one point making a cutting through an embankment of solid rock. There, in the bottom of this lush green valley with beautiful rice terraces climbing up the hillsides, is one of Bali's oldest, and certainly largest, ancient monuments.

Gunung Kawi consists of 10 rock-cut candi, memorials cut out of the rock face in imitation of actual statues – in a similar fashion to the great rock-cut temples of Ajanta and Ellora in India. Each candi is believed to be a memorial to a member of the 11th-century Balinese royalty but little is known for certain. They stand in seven-metre-high sheltered niches cut into the sheer cliff face. There are four on the west side of the river which you come to first. To reach the five on the eastern side, you have to cross the river on a bridge. Each of the sets of memorials has a group of monks' cells associated with it. A solitary candi stands further down the valley to the south; this is reached by a trek through the rice paddies.

Legends relate that the whole group of memorials was carved out of the rock face in one hard working night by the mighty fingernails of Kebo Iwa. It's uncertain who the real builders were but they may date from the Udayana dynasty of the 10th and 11th centuries. It's said that the five monuments on the eastern bank are to King Udayana, Queen Mahendradatta (see the Kutri section in this chapter), their son Airlangga and his brothers Anak Wungsu and Marakata. While Airlangga ruled eastern Java, Anak Wungsu ruled Bali. The four monuments on the western side are, by this theory, to Anak Wungsu's chief concubines. Another theory is that the whole complex is dedicated to Anak Wungsu, his wives, concubines and, in the case of the remote 10th candi, to a royal minister.

Entry to Gunung Kawi is 550 rp. It's another two km to the Tirta Empul temple at Tampaksiring.

Tirta Empul

After Tampaksiring, the road branches. The left fork runs up to the grand palace once used by Sukarno while the right fork leads to the temple at Tirta Empul and continues up to Penelokan. You can look back along the valley and see Gunung Kawi from this road, just before you turn into Tirta Empul. The holy springs at Tirta Empul are believed to have magical powers so the temple here is an important one. The springs are a source of the Pakerisan River, which rushes by Gunung Kawi only a km or so away.

Each year an inscribed stone is brought from a nearby village to be ceremonially washed in the spring. The inscription on the stone has been deciphered and indicates that the springs were founded in 962 AD. The actual springs bubble up into a large, crystal-clear tank within the temple and gush out through waterspouts into a bathing pool. According to legend, the springs were created by the god Indra who pierced the earth to tap the 'elixir of immortality' or *amerta*. Despite its antiquity, the temple is glossy and gleamingly new – it was totally restored in the late '60s.

Overlooking Tirta Empul is the Sukarno Palace, a grandiose structure built in 1954 on the site of a Dutch rest house. Sukarno, whose mother was Balinese, was a frequent visitor to the island.

There is an admission charge (550 rp), parking fee, and you have to wear a temple scarf. Come early in the morning or late in the afternoon to avoid the tour-bus hordes.

Other Sites

There are other groups of candi and monks' cells in the area of Bali encompassed by the ancient Pejeng kingdom, notably at Krobokan and Goa Garba, but none so grand as Gunung Kawi. Between Tirta Empul and Gunung Kawi is the temple of Pura Mengening where you can see a freestanding candi similar in design to those of Gunung Kawi. There is a spring at this temple which also feeds into the Pakerisan River.

Places to Stay & Eat

Apart from the usual selection of warungs there's also the expensive *Tampaksiring Restaurant* for tourist groups; it's some distance below the village. It's not easy to find a place to stay here, but it's an easy day trip from Ubud or Bangli, or a stopover between Ubud and Kintamani.

UBUD TO BATUR

The usual road from Ubud to Batur is through Tampaksiring but there are other lesser roads up the gentle mountain slope. If you head east out of Ubud and turn away from Peliatan, towards Petulu at the junction, this road will bring you out on the crater rim just beyond Penelokan towards Batur. It's a sealed road all the way.

Along this road you'll see a number of woodcarvers producing beautiful painted birds, frogs, garudas and tropical fruit. Tegalalang and the nearby village of Jati, just off the road, are noted woodcarving centres. Further up, other specialists carve stools and there are a couple of places where whole tree trunks are carved into whimsical figures.

East Bali

The eastern end of Bali is dominated by mighty Gunung Agung, the 'navel of the world' and Bali's 'mother mountain'. Towering at over 3000 metres, Agung has not always been a kind mother – witness the disastrous 1963 eruption. Today Agung is quiet but the 'mother temple', Pura Besakih, perched high on the slopes of the volcano, attracts a steady stream of devotees...and tourists.

The route east goes through Klungkung, the former capital of one of Bali's great kingdoms, then close to the coast past Kusamba, the bat-infested temple of Goa Lawah, and past the beautiful port of Padangbai. There are a lots of beachside places to stay between there and Candidasa. The route finally reaches Amlapura, another former capital, from where you can continue

past Tirtagangga to the east coast, or return via a route higher up the slopes of Gunung Agung.

GIANYAR

Gianyar is the administrative centre of the Gianyar district which also includes Ubud, but is of minimal interest in its own right. On the main road from Denpasar, and still in the heavy traffic region of southern Bali, the town has a number of small textile factories on the Denpasar side. You can drop in, see the materials being woven and buy some of the work. Bus-loads of free-spending visitors can push prices up to higher levels than in Denpasar.

Right in the centre of town, across from the large open space known as the alun alun, the old palace is little changed from the time

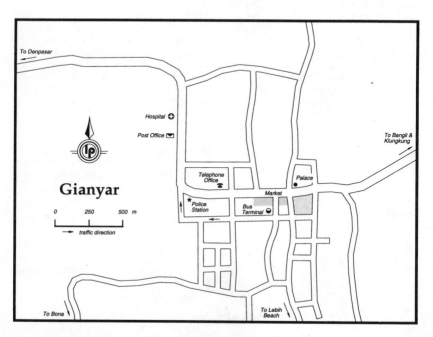

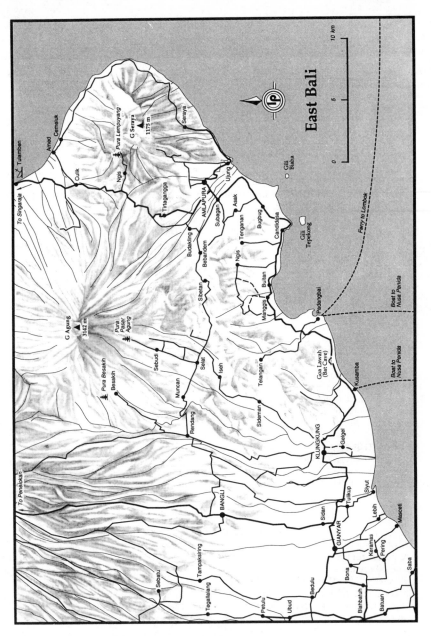

East Bali

the Dutch arrived in the south and the old kingdoms lost their power. The Gianyar royal family saved their palace by capitulating to the Dutch, rather than making a heroic last stand like the other Balinese kingdoms.

Despite its relatively original appearance, the palace, dating from 1771, was destroyed in a conflict with the neighbouring kingdom of Klungkung in the mid-1880s and was rebuilt only to be severely damaged again in the 1917 earthquake. Nevertheless, it's a fine example of traditional palace architecture, surrounded by high brick walls. The royal family of Gianyar still live in the palace, so without a formal invitation you can do no more than look in through the gates.

Gianyar's warungs are noted for their fine roast piglet, babi guling. Eat early, though, as they're usually cleaned out by late morning.

BONA

The village of Bona, on the back road between Gianyar and Blahbatuh, is credited with being the modern home of the Kecak dance. Kecak and other dances are held here every week and are easy to get to from Ubud. Tickets (including transport) from Ubud cost around 5000 rp.

Bona is also a basket-weaving centre and many other articles are also woven from lontar (palm leaves). Nearby Belega, en route to Blahbatuh, is a centre for bamboo work.

LEBIH & THE COAST

South of Gianyar the coast is fringed by black sand beaches and small coastal villages like Lebih. The Pakerisan River, which starts up in the hills at Tampaksiring, reaches the sea near Lebih. Here, and at other coastal villages south of Gianyar, funeral ceremonies reach their conclusion when the ashes are consigned to the sea. Ritual purification ceremonies for temple artefacts are also held on these beaches.

Further west is **Masceti**, site of the Pura Masceti, one of Bali's nine directional temples. On the beach the local villagers have recently erected a huge and somewhat

horrific 'swan' (chicken?) in an attempt to create a tourist attraction! One of the best beaches along this stretch of coast is found to the east of Lebih at **Siyut**, reached via Tulikup.

SIDAN

Continuing east from Gianyar you come to the turn-off to Bangli at Sidan, about two km out of town. Follow this road for about a km until you reach a sharp bend. Here you'll find the Sidan Pura Dalem, a good example of a temple of the dead. Note the sculptures of Durga with children by the gate, and the separate enclosure in one corner of the temple – this is dedicated to Merajapati, the guardian spirit of the dead. If you continue up the Bangli road there's another interesting pura dalem at Penunggekan, just before you reach Bangli. See the Bangli section for more details.

BANGLI

Halfway up the slope to Penelokan, the town of Bangli, once the capital of a kingdom, is said to have the best climate on Bali. It also has a very fine temple and is quite a pleasant place to stay. Bangli is a convenient place from which to visit Besakih, and makes a good base for exploring the area. The town is home to a psychiatric institution and a prison, and is therefore the subject of unkind jokes in other parts of Bali.

Information & Orientation

Bangli has a post office, telephone office (automatic exchange, so it's quite efficient), and a couple of banks. The town is very spread out from north to south; it's nearly 1½ km from the bus stop to the Pura Kehen temple.

Pura Kehen

At the top end of the town, Pura Kehen, the state temple of the Bangli kingdom, is terraced up the hillside. A great flight of steps leads up to the temple entrance, and the first courtyard, with its huge banyan tree, has colourful Chinese porcelain plates set into the walls as decoration. Unfortunately most

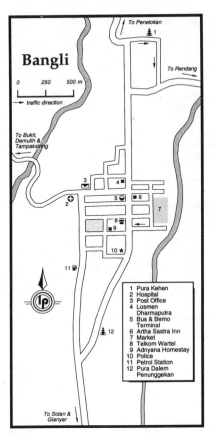

Bangli

0   250   500 m

→ traffic direction

To Penelokan

To Rendang

To Bukit,
Demulih &
Tampaksiring

To Sidan &
Gianyar

1 Pura Kehen
2 Hospital
3 Post Office
4 Losmen
   Dharmaputra
5 Bus & Bemo
   Terminal
6 Artha Sastra Inn
7 Market
8 Telkom Wartel
9 Adnyana Homestay
10 Police
11 Petrol Station
12 Pura Dalem
   Penunggekan

back over Bangli, or you can walk along the ridge line to a viewpoint where all of southern Bali is spread out below. You can see the long sweep of Sanur Beach with the Natour Bali Beach Hotel, a minuscule rectangular box, far away.

Pura Dalem Penunggekan

Just below Bangli, beside the road to Gianyar, there's an interesting temple of the dead, the Pura Dalem Penunggekan. The reliefs on the front illustrate particularly vivid scenes of wrongdoers getting their just desserts in the afterlife.

Places to Stay & Eat

The *Artha Sastra Inn* is a former palace residence and is still run by the grandson of the last king of Bangli. Rooms, some with private bathrooms, cost from 10,000 to 20,000 rp. It doesn't look much from the outside, but it's a pleasant, friendly place, quite popular and very centrally located – right across from the bus terminal and main square.

The *Losmen Dharmaputra*, a short distance up the road towards Kintamani, is a YHA affiliate. It's cheap, but pretty basic and not very attractive. Rather drab singles/doubles cost 5000/7000 rp and you can also get food there. *Adnyana Homestay* (☎ 0366 91244), near the sports ground, is newer and brighter, and costs about 10,000 rp for a room.

Bangli has a good night market (pasar malam) in the square opposite the Artha Sastra and there are some great warungs but they all close early.

KLUNGKUNG

Klungkung was once the centre of Bali's most important kingdom and a great artistic and cultural focal point. The Gelgel dynasty, the most powerful kingdom on Bali at that time, held power for about 300 years, until the arrival of the Dutch. It was here that the Klungkung school of painting was developed. This style, where subjects were painted in side profile (like wayang kulit figures), is still used today, but most of the

of them are now damaged. The inner courtyard has an 11-roofed meru (Balinese shrine) and a shrine with thrones for the three figures of the Hindu trinity – Brahma, Shiva and Vishnu. This is one of the finest temples on Bali.

Bukit Demulih

Three km from Bangli, along the Tampaksiring road, is Bukit Demulih, a hill just off the south side of the road. If you can't find the sign pointing to it, ask local children to direct you. You can make the short climb to the top where there's a small temple and good views paintings are produced in Kamasan, a few km outside Klungkung.

Klungkung is a major public transport junction and a busy market town with pony-drawn carts (dokars) providing an exotic touch. The bus and bemo terminal is a major gathering point, particularly at night when a busy night market (pasar malam) operates there.

Royal Palace

When the ruling Dewa Agung dynasty moved here from Gelgel in 1710, a new palace, the Semara Pura, was established. It was laid out as a large square, believed to be in the form of a mandala, with courtyards, gardens, pavilions and moats, and was built by the best artisans available. Most of the palace and grounds were destroyed during Dutch attacks in 1908, and the two pavilions you see now, and the gateway on the south side of the square west of the Bale Kambang, are all that remains. These remaining struc-

tures are sometimes referred to as Taman Gili, 'island garden', and have been extensively restored and rebuilt. The complex, now surrounded by a stone wall, is on the south side of the road as you reach the centre of town from Denpasar. Entry costs 500 rp, and it costs 200 rp to stop in the carpark across the road.

Kertha Gosa The Kertha Gosa (Hall of Justice) stands in the north-east corner of the Taman Gili, a marked contrast to the busy intersection and modern town. The Kertha Gosa is the open pavilion on the corner of the complex, and a superb example of Klungkung architecture; the roof is completely painted inside with fine paintings in the Klungkung style. The paintings, done on asbestos sheeting, were installed in the 1940s, replacing the cloth paintings which had deteriorated. Further repainting and restoration took place in the '60s and '80s but the style of the paintings appears to have

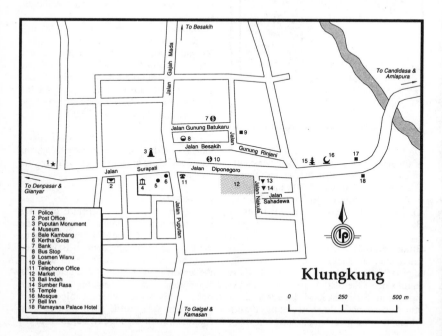

1 Police
2 Post Office
3 Puputan Monument
4 Museum
5 Bale Kambang
6 Kertha Gosa
7 Bank
8 Bus Stop
9 Losmen Wisnu
10 Bank
11 Telephone Office
12 Market
13 Bali Indah
14 Sumber Rasa
15 Temple
16 Mosque
17 Bell Inn
18 Ramayana Palace Hotel

Klungkung

been fairly consistent. Virtually the only record of the earlier paintings was a photograph of the ceiling taken by Walter Spies in the '30s. Given Bali's humid climate there is, of course, rapid deterioration and already the current paintings are looking very second-hand.

This was effectively the 'supreme court' of the Klungkung kingdom, where disputes and cases which could not be settled at the village level were eventually brought. The defendant, standing before the three priests who acted as judges (kerthas), could gaze up at the ceiling and see wrongdoers being tortured by demons and the innocent enjoying the pleasures of Balinese heaven. In the colonial period, the court was used to deal with questions of traditional law (adat) while colonial law was handled by Dutch courts.

Bale Kambang Adjoining the Kertha Gosa in the Taman Gili is the beautiful Bale Kambang (Floating Pavilion), though much of what you see today is the result of rebuilding this century. Its ceiling is painted in Klungkung style, having been repainted in 1945. Around the Kertha Gosa and the Bale Kambang note the statues of top-hatted European figures, an amusing departure from the normal statues you'll see of entrance guardians.

Museum

Across the courtyard to the west of the Bale Kambang is a new museum. It exhibits paintings and handcrafts of Klungkung, and might give you a good introduction to the wayang and Kamasan styles. All exhibits are labelled in English. The museum is open from 7 am to 4 pm, and admission is 500 rp.

Places to Stay & Eat

Few travellers stay overnight in Klungkung as it's only 40 km from Denpasar, even less from Ubud and, in the other direction, only another 16 km to Padangbai or 25 km to Candidasa. If you do want to stop for the night there are a couple of possibilities, the nicest of which is the *Ramayana Palace Hotel* (☎ 0366 21044) on the Candidasa side

of town. It's a pleasant place with a restaurant in a pavilion out the back, far enough from the busy main road to be quiet. The good rooms are quite big and cost 20,000 rp with a bathroom. Small and fairly spartan rooms with shared mandi cost 10,000 rp.

Less attractive alternatives include the *Losmen Wisnu* near the bus terminal in the centre. The upstairs rooms are much brighter than those downstairs. The very basic *Bell Inn* is almost opposite the Ramayana Palace Hotel.

Apart from the Ramayana Palace's restaurant there are several places to eat including the Chinese *Restaurant Bali Indah* and *Restaurant Sumber Rasa*. They're both neat and clean and across from the market.

Things to Buy

There are a number of good shops along Jalan Diponegoro selling Klungkung-style paintings and some interesting antiques. Klungkung is also a good place for buying temple umbrellas – several shops sell them.

Getting There & Away

Bemos bound for Candidasa and Amlapura all pass through Klungkung. Bemos also shuttle up and down the mountain road from Klungkung to Besakih.

KUSAMBA

The road beyond Klungkung was cut by lava flows from the '63 eruption of Agung, but the lava is now overgrown. Turning south off the main road brings you to the coast, and the fishing village of Kusamba, where you'll see lines of colourful fishing prahus (outriggers) lined up on the beach. Fishing is normally done at night and the 'eyes' on the front of the boats help navigation through the darkness. Regular supply trips are made to the islands of Nusa Penida and Nusa Lembongan, clearly visible opposite Kusamba. You could try to get on one of these cargo prahus – departures depend on the weather, tide and demand, but get there early. It's more convenient from Sanur or Padangbai.

Just beyond Kusamba you can see the

thatched roofs of salt-panning huts along the beach. Salt-water-saturated sand from the beach is dried out around these huts and then further processed inside the huts. Although salt processed by machine is cheaper, connoisseurs still demand real sea salt.

GOA LAWAH

Beyond Kusamba the road continues close to the coast and after a few km you come to the Goa Lawah (Bat Cave). The cave in the cliff face here is packed, crammed, jammed full of bats.

The cave, part of a temple, is said to lead all the way to Besakih but it's unlikely anybody would be too enthusiastic about investigating! The bats provide sustenance for the legendary giant snake, Naga Basuki, which is said to live in the cave. A distinctly batty stench exudes from the cave, and the roofs of the temple shrines in front of the cave are also liberally coated with bat droppings. Entry to the bat cave temple is 500 rp (100 rp for children) including hire of a temple scarf. It costs another 200 rp to park in the carpark. The souvenir sellers who besiege visitors are very pushy. It's hard to think of a good reason to stop here.

PADANGBAI

Padangbai is the port for the ferry service between Bali and Lombok. It's off the main Klungkung to Amlapura road, 54 km from Denpasar. The town is a couple of km off the main road, on a perfect little bay, with one of the two main shipping ports in the south of the island. As in some other coastal towns, there's a large Muslim population.

If you walk around to the right from the wharf and follow the trail up the hill, you'll eventually come to the idyllic Pantai Kecil (Little Beach) on the exposed coast outside the bay. There are other pretty and secluded beaches around. Out on the northern corner of the bay is the temple of Pura Silayukti, where Empu Kuturan, who introduced the caste system to Bali in the 11th century, is said to have lived.

Cruise ships visiting Bali use Padangbai but have to anchor offshore outside the harbour as only small ships can actually enter the bay. When the cruise ships are in, Padangbai is temporarily transformed into a cacophonous souvenir market with sellers flocking in from all over the island.

Information

There are moneychangers in the main street, a post office, and a wartel from which you can make international calls at higher than normal prices. The tourist information office is in the carpark near the dock. It's not a great place for shopping, but one interesting speciality is the beautiful model jukungs (outriggers), made by Made Sawela on Jalan Silayukti.

Diving

There's some pretty good diving on the coral reefs around Padangbai, though the water can be a little cold, and visibility is not always good. Most of the Bali dive operations do trips here, but there doesn't seem to be a local firm. The beachfront restaurants cater to dive groups, so ask them for information. You'll need to charter a boat to reach the main sites, Pura Jepun and the Blue Lagoon, both to the north. The coral isn't spectacular, but there's a good variety of fish, and a 40-metre wall at the Blue Lagoon.

Places to Stay

Most visitors to Padangbai stay at one of the pleasant beachfront places – the gentle arc of beach with colourful fishing boats drawn up on the sand is postcard perfect. Closest to the village is the *Rai Beach Inn* which has a collection of two-storey cottages looking rather like traditional rice barns. There's an open sitting area downstairs and a sleeping area with verandah upstairs. They cost 20,000 rp and the only drawback with these cottages is that the high wall which surrounds each one stops you from chatting with your neighbours. The inn also has straightforward single-storey rooms with bathroom at 15,000 rp.

Next along the beach is the *Kerti Beach Inn* with simple rooms at 8000 rp and also double-storey thatched cottages, very

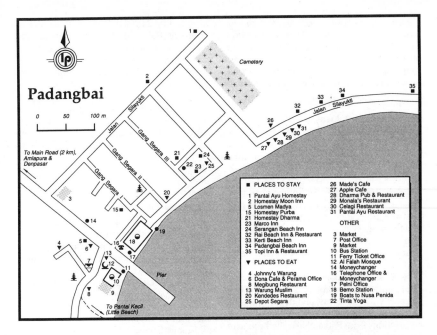

Padangbai

0   50   100 m

To Main Road (2 km),
Amlapura &
Denpasar

Cemetery

To Pantai Kecil
(Little Beach)

Pier

■ PLACES TO STAY	26 Made's Cafe
	27 Apple Cafe
1 Pantai Ayu Homestay	28 Dharma Pub & Restaurant
2 Homestay Moon Inn	29 Monala's Restaurant
5 Losmen Madya	30 Celagi Restaurant
15 Homestay Purba	31 Pantai Ayu Restaurant
21 Homestay Dharma	
23 Marco Inn	OTHER
24 Serangan Beach Inn	
32 Rai Beach Inn & Restaurant	3 Market
33 Kerti Beach Inn	7 Post Office
34 Padangbai Beach Inn	9 Market
35 Topi Inn & Restaurant	10 Bus Station
	11 Ferry Ticket Office
▼ PLACES TO EAT	12 Al Falah Mosque
	14 Moneychanger
4 Johnny's Warung	16 Telephone Office &
6 Dona Cafe & Perama Office	Moneychanger
8 Megibung Restaurant	17 Pelni Office
13 Warung Muslim	18 Bemo Station
20 Kendedes Restaurant	19 Boats to Nusa Penida
25 Depot Segara	22 Tinta Yoga

similar in style to the Rai Beach Inn, at 12,000 rp. The third place in the central beachfront cluster is the *Padangbai Beach Inn*, where rooms are 7000/9000 rp for singles/doubles. The rooms are straight out of the standard losmen design book but, as they all face the sea, they're the best situated rooms in Padangbai.

If you continue along the beach right to the end of the bay, you'll find the *Topi Inn & Restaurant*. It has small rooms upstairs at 8000/10,000 rp for singles/doubles, and dorm beds at 2000 rp.

The beachfront places keep most visitors to Padangbai happy but there are several other alternatives. *Pantai Ayu Homestay* is back from the beach behind the cemetery, but still a good place to stay, with a variety of rooms from 8000/10,000 rp up to 20,000 rp. In the village, *Homestay Dharma* is a plain family compound with very neat and tidy rooms at 9000 rp for a double. Other places in town include *Homestay Purba*, with rooms from 6000/8000 rp to 8000/10,000 rp, *Marco Inn* and *Serangan Beach Inn*.

Places to Eat

Restaurants have been proliferating in Padangbai even faster than hotels. Right across from the Rai Beach Inn there's a line-up of simple beachfront warungs where Ibu Komang, the 'mama' of the *Pantai Ayu Restaurant*, wins the popularity contest hands down. Everyone gets a cheery welcome and the food is simple and well prepared.

Other places in this group on the beach are the long-running *Celagi Restaurant*, *Monala's Restaurant*, the *Dharma Pub & Restaurant* (popular with visiting tour groups), *Apple Cafe* and *Made's Cafe*. At the eastern end of the beach, the *Topi Restaurant* is the fanciest place in Padangbai with an open, sand-floored dining area and a colourful menu featuring fish dishes plus the Indonesian regulars.

In the town but near the beach there's

Depot Segara and *Kendedes Restaurant*, while along the main street there are a host of small Indonesian places including the *Warung Muslim*, in front of the mosque, and *Dona Cafe*. Round past the post office, *Megibung Restaurant* may also be worth a try. None of these places are expensive.

Getting There & Away
To/From Lombok Ferries are scheduled to depart for Lombok every two hours from about 4 am to 10 pm, but they're sometimes late, and sometimes early. The fare is 4800 rp, or 8700 rp in first class. The Getting There & Away chapter for Lombok has more details. The ticket office is down by the pier.

If the fast catamaran service to Bangsal and Senggigi is operating again, get information and a ticket from the office (☎ 234428) near the moneychangers on the main road.

Bus & Bemo Buses direct to Denpasar (Batubulan) cost about 2000 rp. They connect with the ferries and depart from the carpark west of the pier. There are also bus connections from Padangbai right through to Surabaya and Yogyakarta in Java. Bemos leave from the carpark east of the pier, more frequently in the morning. The orange ones go to Candidasa (500 rp) and Amlapura; the blue ones to Klungkung.

Tourist shuttle buses go to most destinations on Bali, and connect with the ferry for destinations on Lombok (10,000 rp to Mataram or Senggigi, about 20,000 rp for the Gili Islands).

To/From Nusa Penida On the beach just east of the pier carpark you'll find the twin-engined fibreglass boats that run across the strait to Nusa Penida (4000 rp).

PADANGBAI TO CANDIDASA
It's 11 km from the Padangbai main road turn-off to Candidasa and between the two is an attractive stretch of coast which is not heavily developed.

After about four km, in the area of **Manggis**, there's an unmarked turn-off to the very exclusive *Amankila* hotel (☎ 0366

21993, fax 21995). One of three Aman resorts on Bali, this one features an isolated seaside location, and understated architecture which complements the environment. The structures are classically simple rectangular shapes with thatched roofs and lots of natural wood and stone. The three main swimming pools appear to step down into the sea, in matching shades of blue. The prices are classically round figures, which step up in elegant US$100 increments – US$300, US$400 and US$500. Most rooms have identical facilities and are of exactly the same size and layout, but you pay US$100 extra for an ocean view, and another US$100 for a private pool.

Balina Beach (Buitan)
Balina Beach is the name bestowed on the tourist development in the village of Buitan, about five or six km from the Padangbai turn-off, just after a substantial girder bridge. The original development here was intended to be a major scuba-diving centre for Bali, and though diving is offered by the two mid-range hotels, it doesn't seem to be overrun with dive groups. It's a quiet, pretty place, in the process of acquiring its first luxury hotel, and losing its beach to erosion.

Diving Diving trips from the Nelayan Village Cottages (see below), including transport and two full tanks, range from US$40 to US$50 on the trips closer to Balina, US$70 for Nusa Penida and US$85 to Pulau Menjangan, on the north coast. You can also go on the same trips to snorkel, from around US$7 to US$10.

Places to Stay *Nelayan Village Cottages* has rooms at a host of prices from as low as US$16/20 for singles/doubles up to US$40/45 for fancier rooms or US$65 for a large family unit. All prices include breakfast but the 15% service and tax charges are extra. This is a quite large and attractive development with a pool and a reasonably good bit of beach. You can fax enquiries or bookings to a Sanur number: 0361 287517 attention

Balina. Nearby, *Homestay Java* asks 10,000 rp for grotty rooms without breakfast.

Directly opposite is *Puri Buitan*, with modern, motel-style rooms from US$30/35 to US$65/75, but they give a good discount.

If you walk east along the remains of the beach for 200 metres, past the construction site, you'll find *Cangrin Beach Homestay* and *Sunrise Homestay*, which have standard losmen rooms for 15,000/20,000 rp a single/double. Only the first one serves lunch and dinner.

Other Beach Areas

Coming from the west, there are hotels and losmen off the main road several km before you reach Candidasa. Even this far out, the beach is still eroded and sea-walls have been constructed to prevent further erosion. Quite a few beachfront swimming pools seem in danger of going out to sea.

Most places to stay are secluded, mid-range to top-end package-tour hotels like the *Candi Beach Cottage* (☎ 0361 751711/2/3/4), with all the mod cons and rooms from US$60/70 to US$70/80. To get there, turn right at the volleyball court about two km or so west of Candidasa. Take a Candidasa-bound bemo from Batubulan and ask to get off at Sengkidu – about 2000 rp.

The same side road leads to the *Amarta Beach Inn Bungalows*, which has a great location, a friendly atmosphere and is good value at 15,000 rp a double, including breakfast. Opposite, *Anom Beach Inn Bungalows* (☎ 0361 233998) are a bit fancier with standard bungalows at US$22/28, and superior air-con bungalows up to US$40/50. In the same area, *Nusa Indah Beach Bungalows* are around 15,000 rp, but they are isolated with no restaurant, so you really need your own transport to get into town for meals. About one km from Candidasa, *Nirwana Cottages* (☎ 0361 236136) has only 10 rooms in a quiet location, with rates from US$35/40 to US$50. Another mid-range place is the *Rama Ocean View Bungalows* (☎ 0361 751864/5), with pool, tennis court, satellite TV etc, for US$33/35 to US$70.

As you approach Candidasa there are a few more cheapies on the beach side of the road. *Sari Jaya Seaside Cottage* is OK and quiet, and costs 10,000 rp for singles or doubles, including breakfast. A group of three cheap places, *Pelangi, Tarura* and *Flamboyant*, is just before the bridge, but not too far to walk into town.

TENGANAN

At the turn-off to Tenganan, just west of Candidasa, a little posse of motorbike riders waits by the junction, ready to ferry you up to the village for 1000 rp. Make a donation as you enter the village. There's also a walking path to Tenganan from Candidasa but the trail is sometimes hard to follow.

Tenganan is a Bali Aga village, a centre of the original Balinese prior to the Majapahit arrival. Unlike the other well-known Bali Aga centre, Trunyan, this is a reasonably friendly place and also much more interesting. Tenganan is a walled village and consists basically of two rows of identical houses stretching up the gentle slope of the hill. The houses face each other across a grassy central area where the village's public buildings are located. The Bali Aga are reputed to be exceptionally conservative and resistant to change but even here the modern age has not been totally held at bay. A small forest of TV aerials sprouts from those oh-so-traditional houses! The most striking feature of Tenganan, however, is its exceptional neatness, the hills behind providing a beautiful backdrop.

Tenganan is full of strange customs, festivals and practices.

A magical cloth known as *kamben gringsing* is also woven here – a person wearing it is said to be protected against black magic. A peculiar, old-fashioned version of the gamelan known as the gamelan selunding is still played here and girls dance an equally ancient dance known as the Rejang.

At the annual Usaba Sambah Festival, held around June or July, men fight with their fists wrapped in sharp-edged pandanus leaves – similar events occur on the island of Sumba, far to the east in Nusa Tenggara. At

The Legend of Tenganan

There's a delightful legend about how the villagers of Tenganan came to acquire their land. The story pops up in various places in Indonesia, but in slightly different forms. The Tenganan version relates how Dalem Bedaulu (the king with a pig's head – see the Bedulu section in the Ubud chapter for details) lost a valuable horse. When its carcass was found by the villagers of Tenganan, the king offered them a reward. They asked that they be given the land where the horse was found – that is, all the area where the dead horse could be smelt.

The king sent a man with a keen nose who set off with the village chief and walked an enormous distance without ever managing to get away from the foul odour. Eventually accepting that enough was enough the official headed back to Bedulu, scratching his head. Once out of sight the village chief pulled a large hunk of dead horse out from under his clothes. ■

this same festival, small, hand-powered ferris wheels are brought out and the village girls are ceremonially twirled round. There are other Bali Aga villages in the vicinity including Asak, where an ancient instrument, the *gamelan gambang*, is still played.

In recent years, festivals have often been cancelled in Tenganan because the village's population has been in steep decline. If a villager marries outside the Tenganan circle he or she loses their Bali Aga status. With such a small population pool and declining fertility, this village and its unique culture may eventually disappear.

CANDIDASA

The road reaches the sea just beyond the turn-off to Tenganan, about 13 km before Amlapura, and runs close to the coast through the small village of Candidasa. Ten

years ago it was just a quiet little fishing village. Two years later a dozen losmen and half a dozen restaurants had sprung up and suddenly it was *the* new beach place on Bali. Now it's shoulder to shoulder tourist development, and many find it overbuilt and unattractive. Nevertheless, many visitors enjoy Candidasa – it's quieter than Kuta, cheaper than Sanur, and a good base from which to explore eastern Bali. It's particularly popular with scuba divers. The main drawback is the lack of a beach, which has eroded away as fast as the new hotels have been erected.

Even the tourist brochures admit that Candidasa's beach disappears at high tide. If they wanted to be scrupulously honest they could add that even at low tide there isn't much of it. So how did a beach resort end up without a beach? The answer lies a few hundred metres offshore where the Candidasa reef used to be. Building all of Candidasa's hotels required large amounts of cement. An essential ingredient of cement is lime, and coral is a convenient source of limestone. So the Candidasa reef was ripped out, ground down and burnt to make the lime for the cement used to build the hotels. Without the protection of the reef the sea soon washed the beach away.

Mining of the coral reef stopped completely in 1991, but the erosion continues, even a dozen km along the coast. A series of large and intrusive T-shaped piers have been built, ironically constructed out of concrete blocks. Sand has started to rebuild itself against these piers, providing some nice, sheltered bathing places if the tide is right. It's quite good for kids, but is not exactly a wide, white palm-fringed beach. Concrete seawalls protect the foreshore from further erosion, but even these are being destroyed in places by the sea. At least it has been a lesson in the fragility of coastal environments, which has not been lost on other would-be beach resorts.

Information

Candidasa has the full complement of shops, moneychangers, travel agencies, bicycle, motorbike and car rental outlets, film developers and other facilities. There are a couple of bookshops and book exchanges and a number of postal agencies where you can buy stamps and mail cards and letters. All of them are easily found along the main street. You can make international phone calls from the private phone office at the Kubu Bali restaurant. Candidasa is in the 0361 phone district; many numbers have changed, and the new ones should have six digits.

Things to See & Do

Candidasa's temple is on the hillside across from the lagoon at the eastern end of the village strip. The fishing village, just beyond the lagoon, has colourful fishing prahus drawn up on the beach. In the early morning you can watch them coasting in after a night's fishing. The owners regularly canvas visitors for snorkelling trips to the reef and the nearby islets.

The main road east of Candidasa spirals up to the Pura Gamang Pass (*gamang* means 'to get dizzy'), from where there are fine views down to the coast. If you follow the beach from Candidasa towards Amlapura a trail climbs up over the headland with fine

views over the rocky islets off the coast. The diving around these islands is good.

Looking inland there's no sign at all of the village below or the road – just an unbroken sweep of palm trees. On a clear day, Agung rises majestically behind the range of coastal hills. Around the headland there's a long sweep of wide, exposed, black sand beach.

Diving

Gili Tepekong, which has a series of coral heads at the top of a sheer drop-off, is perhaps the best site. Other features include an underwater canyon which can be dived in good conditions. It offers the chance to see lots of fish, including some larger marine life. The currents here are strong and unpredictable, the water is cold and visibility is variable – it's recommended for experienced divers only.

Two reliable dive operators are Baruna Water Sports, Bali's biggest and most established operator, with a branch at the Puri Bagus Beach Hotel; and Barrakuda, based at Candidasa Beach Bungalows II, which can offer a full, open-water course with PADI and CAMS certification.

Places to Stay

Candidasa has a number of larger and more luxurious places with air-conditioning, swimming pools and the other accoutrements of the modern travel industry – most of them are on the beach side of the main street. A number of smaller, more tasteful hostelries have also popped up but shoestring travellers needn't worry, for there are still plenty of low-cost places to choose from, particularly in the original fishing village, hidden in the palm trees east of the lagoon. Basic doubles can be found from less than 10,000 rp. If the first price seems excessive, ask for a discount.

Places to Stay – bottom end

Look into a few places before making a decision about where to stay. Starting at the Denpasar side, *Sari Jaya Seaside Cottage*, *Pelangi, Tarura* and *Flamboyant* are cheap

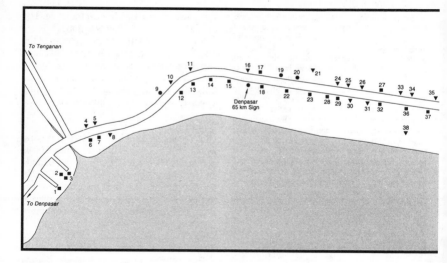

places just before town. On the right, about 200 metres from the Tenganan turn-off as you enter town, *Homestay Geringsing* has cottages from 8500/12,500 rp for singles/doubles, and beachfront cottages at 15,000 rp a double; they're all crammed into a small garden, but are very good for the price. Continuing east, the *Puri Bali* (☎ 229063) has simple, clean and well-kept rooms for 10,000/12,000 rp including breakfast, and the cheap rooms at *Wiratha's Bungalows* (☎ 233973) are also good value at around 10,000 rp.

Further along, also on the beach side,

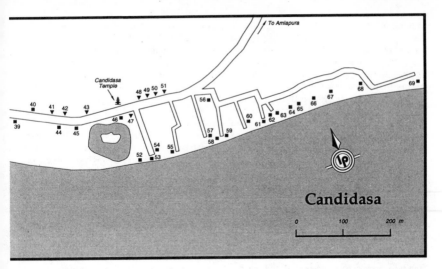

there's the *Puri Pandan* (☎ 235541), at 15,000/20,000 rp for a room with breakfast, and the popular but rock-bottom *Homestay Lilaberata*, at 8000/10,000 rp, with a good location, squat toilets and chickens. The *Pondok Bamboo Seaside Cottages* (☎ 235534) are more fancy, with rooms at

27,000/32,000 rp and a restaurant overlooking the beach.

Homestay Ida, close to the lagoon, is spacious, with pleasantly airy bamboo cottages dotted around a grassy coconut plantation. Smaller rooms are 20,000 rp, and larger rooms with a mezzanine level are 40,000 rp, including breakfast and tax. The *Homestay Kelapa Mas* (☎ 233947), next door, is also well kept and spacious, from 10,000 rp for the smallest rooms to 15,000, 17,000 and 25,000 rp for larger ones – the seafront rooms are particularly well situated.

Beyond the Kelapa Mas is the lagoon, and there are plenty of small losmen further along the beach, as well as some newer, more expensive places. Three fairly standard losmen east of the lagoon are *Dewi Bungalows, Rama Bungalows*, and the *Sindhu Brata Homestay*, all with rooms from 15,000/20,000 rp upwards, and the cheaper *Pandawa Homestay*. Further along the beach, *Barong Beach Inn, Ramayana Beach Inn*, and *Nani Beach Inn* all have basic accommodation from around 10,000/15,000 rp, as well as more expensive rooms. The *Puri Oka* (☎ 224798) has somewhat better standard rooms from 15,000/20,000 rp for singles/doubles, and there's also a swimming pool. Right at the end of the beach, the *Bunga Putri* (Princess Flower) *Homestay* is picturesquely situated with a view back down along the coast, with cheap rooms from 10,000/15,000 rp – it's hard to find and the touts are more a deterrent than an attraction.

Places to Stay – middle

As you come into town from the west, the *Samudra Arirang Hotel* (☎ 234795) is right beside the Tenganan turn-off at the start of Candidasa village. It's a pretty tacky package-tour place with rooms in concrete boxes for US$45 to US$65, plus 15.5% tax and service, minus at least US$10 discount for the asking.

Candidasa Sunrise Beach Bungalows (☎ 235539) are well located with a pool and pleasant rooms, somewhat crowded together, for US$24 to US$27 a double, including tax. Right in the centre of Candidasa the *Candidasa Beach Bungalows II* (☎ 235536) takes considerable liberty with the word 'bungalow': it's a three-storey hotel which gives the distinct impression that the maximum number of rooms has been crammed into the minimum amount of

space. Air-con singles are US$30 and doubles or twins US$35 to US$52; there are some fan-cooled rooms at US$25. Breakfast is included but service and tax are an extra 15%. *Dewa Bharata Bungalows* have a pool, bar and restaurant, and are good value at US$13/15, or US$25/30 with air-con.

Past the lagoon are a number of newer mid-range places, like the *Tinarella Beach Hotel* (☎ 221373, 233971), in a pleasant location with a pool and very elaborate decor, at US$16/20 for singles/doubles. *Ida Beach Village* (☎ 229041) is meant to resemble a traditional Balinese village, and it's very attractive if not authentic – there are not many villages where half the people live in rice barns. Nevertheless, the cottages are very comfortable, well finished and decorated and the garden is pretty. Low-season prices are US$45 to US$50; US$5 more in high season. Prices may rise as they become better known. *Puri Pudak Bungalows* (☎ 233978) are not as attractive or as expensive, but the rooms are OK and there's a pool, so it's not bad value.

Places to Stay – top end

On the side of the road away from the beach *The Watergarden* (☎ & fax 235540) is something delightfully different, with a swimming pool, and fish-filled ponds that wind around the buildings and through the lovely garden. The rooms are tasteful and each one has a verandah area like a jetty, which projects out over the water. They cost US$60/65, plus 15.5% tax and service. Room service offers meals from TJ's restaurant next door.

Another place with a difference is *Kubu Bali Bungalows* (☎ 235531), also on the north side of the road, behind the restaurant of the same name. Beautifully finished individual bungalows, streams, ponds and a swimming pool are landscaped into the steep hillside and offer views over palm trees, the coast and the sea. You'll have to climb a bit to get to your room, but it's worth it. Prices are from about US$55.

Finally the *Puri Bagus Beach Hotel* (☎ & fax 235666) is right at the end of the beach, hidden away in the palm trees which surround the original fishing village, beyond the lagoon. It's a handsome beachfront place in the Kuta/Sanur style but without the neighbours. The nicely designed rooms cost US$60/65 plus service and tax, or try a suite from US$125.

Places to Eat

Quite good food is available in Candidasa, particularly fresh seafood. Restaurants are dotted along the main road, mostly on the inland side, with the price usually corresponding to the size of the place and the quality of the decor. The better hotels also have restaurants; the one at the *Puri Bagus Beach Hotel* is probably the best and the most expensive.

Working along the road from the Denpasar end, some of the more interesting places include *Molly's Garden Cafe* and *TJ's Restaurant*, which is related to the popular TJ's in Kuta, but the food is not as Mexican, or as good. *Ciao Restaurant* serves good Italian food, while *Chez Lilly* is a newer place which already has a reputation for excellent food. *Restaurant Candra* is good for Indian dishes, while *Sumber Rasa* and the *Hawaii Restaurant* are both long-term survivors. *Tirtanadi (The TN) Restaurant* is one of the few eating places on the beach side of the road, with a cheerful atmosphere and a long cocktail list. The beachside restaurant at the *Pura Pandan Losmen* does Balinese feasts and good Chinese dishes.

Back on the north side of the road, the *Kubu Bali Restaurant* is a big place built around a pond with a bright and busy open kitchen area out front, where Indonesian and Chinese dishes are turned out with great energy and panache. It's in the middle price range, but usually worth it. For cheaper eating, try *Warung Srijati* and *Warung Rasmini*, on the same side of the road but closer to the lagoon; the latter is recommended for Indian food. Just beyond the lagoon, the *Pizzeria Candi Agung* and the *Mandara Giri Pizzaria* display different approaches to spelling although pizza is definitely on the menu at both places!

Entertainment

Barong, topeng or legong dance performances take place at 9 pm on Tuesdays and Fridays at the Pandan Harum dance stage in the centre of the Candidasa strip. Entry is 4000 rp. Some of the restaurants have video movies, and there's even music and dancing on some nights, but probably not in the low season when Candidasa is very quiet.

Getting There & Away

Candidasa is on the main route between Amlapura and Denpasar. A bus from the Batubulan terminal should cost about 2500 rp. Tourist shuttle buses also operate to Candidasa; to the airport, Denpasar or Kuta it costs 10,000 rp, to Ubud 7500 rp, or to Singaraja and Lovina beaches, 20,000 rp. Buy tickets from the agents in the main street. Cars, motorbikes and bicycles can be rented in Candidasa.

AMLAPURA

Amlapura is the main town on the eastern end of Bali and the capital of the Karangasem district. The Karangasem kingdom broke away from the Gelgel kingdom in the late 17th century and 100 years later had become the most powerful kingdom on Bali. Amlapura used to be known as Karangasem, the same as the district, but it was changed after the '63 eruption of Agung in an attempt to get rid of any influences which might provoke a similar eruption!

Information

Amlapura is the smallest of the district capitals, a sleepy place which doesn't seem to have fully woken up from its period of enforced isolation after the '63 eruption of Agung cut the roads to the rest of the island. There are banks in Amlapura but it's probably easier to change money in Candidasa. There's also a wartel and a couple of post offices.

Palaces

Amlapura's three palaces are decaying reminders of Karangasem's period as a kingdom. They date from the late 19th and early 20th centuries, but only one of the palaces is open for general inspection. You can study the Puri Gede and Puri Kertasura from the outside but special arrangements must be made for an internal inspection.

Admission to Puri Agung (also known as Puri Kanginan) costs 550 rp, and you can buy an explanation sheet at the entry desk for 200 rp – it's more informative than many 'guides'. There's an impressive three-tiered entry gate and beautiful sculptured panels on the outside of the main building. After you pass through the entry courtyard a left turn takes you to the Bale London, so called because of the British royal crest on the furniture (another version is because it's close to 'Amsterdam', see below). The decrepit building is not open to the public, as a solitary elderly member of the old royal family still lives there.

The main building is known as Maskerdam, after Amsterdam in the Netherlands, because it was the Karangasem kingdom's acquiescence to Dutch rule which allowed it to hang on long after the demise of the other Balinese kingdoms. This may be your best opportunity to view a Balinese palace but it's certainly not impressive. A number of old photographs and paintings of the royal family are displayed on the verandah. Inside you can see into several rooms including the royal bedroom and a living room with furniture which was a gift from the Dutch royal family.

On the other side of this main courtyard is the Bale Kambang, surrounded by a pond like the Bale Kambang in the palace grounds at Klungkung. The ornately decorated Bale Pemandesan, in between Maskerdam and the pool, was used for royal tooth-filing and cremation ceremonies. Opposite this, the Bale Lunjuk was used for other religious ceremonies.

There are other courtyards around the main one. It's said that about 150 members of the old family and their servants still live

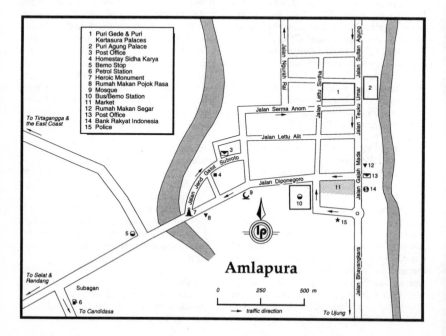

1 Puri Gede & Puri
  Kertasura Palaces
2 Puri Agung Palace
3 Post Office
4 Homestay Sidha Karya
5 Bemo Stop
6 Petrol Station
7 Heroic Monument
8 Rumah Makan Pojok Rasa
9 Mosque
10 Bus/Bemo Station
11 Market
12 Rumah Makan Segar
13 Post Office
14 Bank Rakyat Indonesia
15 Police

To Tirtagangga &
the East Coast

Jalan Nyuang Bali
Jalan Lettu Sintha
Jalan Sultan Agung
Jalan Teuku Umar
Jalan Serma Anom
Jalan Lettu Alit
Jalan Diponegoro
Jalan Gajah Mada
Jalan Jend Gator Subroto
Jalan Bhayangkara

To Selat &
Rendang

Subagan

To Candidasa

Amlapura

0   250   500 m

→ traffic direction

To Ujung

in this slowly deteriorating relic of a now-forgotten era of Balinese history.

Ujung Water Palace

A few km beyond Amlapura, on the road down to the sea, is the Ujung Water Palace, an extensive, picturesque and crumbling ruin of a once-grand palace complex. It has been deteriorating for some time but a great deal more damage has been done to it since the mid-70s, principally by an earthquake in 1979. The last king of Karangasem, Anak Agung Anglurah, was obsessed with moats, pools, canals and fountains; he completed this grand palace in 1921. You can wander around the remnants of the main pool, admire the view from the pavilion higher up the hill above the rice paddies, or continue a little further down the road to the fishing village on the coast.

Places to Stay & Eat

Amlapura has a few places to stay but not many travellers pause here – Candidasa is not far away and it's only another six km to Tirtagangga. If, for some reason, you're intent on staying here there is at least one losmen, on the right after you enter the town. A short distance in towards the centre, *Homestay Sidha Karya* was Amlapura's original losmen, but most visitors deserted it as soon as there was accommodation at Tirtagangga. It's pretty basic, but OK, with rooms at about 10,000 rp.

There's the usual collection of warungs around the bus terminal plus the *Rumah Makan Segar* on Jalan Gajah Mada. Amlapura tends to shut down early so don't leave your evening meal until too late.

Getting There & Away

There are buses from here to Singaraja and the north coast (about 2500 rp), as well as to Denpasar and points in between. Plenty of bemos go to villages in the area, for which Amlapura is a service town.

TIRTAGANGGA

Amlapura's water-loving rajah, having constructed his masterpiece at Ujung, later had another go at Tirtagangga. This water palace, built around 1947, was damaged in the 1963 eruption of Agung and during the political events that wracked Indonesia two years later. It's not grand, but it's still a place of beauty and a reminder of the power the Balinese rajahs once had. The palace has a swimming pool as well as the ornamental ponds. Entrance to the water palace is 550 rp (children 300 rp) and another 2000 rp to use the big swimming pool (children 1000 rp), or 1000 rp for the smaller, lower pool (500 rp for children). These prices have increased a lot lately, but there are some signs that the pools and grounds are being improved.

The rice terraces around Tirtagangga are reputed to be some of the most beautiful on Bali. They sweep out from Tirtagangga almost like a sea surrounding an island. Note how some of the terraces are faced with stones. A few km beyond here, on the road to the east coast, there are more dramatically beautiful terraces, often seen in photographs of Bali.

This is one of the most traditional areas on Bali. Quite a few of the villages have special or unique attractions. There are Buddhist communities near Budakling, and traditional goldsmiths, painters, carvers and so on. Some of the dances and ceremonies are found nowhere else on Bali, and have links with Lombok which was ruled from Karangasem for many years. Ask at your losmen for suggested walks in the surrounding countryside.

Places to Stay & Eat

Actually within the palace compound the *Tirta Ayu Homestay* has pleasant individual bungalows at 20,000/25,000 rp, and two large bungalows with great views for 100,000 rp. Prices include admission to the water palace swimming pools. The restaurant has a superb outlook over the palace pools.

Right by the water palace is the peaceful *Losmen Dhangin Taman Inn* with rooms at 10,000/12,000 to 15,000/20,000 rp including breakfast. The most expensive rooms are large and have an enclosed sitting area. You can sit in the courtyard, gazing across the rice paddies and the water palace while doves coo in the background. The losmen owner here is a character, and the food is not bad.

Across the road from the palace the *Rijasa Homestay* is a small and simple place with extremely neat and clean rooms at 10,000/12,000 rp, including breakfast and tea. A few steps back towards Amlapura the *Taman Sari Inn* has rooms at 8000 and 10,000 rp but it looks rather derelict.

Alternatively you can continue 300 metres beyond the water palace and climb the steep steps to the *Kusuma Jaya Inn*, the 'Homestay on the Hill', with a fine view over the rice paddies. Its prices have increased a lot – it now costs from 25,000 to 45,000 rp, and the staff are not as helpful as they used to be. A km or so further on is a new 'homestay on the hill', with good single/double rooms and outstanding views for 12,000/16,000 rp, including breakfast.

There are several good warungs on the access track to the palace; the one nearest Tirta Ayu does excellent food. Next to the carpark, the *Good Karma* has good food and plays good music.

Getting There & Away

Tirtagangga is about five or six km from the Amlapura turn-off on the main road that runs to the eastern end of Bali. Bemos from Amlapura cost 300 rp. Buses on the main road continue to Singaraja, but you can usually flag them down for transport to Culik or Tulamben – ask at your losmen about the best time.

NORTH OF TIRTAGANGGA

Soon after leaving Tirtagangga, the road starts to climb. Look for the sign to **Pura Lempuyang**, one of Bali's nine directional temples, perched on a hilltop at 768 metres.

Further on, the main road climbs over a small range of hills and descends past some of the most spectacular rice terraces on Bali. They're the last rice paddies for some distance, however, for the east coast is relatively dry and barren, in a rain shadow behind the big mountains.

The road gets back down towards sea level at **Culik** where there's a turn-off to Amed and the road round Bali's south-east corner. The main road goes north to Tulamben and continues round the east coast to Singaraja. The main feature of this route is the superb view of Gunung Agung.

AMED

This corner of Bali is not much visited by tourists, but there is some accommodation now, and there are enough signs on the main road pointing to the Hidden Paradise cottages to ensure that they won't stay hidden for long. Follow these signs from Culik to Amed, and on to where you can stay. The coast has extensive rows of troughs for evaporating sea water to extract salt – one of the main industries here. The coastline is superb and unspoilt, with views across to Lombok and back to Gunung Agung. Apart from the places listed below, tourist facilities are non-existent – bring enough cash. The diving in this area is excellent but there are no local operators; the closest one is in Tulamben. Snorkelling is easy as the coral reef is just offshore.

Places to Stay & Eat

The first place to try is *Kusumajaya Beach Inn* (☎ 0363 21250), a couple of km past Amed proper, but it's hard to be precise about the geography here. It has a restaurant and a few elaborately decorated Bali-style bungalows on a barren slope between the sea and the road – the proprietors are trying to establish a garden. Singles/doubles are 30,000/40,000 rp.

Next are the *Hidden Paradise Cottages* themselves (☎ 0361 231273), which are lovely, isolated and comfortable, with a restaurant, a pool and a great little private beach. It's a surprise to find such a quality place way out here, but with rooms from US$30 to US$65 it's not a low-budget option.

Continuing south along the coast you arrive at *Vienna Beach Bungalows*, a cosy complex with bamboo cottages near the water at 24,000 rp, and others closer to the road for 17,000 rp. They can arrange diving, fishing and sailing trips. Crossing one or two more little hills brings you to *Good Karma*, with classic, basic, bamboo beachside bungalows on stilts at 15,000 and 20,000 rp including breakfast. The main attraction advertised is 'talking and laughing with Baba', the friendly proprietor.

Getting There & Away

It's easy to find these places if you have your own transport. Public transport is easy to Culik, but from there to Amed might be difficult – try to be there early in the day as there are always more bemos then.

The road around the south-east is narrow, winding and hilly, but it's mostly sealed and definitely passable. You might almost be safer with a motorbike than a car, because you'll have more chance of getting out of the way of an oncoming vehicle – be extremely careful. A bemo would be uncomfortable, and you won't see the views. Mostly the road follows the slopes of Gunung Seraya, way above the sea, and there's spectacular coastal scenery. It's a pretty dry area and there are no rice fields, but some places have extensive vineyards so it can look almost Mediterranean. From Amed round to Amlapura is probably only about 30 km, but allow at least two hours to enjoy the trip.

TULAMBEN

The small village of Tulamben has the only places to stay around the east coast. The beach here is composed of pebbles rather than sand but the water is clear and the snorkelling good. In June and July there's good windsurfing. It's an interesting place to pause on a trip around the barren east coast.

The Wreck of the Liberty

Tulamben's prime attraction is the huge WW II wreck of a US cargo ship, the *Liberty*, which is the most popular dive site on Bali. On 11 January 1942 the armed US cargo ship USAT *Liberty* was torpedoed by a Japanese submarine about 15 km south-west of Lombok. It was taken in tow by the destroyers HMNS *Van Ghent* and USS *Paul Jones* with the intention of beaching it on the coast

of Bali and retrieving its cargo of raw rubber and railway parts. When its condition looked perilous the crew were evacuated and, although it was successfully beached, the rapid spread of the war through Indonesia prevented the cargo from being saved.

Built in 1915, the *Liberty* sat on the beach at Tulamben, a prominent east-coast landmark, until 1963 when the violent eruption of Gunung Agung toppled it beneath the surface. Or at least that's one version of the story. Another relates that it sank some distance offshore and the lava flow from the eruption extended the shoreline almost out to the sunken vessel. Whatever the course of events it lies just 40 or 50 metres offshore, almost parallel to the beach with its bow only a couple of metres below the surface.

Diving

To find the wreck simply walk about 100 metres north of the Gandu Mayu Bungalows, the northernmost beach losmen, to the small white toilet-block building by the beach. Swim straight out from the white building and you'll suddenly see the huge wreck rearing up from the depths. It's within easy reach of snorkellers, who can swim without effort around the bow, which is heavily encrusted with coral and a haven for colourful fish.

Of course scuba divers can see a lot more of the wreck; the best parts are between 15 and 30 metres deep. The ship is more than 100 metres long – this is a *big* wreck – but the hull is broken into sections and you can easily get inside it. The bow is in quite good shape, the midships region is badly mangled and the stern is intact. In fact the main attraction is not so much the wreck itself, but the coral which encrusts it and the huge number and variety of fish it supports – as many as 400 species.

Many divers commute to Tulamben from Sanur, Candidasa, and Lovina, and it can get crowded between 11 am and 4 pm, with up to 50 divers on the wreck at a time. It's better to stay the night in Tulamben and dive before or after the crowds. You will want at least two dives to explore the site.

Another dive site here is the coral wall, just east of the Bali Timur Bungalows. It drops over 60 metres to a sandy bottom, and has a wide variety of fish, including some quite unusual species, and various types of sponges.

There is a dive guide, compressor and rental equipment at the Paradise Palm Beach Bungalows. Certified divers pay US$50 for two dives on the wreck, all inclusive.

Places to Stay & Eat

Paradise Palm Beach Bungalows, the village's first place to stay, is a cheerful little losmen with a restaurant right on the beach. Singles/doubles cost 20,000/25,000 rp with breakfast; cheaper rooms are available away from the beach, and closer to the compressor. The bungalows are neat, clean and well kept with bamboo chairs and a table on the verandahs which overlook a pleasant garden.

The *Bali Timur Bungalows*, just on the Amlapura side, are OK at 15,000/20,000 rp, and the *Gandu Mayu Bungalows*, closest to the wreck, charge 25,000 rp. About 1½ km to the south east, there's a new, upmarket place called the *Saya Resort*, which is strictly a package-tour place for divers.

TULAMBEN TO YEH SANIH

Beyond Tulamben the road continues to skirt the slopes of Agung, with frequent evidence of lava flows from the '63 eruption. Beyond Agung, Gunung Abang and then the outer crater of Gunung Batur also slope down to the sea. Shortly before Yeh Sanih (see the North Bali chapter) there's a famous (but not very interesting) horse bath at **Tejakula**. Just before Yeh Sanih you can turn inland to the village of **Sembiran**, noted as a traditional centre for woodcarving. The scenery is stark but an interesting contrast to the rest of Bali, there are frequent vistas of the sea, and the rainfall is so low you can count on sunny weather. None of the towns or villages along this route are set up for tourists.

AMLAPURA TO RENDANG

A back road to Rendang branches off from the Amlapura to Denpasar road, just a km or two out of Amlapura. The road gradually climbs up into the foothills of Gunung Agung, running through some pretty countryside. It's a less-travelled route, which makes it difficult on public bemos. If you have your own wheels (a bicycle is fine), you'll find it very scenic, with some interesting places to stop. At Rendang you can turn north to Besakih, south to Klungkung, or take the very pretty minor road across to Bangli. If you have the time, the energy, and a smattering of Bahasa Indonesia, this would be a wonderful area for trekking. There are very traditional villages between Bebandem and the coast (you could walk down to Tenganan), and there are lovely views everywhere. You can also climb Agung by heading north from Selat (see below).

The road runs through **Abian Soan**, **Bebandem** (which has a busy market every three days), **Sibetan**, **Selat** and **Muncan** before reaching **Rendang**. Sibetan and Rendang are both well known for the salaks grown there. This delicious fruit has a curious 'snakeskin' covering. It's worth diverting a km or so at **Putung** to enjoy the fantastic view down to the coast. Only here do you realise just how high up you have climbed.

Shortly before Selat you can take a road that runs south-west through **Iseh** and **Sideman** to meet the Amlapura to Klungkung road. The German artist Walter Spies lived in Iseh for some time from 1932. Later, the Swiss painter Theo Meier, nearly as famous as Spies for his influence on Balinese art, lived in the same house. Sideman was a base for Swiss ethnologist Urs Ramseyer, and is also a centre for traditional culture and arts, particularly weaving of songket with threads of silver and gold.

Places to Stay

Three km along the Rendang road from the junction as you leave Amlapura, *Homestay Lila* is a very pretty little place in the rice paddies at Abian Soan. It's a half-hour walk from the homestay to Bukit Kusambi, which has a great panorama.

Further along towards Rendang, you can

turn off the road a km or so to the superbly situated *Putung Central Country Club*, a set of government-run bungalows with a restaurant, tennis court and brilliant view. It's somewhat run down, and charges 25,000/30,000 rp for two-storey bungalows, with a bathroom and small sitting area downstairs, but if you don't fall for this they might offer you a cheaper room. Set on the edge of a ridge, the bungalows overlook the coast far, far below. You can see large ships anchored off Padangbai and across to Nusa Penida.

The *Homestay Sideman* is a delightful place to stay at Sideman, but it's a bit expensive at around 45,000 rp per person, though that includes all meals. It's pleasantly old fashioned, with four-poster beds, interesting decorations and lots of books to read.

BESAKIH

Perched nearly 1000 metres up the side of Gunung Agung is Bali's most important temple, Pura Besakih. In all, it comprises about 30 separate temples in seven terraces up the hill, all within one enormous complex.

The temple was probably first constructed more than 1000 years ago; 500 years later, it became the state temple of the powerful Gelgel and Klungkung kingdoms. Today, it's the 'mother temple' of all Bali – every district on Bali has its own shrine or temple at Besakih and just about every Balinese god you care to name is also honoured there. In addition, there are also family temples, mostly for local families, with shrines and memorials going back several generations. Apart from its size and majestic location, Besakih is also probably the best kept temple you'll see on the island. This is not a temple simply built and then left to slowly decay.

As well as being the Balinese mother temple, Besakih is also the mother of Balinese financial efforts. You pay to park (300 rp per car; 100 rp for a motorbike), pay to enter (550 rp per person), pay to rent a scarf (1000 rp!) and then brave the usual large collection of souvenir sellers.

The temple is definitely impressive, but you do not need a guide to see it. So if someone latches on to you and begins to tell you about the temple, let them know quickly whether you want their services.

Places to Stay

About five km below Besakih the *Arca Valley Inn* has a restaurant and rooms for about 12,000/15,000 rp. It's prettily situated in a valley by a bend in the road. This is a

Pura Besakih

good place to stay if you want to climb Gunung Agung from Besakih and want an early start. There is also a losmen close to the temple entrance.

Getting There & Away

The usual route to Besakih is by bus or bemo to Klungkung from where there are regular bemos up the hill to the temple for about 1000 rp. If there are no direct bemos about to depart, get one to Rendang or Menanga, then another to Besakih. After about 2 pm you may have trouble getting a bemo back, so leave early or be prepared to charter or hitch.

GUNUNG AGUNG

Gunung Agung is Bali's highest and most revered mountain, an imposing peak from most of southern and eastern Bali, though it's often obscured by cloud and mist. Though most books and maps give its height as 3142

The 1963 Eruption

The most disastrous volcanic eruption in Bali this century took place in 1963 when Agung blew its top in no uncertain manner and at a time of considerable prophetic and political importance.

March 8, 1963 was to be the culmination of Eka Desa Rudra, the greatest of all Balinese sacrifices and an event which only takes place every 100 years according to the Balinese calendar. At the time of the eruption, it had been more than 100 Balinese years (115 years on the lunar calendar) since the last Eka Desa Rudra, but there was some dispute amongst the priests as to the correct and most propitious date.

Naturally the temple at Besakih was a focal point for the festival but Agung was already acting strangely as preparations were being made in late February. The date of the ceremony was looking decidedly unpropitious, but Sukarno, then the president of Indonesia, had already scheduled an international conference of travel agents to witness the great occasion as a highlight of their visit to the country, and he would not allow it to be postponed. Agung had been dormant since 1843 but by the time the sacrifices commenced, the mountain was belching smoke and ash, glowing and rumbling ominously. The travel agents saw what must have been one of the great sights of history – a once-a-century Balinese celebration with a near-erupting volcano as a backdrop. Strangely – perhaps wisely – Sukarno did not attend, but in any event, Gunung Agung contained itself until the travel agents had flown home.

On 17 March Agung exploded. The catastrophic eruption killed more than 1000 people (some estimate 2000) and destroyed entire villages – 100,000 people lost their homes. Streams of lava and hot volcanic mud poured right down to the sea at several places, completely covering roads and isolating the eastern end of the island for some time. The entire island was covered in ash, and crops were wiped out everywhere. The torrential rainfall that followed the eruptions compounded the damage as boiling hot ash and boulders known as *lahar* were swept down the mountain side, wreaking havoc on many villages like Subagan, just outside Amlapura, and Selat, further along the road towards Rendang. The whole of Bali suffered a drastic food shortage and many Balinese, whose rice land was completely ruined, had to be resettled in west Bali and Sulawesi.

Although Besakih is high on the slopes of Agung, only about six km from the crater, the temple suffered little damage from the eruption. Volcanic dust and gravel flattened timber and bamboo buildings around the temple complex but the stone structures came through unscathed. The inhabitants of the villages of Sorga and Lebih, also high up on Agung's slopes, were all but wiped out. Most of the people killed at the time of the eruption were burnt and suffocated by searing clouds of hot gas that rushed down the volcano's slopes. Agung erupted again on 16 May, with serious loss of life although not on the same scale as the March eruption.

The Balinese take signs and portents seriously – that such a terrible event should happen as they were making a most important sacrifice to the gods was not taken lightly. Sukarno's political demise two years later, following the failed communist coup, could be seen as a consequence of his defying the power of the volcanic deity. The interrupted series of sacrifices finally recommenced 16 years later, in 1979. ■

metres, some say it lost its top in the 1963 eruption and it is now only 3014 metres. The summit is an oval crater, about 500 metres across, with its highest point on the western edge above Besakih.

It's possible to climb Agung from various directions, but the two shortest and most popular routes are from the temple at Besakih, and up the southern flank from Selat, via Sebudi. The latter route goes to the lower edge of the crater rim, and you can't make your way from there round to the very highest point. If that's important to you, climb from Besakih. Try to get to the top before 8 am, to have the best chance of seeing the view before the clouds form. This means starting well before dawn, so plan your climb when there will be some moonlight, and take a torch (flashlight). Also take plenty of water and food, waterproof clothing, a warm woollen sweater and extra batteries – just in case.

You should take a guide for either route. Before you start, or early in the climb, the guide will stop at a shrine and make an offering and some prayers. This is a holy mountain and you should show respect. Besides, you will want to have everything going for you on the climb.

Climb from Selat

This route involves the least walking because there is a serviceable road from Selat to the Pura Pasar Agung temple, high on the southern slopes of the mountain. From there you can climb to the top in as little as two hours, but allow at least three or four. Selat is on the Amlapura to Rendang road, and you should report to the police station here before you start, and again when you return. If you haven't already arranged transport and a guide, the police will be able to help. One recommended guide is Ketut Uriada, a primary school teacher at Muncan, a few km west of Selat. He's well known in Muncan, and he can help arrange the practicalities. He'll charge around 20,000 rp, plus whatever it costs for transport, food etc.

The road climbs from Selat to Sebudi, then very steeply to the temple. You can stay the night in Selat and drive up early in the morning, or drive up the day before and stay overnight at the temple. A donation and some devotions may be appropriate here. Pura Pasar Agung (Agung Market Temple) has been greatly enlarged and improved, in part as a monument to the 1963 eruption which devastated this area – evidence of the eruption is still clear beside the road from Sebudi.

Start climbing from the temple at around 3 or 4 am. There are numerous trails through the pine forest – this is where you need your guide – but after an hour or so you'll climb above the tree line. The ground is stony and can be loose and broken towards the summit. Allow plenty of time to get down again. From the temple you can walk down to Sebudi, from where there are bemos, or arrange for a chartered bemo to pick you up at the temple.

Climb from Besakih

If you want to climb Gunung Agung from Besakih you must leave no later than 6.30 am if you want to get down before nightfall; much earlier if you want a clear view from the top. Allow five to six hours for the climb, and four to five for the descent. It's easy to get lost on the lower trails so hire a guide at Besakih – the cost could be anything from 20,000 to 30,000 rp depending on the size of your party, plus a few thousand rp as a tip. Arrange the details the day before, and stay in a losmen near Besakih so you can start early.

South-West Bali

Most of the places regularly visited in south-western Bali, like Sangeh or Tanah Lot, are easy day trips from Denpasar, Kuta or Ubud. The rest of the west tends to be a region travellers zip through on their way to or from Java. A few places are worth a stop though, including some quiet beaches, a few out-of-the-way places to stay, and the southern regions of the Bali Barat National Park.

In the latter half of the last century this was an area of warring kingdoms. With the Dutch takeover in the early 20th century, however, the princes' lands were redistributed among the general population. With this bounty of rich agricultural land the region around Tabanan quickly became one of the wealthiest parts of Bali, and has some fine rice-field scenery.

Further west, spectacular roads head inland across the central mountains to the north coast. Along the southern coast there are long stretches of wide black sand beach and rolling surf. Countless tracks run south of the main road, usually to fishing villages which rarely see a tourist despite being so close to a main transport route.

SEMPIDI, LUKLUK & KAPAL
Kapal is the garden gnome and temple curlicue centre of Bali. If you're building a new temple and need a balustrade for a stairway, a capping for a wall, a curlicue for the top of a roof, or any of the other countless standard architectural motifs then the numerous shops which line the road through Kapal will probably have what you need. Or if you want some garden ornamentation, from a comic-book deer to a brightly painted Buddha, then again you've come to the right place.

Kapal's Pura Sadat is the most important temple in the area. Although it was restored after WW II (it was damaged in an earthquake earlier this century), the Sadat is a very ancient temple, possibly dating back to the 12th century.

TANAH LOT
The spectacularly located Tanah Lot is pos-

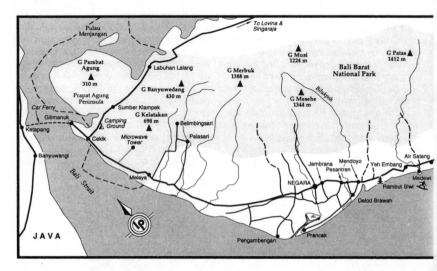

sibly the best known and most photographed temple on Bali. The tourist crowds here are phenomenal, especially at sunset, and the commercial hype is terrible. Tanah Lot sunset tours are heavily promoted in all the tourist areas. The temple, perched on a little rocky islet, looks superb whether delicately lit by the dawn light or starkly outlined at sunset. But can it ever live up to the hype?

It's a well-organised tourist trap – you pay the parking attendants (350 rp) and they show you where to park. Dozens of souvenir shops are in a sort of sideshow alley, which you can easily bypass. There's a ticket office to collect the entry fee (550 rp), then you follow the crowd down the steps to the sea. You can walk over to the temple itself at low tide, or climb up to the left and sit at one of the many tables along the cliff top. Order a drink (5000 rp for a beer!) or dinner, get your camera ready, and wait for 'The Sunset'.

By this stage a lot of the tourists are muttering things like 'this had better be good', and are ready to demand their money back if the sunset isn't suitably spectacular.

For the Balinese, Tanah Lot is one of the important and venerated sea temples. Like Pura Luhur Ulu Watu, at the southern end of the island, Tanah Lot is closely associated with the 16th-century Majapahit priest, Nirartha. It's said that Nirartha passed by here and, impressed with the tiny island's superb setting, suggested to local villagers that this would be a good place to construct a temple.

Places to Stay & Eat
The *Dewi Sinta Cottages* (☎ 0361 23545) are in souvenir shop alley, not far from the ticket office. They're new, clean and unexciting, with standard rooms at US$12/16, air-con rooms with 'hot and cold raining shower' for US$23/25.

Getting There & Away
Tanah Lot is reached by turning off the Denpasar to Gilimanuk road near Kediri and heading down to the coast – it's very well signposted. By bemo you start from Ubung terminal at Denpasar. From there go to Kediri (1000 rp) then get another bemo to the coast (about 350 rp). There is no regular service out of Tanah Lot, so if you stay for the sunset, your only options may be to stay the night, charter a bemo or walk.

If you have your own wheels, leave early

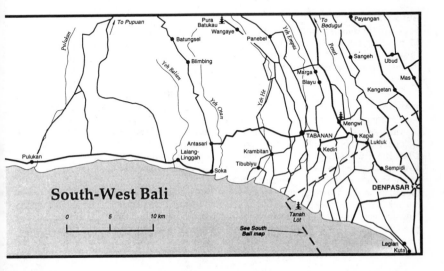

South-West Bali

to miss the tourist jam, or hang around till it's finished. Tours to Tanah Lot usually take in a few other sites like Bedugul, Mengwi or Sangeh; a basic half-day excursion will cost from 20,000 rp, an upmarket tour with dinner, US$28.

MENGWI

The huge state temple of Pura Taman Ayun, surrounded by a wide moat, was the main temple of the Mengwi kingdom, which survived until 1891 when it was conquered by the neighbouring kingdoms of Tabanan and Badung. The temple was originally built in 1634 and extensively renovated in 1937. It's a very large, spacious temple and the elegant moat gives it a very fine appearance. The first courtyard is a large, open grassy expanse and the inner courtyard has a multitude of merus (multi-tiered shrines).

In a beautiful setting across the moat from the temple is a rather lost-looking arts centre. There's also a small museum with models and dioramas of Balinese festivals, which are unspectacular and not very informative. The *Water Palace Restaurant* overlooking the moat is not a bad place for lunch, but service is not quick.

BELAYU

In Belayu (or Blayu), a small village between Mengwi and Marga, traditional songket sarongs are woven with intricate gold threads. These are for ceremonial use only, not for everyday wear.

MARGA

Near Marga, west of the road three km north of Mengwi, is a peculiar memorial to Lt Colonel I Gusti Ngurah Rai, a local hero. In 1946 Rai led his men in a futile defence against a larger and better armed Dutch force trying to recover Bali after the departure of the Japanese. The Dutch called in air support but the Balinese refused to surrender. The outcome was similar to the puputans of 40 years before; all 94 of Ngurah Rai's men were killed. Denpasar's airport is named in his memory.

SANGEH

About 20 km north of Denpasar, near the village of Sangeh, stands the monkey forest of Bukit Sari. It is featured, so the Balinese say, in the *Ramayana*.

To kill the evil Rawana, king of Lanka, Hanuman had to crush him between two halves of Mahameru, the holy mountain. Rawana, who could not be destroyed on the earth or in the air, would thus be squeezed between the two elements. On his way to performing this task, Hanuman dropped a piece of the mountain near Sangeh, complete with a band of monkeys.

Of course, this sort of legend isn't unique – Hanuman dropped chunks of landscape all over the place!

There's a unique grove of nutmeg trees in the monkey forest and a temple, Pura Bukit Sari, with an interesting old garuda statue. Plus, of course, there are lots of monkeys. Take care, for the monkeys will jump all over you if you've got a pocketful of peanuts and don't dispense with them fast enough. The Sangeh monkeys have also been known to steal hats, sunglasses and even thongs from fleeing tourists! A new variation on this mischief has been created by some local people, who reclaim the items from the monkeys and then charge a ransom for their return.

This place is touristy, but the forest is cool, green and shady, and the monkeys are cute as well as cheeky. The souvenir sellers are restricted to certain areas and are easy to avoid. There's a charge for parking and for entry.

Getting There & Away

You can reach Sangeh by bemos which run direct from Denpasar – they leave from a terminal at Wangaya, on Jalan Kartini a block north of Gajah Mada, which seems to serve only one destination. There is also road access from Mengwi and from Ubud.

TABANAN

The town of Tabanan is the capital of the district of the same name. It's at the heart of the rice belt of southern Bali, the most fertile and prosperous rice-growing area on the island. It's also a great centre for dancing and

Top: Rice fields near Sideman, East Bali (GA)
Left: Swimming pool at the Amankila Hotel, East Bali (JL)
Right: Collecting fodder, Bugbug, East Bali (GA)

Top: Sunrise, Padangbai, East Bali (GE)
Bottom: Gunung Agung, East Bali (PL)

gamelan playing. Mario, the renowned dancer of the prewar period, who perfected the Kebyar dance and is featured in Covarrubias' classic guide to Bali, was from Tabanan.

It's quite a large town, with shops, banks, hospital, market etc. You could probably find a place to stay here, but no-one does. The only attraction is the **Subak Museum**, with exhibits on the irrigation and cultivation of rice, and the intricate social systems which govern it. The museum is on the left, just before you come into town, and is easy to miss. It's open from 8 am to 2 pm Monday to Thursday, closing at 11 am Friday and 12.30 pm Saturday.

AROUND TABANAN

There's not a lot of tourist activity in the southern part of Tabanan district, but it's very accessible, and a good area to see some more of Bali's most important industry, which is still agriculture rather than tourism. At nearby **Kediri**, the Pasar Hewan is one of Bali's busiest markets for cattle and other animals.

A little west of Tabanan a road turns down to the coast through **Krambitan** (or Kerambitan), a village noted for its beautiful old buildings, including two 17th-century palaces, its tradition of wayang-style painting, and its own styles of music and dance. One of the palaces provides accommodation and meals for visitors – they specialise in handling groups who are welcomed as VIPs, entertained at a Balinese feast and housed in a traditional palace bale – all for a price. It's very well done, but it must be arranged in advance, and it's usually for groups only. Phone 0361 92667 for details.

A nice, secluded place to stay is *Bee Bees Bungalows & Restaurant*, at Tibubiyu, four km south-west of Krambitan. They charge 32,000/40,000 rp, plus 10,000 rp for an extra bed, including breakfast – simple rural tranquillity doesn't come dirt cheap, but if you want somewhere that's reasonably comfortable but untouristed, this is the place.

About 10 km south of Tabanan is the village of **Pejaten**, which is a centre for the production of traditional pottery, including elaborate, ornamental roof tiles. Porcelain clay objects, which are made for purely decorative use, can be seen in the Pejaten Ceramics Workshop.

Lalang-Linggah

About 29 km from Tabanan on the road to Gilimanuk, near the village of Lalang-Linggah, the *Balian Beach Bungalows* overlook the Balian River (Yeh Balian), close to the sea and surrounded by coconut plantations. Most of the accommodation is in pavilions sleeping from three to six, costing between 35,000 and 50,000 rp. It's not really a low-budget place, but there are a few cheap bunk beds, and some rooms from 20,000 rp. There are some surf breaks round here, and safe swimming in the river. It's very peaceful, well run and friendly. Families are welcome. To get there from Denpasar, take any Negara or Gilimanuk bus and ask the driver to stop at Lalang-Linggah, near the 49-km post just before the road descends to the bridge over the Balian River.

JEMBRANA COAST

About 34 km north-east of Tabanan you cross into Bali's most sparsely populated district, Jembrana. There are some interesting backroads to the north coast, but the main road follows the north coast most of the way to Negara, the district capital. There's some beautiful scenery but little tourist development along the way.

Medewi

About 30 km from Soka, and 25 km before Negara, a large but faded sign announces the side road south to 'Medewi Surfing Point'. The turn-off is just west of Pulukan village. The beach is nothing, but Medewi is noted for its *long* left-hand wave. It works best at mid to high tide on a two-metre swell – get there early before the wind picks up.

Go down the side road to the *Hotel Nirwana*, on the right, and the fancier *Medewi Beach Cottages*, on the left, now under the same management. The cottages have a swimming pool and restaurant, and very comfortable rooms with air-con, hot water and TV for 47,000 to 100,000 rp. Rooms in the two-storey block opposite are more basic, and expensive for what they offer at 23,000/30,000/42,000 rp for singles/doubles/triples, but you can use the pool over the road. There's a restaurant overlooking the beach, and a more attractive one at the cottages, but both have only standard fare at slightly higher than standard prices. For bottom-end accommodation, there's a couple of very basic bamboo huts nearby for 10,000/15,000 rp. Turn left off the main road a little further west to the *Tinjaya Bungalows*, with quite pleasant rooms in two-storey grass-and-bamboo cottages, but still no bargain at 20,000 rp downstairs and 25,000 rp upstairs.

Rambut Siwi

Between Air Satang and Yeh Embang, a short diversion off the main road leads to the beautiful coastal temple of **Pura Luhur** at Rambut Siwi. Picturesquely situated on a cliff top overlooking a long, wide stretch of beach, this superb temple with its numerous shady frangipani trees is one of the important coastal temples of southern Bali. It is another of the temples established in the 1500s by the priest Danghyang Nirartha who had such a good eye for ocean scenery (see also Tanah Lot and Ulu Watu).

NEGARA

Negara, the capital of the Jembrana district, comes alive each year when the **bull races** take place around September and October (ask at the tourist office in Denpasar for the exact dates). The racing animals are actually water buffaloes, normally docile creatures, which charge down a two-km stretch of road pulling tiny chariots. Riders stand on top of the chariots forcing the bullocks on, sometimes by twisting their tails. The winner, however, is not necessarily first past the post. Style also plays a part and points are awarded for the most elegant runner! Gambling is not legal on Bali but...

Places to Stay & Eat

Hotel Ana, on Jalan Ngurah Rai, the main street through town, is a standard, cheap losmen with rooms for less than 10,000 rp. Nearby is the *Hotel & Restaurant Wira Pada*

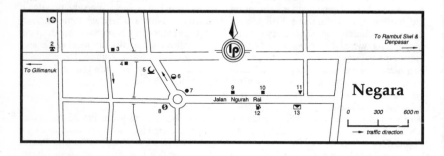

1	Hospital
2	Telephone
3	Losmen & Rumah Makan Taman Sari
4	Hotel Ijo Gading
5	Mosque
6	Bus Station
7	Market
8	Bank
9	Hotel Ana
10	Hotel & Restaurant Wira Pada
11	Rumah Makan Puas
12	Petrol Station
13	Post Office

(☎ 0365 41161), at Jalan Ngurah Rai 107, which costs 10,000/12,500 rp including breakfast, 15,000/18,000 rp for a room with a shower, or 25,000/30,000 rp with air-con. The Wira Pada serves good food, as does the *Rumah Makan Puas*, a little further east on the same street.

The Denpasar to Gilimanuk road, which bypasses the town centre, has several cheap accommodation possibilities, including *Hotel Ijo Gading*, west of the town, which is clean and friendly, and the *Losmen & Rumah Makan Taman Sari* (☎ 0365 41154), on the other side of the road. Most of these places seem to be deserted much of the time, but presumably they increase their prices and their occupancy rates in the racing season.

Getting There & Away
Public transport from Denpasar's Ubung terminal costs around 3500 rp – try to get a direct bus rather than a bemo that will stop at every village en route. For the bull races, agents in the southern tourist areas offer day tours at various prices.

AROUND NEGARA
There's a bulge in the coastline south of Negara, which has quite a few beaches, though none is particularly attractive, some are dangerous, and there are no tourist hotels. Prancak is the site of Nirartha's arrival on Bali in 1546, commemorated by a small temple, the Pura Gede Prancak.

Jembrana
Jembrana, once capital of the region, is the centre of the *gamelan jegog*, a gamelan using huge bamboo instruments that produce a very low-pitched, resonant sound. Performances often feature a number of gamelan groups engaging in musical contest. To see and hear them in action, time your arrival with a local festival, or ask in Negara where you might find a group practising.

Belimbingsari & Palasari
Christian evangelism on Bali was discouraged by the Dutch administration, but sporadic missionary activity resulted in a number of converts, many of whom were rejected by their own communities. There was little room for them in Denpasar, so in 1939 they were encouraged to re-settle in Christian communities in the wilds of west Bali.

Belimbingsari was established as a Protestant community, and now has the largest Protestant church on Bali. It's an amazing structure with features of church architecture rendered in a distinctly Balinese style – there is a kulkul in place of a church bell, an aling-aling entrance gate and some very attractive Balinese angels. Come on Sunday to see inside.

Palasari is the Catholic community. They are still working on their cathedral, but the structure is already large and impressive (there could be some competition here). It also shows Balinese touches, in the spires which resemble the multi-roofed meru in a Balinese temple, and a facade with the same shape as a temple gate.

These villages are north of the main road, and the best way to see them is with your own transport, by doing a loop starting from Melaya.

Other Immigrant Communities
Jembrana also has a substantial Muslim population, descended from seafaring people from Java, Madura and Sulawesi. Mosques are a common sight. **Loloan Timur**, just south of Negara, is a largely Bugis community, retaining 300-year-old traditions. Look for their distinctive, rectangular houses.

Being sparsely populated, the district has attracted other, more recent immigrant communities. As well as the Christians, entire villages from east Bali re-settled here after volcanic eruptions destroyed their homes.

CEKIK
About a km before Gilimanuk, Cekik is the point at which the road to the north coast branches off to the right. On the Denpasar side of the junction, the curious pagoda-like structure with a spiral stairway around the outside is a **War Memorial**. It commemorates the landing of republican forces on Bali

to oppose the Dutch who were trying to reassert control of Indonesia after WW II. Between April and July 1946, several republican units were ferried across the Bali Strait in outrigger canoes and fishing boats. One of these fleets encountered Dutch patrol boats, and actually managed to sink one in the new country's first sea battle.

Archaeological excavations at Cekik during the 1960s yielded the oldest evidence of human life on Bali. Finds include burial mounds with funerary offerings, bronze jewellery, axes, adzes and earthenware vessels from around 1000 BC, give or take a few centuries.

BALI BARAT NATIONAL PARK

Also in Cekik, on the south side of the road, is the headquarters of the West Bali National Park (Taman Nasional Bali Barat), open 7.30 am to 2 pm Monday to Saturday. The visitors' centre does not have much information about the park, but is the place to make arrangements for trekking in its southern regions. For information about the northern part of the park, and diving trips to Menjangan Island, go to the other park office at Labuhan Lalang (see the North Bali chapter for information and some background on the park's flora and fauna).

Trekking

All trekking groups must be accompanied by an authorised guide, and you will also need to organise transport to the starting point of the trek. There's a park entry fee of 2000 rp per person. The usual starting points are the village of Belimbingsari, the microwave tower on the south-west slopes of Gunung Kelatakan, or the road going through Labuhan Lalang.

A short two-hour trek can be made from Belimbingsari, through thick forest and fruit plantations. The guide will cost about 10,000 rp, and you will have to pay for transport to and from Belimbingsari. A longer trek, about four hours, can be made from the microwave tower to Ambyasari, between Belimbingsari and the main road. The guide will cost about 15,000 rp, plus transport. A full-day trek,

around seven hours, would be from Belimbingsari to Labuhan Lalang on the north coast; about 30,000 rp for the guide.

Some other possibilities include longer treks staying overnight in rustic shelters; exploring the mangroves of Gilimanuk Bay by boat; and observing birds and wildlife in the area round Sumber Klampek. Treks on the Prapat Agung Peninsula are currently restricted.

It's best to arrive the day before you want to trek, make your arrangements at park headquarters, then stay the night, either at the campground in the park about one km from Cekik, or in a losmen in Gilimanuk, ready for an early start. Alternatively, you could just arrive at the park headquarters by 7 am – there will probably be a guide available.

GILIMANUK

At the far western end of the island, Gilimanuk is the terminus for ferries which shuttle back and forth across the narrow strait to Java. There's a bus station and a market on the main street about a km from the ferry port, as well as shops, cheap restaurants and a couple of places to change money. Most travellers buy combined bus and ferry tickets and don't need to stop in Gilimanuk. There's little of interest here for the traveller anyway, though it does have the closest accommodation to the national park, if you want to start a trek there early in the morning.

Places to Stay

There are several places to stay along Jalan Raya, the main road into the port. *Homestay Surya*, *Lestari Homestay* and *Nirwana* are all cheap, basic losmen which have rooms for less than 10,000 rp. *Nusantara II* is 100 metres east of the main drag, through a split gate to the south of the ferry port. It's also basic, and no cheaper, but it's better located away from the busy road, near the bay.

Getting There & Away

The bus and bemo terminal is about a km south of the ferry port, on the east side of the road. In one of those mysteries of Bali's public transport system, the posted fare at

Gilimanuk to Ubung terminal in Denpasar is only 3200 rp, while the fares posted at Ubung for Gilimanuk are 4500 rp. It's not uncommon to have small differences in the fares in each direction, but in this case it's likely that the fare from Gilimanuk will soon rise. The fare to Singaraja is about 2500 rp.

To/From Java The ferries to Java leave every 15 to 30 minutes, 24 hours a day. One-way fares are 650 rp for an adult, 450 rp for a child, 950 rp for a bicycle, 1800 rp for a motorbike, and 7400 rp for a car. Car rental contracts usually prohibit rental vehicles being taken out of Bali.

Central Mountains

Bali, as you'll quickly realise from a glance at one of the three-dimensional terrain models so common in Balinese hotels, has lots of mountains. Most are volcanoes, some dormant, some definitely active. The mountains divide the gentle sweep of fertile rice land to the south from the narrower strip to the north. In eastern Bali there's a small clump of mountains right at the end of the island, beyond Amlapura. Then there's the mighty volcano Gunung Agung (3142 metres), the island's mother mountain (see the East Bali chapter). North-west of Agung is the stark and spectacular caldera which contains the volcanic cone of Gunung Batur, Lake Batur, and numerous smaller craters. In central Bali, around Bedugul, is another complex of volcanic craters and lakes, with much lusher vegetation. A string of smaller mountains stretches off to the sparsely inhabited western region.

The popular round trip to the north coast crosses the mountains on one route (eg via Gunung Batur), and returns on the other (from Singaraja on the coast via Bedugul), thus covering the most interesting parts of the central mountain region. You can do the circuit easily in either direction.

Gunung Batur Area

PENELOKAN

Penelokan appropriately means 'place to look', and has superb views across to Gunung Batur and down to Lake Batur at the bottom of the crater. The road runs around the narrow rim of the crater to Penulisan, where you can look back into the crater or turn the other way and see Bali's northern coastline spread out at your feet, far below. You can stay in Penelokan, but those intending to tour the lake or climb Gunung Batur might find it more convenient to stay at the

bottom of the crater, in either Kedisan or Toyah Bungkah.

Information

It costs 500 rp per person to enter the crater rim area, plus 400 rp for a car, and another 50 rp for insurance. Keep the tickets if you plan to drive back and forth around the crater rim or you may have to pay again. You can change money at the Lakeview restaurant.

Penelokan has a reputation as a money-grubbing place where you're constantly importuned to buy things and where you need to keep an eye on your gear. Many day tours come to Gunung Batur, stopping for lunch at Penelokan. The hawkers have trained themselves to make their pitch and close the deal quickly. The only thing sure to discourage them is the arrival of a bus-load of tourists more affluent than yourself.

It can get surprisingly chilly up here so come prepared. Clouds often roll in over the crater, sometimes getting hung up along the rim, obscuring the view and making the crater rim towns cold and miserable places to be.

Places to Stay

There are a couple of places to stay in Penelokan, teetering right on the edge of the crater. Apart from the views, these are just basic losmen with somewhat more than basic prices, depending on what the owners reckon the market will bear.

If you arrive from the south, the first place to stay in Penelokan is the *Lakeview Restaurant & Homestay* (☎ 32023), which has economy rooms for US$8 and more comfortable bungalow-style rooms with bathroom for US$15. It's not a very clean place, and the economy rooms are impossibly small – but the view, the view...!

Continuing past the side road down into the crater, you come to *Losmen & Restaurant Gunawan*, which may be slightly better value. Again, the view is terrific, the

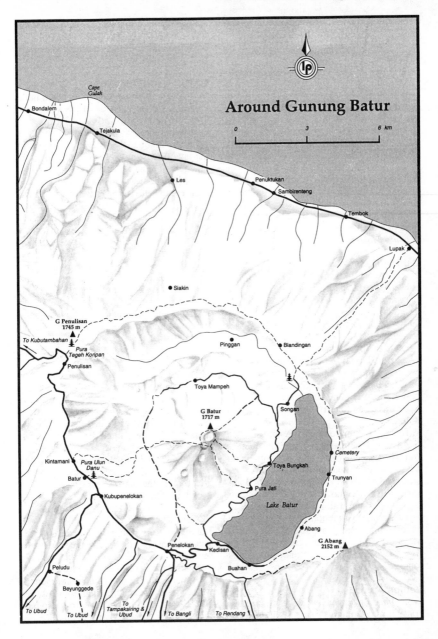

Around Gunung Batur

0   3   6 km

Cape Gulah

Bondalem
Tejakula
Les
Penuktukan
Sambirenteng
Tembok
Lupak
Siakin
G Penulisan 1745 m
To Kubutambahan
Pura Tegeh Koripan
Penulisan
Pinggan
Blandingan
Toya Mampeh
G Batur 1717 m
Songan
Kintamani
Pura Ulun Danu
Batur
Kubupenelokan
Toya Bungkah
Cemetery
Trunyan
Pura Jati
Lake Batur
Penelokan
Kedisan
Abang
G Abang 2152 m
Peludu
Buahan
Beyunggede
To Ubud
To Ubud
To Tampaksiring & Ubud
To Bangli
To Rendang

economy rooms are tiny at 20,000 rp and there is a bigger bungalow at 25,000 rp.

Places to Eat

Along the road from Penelokan towards Kintamani you'll find a crowd of restaurants which are geared to bus-loads of tour groups. All the restaurants have fine views and all prepare buffet-style lunches at international tourist prices. The restaurants, from Penelokan to Kintamani, include the *Caldera Batur, Lakeview, Batur Garden, Gunawan, Puri Selera, Puri Aninditha* and the *Kintamani Restaurant*. Lunch costs from around 10,000 rp if you order from the menu. The *Restaurant Mutiara* is better value, and there are also cheap warungs along the main road like the *Warung Makan Ani Asih* or the *Warung Makan Sederhana*.

Getting There & Away

To get to Penelokan from Denpasar, you can either get a Kintamani-bound bemo from Batubulan station (1800 rp) which will pass through Penelokan, or you can take one of the more frequent bemos to Gianyar (1000 rp) or Bangli (1200 rp) first and then another from there up the mountain. To get to Penelokan from Ubud, go first to Gianyar. Orange bemos shuttle back and forth fairly regularly between Penelokan and Kintamani (300 rp). Less frequently bemos go down to the lakeside at Kedisan (500 rp or more) and Toyah Bungkah.

The two main routes to Penelokan, via Gianyar and Tampaksiring, meet just before you get to Penelokan and are both good roads. The other roads are OK but have very little public transport. (See the Ubud to Batur section in the Ubud & Around chapter for details.) You could also take the rougher road east from the Y-junction below Penelokan, which joins the Rendang to Besakih road at Menanga. If the weather's clear you'll have fine views of Gunung Agung along this route.

Getting Around

From Penelokan you can hike around the crater rim to Gunung Abang (2152 metres),

the high point of the outer rim, though trees hide the view almost to the top. You can't continue hiking in this anticlockwise direction as the trail stops.

BATUR & KINTAMANI

The village of Batur used to be down in the crater. A violent eruption of the volcano in 1917 killed thousands of people and destroyed more than 60,000 homes and 2000 temples. Although the village was wiped out, the lava flow stopped at the entrance to the villagers' temple.

Taking this as a good omen, the village was rebuilt, only to have Batur erupt again in 1926. This time the lava flow covered all but the loftiest temple shrine. Fortunately, the Dutch administration anticipated the eruption and evacuated the village, partly by force, so very few lives were lost. The village was relocated up on the crater rim, and the surviving shrine was also moved up and placed in the new temple, Pura Ulun Danu. Construction on the new temple commenced in 1927. Gunung Batur is the second most important mountain in Bali – only Agung outranks it – so the temple here, one of the island's nine directional temples, is of considerable importance.

The villages of Batur and Kintamani now virtually run together – it's basically one main street spread out around the western rim of the crater. Although often cold and grey, it is famed for its large and colourful market, held every three days. It starts and ends early – by 11 am it's all over. The high rainfall and cool climate up here make this a very productive fruit and vegetable growing area though the orange crops have recently been depleted by disease.

Places to Stay & Eat

Losmen along the main street of this volcano-rim town don't have the spectacular setting of the places at Penelokan.

Nearest the Penelokan end of town (about 4½ km away) is *Losmen Superman's*, on the west side of the road, which asks between 10,000 and 20,000 rp for pretty squalid rooms. They may take less, but don't bother.

About two km further north on the same side of the road, the *Hotel Miranda* has rooms from 6000 to 10,000 rp for singles/doubles, including breakfast; the most expensive rooms have bathrooms. It has good food and an open fire at night. Made Senter, who runs it, is very friendly and informative and also acts as a guide for treks into the crater and around Gunung Batur.

Continuing along the road for a few hundred metres you come to *Losmen Sasaka* on the right. It appears to be new, even modern, but a closer look reveals that the washbasin has no taps, the toilet has to be flushed with a bucket and the hot-water tap is mostly for decoration. Nevertheless, the rooms are large, the place is clean, the views are great and the price (15,000/20,000 rp for singles/doubles) includes breakfast.

Further along again, a sign points off the road to the *Puri Astini Inn* – it says 400 metres, but the distance is more like 800 metres, down quite a rough track. The rooms have a minimal bathroom, no view and cost 12,000 to 20,000 rp including breakfast. It's a convenient spot from which to start a trek into the crater, but has nothing else to recommend it.

Getting There & Away

From Denpasar (Batubulan station) a bemo to Kintamani is about 2000 rp, though there will be more frequent bemos from Gianyar or Bangli. Buses run between Kintamani and Singaraja on the north coast for 2000 rp.

PENULISAN

The road continues along the crater rim beyond Kintamani, gradually climbing higher and higher. Sometimes, if you come up from the south, you'll find yourself ascending through the clouds around Penelokan and Kintamani then coming out above them as you approach Penulisan. If it's clear, there are more fine views down over the crater.

At a bend in the road at Penulisan, a steep flight of steps leads to Bali's highest temple, Pura Tegeh Koripan, at 1745 metres. Inside the highest courtyard are rows of old statues and fragments of sculptures in the open bale (pavilions). Some of the sculptures date back as far as the 11th century. The views from this hilltop temple are superb: facing north you can see down over the rice terraces clear to the Singaraja coast.

Towering over the temple, however, notice the shrine to a new and powerful god – Bali's TV repeater mast!

GUNUNG BATUR & LAKE BATUR

The views from the crater at Penelokan, Batur, Kintamani and Penulisan are superb, but for a closer look you can descend into the massive outer crater, take a boat across the lake and/or climb the dormant Gunung Batur volcano.

A hairpin-bend road winds its way down from Penelokan to Kedisan on the shore of the lake. To get to the hot springs at Toya Bungkah, take the quaint little road which

winds around the lakeside from Kedisan, over many turns and switchbacks, through the lava field. The road continues to Songan, under the north-eastern rim of the crater, and a side road goes around to the north side of Gunung Batur until it is stopped near Toya Mampeh by a huge 'flow' of solidified black lava from the 1974 eruption. You can climb to the summit of Gunung Batur in just a few hours from either Kedisan or Toya Bungkah, or make longer treks over and around the central volcano and up the crater rim.

Expect to be hassled by touts from top to bottom, and around the lakeshore. They will offer to take you to a place to stay, but their real objective is to act as your guide for a trek in the area. Finding a room yourself is not difficult.

Kedisan

Coming into Kedisan from Penelokan you reach a T-intersection. Turning left towards Toya Bungkah you come first to the *Segara Bungalows*, where basic singles/doubles cost from 8000/10,000 rp and more comfortable rooms are 15,000/25,000 rp, including breakfast. A bit further on is the *Surya Homestay & Restaurant* with rooms from 10,000 to 25,000 rp. The cheapest rooms are not fancy, but definitely OK. They ask up to 40,000 rp for rooms with hot water. Turning right as you come into town will bring you to the *Segara Homestay* which has the same owner as the Segara Bungalows, but cheaper and more basic rooms from 6000 rp.

Buahan

A little further around the lake is Buahan, a small place with market gardens right down to the lakeshore. *Baruna Cottages* is a more peaceful place to stay, but not without its hustlers. It has a restaurant and singles/doubles with mandi from 8000/10,000 rp to 10,000/15,000 rp.

Trunyan & Kuban

The village of Trunyan, on the shore of Lake Batur, is squeezed tightly between the lake and the outer crater rim. This is a Bali Aga village, inhabited by remnants of the original

Balinese, the people who predate the Majapahit arrival. Unlike the other well-known Bali Aga village, Tenganan, this is not an interesting and friendly place. It's famous for its four- metre high statue of the village's guardian spirit, Ratu Gede Pancering Jagat, but you're not allowed to see it. There are only a couple of the traditional Bali Aga style dwellings, some old structures in the temple, and a huge banyan tree, said to be over 1100 years old.

A little beyond Trunyan, and accessible only by the lake (there's no path) is the village cemetery at Kuban. The people of Trunyan do not cremate or bury their dead – they lie them out in bamboo cages to decompose, though strangely there is no stench. A collection of skulls and bones lies on a stone platform. This is a tourist trap for those with macabre tastes.

Getting There & Away Getting across the lake from Kedisan was once one of Bali's great rip-offs. After negotiating a sky-high price, your boatman would then want to renegotiate halfway across. Meanwhile, your motorbike was being stripped back at Kedisan. It got so bad that the government took over and set prices. Now the boats leave from a jetty near the middle of Kedisan, where there is a ticket office and a secure carpark (and a few persistent hawkers of second-rate souvenirs). The listed price for a boat for a round trip stopping at Trunyan, the cemetery at Kuban, the hot springs at Toya Bungkah, and returning to Kedisan is around 38,000 rp depending on the number of passengers (the maximum is eight). With four people it works out at 9500 rp each, including entry fees, insurance, and a not-very-informative guide. It's cheaper with more passengers, but still not worth it. The first boat leaves at 8 am and the last at 4 pm; the complete trip takes about two hours.

If you want to do it on the cheap don't consider the alternative of hiring a dugout canoe and paddling yourself – the lake is bigger than it looks from the shore and it can get very choppy. A better alternative is to walk to Buahan and from there, follow the good footpath around the lakeside to Trunyan, an easy hour or two's walk. The walk will be the best part of the trip. From Trunyan you may be able to negotiate a cheaper boat to the cemetery and hot springs, but don't count on it.

Toya Bungkah (Tirta)

Directly across the lake from Trunyan is the small settlement of Toya Bungkah, also known as Tirta, with its hot springs – *tirta* and *toya* both mean 'water'. The hot springs *(air panas)* bubble out in a couple of spots and are used to feed an unattractive bathing pool before flowing out into the lake. It costs 1000 rp to bathe in the pool. You can use soap and shampoo under the shower heads where the water flows out. The water is soothingly hot, ideal for aching muscles after a volcano climb, but you are stared at by locals, hassled by hawkers and surrounded by litter.

Toya Bungkah is a grubby little village, but despite this, many travellers stay here so that they can climb Gunung Batur in the early morning – and most get out as quickly as possible afterwards.

Information There's a ticket office as you enter, which charges 550 rp for entry into the hot springs area, plus 400 rp for a car and 50 rp for insurance.

If you want to find out about trekking, look for the sign of Jero Wijaya, who has excellent information about the area, and can arrange a guide at a reasonable rate if you think you need one. He has some useful maps showing the whole crater area, with a variety of treks on Gunung Batur, up to the outer rim and beyond to the east coast. His knowledge of the history and geology of the area is way ahead of some of the local amateur guides, who can do little more than show you the path.

Places to Stay There are quite a few places to stay in Toya Bungkah, most of them pretty basic. More are being built, including a big place to cater for package tourists.

On the left as you enter, *Arlina Bungalows* is a new place, clean and well run, and soon to have a restaurant. Good-size rooms with fanciful fairy grotto bathrooms cost 10,000/ 15,000 rp for singles/doubles, 10,000 rp more with hot water. Next on the left, *Under the Volcano Homestay* (one of two by that name) has basic singles/doubles from around 12,000 rp.

Nyoman Pangus Homestay & Restaurant, on the right as you come in from Kedisan, is one of the originals here, clean and friendly with rooms at 10,000 to 15,000 rp. Next on the right are *Amertha's Bungalows*, which look OK but are not always clean. They ask US$6/10 for singles/doubles.

The *Balai Seni Toyabungkah* (Toya Bungkah Arts Centre), up the hill on the western side of the village, is a 'centre for international understanding and co-operation based on the arts', but for most of the time it is just a slightly better place to stay, with rooms from 15,000 rp and bungalows from 25,000 rp, sometimes with hot water. There's also a library there. The three *Putu Bungalows*, with Bali-style decorations, are behind Nyoman Mawa's restaurant. Doubles cost 25,000 rp, and you'll have to ask around to find someone to take your money and let you in.

Awangga Bungalows, at the other end of the village near the lake, advertises itself as the 'cheapest', with simple rooms from 10,000 rp including breakfast. The nearby *Wisma Tirta Yastra*, right by the lake, asks only 8000/10,000 rp with breakfast, and looks quite OK with a very good position. Around 10,000 rp is the going rate for basic rooms with a basic breakfast, give or take 2000 rp. Places in this category include the *Black Lava Homestay*, *Siki Inn* and *Puri Bening Hayato Hotel*. The second *Under the Volcano*, at the far end of town, asked 15,000/20,000 rp for an ordinary room, but may have been just trying it on.

Places to Eat Fresh fish from the lake is the local speciality, usually barbecued with onion and garlic. The fish are tiny but tasty, and sometimes you get three or four for a meal as there is not much meat on them. There are a number of warungs and restaurants, mostly with similar menus and prices. *Nyoman Pangus Restaurant* (it used to be called a warung) does a good version of the barbecued fish.

Trekking

Soaring up in the centre of the huge outer crater is the cone of Gunung Batur (1717 metres). It has erupted a number of times this century, most recently in 1971 and 1974. The crater has a number of volcanic features including lava flows, lava tubes, parasitic cones and craters-within-craters. There are at least three main routes up, and some interesting walks around the summit. You can take one route up and another one down, then get a bemo back to your starting point. A bemo from Kedisan to Toya Bungkah should cost about 500 rp. Start very early in the morning, before mist and cloud obscure the view. Ideally you should get to the top for sunrise – it's a magnificent sight, though it can get crowded up there. In the rainy season it may be cloudy in the morning and clear somewhat during the day.

Guides In and around Toya Bungkah you will be hassled by people offering to guide you up the mountain, sometimes asking outrageous prices, starting at 24,000 rp. About 6000 rp would be a fair price for guiding you up and back on one of the standard routes. If you want to explore the crater, or take an unusual route up the mountain, then you may need a guide with more expertise than the kids who hassle you in town. There are plans to provide a relatively easy, well-marked trail, with a moderate trail fee which will benefit the whole community and support environmental and safety improvements.

If you have a reasonable sense of direction, and it's not totally dark when you start climbing, you won't need a guide at all for the usual routes. If you're not confident about it, take a guide.

Eggs Would-be guides will offer to provide breakfast on the summit, and this often includes the novelty of cooking eggs (more recently, bananas) in the steaming holes at the top of the volcano. Some of these holes are extremely hot, and it is indeed possible to cook eggs in them. Unfortunately, the practice has resulted in an accumulation of litter – egg shells, banana peels etc – around the summit. By all means take some food to the top, but make sure it does not result in any more rubbish, and discourage your guide from using the volcano as a stove.

Routes The easiest route is from the northeast, where a new track enables you to take a car to within about 45 minutes' walk from the top. From Toya Bungkah take the road north-east towards Songan, and take the left fork after about 3½ km. Follow this small road for another 1.7 km to a well-signed track on the left, which climbs another km or so to a parking area. From here the walking track is easily followed to the top. One of the guides should be able to arrange transport, for a price. You may decry the new vehicle access track, but this is hardly a wilderness area. If you want a more challenging climb, take another route.

There is also a pretty straightforward route from Toya Bungkah. Walk out of town on the road to Kedisan and turn right just after the office where you buy the entry ticket. There are quite a few paths at first but they all rejoin sooner or later – just keep going uphill, tending south-west and then west. After half an hour or so you'll be on a ridge with quite a well-defined track; keep going up. It gets pretty steep towards the top, and it can be hard walking over the loose volcanic sand – climbing up three steps and sliding back two. It takes about two hours to get to the top.

At the summit it's possible to walk right around the rim of the volcanic cone, or descend into the cone from the southern edge. Wisps of steam issuing from cracks in the rock, and the surprising warmth of the ground, indicate that things are still happening down below.

Other popular routes are from Kedisan or from Pura Jati, the ruined village on the Kedisan to Toya Bungkah road. Another possible route is from Kintamani, first descending the outer crater rim and then climbing the inner cone. For an interesting round trip, you can climb Gunung Batur from Toya Bungkah, follow the rim around to the other side, then descend on the route back to Kedisan. Climbing up, spending a reasonable time on the top and then strolling back down can all be done in four or five hours.

There are several refreshment stops along the way, and people with ice buckets full of cold drinks. It'll cost you more than 2500 rp for a small coke, but it's been carried a long way. The warung at the top has tea and coffee (1500 rp), sometimes jaffles (2500 rp) and a brilliant view (free).

Songan

The road continues from Toya Bungkah around the lake to Songan, quite a large village with some old buildings, and market gardens which extend to the edge of the lake. Not many tourists come this far but there is one place to stay, the *Restiti Inn Homestay & Restaurant*, on the left side of the road past the main part of the village, which looks quite OK and costs 10,000/15,000 rp for a room with a mandi.

At the end of the road there's a temple at the crater edge – from there you can climb to the top of the outer crater rim in just 15 minutes, and see the east coast, only about five km away. It's an easy downhill stroll to the coast road at Lupak but, unless you want to walk back, remember to take your stuff with you – there's no direct public transport back to Toya Bungkah.

Lake Bratan Area

Approaching Bedugul from the south, you gradually leave the rice terraces behind and ascend into the cool, damp mountain country. There are several places to stay on the southern slopes and near the lake, and Bedugul can be an excellent base for walking trips around the other lakes and surrounding hills. There is also an interesting temple, botanical gardens, a colourful market, an excellent golf course and a variety of activities on Lake Bratan itself.

BEDUGUL
Taman Rekreasi Bedugul

The Bedugul Leisure Park (Taman Rekreasi Bedugul) is at the southern end of the lake. It's along the first road to the right as you come in from the south, and it costs 500 rp to get into the lakeside area. Along the waterfront are an expensive restaurant, souvenir shops, a hotel, and facilities for a number of water activities. You can hire a canoe and paddle across to the temple – it costs 20,000 rp at the ticket office for a canoe for half an hour, but independent touts come down to 15,000 rp for 'a long time'; it's cheaper if you go round the lake past the Ashram Guesthouse.

You can also hire a motor-boat (17,500 rp per person for an hour if you have four people) or a jet-ski. Water-skiing and parasailing are also available. What was described as 'the serene calm of Lake Bratan' is often shattered by the din of these motorised craft, and the loudspeaker blaring that their time is up. Though this is the prettiest end of the lake, it's hard to appreciate it whilst surrounded by such an over-commercialised tourist facility.

Botanical Gardens

North of Bedugul the road climbs a hill and descends again to an intersection, conspicuously marked with a large, phallic sculpture of a sweet corn cob. The smaller road leads west up to the entrance of the Kebun Raya Bali, the botanical gardens. The gardens were established in 1959 as a branch of the national botanical gardens at Bogor, near Jakarta. They cover more than 120 hectares on the lower slopes of Gunung Pohon, and have an extensive collection of trees and some 500 species of orchid. It's a lovely place, cool, shady and scenic. Usually there are very few visitors, but groups of Balinese like to come for picnics, especially on Sunday when the atmosphere is more festive.

Some plants are labelled with their botanical names, but apart from that there is almost

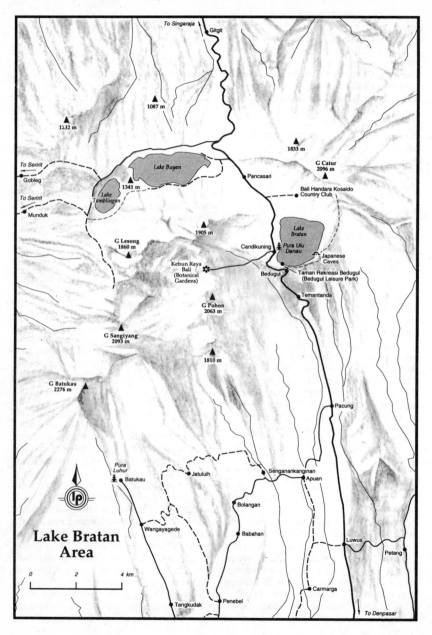

To Singaraja
Gitgit

1087 m

1232 m

1833 m

To Seririt
Gobleg
Lake Buyan
Pancasari
G Catur
2096 m

1341 m
To Seririt
Lake
Tamblingan
Munduk
Bali Handara Kosaido
Country Club

1905 m
Lake
Bratan
Pura Ulu
Danau
G Lesong
1860 m
Candikuning
Japanese
Caves
Kebun Raya
Bali
(Botanical
Gardens)
Bedugul
Taman Rekreasi Bedugul
(Bedugul Leisure Park)
G Pohon
2063 m
Temantanda

G Sangiyang
2093 m

1810 m

G Batukau
2276 m
Pacung

Pura
Luhur
Batukau
Jatuluih
Senganankanginan
Apuan

Bolangan

Lake Bratan
Area
Wangayagede
Babahan

Luwus
Petang

0   2   4 km

Carmarga

Tengkudak   Penebel
To Denpasar

nothing in the way of visitor information. Some visitors have been annoyed here by stray dogs – carry a stick to deter them. The gardens open every day, from 7 or 8 am to 4.30 pm. Entry is 500 rp and parking is 500 rp for a car, 150 rp for a motorbike. You can drive a car right into the gardens for 2500 rp, but it's better to walk.

Candikuning

Continuing north towards Singaraja from the botanical gardens turn-off you pass the turn-off to the flower and produce market on the left. It's very colourful and well recommended, and is at its best early in the morning when truck loads of flowers, fruit and vegetables are dispatched to the hotels and restaurants in south Bali.

The road swings back to the lakeside past the Ashram Guesthouse, and there's a small landing where you can hire canoes more cheaply than in Bedugul – 7500 rp for half an hour, 10,000 rp for 'a long time', which should enable you to paddle yourself round most of the lake. See the aside in this section for details.

Pura Ulu Danau Also at Candikuning, a few km north of Bedugul, and actually projecting into the lake, is the Hindu/Buddhist temple of Pura Ulu Danau. It's very picturesque, with a large banyan tree at the entrance, attractive gardens and one courtyard isolated on a tiny island in the lake. The temple, founded in the 17th century, is dedicated to Dewi Danau, the goddess of the waters. It is the focus of ceremonies and pilgrimages to ensure the supply of water. Ulu Danau has classical Hindu thatched-roof merus and an adjoining Buddhist stupa. There are the usual admission and parking charges.

Around the Lakes

North of Candikuning, the road descends past the Bali Handara Kosaido Country Club, with its beautifully situated, world-class **golf course**. Green fees are US$57.75 for 18 holes, and you can hire a half-set of clubs for US$10.

If you continue to Lake Buyan, there's a fine walk around the southern side of Buyan, then over the saddle to the adjoining, smaller **Lake Tamblingan**. From there you can walk uphill, then west to the village of **Munduk** (about two to three hours) and then take the road around the northern side of the lakes back to Bedugul. Alternatively, you can follow the road west from Munduk, and then north, descending through picturesque villages to Seririt on the north coast.

Places to Stay

There are some new places along the road up to Bedugul from the south, starting at Pacung on the southern slopes with a wonderful panorama of southern Bali. The *Pacung Mountain Hotel* (☎ 0361 262460/1/2) is a top-end place perched on a steep hillside looking west to Gunung Batukau. It has a pool, restaurant, and comfortable rooms from US$65/70 to US$80. The *Green Valley*

It's possible to paddle across Lake Bratan to some caves which the Japanese used during WW II. You can also walk there in about an hour. From there a very well marked path ascends to the top of Gunung Catur (2096 metres). It takes about two hours for the climb up and an hour back down. The final bit is steep and you should take some water but it is well worth the effort. There is an old temple on the summit with lots of monkeys.
Anne Whybourne & Peter Clarke, Australia

An interesting two-to-three hour circuit walk is from the Bedugul Hotel up to the market, through to the Botanical Gardens the back down the road to the lakeside and through the grounds of the Ashram Guesthouse to skirt the lakeside back to the Bedugul Hotel. This walk takes in great views of the countryside and Balinese lifestyle. A visit to the market is an absolute must.
Justin Dabner & Angela Johnson, Australia

Hotel (☎ 0368 21020, 21207) is on the other side of the road, with great views east to Gunung Agung, and rooms from 25,000/ 30,000 rp.

Opposite the turn-off to the Taman Rekreasi, the *Hadi Raharjo* (☎ 0362 23467) is an OK losmen with a restaurant and rooms at 15,000/20,000 rp (it threatens to become a mid-range place and change its name to 'Strawberry'). Inside the Taman Rekreasi area, the *Bedugul Hotel* (☎ 0361 226593) has motel-style rooms next to the lake for 45,000 rp, and older rooms on the slope behind from 35,000 rp. The ones next to the lake have less character and more noise, especially at weekends.

Continuing north, the road climbs higher up the hillside to the turn-off for the pricey *Bukit Permai Hotel* (☎ 0362 23662). 'Deluxe' rooms cost US$22.50, 'executive' rooms are US$30 and suite rooms US$35. Prices include tax, breakfast, TV, hot water, a fireplace and a great view. It's OK, but doesn't look like a fun place to stay. On the side road to the botanical gardens you'll find the ugly and overpriced *Losmen Mawa Indah* which asks 15,000 rp but should take less.

Back on the lakeside road you come to the *Lila Graha* (☎ 0362 23848), up a steep drive on the left, with singles/doubles from 25,000/30,000 rp, or 60,000 rp for a suite. It is well located, clean and comfortable, and the accommodation incorporates an old Dutch rest house. On the other side of the road, right by the lake, is the popular *Ashram Guesthouse* (☎ 0362 22439), with ordinary rooms from 15,000 rp, up to 60,000 rp for bigger rooms with hot water. People enjoy staying here.

Top-end accommodation can be found at the *Bali Handara Kosaido Country Club* (☎ 0361 288944, 0362 22646; fax 0361 287358), north of Candikuning, where the cheapest room is a 'standard bungalow' at US$65, and the most expensive is an 'executive suite' at US$350, plus 15.5% tax and service, but there are lots of options in between. The view from the bar might be worth the price of a drink. As well as the golf

course, there are tennis courts, a gym and a Japanese bath.

Further north, a driveway goes west of the road to *Lake Buyan Cottages*, an expensive package-tour place with cottages at US$80, and a Japanese-style cottage at US$200.

Places to Eat

The lakeside restaurant at the Taman Rekreasi is a bit expensive – 3750 rp for a mie goreng! The restaurant at the Bedugul Hotel does buffet lunches for tour groups. In Candikuning you'll find the *Restaurant Pelangi, Rumah Makan Mini Bali* and others in the same area. Further north, the lakeside *Taliwang Restaurant* has food which is not so tourist-oriented, and is one of the best options. There are a few places near the Ulu Danau temple which should provide a reasonable meal at a reasonable price. The restaurants at the Bali Handara and the Pacung Mountain hotels probably have the best food, at a price.

Getting There & Away

Bedugul is on the main north-south road so is easy to get to from either Denpasar or Singaraja. It costs 1800 rp from Denpasar's Ubung bus terminal, a bit less from the western bus station in Singaraja. The road is sealed all the way and signposted, so it's easy to follow if you have your own transport.

BEDUGUL TO SINGARAJA

Heading north from the Lake Bratan area, on the scenic main road, you come to the coastal town of Singaraja, about 30 km away (see the North Bali chapter). On the way there's the beautiful **Gitgit Waterfall**, west of the road just past Gitgit village, about 10 km north of Bedugul. There are plenty of signs and a carpark. You buy a ticket (450 rp) at the office near the west side of the road, and follow the concrete path between the rows of souvenir stalls for about 500 metres. It's quite pretty when you get there, a great place for a swim or a picnic, but far from pristine.

The new *Gitgit Hotel* has clean but uninteresting rooms at 25,000/35,000 rp, or 10,000 rp more with hot water. There's a lovely view from here, but this hotel doesn't take advantage of it.

GUNUNG BATUKAU

West of the Mengwi-Bedugul-Singaraja road rises 2276-metre Gunung Batukau, the 'coconut-shell mountain'. This is the third of Bali's three major mountains and the holy peak of the western end of the island.

Pura Luhur

Pura Luhur, on the slopes of Batukau, was the state temple when Tabanan was an independent kingdom. The temple has a seven-roofed meru to Maha Dewa, the mountain's guardian spirit, as well as shrines for the three mountain lakes: Bratan, Tamblingan and Buyan.

There are several routes to Pura Luhur but none of them are particularly high-class roads – it's a remote temple. You can reach it by following the road up to Penebel from Tabanan. Or turn off the Mengwi to Bedugul road at Baturiti near the 'Denpasar 40 km' sign and follow the convoluted route to Penebel. Wangayagede, the nearest village to the temple, is surrounded by forest and is often damp and misty.

Jatuluih

Also perched on the slopes of Gunung Batukau, but closer to Bedugul and the Mengwi to Bedugul road, is the small village of Jatuluih, whose name means 'truly marvellous'. The view truly is – it takes in a huge chunk of southern Bali.

ROUTES THROUGH PUPUAN

The two most popular routes between the south and north coast are the roads via Kintamani or Bedugul, but there are two other routes over the mountains. Both branch north from the Denpasar to Gilimanuk road, one from Pulukan and the other from Antasari, and meet at Pupuan before dropping down to Seririt, to the west of Singaraja.

The Pulukan to Pupuan road climbs steeply up from the coast providing fine views back down to the sea. The route runs through spice-growing country and you'll often see spices laid out on mats by the road to dry – the smell of cloves rises up to meet you. At one point, the narrow and winding road actually runs right through an enormous banyan tree which bridges the road. Further on, the road spirals down to Pupuan through some of Bali's most beautiful rice terraces.

The road from Antasari starts through rice paddies, climbs into the spice-growing country, then descends through the coffee growing areas to Pupuan.

If you continue another 12 km or so towards the north coast you reach Mayong, where you can turn east to Munduk and on to Lake Tamblingan and Lake Buyan. The road is rough but passable, and offers fine views of the mountains, lakes and out to the northern coast. Munduk is a traditional village, and there are some interesting walks in the area.

North Bali

Northern Bali, the district of Buleleng, makes an interesting contrast with the south of the island. The Lovina beaches, west of Singaraja, are popular with budget travellers, with a good variety of places to stay and eat, but nothing like the crowding and confusion of Kuta. Many travellers arriving from Java go straight from Gilimanuk to the north coast, rather than taking the south-coast road which would leave them in Denpasar or, horror of horrors, Kuta Beach. Apart from the peaceful beaches, there are a number of other features worth visiting.

The north coast has been subject to European influence for longer than the south. Although the Dutch had established full control of northern Bali by 1849, it was not until the beginning of this century that their power extended to the south. Having first encountered Balinese troops in Java in the 18th century, the Dutch were the main purchasers of Balinese slaves, many of whom served in the Dutch East India Company armies.

Although the Netherlands did not at first become directly involved in the island's internal affairs as it had in Java, in 1816 it made several unsuccessful attempts to persuade the Balinese to accept Dutch authority. Various Balinese kings continued to provide the Dutch with soldiers but, in the 1840s, disputes over the looting (salvaging?) of shipwrecks, together with fears that other European powers might establish themselves on Bali, prompted the Dutch to make treaties with several of the Balinese rajahs. The treaties proved ineffective, the plundering continued and disputes arose with the rajah of Buleleng.

In 1845 the rajahs of Buleleng and Karangasem formed an alliance, possibly to conquer other Balinese states or, equally possibly, to resist the Dutch. In any case, the Dutch were worried, and attacked Buleleng and Karangasem in 1846, 1848 and 1849, seizing control of the north in the third attempt. The western district of Jembrana came under Dutch control in 1853, but it was

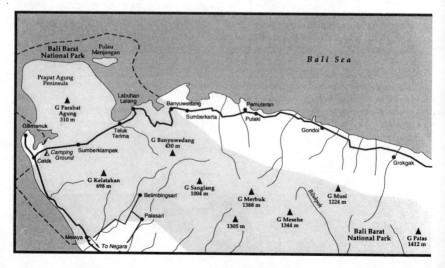

not until 1906 that the south was finally subdued.

From the time of their first northern conquests, the Dutch interfered increasingly in Balinese affairs. It was here that Balinese women first covered their breasts – on orders from the Dutch to 'protect the morals of Dutch soldiers'.

Buleleng has a strong artistic and cultural tradition. Its dance troupes are highly regarded and a number of dance styles have originated here, including Joged and Janger. Gold and silver work, weaving, pottery, musical-instrument making, and temple design all show distinctive local styles. The Sapi Gerumbungan is a bull race in which style is as important as speed. This is a Buleleng tradition, and quite different from the races of Negara, in south-west Bali. Events are held at Kaliasem, near Lovina, on Independence Day (August 17), Singaraja Day (March 31) and other occasions.

SINGARAJA

Singaraja was the centre of Dutch power on Bali and remained the administrative centre for the islands of Nusa Tenggara (Bali through to Timor, called the Lesser Sunda Islands during the Dutch colonial years) until 1953. It is one of the few places on Bali where there are visible reminders of the Dutch period, but there are also Chinese and Muslim influences. With a population of around 85,000 Singaraja is a busy town, but orderly, even quiet, compared with Denpasar. Dokars are still used on the pleasant tree-lined streets, and there are some interesting Dutch colonial houses. The 'suburb' of Beratan, south of Singaraja, is the silver-work centre of northern Bali.

For years the port of Singaraja was the usual arrival point for visitors to Bali – it's where all the prewar travel books started. Singaraja is hardly used as a harbour now, due to its lack of protection from bad weather. Shipping for the north coast generally uses the new port at Celukanbawang, and visiting cruise ships anchor at Padangbai in the south. Singaraja has a conspicuous monument on its waterfront, with a statue pointing to an unseen enemy out to sea. It commemorates a freedom fighter who was killed here by gunfire from a Dutch warship early in the struggle for independence.

Singaraja is still a major educational and

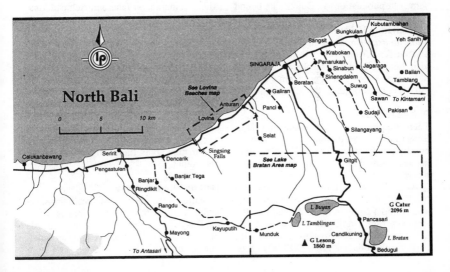

cultural centre, and two university campuses give the city a substantial student population.

Orientation & Information

It's easy to find your way around. The main commercial area is in the north-east part of town behind the old harbour, on Jalan Diponegoro, Jalan Imam Bonjol, Jalan Erlangga and Jalan Jen Achmad Yani. Traffic does a one-way loop, clockwise around this block.

The helpful tourist office (☎ 61141) is on Jalan Veteran, on the south side of town. It's open from 8 am to 2 pm, closing at noon on Friday, 1 pm Saturday.

The post office and telephone office are near each other on Jalan Imam Bonjol. The telephone code for Singaraja, and all of Buleleng district, is 0362.

Gedung Kirtya Historical Library,

This small institution has a collection of around 3000 old Balinese manuscripts inscribed on lontar (palm). These lontar books include literary, mythological, historical and religious works. Even older written works, in the form of inscribed metal plates, are kept here, but most valuable works have been transferred to Denpasar. There are also some old publications in Dutch, like bound copies of *Kolonial Tidschrit* (Colonial Journal) from 1934 to 1940, and a *Javaansch Nederlandsch Handwoordenboek*, in Dutch and Sanskrit, from 1901. You're welcome to visit, but you'll find this a place for scholars rather than tourists. It opens from 7 am to 1 pm Monday to Friday – donation requested.

Places to Stay

There are plenty of places to stay and eat in Singaraja but most tourists go straight to the beaches, only a few km away. It's a pity because Singaraja is quite an interesting place.

As in Denpasar, most of the hotels are principally used by local business travellers. You'll find a string of hotels along Jalan Jen Achmad Yani, starting in the east with the *Hotel Sentral* (☎ 21896) a good choice with basic singles/doubles at 7000/10,000 rp, or

22,500/30,000 rp with air-con. The *Hotel Garuda* (☎ 41191), further west at No 76, has rooms from 7500 to 12,500 rp including breakfast, while the *Hotel Duta Karya* (☎ 21467), across the road, is OK at 12,500/14,000 rp for singles/doubles, or 25,000/30,000 rp with air-con. Further west again, and handy to the bus station, are the *Hotel Saku Bindu* (15,000 rp a double) and the *Hotel Gelar Sari*.

On the western side of Jalan Gajah Mada, the street that continues south to Bedugul and Denpasar, Jalan Gajah Mada, is the *Tresna Homestay* (☎ 21816). It's cheap, with basic rooms at 5000 rp and better rooms at 10,000/12,500 rp. The proprietors are very friendly, interesting and informative, and the place has an amazing collection of antiques and old junk, some of it for sale.

Wijaya Hotel (☎ 21915), a few hundred metres from the Western bus terminal on the east side of Jalan Sudirman, is the most comfortable place, with standard rooms at 11,500/14,000 rp, up to 62,000/69,000 rp for the best room with air-con and hot water.

Places to Eat

There are plenty of places to eat in Singaraja, including a batch of places in the small Mumbul market on Jalan Jen Achmad Yani. You'll find the popular *Restaurant Gandhi* here, with a good Chinese menu and glossy, clean surroundings. Across the road is the *Restaurant Segar II*, where a good Chinese meal will run to about 6000 rp. There are also a few restaurants along Jalan Imam Bonjol, and some warungs near the two bus stations. *Gaguk Cafe*, an open-fronted place just west of the western bus terminal, is very friendly and popular with local students, and great for a snack or a meal. It's also a good place for information about things to see and how to get around.

Getting There & Away

Singaraja is the north coast's main transportation centre with two bus terminals. From the Banyuasri terminal, on the western side of town, buses to Denpasar (Ubung terminal) via Bedugul leave about every half hour

Singaraja

0   0.5   1 km

→ traffic direction

Jalan Surapati

To East Bus
Terminal &
Kubutambahan

Jalan Erlangga

Jalan Diponegoro

Jalan Rajawali

Jalan Dewi Sartika

Jalan Skip

Jalan Jen Achmad Yani

Jalan Dewi Sartika

Jalan Kartini

Jalan Imam Bonjol

Jalan Pramuka

Jalan Udayana

To Lovina &
Gilimanuk

Jalan Ngurah Rai

Jalan Gajah Mada

Jalan Sudirman

Jalan Pahlawan

Jalan Veteran

To Beratan,
Gitgit &
Bedugul

1 Gaguk Cafe
2 West Bus Terminal -
   Kalibukbuk, Gilimanuk & Denpasar
3 Hotel Saku Bindu
4 Petrol Station
5 Hotel Gelar Sari
6 Wijaya Hotel
7 Hotel Garuda
8 Hotel Duta Karya
9 Mosque
10 Bank Bumi Daya
11 Bank Dagang Negara
12 Hotel Sentral
13 Restaurant Gandhi
14 Bank Central Asia
15 Post Office
16 Telephone & Telegraph Office
17 Police
18 Jagatnartha Temple
19 Tresna Homestay
20 Gedung Kirtya - Historical Library
21 Tourist Office

from 6 am to 4 pm and cost around 2000 rp. Buses to Gilimanuk cost 2500 rp (about two hours), and bemos to Lovina should be 500 rp, but it may be easier to get this price along the road than at the terminal. The eastern terminal, Terminal Penarukan, is a couple of km east of town, and has minibuses to Kintamani (2,500 rp) and Amlapura (via the coast road; 2500 rp).

There are also direct night buses to Surabaya (Java) from the Banyuasri terminal. They leave at about 5 pm and arrive at about 3 am (about 20,000 rp). You can also arrange tickets from the Lovina Beach places. There are no direct buses to Yogyakarta but it is possible to arrange to connect with a Denpasar to Yogyakarta bus departing from Gilimanuk.

LOVINA

West of Singaraja is a string of coastal villages – Pemaron, Tukad Mungga, Anturan, Lovina, Kalibukbuk and Bunut Panggang – which have become popular beach resorts collectively known as Lovina. The shops, bars and other tourist facilities don't dominate the place as they do at Sanur or Kuta. Visitors are hassled with people trying to sell dolphin trips, snorkelling, sarongs, and so on, but they don't seem to sell as hard as at Kuta, and the intensity of the harassment seems to wax and wane. It's a good place to meet other travellers, and there's quite an active social scene.

The beaches here are black volcanic sand, not the white stuff you find in the south. It doesn't look as appealing but it's perfectly clean and fine to walk along. Nor is there any surf – a reef keeps it almost flat calm most of the time. The sunsets here are every bit as spectacular as those at Kuta, and as the sky reddens, the lights of the fishing boats appear as bright dots across the horizon. Earlier in the afternoon, at fishing villages like Anturan, you can see the prahus (outriggers) being prepared for the night's fishing. It's quite a process bringing out all the kerosene lamps and rigging them up around the boat.

Orientation & Information

Going along the main road, it's hard to know where one village ends and the next one begins, so note the km posts which show distances from Singaraja. These are marked on the map. The tourist area stretches out over seven or eight km, but the main focus is at Kalibukbuk, about 10½ km from Singaraja. This is where you'll find the tourist office and the police station, which share the same premises. The tourist office is open Monday to Thursday and Saturday from 7 am to 5.30 pm, Friday from 7 am to 1 pm. If you need information outside these times the police may be able to help. There's a moneychanger nearby, and some of the hotels also change money.

There's a postal agent on the main road near Khie Khie restaurant, and you can also buy stamps and post letters at the Hotel Perama. Local and long-distance telephone calls can be made from the postal agent, and also at Aditya Bungalows, but international calls are much cheaper at the telephone office in Singaraja.

East of Arya's Cafe you'll find Beny Tantra's Air-Brush T-shirt shop. It's not cheap, but it's worth a look because his designs are so good – brilliant in fact. He'll also make T-shirts to order, and some of his cartoons are available as postcards.

Dolphins

Seeing the dolphins at Lovina is quite an experience, and one not to be missed. You take a boat out before dawn, and see the sun burst over the volcanoes of central Bali. Then you notice that, despite the ungodly hour, dozens of other boats have gathered beyond the reef and lie there waiting. Suddenly a dolphin will leap from the waves, to be followed by several more and then a whole school, vaulting over the water in pursuit of an unseen horde of shrimps. The boats all turn and join the chase, sometimes surrounded by dozens of dolphins, till the animals unaccountably cease their sport, and the boats wait quietly for the next sighting.

At times tourists are hassled by touts selling dolphin trips, but the problem seems to vary. The price of a dolphin trip is now supposedly fixed by the boat owners' cartel at 10,000 rp per person, and you buy a ticket from an office on the beach, or perhaps from your hotel. Occasionally a tout will sell a dolphin trip for more than this rate (maybe 15,000 rp) and pocket the difference, prompting a new round of direct marketing which can be a major annoyance.

There are reports that the number of dolphins in the morning show has declined, perhaps because of too much attention. It's not clear whether this is a temporary, seasonal or long-term decline.

Snorkelling & Diving

Generally, the water is very clear and the reef is terrific for snorkelling. It's not the best coral you'll find but it's certainly not bad and getting out to it is very easy. In many places you can simply swim out from the beach, or get a boat to take you out; the skipper should know where the best coral is. The snorkelling trips are controlled by the same cartel of boat owners which does the dolphin trips, and prices are fixed at 5000 rp per person for an hour, including the use of mask, snorkel and fins. There is some technicality about whether or not you can see dolphins and snorkel on the one trip for a special rate, or whether you have to return to shore and do a separate trip to snorkel.

Scuba diving on the reef is nothing special, but it is a good area for beginners. The only locally based diving operation which is qualified to run open-water courses for beginners to PADI, CMAS or BSAC standards is Spice Dive (☎ 23305), in new purpose-built premises on the south side of the main road near Johni's restaurant. It's a small, well-run operation and the owners, Imanuel and Nancy, are friendly and very informative. They also offer an introductory dive, and for certified divers they do trips on Lovina reef (from US$45), and to Amed, the wreck at Tulamben (US$55), and to the island of Pulau Menjangan in the Bali Barat National Park (US$60). Costs are lowest if you can arrange a group of around six people. Menjangan offers probably the best diving on Bali, but transport costs make it an expensive dive and a long day if organised through operators from anywhere else on Bali. Barrakuda, a Sanur-based operator, has a branch at Baruna Beach Cottages, at the Singaraja end of the Lovina strip. Baruna Water Sports has a base at the Palma Beach Hotel.

Places to Stay

There are now so many places to stay along the Lovina Beach strip that it's impossible to list them all, or to keep the list up to date. The first hotel is north of the main road just after the six-km marker, the last is nearly 14 km from Singaraja. Places are usually clustered in groups on one of the side roads to the beach, then there might be nothing for half a km or so.

During peak times (mid-July to the end of August and mid-December to mid-January) accommodation can be tight and prices are somewhat higher. Generally the cheapest places are away from the beach, some on the south side of the main road. Upstairs rooms are cooler and a bit more expensive, especially if they have a view. There's a 5% tax on hotel accommodation, but not on the cheaper homestays, and the fancier places

have a 10% service charge as well. Mostly it's budget accommodation, but there are a few mid-range places – generally they're the ones with phone numbers. They are all in the 0362 zone.

Singaraja to Anturan Starting from the Singaraja end, the first place is the *Aldian Palace Hotel* (☎ 23549), a mid-range place but not well located, with double rooms from US$16 to US$35. Then there's the nice looking *Baruna Beach Cottages* (☎ 22252), with individual cottages and rooms in a larger two-storey block. All have bathrooms, and prices range from US$17 for losmen-style rooms, US$24 for cottage-style rooms, up to US$52 for beachfront rooms with air-con, plus 15.5% tax and service. There's a swimming pool, a bar/restaurant on the beach, and you can also rent water-sports equipment and arrange diving trips.

On the next side road, the *Jati Reef Bungalows*, in the rice paddies close to the beach, look a bit like concrete bunkers. Comfortable double rooms with private, open-air bathrooms cost around 12,000 to 15,000 rp. The nearby *Happy Beach Inn* is in fact a cheerful place, with good food and rooms from 7000 to 10,000 rp. In between those two, *Puri Bedahulu* is right on the beach and has some Balinese-style features for 20,000 rp, or 35,000 rp with air-con. Further inland are the *Permai Beach Bungalows*, where basic rooms cost from 10,000/15,000 rp and rooms with hot water and air-con cost from 30,000 rp. The reef off the beach here is reputed to be the best along the Singaraja to Lovina coastal strip.

Fronting onto the main road, but extending all the way down to the beach, is the upmarket *Bali Taman Beach Hotel* (☎ 22126). Standard singles/doubles cost US$22.50/27.50 and air-con rooms cost US$45/55.

Anturan Continuing along the road, you come to the turn-off to the scruffy little fishing village of Anturan, where there are a few places to stay. *Mandhara Cottages* have

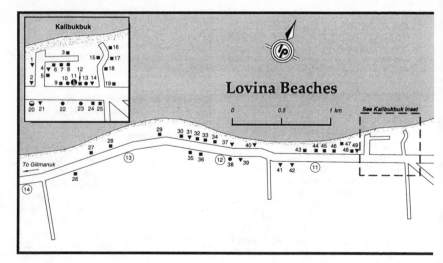

Kallbukbuk

Lovina Beaches

0   0.5   1 km

See Kallbukbuk Inset

To Gilimanuk

basic singles/doubles with bathroom for 8000/10,000 rp, 2000 rp more for bigger rooms, including breakfast. The friendly *Gede Homestay*, just behind, costs 7000/10,000 rp for smaller rooms and 12,000/20,000 rp for the best rooms. Gede is a musician, and also provides entertainment, information and good Balinese food. Walk a short distance east along the beach to the refurbished *Simon's Seaside Cottages* (☎ 41183), with comfortable rooms for US$20. There's actually a little track leading

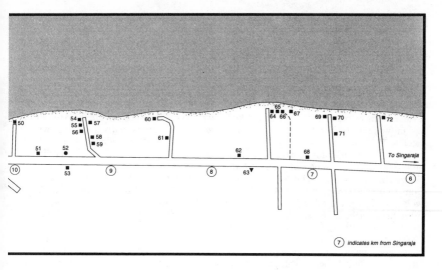

60	Lila Cita	31	Karina Restaurant
61	Celuk Agung Cottages	37	Johni's Restaurant
62	Hotel Perama & Postal Agency	39	Restaurant Adi Rama
64	Mandhara Cottages	40	Marta's Warung
65	Gede Homestay	41	Superman Restaurant
66	Simon's Seaside Cottages	42	Singa Pizza Restaurant
67	Homestay Agung & Restaurant	49	Wina's Bar & Restaurant
68	Bali Taman Beach Hotel	63	Harmoni Restaurant
69	Happy Beach Inn		
70	Jati Reef Bungalows		OTHER
71	Permai Beach Bungalows		
72	Baruna Beach Cottages	10	Perama Office
		11	Tourist Office & Police Station
▼	PLACES TO EAT	13	Malibu Club
		20	Bus Stop
1	Bali Bintang Restaurant	22	Moneychanger
2	Puri Taman Restaurant	23	Air-Brush T-Shirt Shop
4	Kakatua Bar & Restaurant	38	Spice Dive
14	Surya Restaurant	52	Radio Mast
21	Arya's Cafe		

from the main road directly to Simon's, but it's hard to spot. The beach here is a bit nicer than at Mandhara, at the end of the Anturan road. Next door to Simon's is *Homestay Agung*, at around 10,000 rp, which gets mixed reports, but some people like it.

Anturan to Kalibukbuk Continuing west from Anturan you pass the *Hotel Perama* (☎ 21161) on the main road, with basic rooms from 6000/8000 rp, including breakfast. This is also the office for the Perama bus company, and a good source of information for tours. The next turn-off goes down to the *Lila Cita*, right on the beachfront. It's simple and reasonably clean, with singles/doubles at 8000/10,000 rp, or 15,000/20,000 rp with private mandi, and the sea is just outside your window. On the way there you'll pass the *Celuk Agung Cottages* (☎ 23039), with rooms from US$20/25, up to US$50/55 for a suite room with air-con, fridge and 'lukewarm water'. Other facilities include satellite TV, tennis courts and a pool.

The next side road down to the beach has quite a few places to stay. The pleasant *Kali Bukbuk Beach Inn* (☎ 21701) has rooms from 15,000/20,000 rp to 30,000/35,000 rp with air-con. On the other side, back a bit from the beach, is *Banyualit Beach Inn* (☎ 25889), with fan-cooled doubles at 22,000 rp, up to 40,000 rp with air-con – it's pretty good value for the location and the facilities it offers. Other budget places here include *Yudhistra Inn*, *Indra Pura*, *Awangga Inn* and *Janur's Dive Inn*.

Back on the main road, on the side away from the beach, is the *Adi Homestay*, with ordinary rooms from 9000 to 20,000 rp, which seems steep for a plain losmen in this location. On the beach side of the main road is the new *Palma Beach Hotel* (☎ 23775, fax 23659), with a big pool and air-con rooms with fridge, hot water and TV, from US$60/67.50 to US$78/85; you can use the pool for just 5000 rp.

Kalibukbuk A little beyond the 10-km marker is the 'centre' of Lovina – the village of Kalibukbuk. Here you'll find *Ayodya Accommodation*, a traditional place in a big old Balinese house. Rooms cost from 7000 to 8000 rp and are bare and functional, but you sit outside and take your meals there. It's very pleasant in the evening, although the traffic noise can be annoying.

Follow the track beside Ayodya down towards the beach and you'll come to the delightful *Rambutan Cottages* (☎ 23388). The beautifully finished rooms cost from 30,000 to 45,000 rp, or 55,000 rp with hot water; 5000 rp more in the peak season. They have a new swimming pool set in a pretty

garden, and a spacious restaurant with ace food. Next along is the *Puri Bali Bungalows* where singles/doubles cost 8000/10,000 rp, good value for this location. Closest to the beach is the super-clean and well-run *Rini Hotel* (☎ 23386), with a variety of comfortable rooms from 25,000 rp. There's a good restaurant, and families and children are welcome. Opposite Rini are the *Astina Cottages*, in a pretty garden setting, with a variety of rooms and bungalows from 9000 to 15,000 rp; prices are a bit higher in the peak season.

On the south side of the main road, west of Ayodya, you'll find the *Khie Khie Hotel & Restaurant*, with a not-very-attractive pool, and rooms at 20,000 rp. A bit further along is the small *Wisata Jaya Homestay*, one of the cheapest around, with basic but satisfactory rooms for 8000 rp. On the beach side of the road is the *New Srikandi Hotel Bar & Restaurant*, which is also cheap, and *Chono Beach Cottages*, which are more expensive.

The next turn-off, just beyond the 11-km marker, takes you down a driveway to *Nirwana Cottages* (☎ 22288). This is the biggest development at Lovina, with a large slab of beachfront property and double rooms from 20,000 to 45,000 rp; some people think it's overpriced, and have found that the cleaning and the management are not as good as the location.

Right behind Nirwana is *Angsoka Cottages* (☎ 22841), which has a pool and advertises 'luxury on a shoestring' but only has a couple of cheap rooms – most are over 35,000 rp, up to 65,000 rp with air-con and hot water. *Susila Beach Inn 2*, beside the Angsoka, is a small, straightforward losmen with cheap rooms for 7000/8000 rp. The *Ray Beach Inn*, next door, has rooms at 8000/10,000 rp in the cell-block style. *Palestis Hotel*, on the road to the beach, is new and very colourful, with quite good rooms for 20,000 rp, including breakfast.

Back on the main road there's a string of cheaper places with prices from about 8000 rp. They include the *Purnama Homestay*, *Mangalla Homestay* and *Susila Beach Inn* which are all grouped together on the north side of the road. Some of the places here extend through to the beach so you can get away from the road noise. *Lovina Beach Hotel* (☎ 23473) has a variety of rooms extending to the beach – pretty basic ones are US$5; better ones are up to US$25 with air-con and hot water. *Puri Tasik Madu* costs 12,000 rp for downstairs rooms, 15,000 rp upstairs, and is close to the beach.

Beyond Kalibukbuk Continuing further along there's *Aditya Bungalows & Restaurant* (☎ 22059), a big mid-range place with beach frontage, pool, shops and a variety of rooms with TV, phone, fridge etc. Some of the rooms are right on the beach and costs range from US$20 to US$60. Next, there's the friendly *Parma Beach Homestay*, with cottages from 10,000/12,000 rp to 20,000/25,000 rp, set in a garden extending down to the beach. *Bali Dewata* is on the south side of the road, a basic but clean and friendly place for 10,000/15,000 rp. The *Toto Homestay* is another bottom-end place, near the road at the end of town but right on the beach. Spartan rooms are 7500 rp a double. *Samudra Cottages*, with a secluded location further along the road, are from 10,000/15,000 rp, and have a new hotel building growing beside them. *Krisna Beach Inn* is the next one, at 10,000/15,000 rp for singles/doubles, and there are now even more places extending west of here. The *Adirama Beach Hotel* (☎ 23759) offers a pool, beachfront location and not much in the way of style, with rooms from US$22, US$30 with air-con, or US$45 with TV.

Places to Eat

Most of the places to stay along the beach strip also have restaurants. Many of the restaurants are also bars, depending on the time of night, and you can stop at any of them just for a drink. With all these places, plus a handful of warungs, there are dozens of places to eat. Some of them are listed here, but you'll do well just looking around and eating anywhere that takes your fancy.

Starting from the Singaraja end, the *Harmoni Restaurant*, on the main road, has great fresh fish and other seafood dishes, but service can be slow in between meal times. The restaurant at *Happy Beach Inn* is good, with friendly service – order Balinese roast duck a day in advance. In Kalibukbuk village, the *Surya Restaurant* is very well regarded, and will also do good Balinese dishes. The *BU Warung*, next to the tourist office, is good value, or you could try *Chono's*, a little bit to the west. Across the road, *Arya's Cafe* is a favourite with locals – everyone recommends it; try their cakes and desserts.

On the road down to Nirwana there's the *Kakatua Bar & Restaurant*, which offers a good meal in a very convivial atmosphere. The restaurant at *Nirwana* is pricey, and it's been redesigned so it doesn't overlook the beach as nicely as it used to.

Further along are *Singa Pizza Restaurant*, the *Superman Restaurant*, *Marta's Warung* and then *Johni's Restaurant*. All these places are popular, and their menus and prices are similar so it's impossible to single out individual places. *Wina's Bar & Restaurant* is more of a nighttime hangout, as is the *Malibu Club*, but they both serve meals.

Entertainment

Some of the hotel restaurants have special nights with an Indonesian buffet meal and Balinese dancing. At about 6000 rp for entertainment and all you can eat, this can be very good value. *Rambutan* does a good one, usually on Wednesdays and Sundays. *Aditya*, the *New Srikandi* and *Angsoka* also have buffet nights which are well advertised by leaflets that circulate around the beach and the bars. There's often live music at the *Malibu Club*, and they also have video movies.

Quite a few Balinese guys hang round the bars in Lovina. Most of them are pretty harmless, and some of them are a lot of fun. The shameless con-artists of a few years ago have mostly moved on. Nevertheless, you should be sceptical if local guys offer elaborate pretexts for wanting large amounts of money.

Getting There & Away

To get to Lovina from the south of Bali by public transport, you first have to get to Singaraja, then take a bemo out from there. The regular bemo fare from Singaraja to the middle of Lovina's beach strip is 500 rp.

There are direct public buses between Surabaya (Java) and Singaraja, but if you're coming in from the west you can get off along the Lovina beach strip, rather than have to backtrack from Singaraja. Public buses to Surabaya leave Singaraja at 5 pm; call the ticket office on 25141 to arrange a pick up, or get the staff at your losmen to help. Alternatively, there are frequent buses to Gilimanuk, where you can take the ferry to Java, and arrange onward transport. If you're just going a short way west, to Sing Sing, Banjar or Seririt, you can flag down a bemo in the main drag.

The Perama bus company's office (☎ 21161) and bus stop is at the Perama Hotel in Anturan, about eight km from Singaraja. Fares are 12,500 rp to Kuta or Ubud, 20,000 rp to Candidasa or Padangbai, 30,000 rp to Lombok, 20,000 rp to Surabaya and 38,000 rp to Yogyakarta.

Getting Around

The Lovina strip is very spread out, but you can get back and forth on bemos, which should cost 300 rp for a short trip (two or three km), or 500 rp all the way to Singaraja – they will try to charge you more if they can. You can also rent bicycles (3000 rp per day), motorbikes (around 10,000 rp per day), and cars (about 40,000 rp per day without insurance; less for longer). Enquire at the places in Kalibukbuk, or ask at your losmen. For a charter bemo, try at the Banyuasri terminal in Singaraja where there might be a few to compete for your business.

WEST OF SINGARAJA

The road west of Singaraja follows the coast through Lovina then cuts through the Bali Barat National Park to join the south-coast road near Gilimanuk, the port for ferries to Java. There are several places along this road, or near to it, which are worth a visit.

Waterfalls

At the village of **Labuhan Haji**, five km from the middle of the Lovina beach strip, there's a sign to Singsing Air Terjun ((Daybreak Waterfall). About one km from the main road there's a warung on the left and a carpark on the right – you may be asked to pay for parking. Walk past the warung and along the path for about 200 metres to the lower falls. The waterfall is not huge, dropping about 12 metres into a deep pool which is good for a swim. The water isn't crystal clear, but it's much cooler than the sea and very refreshing.

You can clamber further up the hillside to the second waterfall (Singsing Dua), which is slightly bigger and has a mud bath which is supposedly good for the skin. This one also cascades into a deep pool in which you can swim. It's a pretty setting and makes a nice day trip from Lovina. There are some other falls in the area which you have to walk to – ask at your losmen for details. Waterfalls are more spectacular in the wet season, and may be just a trickle in the dry season.

Banjar

Buddhist Monastery Bali's only Buddhist monastery *(wihara)* is about half a km beyond the village of **Banjar Tega**, which is about three km up a steep track from the main coast road – get a lift on the back of a motorbike for about 500 rp. It is vaguely Buddhist-looking, with colourful decoration, a bright orange roof and statues of Buddha, but overall it's very Balinese with the same decorative carvings and door guardians. It's quite a handsome structure, in a commanding location with views down the valley and across the paddy fields to the sea. The road continues past the monastery, winding further up into the hills.

Hot Springs The hot springs (air panas) are only a short distance west of the monastery if you cut across from Banjar Tega, rather than return to the main road. From the monastery, go back down to Banjar Tega and turn left in the centre of the village. The small road runs west for a km or so to the village of Banjar. From there it's only a short distance uphill before you see the 'air panas 1 km' sign on the left. Follow the road to the carpark where you'll be shown a place to park. Buy your ticket from the little office (400 rp, children 200 rp) and cross the bridge to the baths. There are changing rooms under the restaurant, on the right side.

Eight carved stone nagas (mythological serpents) spew water from a natural hot spring into the first bath, which then overflows (via the mouths of five more nagas), into a second, larger pool. In a third pool, water pours from three-metre-high spouts to give you a pummelling massage. The water is slightly sulphurous and pleasantly hot, so you might enjoy it more in the morning or the evening than in the heat of the day. You must wear a swimsuit and you shouldn't use soap in the pools, but you can do so under an adjacent outdoor shower.

The whole area is beautifully landscaped with lush tropical plants. The restaurant, a striking Balinese-style building, is not too expensive and has good Indonesian food.

Getting There & Away The monastery and hot springs are both signposted from the main road. If you don't have your own transport, it's probably easiest to go to the hot springs first. Heading west from Singaraja, continue beyond the turn-off to Banjar Tega to the Banjar turn-off (around the 18 km marker) where there are guys on motorbikes who will take you up to the air panas for 500 rp one-way. From the springs you can walk across to the monastery and back down to the main road.

Seririt
Seririt is a junction town for the roads that run south over the mountains to Pulukan or Bajera, on the way to Denpasar. The road running west along the coast towards Gilimanuk is quite good, with some pretty coastal scenery and few tourists.

Seririt has a petrol station and a reasonable selection of shops. If you need to stay there, the *Hotel Singarasari* (☎ 92435), near the bus and bemo stop, has rooms for 8000 rp, or 20,000 rp with air-con and TV. There are

places to eat in the market area, just north of the bemo stop.

Celukanbawang
Celukanbawang, the main port for northern Bali, has a large wharf. Bugis schooners, the magnificent sailing ships which take their name from the seafaring Bugis people of Sulawesi, sometimes anchor here. The *Hotel Drupadi Indah*, a combination losmen, cinema, bar and restaurant, is the only place to stay; it costs 15,000 rp for an ordinary room.

Pulaki
Pulaki is famous for its Pura Pulaki, a coastal temple which was completely rebuilt in the early '80s. The temple has a large troop of monkeys. Pulaki itself seems to be entirely devoted to grape growing and the whole village is almost roofed over with grapevines. A local wine is made which tastes a little like sweet sherry – mixed with lemonade it's drinkable, sort of. The grapes are also exported as dried fruit.

Pemuteran
One km past Pulaki is the Pemuteran temple, with hot springs just outside, but neither is particularly interesting. North of the road near here is the *Pondok Sari Accommodation & Restaurant*, all by itself with its own little beach. It's used as base for diving trips to Menjangan Island, about 16 km away, but it would also be a nice place to get away from it all. Very comfortable, attractive rooms cost 35,000 rp without breakfast, plus 10% tax and service. There's a Sanur number for bookings (☎ 289031).

BALI BARAT NATIONAL PARK
The Bali Barat (West Bali) National Park covers nearly 20,000 hectares of the western tip of Bali. In addition, 50,000 hectares are protected in the national park extension, as well as nearly 7000 hectares of coral reef and coastal waters. On an island as small and densely populated as Bali, this represents a major commitment to nature conservation.

The park headquarters is at Cekik, near

Gilimanuk, and some treks can be done from there (see the South-West Bali chapter for details). Coming from the north coast, there is a visitors centre at Labuhan Lalang (open from 7 am to 4 pm every day), with some information and a good relief model of the national park. There are a couple of trekking possibilities here, but the main attraction is diving and snorkelling on Menjangan Island. The standard of facilities and information for visitors is quite limited.

The main north-coast road connects with Gilimanuk through the national park, and you don't have to pay any entrance fees just to drive through. If you want to visit any places of interest (they're called 'visitor objects'), then you have to buy an entry ticket – 2000 rp for the day. In addition you pay for parking at some of the visitor objects.

Flora & Fauna

Most of the natural vegetation in the park is not tropical rainforest, which requires rain all year, but a coastal savannah, with deciduous trees which become bare in the dry season. The southern slopes have more regular rainfall, and hence more tropical vegetation, while the coastal lowlands have extensive mangroves. Over 200 species of plants inhabit the various environments.

Animals include black monkey, leaf monkey and macaque; barking deer, sambar deer, mouse deer, Java deer and muncak; squirrel, wild pig, buffalo, iguana, python and green snake.

The bird life is prolific, with many of Bali's 300 species represented. The most famous bird is the Bali starling (*Leucopsar rothschildi*), also known as the Bali mynah, Rothschild's mynah, or locally as *jalak putih*; it's Bali's only endemic. This striking white bird, with black tips on wings and tail and a distinctive bright blue mask, is greatly valued as a caged bird. Its natural population fell as low as 40 pairs, but efforts are being made to rebuild the population by re-introducing captive birds to the wild. Initially this is taking place on Menjangan Island and the Prapat Agung Peninsula, so trekking in both these areas is currently restricted.

Banyuwedang Hot Springs

Coming from the north coast, this is the first 'visitor object' you will encounter. There is a Balinese temple and, according to one brochure, water from these springs will 'strengthen the endurance of your body against the attack of skin disease'. The place is smelly and unattractive.

Labuhan Lalang & Pulau Menjangan

At Labuhan Lalang you have to purchase the 2000 rp ticket to enter the park, even if you just want to look at the foreshore area, and parking a car costs 2000 rp whether you're there for the day or just half an hour. There's a jetty for the boats to Menjangan, a warung with the usual sort of menu and a pleasant white sand beach 200 metres to the east. There are coral formations close to the shore which are good for snorkelling.

Excursions from Labuhan Lalang to Pulau Menjangan (Menjangan Island) start at 42,000 rp per person, for the half-hour boat trip, three hours on or around the island, and the return trip. If you want to stay longer, each additional hour costs about 5000 rp. Both snorkelling and scuba diving are excellent around the island, with great visibility, superb unspoiled coral, caves, lots of tropical fish and a spectacular drop-off. Boats should use fixed moorings, which have been installed to prevent the coral being damaged by anchors. Diving is usually best in the early morning. Diving trips to the island can be arranged with various dive operators on Bali, but it's a long way to come for a day trip from the south. The closest dive operation is at Lovina Beach.

Trekking on the island is not permitted at the moment, because of a project to re-establish the Bali Starling population.

Trekking

Three-hour guided treks around the Labuhan Lalang area can be arranged at the visitors centre. You must take a guide, who will cost about 15,000 rp with from one to four people. Either arrange things the day before, or just turn up at the visitors centre at 7.30 am. Early morning is the best time to go.

A seven-hour trek across to Belimbingsari is also possible. Prapat Agung, the peninsula north of the Terima to Gilimanuk road, has some good places to see wildlife, but access is currently restricted because of the Bali starling project. Some overnight treks in the national park can be arranged from the headquarters in Cekik.

Jayaprana's Grave

A 10-minute walk up some stone stairs from the south side of the road, a little way west of Labuhan Lalang, will bring you to this site. The foster son of a 17th-century king, Jayaprana, planned to marry Leyonsari, a beautiful girl of humble origins. The king, however, also fell in love with Leyonsari and had Jayaprana killed. In a dream, Leyonsari learned the truth of Jayaprana's death, and killed herself rather than marry the king. This Romeo and Juliet story is a common theme in Balinese folklore, and the grave is regarded as sacred even though the ill-fated couple were not deities.

From the site, there's a fine view to the north and, according to a national park pamphlet, '...you will feel another pleasure which you can't get in another place'.

Places to Stay

There are no lodgings at all in the national park area. The closest places are in Gilimanuk (see the South-West Bali chapter), or at Pemuteran on the north coast (see the entry earlier in this chapter). For overnight treks there are some rough shelters, and you need to bring your own food, cooking and sleeping gear. There is a campground near Cekik.

Getting There & Away

The road east follows the coast to Lovina and Singaraja. The road west goes to Cekik, where there is a T-intersection – if you turn right, it's three km to Gilimanuk; turning left will take you to Negara and Denpasar.

EAST OF SINGARAJA

Interesting sites east of Singaraja include some of Bali's best known temples. The north-coast sandstone is very soft and easily carved, allowing local sculptors to give free rein to their imaginations. You'll find some delightfully whimsical scenes carved into a number of the temples here.

Although the basic architecture of the temples is similar in both regions, there are some important differences. The inner courtyard of southern temples usually houses a number of multi-roofed shrines (merus) together with other structures, whereas in the north, everything is grouped on a single pedestal. On the pedestal you'll usually find 'houses' for the deities to use on their earthly visits and also for storing important religious relics. Also, there will probably be a *padmasana* or 'throne' for the sun god.

At Kubutambahan there is a turn-off to the south which takes you up to Penulisan and Kintamani, or you can continue east to the lovely spring-fed pools at Yeh Sanih. From there the road continues right around the east coast to Tulamben and Amlapura (see the East Bali chapter).

Sangsit

At Sangsit, only a few km beyond Singaraja, you'll find an excellent example of the colourful architectural style of northern Bali. Sangsit's **Pura Beji** is a subak temple, dedicated to the spirits that look after irrigated rice fields. It's about half a km off the main road towards the coast. The sculptured panels along the front wall set the tone with their Disneyland-like demons and amazing nagas. The inside also has a variety of sculptures covering every available space, and the inner courtyard is shaded by a frangipani tree.

Sangsit's **Pura Dalem** shows scenes of punishment in the afterlife, and other pictures which are humorous and/or erotic.

If you continue beyond Sangsit to **Bungkulan**, you'll find another fine temple with an interesting kulkul (warning drum). The *Sara & Dewa Guesthouse* in Bungkulan is a cheap and interesting place to stay. It's the only place to stay, so it's easy to find.

Jagaraga

The village of Jagaraga, a few km off the main road, has an interesting **Pura Dalem**. The small temple has delightful sculptured panels along its front wall, both inside and out. On the outer wall look for a vintage car driving sedately past, a steamer at sea and even an aerial dogfight between early aircraft. Jagaraga is also famous for its legong troupe, said to be the best in northern Bali.

It was the capture of the local rajah's stronghold at Jagaraga that marked the arrival of Dutch power on Bali in 1849. A few km past Jagaraga, along the right-hand side as you head inland, look for another small temple with ornate carvings of a whole variety of fish and fishermen.

Sawan

Several km further inland, Sawan is a centre for the manufacture of gamelan gongs and complete gamelan instruments. You can see the gongs being cast and the intricately carved gamelan frames being made.

Kubutambahan

Only a km or so beyond the Kintamani turn-off at Kubutambahan is the **Pura Maduwe Karang**. Like Pura Beji at Sangsit, the temple is dedicated to agricultural spirits, but this one looks after unirrigated land.

This is one of the best temples in northern Bali and is particularly noted for its sculptured panels, including the famous bicycle panel depicting a gentleman riding a bicycle with flower petals for wheels. The cyclist may be Nieuwenkamp, one of the first Dutch people to explore Bali, who did actually get around by bicycle. It's on the base of the main plinth in the inner enclosure, and there are other panels worth inspecting.

Yeh Sanih

About 15 km east of Singaraja, Yeh Sanih (also called Air Sanih) is a popular local spot where freshwater springs are channelled into some very pleasant swimming pools before flowing into the sea. Yeh Sanih is right by the sea and the area with the pools is attractively

Temple guardian, Kubutambahan

laid out with pleasant gardens, a restaurant and a couple of places to stay. It's well worth a visit and admission to the springs and pool is 400 rp (children 200 rp). On the hill overlooking the springs is the Pura Taman Manik Mas temple.

Places to Stay & Eat There are a couple of places to stay near the springs. In fact, the *Bungalow Puri Sanih* is actually in the springs complex, with a restaurant overlooking the pretty gardens. It has doubles for 15,000 to 20,000 rp – the more expensive rooms are upstairs in little two-storey bungalows. Also at the springs, on the east side, *Yeh Sanih Seaside Cottages* has rooms at 30,000 rp and cottages near the sea at 40,000 rp. Up the steep stairs opposite, *Puri Rena* has double rooms at 15,000 and 20,000 rp, and a restaurant with great views. There are also a number of warungs across the road from the springs. *Tara Beach Bungalows* are one km east of Air Sanih, with basic bungalows at 7000/10,000 rp and better ones at 10,000/20,000 rp.

Top: Lake Batur from Kintamani, Central Mountains, Bali (MJ)
Bottom: Pura Ulu Danau, on the shores of Lake Bratan, Bali (GA)

Top: Lake Batur sunrise, Bali (JL)
Left: View of Gunung Agung from Toyapakeh, Nusa Penida (JL)
Right: Young man on Nusa Lembongan (JL)

Nusa Penida

Nusa Penida, an administrative region within the Klungkung district, comprises three islands – Nusa Penida itself, the smaller Nusa Lembongan to the north-west, and tiny Nusa Ceningan between them. Nusa Lembongan attracts visitors for its surf, seclusion and snorkelling. The island of Nusa Penida is right off the tourist track and has few facilities for visitors, while Nusa Ceningan is virtually uninhabited. There is increased tourist interest, with some people staying on Lembongan, but many visit only on expensive day cruises from the mainland, diving, snorkelling or surfing from their boat, or making brief forays ashore.

Economic resources are limited on Nusa Penida. It has been a poor region for many years and there has been some transmigration from here to other parts of Indonesia. Thin soils and a lack of water do not permit the cultivation of rice, but other crops are grown – maize, cassava and beans are staples here. Tobacco is grown for export to mainland Bali. Fishing is another source of food, and some sardines and lobster are also sold to Bali. The cultivation of seaweed is a recent development but now quite well established, and the underwater fences on which it is grown can be seen off many of the beaches. After harvesting, the seaweed is spread out on the beach to dry, then exported to Hong Kong, Japan and Europe where it is used as a thickening agent in processed foods and cosmetics.

Diving

There are some great diving possibilities around, and between, the islands, but no dive operations at all. You have to organise it all from the mainland. Enquire with the diving operators in Sanur or Candidasa, and stick with the most reputable ones. Diving here is demanding, with cold water and difficult currents, and local knowledge is essential. A particular attraction is large marine animals, including turtles, sharks and rays.

NUSA LEMBONGAN
Jungutbatu

Most visitors to Nusa Lembongan come for the quiet beach or the surf that breaks on the reef, and they stay around the beach at Jungutbatu. The reef protects the beach, a perfect crescent of white sand with clear blue water, and there are superb views across the water to Gunung Agung on mainland Bali. There's also good snorkelling on the reef, with some spots accessible from the beach. To reach other snorkelling spots you need to charter a boat, which costs about 5000 rp per hour.

There's no jetty – the boats usually beach at the village of Jungutbatu and you have to jump off into the shallows. Your boat captain might be able to leave you at the north-eastern end of the beach where most of the bungalows are, but otherwise you'll have to walk a km to reach them.

Information Apart from a few basic bungalows and restaurants there are virtually no tourist facilities, though some of the cruise boat operators are planning improvements at the beaches they visit. There's no post office and the bank doesn't change travellers' cheques. The notice board at the Main Ski restaurant advertises excursions and day trips to various locations around the three islands, as well as the cost of bicycle and motorbike hire. The restaurant owners also know the name and address of a local doctor who seems to specialise in coral cuts and surfing injuries.

Surfing Surfing here is best in the dry season, May to September, when the winds come from the south-east. There are three main breaks on the reef, all aptly named. Off the beach where the bungalows are is **Shipwreck**, a right-hand reef break named for the remains of a wreck which is clearly visible from the shore. To the south-west of this is **Lacerations**, a fast hollow right which breaks over shallow coral – did you bring a helmet? Further south-west again is **Playground**, an undemanding left-hander.

You can paddle out to Shipwreck, but for the other two it's better to hire a boat. Prices are negotiable depending on time and numbers, but it's about 3000 to 5000 rp to be taken out and back, with an hour's surfing in between. Strangely, the surf can be crowded even when the island isn't, as charter boats often bring groups of surfers for day trips from the mainland.

Places to Stay & Eat In the village, *Johnny's Losmen* was the first place on Lembongan to accommodate visitors. It's basic but quite OK, and cheap at 4000/5000 rp for singles/doubles, although not many people stay here. There are some other small places near the village – *Bungalow Number 7* is also OK, and cheap. These days most of the accommodation is further along the beach to the north-east, and that's where most of the visitors go. Don't deal with the touts here – go to the desk of the losmen yourself, and don't give any money to anyone else.

Heading north-east you'll reach the conspicuous *Main Ski Inn & Restaurant* ('main ski' is Indonesian for surfing). The two-storey restaurant, right on the beach, is a little more expensive than some of the others, but serves good food and has a great view. Binoculars are provided so you can watch the surf while you're waiting for lunch. Upstairs rooms are 12,000/15,000 rp for singles/doubles, rooms downstairs are 10,000/12,000 rp.

Agung's Lembongan Lodge has cheap double rooms from 6000 rp, and better ones at 15,000 rp. Its restaurant has cheap but tasty food. Next to that is the more expensive *Nusa Lembongan Bungalows & Restaurant*. Finally there's *Ta Chi Cottages* (or Tarci) with rooms from 12,000 to 15,000 rp and reputedly the best cook on the island.

Lembongan Village

It's about three km south-west along the sealed road from Jungutbatu to Lembongan village, the island's other town. Leaving Jungutbatu you pass a Balinese-style temple with an enormous banyan tree, then climb up a knoll with a nice view back over the beach. After crossing the knoll you descend to the outskirts of Lembongan village and soon get the feeling that tourists are a rarity here. The

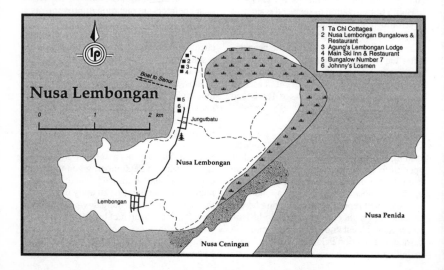

Nusa Lembongan

1 Ta Chi Cottages
2 Nusa Lembongan Bungalows & Restaurant
3 Agung's Lembongan Lodge
4 Main Ski Inn & Restaurant
5 Bungalow Number 7
6 Johnny's Losmen

Boat to Sanur

Jungutbatu

Nusa Lembongan

Lembongan

Nusa Penida

Nusa Ceningan

people aren't hostile, but neither do they display the welcoming smiles that greet you elsewhere on Bali. Following the road downhill brings you to the lagoon which separates Nusa Lembongan from Nusa Ceningan. It's possible to continue right around the island, following the rough track which eventually comes back to Jungutbatu.

The Underground House As you enter Lembongan you'll pass a warung on the right with a couple of pool tables. For 1000 rp the kids here will offer to take you through the labyrinthine underground 'house', 100 metres back off the road. It's a crawl and scramble through many small passages, rooms and chambers, supposedly dug by one man.

The story goes that the man lost a dispute with an evil spirit and was condemned to death, but pleaded to be allowed to finish his house first. The spirit relented, and the man started excavating his cave with a small spoon. He always started a new room before he finished the last one, so of course the house was never completed, and thus his death sentence was postponed indefinitely.

The kids provide a candle but it would be a good idea to bring your own torch (flashlight). Be very careful as there are big holes in unexpected places. On your way back to the road, have a look down the well and see from how far down the villagers must draw their water.

Getting There & Away
To/From Sanur Boats leave from the northern end of Sanur Beach, in front of the Ananda Hotel. There's a ticket office there; don't buy from a tout. The boat captains – that's what they're called – have fixed the tourist price to Lembongan at 15,000 rp. The strait between Bali and the Nusa Penida islands is very deep and huge swells develop during the day, so the boats leave before 8.30 am. Even so, you may get wet with spray, so be prepared. The trip takes at least 1½ hours, more if conditions are unfavourable.

To/From Kuta Some agencies in Kuta sell a ticket through to Lembongan via Sanur. Perama charges 22,500 rp.

To/From Kusamba Most boats from Kusamba go to Toyapakeh on Nusa Penida, but sometimes they go to Jungutbatu on Lembongan. Boats from Sanur are safer and quicker.

To/From Nusa Penida Boats take locals between Jungutbatu and Toyapakeh on Nusa Penida, particularly on market days. You'll have to ask around to find when they leave, and discuss the price. The public boats will be chock full of people, produce and livestock. A charter boat will run to about 30,000 rp, which would be OK between six or eight people.

Getting Around
The island is fairly small and you can easily walk around it in a few hours. You can also hire a motorbike or get a lift on the back of one.

NUSA PENIDA
Clearly visible from Sanur, Padangbai, Candidasa or anywhere else along Bali's south-eastern coast, the hilly island of Nusa Penida has a population of around 40,000 and was once used as a place of banishment for criminals and other undesirables from the kingdom of Klungkung.

Nusa Penida is also the legendary home of Jero Gede Macaling, the demon who inspired the Barong Landung dance. Many Balinese believe the island to be a place of enchantment and evil power *(angker)* – paradoxically, this is an attraction. Although foreigners rarely visit here, thousands of Balinese come every year for religious observances aimed at placating the evil spirits. The island has a number of interesting temples dedicated to Jero Gede Macaling, including Pura Ped near Toyapakeh and Pura Batukuning near Sewana.

There is also a huge limestone cave, Goa Karangsari, on the coast about four km from Sampalan. The mountain village of Tanglad

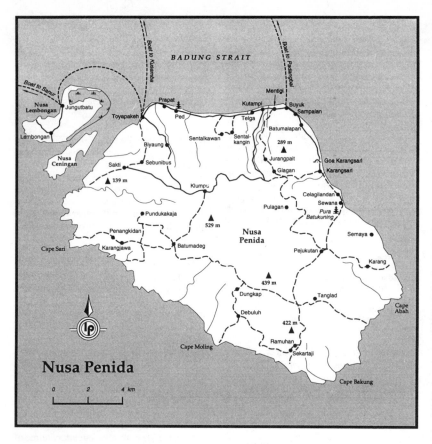

Nusa Penida

0   2   4 km

in the south-east, with its throne for the sun god, Surya, is also interesting.

The north coast has white sand beaches and views over the water to the volcanoes on Bali. This coastal strip, with the two main towns of Toyapakeh and Sampalan, is moist and fertile, almost lush. The south coast has limestone cliffs dropping straight down to the sea – a spectacular sight if you're coming that way by boat. Rickety bamboo scaffolds enable fresh water to be collected from springs near the base of the cliffs.

The interior is a hilly, rugged landscape with sparse-looking crops and vegetation

and unsalubrious villages. Rainfall is low, and there are large square concrete tanks called *cabangs* in which water is stored for the dry season. The hillsides are terraced, but they are not like the wet rice paddies of Bali. The terraces are supported with stone walls and the crops include sweet potatoes, cassava, corn and soybeans, but not rice, which is brought in from the mainland.

The population is predominantly Hindu, though there are some Muslims, and a mosque, in Toyapakeh. The culture is distinct from that of Bali. The language is an old form of Balinese no longer heard on the mainland, and there are also local types of dance, architecture and craft, including a unique type of red ikat weaving. The people have had little contact with foreign visitors and the children are more likely to stare than shout 'hello mister'. They are not unfriendly, just bemused. Many people do not speak Indonesian and almost no-one speaks English.

Sampalan

There's nothing inspiring about Sampalan, but it's pleasant enough, with a market, warungs, schools and shops strung out along the coast road. The market area, where the bemos congregate, is on the northern side of the road, by definition almost in the middle of the town. Buyuk Harbour, where the boats leave for Padangbai, is a few hundred metres west of the market. The town's only losmen is opposite the police station, a few hundred metres in the opposite direction.

Goa Karangsari

If you follow the coast road south-east from Sampalan for about six km, you'll see the cave entrance up the hill on the right side of the road, just before the village of Karangsari. You might have to ask for directions. The entrance is a small cleft in the rocks, but the cave is quite large, extending for over 200 metres into the hillside. It is inhabited by many small bats which are noisy but harmless. During the Galungan Festival there is a torch-lit procession into the cave, followed by ceremonies at a temple by the lake in one of the large chambers. If you want to do more than put your head in the entrance, bring a good torch.

Toyapakeh

If you come by boat from Nusa Lembongan you'll probably be dropped on, or just off, the beach at Toyapakeh. It's a pretty town with lots of shady trees. The beach has clean white sand, clear blue water, a neat line of prahus and Bali's Gunung Agung as a backdrop. Step up from the beach and you're at the roadhead, where there will be bemos to take you to Ped or Sampalan (about 400 rp).

Few travellers stay here, but if you want to you'll find the *Losmen Terang* on your right, which has rooms for about 5000 rp.

Pura Dalem Penetaran Ped

This important temple is near the beach at the village of Ped, a few km east of Toyapakeh. It houses a shrine for Jero Gede Macaling, the source of power for the practitioners of black magic, and it's a place of pilgrimage for those seeking protection from sickness and evil. The temple structure is crude, even ugly, which gives it an appropriately sinister ambience.

Getting There & Away

The strait between Nusa Penida and southern Bali is very deep and subject to heavy swells – if there is a strong tide running the boats may have to wait. You may also have to wait a while for a boat to fill up with passengers.

From Padangbai Fast, twin-engine fibre-glass boats operate between Padangbai and Nusa Penida. The boats are about eight or 10 metres long and look pretty seaworthy. They're well-supplied with life jackets, which is unusual for small Indonesian craft, but reassuring. The trip takes less than an hour and costs 4000 rp. It's an exciting ride as the boat bounces across the water beneath the looming volcano of Agung. At Padangbai, the boats land on the beach just east of the carpark for the Bali to Lombok ferry. On Nusa Penida, they land at the beach at Buyuk Harbour, just west of Sampalan, or on the beach at Toyapakeh.

From Kusamba Prahus carry produce and supplies between Nusa Penida and Kusamba, which is the closest port to Klungkung, the district capital. The boats leave when they're full, weather and waves permitting, and cost about 2500 rp one-way. They are slower than the boats from Padangbai, and may be heavily loaded (overloaded?) with provisions.

From Nusa Lembongan The boats that carry local people between the islands usually land at Toyapakeh. Ask around the beachfront area to find when the next one is leaving, and discuss the price. Get there early. You may have to wait quite a while, or charter a boat.

Getting Around

There are regular bemos on the sealed road between Toyapakeh and Sampalan, on to Sewana and up to Klumpu, but beyond these areas the roads are rough or nonexistent and transport is uncertain. If you want to charter a bemo try to find Wayan Patra, from Banjar Sentral Kanjin in Ped. He knows Nusa Penida well, and speaks English. You may be able to get someone to take you on the back of a motorbike, although this can be a high-risk form of transport. If you really want to explore the island bring a mountain bike from the mainland (but remember Nusa Penida is hilly), or plan to do some walking.

LOMBOK

Facts about Lombok

HISTORY

The earliest recorded society on Lombok was the relatively small kingdom of the Sasaks. The Sasaks were agriculturalists and animists who practised ancestor and spirit worship. The original Sasaks are believed to have come overland from north-west India or Burma in waves of migration that pre-dated most Indonesian ethnic groups. Few relics remain from the old animist kingdoms and the majority of Sasaks today are Muslim, although animism has left its mark on the culture. Not much is known about Lombok before the 17th century, at which time it was split into numerous, frequently squabbling states each presided over by a Sasak 'prince' – disunity which the neighbouring Balinese exploited.

Balinese Rule

In the early 1600s, the Balinese from the eastern state of Karangasem established colonies and took control of western Lombok. At the same time, the roving Makassarese crossed the strait from their colonies in western Sumbawa and established settlements in eastern Lombok. This conflict of interests ended with the war of 1677-78, which saw the Makassarese booted off the island, and eastern Lombok temporarily reverting to the rule of the Sasak princes. Balinese control soon extended east and by 1740 or 1750 the whole island was in their hands. Squabbles over royal succession soon had the Balinese fighting amongst themselves on both Bali and Lombok, and Lombok split into four separate kingdoms. It was not until 1838 that the Mataram kingdom subdued the other three, reconquered eastern Lombok (where Balinese rule had weakened during the years of disunity) and then crossed the Lombok Strait to Bali and overran Karangasem, thus reuniting the 18th-century state of Karangasem-Lombok.

While the Balinese were now the masters of Lombok, the basis of their control in western and eastern Lombok was quite different and this would eventually lead to a Dutch takeover. In western Lombok, where Balinese rule dated from the early 17th century, relations between the Balinese and the Sasaks were relatively harmonious. The Sasak peasants, who adhered to the mystical Wektu Telu version of Islam, easily assimilated Balinese Hinduism, participated in Balinese religious festivities and worshipped at the same shrines. Intermarriage between Balinese and Sasaks was common.

The western Sasaks were organised in the same irrigation associations (subaks) that the Balinese used for wet-rice agriculture. The traditional Sasak village government, presided over by a chief who was also a member of the Sasak aristocracy, was done away with and the peasants were ruled directly by the rajah or a land-owning Balinese aristocrat.

Things were very different in the east, where the recently defeated Sasak aristocracy hung in limbo. Here the Balinese had to maintain control from garrisoned forts and, although the traditional village government remained intact, the village chief was reduced to little more than a tax collector for the local Balinese district head *(punggawa)*.

The Balinese ruled like feudal kings, taking control of the land from the Sasak peasants and reducing them to the level of serfs. With their power and land-holdings slashed, the Sasak aristocracy of eastern Lombok was hostile to the Balinese. The peasants remained loyal to their former Sasak rulers, and supported rebellions in 1855, 1871 and 1891.

Dutch Involvement

The Balinese succeeded in suppressing the first two revolts, but the third uprising, in 1891, was a different story. Towards the end of 1892 it too had almost been defeated, but the Sasak chiefs sent envoys to the Dutch resident in Buleleng (Singaraja) asking for help and inviting the Dutch to rule Lombok.

Although the Dutch planned to take advantage of the turmoil on Lombok they backed off from military action – partly because they were still fighting a war in Aceh (in Sumatra) and partly because of the apparent military strength of the Balinese on Lombok.

Dutch reluctance to use force began to dissipate when the ruthless Van der Wijck succeeded to the post of Governor General of the Dutch East Indies in 1892. He made a treaty with the rebels in eastern Lombok in 1894 and then, with the excuse that he was setting out to free the Sasaks from tyrannical Balinese rule, sent a fleet carrying a large army to Lombok. Though the Balinese rajah quickly capitulated to Dutch demands, the younger Balinese princes of Lombok overruled him and attacked and routed the Dutch. It was a short-lived victory; the Dutch army dug its heels in at Ampenan and in September reinforcements began arriving from Java. The Dutch counterattack began, Mataram was overrun and the Balinese stronghold of Cakranegara was bombarded with artillery. The rajah eventually surrendered to the Dutch and the last resistance collapsed when a large group of Balinese, including members of the aristocracy and royal family, were killed in a traditional puputan, deliberately marching into the fire from Dutch guns.

Dutch Rule

Dutch rule of Lombok is a case study in callous colonial rule. New taxes resulted in the impoverishment of the majority of peasants and the creation of a new stratum of Chinese middlemen. The peasants were forced to sell more and more of their rice crop in order to pay the taxes; the amount of rice available for consumption declined by about a quarter between 1900 and the 1930s. Famines took place from 1938 to 1940 and in 1949.

For nearly half a century, by maintaining the goodwill of the Balinese and Sasak aristocracy and using a police force that never numbered more than 250, the Dutch were able to maintain their hold on more than 500,000 people. The peasants wouldn't act against them for fear of being evicted from their land and losing what little security they had. There were several failed peasant uprisings but they were never more than localised rebellions, the aristocracy never supported them, and the peasants themselves were ill-equipped to lead a widespread revolt. Even after Indonesia attained its independence, Lombok continued to be dominated by its Balinese and Sasak aristocracy.

Post-Colonial Lombok

Under Dutch rule the eastern islands of Indonesia, from Bali on, were grouped together as the Lesser Sunda Islands. When Sukarno proclaimed Indonesian independence on 17 August 1945, the Lesser Sunda Islands were formed into a single province called Nusa Tenggara, which means 'islands of the southeast'. This proved far too unwieldy to govern and it was subsequently divided into three separate regions – Bali, West Nusa Tenggara and East Nusa Tenggara. Thus Lombok became part of West Nusa Tenggara in 1958.

GEOGRAPHY

Lombok is one of the two main islands of the province of West Nusa Tenggara (Nusa Tenggara Barat, or NTB), about halfway along the Indonesian archipelago. Sumbawa is the other main island of West Nusa Tenggara province. Lombok is 8° south of the equator and stretches some 80 km east to west and about the same distance north to south.

Lombok is dominated by one of the highest mountains in Indonesia, Gunung Rinjani, which soars to 3726 metres. A dormant volcano, Rinjani last erupted in 1901. It has a large caldera with a crater lake, Segara Anak, 600 metres below the rim and a new volcanic cone which has formed in the centre.

Central Lombok, south of Rinjani, is similar to Bali, with rich alluvial plains and fields irrigated by water flowing from the mountains. In the far south and east it is drier, with scrubby, barren hills resembling parts of Australia's outback. This area gets little rain, and often has droughts which can last for months. In recent years, a number of

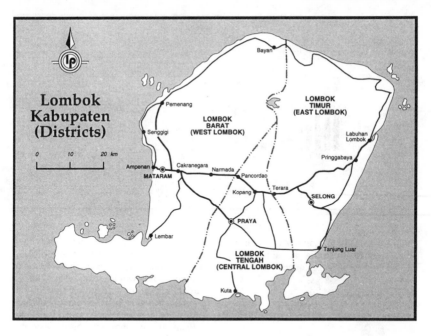

dams have been built, so the abundant rainfall of the wet season can be retained for year-round irrigation. The majority of the population is concentrated in the fertile but narrow east-west corridor sandwiched between the dry southern region and the slopes of Rinjani to the north.

Districts

Lombok is divided into three kabupaten (districts): Lombok Barat (West Lombok; capital Mataram); Lombok Tengah (Central Lombok; capital Praya); and Lombok Timur (East Lombok; capital Selong). Mataram is also the administrative capital of the West Nusa Tenggara Province.

CLIMATE

In Lombok's dry season – from June to September – the heat can be scorching. At night, particularly at higher elevations, the temperature can drop so much that a jumper (sweater) and light jacket are necessary. The wet season extends from October to May, with December and January the wettest months.

FLORA & FAUNA

Apart from banana and coconut palms, which grow in profusion over most of Lombok, the forests are confined largely to the mountain regions where they are extensive and dense, though logging is taking its toll. Teak and mahogany are among the forest timbers. Other native trees include bintangur, kesambi, bungur and fig, all of which are used widely for building houses and furniture. Much of the rest of the island is devoted to rice cultivation and the rice fields are every bit as picturesque as Bali's – including the ducks, which are becoming more common.

Several species of deer, including barking deer, as well as wild pigs, porcupines, snakes, numerous kinds of lizards, frogs, turtles, long-tailed monkeys, civets and feral

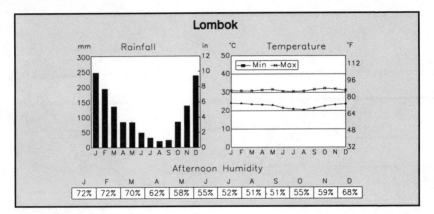

Lombok

Rainfall / Temperature / Afternoon Humidity

	J	F	M	A	M	J	J	A	S	O	N	D
	72%	72%	70%	62%	58%	55%	52%	51%	51%	55%	59%	68%

cattle are found here. Lombok is the furthest point west of Australia that the sulphur-crested cockatoo can be found.

Sulphur-crested cockatoo

The Wallace Line

The 19th-century naturalist, Sir Alfred Wallace (1822-1913), observed great differences in fauna between Bali and Lombok – as great as the differences between Africa and South America. In particular, there were no large mammals (elephant, rhino, tiger etc) east of Bali, and very few carnivores. He postulated that, during the ice ages when sea levels were lower, animals could have moved by land from what is now mainland Asia all the way to Bali, but the deep Lombok Strait would always have been a barrier. Thus he drew a line between Bali and Lombok, which he believed marked the biological division between Asia and Australia.

Plant life, on the other hand, does not reveal such a sharp division, but a gradual transition from predominantly Asian rainforest species to mostly Australian plants like eucalypts and acacias, better suited to long dry periods. This is associated with the lower rainfall as one moves east of Java. Environmental differences, including those in the natural vegetation, are now thought to provide a better explanation of the distribution of animal species than Wallace's theory about limits to their original migrations.

Modern biogeographers do recognise a distinction between Asian and Australian fauna, but the boundary between the regions is regarded as much fuzzier than Wallace's line. This transitional zone between Asia and Australia is nevertheless referred to as 'Walacea'.

ECONOMY

Lombok's economy is based on agriculture and the rice grown here is noted for its excellent quality. However, the climate on Lombok is drier than Bali's and, in many areas, only one crop can be produced each year. In some years water shortages caused by poor rains can limit rice production, or even cause a complete crop failure, leading to rising prices and unstable markets. The last major crop failure was caused by drought in 1966, and as many as 50,000 people perished for want of food. In 1973 there was another bad crop, and though the outcome was not as disastrous, rice on Lombok rose to double the price it was on Bali.

Dam building and the improvement of agricultural techniques, some supported by foreign-aid projects, will hopefully ensure better and more reliable crops in the future. Though rice is the staple crop there are small and large plantations of coconut palms, coffee, kapok and cotton. Tobacco is a common cash crop, and the square brick drying towers are often seen. In the fertile areas the land is intensively cultivated, often with a variety of crops planted together. Look for the vegetables and fodder trees planted on the levees between the paddy fields. Crops such as cloves, vanilla, pepper and pineapples are being introduced. Where possible, two rice crops are grown each year, with a third crop, perhaps of pineapples, grown for cash.

Fishing is widespread along the coastline which, edged by coral, has many good spawning areas. Stock-breeding on Lombok is done only on a small scale. Pumice stone is a profitable export, especially when stone-washed denim is in fashion.

Tourism

Lombok is keen to develop its tourist industry, perhaps inspired by Bali's obvious success. The first step in this direction was the development of Senggigi Beach and particularly the upmarket Senggigi Beach Hotel, owned by Garuda, the national airline. Both the Indonesian and the West Nusa Tenggara governments want to attract 'quality' tourists, and are promoting the establishment of expensive resort hotels. Most of the initial development is at Senggigi, but large tracts of beachfront land

all round the island have been acquired for 'co-developments' with Javanese and foreign interests. Some local people who sold their land used the money for a pilgrimage to Mecca and now live in poverty.

Regulations make it increasingly difficult to establish budget accommodation on the many beautiful but undeveloped beaches. There is some conflict of interest between big development interests and the operators of small, low-budget tourist facilities, for example on the Gili Islands. On the bright side, stringent environmental standards are being imposed on new developments.

After a rash of speculation, development has slowed somewhat, in the face of hard economic reality. With more and more deluxe hotels on Bali, and a depressed international economy, there are second thoughts about how many fancy hotel rooms can be filled. Lombok's airport does not have the capacity for large numbers of arrivals, and though there is talk of a new international airport in southern Lombok, investors are unlikely to put up the large sums necessary for luxury hotels until there is something concrete. Other improvements in infrastructure, like reliable electricity and water supplies, are also necessary. In the meantime, Lombok should continue as a relatively unspoiled and affordable destination – at least for a while.

POPULATION & PEOPLE

Lombok has a population of 2.4 million (1990 census), the majority living in and around the main centres of Ampenan, Cakranegara, Mataram, Praya and Selong. Almost 90% of the people are Sasak, about 10% are Balinese and there are minority populations of Chinese, Javanese and Arabs.

Sasaks

The Sasaks are assumed to have originally come from north-western India or Burma, and the clothing they wear even today – particularly the women – is very similar to that worn in those areas. Sasak women traditionally dress in long black sarongs called *lambung* and short-sleeved blouses with a V-

neck. The sarong is held in place by a four-metre long scarf known as a *sabuk*, trimmed with brightly coloured stripes. They wear very little jewellery and never any gold ornaments. Officially, most Sasaks are Muslims, but unofficially, many of the traditional beliefs have become interwoven with Muslim ideology.

Balinese

The Balinese originally settled in the west and the majority of Lombok's Balinese still live there today and retain their Hindu customs and traditions intact. Historically, as feudal overlords of Lombok, they earned the ill will of the Sasaks. Even today, the Sasaks regard the Dutch as liberating them from an oppressive power, but by and large the Balinese and Sasaks co-exist amicably. The Balinese contributed to the emergence of Lombok's Wektu Telu religion, and Balinese temples, ceremonies and processions are a colourful part of west Lombok's cultural life.

The Balinese are also involved in commercial activities, particularly the tourist industry. Many of the cheap and mid-range hotels are run by Balinese, with the same friendliness and efficiency you find on Bali itself.

Chinese

The Chinese first came to Lombok with the Dutch as a cheap labour force and worked as coolies in the rice paddies. Later they were given some privileges and allowed to set up and develop their own businesses, primarily restaurants and shops. Most of the Chinese living on Lombok today are based in Ampenan and Cakranegara. Almost every shop and every second restaurant in Cakra is run or owned by the Chinese.

Arabs

In Ampenan there is a small Arab quarter known as Kampung Arab. The Arabs living here are devout Muslims who follow the Koran to the letter, and marry amongst themselves. They are well educated and relatively affluent; many follow professions such as teaching and medicine, while others are insurance agents or office workers.

Buginese

In the late 19th century, seafaring immigrants from southern Sulawesi started to settle on the coastal areas of Lombok. Their descendants still operate much of the fishing industry. In Labuhan Lombok, Labuhan Haji and Tanjung Luar, Bugis-style houses are a common sight, constructed on stilts with low-pitched roofs and sometimes carved decorations on the verandahs and gables.

ARTS
Weaving

Lombok is renowned for its traditional weaving, the techniques being handed down from mother to daughter. Each piece of cloth is woven on a handloom in established patterns and colours. Some fabrics are woven in as many as four directions and interwoven with gold thread, and many take at least a month to complete. Flower and animal motifs of buffaloes, dragons, lizards, crocodiles and snakes are widely used to decorate this exquisite cloth. Several villages specialise in this craft, particularly Sukarara and Pringgasela.

Lombok also has a fine reputation for plaited basketware, bags and mats. Loyok and Kotaraja are two villages where this ancient Sasak craft is still practised. See the Arts & Crafts section for more information.

Music & Dance

Lombok has some brilliant dances found nowhere else in Indonesia. But unlike Bali which encourages – in fact hustles – Westerners to go along to its dances, getting to see any on Lombok previously depended on word of mouth or pure luck. For good or ill, performances are starting to be staged for tourists in some of the luxury hotels, and in the village of Lenek, which is known for its dance traditions.

Cupak Gerantang This is a dance based on one of the Panji stories, an extensive cycle of written and oral stories originating in Java in the 15th century. Like Arjuna, Panji is a romantic hero and this dance is popular all over Lombok. It is usually performed at traditional celebrations, such as birth and marriage ceremonies, and at other festivities.

Kayak Sando This is another version of a Panji story but here the dancers wear masks. It is only found in central and east Lombok.

Gandrung This dance is about love and courtship – *gandrung* means 'being in love' or 'longing'. It is a social dance, usually performed outdoors by the young men and women of the village. Everyone stands around in a circle and then, accompanied by a full gamelan orchestra, a young girl dances dreamily by herself for a time, before choosing a male partner from the audience to join her. The Gandrung is common to Narmada (west Lombok), Suangi and Lenek (east Lombok) and Praya (central Lombok).

Oncer This is a war dance performed by men and young boys. It is a highly skilled and dramatic performance which involves the participants playing a variety of unusual

musical instruments in time to their movements. The severe black of the costumes is slashed with crimson and gold waist bands, shoulder sashes, socks and caps. It's performed with great vigour at adat festivals, both in central and eastern Lombok.

Rudat Also a traditional Sasak dance, the Rudat is performed by pairs of men dressed in black caps and jackets and black-and-white checked sarongs. The dancers are backed by singers, tambourines and cylindrical drums called *jidur*. The music, lyrics and costume used in this dance show a mixture of Islamic and Sasak cultures.

Tandak Gerok Traditionally a performance from eastern Lombok, the Tandak Gerok combines dance, theatre and singing to music played on bamboo flutes and the bowed lute called a rebab. Its unique and most attractive feature is that the vocalists imitate the sound of the gamelan instruments. It is usually performed after harvesting or other hard physical labour, but is also put on at adat ceremonies.

Genggong Seven musicians are involved in this particular performance. Using a simple set of instruments which includes a bamboo flute, a rebab and knockers, they accompany their music with dance movements and stylised hand gestures.

Barong Tengkok This is the name given to the procession of musicians who play at weddings or circumcision ceremonies.

Contemporary Music The Sasak enjoyment of music and dance extends to rock, and you're most likely to encounter it blaring from the cassette player in a taxi, bus or bemo. Indonesian performers, mostly from Java, do some pretty good cover versions of Western hits, as well as original rock songs, mostly in Indonesian and often with a strong reggae influence. Shops in Mataram have thousands of cassettes in stock, so if you hear something you like, note down the details and buy a copy to take home. Lombok bands can be heard at Senggigi, and young locals are enthusiastic on the dance floor.

Architecture

Traditional laws and practices govern Lombok's architecture, as they do any other aspect of daily life. Construction must commence on a propitious day, always with an odd-numbered date, and the frame of the building must be completed on that same day. It would be bad luck to leave any of the important structural work to the following day.

In a traditional Sasak village there are three types of buildings: the communal meeting hall or *beruga*, family houses or *bale tani*, and rice barns or *lumbung*. The beruga and the bale tani are both rectangular, with low walls and a steeply pitched thatched roof, though of course the beruga is larger. The arrangement of rooms in a family house is also very standardised – there is an open verandah or *serambi* in front, and two rooms on two different levels inside: one for cooking and entertaining guests, the other for sleeping and storage.

Lumbung The lumbung, with its characteristic horseshoe shape, has become something of an architectural symbol on Lombok. You'll see rice-barn shapes in the design of hotel foyers, entrances, gateways and even phone booths. A lumbung design is often used for tourist bungalows. On an island that has been regularly afflicted with famine, a rice barn must be a powerful image of prosperity. Ironically, the new strains of high-yield rice, which have done so much to increase the food supply in Indonesia, cannot be stored in a traditional rice barn. It is said that the only lumbung built these days are for storing tourists.

CULTURE & CUSTOMS

Traditional law (adat) is still fundamental to the way of life on Lombok today, particularly customs relating to courting and marriage rituals, and circumcision ceremonies. In western Lombok you can see Balinese dances, temple ceremonies, and colourful processions with decorative offerings of flowers, fruit and food. Sasak ceremonies are often less visible though you may see colourful processions. Ask around and you can probably find when and where festivals and celebrations are being held.

Birth

One of the Balinese rituals adopted by the Wektu Telu religion is a ceremony which takes place soon after birth and involves offerings to, and the burial of, the placenta. This ceremony is called *adi kaka* and is based on the belief that during the process of each birth, four siblings escape from the womb, symbolised by the blood, the fertilised egg, the placenta and the amniotic fluid that protects the foetus during pregnancy. If the afterbirth is treated with deference and respect, these four siblings will not cause harm to the newborn child or its mother. The priest then names the newborn child with a ritualistic scattering of ashes known as *buang au*. When the child is 105 days old it has its first haircut in another ceremony called the *ngurisang*.

Circumcision

The laws of Islam require that all boys be circumcised *(nyunatang)* and in Indonesia this is usually done somewhere between the ages of six and 11. Much pomp and circumstance mark this occasion on Lombok. The boys are carried through the village streets on painted wooden horses and lions with tails of palm fronds. The circumcision is performed without anaesthetic as each boy must be prepared to suffer pain for Allah, and as soon as it is over they all have to enact a ritual known as the *makka* – a kind of obeisance involving a drawn kris dagger which is held unsheathed.

Courting

There's much pageantry in Sasak courting mores. Traditionally, teenage girls and boys are kept strictly apart except on certain festival occasions – weddings, circumcision feasts and the annual celebration of the first catch of the strange *nyale* fish at Kuta. On

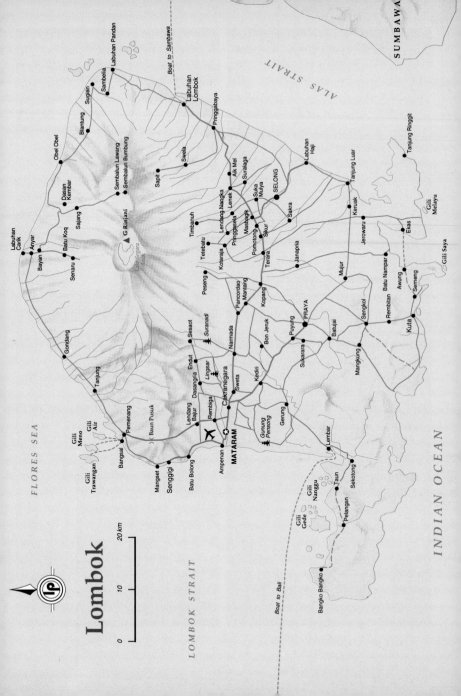

Top Left: Calf (MJ)
Top Right: Canna (JL)
Bottom Left: Hibiscus (JL)
Bottom Right: Ducks (GA)

these occasions they are allowed to mingle with each other freely. However, if at one of these occasions a girl publicly accepts a gift from a boy – food for example – she is committed to marrying him.

Harvest time is another opportunity for courting. Traditionally the harvesting of rice was women's work, and the men carried the sheaves away on shoulder-poles. Under the watchful eyes of the older men and women, a group of girls would approach the rice paddy from one side, a group of boys from the other. Each group would sing a song, each would applaud the other and do some circumspect flirting. This courtship ritual is still carried on in the more isolated, traditional villages.

Marriage Rituals

Young couples have a choice of three rituals: the first is an arranged marriage, the second a union between cousins and the third elopement. The first two are simple and uncomplicated: the parents of the prospective bridal couple meet to discuss the bride's dowry and sort out any religious differences. Having handled the business arrangements, the ceremony, *sorong serah*, is performed.

The third method is far more complicated and dramatic. Theoretically a young girl is forbidden to marry a man of lower caste, but this rule can be broken through kidnapping and eloping. As a result, eloping is still a widespread practice on Lombok, despite the fact that in most instances the parents of the couple know what's afoot. Originally it was used as a means of eluding other competitors for the girl's hand or in order to avoid family friction, but it also minimised the heavy expenses of a wedding ceremony!

The rules of this ritual are laid down and must be followed step by step. After the girl is spirited away by the boy, he is required to report to the kepala desa (head of the village) where he has taken refuge. He receives 44 lashes for such a 'disrespectful' action and has a piece of black cotton string wound around his right wrist to indicate to all that he has kidnapped his future bride. The kepala desa then notifies the girl's family through the head of their village. A delegation from the boy's family visits the girl's parents, and between them they settle on a price for the bride, which is distributed among members of the bride's family in recompense for losing her.

Traditional dowries are worked out according to caste differences; the lower his caste and the higher hers, the more he has to pay. Payment is in old Chinese coins *(bolong)* and other ceremonial items, rather than in cash. Once this has been settled the wedding begins. Generally the bride and groom, dressed in ceremonial clothes, are carried through the streets on a sedan chair on long bamboo poles. The sounds of the gamelan (known as the *barong tengkok)* mingle with the shouts and laughter of the guests as the couple are swooped up and down and around on their way to the wedding place. Throughout the whole ceremony the bride must look downcast and unhappy at the prospect of leaving her family.

Death

The Balinese inhabitants of Lombok hold cremation ceremonies identical to those on Bali. Members of the Wektu Telu religion have their own rituals. The body is washed and prepared for burial by relations in the presence of a holy man, and then wrapped in white sheets and sackcloth. The corpse is placed on a raised bamboo platform while certain sections of the Koran are read out and relations pray to Allah and call upon the spirits of their ancestors. The body is then taken to the cemetery and interred with the head facing towards Mecca. During the burial, passages of the Koran are read aloud in Sanskrit and afterwards more quotations from the Koran are recited in Arabic.

Relatives and friends of the dead place offerings on the grave – pieces of hand-carved wood if it's a man or decorative combs if it's a woman. Various offerings which include combs and cloth are also made in the village. Several ceremonies, involving readings from the Koran, are performed on the third, seventh, 40th and 100th days after the death. A special ceremony, known as *nyiu*, is carried out after 1000 days have elapsed – the grave is sprinkled with holy water and the woodcarvings or combs removed and stones put in their place.

A Muslim cemetery is typically a low hill covered with gnarled and twisted frangipani trees. Small 'headstones', about 40 cm high, stand under the trees. You'll see these cemetery mounds all over Lombok, and you might find them spooky places even if you're not superstitious.

There's also an interesting Chinese cemetery just north of Ampenan. Some of the graves are quite large and elaborately decorated. Wealthy Chinese are buried with many of the material possessions which they enjoyed during their life. Clothes, cooking equipment, radios, TV sets and even motorbikes are said to be interred with their owners in this cemetery.

Contests

The Sasaks are fascinated by physical prowess and heroic trials of strength, fought on a one-to-one level. As a result they have developed a unique contest of their own and adapted others from nearby Sumbawa. These contests are most frequently seen in July, August and September – August is the best month.

Peresehan This peculiar man-to-man combat is a great favourite all over Lombok. Usually held in the late afternoon in the open air, a huge crowd – all men apart from the occasional curious female traveller – gather together to watch two men battle it out with long rattan staves, protected only by small rectangular shields made from cow or buffalo hide. The staves are ceremoniously handed around the crowd. With great drama the gamelan starts to play and two men, dressed in exquisite finery featuring turbans or head scarves and wide sashes at the waist, feign the movements of the contest about to be fought.

Having shown everyone how it is supposed to be done, the two men look around the crowd for contestants, who are carefully chosen to match each other as closely as possible in height and strength. Anyone can be chosen; some perform several times during the afternoon, others refuse to take part at all. While it is quite permissible to refuse, it is clearly of great status to win. Those who agree to participate must quickly find scarves to wrap around their heads and waists if they aren't already wearing them (the head gear and waist sash are supposed to have magical protective powers) then they take off their shirts and shoes, roll up their trousers, pick up their staves and shields and begin laying into each other.

If either of the fighters loses his headscarf or waistband the contest is stopped immediately until he puts it back on. It goes for three rounds – often five with more experienced fighters – or until one of the two is bleeding or surrenders. The *pekembar* (umpire of the contest) can also declare the contest over if he thinks things are getting too rough. This often happens, for though the movements are very stylised, there is absolutely nothing carefully choreographed or rigged about the Peresehan. Both contestants generally finish with great welts all over them, the crowd gets wildly excited and each fighter has his own groupies cheering him on. At the end of each contest the winner is given a T-shirt or sarong, and the loser also gets some small token.

Before the event, as part of the spectacle and atmosphere, a greasy pole contest is often held. Two tall poles are erected, topped by a gaily decorated, large wooden wheel with a number of goodies dangling from it, such as cloth, bags and shorts. Amid much mirth and merriment two small boys attempt to clamber up the slippery pole and untie the loot.

Lanca This particular trial of strength originated in Sumbawa, but the Sasaks have also adopted the *lanca* and perform it on numerous occasions, particularly when the first rice seedlings are planted. Like peresehan it is a contest between two well-matched men, who use their knees to strike each other. It involves a fair amount of skill and a lot of strength.

Avoiding Offence

Most of Lombok is conservative, and immodest dress and public displays of affection between couples can cause offence. Both men and women should cover their knees, upper arms and shoulders – shorts and tank tops should not be worn away from the beach areas. Nude or topless bathing is also offensive.

Sport

Sasaks (males anyway) are keen on competitive sports. There's quite a large football (soccer) stadium near Cakranegara, and every town has a football field. Volleyball, badminton and table tennis are also popular. In the late afternoon in almost any village you will find young men enjoying an enthusiastic game of volleyball or soccer, often with an enthusiastic audience as well. Just north of Mataram is a substantial horse-racing track, where young bareback riders compete furiously.

RELIGION
Wektu Telu

This unique religion originated in the village of Bayan, in northern Lombok. Officially only a very small proportion of the population belongs to this faith, which is not one of Indonesia's 'official' religions. More and more young people turn to Islam.

The word *wektu* means 'result' in the Sasak language, while *telu* means 'three' and signifies the complex mixture of the three religions which comprise Wektu Telu: Balinese Hinduism, Islam and animism. Members of the Wektu Telu religion regard themselves as Muslims, although they are not officially accepted by the Muslims as such.

The fundamental tenet of Wektu Telu is that all important aspects of life are underpinned by a trinity. One example of this principle is the trinity of Allah, Mohammed and Adam. Allah symbolises the one true God, Mohammed is the link between God and human beings and Adam represents a

being in search of a soul. The sun, the moon and the stars are believed to represent heaven, earth and water. The head, body and limbs represent creativity, sensitivity and control.

On a communal basis the Wektu Telu hold that there are three main duties which they must fulfil: belief in Allah, avoiding the temptations of the devil and cooperating with, helping and loving other people. The faithful must also pray to Allah every Friday, meditate and undertake to carry out good deeds.

The Wektu Telu do not observe Ramadan, the month-long period of abstinence so important in the Islamic faith. Their concession to it is a mere three days of fasting and prayer. They also do not follow the pattern of praying five times a day in a holy place, one of the basic laws of Islam. While prayer and meditation are of supreme importance in their daily rituals, the Wektu Telu believe in praying from the heart when and where they feel the need, not at appointed times in places specifically built for worship. According to them, all public buildings serve this purpose and all are designed with a prayer corner or a small room which faces Mecca. Wektu Telu do not make a pilgrimage to Mecca, but their dead are buried with their heads facing in that direction.

As for not eating pork, the Wektu Telu consider everything which comes from Allah to be good.

Castes Unlike the Muslims, the Wektu Telu have a caste system. There are four castes, the highest being Datoe, the second Raden, the third Buling and the fourth Jajar Karang.

Islam

The great majority of Lombok's population are Muslims. Islam reached Indonesia in the 13th century through peaceful Gujarati merchants arriving on the eastern coast of Lombok via Sulawesi (the Celebes), and on the west coast via Java. Today it is the professed religion of 90% of the Indonesian people and its traditions and rituals affect all aspects of their daily life. Friday afternoon is the officially decreed time for believers to worship and all government offices and many businesses are closed as a result. Arabic is taught in all Indonesian schools so the Koran can continue to be read and studied by successive generations. Scrupulous attention is given to cleanliness, including ritualistic washing of hands and face. The pig is considered to be unclean and is not kept or eaten in strict Muslim regions. Indonesian Muslims may have more than one wife though this is not common on Lombok, partly because few men can afford to keep a second wife. Those who make the pilgrimage to Mecca are known as *haji* if they are men, *haja* if they're women, and are deeply respected.

Islam not only influences routine daily living and personal politics but also affects the politics of government. Orthodox Muslims demand that the government protects and encourages Islam. Power brokers around Suharto view the idea of a strong Islamic bloc in the People's Representative Council, the country's most influential policy-making body, as a security risk and a situation to be avoided at all costs.

The founder of Islam, Mohammed, was born in 571 AD and began his teachings in 612. He forged together an early Hebraic kind of monotheism and a latent Arab nationalism, and by 622 was beginning to gain adherents. Mohammed did not demonstrate supernatural powers, but he did claim he was God's only teacher and prophet, charged with the divine mission of interpreting the word of God. Mohammed's teachings are collated and collected in the scripture of Islam, the Koran, which was compiled from his oral and written records shortly after his death. It is divided into 14 chapters and every word in it is said to have emanated from Mohammed and been inspired by God himself, in the will of Allah.

The fundamental tenet of Islam is 'there is no god but Allah and Mohammed is his prophet'. The word 'Islam' means submission, and the faith demands unconditional surrender to the wisdom of Allah, not just adherence to a set of beliefs and rules. It involves total commitment to a way of life, philosophy and law. Aspects of Islam have been touched by animist, Hindu and Buddhist precepts, influencing both peripheral details like mosque architecture and fundamental beliefs like the attitudes to women.

Muslim women in Indonesia are allowed more freedom and shown more respect than women in some other Islamic countries. They do not have to wear veils, nor are they segregated or considered to be second-class citizens. There are a number of matrilineal and matriarchal societies and sometimes special mosques are built for women. Muslim men in Indonesia are only allowed to marry two women and must have the consent of their first wife to do so. Throughout Indonesia it is the women who initiate divorce proceedings where necessary, under the terms of their marriage agreement.

LANGUAGE

Most people on Lombok are bilingual, speaking their own ethnic language, Sasak, as well as the national language, Bahasa Indonesia, which they are taught at school and use as their formal and official mode of communication.

Apart from those working in the tourist industry, few people on Lombok speak English, and this includes police and other officials. Nevertheless, English is becoming more widely spoken on Lombok. Travellers without a grasp of Bahasa Indonesia can get by, but some knowledge of it enhances an understanding of the island and could also be invaluable in an emergency. Outside the main centres, finding anyone who can say more than a few phrases of English is extremely rare. If you can't speak Indonesian, arm yourself with a phrasebook and dictionary.

Sasak

Sasak is not derived from Malay, so don't expect to be able to understand Sasak if you can speak Bahasa Indonesia. Nevertheless, some words are similar, and Sasak speakers use Indonesian words when there are no Sasak equivalents. Sasak only expresses what is important in traditional contexts, but in these it can be precise and subtle. For example, where English has one word for rice, Indonesian has three – *padi* for the growing rice plant, *beras* for uncooked grain, and *nasi* for cooked rice. Sasak has equivalents for those *(pare, menik* and *me)*, and it also has *gabah*, for rice grains with their husks ready for planting, *binek* for a rice seedling up to three days old, *ampar* for small rice plants up to 20 days old, and *lowong* for rice plants which are ready to be transplanted from the seed beds into the flooded paddy field.

Sasak would be a difficult language to learn – it is not a written language so its usages are not well documented, and there are substantial variations from one part of Lombok to another. There is no English-Sasak dictionary. Learning Bahasa Indonesia would be a much more practical option for a visitor to Lombok, but some of the following expressions may be useful. Pronounce the words as if they were written in Bahasa Indonesia. (Thanks to Hadji Radiah of Lendang Nangka for help in preparing this section.)

Greetings & Civilities Sasak does not have greetings such as 'Good morning'. A Sasak approaching a friend might ask, in the local language, 'What are you doing?' or 'Where are you going?' simply as a form of greeting. Local people will frequently ask foreigners questions like this in English (it may be their only English!) as a greeting. Don't get annoyed – they are just trying to be polite. A smile and a 'hello', or a greeting in Indonesian, is a polite and adequate response.

Useful Words

good	*solah*
big	*belek*
small	*kodek*
cold	*enyet*
hot	*beneng*
north	*daya*
south	*lauk*
east	*timuk*
west	*bat*
day	*jelo*
Monday	*senen*
Tuesday	*selasa*
Wednesday	*rebo*
Thursday	*kmis*
Friday	*jumat*
Saturday	*saptu*
Sunday	*ahat*

Useful Phrases

Where are you going?
Wah me aning be?
I am going to Sweta.
Sweta wah mo ojak ombe.
How are you?
Berem be khabar?
Where is the way to Sweta?
Embe langan te ojok Sweta?
How far is it from here to Sweta?
Berembe kejab ne olek te ojok Sweta?
Where is Radiah's place?
Embe tao' balem Radiah?
I want to go to the toilet.
Tiang melet ojok aik.
Leave me alone!
Endotang aku mesak.
Endotang aku mesak mesak! (stronger)
Go away!
Nyeri to! (say it forcefully, emphasising the 'to')

People & Families

person	*dengan*
woman	*dengan mine*
man	*dengan mama*
baby	*bebeak*
child	*kanak*
boy	*kanak mama*
girl	*kanak mine*
young unmarried woman	*dedera*
widow	*bebalu mine*
widower	*bebalu mama*
father	*amak*
mother	*inak*
wife	*senine*
husband	*semama*

Numbers

1	*skek*	20	*dua pulu*
2	*dua*	30	*telung dasa*
3	*telu*	40	*petang dasa*
4	*empat*	50	*seket*
5	*lima*	60	*enam pulu*
6	*enam*	70	*pituk pulu*
7	*pituk*	100	*satus*
8	*baluk*	200	*satak*
9	*siwak*	300	*telungatus*
10	*sepulu*	400	*samas*
11	*solas*	500	*limangatus*
12	*dua olas*	700	*pitungatus*
13	*telu olas*	800	*bali ratus*
14	*empat olas*	900	*siwak ratus*
		1000	*sia*

Facts for the Visitor

Most of the information in the chapter on Facts for the Visitor to Bali is also relevant for Lombok. This chapter includes additional information which is specific to Lombok.

VISAS

Visa requirements are the same as for Bali. There is an immigration office (kantor imigrasi) in Mataram but no consulates at all.

DOCUMENTS

An International Driving Permit is necessary if you want to hire a car or motorbike. You can't get a local licence for motorbikes.

MONEY

US dollars are the most readily exchanged, though other currencies are negotiable in the banks. Exchange rates on Lombok are a couple of points lower than on Bali. Travellers' cheques can be changed in the main towns and tourist areas, but US$ cash is more negotiable in remote areas. In Mataram there are a number of big banks and a few moneychangers. You can also change travellers' cheques at Senggigi, Kuta, the Gili Islands, and at the bank in Praya, but don't go further afield without making sure you have enough currency. When you get money changed, make sure you are given plenty of smaller denomination notes. In the villages it's often very difficult to get change for big notes.

You can have money transferred to the Bank Ekspor-Impor in Cakranegara.

Costs

Costs are similar to those on Bali for equivalent standards of food and accommodation, but there are not as many mid-range places in which to stay or eat, not as many people hassling you to buy things and generally not as many temptations, so you'll probably spend less on Lombok. Entry charges, a few places like Narmada apart, are not so common on Lombok, but you will often be requested for a donation on some pretext, and it's good manners to make one.

Begging is virtually unknown on Lombok, but if children think you're going to give something away, you'll see nothing but outstretched palms.

Some shops on Lombok have fixed prices, but usually you are expected to bargain, particularly for items like antiques, cloth or basketware. If you bargain hard you may end up paying half to two-thirds of the starting price, but sometimes you may only be able to get a nominal amount knocked off the starting figure.

Restaurant prices on Lombok are invariably fixed. Hotels are not likely to drop their prices as the competition is not as fierce as on Bali, and the asking price is rarely inflated.

WHEN TO GO

The dry season is better for trekking and travel to remote areas, particularly from June to October. The wet season is a little hotter and considerably more humid, but quite OK for travelling; in some ways it's more pleasant than dry dusty conditions, and the landscape is greener and more attractive.

The Muslim fast of Ramadan applies to Lombok and it's not the best time to visit, particularly if you want to travel to traditional rural areas (see Holidays & Festivals, below).

TOURIST OFFICE

The West Nusa Tenggara regional tourist office is at Jalan Langko 70, Ampenan (☎ 21866, 31730). It has a couple of coloured brochures with useful information, and quite a good map. The staff are great – very friendly and informative.

BUSINESS HOURS

Government offices open from 7 am to 2 pm Monday to Thursday, closing at 11 am Friday and 12.30 pm Saturday. Post offices open at 8 am and close at 11 am Friday and 1 pm Saturday. Most businesses open from 8 am to 4 pm Monday to Friday, 8 am to noon on Saturday, often closing for an hour or so at lunch time.

HOLIDAYS & FESTIVALS

All three Lombok religions have their own holidays and festivals. Other national holidays are also observed – New Years Day, Good Friday, Ascension, Independence Day (August 17) and Christmas Day.

Most of Lombok's own festivals take place at the beginning of the rainy season around October to December, or at harvest time around April to May. During these periods there are celebrations in villages all over the island, and people dress in their most resplendent clothes and flaunt status symbols such as sunglasses and watches. Wooden effigies of horses and lions are carried in processions through the streets and the sound of the gamelan reaches fever pitch. While most of these ceremonies and rituals are annual events, most of them do not fall on specific days in the Western calendar.

The Muslim year is shorter than the Western one so their festivals and events fall at a different time each year (see the table below).

Ramadan

Ramadan is the ninth month of the Muslim calendar, the month of fasting or *puasa*. During Ramadan people rise early for a big breakfast, then abstain from eating, drinking and smoking until sunset. Many visit family graves and royal cemeteries, recite extracts from the Koran, sprinkle the graves with holy water and strew them with flowers. Special prayers are said at mosques and at home. During this time many restaurants are closed, and foreigners eating or smoking in public are regarded with contempt that can border on aggression. During Ramadan, Muslims may be preoccupied with the fast or their religious obligations. The end of Ramadan is a major celebration and holiday, so transport and accommodation is crowded, but it's an interesting time to be on Lombok. Don't plan on travelling anywhere – stay put, preferably in a Balinese-run hotel, but don't miss the celebrations on the streets.

Other Religious Festivals

Other occasions observed on Lombok include:

Puasa – this Wektu Telu festival is held in deference to the Muslim period of abstinence. The three days of fasting and prayer begin at the same time as Ramadan.

Idul Fitri – also called Hari Raya, this is the first day of the 10th month of the Muslim calendar and the end of Ramadan. This climax to a month of austerity and tension is characterised by wild beating of drums all night, fireworks and no sleep. At 7 am everyone turns out for an open-air service. Women dress in white and mass prayers are held followed by two days of feasting. Extracts from the Koran are read and religious processions take place. Gifts are exchanged and pardon is asked for past wrongdoings. Everyone dresses in their finest and newest clothes and neighbours and relatives are visited with gifts of specially prepared food. It is traditional to return to one's home village, so many Indonesians travel at this time. At each house visited, tea and sweet cakes are served and visiting continues until all the relatives have been seen.

Hari Raya Ketupat – this is a Wektu Telu celebration held at Batulayar, near Senggigi, seven days after the end of Ramadan.

Idul Adha – this day of sacrifice is held on the 10th day of the 11th month of the Muslim calendar. People visit the mosque and recite passages from the Koran.

Maulid Nabi Mohammed – also called Hari Nata, Mohammed's birthday is held on the 12th day of the 12th month of the Arabic calendar.

Festival	1994	1995	1996	1997
Ramadan Begins	12 February	1 February	22 January	10 January
Idul Fitri	15 March	4 March	22 February	10 February
Maulid Nabi	19 August	9 August	28 July	18 July

Mi'raj Nabi Mohammed – this festival celebrates the ascension of Mohammed.

Pujawali – this is a Bali Hindu celebration held every year at the Kalasa Temple at Narmada in honour of the god Batara, who dwells on Lombok's most sacred mountain, Gunung Rinjani. At the same time the faithful who have made the trek up the mountain and down to Lake Segara Anak hold a ceremony called *pekelan*, where they throw gold trinkets and objects into the lake.

Perang Ketupat – this annual rain festival is held at Lingsar, between October and December. Adherents of the Wektu Telu religion and Balinese Hindus give offerings and pray at the temple complex, then come out and pelt each other with *ketupat*, sticky rice wrapped in banana leaves (see the Lingsar section in the West Lombok chapter).

Harvest Ceremony – held at Gunung Pengsong some time around March or April as a thanksgiving for a good harvest, this Bali Hindu ceremony involves a buffalo being dragged up a steep hill and then sacrificed.

Pura Meru – a special Bali Hindu ceremony held every June at full moon in the Balinese temple in Cakranegara.

Bersih Desa – this festival occurs at harvest time. Houses and gardens are cleaned, fences whitewashed, roads and paths repaired. Once part of a ritual to rid villages of evil spirits, it is now held in honour of Dewi Sri, the rice goddess.

POST & TELECOMMUNICATIONS

The main post office in Mataram is the only one that will keep poste restante mail. There are other post offices on Lombok, but poste restante mail is always redirected to Mataram.

Telephone services have improved greatly on Lombok. You can make international calls from private or Telkom wartels in most larger towns. They are routed through Jakarta and it's sometimes difficult to get through. Costs are the same as from Bali. All of Lombok is in the 0364 phone district.

TIME

Lombok is in the same time zone as Bali, eight hours ahead of GMT.

ELECTRICITY

In most towns the electricity supply is 220 volts, but some smaller places still have 110 volts. In less developed parts of Lombok, electricity supply may be erratic or nonexistent. Small generators are sometimes used too. Outside the main towns and Senggigi you should check before you plug in.

BOOKS & MAPS

Western publications written about Lombok are a rarity compared with the many works available which focus on Bali. Most of the information about Lombok can be found in more general works about Nusa Tenggara or Indonesia.

Lombok: Conquest, Colonisation & Underdevelopment, 1870-1940 by Alfons van der Kraan (Heinemann, 1980) is a history of the colonial period. *East of Bali* (Periplus Editions) is a travel guide to Nusa Tenggara with some good background material on Lombok, and nice colour photos.

A few interesting maps are available. One published by Periplus has the best map of Mataram and shows the topography well, but the roads aren't always accurate. *Indonesia III*, a map of Lombok published by Travel Treasure Maps (Knaus Publications, distributed in Indonesia by Periplus), is not super detailed, but has interesting notes, and useful maps of the main tourist areas on the back.

There are a couple of bookshops on Jalan Pabean in Ampenan and others in Cakranegara but it's hard to pick up new books in English. Senggigi has a fair selection at the supermarket, and also a second-hand bookshop. A few of the popular losmen have selections of second-hand paperbacks.

FILM & PHOTOGRAPHY

On Lombok colour print film is readily available at numerous outlets in Ampenan, Mataram and Cakranegara, including general stores and chemists (drugstores) as well as specialist film and camera shops. There is some colour transparency film around, but it's not easy to find. The price of film on Lombok is similar to Bali, but Lombok does not have as many facilities for developing and printing.

Most people on Lombok are happy to have their photo taken, but ask anyway. If they're reluctant, it may be because they don't think they look their best. If someone's dressed up for a ceremony, they may be disappointed if you don't offer to photograph them.

HEALTH

Most of the health considerations are the same as for Bali, except that malaria is a real risk on Lombok, despite some recent success in controlling mosquito numbers. The risk is greatest in the wet months and in remote areas. It is the serious *P. falciparum* strain and may be Chloroquine resistant (see below). Malaria is spread by mosquito bites, and symptoms include headaches, fever, chills and sweating which may subside and recur. Without treatment malaria can develop more serious, potentially fatal, effects.

Start a course of antimalarials before you get to Lombok (a week or two weeks before is usual). Your doctor will probably have a personal recommendation for one form or another. Antimalarial drugs do not actually prevent the disease but suppress its symptoms. Chloroquine is the usual malarial prophylactic; Mefloquine and Doxycycline are becoming more common, Maloprim and Fansidar are now less frequently prescribed. There have been some failures of Chloroquine and Maloprim on Lombok; your doctor should confirm that multi-drug resistant strains of malaria, which are spreading in eastern Nusa Tenggara, have not appeared on Lombok. Side effects are another consideration which your doctor should explain.

Regardless of the drugs, your first and best defence against malaria is to prevent mosquito bites. Use a good repellent with DEET. Cover up at dusk. Burn mosquito coils. A mosquito net is effective if there are no gaps, you're not actually touching it, and there are no mosquitoes inside it with you.

Medical Treatment

The general hospital (☎ 21354) in Mataram is the biggest. Let them know you can pay cash for a private doctor and any drugs you need. The Catholic hospital in Ampenan might be better for visitors. For anything really serious, get to Denpasar, or even Singapore or Darwin. You do have travel insurance don't you?

WOMEN TRAVELLERS

On Lombok, people are pretty reserved, and women are generally treated with respect. The sort of harassment which Western women often experience in Muslim countries is very unusual, though not totally unheard of, on Lombok. Boys sometimes try to touch foreign women on the breasts or bum, probably as much from curiosity as lust. Western films and TV, as well as the 'promiscuous' behaviour of many visitors (eg kissing in public) has created fanciful ideas about Western sexual mores. Respectful dressing is a good idea – beachwear should be reserved for the beach, and basically the less skin you expose the better. Attitude can be as important as what you wear.

DANGERS & ANNOYANCES

There are few reports of theft or pickpockets. The traffic is much lighter on Lombok than on Bali, but there is still a danger of traffic accidents. Trekkers sometimes hurt themselves, and there have been some deaths from falls on Gunung Rinjani, or drowning in the crater lake.

Generally you are less likely to be hassled by people selling things than you are on Bali, and more likely to be annoyed by curious locals, especially youngsters in less touristed areas.

TAKING THE CHILDREN

Lombok is generally quieter than Bali, and much less dangerous. People are fond of kids, though perhaps more reserved about it than the Balinese. The main reservation about bringing kids here is the risk of malaria. Discuss malaria prevention with your doctor. Weekly tablets are probably easier for kids than daily ones. You can also get antimalarials for children in syrup form. Protection against mosquitoes is the most important preventive measure, for malaria and other illnesses.

ACTIVITIES

Trekking

A climb up Gunung Rinjani (3726 metres) is the big challenge for trekkers. This involves at least two nights camping out, but the necessary equipment can be hired in Batu Koq, where most people start walking. There are several routes up, and a world of possibilities for those who want to spend some days hiking in a relatively remote area.

If you just want to explore the countryside on foot, visiting a number of villages, the area of central Lombok, between the main east-west road and the southern slopes of Rinjani, is recommended.

Surfing

The southern and eastern coasts of Lombok get the same swells that generate the big breaks on Bali's Bukit Peninsula. The main problem is getting to them. Lombok's Kuta Beach is the most accessible beach by road. There are places to stay and eat there, and boat owners will take you out to the reef breaks. Other south-coast places which you can get to by land, with a little difficulty, include Selong Blanak, Mawun and Ekas – there are lots of reef breaks accessible by boat from these areas. Desert Point, near Bangko Bangko, on the south-western peninsula, is Lombok's most famous break. It's a classic wave, and you can reach it by land, but there are virtually no visitor facilities. The easiest way to reach it is with a surf tour on a chartered yacht, usually from Bali, though boats can be chartered from Lembar. Desert Point does not work regularly and needs a good size swell.

Diving & Snorkelling

There is quite good snorkelling off the Gili Islands, and some possibilities for scuba diving. A few dive operations are located on these islands and on the Senggigi tourist strip, some more reliable than others. New diving areas are still being explored on Lombok, such as Gili Petangan off the east coast, but you'll need the help of a good operator and guide.

Diving operations on Lombok include:

Albatross Diving
At Mataram (☎ 22127), Senggigi Beach and Paradise Bungalows on Gili Trawangan, this is one of the longest established operators, conducting dive trips for certified divers.

Baruna Water Sports
This big Bali-based operation has an office at the Senggigi Beach Hotel (☎ 23430).

Blue Marlin Dive Centre
Gili Air (☎ 36341), with information counters on Gili Trawangan, Gili Meno, Senggigi (at NZ Tours, ☎ 93033) and Jalan Koperasi 81 Ampenan. This is the only Lombok-based operation which has PADI-qualified instructors offering a full open-water course, and guides with good local knowledge. See the Gili Islands chapter for details.

ACCOMMODATION

There are a few big 'international' hotels in the Senggigi Beach area, and a good selection of budget to mid-range accommodation in Ampenan, Mataram and Cakranegara. There is some basic accommodation in the Senggigi area, lots of cheap bungalows on the Gili Islands and more at Lombok's Kuta Beach. The villages around Tetebatu also have some simple places to stay.

Typically, a Lombok beach bungalow is a hut on stilts, with a small verandah out the front. Almost all of them are at the bottom of the price range, about 10,000/15,000 rp for singles/doubles, including a light breakfast. The growth of budget accommodation may be limited by restrictions aimed at preserving the best beach areas for more upmarket developments. Some places are depressing and dirty while others are attractive and bright.

Outside the areas mentioned above, accommodation can be scarce, but you can make day trips to most other parts of the island quite easily. If you are stuck in a remote area, you can usually stay with the kepala desa (headman of a village), as on Bali.

FOOD

There are fewer tourist restaurants on Lombok, which means you'll be eating Indonesian or Chinese dishes in most places, though simple Sasak food and Padang food is also available. In Bahasa Indonesia the word *lombok* means chilli pepper and they're used liberally in the local cooking. Unless you like having your mouth on fire beware of adding even more.

By and large the Chinese restaurants on Lombok are cleaner and have more variety and tastier food than the Indonesian rumah makan. As with Bali there is no question that you will eat well and cheaply.

Sasak food uses white rice as a staple, served with vegetables and hot chilli. A little chicken is used, some fish, very little meat and no pork. Some specialities include:

ares – a dish made from the pith of a banana tree stem, with coconut juice, garlic and bumbu, sometimes mixed with chicken or meat

ayam Taliwang – this dish of fried or grilled chicken with chilli sauce is originally from Taliwang on Sumbawa, but it has almost become a Lombok speciality

bumbu – a hot spice

kangkung – water convolvulus, the leaves are used as a green vegetable like spinach; you can see it growing in the river at Ampenan

pelecing – a sauce made with chilli, fish paste *(trassi)*, tomato, salt and bumbu

pelecing manuk – fried chicken with pelecing

sate pusut – a snack with a sausage-shaped mixture of grated coconut, meat, bumbu and brown sugar wrapped onto a sate stick; try it at the market

serebuk – a dish of grated coconut, sliced vegetable and kangkung

timun urap – sliced cucumber with grated coconut, onion and garlic

DRINKS

Bottled water is widely available. Tea (teh) is commonly served with meals. Alcohol is not common on Lombok, because the population is predominantly Muslim, but beer and even spirits are available at bars and restaurants in Senggigi and the Gili Islands. Brem, (rice wine) and tuak (palm beer) are made locally, but are not conspicuous. In the isolated villages, or stricter Muslim towns like Labuhan Lombok, forget it.

For a mild intoxicant, some people chew betel nut. It's mainly used by older men in the more isolated villages, but is becoming less common.

ENTERTAINMENT

The local population is not big on nightlife – cinemas (bioskop) in the larger towns are about as exciting as it gets. The tourist office should be able to tell you where to find a performance of traditional dancing at which you will be welcome, though dances are not usually performed for tourists.

There is some action at Senggigi, with local bands doing good rock and reggae-style dance music. When hundreds of young Europeans descend on Gili Trawangan there's lots of dancing, drinking and late-night loitering in the beachside bars and restaurants.

THINGS TO BUY

Handcrafts on Lombok are traditional, practical articles like boxes, basketware and pottery, hand-made from natural materials like palm leaf, bamboo, grass fibres and rattan. Hand-woven sarongs and fabrics are especially interesting and attractive. For more details, see the Arts & Crafts section. Villages often specialise in certain crafts, though tourist shops stock items from all over Lombok, as well as from other parts of Indonesia.

Nearly every village on Lombok has a market at least once a week where there are numerous stalls selling food, clothes, handcrafts and many other items. The biggest market with the best variety is at Sweta. Supermarkets in Cakranegara and Senggigi have the best range of Western-type goods.

Getting There & Away

There is no international airport on Lombok, but it's quite accessible by air and sea from the neighbouring islands. The vast majority of travellers arrive from Bali, less than 100 km away, while those island-hopping from the east will reach Lombok from Sumbawa. It's also possible to fly direct to Lombok from Java or Sulawesi.

AIR

Lombok's Selaparang Airport is at Rembiga, just north of Mataram. Note that all air tickets purchased in Indonesia are subject to a 10% tax, in addition to the fares quoted below. The airport tax is included in the ticket price. The airlines serving Lombok are Garuda-Merpati (☎ 23235) and Sempati (☎ 21226, 24844/5). A number of agents in Mataram and Senggigi can sell tickets and reconfirm flights. It's important to reconfirm, as the flights are on quite small planes and it's easy to get bumped. See the Air Travel Glossary in the Bali Getting There & Away chapter for more details.

To/From Bali

Merpati has eight flights per day in each direction between Denpasar and Mataram, at 47,500 rp. Sempati has two flights a day each way, at the same price. It's a very short flight, about 25 minutes, with fine views of Nusa Penida, the south-eastern coast of Bali and the Gili Islands. Though the ferry is much cheaper, many low-budget travellers still fly to save the long ferry trip and the time and expense of getting to and from the ports of Padangbai (Bali) and Lembar (Lombok).

To/From Sumbawa

There is one Merpati flight a day between Mataram and Sumbawa Besar (54,500 rp), continuing to Bima (90,500 rp).

To/From Java

There are several flights per day between Mataram and Surabaya (118,000 rp), Yogyakarta (135,500 rp), Semarang, and Jakarta (228,000 rp).

To/From Sulawesi

There is one Sempati flight per day to Ujung Pandang (158,000 rp), and several if you go via Denpasar.

SEA

To/From Bali

Ferry There are ferries every two hours between Padangbai (Bali) and Lembar (Lombok). Scheduled departure times from both ports are 6, 8 and 10 am, noon, 2, 4, 6, 8 and 10 pm. Sometimes they leave later, or even earlier, than the scheduled times. *Ekonomi* costs around 4800 rp (2500 rp for children), 1st class is 8700 rp (4700 rp for children). You can take a bicycle (800 rp), motorbike (5300 rp) or car (price depends on size – over 50,000 rp for a Suzuki Jimny).

For 1st-class passengers there's an air-conditioned cabin with aircraft-type seats, a snack bar and video entertainment. Ekonomi passengers sit on bench seats or wherever they can find a spot. Food and drinks are available on board or from the numerous hawkers who hang around the wharf until the ferry leaves. The trip takes at least four hours, sometimes up to seven.

Mabua Express The luxury jet-powered *Mabua Express* provides a fast boat service between Lembar Harbour on Lombok and Benoa Port on Bali. The *Mabua Express* leaves Benoa Port at 8.30 am and 2.30 pm, and leaves Lembar at 11.30 am and 5 pm. The trip takes about two hours. It costs US$17.50 for 'Emerald Class' and US$25 for 'Diamond Class'; the latter includes transfer from the port of arrival, and drinks and a snack on the boat. It's not much cheaper than the airfare, but it's a fun trip and it may be more reliable than Merpati's service.

If you book your ticket through an agent

such as Perama, they should be able to arrange transfers to and from the ports, but otherwise you do it yourself. Children between two and 12 are charged half price, but may be subjected to two hours of violent video entertainment. For the latest details, telephone Mabua's office on Bali (☎ 0361 72370, 72521) or Lombok (☎ 0364 25895, 37224).

Other Fast Boat Services A small, fast boat service used to run between Padangbai and Bangsal (the place on Lombok where you get boats to the Gili Islands), Senggigi or Lembar. It charged 20,000 rp and supposedly took two hours, but sometimes it took much longer and wasn't very reliable. The service was suspended in late 1993, but it may resume. Enquire in Padangbai (☎ 0361 234428), Senggigi (☎ 0364 93045 ext 339) or Mataram (☎ 0364 27295).

Tourist Shuttle The main advantage in taking one of the shuttle bus services is that it saves the hassle of the bemo connections to the ports at each end. Perama has services running to/from Lembar, Mataram, Senggigi, the Gili Islands, Labuhan Lombok, and Kuta Beach on Lombok, and various tourist centres on Bali, and also connections to Java and Sumbawa. Other companies have similar services at similar prices. For example, a ticket from Ubud to Gili Meno costs 27,500 rp, including the ferry to Lombok and a boat to the island, with all the connections in between. On public transport you could probably do this trip for about 10,000 rp (if you weren't overcharged) but it would involve five bemo connections, a pony cart, the ferry and a boat. It would probably take longer and, if you missed a connection, you might have to spend a night somewhere in between.

To/From Sumbawa

Ferry Passenger ferries leave Labuhan Lombok (in eastern Lombok) for Poto Tano

(Sumbawa) about every hour from 7 am to 6 pm, but the exact times vary in practice. In the other direction they're scheduled to depart at half past the hour. The trip takes about 1½ hours and costs 3100 rp in Ekonomi A (1600 rp for a child), 2000 rp in Ekonomi B (1300 rp for a child), 2500 rp for a bicycle, 3200 rp for a motorbike and 32,000 rp for a small car.

Bus Direct buses run from Sweta terminal on Lombok to destinations on Sumbawa, including Sumbawa Besar (five buses per day, 9000 rp, 10,000 rp with air-con), Dompu (at 6 am and 4 pm, 15,000 rp, 21,000 rp with air-con), and Bima (8 am and 2 pm, 18,000 rp, 22,000 rp with air-con). Fares include the ferry.

Tourist Shuttle Perama has bus-ferry-bus connections between Lombok and Sumbawa Besar, Dompu and Bima on Sumbawa, which are a little more expensive than the direct buses.

To/From Other Islands

The national shipping line, Pelni, has passenger ships doing regular loops through the islands of Indonesia, with the *Kelimutu* typically calling at Lembar once a fortnight, usually on a Wednesday or Thursday. The usual stops before and after Lembar are Bima (Sumbawa) and Surabaya (Java), but the *Kelimutu* continues to other ports. The exact dates and routes can change, so enquire well in advance. The Pelni office on Lombok is at Jalan Industri 1 in Ampenan (☎ 21604).

TOURS

A number of agents on Bali offer tours of Lombok, which may be worthwhile if your time is limited. They tend to be expensive, with air transport there and back and accommodation in upmarket hotels. A tour of three days and two nights would be around US$150.

Getting Around

Lombok has an extensive network of roads, although there are many outlying villages that are difficult to get to by public transport. There is a good main road across the middle of the island between Mataram and Labuhan Lombok, and quite good roads to the south of this route. The road round the north coast is rough but usable, while roads to the extreme south-west and south-east are very rough or nonexistent.

Public buses and bemos are generally restricted to main routes. Away from these, you have to hire a pony cart, get a lift on a motorbike, or walk. In the north-east and the south there is usually some public transport between the bigger towns, but it might mean waiting a long time and riding in the back of a truck. Most public transport stops before 10 pm, often earlier in more isolated areas. If you find yourself out in the sticks without your own wheels you can try to charter a bemo or just make yourself as comfortable as you can until sunrise.

You can get around the whole island and to most of the remote locations if you have your own transport. A motorbike is the cheapest and most versatile option. A rented car with good ground clearance will get you to most places where there's a road. A bicycle, especially a mountain bike, would be ideal as you could put it on boats for coastal hops or to visit small islands. If you are exploring remote regions, remember that food and drinking water are often scarce so it's a good idea to carry your own.

During the wet season many unsealed roads are flooded or washed away, and others are impassable because of fallen rocks and rubble, making it impossible to get to many out-of-the-way places. The damage may not be repaired until the dry season.

Lombok has the usual Indonesian methods of transport: bemos, buses, minibuses, pony carts, outrigger canoes (prahus) or small boats for short sea voyages. A few taxis are available, and charge either by the hour, or a fixed sum for a particular distance such as from the airport to Senggigi. They're not common and they don't have meters.

Warning

Like many Indonesians, people on Lombok don't travel well, and often suffer from travel sickness on buses and boats. This might be a problem for you as well as them!

BEMO & BUS

The cheapest and most common way of getting around is by bemo or minibus (both of these terms, or sometimes 'colt', are used) for shorter distances, or bus for longer stretches. On rough roads in remote areas trucks may be used as public transport vehicles. There are several bus/bemo terminals on Lombok. The main one is at Sweta, a couple of km out of Cakranegara. Other terminals are at Praya, Kopang and Selong, and you may have to go via one or more of these transport hubs to get from one part of Lombok to another.

Public transport fares are fixed by the provincial government and at Sweta there is a prominently displayed list of fares to most places on the island. This does not stop the bus and bemo boys from trying to overcharge, so check the notice board before setting off. Children on a parent's knee are free, and up to the age of 11 they cost around half price. You may have to pay more if you have a big bag.

As with all public transport in Indonesia, drivers wait until their vehicles are filled to capacity before they contemplate moving. The maximum permitted number of passengers is usually written somewhere in or on the vehicle. The limit is enforced, but still permits pretty cramped conditions, especially if there is all sorts of other stuff being carried. More often than not you won't be able to see the countryside. However, people are very friendly, many offer to share their food with you, and most ask where you come from *(Dari mana?)* and generally want to find out all they can.

Chartering a Bemo

Many trips involve several changes and a lot of waiting around. If you're pressed for time, and you can get a few people together, hiring a bemo (or a taxi) by the day, or even from one village to the next, can be cheap and convenient. One limitation is that drivers may be reluctant to venture off sealed roads. They don't want to damage their vehicles and, if the truth be known, some of them are not very skilled drivers.

Some bemos are restricted to certain routes or areas, for example the yellow ones which shuttle around the main town cannot be chartered for a trip to Lembar. The white minibus bemos can go anywhere, and can be chartered for 50,000 to 60,000 rp per day (8 am to 5 pm), including petrol and an English-speaking driver. Work out where you want to go and be prepared for some hard bargaining. If you detour to somewhere else on the way, be prepared to pay extra.

You can probably arrange to charter a bemo through your losmen or hotel, through the tourist office in Ampenan or the transport co-operative (Koprasi) in Senggigi. Alternatively you can simply go to a bemo stop and ask the drivers. Check that the vehicle is roadworthy. A straightforward trip can quickly turn into a nightmare when you find yourself out after dark, in the rain, with a wiperless and lightless bemo!

DRIVING
Motorbike Rental

There's a place in Mataram (see the West Lombok chapter) where the renters of motorbikes congregate, and also a few losmen which rent them. The bikes and the rental charges are very similar to Bali – for a 100 cc Honda Astrea with automatic clutch, it's about 12,000 rp for one day, 9000 rp per day for a longer period. Yamaha trail bikes (110 cc) are also available for slightly more. The owners want to see an International Driving Permit (one for cars only is OK by them, if

not strictly legal) and sometimes want you to leave a passport for security (they give you a receipt for it, but change plenty of cash first because it may be difficult to get cash later without a passport). Check the condition of the motorbike. Some are not well maintained, and you can quickly get into areas where there's no spare parts or mechanical help.

In remote areas a motorbike can get by on tiny, rough roads which would be difficult or impassable by car. Once you get out of the main centres there's not much traffic on the roads, apart from people, dogs and water buffaloes, but you do have to contend with numerous potholes and people at work upgrading the roads. This can be particularly hazardous at night when you round a corner and come slap up against a grader, rocks piled into the middle of the road and 44-gallon drums of tar. Warning signs are rarely, if ever, put up when roadworks are in progress. Up in the mountains there are unprotected drops down sheer cliff faces.

There are petrol stations around the larger towns; out in the villages, petrol is often available from plastic containers at small wayside shops – look out for signs that read *premium*, or *press ban* (literally 'tyre repair'). If you intend going to out-of-the-way places it may be advisable to take some with you, if you can carry it safely. Petrol is 700 rp a litre at petrol stations; 750 rp from roadside vendors. Tyre repair should cost 500 rp for each hole, but you won't be in a good bargaining position.

Car Rental

Car hire on Lombok is usually a less formal arrangement than on Bali – basically you arrange to borrow a car from a private owner. The owners may insist on a licence and sometimes want you to leave a passport for security. There is sometimes an insurance cover for theft or damage of the car (you may have to pay the first US$250), but not for injury to other people or property. It costs about 35,000 to 50,000 rp per day for a small vehicle such as a Suzuki Jimny, depending on the insurance cover, where you get it and how you bargain. If you take the vehicle for a few days or a week you should get a discount. Large Toyota 4WD vehicles are actually cheaper (around 35,000 rp) but you will pay more for petrol. Between four people it can be quite a cheap way to get around.

Hotels in Ampenan, Mataram or Senggigi can often arrange car or motorbike hire, as can some of the tourist-type shops. There are some 'official' car rental companies in Mataram which have a wider range of vehicles, but these tend to be more expensive.

Town	Distance from Sweta (km)
Narmada	6
Kopang	25
Selong	47
Pringgabaya	60
Labuhan Lombok	69
Sambelia	89
Airport	7
Senggigi	12
Pemenang	31
Bayan	79
Lembar	22
Ampenan	7
Suranadi	13
Sesaot	15
Praya	27
Tetebatu	46
Lingsar (via Narmada)	10
Gunung Pengsong	8
Kuta	54
Batu Bolong	10

BICYCLE

Bicycles are available for rent in and around the main tourist centres of Lombok. Near the Cirebon Restaurant in Ampenan they have very good bikes for 5000 rp per day. Old bikes cost from 3000 rp.

CIDOMO

The type of pony cart used on Lombok is locally known as a *cidomo*, and has car tyres instead of the spoked wooden wheels on a Balinese dokar. 'Cidomo' is a contraction of *cika* (a traditional handcart), *dokar* (the usual Indonesian word for a pony cart) and *mobil* (because motor-car wheels and tyres are used). They are usually brightly coloured

Cidomo

with decorative motifs, and are fitted out with bells that chime when they're in motion. The small ponies that pull them often have long colourful tassels attached to their gear. A typical cidomo has bench seating on either side which can comfortably fit three people, four if they're all slim. It's not unusual, however, to see a dozen or more passengers, plus several bags of rice and other paraphernalia piled up in a cart.

Some visitors are upset that the ponies seem to be heavily laden and harshly treated, but usually they're looked after reasonably well, as the owners depend on them for their livelihood. Cidomos are a very popular form of transport in many parts of Lombok, and often go to places that bemos don't, won't or can't.

The minimum price is 150 rp but it's unlikely that you'll be taken anywhere for less than 200 rp. Count on paying around 250 rp per person for up to two or three km, or maybe 750 rp for the whole cidomo. If you're alone, you'll have to wait for others or pay for the whole thing yourself.

OJEK

An *ojek* is a motorbike on which you ride as a paying pillion passenger. The cost is around 500 to 600 rp for up to five km, and you can't take much luggage. It's not quite as hair-raising on Lombok as it is on Bali.

PRAHU

These elegant, brilliantly painted, outrigger fishing boats, are used for short inter-island hops, like travelling from Bangsal Harbour to the Gili Islands. Mostly they use a small outboard motor, though sail-powered ones are still very common. A jukung is a slightly larger version of a prahu.

TOURS

Specialised tours, such as a 'nature tour' or a 'handcraft tour', will give a quick introduction to a specific aspect of the island, and you can re-visit your favourite places indepen-

dently. Costs are from US$10 for a half-day tour, and from US$15 for a full day. The tourist office can advise you – hotels usually have an arrangement with a tour operator. Generally, however, the real attractions of Lombok are the landscapes, the people, and the relaxed pace of life, which you won't appreciate on a whirlwind tour of the main 'sights'.

West Lombok

AMPENAN, MATARAM, CAKRANEGARA & SWETA

Although officially four separate towns, Ampenan, Mataram, Cakranegara and Sweta actually run together, so it's virtually impossible to tell where one stops and the next starts. Collectively they're the main 'city' on Lombok, and travellers often use them as a base to organise trips elsewhere on the island. However, many visitors head straight to Senggigi or the Gili Islands and don't stay in the town at all. There are banks, travel agents, some interesting shops and markets, and a few things to see, but the towns are not a major attraction.

Ampenan

Once the main port of Lombok, Ampenan is now not much more than a small fishing harbour. It's a bit run down and dirty, but it has character. The main road does not actually reach the coast at Ampenan, but simply fades out just before it gets to the port's grubby beach.

Ampenan has a curious mixture of people. Apart from the Sasaks and Balinese, there are also some Chinese, and a small Arab quarter known as Kampung Arab (*kampung* means 'district' or 'quarter'). The Arabs living here are devout Muslims, usually well educated and friendly towards foreigners.

Mataram

Mataram is the administrative capital of the province of Nusa Tenggara Barat (West Nusa Tenggara). Some of the public buildings, such as the Bank of Indonesia, the post office and the governor's office and residence, are substantial. The large houses around the outskirts of town are the homes of Lombok's elite.

Cakranegara

Now the main commercial centre of Lombok, bustling Cakranegara is usually referred to as Cakra. Formerly the capital of

Lombok under the Balinese rajahs, Cakra today has a thriving Chinese community as well as many Balinese residents. Most of the shops and restaurants in Cakranegara are run or owned by Chinese, and there are friendly losmen run by Balinese.

Sweta

Seven km from Ampenan and only about 2½ km beyond Cakra is Sweta, the central transport terminal of Lombok. This is where you catch bemos and buses to other parts of the island and on to Sumbawa. There are several warungs here, and numerous food, tobacco and drink vendors. Stretching along the eastern side of the terminal is a vast, covered market, the largest on Lombok. If you wander through its dim alleys you'll see stalls spilling over with coffee beans, eggs, rice, fish, fabrics, crafts, fruit and hardware. There's also a bird market.

Orientation

The 'city' is effectively divided into four functional areas: Ampenan, the port; Mataram, the administrative centre; Cakranegara, the trading centre; and Sweta, the transport centre. The towns are spread along one main road which starts as Jalan Pabean in Ampenan, quickly becomes Jalan Yos Sudarso, then changes to Jalan Langko, then to Jalan Pejanggik and finishes up in Sweta as Jalan Selaparang. It's a one-way street, running west to east. It's difficult to tell where the road changes names. Indeed, it seems that they overlap, since some places appear to have more than one address.

A second one-way street, Jalan Sriwijaya/Jalan Majapahit, brings traffic back in the other direction. Bemos run a shuttle service between the smaller bemo terminal in Ampenan and the main terminal in Sweta, about seven km away. Getting back and forth is therefore dead easy. You can stay in Ampenan, Mataram or Cakra since there are hotels and restaurants in all three places.

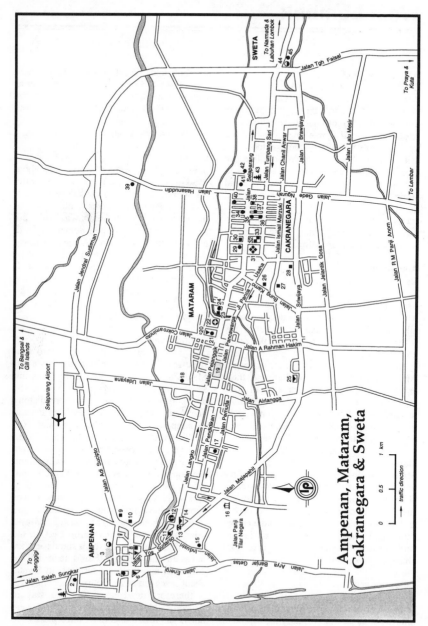

Ampenan, Mataram,
Cakranegara & Sweta

■   PLACES TO STAY

8	Hotel Zahir
9	Losmen Wisma Triguna
10	Losmen Horas
11	Nitour Hotel & Restaurant
23	Hotel Kertajoga
26	Hotel Granada
27	Graha Ayu
28	Puri Indah Hotel
30	Selaparang Hotel
32	Hotel & Restaurant Shanti Puri
33	Oka Homestay
36	Losmen Ayu
37	Adiguna Homestay

▼   PLACES TO EAT

6	Pabean & Cirebon restaurants
7	Kiki Restaurant
20	Garden House Restaurant
38	Sekawan Depot Es

OTHER

1	Pura Segara Temple
2	Sudirman Antiques
3	Ampenan Market
4	Ampenan Bemo Terminal
5	Moneychangers
12	Tourist Office
13	Telephone Office
14	Post Office
15	Pelni Office
16	Museum
17	Mataram University
18	Immigration Office
19	Main Square (Lampangan Mataram)
21	Governor's Office
22	Hospital
24	Perama Office
25	GPO (poste restante)
29	Rinjani Hand Woven
31	Cilinaya Shopping Centre
34	Bank Ekspor-Impor
35	Merpati Office
39	Lombok Handicraft Centre
40	Motorbike Rental
41	Selamat Riady
42	Mayura Water Palace
43	Pura Meru Temple
44	Sweta Bus/Bemo Terminal
45	Sweta Market

Mataram has a small commercial 'centre' near the river and a larger shopping area past the Jalan Selaparang/Jalan Hasanuddin intersection. You'll find the Cakra market just east of here, south of the main road. The Mataram government buildings are chiefly found along Jalan Pejanggik. The main square, Lampangan Mataram, is on the south side of Jalan Pejanggik. Art exhibitions, theatre, dance and wayang kulit performances are held in the square, but you'll only find out about these shows by word of mouth. Alternatively, look for the swarms of police and military personnel that are the most obvious sign of such an occasion.

Information
Tourist Office The main government tourist office, the Kantor Dinas Pariwisata Daerah or DIPARDA (☎ 21866, 31730), is in Mataram at Jalan Langko 70, on the north side, almost diagonally opposite the telephone office. The people at the tourist office are friendly, helpful and well informed. They keep standard government office hours – 7 am to 2 pm most days, closing 11 am Friday and 12.30 pm Saturday.

The Perama office (☎ 22764, fax 23368) is at Jalan Pejanggik 66. The staff are very helpful and provide good information, organise shuttle bus connections, change money (unless they're out of cash), arrange day tours around Lombok, and try to sell Land-Sea Adventure tours to Komodo and Flores.

Money There are a number of banks along the main drag, all in large buildings. Most will change travellers' cheques, although it can take some time. The Bank Ekspor-Impor seems to have longer opening hours than other banks: weekdays from 7.30 am to noon and from 1 to 2 pm. There are also moneychangers in Ampenan, and in Mataram's Cilinaya shopping centre, on the south side of Jalan Pejanggik. They're efficient, open for longer hours, and have rates similar to the banks. You can also change travellers' cheques at the airport and at the Perama office.

Post Mataram's main post office, on Jalan Sriwijaya, has the only poste restante service. It's open from 8 am to 2 pm Monday to Thursday and on Saturday, and from 8 to 11 am on Friday. Mail sent from Lombok goes to Bali first, so it can take some time to get through.

Telecommunications The Telkom telephone office, at the Ampenan end of Mataram on Jalan Langko, has telegram and fax services; it's open 24 hours every day. The international telephone service from here is very efficient, and you can usually get an overseas call through in minutes. There's another wartel in the Cilinaya shopping centre in Cakra. All of Lombok is in the 0364 telephone district.

Immigration Lombok's kantor imigrasi (immigration office) is on Jalan Udayana, the road out to the airport.

Bookshops There are a number of bookshops along the main road through the towns. Toko Buku Titian in Ampenan has some English magazines and maps. The bookshop in the Cilinaya shopping centre also has some English titles. The daily *Jakarta Post* usually arrives at 2 pm the day after publication.

Weaving Factories
A few weaving factories operate in Mataram, where you can see dyeing and weaving, and buy ikat cloth or handwoven songket sarongs. In fixed-price shops they charge around 15,000 rp per metre (1200 mm width) for ikat woven in mercerised cotton. The hand-and-foot powered looms are amazing contraptions that look as if they haven't altered since the Majapahit dynasty. Places to look at include Selamat Riady, off Jalan Hasanuddin. A bemo will drop you within a few metres of the factory and you're welcome to wander around. Rinjani Hand

Woven, at Jalan Pejanggik 44-46, beside the Selaparang Hotel, also has an interesting collection of woven materials. Another place to try is Sari Kusuma, Jalan Selaparang 45, Cakranegara, open from 8 am to 4 pm.

Pura Segara
This Balinese sea temple is on the beach a km or so north of Ampenan. Nearby are the remnants of a Muslim cemetery and an old Chinese cemetery – worth a wander through if you're visiting the temple.

Museum Negeri
The Museum Negeri Nusa Tenggara Barat is on Jalan Panji Tilar Negara in Ampenan. With exhibits on the geology, history and culture of Lombok and Sumbawa, it's well worth browsing around if you have a couple of free hours. If you intend buying any antiques or handcrafts have a look at the krises, songket, basketware and masks to give you a starting point for comparison. It's open from 8 am to 2 pm Tuesday to Sunday. Admission is 200 rp, 100 rp for children.

Mayura Water Palace
On the main road through Cakra, this 'palace' was built in 1744 and was once part of the royal court of the Balinese kingdom on Lombok. The centrepiece is a large artificial lake with an open-sided pavilion in the centre, connected to the shoreline by a raised footpath. This Bale Kambang (Floating Pavilion) was used as both a court of justice and a meeting place for the Hindu lords. There are other shrines and fountains dotted around the surrounding park. The entrance to the walled enclosure of the palace is on the western side (entry 500 rp). Today the palace grounds are used as a place to unleash fighting cocks and make offerings to the gods. It's a pleasant retreat from Cakra, although less than a century ago it was the site of bloody battles with the Dutch.

In 1894 the Dutch sent an army to back the Sasaks in a rebellion against their Balinese rajah. The rajah quickly capitulated but the crown prince decided to fight on while the Dutch-backed forces were split between various camps.

The Dutch camp at the Mayura Water Palace was attacked late at night by a combined force of Balinese and western Sasaks. The camp was surrounded by high walls, and the Balinese and Sasaks took cover behind them as they fired on the exposed army, forcing the Dutch to take shelter in a nearby temple compound. The Balinese also attacked the Dutch camp at Mataram, and soon after the entire Dutch army on Lombok was routed and withdrew to Ampenan where, according to one eyewitness, the soldiers 'were so nervous that they fired madly if so much as a leaf fell off a tree'. The first battles resulted in enormous losses of men and arms for the Dutch.

Although the Balinese had won the battle they had just begun to lose the war. Now they would not only have to continue to fight the eastern Sasaks but also the Dutch, who were quickly supplied with reinforcements from Java. The Dutch attacked Mataram a month after their initial defeat, fighting street to street not only against Balinese and west Sasak soldiers but also the local population. The Balinese crown prince was killed in the battle for the palace and the Balinese retreated to Cakranegara, where they were well armed and where the complex of walls provided good defence against infantry. Cakra was attacked by a combined force of Dutch and eastern Sasaks and, as happened in Mataram, Balinese men, women and children staged repeated suicidal lance attacks, to be cut down by rifle and artillery fire. The rajah and a small group of *punggawas* (commanders) fled to the village of Sasari near the pleasure gardens at Lingsar. A day or two later the rajah surrendered to the Dutch, but even his capture did not lead the Balinese to surrender.

In late November the Dutch attacked Sasari and a large number of Balinese chose the suicidal puputan. With the downfall of the dynasty the local population abandoned its struggle against the Dutch. The conquest of Lombok, thought about for decades, had taken the Dutch barely three months. The old rajah died in exile in Batavia in 1895.

Pura Meru

Directly opposite the water palace on the main road is the Pura Meru, the largest temple on Lombok. It's open every day, and a donation is expected (about 500 rp or 'up to you'). It was built in 1720 under the patronage of the Balinese prince, Anak Agung Made Karang of the Singosari kingdom, as an attempt to unite all the small kingdoms on Lombok. Although built as a symbol of the universe, and dedicated to the Hindu trinity of Brahma, Vishnu and Shiva, it's not a great-looking temple.

The outer courtyard has a hall housing the wooden drums that are beaten to call believers to festivals and special ceremonies. In the middle courtyard are two buildings with large raised platforms for offerings. The inner court has one large and 33 small shrines, as well as three meru (multi-roofed shrines), which are in a line: the central one, with 11 tiers, is Shiva's house; the one in the north, with nine tiers, is Vishnu's and the seven-tiered one in the south is Brahma's. The meru are also said to represent the three great mountains, Rinjani, Agung and Bromo. A festival is held here each June.

Places to Stay – bottom end

The most popular cheap places to stay are in Ampenan and Cakranegara. Jalan Koperasi branches off Jalan Yos Sudarso in the centre of Ampenan. Only a short stroll from the centre is the *Hotel Zahir* (☎ 22403) at Jalan Koperasi 12. It's a straightforward place with singles/doubles at 6000/7500 rp, or 8000/10,000 rp with bathroom. Prices include breakfast, and tea or coffee throughout the day. The rooms at this popular, convenient and friendly losmen each have a small verandah and face a central courtyard. The owners can arrange motorbike rental for about 10,000 rp per day.

Continue along the road to Jalan Koperasi 65 where *Losmen Horas* (☎ 21695) is pretty basic, but has singles/doubles with Indonesian-style bathrooms for 5000/7500 rp. Continuing further east you come to *Losmen Wisma Triguna* (☎ 31705), which is operated by the same people as the Horas. It's a little over a km from central Ampenan and is a quiet, relaxed place. Spacious rooms opening onto a bright verandah or the garden cost from 10,000 rp, including breakfast. The people at Horas or Wisma Triguna have good information on climbing Gunung Rinjani. The nearby *Losmen Angi Mammire* is cheaper and not as roomy, but quite OK.

Back in the centre of Ampenan is *Losmen Pabean* (☎ 21758) at Jalan Pabean 146, the eastern end of Jalan Yos Sudarso. It's basic but a bit better inside than it looks from the outside. Rooms are 4500/7000 rp for singles/doubles with shared mandi.

In Mataram, *Hotel Kambodja* (☎ 22211), on the corner of Jalan Supratman and Jalan Arif Rahmat, is pleasant and has rooms for about 8500 rp.

At the Cakranegara end of Mataram, south of the main drag and just north of Jalan Panca Usaha, are a number of Balinese-style losmen which are quite good places to stay. The *Oka Homestay*, on Jalan Repatmaja, has a quiet garden and singles/doubles at 8000/10,000 rp with breakfast. The *Astiti Guest House* (☎ 27988), in the same area on Jalan Subak, has rooms from 6000/8000 rp with shared bathroom, 8000/10,000 rp with private bath and 35,000 rp with air-con, including breakfast, and tea anytime. It's popular with surfers and the staff can help with transport information, rental cars etc.

Adiguna Homestay, on Jalan Nursiwan, is another good budget place with rooms from 8000/11,000 rp. The very friendly *Losmen Ayu* (☎ 21761), in the same street, has cheap rooms at about 10,000 rp a double. The bemos from Lembar come close to this area; get off on Jalan Gede Ngurah and walk west on Jalan Panca Usaha.

In the same area, at Jalan Maktal 15, the *Hotel & Restaurant Shanti Puri* (☎ 32649) is almost mid-range quality, but has cheap singles/doubles for 5000/7000 rp. Very comfortable rooms cost up to 12,000/15,000 rp. It's run by a friendly and helpful Balinese family who can also arrange motorbike and car hire.

Places to Stay – middle

There are quite a few good-value, mid-range places in the Mataram-Cakra area. The *Selaparang Hotel* (☎ 32670) is at Jalan Pejanggik 40-42 in Mataram. Air-con rooms cost 42,500/47,500 rp for singles/doubles, and fan-cooled rooms about half this. Across the road at 105 is the *Mataram Hotel* (☎ 23411) with double rooms at 25,000 rp, or rooms with air-con, TV, hot water and other mod cons for up to 50,000 rp. Both these mid-range hotels have pleasant little

restaurants. At Jalan Pejanggik 64, just west of the Perama office, is the *Hotel Kertajoga* (☎ 21775). It's good value, with fan-cooled rooms at 15,000/18,500 rp, and 20,500/25,500 rp with air-con.

Hotel Pusaka (☎ 33119), at Jalan Hasanuddin 23, is mainly for Indonesian travellers, but has a variety of quite good rooms from 12,500/15,000 rp up to 45,000/60,000 rp with air-con, including tax and breakfast. The cheap rooms are pretty basic but OK, and the mid-range rooms are quite good. It's close to the mosque.

Places to Stay – top end

At Jalan Yos Sudarso 4 in Ampenan, the *Nitour Hotel & Restaurant* (ex Wisma Melati; ☎ 23780, fax 36579) is quiet and comfortable, with carpets, air-con, telephone etc. 'Superior' rooms are US$30, 'deluxe' rooms US$35.

The heavily advertised *Hotel Granada* (☎ 22275) is on Jalan Bung Karno, south of the shopping centre in Mataram. There's a swimming pool and all rooms are air-conditioned. It has vaguely Iberian architecture and a caged menagerie. The prices include breakfast, and start at 59,000 rp a double plus 10% tax; ask for a low-season discount. If you want this kind of comfort, the *Puri Indah Hotel* (☎ 37633) on Jalan Sriwijaya also has a restaurant and a pool but is much better value at 15,000/20,000 rp, or 25,000/30,000 rp for air-con singles/doubles. The nearby *Graha Ayu* has rooms from 50,000 rp with all mod cons, but doesn't look appealing.

Places to Eat

Ampenan has several Indonesian and Chinese restaurants including the very popular *Cirebon*, at Jalan Pabean 113, with a standard Indonesian/Chinese menu and most dishes from around 2000 rp. Next door at No 111 is the *Pabean*, with similar food. *Poppy*, in the same area, is also recommended. On the other side of the intersection, upstairs from the art shop, *Kiki Restaurant* has a pleasant atmosphere and very good food for reasonable prices. The tables on the balcony overlooking the town centre are fun. *Rumah Makan Arafat*, at Jalan Saleh Sungkar 23, has good, cheap Indonesian food. Other alternatives are the *Setia* at Jalan Pabean 129 and the *Depot Mina* at Jalan Yos Sudarso 102. *Timur Tengah*, at Jalan Koperasi 22 right across from the Hotel Zahir, is popular but closed on Sundays and during Ramadan.

There are a couple of interesting restaurants in Mataram. The *Garden House Restaurant* is a pleasant open-air place with inexpensive nasi campur, nasi goreng and other standard meals. *Denny Bersaudra*, a bit further east, is well known for Sasak-style food. The nearby *Taliwang* also offers local dishes. *Flamboyan Restaurant*, on the south side of Pejanggik, is a good place for Indonesian and seafood. *Flamboyan Restaurant II*, on the road to Senggigi, also has good food.

In Cakra the *Sekawan Depot Es* has cold drinks downstairs and a seafood and Chinese restaurant upstairs. Around the corner on Jalan Hasanuddin is the *Rumah Makan Madya*, which serves very good, cheap food in authentic Sasak style. There are a number of other restaurants in this area, a handful of bakeries and, of course, plenty of places to buy food at the market.

Things to Buy
Sudirman Antiques, on Jalan Saleh Sungkar (the road north to Senggigi), is one of the biggest and best known antique and handcraft shops. There's a few others nearby, so this is a good area to look around. Rora Antiques, in Ampenan at Jalan Yos Sudarso 16A, sells some excellent woodcarvings, baskets and traditional Lombok weavings (songket and so on). Renza Antiques, at Jalan Yos Sudarso 92, is also a good place to browse. Musdah, at Dayan Penen, Jalan Sape 16, also has an interesting collection of masks, baskets, krises and carvings for sale.

The Lombok Handicraft Centre, at Sayang Sayang north of Cakra, has a number of shops with a good selection of crafts from Lombok and elsewhere. An excellent place to look for local products is the Sweta market, next to the Sweta bemo terminal. For handwoven fabrics, see the weaving factories mentioned earlier.

Getting There & Away
Air There's a Garuda/Merpati office (☎ 23762) close to the Nitour Hotel which can book and reconfirm flights. It's at Jalan Yos Sudarso 6 in Ampenan (open 8 am to 5 pm Monday to Saturday). The main Merpati office (☎ 32226, 36745) is on Jalan Selaparang in Cakra.

A third office (☎ 22670, 23235) is at the Selaparang Hotel, Jalan Pejanggik 40-42 in Mataram. The Sempati office (☎ 21226, 24844, 24845) is in the Cilinaya shopping centre in Mataram.

Bus Sweta has the main bus terminal for the entire island. It's also the eastern terminus for the local bemos which shuttle back and forth to Ampenan. There's an office in the middle of the place, with a notice board on which you can check the fare before you're hustled on board one of the vehicles. Some distances and approximate bemo fares from Sweta to other parts of Lombok include:

Destination	Fare
East (Jurusan Timor)	
Narmada (6 km)	200 rp
Mantang (17 km)	600 rp
Kopang (25 km)	700 rp
Terara (29 km)	800 rp
Sikur (33 km)	900 rp
Pomotong (34 km)	950 rp
Masbagik (36 km)	1000 rp
Selong (47 km)	1400 rp
Labuhan Haji (57 km)	1800 rp
Labuhan Lombok (69 km)	2000 rp
South & Central	
(Jurusan Selatan & Tenggara)	
Kediri (5 km)	500 rp
Lembar (22 km)	700 rp
Praya (27 km)	700 rp
Mujur (36 km)	1100 rp
Kuta (54 km)	1500 rp
North (Jurusan Utara)	
Senggigi (12 km)	500 rp
Pemenang (31 km)	700 rp
Tanjung (45 km)	900 rp
Bayan (79 km)	1800 rp

Boat The ferry docks at Lembar, 22 km south of Ampenan (see below for details). The Bali ferry office is at Jalan Pejanggik 49 in Mataram. The *Mabua Express* office is in Lembar (☎ 25895, 37224). The office of Pelni, the national shipping line, is at Jalan Industri 1 in Ampenan (☎ 21604).

Getting Around
To/From the Airport Lombok's Selaparang Airport is only a couple of km from Ampenan. Taxis from there cost about 5000 rp to Ampenan, Mataram and Cakra, 6000 rp to Sweta, 8000 rp to Senggigi, and 15,000 rp to Bangsal. Alternatively, you can walk out of the airport carpark to the main road, and take one of the frequent No 7 bemos which run straight to the Ampenan bemo stop for 250 rp.

Bemo & Cidomo Ampenan-Mataram-Cakra-Sweta is very spread out, so don't plan to walk from place to place. Bemos shuttle back and forth along the main route between the Ampenan terminal at one end and the Sweta terminal at the other. The fare is a standard 250 rp regardless of the distance. There are also plenty of cidomos to rent for shorter trips around town, although these are not permitted on the main streets. The bemo terminal in Ampenan is a good place to charter a bemo.

Car Hotels in town can often arrange car hire. Metro Photo (☎ 32146) at Jalan Yos Sudarso 79 in Ampenan can arrange pretty cheap rental cars.

There are some 'official' car rental companies, but these tend to be more expensive. Rinjani Rent Car (☎ 21400), in Mataram opposite the Hotel Granada on Jalan Bung Karno, has Suzuki Jimnys for 50,000 rp per day without insurance. Yoga Rent Car (☎ 21127), in the Cilinaya shopping centre in Mataram, has similar cars for 45,000 rp per day.

Motorbike Your hotel might be able to get you a rental motorbike. If not, go to Jalan Gelantik, off Jalan Selaparang near the junc-tion with Jalan Hasanuddin, at the Cakranegara end of Mataram. The motor-bike owners who hang around there have bikes to rent for 10,000 to 12,500 rp a day. As usual, the more you pay the better bike you get and it's wise to check a bike over carefully before taking it.

Bicycle You can rent good bicycles from the Cirebon Restaurant in Ampenan for about 5000 rp per day.

GUNUNG PENGSONG
This Balinese temple is built – as the name suggests – on top of a hill. It's nine km south of Mataram and has great views of rice fields, the volcanoes and the sea. Try to get there early in the morning before the clouds envelop Gunung Rinjani. Once a year, gen-erally in March or April, a buffalo is taken up the steep 100-metre slope and sacrificed to give thanks for a good harvest. The Bersih Desa Festival also occurs here at harvest time – houses and gardens are cleaned, fences whitewashed, roads and paths repaired. Once part of a ritual to rid the village of evil spirits, it is now held in honour of the rice goddess Dewi Sri. There's no set admission charge, but you will have to pay the caretaker 200 rp or so, especially if you use the carpark.

LEMBAR
Lembar, 22 km south of Ampenan, is the main port on Lombok. The ferries to and from Bali dock here, as does the *Mabua Express*. There's a canteen at the harbour where you can buy snacks and drinks while waiting to catch the ferry. The only place to stay, the *Serumbung Indah* (☎ 37153), has a restaurant and rooms from around 15,000 rp, but it's not very convenient, being about two km north of the harbour on the main road.

Getting There & Away
You can buy your tickets to Bali at the wharf on the day, or from the offices in Mataram. Ferries leave every two hours from 6 am. The *Mabua Express* leaves at 11.30 am and 5 pm.

In theory you should be able to get a bemo

from Lembar to Sweta for about 700 rp; in practice they will try to get you on a special charter bemo, or otherwise manage to charge you more – maybe 1000 rp. If you come on the *Mabua Express* and want a public bemo to town, you have to leave the dock area and walk 200 metres to the left, then turn right to find the bemos waiting at the roadside. There are set fares for 'taxis'; the price per person depends on the number of passengers. To Mataram it's 7000 rp each with two people, or 12,000 rp by yourself. Minibuses from the hotels in town sometimes meet the ferry.

Regular buses and bemos to Lembar from Sweta cost 700 rp during the day. If you don't have a ticket, ask to be dropped off near the ferry office.

SOUTH-WESTERN PENINSULA

If you approach Lembar by ferry you'll see a hilly and little-developed peninsula on your right. A road from Lembar runs on to this peninsula in Lombok's south-west, but it's pretty rough after Sekotong, and impassable for ordinary cars after Taun. Bangko Bangko is at the end of the track, and from there it's two or three km to Desert Point, which has great surf but no places to stay or eat. There are a number of picturesque islands off the north coast of the peninsula and one of them, Gili Nanggu, has some tourist bungalows. *Istana Cempaka* charges US$11 per person including all meals. Enquiries and bookings can be made by phoning a Cakra number (☎ 22898).

SENGGIGI

On a series of sweeping bays, between three and 12 km north of Ampenan, Senggigi has become the most developed tourist area on Lombok. All the tourist facilities are here, and a range of top-end and mid-range accommodation. There are still some budget places too. One day Senggigi might be a pleasant, mid-range beach resort in the Sanur mould, but at its present stage of development it's more like a construction site, with lots of new buildings which have not yet been softened by landscaping, and without the unspoiled beauty of a few years ago. The

nicest places are the isolated groups of bungalows north of the central area.

Senggigi has fine beaches, although they slope very steeply into the water. There's some snorkelling off the point and in the sheltered bay around the headland. There are beautiful sunsets over the Lombok Strait and you can enjoy them from the beach or from one of the beachfront restaurants. As it gets dark the fishing fleet lines up offshore, each boat with its bright lanterns (new arrivals wonder which Balinese city is across the water). Senggigi has the only nightlife on Lombok, and it can be good fun.

Orientation

The area known as Senggigi is spread out along nearly 10 km of coastal road. Most of the shops, travel agents and other facilities, and a fair concentration of the accommodation, are on the stretch of road near the Senggigi Beach Hotel, about six km north of Ampenan.

Information

Kotasi is the tourist office of the local cooperative, and is good for transport information. Nearby is a private telephone office and a postal agent. You can change money or travellers' cheques at the Graha Beach Hotel, in the middle of the Senggigi strip, and at most of the big hotels, if they have the cash. The staff at the Graha Beach can also make bookings and reconfirm flights for Garuda and Merpati, as can a number of travel agents, such as Nazareth Tours & Travel (☎ 93033). There's a Perama office (☎ 93007/8/9) a bit further north which runs tours and tourist transport and will also provide information and change money, and some other agencies for tourist shuttle buses, like Lombok Independent. Other facilities include the supermarket, a Telkom telephone office and some photo-processing places.

Batu Bolong Temple

This temple is on a rocky point which juts into the sea about a km south of Senggigi Beach, five km north of Ampenan. The rock

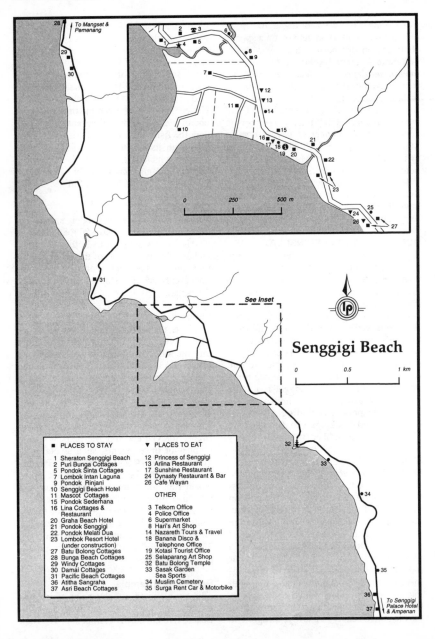

To Mangset & Pemenang

See Inset

Senggigi Beach

0   0.5   1 km

0   250   500 m

To Senggigi
Palace Hotel
& Ampenan

■ PLACES TO STAY   ▼ PLACES TO EAT

1 Sheraton Senggigi Beach   12 Princess of Senggigi
2 Puri Bunga Cottages   13 Arlina Restaurant
5 Pondok Sinta Cottages   17 Sunshine Restaurant
7 Lombok Intan Laguna   24 Dynasty Restaurant & Bar
9 Pondok Rinjani   26 Cafe Wayan
10 Senggigi Beach Hotel
11 Mascot Cottages   OTHER
15 Pondok Sederhana
16 Lina Cottages &   3 Telkom Office
    Restaurant   4 Police Office
20 Graha Beach Hotel   6 Supermarket
21 Pondok Senggigi   8 Hari's Art Shop
22 Pondok Melati Dua   14 Nazareth Tours & Travel
23 Lombok Resort Hotel   18 Banana Disco &
    (under construction)   Telephone Office
27 Batu Bolong Cottages   19 Kotasi Tourist Office
28 Bunga Beach Cottages   25 Selaparang Art Shop
29 Windy Cottages   32 Batu Bolong Temple
30 Damai Cottages   33 Sasak Garden
31 Pacific Beach Cottages   Sea Sports
36 Atitha Sangraha   34 Muslim Cemetery
37 Asri Beach Cottages   35 Surga Rent Car & Motorbike

on which it sits has a natural hole in it which gives the temple its name – *batu bolong* means literally 'rock with hole'. Being a Balinese temple, it's oriented towards Gunung Agung, Bali's holiest mountain, across the Lombok Strait. There's a fantastic view and it's a good place to watch the sunsets. Legend has it that beautiful virgins were once thrown into the sea from the top of the rock. Locals like to claim that this is why there are so many sharks in the water here.

Places to Stay – bottom end
Senggigi is moving upmarket. Although there's plenty of mid-range accommodation, and an increasing number of expensive places, there's not that much for shoestring travellers. The most popular travellers' centre at Senggigi is the *Pondok Senggigi* (☎ 93273). It's expanded quite a bit, but still has some cheaper rooms at 10,000/13,000 rp for singles/doubles with shared bathroom. Rooms with Western-style bathrooms go from 15,000/20,000 rp, and deluxe air-con rooms are 70,000/80,000 rp. There's also an extra 15% tax and service charge. The rooms run off a long verandah with a pleasant garden area in front. There's a good restaurant which is very popular, and sometimes live music, so it's not the most serene place to stay.

About the cheapest place to stay is *Pondok Sederhana*, north-west of Pondok Senggigi. The rooms are a bit dirty, but dirt cheap from about 7000 rp with shared mandi and toilet, and the position is good. There are some small places off the main road away from the beach, like the *Astiti Guesthouse* with singles/doubles at 8000/10,000 rp and 10,000/14,000 rp. They're not far from the centre of things but still quiet and pretty good value.

The *Pondok Sinta Cottages* are further north and closer to the beach, and they're cheap at 6000/7500 rp, or 10,000/12,000 rp with private bathroom, including breakfast and tax. *Damai Cottages*, way north in an area known as Mangset, are moderately cheap at 13,000/16,000 rp.

Places to Stay – middle
One of the first places you'll strike coming in from Ampenan is *Asri Beach Cottages*, with standard rooms at 12,500 rp and bungalows at 17,500 rp, including tax and breakfast. They're basic but clean, and near the beach. Just north of Asri is *Atitha Sangraha*, a nice place with spotlessly clean cottages near the beach from around 20,000 rp.

Batu Bolong Cottages (☎ 24598) has bungalows on both sides of the road. On the beach side they cost from 35,000 rp, and on the other side from 30,000 rp, including tax.

The small *Pondok Melati Dua* (☎ 93288), on the right as you enter Senggigi central, has standard rooms at 20,000/22,000 rp and cottages at 30,000/32,500 rp, including tax and breakfast. It's a short walk to the beach, and generally a nice place.

Lina Cottages (☎ 93237), with rooms at 25,000/35,000 rp, is central, friendly, and good value and its restaurant has a good reputation. A little further north, *Pondok Rinjani* has cottages with private bathrooms at 22,000/28,000 rp plus tax.

Windy Cottages are out by themselves, north of Senggigi in Mangset. It's a great location if you want to get away from it all, and the restaurant has good food. There are only eight rooms, at 20,000 rp for standard rooms and 35,000 rp for bungalows.

Places to Stay – top end
The first place you see coming north from Ampenan is the new *Senggigi Palace Hotel* (☎ 93045/6/7/8/9, fax 93043), and you'll certainly see it – the central lobby building is massive. The rooms are plain and clean (sterile?), with fridge, phone, TV and video, and cost US$60/70, or US$75/85 with an ocean view. It has a vast swimming pool, and may look prettier when the garden is established.

Senggigi's first big 'international standard' hotel is right on the headland. Operated by Garuda, the *Senggigi Beach Hotel* (☎ 93210, fax 93200) charges from US$60/75 for an air-con room and up to US$160 for a deluxe bungalow. The hotel has a beautiful setting, a swimming pool and other mod cons, though it's almost old enough to need a facelift. At least as classy is the *Lombok Intan Laguna* (☎ 93090, fax 93185), a large and handsome luxury hotel with a big pool and rooms from US$80/95 and suites from US$200, plus 21% tax and service. (Rumour has it that the Intan Laguna was recently downgraded from three stars to two on some pretext, but it still looks good. If you can feel sorry for a luxury hotel, give this one a sympathy vote.)

Mascot Berugaq Elen Cottages (☎ 93365, fax 22314), near the Senggigi Beach Hotel, are pleasant individual cottages from US$29 to US$33, plus 21% service and tax. (Formerly they were just 'Mascot Cottages'.) The *Graha Beach Hotel* (☎ 93101, fax 93400) has singles/doubles from US$40/45 (US$5 more for an ocean view), with air-con, TV and a beachfront restaurant.

Puri Bunga Cottages (formerly Ida Beach Cottages; ☎ 93013, fax 93286) are stepped up the hillside on the east side of the road with great views, but it's a bit of a trek to the higher rooms and to the beach. They have air-con, telephone, TV, hot water, swimming pool, restaurant and indifferent staff. The published rate is US$60/65, but it must be overpriced as they offer a 50% discount.

Further north, the new *Sheraton Senggigi Beach* (☎ 93333, fax 93140) is the best hotel in Senggigi, and also the most expensive, with rooms from US$105 to US$125, suites from US$275 to US$800, plus 21% tax and service. The rooms are comfortable, stylish and tastefully decorated with local handcrafts. The pool and gardens are lovely, and the staff are friendly and efficient. There's a children's pool and playground and special family packages. The Sheraton is making an effort to train local staff, and promote local crafts and culture, and is one of the first places to recycle some of their waste water for the gardens.

At the northern end of Senggigi, *Pacific Beach Cottages* (☎ 93006, fax 93027) has all the standard luxuries – air-con, TV, hot water, swimming pool – but the rooms are ordinary and it has no character at all. Stan-

dard rooms cost US$25/30 for singles/doubles; add US$5 for deluxe rooms, or US$20 for 'executive deluxe' bungalows, plus 21% tax and service. Even further north in Mangset you'll find the well-run *Bunga Beach Cottages*, with a splendid beachfront position, a pool and 28 comfortable, air-conditioned bungalows in a pretty garden from US$42/45 to US$52/55.

Other top-end places under construction include the *Lombok Resort Hotel* and a *Holiday Inn*.

Places to Eat

Most of the places to stay have their own restaurants and you can eat at any one you like. The restaurant at *Pondok Senggigi* is popular from breakfast time until late at night. It's not the cheapest (nasi goreng is 2500 rp, a main course of fish is around 5000 rp), but the food and the atmosphere are good. The restaurant at *Lina Cottages* has some very tasty dishes and is also popular.

There's not much at the bottom end of the scale; local warungs seem to have been priced out of the real estate market. *Cafe Wayan*, south of the centre, is related to the excellent Cafe Wayan in Ubud, which should be recommendation enough. The centrally located *Princess of Senggigi* is also a good eatery. The *Sunshine Restaurant* has a typical tourist menu and good Chinese food. Further north is the *Arlina Restaurant*, another good-value place. At the other end of the Senggigi strip, the restaurant at *Windy Cottages* serves very good food at reasonable prices in a delightful seaside setting.

Entertainment

Pondok Senggigi, the *Graha Beach Hotel* and *Dynasty Restaurant & Bar* have live music on occasions, with both tourists and young locals crowding the dance floor. The local bands do good rock and reggae music with an Indonesian flavour, as well as covers of popular Western numbers.

Getting There & Away

A public bemo from Ampenan to Senggigi is about 500 rp. To get to Senggigi from the airport, first get a bemo to the Ampenan terminal (250 rp), then another to Senggigi. Officially a taxi from the airport to Senggigi is 8000 rp, but you can walk out of the airport and charter a bemo for about 7000 rp.

To charter a bemo in Senggigi, go to the transport co-operative (Koprasi), on the main road, near the Banana Disco.

The fast catamaran from Padangbai used to call at Senggigi, and may resume service. Other boats run directly to the Gili Islands, which is not a cheap option, but very scenic.

NARMADA

Laid out as a miniature replica of the summit of Gunung Rinjani and its crater lake, Narmada is a hill about 10 km east of Cakra, on the main east-west road crossing Lombok. It takes its name from a sacred river in India. The temple, Pura Kalasa, is still used, and the Balinese Pujawali celebration is held here every year in honour of the god Batara, who dwells on Gunung Rinjani.

Narmada was constructed by the king of Mataram in 1805, when he was no longer able to climb Rinjani to make his offerings to the gods. Having set his conscience at rest by placing offerings in the temple, he spent at least some of his time in his pavilion on the hill, lusting after the young girls bathing in the artificial lake.

Along one side of the pool is the remains of an aqueduct built by the Dutch and still in use. Land tax was tied to the productivity of the land so the Dutch were keenly interested in increasing agricultural output. They did this by extending irrigation systems to increase the area under cultivation. The Balinese had already built extensive irrigation networks, particularly in the west of Lombok.

It's a beautiful place to spend a few hours, although the gardens are neglected. Don't go there on weekends, when it tends to become very crowded. Apart from the lake there are two other pools in the grounds. Admission is 500 rp, and there's an additional charge to swim in the pool.

Places to Eat

Right at the Narmada bemo station is the local market, which sells mainly food and clothing and is well worth a look. There are a number of warungs scattered around offering soto ayam (chicken soup) and other dishes.

Getting There & Away

There are frequent bemos from Sweta to Narmada, costing around 200 rp. When you get off at the bemo station at Narmada, you'll see the gardens directly opposite. If you cross the road and walk 100 metres or so south along the side road you'll come to the entrance. There are parking fees for bicycles, motorbikes and cars.

LINGSAR

This large temple complex, just a few km north of Narmada, is said to have been built in 1714. The temple combines the Bali Hindu and Wektu Telu religions in one complex. Designed in two separate sections and built on two different levels, the Hindu pura in the northern section is higher than the Wektu Telu temple in the southern section.

The Hindu temple has four shrines. On one side is Hyang Tunggal, which looks towards Gunung Agung, the seat of the gods on Bali. The shrine faces north-west rather than north-east as it would on Bali. On the other side is a shrine devoted to Gunung Rinjani, the seat of the gods on Lombok. Between these two shrines is a double shrine symbolising the union between the two islands. One side of this double shrine is named in honour of the might of Lombok, and the other side is dedicated to a king's daughter, Ayu Nyoman Winton who, according to legend, gave birth to a god.

The Wektu Telu temple is noted for its small enclosed pond devoted to Lord Vishnu. It has a number of holy eels that look like huge swimming slugs and can be enticed from their hiding places by the use of hard-boiled eggs as bait. The stalls outside the temple complex sell boiled eggs – expect to pay around 200 rp or so. Get there early to see the eels, because they've had their fill of eggs after the first few tour groups. Next to the eel pond is another enclosure with a large altar or offering place, bedecked in white and yellow cloth and mirrors. The mirrors are offerings from Chinese business people asking for good luck and success. Many local farmers also come here with offerings.

At the annual rain festival at the start of the wet season – somewhere between October and December – the Hindus and the Wektu Telu make offerings and pray in their own temples, then come out into the communal compound and pelt each other with ketupat – rice wrapped in banana leaves. The ceremony is to bring the rain, or to give thanks for the rain. Be prepared to get attacked with ketupat from both sides if you visit Lingsar at this time!

Getting There & Away

Lingsar is off the main road. First take a bemo from Sweta to Narmada (200 rp), then catch another to Lingsar village (also 200 rp), and walk the short distance from there to the temple complex. It's easy to miss the temple, which is set back off the road behind the school.

SURANADI

A few km east of Lingsar, Suranadi has one of the holiest temples on Lombok. This small temple, set in pleasant gardens, is noted for its bubbling, icy cold spring water and restored baths with ornate Balinese carvings. The eels here are also sacred and seldom underfed – how many hard-boiled eggs can an eel eat? You can also bathe here (it's polite to ask first), or use the swimming pool at the hotel (1000 rp, kids 500 rp).

Hutan Wisata Suranadi

Not far from Suranadi, on the road towards Sesaot, there's a small jungle sanctuary, the Hutan Wisata Suranadi (*hutan* means 'forest' or 'jungle'), but it's sadly neglected.

Places to Stay & Eat

The *Suranadi Hotel* (☎ 33686) has rooms and cottages which are grossly overpriced at US$12 to US$50, plus 21% tax and service. It's an old Dutch building, originally an administrative centre, although it's no great example of colonial architecture. There are two swimming pools, tennis courts, a restaurant and a bar. There's a cheaper *homestay* nearby for 10,000/12,000 rp including breakfast – ask at the warungs in the main street.

SESAOT

About five km from Suranadi, and also worth a visit, is Sesaot, a small quiet market town on the edge of a forest where wood-felling is the main industry. There's regular transport from Suranadi to Sesaot and you can eat at the warung on the main street, which has simple but tasty food.

Go up the main street and turn left over the bridge. There are some nice places for picnics, popular with locals on holidays, and you can swim in the river. The water is very cool and is considered holy as it comes straight from Gunung Rinjani. You can continue up the road about three km to Air Nyet, a small village with more places for swimming and picnics.

Top: Kuta Beach, South Lombok (JL)
Middle: Sulawesi-style houses, Labuhan Lombok (JL)
Bottom: Rice cultivation, Central Lombok (JL)

Top: Narmada, West Lombok (JL)
Left: Sendang Gila Waterfall, near Senaru, North Lombok (JL)
Right: Selling chillis, West Lombok (JL)

Central, South & East Lombok

Central Lombok, or Lombok Tengah, is the name of one of the three administrative districts (kabupaten) on Lombok, but for the first section of this chapter the term is used more generally, to cover the inland towns and villages in the rich agricultural area south of Gunung Rinjani. The second section covers the towns further south and the beautiful south coast, an area of much speculation but little development, so far. The third section covers the east coast, an area scarcely visited by foreigners except for those using the ferry port at Labuhan Lombok.

Central Lombok

The area on the southern slopes of Gunung Rinjani is well watered and lush, and offers opportunities for scenic walks through the rice fields and the jungle. Towards the south coast the country is drier, and dams have been built to provide irrigation during the dry season. Most of the places in central Lombok are more or less traditional Sasak settlements, and several of them are known for particular types of local handcrafts.

TETEBATU

A mountain retreat at the foot of Gunung Rinjani, Tetebatu is 50 km from Mataram and about 10 km north of the main east-west road. It's quite a bit cooler here, and it can be misty and rainy, particularly between November and April.

There are magnificent views over southern Lombok, east to the sea and north to Gunung Rinjani. You can climb part way up Rinjani from here but the formerly magnificent stands of mahogany trees have virtually disappeared. Other destinations for walks include Jukut Waterfall, six km to the east, and the *hutan* (forest), four km north-west, where lots of jet-black monkeys will shriek at you.

Places to Stay & Eat

The original place to stay is *Wisma Soedjono*, an old colonial house that was once a country retreat for a Dr Soedjono. A number of rooms and lumbung-like bungalows have been added as well as a restaurant and a good-sized swimming pool. In the simplest rooms, prices start at 15,000 rp for a double, and peak at 35,000 rp for 'VIP' accommodation. The better rooms have Western-style toilets and showers with hot water, and all prices include continental breakfast. The staff provide good information about walks in the area. Food here is excellent, but costs extra – you can even get a packed lunch if you want to spend the day out walking. There are also two or three warungs in the town.

Some cheap places to stay are sprouting in the lovely rice fields. One such place is *Diwi Enjeni*, on the south side of town with a nice outlook. Bungalows cost 7500 rp, including breakfast, and there's a small restaurant. *Pondok Tetebatu* is nearby, at a similar price. Turn right in Tetebatu to the *Green Ory* bungalow which costs 25,000 rp but could sleep several people. Continue on the road to the waterfall to find *Wisma Paradiso*, another nice cheapie.

Getting There & Away

Getting to Tetebatu involves a number of changes if you haven't got your own wheels. There is a direct bus from Sweta to Pomotong (950 rp), but as you may have to wait around for a while, it may actually be quicker to take a bemo to Narmada then another to Pomotong. From Pomotong take a bemo or cidomo to Kotaraja (400 rp), and from there another bemo or cidomo to Tetebatu. Or go straight there on the back of a motorbike for 1000 rp or so. If you're not in a hurry and you're not carrying too much, you can walk from Pomotong to Tetebatu. It's an easy 2½ to three hours, through attractive country patched with rice fields.

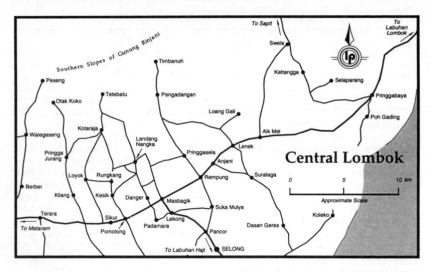

To Sapit

Swela

Kettangga

Selaparang

To Labuhan Lombok

Pringgabaya

Poh Gading

Southern Slopes of Gunung Rinjani

Timbanuh

Peseng

Tetebatu

Pengadangan

Loang Gali

Otak Koko

Aik Mel

Kotaraja

Lenek

Waiegeseng

Lendang Nangka

Pringgasela

Anjani

Central Lombok

Pringga Jurang

Rempung

Suralaga

0   5   10 km

Loyok

Rungkang

Approximate Scale

Berber

Kesik

Danger

Kilang

Masbagik

Suka Mulya

Koleko

Terara

Sikur

Lekong

Dasan Geres

To Mataram

Pomotong

Padamara

Pancor

To Labuhan Haji   SELONG

KOTARAJA

Kotaraja means 'city of kings', although no kings ruled from here, and it's hardly a city. Apparently, when the Sasak kingdom of Langko (located at Kopang in central Lombok) fell to the Balinese invaders, the rulers of Langko fled to Loyok, the village south of Kotaraja. After the royal compound in that village was also destroyed, two sons of the ruler of Langko went to live in Kotaraja. The aristocracy of Kotaraja can trace their ancestry back to these brothers, although the highest caste title of *raden* has now petered out through intermarriage.

The area round Kotaraja is noted for blacksmithing and basketware. Traditional blacksmiths still use an open hearth and human-powered bellows, but old car springs are the favoured 'raw material' for knives, farm implements and other tools.

Getting There & Away

There are no losmen in Kotaraja, so visit from Tetebatu or Lendang Nangka. With your own transport you can make a day trip from the capital – it's only 32 km from Sweta.

LOYOK

Loyok, a tiny village just a few km from Kotaraja, is also noted for its fine handcrafts, particularly basketware and weaving with natural fibres. Most of the craftspeople work from their homes, but the cidomo drivers will be able to take you to where the basket weavers work. There's a place in the main street where you can buy some of the excellent basketware, and also a Handcraft Centre with some work on display. You can stay at the *Wisma Loyok* for 12,500 rp with dinner and breakfast.

Getting There & Away

To get to Loyok, you can get a bemo from Pomotong to take you as far as Rungkang, the turn-off to the village, and then either walk the last km, or get a cidomo for 250 rp per person. If you're setting out from Kotaraja for Loyok you have the same options – either take a cidomo or walk. It's a very pretty drive, with traditional thatched Sasak huts and lush rice terraces along the way.

RUNGKANG

This small village, less than a km east of

Loyok, is known for its pottery, which is made from a local black clay. The pots are often finished with attractive cane work, which is woven all over the outside for decoration and for greater strength. Similar pottery is made in a number of other villages in the area south of the main road.

MASBAGIK

Quite a large town on the main road at the turn-off to Selong, Masbagik has a market on Monday morning. It's well known for production of pottery and ceramics. There's a post office and a Telkom wartel here. Just east of the wartel, follow the track to the left for 500 metres to Repo village, where you can stay at *Sasak House* for 12,000/15,000 rp with three meals. It's not very well located but Gep, the guy who runs it, was looking for a better place so it may be worth asking about. A bemo from Sweta to Masbagik (42 km) costs 1000 rp, and you can hire a motorbike to get around.

LENDANG NANGKA

Seven km from Tetebatu, this traditional Sasak village has similar surroundings to those of Tetebatu. In and around the village you can see blacksmiths who still make knives, hoes and other tools using traditional techniques. Silversmiths are also starting to work here. **Jojang**, the biggest freshwater spring in Lombok, is a few km away. Or you can walk to a waterfall with beautiful views, and look for black monkeys in a nearby forest. In August you should be able to see traditional Sasak stick fighting at Lendang Nangka. It's a violent affair with leather-covered shields and bamboo poles. Local dances are a possibility at **Batu Empas**, one km away.

Hadji Radiah is a local primary school teacher who has been encouraging people to stay in Lendang Nangka. Since Radiah originally wrote to us about the first edition of the *Bali & Lombok* guidebook, his family homestay has become quite popular among travellers who want an experience of typical Lombok village life. He speaks English very well, and is a mine of information on the

surrounding countryside and customs. He has a map for local walks and enjoys acting as a guide.

Places to Stay

Staying with Radiah will cost about 10,000/15,000 rp for a basic single/double, including three excellent meals per day of local Sasak food, and tea or coffee. You will get customary Sasak cake and fruit for breakfast – it's not luxury, but is good value and highly recommended. His house is fairly easy to find (see the map, but everyone knows him), and has 12 bedrooms for guests. There's a new place to stay on the west side of Lendang Nangka, *Wisma Ewira*, which is quite nice and also costs 10,000/15,000 rp with three meals.

Getting There & Away

Take a bemo from Sweta to Masbagik (42 km, 1000 rp) and then take a cidomo to Lendang Nangka (about four km), which should cost 350 rp per person, but the driver will want at least three passengers, or 1000 rp for the whole cart. Lendang Nangka is about five km from Pomotong and connected by a surfaced road – take a cidomo for 400 rp (500 rp if you have a heavy load).

PRINGGASELA

This village is a centre for traditional weaving, such as sarongs, blankets etc. You can see the weavers in action, and buy some of their beautiful work at a bargain price – that is, you'll have to bargain.

LENEK

Lenek has a traditional music and dance troupe which performs for tourists on a more-or-less regular basis. Ask at the tourist office in Mataram for the times. A little north and east of Lenek is the village of Loang Gali, where a room and three meals at the *Loang Gali Cottages* costs 12,500 rp per person.

SAPIT

At Aik Mel, near Lenek, a side road heads north up the shoulder of Gunung Rinjani, past Swela to Sapit. This place offers cool air, stunning views and the attractive forest area of Lemor. You can walk from Sapit to Sembalun Bumbung, and from there do a climb up Rinjani from the east side. The road north of Sapit is not driveable. The *Hati Suci Homestay* in Sapit has bungalows at 10,000 to 12,000 rp, and bunk beds at 4000 rp, including breakfast. There's a restaurant, and the staff can help with information about climbing Rinjani. Get there by bemo from Masbagik (1000 rp).

South Lombok

SUKARARA

Twenty-five km south of Mataram, not far off the Kediri to Praya road, is the small village of Sukarara. On the way to this traditional weaving centre you'll pass picturesque thatched-roof villages surrounded by rice fields. More unusual are the houses built from local stone found in Sukarara.

Nearly every house in Sukarara has an old wooden handloom. Along the main street there are lots of places with looms set up outside, and displays of sarongs hanging in bright bands. Typically they have attractive young women working out the front, in the traditional black costume with brightly coloured edgings. More women work inside, often wearing jeans and watching TV as they work, but most of the material is actually made in homes in surrounding villages.

Before you go to Sukarara it may be a good idea to check prices in the Selamat Riady weaving factory in Cakranegara, and get some idea of how much to pay and when to start bargaining. There's such a range in quality and size that it's impossible to give a guide to prices, but the best pieces are magnificent and well worth paying for. If you're accompanied by a guide to Sukarara it will inevitably cost you more due to the addition of commissions. The village is a regular stop for tour groups, but don't let that deter you from visiting.

Getting There & Away

Get a bemo from Sweta towards Praya, and get off at Puyung (about 600 rp). From Puyung you can hire a cidomo for about 250 rp to take you the two km to Sukarara.

PENUJAK

This small village, six km south of Praya, is well known for its traditional *gerabah* pottery made from a local red clay. You'll see the pottery places from the road, and you can watch the pots being made by hand and fired in traditional kilns. There's a lot worth buying, but the bigger pieces will be hard to carry.

Pots range in size up to a metre high, and there are kitchen vessels of various types, and decorative figurines, usually in the shape of animals. The local industry has formed a partnership with a New Zealand organisation to develop export markets for its products, so hopefully this distinctive pottery will become more widely known.

REMBITAN & SADE

The area from Sengkol down to Kuta Beach is a centre of traditional Sasak culture, and there are many relatively unchanged Sasak villages where the inhabitants still live in customary houses and engage in traditional craftwork.

The village of Rembitan is a few km south of Sengkol and has a population of about 750. It's a slightly sanitised Sasak village where tourists are welcome to look around, with one of the local kids as a guide. Masjid

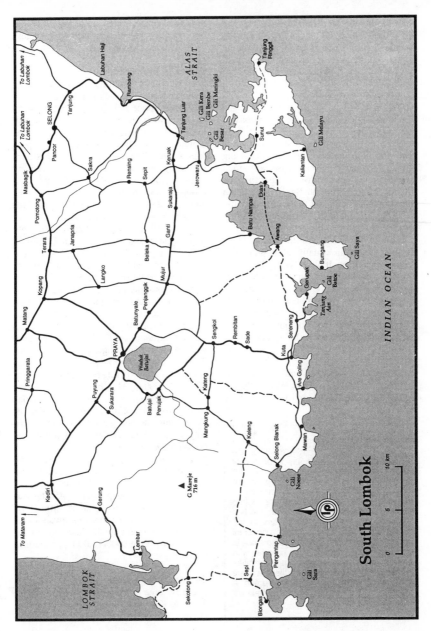

South Lombok

Kuno, an old thatched-roof mosque, tops the hill around which the village houses cluster. A little further south is Sade, a traditional village which was apparently constructed just for tourists. Hawkers here give the hard sell.

KUTA BEACH

The best-known place on the south coast is Lombok's Kuta Beach (sometimes spelt Kute Beach), a magnificent stretch of white sand and blue sea with rugged hills rising around it, but not much else. It is a very small development with far fewer tourists than the famous (infamous?) Kuta Beach on Bali, but there are perennial plans to develop not only Kuta, but a whole stretch of the superb south coast with luxury hotels.

People flock to Kuta for the annual nyale fishing celebration, usually falling in February or March each year, with thousands sleeping on the beach, visiting celebrities and TV crews. For the rest of the year it's very quiet. There are surf breaks on the reefs round here, but they're still 'secret' – the local boatmen will take you out; the charter rate is about 40,000 to 50,000 rp per day.

Information

You can change money at Anda Cottages, but the rates are not very good. Wisma Segara Anak is a postal agent, and has a booking desk for Perama. There are phones in Kuta, but no wartel. There's a market twice a week, on Sunday and Wednesday.

Places to Stay & Eat

Most of Kuta's accommodation is along the beachfront road to the east of the village – all of a similar price and quality. The following are the low-season prices; expect to pay up to 5000 rp more if there are other tourists around. After the police station you pass *Rambutan*, with rooms at 6000 and 8000 rp, including tea and breakfast. The *Wisma Segara Anak* next door has a restaurant, and rooms at 4000/6000 rp for singles/doubles and bungalows at 12,000/15,000 rp including breakfast. Next along, *Pondok Sekar Kuning* (Yellow Flower Cottage) has double rooms downstairs for 5000 rp; and upstairs, with a nice view, for 10,000 rp; 10,000 and 15,000 rp in the high season. *Anda Cottages* (☎ 54836), next door, is the original place at Kuta. It has some pleasant trees and shrubs, a good restaurant with Indonesian, Chinese and Western dishes, and rooms from 8000 to 10,000 rp including breakfast.

A bit further along is *Florida Bungalows*, with good food and singles/doubles at 5000/8000 rp, and the *Rinjani Agung Beach Bungalows* with standard rooms from 12,000/15,000 rp. *Mascot* is only a place for a beer and music – it's almost a pub. Continue to the *Cockatoo Cottages & Restaurant*, the last place along the beach, with a nice restaurant area and rooms for 6000/10,000 rp, including breakfast.

Kuta Beach Bungalows are on the edge of the village at the west end of the beach, and charge 6000/8000 rp including breakfast. There are a few cheap, basic homestays in the village, and also the *Losmen Mata Hari*, near the market on the road to Mawan. It has a restaurant and nine small, clean rooms with private showers at 8000/10,000 rp, including breakfast.

Getting There & Away

There is some direct public transport from Sweta to Kuta for 1500 rp, or get a bemo to Praya (700 rp) and another from there to

---

Nyale Fishing Festival
On the 19th day of the 10th month in the Sasak calendar – generally February or March – hundreds of Sasaks gather on the beach. When night falls, fires are built and the young people sit around competing with each other in rhyming couplets called *pantun*. At dawn the next morning, the first nyale are caught, after which it is time for the Sasak teenagers to have fun. In a colourful procession boys and girls put out to sea – in different boats – and chase one another with lots of noise and laughter. The worm-like nyale fish are eaten raw or grilled, and are believed to have aphrodisiac properties. A good catch is a sign that the rice harvest will also be good. ■

Sengkol (500 rp) and a third down to Kuta (300 rp). Travel early or you may get stuck and have to charter a vehicle. Market day in Sengkol is Thursday, so there may be more transport then. Perama has connections to Kuta from Mataram and Senggigi (10,000 rp) and other tourist areas. Lombok Independent shuttle buses from Senggigi cost the same. If you have your own transport it's easy – the road is sealed all the way. The final five km to Kuta is a steep and winding descent which suddenly leaves the hills to arrive at the coast.

EAST OF KUTA

Quite good roads go round the coast to the east, passing a series of beautiful bays punctuated by headlands. There's some public transport, but you will see more with your own transport – a bicycle would be good. All the beachfront land has been bought by speculators for planned tourist resorts. **Segar Beach** is about two km east around the first headland, and you can easily walk there. An enormous rock about four km east of the village offers superb views across the countryside if you climb it early in the morning. The road goes five km east to **Tanjung Aan** (Cape Aan) where there are two classic beaches with very fine, powdery white sand. This is an area slated for upmarket resort hotels.

The road continues another three km to the fishing village of **Gerupak**, where there's a market on Tuesday. From there you can get a boat across the bay to **Bumgang**. Alternatively, turn north just before Tanjung Aan and go to **Sereneng**. Beyond here the road deteriorates, but you can get to **Awang** with a motorbike or on foot, then get a boat across to **Ekas**, a not-so-secret surf spot (see the East Lombok section below).

WEST OF KUTA

The road west of Kuta has recently been sealed as far as **Selong Blanak**, a lovely sandy bay. It doesn't follow the coast closely, but there are regular and spectacular ocean vistas. In between are more fine beaches like **Mawan**, **Tampa**, **Rowok** and **Mawi**, but you

have to detour to find them. They are all known to have surfing possibilities in the right conditions. *Selong Blanak Cottages* are by themselves, 1½ km north of Selong Blanak Beach, but the management provide transport to the beach and back for nothing, and to more isolated spots for a small price. It's a very nice place to stay, with a restaurant and a variety of rooms from 15,000/20,000 rp; 5000 rp more in high season. The road between Selong Blanak and Penujak is mostly sealed and quite passable.

The coast road continues west to **Pengantap**, but beyond there it gets very rough. In the dry season, with a motorbike or 4WD, you might make it through to **Blongas** and north to **Sekatong** and **Lembar**. Don't try it in the wet season.

East Lombok

For most travellers, the east coast is just Labuhan Lombok, the port for ferries to Sumbawa, but improvements to the road around the north coast make a round-the-island trip quite feasible. Similarly, the once-remote south-eastern peninsula is becoming more accessible, particularly to those with their own transport.

LABUHAN LOMBOK

There are fantastic views of mighty Gunung Rinjani from the east-coast port of Labuhan Lombok. From Khayangan Hill on the south side of the harbour you can look across the Alas Strait to Sumbawa. The town is a sleepy little place with concrete houses, thatched shacks and stilt bungalows in the Sulawesi style. Ferries to Sumbawa leave from the jetty on the east side of the bay.

If you're just passing through Labuhan Lombok on your way to Sumbawa there's no need to stay overnight. A bus from Sweta only takes a couple of hours, and there are regular ferries.

Places to Stay & Eat

In the village of Labuhan Lombok you can

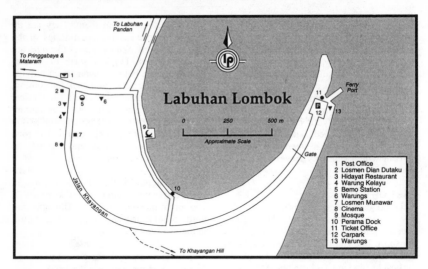

Labuhan Lombok

To Labuhan Pandan

To Pringgabaya & Mataram

Ferry Port

0   250   500 m
Approximate Scale

Jalan Khayangan

Gate

To Khayangan Hill

1 Post Office
2 Losmen Dian Dutaku
3 Hidayat Restaurant
4 Warung Kelayu
5 Bemo Station
6 Warungs
7 Losmen Munawar
8 Cinema
9 Mosque
10 Perama Dock
11 Ticket Office
12 Carpark
13 Warungs

stay at the very basic *Losmen Dian Dutaku*, on the main road coming into town, with rooms at 2600/3600 rp for singles/doubles. On Jalan Khayangan, the road that runs round to the ferry port, the *Losmen Munawar* is a better place with rooms at 3000/5500 rp; it's pretty basic but quite OK. There are a few warungs around the bemo terminal.

Getting There & Away

There are regular buses and bemos between Labuhan Lombok and Sweta. The 69-km trip costs about 2000 rp and should take a bit less than two hours. If you're zipping straight across Lombok and bound for Bali, you can take a bus via Sweta to Lembar. Other road connections go to Masbagik (1000 rp) and Kopang (1500 rp).

Regular passenger ferries leave Labuhan Lombok for Poto Tano (Sumbawa). According to one schedule they leave at 7, 8.30, 11 and 11.30 am, and 2.30, 4 and 5 pm, but at the harbour the staff said they depart every hour on the hour from 7 am to 6 pm. If you get a through bus from Sweta you won't have to worry about it; if you're travelling independently, try to get to the port before 11 am,

to make the 1½ hour crossing and the two-hour bus trip to Sumbawa Besar before dark.

The ferry costs 3100 rp in Ekonomi A (children 1600 rp), 2000 rp in Ekonomi B, 2500 rp for a bicycle, 3200 rp for a motorbike and 32,000 rp for a small car. There's a 300 rp harbour tax as well. Ekonomi A has air-con, which may be worth it – it can be a bloody hot trip! If you go on Ekonomi B, take drinking water and a hat, and arrive at the dock early to get a seat. The ferries can get very crowded, especially at times such as Ramadan when local people travel.

The boats depart from a new port on the east side of the harbour. It's about two or three km from the port to the town of Labuhan Lombok, on the road which skirts the south side of the bay. It will be too hot to walk, so take a bemo for 250 rp. The ticket office is beside the carpark. There are a couple of food stalls and warungs at the port, and food vendors come on board the boat.

NORTH OF LABUHAN LOMBOK

Foreigners are still a curiosity along this coast. Look for the giant trees about five km north of the harbour. **Pulu Lampur**, 14 km north, has a black sand beach and is popular with locals on Sundays and holidays.

Another few km to the north you can stay at the pleasant and secluded *Siola Cottages*, just before the village of **Labuhan Pandan**. They're by themselves in a coconut grove on the seashore, for 12,000/20,000 rp for singles/doubles with three meals; or just stop for a meal or a snack. From here you can charter a boat to the uninhabited islands of **Gili Sulat** and the **Gili Petangan** group, with lovely white beaches and good coral for snorkelling, although there are no facilities on them. A boat costs about 30,000 rp for up to five passengers, for a day trip out and back, with a few hours on an island. Take drinking water and a picnic lunch.

Perama has a camp on one of the islands, which is a stopover on its expensive Land-Sea Adventure tours. A short trip to the so-called **Perama Island** from Labuhan Lombok costs about 25,000 rp, including transport, snorkelling gear and three meals. It's best to arrange it with Perama in Mataram.

The road continues through **Sambelia** and **Sugian** to the north coast (see the next chapter). It's in the process of being sealed, and new bridges are under construction, but it's quite passable on a motorbike or Suzuki jeep, at least in the dry season. By public transport, you can get a bemo to Anyar (near Bayan) from Labuhan Lombok.

SOUTH OF LABUHAN LOMBOK

The capital of the East Lombok administrative district is **Selong**, which has some old buildings from the Dutch period. It has grown a lot in recent years, and there is an almost continuous urban strip from Pancor to Tanjung. Pancor is a bus and bemo terminal for the region, and you can change money at the BPD Bank. The *Wisma Erina*, on the east side of the main road, is not a bad place to stay.

On the coast is **Labuhan Haji**, accessible from Selong and Tanjung by bemo. Formerly a port for those departing on a *haji*, or pilgrimage to Mecca, the port buildings are abandoned and in ruins. The black sand beach here is a bit grubby but OK for swimming. There's accommodation at *Melewi's Beach Cottages*, on the beach just north of where the road from Selong comes in. Doubles are 20,000 rp including breakfast and other meals can be arranged. It doesn't appear to be a very well-run place, but it's isolated and has great views across to Sumbawa. It would be a good place to feed mosquitoes, so take precautions.

Further south you come to **Tanjung Luar**, one of Lombok's main fishing ports with a strong smell of fish and lots of Sulawesi-style houses on stilts. From there the road swings west to **Keruak**, and continues to **Sukaraja**, a very traditional Sasak-style village that tourists are welcome to visit.

Just west of Keruak there's a road south to Jerowaru (3.6 km) and the south-eastern peninsula, which was inaccessible until recently. This peninsula is sparsely populated with a harsh climate and scrubby vegetation, but the coastline has some interesting features. Turn right at Jerowaru and follow the road about 16 km to **Kaliantan** on the south coast, which has no places to stay, but there's a wonderful white beach and brilliant ocean views.

A sealed road branches west 6.4 km past Jerowaru – it gets pretty rough but eventually reaches **Ekas**. There's no accommodation there, but you can get a small boat to take you a few km south to *Laut Surga Cottages*. In the dry season you can get to the cottages by road, turning left after 5.2 km on the Ekas road and following the small blue signs. Laut Surga is mainly a place where surfers stay, but it has a lovely little beach. 'Laut Surga' means 'heaven sea', but it's hell to get to. You might make it to Ekas by bemo from Keruak, and you can also get there by boat from Awang (see the section on South Lombok).

On the east coast of the peninsula, **Tanjung Ringgit** has some large caves which, according to local legend, are home to a demonic giant. Tanjung Ringgit is a day's walk from the nearest road, or you might be able to charter a boat from Tanjung Luar. There's a cultivated pearl operation at **Sunut**, on the north coast of the peninsula.

North Lombok

AROUND THE NORTH COAST

It's possible to go by road around the north coast, though it's pretty rough between Bayan and Sambelia. It's very scenic, with a variety of landscapes and seascapes, but there are few tourists and even fewer facilities. You'll need a reliable motorbike, or a vehicle with good ground clearance – you're unlikely to make it in a normal car. You can do it on public transport, but east of Bayan that probably means standing in the back of a truck rather than sitting on a bus or a bemo. The road is being improved all the time, but the improvements are an obstacle in themselves, with long sections piled with stones or covered in loose gravel, and rough detours over creeks while the new bridge is under construction.

From Ampenan, a road goes north to Senggigi and Mangset, and now continues to Pemenang. It's a winding and wonderfully scenic coastal route, but it does not yet have a regular bemo service. The inland route going north from Mataram is a good road, through Lendang Bajur and the Pusuk Pass (Baun Pusuk) to Pemenang. It's also a scenic route, and it's worth stopping on the pass for the view, and the monkeys. A bemo for the 31-km trip is about 700 rp. Pemenang is where you turn off for Bangsal and the Gili Islands (see the next chapter), but you can keep going to Sira and the north coast.

Sira

Just a few km north of Pemenang, on the coast facing Gili Air, Sira has a white sand beach and good snorkelling on the nearby coral reef. There is a proposal to develop a big three-star hotel here but at the moment there's no accommodation.

Tanjung

This town is quite large and attractive, and has a big cattle market on Sundays. Further on is Karang Kates (Krakas for short) where freshwater bubbles from the sea bed 400 metres offshore – the people here collect their drinking water from the sea. From **Gondang** you can walk about four km to the Tiu Pupas Waterfall. There are a number of traditional villages south and west of here, where Wektu Telu is the prevailing religion. Tanjung is 45 km from Sweta and a bemo costs about 900 rp.

Bayan

Bayan, near the northernmost part of Lombok's coast, is the birthplace of the Wektu Telu religion, and also a home for traditional Muslims. The mosque here is 300 years old, and is said to be the oldest on Lombok. Bayan is at the the turn-off to Batu Koq and Senaru, the usual route for climbing Rinjani – see the next section for details. There are a couple of warungs here, and accommodation a few km away in Batu Koq.

There are several buses daily from Sweta to Bayan, the first leaving at around 9 am. It's a 79-km, three-hour trip, costing about 1800 rp, and you should try to get on an early bus. There may be more frequent bemos to intermediate places like Pemenang or Tanjung.

East of Bayan

The north-coast road continues about nine km to a junction. The road south goes to **Sembalun Bumbung** and **Sembalun Lawang**, traditional villages which can also be used as approaches to Rinjani.

Continue 35 km east on a winding road, through landscapes alternately lush and arid, to reach **Sambelia** and **Labuhan Pandan** on the east coast. There's one place to stay there (see the previous chapter) or you can continue to Labuhan Lombok.

GUNUNG RINJANI

Rinjani is the highest mountain on Lombok and, outside Irian Jaya, about the highest in Indonesia. At 3726 metres it soars above the island and dominates the landscape, but by

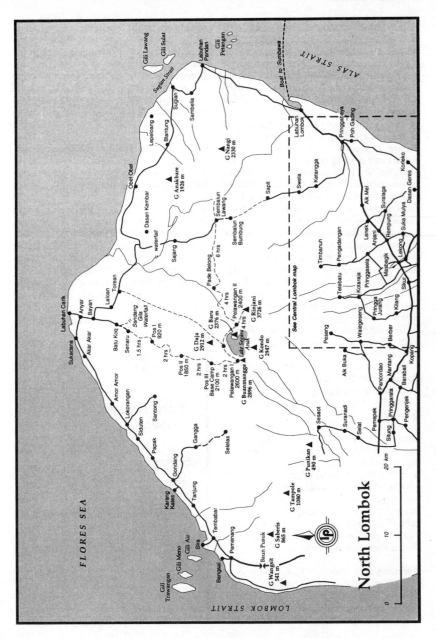

North Lombok

mid-morning on most days the summit is shrouded in cloud. The mountain is actually an active volcano – its last eruption was in 1901. There's a huge crater containing a large green crescent-shaped lake, Segara Anak, which is about six km across at its widest point. There's a series of natural hot springs on the north-eastern side of the caldera, a testimony to the fact that Rinjani is still geologically active. These springs, known as Kokok Putih, are said to have remarkable healing powers, particularly for skin diseases. The lake is 600 vertical metres below the caldera rim, and in the middle of its curve there's a new cone, Gunung Baru (also known as Gunung Barujari), only a couple of hundred years old.

Both the Balinese and Sasaks revere Rinjani. To the Balinese it is equal to Gunung Agung, a seat of the gods, and many Balinese make a pilgrimage here each year. In a ceremony called pekelan the people throw jewellery into the lake and make offerings to the spirit of the mountain. Some Sasaks make several pilgrimages a year – full moon is the favourite time for paying their respects to the mountain and curing their ailments by bathing in its hot springs.

The main approaches to Rinjani are from Batu Koq and Senaru, on a northern ridge, or from Sembalun Lawang to the east.

Batu Koq

Batu Koq is the usual starting point for a climb up Gunung Rinjani. There are several homestays in the village, some of which have superb views over the valley to the east, and up to the rim of Rinjani. They cost around 8000/12,000 rp for singles/doubles with a private bathroom. Most of them have places to eat and there are a few which sell biscuits, canned fish, eggs, chocolate and other food you can take trekking. There are also places to rent equipment for trekking.

Sendang Gila Waterfall Make sure you go to this magnificent waterfall. It's a very pleasant half-hour walk, partly through forest, and partly alongside an irrigation canal which follows the contour of the hill, occasionally disappearing into tunnels where the cliffs are too steep. Watch for the sleek black monkeys swinging through the trees. Splash around near the waterfall – the water cascades down the mountain slope so fast that it's strong enough to knock the wind out of you. A much longer walk takes you through more forest to the upper part of the falls.

Getting There & Away There are bemos from Bayan to Batu Koq for about 700 rp. There are even Perama buses going direct to Batu Koq from Mataram.

Senaru

Perched high in the foothills of Rinjani, about seven km from Bayan, the small, traditional village of Senaru has an air of untainted antiquity. The villagers of Senaru did not encounter Westerners until the 1960s. Before then they lived completely isolated from the rest of the world. Even though

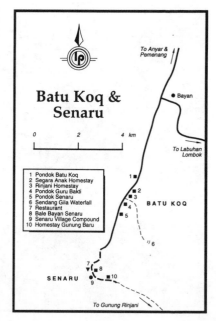

Batu Koq & Senaru

To Anyar & Pemenang

• Bayan

0   2   4 km

To Labuhan Lombok

1 Pondok Batu Koq
2 Segara Anak Homestay
3 Rinjani Homestay
4 Pondok Guru Bakti
5 Pondok Senaru
6 Sendang Gila Waterfall
7 Restaurant
8 Bale Bayan Senaru
9 Senaru Village Compound
10 Homestay Gunung Baru

BATU KOQ

SENARU

To Gunung Rinjani

trekkers pass by all the time and are welcome to visit, it still seems so different and so timeless that it retains a sense of isolation, as if modern civilisation is a world away. The village is surrounded by a high wooden paling fence and comprises about 20 thatched wooden huts, some on stilts, others low to the ground. As you enter there is a visitors book and a donation tin, and a notice indicating how proceeds are used to benefit the village. For all its quaintness, it is obviously a poor village, and you should give something, though no-one hassles you at all.

This is as close as you'll get to Rinjani in a vehicle, and there are a couple of places to stay. The *Bale Bayan Senaru* has quite adequate rooms for 5000/10,000 rp, including breakfast, and there's a warung opposite. The basic *Homestay Gunung Baru* asks the same amount, and it's a bit higher up the ridge so you can see the sunset as well as the sunrise, and be 500 metres closer to the summit when you start walking. It's only a km or so from Batu Koq to Senaru so you can easily walk.

Sembalun Bumbung & Sembalun Lawang

High up on the eastern slopes of Gunung Rinjani is the cold but beautiful Sembalun Valley. The inhabitants of the valley claim descent from the Hindu Javanese, and a relative of one of the Majapahit rulers is said to be buried here. While it seems unlikely that Java ever controlled Lombok directly, similarities in music, dance and language suggest that Lombok may have come under some long-lasting Javanese influence several hundred years ago.

In the valley are the traditional Sasak villages of Sembalun Bumbung and Sembalun Lawang. It's only a 45-minute walk from one village to the other and there are many pleasant walks in the surrounding area. From Sembalun Bumbung there is a steep 1½-hour climb to a saddle with a beautiful panoramic view.

In Sembalun Lawang you may be able to stay with the kepala desa for about 5000 rp per person. Accommodation with the kepala

desa in Sembalun Bumbung is more basic. Bring food and camping gear for your trek as none is available here.

Getting There & Away From the north-coast road nine km east of Bayan, a rough but usable road climbs to Sembalun Lawang and continues to Sembalun Bumbung. There may be public transport up this road but there won't be much and you'll have to start early.

From the south you can reach Sembalun Bumbung in a beautiful five-hour walk from Sapit, through coffee, paw paw, rice and vegetable fields, then through forest. Sapit has bemo connections to Pringgabaya on the main east-west road.

Climbing Rinjani

Many people climb up to Rinjani's crater lake every year. They are mostly local people making a pilgrimage or seeking the curative powers of the hot springs. Many foreign visitors make the climb too, though very few people go the extra 1700 or so metres to the very summit of Rinjani. Even the climb to the crater lake is not to be taken lightly. Don't try it during the wet season as the tracks will be slippery and very dangerous; in any case you would be lucky to see any more than mist and cloud. During the full moon it will be very crowded.

There are a few possibilities, from a quick dash to the rim and back, to a four or five-day trek around the summit. Most visitors stay in Batu Koq or Senaru, climb from there to the crater lake and return the same way. The other main route is from Sembalun Lawang on the eastern side. The northern route is more easily accessible and has facilities for trekkers.

The people at the Wisma Triguna losmen in Ampenan can give good information about the climb. For a price (over US$100) they will organise the complete trip for you – food, tent, sleeping bag and a guide. But if you don't come at that they can tell you how to go about it on your own. A number of agencies in Mataram or Senggigi organise guided all-inclusive treks, from US$100 and upwards. A sleeping bag and tent are abso-

in), tea, biscuits or bread, some tins of fish or meat (and a can opener!), onions, fruit, and anything else that keeps your engine running. Take plenty of water; the bottles you buy it in are adequate containers. Don't forget matches, a torch (flashlight), and some cigarettes – even if you don't smoke, the guides really appreciate them. It's better to buy most of these supplies in Mataram or the supermarket in Senggigi as there's more choice, but you can get a fair range in Batu Koq.

Environmental Care A lot of rubbish is dropped along the route. The only reason it doesn't look worse is that student groups from the university come and clean it up every few months. Bring all rubbish out. Don't try to burn it or bury it. The other problem is firewood – there's none left up by the lake, so people have burned the floors of the shelters and are now destroying live trees. Bring a stove and fuel for cooking, and enough clothing to keep warm.

Northern Route This is the most popular route taken by visitors, ascending via Batu Koq and Senaru and returning the same way. It takes about three days. The walking times given are pretty slow.

Day 1 Depart Batu Koq at about 8 am for Senaru (altitude 600 metres). From there it's about 1½ hours to the first post, Pos I (920 metres), then another two hours to Pos II (1850 metres), where there is a hut and a water supply (sterilise the water). A further two hours brings you to the base camp at Pos III (2100 metres), where there is also water. The climb is relatively easy going through dappled forest, with the quiet broken only by the occasional bird, animal, bell or wood-chopper. At base camp pitch your tent, collect wood and water and, if you have enough energy left, climb up to the clearing and watch the sunset. The ground is rock hard at base camp and it's very cold.

Day 2 Set off very early, to arrive at the crater rim for sunrise. It takes about two hours to

lutely essential, but you can rent them in Batu Koq.

Guides You can do the trek from Batu Koq without a guide, but in some places there's a number of trails which branch off and you could get lost. Guides can also be informative, good company, and act as porters, cooks and water collectors. When you're doing this walk with a guide, make sure you set your own pace – some guides climb Rinjani as often as 20 or 30 times a year and positively gallop up the slopes! A guide will cost about 15,000 rp per day, porters about 10,000 rp per day. From Sembalun Lawang you'll definitely need a guide; again about 15,000 rp per day.

Equipment There are some very crude shelters on the way but don't rely on them. In Batu Koq you can rent a two or three-person tent (12,500 rp for up to five days), a stove and cooking gear (2500 rp) and a sleeping bag (10,000 rp). You could probably get the whole lot for about 20,000 rp for three days. Check the equipment before you take it. It gets cold, so bring thick woollen socks, a sweater and a groundsheet as well.

Food & Supplies You need to take enough food to last three days – including food for your guide. Take rice, instant noodles, sugar, coffee, eggs (get a container to carry them reach Pelawangan I, on the rim of the volcano, at an altitude of 2600 metres. Rinjani is covered in dense forest up to 2000 metres, but at around this height the vegetation changes from thick stands of mahogany and teak trees to the odd stand of pine. As you get closer to the rim the pines become sparser and the soil becomes rubbly and barren. The locals cut down the mahogany and teak trees with axes and then carry the huge logs down the steep slopes, by hand!

Monkeys, wild pigs, deer and the occasional snake inhabit the forest. Once you get above the forest and up to the clearing the going is hot as there's not much shade – the land here is harsh and inhospitable – but you have superb views across to Bali and Sumbawa.

From the rim of the crater, it takes up to six hours to get down to Segara Anak and around to the hot springs, though some people say it takes as little as two. The descent from the rim into the crater is quite dangerous – for most of the way the path down to the lake clings to the side of the cliffs and is narrow and meandering. Watch out for rubble – in certain spots it's very hard to keep your footing. Close to the lake a thick forest sweeps down to the shore. There are several places to camp along this lake, but if you head for the hot springs there are many more alternatives. The track along the lake is also narrow and very slippery – be careful and take it slowly. There are several species of small water bird on the lake, and it has been stocked with fish over the last few years.

After setting up camp at the lake, it's time to soak your weary body in the springs and recuperate. It's not as cold here as it is at base camp, but it is damp and misty from the steaming springs. Even with hundreds of local people around, it can still be an eerie place. Watch your step on the paths – although this is a holy place, some people have few inhibitions or qualms about relieving themselves when and wherever they need to.

Day 3 Start early to do the hard climb back to the crater rim before it gets too hot. Then it's all downhill to Senaru. It's a full day's walk, between eight and 10 hours, and you'll arrive back in Batu Koq in the afternoon. The last bemo down the mountain from Senaru leaves at 4 pm.

Eastern Route You can climb to the crater of Rinjani directly from Sembalun Lawang, but you must come prepared with a sleeping bag, tent, food and other supplies. You can hire a guide in Sembalun Lawang – and you'll need one to get through the maze of trails as you climb west from the village. It will take about six hours to get to the village of Pade Belong, and another four hours to get to Pelawangan II on the crater rim at 2400 metres. Near here there's a crude shelter and a trail junction, with one track climbing southwards to the summit of Rinjani and the other heading west, to much more comfortable camp sites near the hot springs or the lake, about four hours away.

Going the other way, you can get from the crater rim down to Sembalun Lawang in about seven hours. It's quite possible to ascend by the northern route and descend by the eastern route, or vice versa, but you'll have to work out how to get yourself, and particularly your guide, back to your starting point.

A Night Climb If you travel light and climb fast, you can reach the crater rim from Senaru in about six hours or even less – it's an 800-metre altitude gain in 10 km, approximately. With a torch and some moonlight, and/or a guide, set off at midnight and you'll be there for sunrise. Coming back takes about four hours, so you'll be down in time for lunch. Take lots of snack food and a litre of water.

Other Routes on Rinjani You can climb up to the crater from Torean, a small village just south-east of Bayan. The trail follows Sungai Kokok Putih, the stream that flows from Lake Segara and the hot springs, but it's hard to find; you'll need a guide.

You can also climb the south side of Rinjani, from either Sesaot or Tetebatu.

Either route will involve at least one night camping in the jungle, and you may not see any views at all until you get above the tree line. Again, a guide is essential.

Gunung Baru, the 'new' cone in the middle of lake Segara Anak, may look tempting, but it's a very dangerous climb. The track around the lake to the base of Baru is narrow, and people have drowned after slipping off the it. The climb itself is over a very loose surface, and if you start sliding or falling there is nothing to stop you and nothing to hang on to.

To the Very Top The path to the summit branches off the Sembalun Lawang track near Pelawangan II. From the shelter there, allow four hours to reach the summit. Start early in the morning because you have to get to the top within an hour or so of sunrise if you want to see more than mist and cloud.

The first two days were pretty much as described [in the section on the Northern route], but on the third day we warmed up in the springs before making a three-hour climb to a shelter by the path just before the junction with the summit route. This shelter is just a hollow scooped out of the ground and lined with dry grass. A few old sheets of iron serve as a roof. It fits three people, or maybe an intimate four.

The next morning we watched the sun rise over Sumbawa from the junction of the paths, before starting the final ascent. The view from the rim is great, but it's nothing compared with the view from the very top! From the top, you look down into the crater which fills up with 'cotton wool' cloud streaming through the gap in the crater wall at the hot springs. In the distance, you look over Bali in one direction and Sumbawa in the other.

It's a difficult three-hour climb from the shelter; the air gets thinner and the terrain is horrible to walk on. It's powdery to start with, then you find loose stones on a steep slope (offering little support for your weight). It's a case of climbing one step up, then sliding two-thirds of a step back down, and the peak always looks closer than it is! Climbing without strong-toed shoes or boots would be masochistic.

Richard Tucker, England

The Gili Islands

Off the north-west coast of Lombok are three small, coral-fringed islands – Gili Air, Gili Meno and Gili Trawangan – each with superb, white sandy beaches, clear water, coral reefs, brilliantly coloured fish and the best snorkelling on Lombok. Although known to travellers as the 'Gili Islands', *gili* actually means 'island', so this is not a local name. There are lots of other gilis around the coast of Lombok.

A few years ago, descendants of Bugis immigrants were granted leases to establish coconut plantations. The main economic activities are fishing, raising livestock, and growing corn, tapioca, peanuts and, of course, coconuts. As tourists started to visit Lombok, many people on the Gilis found the most profitable activity was 'picking white coconuts' – a local expression for providing services to tourists.

The islands have become enormously popular with visitors, especially young Europeans, who come for the very simple pleasures of sun, snorkelling and socialising. It's cheap, and the absence of cars, motor-bikes and hawkers adds greatly to the pleasure of staying on the Gilis.

Their very popularity may be a problem, as numbers sometimes exceed the available rooms and put pressure on the island environments, especially the supply of fresh water and the capacity of septic systems to cope with waste. The local population is aware of environmental issues, and is trying to retain the unspoilt quality of the islands while improving the facilities, but there is always the temptation to put up just one more bungalow.

Big business interests are trying to cash in on the popularity of the Gili Islands. There is a proposal to build a luxury resort on the mainland at Sira, and golf courses on Gili Air and Gili Trawangan. This would effectively destroy the simple charm that makes these islands so attractive to current visitors, and would have substantial environmental implications, like a pipeline from the mainland, over the coral reefs, to supply fresh water for the fairways. The proposal is not supported by many of the local people who lease the land, on which they've built tourist bungalows and restaurants.

In 1992 a number of bungalows on Trawangan were closed down and/or relocated by the government authorities; it's not clear whether this was to make way for a grandiose development project, or because the bungalows contravened the lease conditions, or because they did not meet environmental and health standards.

The owners were told to vacate the leased land, and offered new sites and compensation (the adequacy of the compensation is another question). Some of the owners did not move and, after repeated requests, the authorities closed down their bungalows by the simple but effective means of cutting the legs off with chainsaws.

Most of the businesses have now been re-established at the south end of Gili Trawangan, and others are to be set up at the north end, but not right on the beach – the plan seems to be to build the golf course in a 'U' shape around them. The changes to date have left the northern end of the beach looking bare and desolate, and the southern end crowded with shoulder to shoulder bungalows and restaurants. A few bungalows on the south-west side of Gili Air are also to be removed to make way for the golf course.

Other problems in this paradise include occasional outbreaks of illness – bouts of food poisoning, typhoid and cholera have been reported, and the islands are definitely in a malaria risk area.

In 1993, 15 or 20 bungalows were destroyed in a fire, apparently caused by a candle left burning in a bungalow – be careful with candles and mosquito coils.

Avoiding Offence

The islanders are Muslims, and visitors should respect their sensibilities. In particular, topless (for women) or nude sunbathing is offensive to them, although they won't say so directly. Away from the beach, it is polite for both men and women to cover their shoulders and knees.

Information

You can change money and make inter-

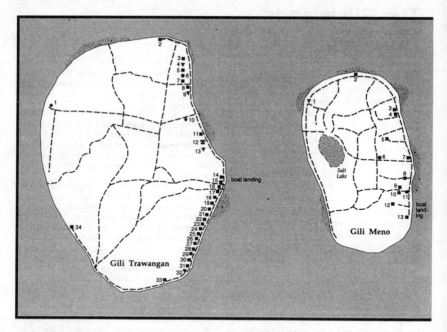

GILI TRAWANGAN

1 Navigation Light
2 Nusa Tiga
3 Coral Beach *
4 Borobudur Restaurant *
5 Good Heart *
6 Mountain View *
7 Creative *
8 Sudi Nampir
9 Excellent Restaurant
10 Blue Marlin Dive Centre
11 Mountain View
12 Wartel
13 Borobudur Restaurant
14 Danau Hijau Bungalows
15 Fantasi Bungalows
16 Pak Majid's
17 Sandy Beach Bungalows
18 Dua Sekawan I
19 Paradise Cottages
20 Damai Indah
21 Rudy's Pub & Cottages
22 Dua Sekawan II
23 Trawangan Cottages

24 Halim
25 Holiday Inn
26 Pasir Putih
27 Homestay Makmur
28 Melati Losmen
29 Majestic Cottages
30 Rainbow Cottages
31 Mawar Accommodation
32 Simple Food
33 Pondok Santi
34 Mawar II

GILI MENO

1 Good Heart Restaurant
2 Blue Coral Bungalows
3 Pondok Meno
4 Zoraya Pavillion
5 Casa Blanca
6 Pondok Wisata
7 Janur Indah Bungalows
8 Matahari Bungalows
9 Fantastic Cottages
10 Rawa Indah
11 Malia's Child Bungalows

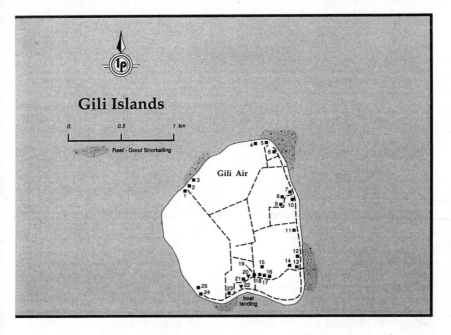

Gili Islands

0.   0.5   1 km

Reef - Good Snorkelling

Gili Air

boat landing

12	Gazebo Hotel
13	Kontiki Cottages & Restaurant
	GILI AIR
1	Hink Bungalows *
2	Muksin Cottages *
3	Rose Cottages
4	Lombok Indah
5	Han's Bungalows & Restaurant
6	Gusung Indah Bungalows
7	Fantastic Bungalows
8	Coconut Cottages
9	Gili Air Cottages
10	Ozzy's Shop
11	Bulan Madu
12	Gita Gili Sunrise

13	Corner Cottages
14	Nusa Tiga Bungalows
15	Bupati's Cottages
16	Sederhana Losmen
17	Resorta Cottages
18	Garden Cottages
19	Pondok Gili Air
20	Go Go Pub
21	Bamboo Cottages
22	Fanta Pub
23	Gili Indah Cottages & Perama Office
24	Lucky Cottages *
25	Salabose Cottages *

* These businesses will be re-established in the positions indicated

national phone calls at any of the islands. Most places have electricity, sometimes from their own generators, but the supply is sometimes erratic and usually stops at about 10 pm. There are small shops with a bare minimum of supplies, second-hand books and some handcrafts, clothing and souvenirs.

Activities

You don't have to be totally inactive. A few places rent paddle boards (called canoes) – some boards even have a window so you can see the coral. Some windsurfers are available on Trawangan and Meno, and you can rent a boat to go fishing.

Diving The coral round the islands is good for snorkelling, but much has been damaged by fish bombing. Ask locally to find the best spots, most of which you can reach from the shore. For scuba divers, the visibility is fair to good (best in the dry season), and there is some very good coral reef accessible by boat. Marine life includes some turtles, rays, sharks (harmless) and a giant clam. There are a number of scuba diving operations, some more reliable than others. Albatross is the longest-established outfit, and can take out certified divers. Blue Marlin Dive Centre, on Gili Trawangan, is the only one with an instructor qualified to PADI standards, and can offer a full range of diving courses from beginners to advanced level. A complete PADI open-water course costs about US$290.

Accommodation & Food

Most places to stay come out of a standard mould – you get a plain little bungalow on stilts, with a small verandah out the front and a concrete bathroom block out the back. (It's very easy to see which bungalows have their own bathroom.) Inside, there will be one or two beds with mosquito nets.

Accommodation prices are pretty well fixed, though there is some cost-cutting in the low season and some places charge more because they're a bit better, or think they are. The low-season price is about 9000/15,000 rp for singles/doubles with bed and breakfast only, or 15,000/22,000 rp with three meals. Add 2000/5000 rp for the high season. Most places provide only bed & breakfast these days; you can order dinner as an extra, or eat somewhere else. Rooms with shared bathroom are cheaper, but becoming rare.

Getting There & Away

From Ampenan or the airport, you can get to one of the islands and be horizontal on the beach within a couple of hours. Start with a short bemo ride north to Rembiga (about 200 rp), then a scenic bus trip to Pemenang (600 rp). Alternatively, you may be able to get a bemo from Sweta direct to Pemenang for about 700 rp. From there it's a km or so off the main road to the harbour at Bangsal, 200 rp by cidomo.

There's a small information office at Bangsal Harbour which charges the official fares out to the islands – 900 rp to Gili Air, 1000 rp to Gili Meno and 1200 rp to Gili Trawangan. It's a matter of sitting and waiting until there's a full boat load, about 20 people. If you have almost that number waiting, the boat will leave if you can pay the extra fares between you. As soon as you do this, you'll be amazed at how many local people appear from nowhere to fill the boat. Try to get to Bangsal by 10 am. It's not an unpleasant place to hang around while you're waiting for a boat, and the shaded warungs like the *Parahiangan Coffee House* have good food and coffee. You can charter a whole boat to any of the islands, or any combination, but it's expensive – 60,000 rp to visit all three islands.

Perama shuttle buses go from Mataram or Senggigi to Bangsal (5000 rp) and the Gili Islands (about 10,000 rp, including the boat). Lombok Independent has a slightly cheaper service – around 6500 rp from Senggigi.

Getting Around

There is now a shuttle service between the islands, so you can stay on one and have a look, or a snorkel, around the others. The boat fares for 'island hopping' are 4000 rp between Gili Air and Gili Trawangan; 3000 rp between Gili Meno and either of the other two islands. They do two runs a day, one between 9 and 10 am, and the other between 3 and 4 pm.

On the islands themselves there are cidomos trotting round the tracks (500 rp is the usual charge). If you're in a hurry (almost inconceivable on the Gilis) you can rent a bicycle, but the main mode of transport is walking.

GILI AIR

Gili Air is the closest island to the mainland and has the largest population, with about 1000 people. There are beaches around most of the island and a small village at the southern end. Homes and small farms are dotted amongst the palm trees, along with a few losmen and a couple of 'pubs'. Because the buildings are so scattered, the island has a pleasant, rural character and is delightful to wander around. There are plenty of other people to meet, but if you stay in one of the more isolated places, socialising is optional. Gili Indah Cottages is where you'll find the Perama office, telephone office, and moneychanger. You can also change money at Gita Gili Sunrise, which may give a better rate.

Places to Stay & Eat

Most of the accommodation is scattered round the southern end of the island at the harbour, though there are losmen near the east, north and west coasts. Most of the places, about 15 of them, charge the standard rates (9000/15,000 rp with breakfast) and are so similar that it seems hardly fair to mention any in particular. Pick one that appeals to you in a location you like, or one that's been recommended by other travellers.

Coconut Cottages are very nice with great food, and only slightly more expensive than average. *Gili Indah* (☎ 36341) is the biggest place on Gili Air, with rooms from US$7/10 up to US$20/30 for very nice, spacious, pavilion-style rooms. Up north, at the other end of the island, *Han's Bungalows* are above average in price at 15,000/20,000 rp, though they do have a beautiful outlook and a swimming pool is planned. (Often spelled without the apostrophe, these bungalows are popular with German visitors though the owner, Han, is actually a local.) *Bulan Madu* has a few very attractive and comfortable rooms, but it's much pricier at 50,000/60,000 rp.

GILI MENO

Gili Meno, the middle island, has the smallest population – about 500. It is also the quietest of the islands, with the fewest tourists. There's a salt lake in the middle of the island which produces salt in the dry season and mosquitoes in the wet season. The mozzies are probably no worse than in other places at that time of year, but the usual precautions are called for – mosquito net, repellent, long sleeves and long pants around dusk. You can change money and make phone calls at the Gazebo Hotel.

Places to Stay & Eat

The accommodation here is mostly on the east beach, with a few places which are pretty upmarket by Gili standards. The *Zoraya Pavillion* (☎ 33801) has a variety of rooms from 15,500 to 40,000 rp a double, with various water sports and a tennis court. The *Gazebo Hotel* (☎ 35795) has tastefully decorated Bali-style bungalows with private bathrooms, air-con and electricity (if it's working). It costs about US$45 a double for bed & breakfast. Anyone can eat in the fancy balcony restaurant. *Casa Blanca* seems overpriced at US$25/30, even with its tiny swimming pool. *Kontiki* (☎ 32824) has both standard price and more expensive rooms – look at them first to make sure they're worth the extra rupiah. The other half-dozen places have pretty much standard Gili Islands bungalows (perhaps a little more spacious than on the other two islands) and charge standard prices.

GILI TRAWANGAN

The largest island, with a local population of about 700, Trawangan also has the most visitors and the most facilities, and a reputation as the 'party island' of the group. The accommodation and restaurants/bars are all along the south and south-east coast beaches, where some of them were forced to shift. It's a compact layout, perhaps a little too compact, though there are a couple of places away from the others. Some places may be rebuilt on the north-east of the island, but not right on the beach. There's a wartel in the middle of the beach strip. Lots of places will change money, but you'll get a better rate on the mainland. The Blue Marlin Dive Centre will give a cash advance on your credit card. You can rent windsurfers here too.

A hill at the south of the island has traces of two Japanese WW II gun emplacements. At sunset, it's a good place to enjoy the view across the straits to Bali's Gunung Agung. The sunrise over Gunung Rinjani is also impressive; one islander described Trawangan's three main attractions as 'sunrise, sunset and sunburn'!

Places to Stay & Eat

The accommodation and prices here are even more standardised than on the other islands. Typical basic bungalows cost 10,000/15,000/20,000 rp for singles/doubles/triples, with breakfast and private mandi. *Pondok Santi* is a bit more expensive, but probably worth the extra. Pick a place you like the look of (some have prettier gardens), or one recommended by a recent visitor, or go with one of the friendly people who will meet you when the boat comes in.

Most of the places to stay also serve food, but there's a few convivial restaurants which are more like bars in the evening. There's usually music and dancing in at least one of them. *Pasih Putih* and *Halim* are reputed to have the best food.

Glossary

adat – tradition; manners and customs

air panas – hot springs

aling aling – guard wall behind the entrance gate to a Balinese family compound. Demons can only travel in straight lines so the aling aling prevents them from coming straight in through the front entrance.

alun alun – main public square of a town or village

angklung – portable form of the gamelan used in processions as well as in other festivals and celebrations

anjing – dog

arak – colourless, distilled palm wine; the local firewater

arja – refined form of Balinese theatre, like an opera

Arjuna – a hero of the *Mahabharata* epic and a popular temple gate guardian image

bahasa – language

bale – house, building, pavilion

bale banjar – communal meeting place of the village banjar (a sort of community club which organises activities including the gamelan)

bale gede – reception room or guesthouse in the home of a wealthy Balinese

bale kambang – floating pavilion; a building surrounded by a moat

Bali Aga – the 'original' Balinese; these people managed to resist the new ways brought in with the Majapahit migration

balian – see dukun

banjar – local division of a village represented by all the married adult males

banyan – holy tree; see waringin

bapak – father; also a polite form of address to any older man

baris – warrior dance

Barong – mythical lion-dog creature, star of the Barong & Rangda dance and champion of the good

Barong Landung – literally 'tall barong', these enormous puppet figures are seen at the annual festival on Pulau Serangan

Barong Tengkok – name for the portable gamelan used for wedding processions and circumcision ceremonies on Lombok

Baruna – god of the sea

Batara – title used to address a deceased spirit, particularly that of an important person

batik – process of printing fabric by coating part of the cloth with wax, then dyeing it and melting the wax out. The waxed part is not coloured and repeated waxings and dyeings build up a pattern. Although a Javanese craft, the Balinese also produce batik.

Bayu – god of the air

Bedaulu, Dalem – legendary last ruler of the Pejeng dynasty

bemo – popular local transport on Bali and Lombok, traditionally a small pick-up truck with a bench seat down each side in the back. Small minibuses are now commonly used as bemos.

bensin – petrol (gasoline)

Bima – another hero of the *Mahabharata*, the biggest and strongest of the Pandava brothers

bioskop – cinema

Boma – son of the earth, a temple guardian figure

Brahma – the creator, one of the trinity of Hindu gods

brahmana – the caste of priests and highest of the Balinese castes; although all priests are brahmanas, not all brahmanas are priests

brem – rice wine

bu – shortened form of ibu (mother)

bukit – hill; also the name of the southern peninsula of Bali

bupati – government official in charge of a district (kabupaten)

buta – demon or evil spirit

camat – government official in charge of a subdistrict (kecamatan)

candi – shrine, originally of Javanese design; also known as prasada

candi bentar – split gateway entrance to a temple

caste – the Balinese caste system is nowhere near as important or firmly entrenched as India's caste system. There are four castes: three branches of the 'nobility' (Brahmana, Wesia, Satria) and the common people (Sudra).

catur yoga – ancient manuscript on religion and cosmology

cidomo – on Lombok, pony cart with car wheels

Cokorda – male title of a person of the Satria caste

dalang – puppet master and storyteller in a wayang kulit performance; a man of varied skills and considerable endurance

danau – lake

desa – village

dewa – deity or supernatural spirit

dewi – goddess

Dewi Danau – goddess of the lakes

Dewi Sri – goddess of rice

dokar – pony cart; still a popular form of local transport in many towns and larger villages throughout Bali – known as a cidomo on Lombok

dukun – 'witch doctor', actually a faith healer and herbal doctor

Durga – goddess of death and destruction and consort of Shiva

durian – fruit that smells like hell and tastes like heaven

Gajah Mada – famous Majapahit prime minister who defeated the last great king of Bali and extended Majapahit power over the island

Galungan – great Balinese festival, an annual event in the 210-day Balinese wuku calendar

gambang – gamelan orchestra from Jakarta

gamelan – traditional Balinese orchestra, usually percussion with large xylophones and gongs

Ganesh – Shiva's elephant-headed son

gang – alley or footpath

Garuda – mythical man-bird creature, the vehicle of Vishnu and the modern symbol of Indonesia

gili – small island (Lombok)

goa – cave

gringsing – rare double ikat woven cloth (made only in the Bali Aga village of Tenganan)

gunung – mountain

gusti – polite title for members of the Wesia caste

Hanuman – monkey god who plays a major part in the *Ramayana*

harga biasa – standard price

harga turis – inflated price for tourists

homestay – small, family-run losmen

ibu – mother; also polite form of address to any older woman

Ida Bagus – honourable title for a male Brahman

iders-iders – long scrolls painted in the wayang style, used as temple decorations

ikat – cloth where a pattern is produced by dyeing the individual threads before weaving. Ikat is usually of the warp or the weft, although the rare 'double ikat' technique is found in Tenganan (see gringsing).

Indra – king of the gods

jalan – street

jalan jalan – to walk

jidur – large cylindrical drums played throughout Lombok

jukung – see prahu

kabupaten – districts (known as regencies during Dutch rule)

kain – wraparound article of clothing which resembles a sarong

kaja – Balinese 'north' which is always towards the mountains. The most important shrines are always on the kaja side of a temple; see also kelod.

kala – demonic face often seen over temple gateways. The kalas' outstretched hands are to stop evil spirits from entering, although they are themselves evil spirits.

kali – rivulet

kampung – district, neighbourhood

kantor – office

kawi – classical Javanese, the language of poetry

kawin – married

kebaya – Chinese, long-sleeved blouse with low neckline and embroidered edges

kecamatan – subdistrict

kelod – opposite of kaja; the side of a temple oriented away from the mountains and toward the sea

kemban – woman's breast cloth

kepala desa – village headman

kepeng – old Chinese coins with a hole in the centre; these were the everyday currency during the Dutch era and can still be obtained quite readily from shops and antique dealers

ketupat – kind of sticky rice cooked in a banana leaf. Balinese Hindus and adherents of the Wektu Telu religion pelt each other with ketupat in a mock war held annually at Lingsar on Lombok – the ceremony is to honour the rainy season.

kretek – Indonesian clove cigarettes; a very familiar odour on Bali

kris – traditional dagger, often held to have spiritual or magical powers

kulkul – hollow tree-trunk drum used to sound a warning or call meetings

Kuningan – holy day celebrated throughout Bali on the 10th day of the Galungan Festival

labuhan – harbour

lamak – long, woven palm-leaf strips hung in temples during festivals

lambung – rice barn with a round roof; an architectural symbol of Lombok

langse – rectangular decorative hangings used in palaces or temples

Legong – classic Balinese dance, performed by young girls who are also known as Legong.

leyak – evil spirit which can assume fantastic forms by the use of black magic

lontar – type of palm tree; traditional books were written on the dried leaves of lontar

losmen – small Balinese hotel, often family-run and similar in design to a traditional Balinese house

Mahabharata – one of the great Hindu holy books, tells of the battle between the Pandavas and the Korawas

main ski – surfing

Majapahit – last great Hindu dynasty in Java. The Majapahit were pushed out of Java by the rise of Islamic power, and moved into Bali.

malam – night

mandi – Indonesian 'bath' consisting of a large water tank from which you ladle water over yourself

manusa yadnya – ceremonies which mark the various stages of Balinese life from before birth to after cremation

mapadik – marriage by request, as opposed to ngrorod

meru – multi-roofed shrines in Balinese temples. The name meru comes from the Hindu holy mountain Mahameru

naga – mythical snake-like creature

nasi – cooked rice

ngrorod – marriage by elopement; a traditional 'heroic' way of getting married on Bali

nusa – island

nyale – worm-like fish caught off Kuta Beach, Lombok; a special ceremony is held each year around February/March in honour of the first catch of the season

Nyepi – major annual festival in the Hindu saka calendar, this is a day of complete stillness and rest in preparation for a night of chasing out evil spirits

odalan – Balinese 'temple birthday' festival held in every temple annually (according to the weku calendar, ie once every 210 days)

ojek – motorbike which carries paying pillion passengers

padi – growing rice plant; hence the English paddy field

padmasana – temple shrine, a throne for the sun god Surya

paduraksa – covered gateway to a temple

paibon – shrine in a state temple for the royal ancestors

pak – shortened form of bapak (father)

palan palan – slowly

palinggihs – temple shrines consisting of a

simple little throne. Palinggihs are intended as resting places for the gods when they come down for festivals.

pandanus – palm plant used in weaving mats etc

pande – blacksmiths; they are treated somewhat like a caste in their own right

pantai – beach

pantun – ancient Malay poetical verse in rhyming couplets

pasar – market

pasar malam – night market

patih – prime minister

pedanda – high priest

pekembar – umpire or referee in the traditional Sasak trial of strength known as peresehan

pemangku – temple guardian and priest for temple rituals, not necessarily of high caste

pendet – formal offering dance performed at temple festivals

penjors – long bamboo poles with decorated ends arched over the road or pathway during festivals or ceremonies

perbekel – government official in charge of a village (desa)

peresehan – popular form of one-to-one physical combat peculiar to Lombok in which two men fight each other armed with a small hide shield for protection and a long rattan stave as a weapon

prahu – traditional Indonesian outrigger

prasada – see candi

pratima – figure of a god used as a 'stand-in' for the actual god's presence during a ceremony

propinsi – province; Indonesia has 27 propinsi, of which Bali is one

puputan – warrior's fight to the death; honourable but suicidal option when faced with an unbeatable enemy

pura – temple

pura dalem – temple of the dead

pura desa – temple of the village for everyday functions

pura puseh – temple of the village founders or fathers, honouring the village's origins

pura subak – temple of the rice growers association

puri – palace

puseh – place of origin

rajah – lord or prince

Ramadan – Muslim month of fasting

Ramayana – one of the great Hindu holy books, stories from which form the keystone of many Balinese dances and tales

Rangda – widow-witch who represents evil in Balinese theatre and dance

rattan – hardy, pliable vine used for handcrafts, furniture and weapons

rebab – bowed lute

rudat – traditional Sasak dance, with some Islamic influence

rumah makan – restaurant; literally 'house to eat'

saka – local Balinese calendar which is based on the lunar cycle; see also wuku

sakti – magical power

sampan – small sailing vessel used primarily for island hops or short journeys

sanghyang – trance dance in which the dancers impersonate a local village god

Sanghyang Widi – Balinese supreme being; this deity is never actually worshipped as such; one of the 'three in one' or lesser gods stand in

Sasak – native of Lombok; also the language

satria – second Balinese caste

sawah – individual rice field

sebel – polluted, spiritually unclean

selat – strait

Shiva – the creator and destroyer, one of the three great Hindu gods

sirih – betel nut, chewed as a mild narcotic

songket – silver or gold-threaded cloth, hand woven using a floating weft technique

subak – village association that organises rice terraces and shares out water for irrigation. Each sawah owner must be a member of the subak.

sudra – lowest or common caste to which the majority of Balinese belong

sungai – river

taman – ornamental garden; literally 'garden with a pond'

tanjung – cape or point

teluk – gulf or bay
Trisakti – 'three in one' or trinity of Hindu gods: Brahma, Shiva and Vishnu

uang – money

Vishnu – the preserver, one of the three great Hindu gods

wantilan – open pavilion used to stage cock-fights
waringin – banyan tree. This large, shady tree, found at many temples, has drooping branches which root to produce new trees.
wartel – public telephone office; contraction of warung telekomunikasi
warung – food stall, a sort of Indonesian equivalent to a combination corner shop and snack bar
wayang kulit – leather puppet used in shadow puppet plays
wayang wong – masked drama playing scenes from the *Ramayana*
Wektu Telu – religion peculiar to Lombok which originated in Bayan and combines many tenets of Islam and aspects of other faiths
wesia – military caste and most numerous of the Balinese noble castes
wihara – monastery
wuku – local Balinese calendar made up of 10 different weeks, between one and 10 days long, all running concurrently; see also saka

yeh – water (Balinese); also river

Index

THANKS

To those travellers who took the time and energy to write to us with corrections and additions – thank you! Apologies if we've misspelt your names:

Nancy Abadilla (USA), Duncan & Pamela Ainslie (C), Anak Agung Ariawan (Indo), Marie-Emilie Auscher (F), Janet Backlious (Aus), Charlie Badenhop, Vicky Bargmann (Aus), Helen Barry (Aus), A Bleisch (CH), Hilary Bowen (UK), Marc Brierty (Aus), Glenn Brown (Aus), Bill Bryant (Aus), Michelle Byatt (Aus), Kathryn Campbell, Jeannine M Carroll, Bud Carroll (USA), Julian Childs (UK), Irene Chong (Sin), Charlotte Clark (Aus), Alex Cobbold (UK), Gary Collinson (Aus), Colin Conway (UK), Alison Cooper (Aus), Dan & Karen Curran (USA), Justin Dabner (Aus), Susan Dahinten (C), Jane Dalsgaard, Jeanette M Debney (Aus), J Dekker (NL), Martin Ditcham, Alistair Dow, Piers & Joy Dunkley (Aus), L Dyson (Aus), Cass Edwards (Aus), Sam Eldred, Frederic Febvre (F), P Gedge (UK), Anna Gelander (CH), Kimberly Gray (USA), Paul Gurry (Aus), Brian Hall (UK), Simon Hallam (Aus), Sally Ann Hillson (UK), Dr Finngeir Hiorth (NL), Mark Hommel, Richard & Tina Hood, David Irwan, Kullmann J, Tim Jackson (NZ), Hartley Johnson (USA), Claus W Jorgensen (DK), Jane Kent (Aus), Gunilla Kirchner (UK), Ellen & Henry Laning (NL), Peter Lawrenson (NZ), Karen & Paul Leib (USA), Kay Lewisohn (Aus), Karen List (DK), Mark Mackintosh (UK), Heather Magstadt, Janet Maier (C), Lyn & Julie Manning (NZ), Gren Manuel (UK), Joan Marso (USA), Angela McCrory (Aus), Dudley McFadden Jr (USA), John & Miki McGehee (USA), Dan Mchargue (USA), Sean McQuillam (UK), Mandy Mealing, George L Melekin (USA), Andonea Michael (UK), Letizia Barbi Migliavacca (I), Renee Miles (Aus), Tommy Miller (USA), Phil Montague (Aus), Nancy & Liz Muller (USA), Shelley Muzzy (USA), Simon Nally (Aus), Gae Nastasi (Aus), Deborah Nixon (Aus), Trevor Ockenden (Aus), I Made Patera (Indo), Richard Piggott (UK), Ken Rabehl (C), Tim Ramey (USA), Rasmussen Family (DK), Diana Reed (Aus), Jessica Reynolds, Rainer Ruhnow (D), E Ryckmans (UK), Tem Samson (UK), Wayan Sarjana (Indo), Deborah Slinger (Aus), Joan Stein (USA), Dr I Wayan Sumantera (Indo), M Tervoort (NL), I Ketut Uriada, C Uteda (USA), Diederik Van Der Molen (NL), Maarten Van Zanen (NL), David Varney (UK), T J M Vis (NL), John and Pat Walker (Aus), Fero Wijaya (Indo), Alison Wood, Alan Wood (UK), Matt Wright (UK)

Aus – Australia, C – Canada, CH – Switzerland, D – Germany, DK – Denmark, F – France, I – Italy, Indo – Indonesia, NL – Netherlands, NZ – New Zealand, UK – United Kingdom, USA – United States of America

Guides to South-East Asia

South-East Asia on a shoestring
The well-known 'yellow bible' for travellers in South-East Asia covers Brunei, Myanmar (Burma), Cambodia, Hong Kong, Indonesia, Laos, Macau, Malaysia, the Philippines, Singapore, Thailand and Vietnam.

Cambodia – a travel survival kit
As one of the last nations in the region opens its doors to travellers, visitors will again make their way to the magnificent ruins of Angkor. Another first for Lonely Planet!

Indonesia – a travel survival kit
Some of the most remarkable sights and sounds in South-East Asia can be found amongst the 13,000 islands of Indonesia – this book covers the entire archipelago in detail.

Laos – a travel survival kit
From the fertile lowlands of the Mekong River Valley to the rugged Annamite highlands, Lao hospitality, natural scenery and the attractive capital of Vientiane have survived decades of war and now offer travellers an unparalled glimpse of old Indochina.

Malaysia, Singapore & Brunei – a travel survival kit
Three independent nations of amazing geographic and cultural variety – from the national parks, beaches, jungles and rivers of Malaysia, to the tiny oil-rich Brunei and the urban prosperity and diversity of Singapore.

Myanmar (Burma) – a travel survival kit
Myanmar is one of Asia's most interesting countries. This book shows how to make the most of a trip around the main triangle route of Yangon–Mandalay–Bagan, and explores many lesser-known places such as Bago and Inle Lake.

Philippines – a travel survival kit
The friendly Filipinos, colourful festivals and superb natural scenery make the Philippines one of the most interesting countries in South-East Asia for adventurous travellers and sun-seekers alike.

Thailand – a travel survival kit
This authoritative guide includes Thai script for all place names and the latest travel details for all regions, including tips on trekking in the remote hills of the Golden Triangle.

Vietnam – a travel survival kit
From the wide avenues and pavement restaurants of Hanoi and Saigon to the spectacular verdant countryside, travelling in Vietnam is packed with challenges and surprises. A comprehensive and informative guide to one of the region's most popular destinations.

Singapore – city guide
Singapore offers a taste of the great Asian cultures in a small, accessible package. This compact guide will help travellers discover the very best that this city of contrasts can offer.

Bangkok – city guide

Bangkok has something for everyone: temples, museums and historic sites; an endless variety of good restaurants, clubs, international culture and social events; a modern art institute; and great shopping opportunities. This pocket guide offers you the assurance that you will never be lost...or lost for things to do in this fascinating city!

Also available:

Thai phrasebook, *Thai Hill Tribes* phrasebook, *Burmese* phrasebook, *Pilipino* phrasebook, *Indonesian* phrasebook, *Papua New Guinea Pidgin* phrasebook, *Mandarin Chinese* phrasebook and *Vietnamese* phrasebook.

Lonely Planet Guidebooks

Lonely Planet guidebooks cover every accessible part of Asia as well as Australia, the Pacific, South America, Africa, the Middle East, Europe and parts of North America. There are five series: *travel survival kits*, covering a country for a range of budgets; *shoestring guides* with compact information for low-budget travel in a major region; *walking guides*; *city guides* and *phrasebooks*.

Australia & the Pacific
Australia
Australian phrasebook
Bushwalking in Australia
Islands of Australia's Great Barrier Reef
Outback Australia
Fiji
Fijian phrasebook
Melbourne city guide
Micronesia
New Caledonia
New South Wales
New Zealand
Tramping in New Zealand
Papua New Guinea
Bushwalking in Papua New Guinea
Papua New Guinea phrasebook
Rarotonga & the Cook Islands
Samoa
Solomon Islands
Sydney city guide
Tahiti & French Polynesia
Tonga
Vanuatu
Victoria
Western Australia

North-East Asia
Beijing city guide
China
Cantonese phrasebook
Mandarin Chinese phrasebook
Hong Kong, Macau & Canton
Japan
Japanese phrasebook
Korea
Korean phrasebook
Mongolia
North-East Asia on a shoestring
Seoul city guide
Taiwan
Tibet
Tibet phrasebook
Tokyo city guide

Middle East
Arab Gulf States
Egypt & the Sudan
Arabic (Egyptian) phrasebook
Iran
Israel
Jordan & Syria
Middle East
Turkey
Turkish phrasebook
Trekking in Turkey
Yemen

South-East Asia
Bali & Lombok
Bangkok city guide
Cambodia
Indonesia
Indonesian phrasebook
Jakarta city guide
Laos
Malaysia, Singapore & Brunei
Myanmar (Burma)
Burmese phrasebook
Philippines
Pilipino phrasebook
Singapore city guide
South-East Asia on a shoestring
Thailand
Thai phrasebook
Thai Hill Tribes phrasebook
Vietnam
Vietnamese phrasebook

Indian Ocean
Madagascar & Comoros
Maldives & Islands of the East Indian Ocean
Mauritius, Réunion & Seychelles

Mail Order

Lonely Planet guidebooks are distributed worldwide. They are also available by mail order from Lonely Planet, so if you have difficulty finding a title please write to us. US and Canadian residents should write to Embarcadero West, 155 Filbert St, Suite 251, Oakland CA 94607, USA; European residents should write to 10 Barley Mow Passage, Chiswick, London W4 4PH; and residents of other countries to PO Box 617, Hawthorn, Victoria 3122, Australia.

Indian Subcontinent
Bangladesh
India
Hindi/Urdu phrasebook
Trekking in the Indian Himalaya
Karakoram Highway
Kashmir, Ladakh & Zanskar
Nepal
Trekking in the Nepal Himalaya
Nepali phrasebook
Pakistan
Sri Lanka
Sri Lanka phrasebook

Africa
Africa on a shoestring
Central Africa
East Africa
Trekking in East Africa
Kenya
Swahili phrasebook
Morocco
Arabic (Moroccan) phrasebook
North Africa
South Africa, Lesotho & Swaziland
Zimbabwe, Botswana & Namibia
West Africa

Europe
Baltic States & Kaliningrad
Britain
Central Europe on a shoestring
Central Europe phrasebook
Czech & Slovak Republics
Dublin city guide
Eastern Europe on a shoestring
Eastern Europe phrasebook
Finland
France
Greece
Greek phrasebook
Hungary
Iceland, Greenland & the Faroe Islands
Ireland
Italy
Mediterranean Europe on a shoestring
Mediterranean Europe phrasebook
Poland
Prague city guide
Scandinavian & Baltic Europe on a shoestring
Scandinavian Europe phrasebook
Switzerland
Trekking in Spain
Trekking in Greece
USSR
Russian phrasebook
Vienna city guide
Western Europe on a shoestring
Western Europe phrasebook

Central America & the Caribbean
Baja California
Central America on a shoestring
Costa Rica
Eastern Caribbean
Guatemala, Belize & Yucatán: La Ruta Maya
Mexico

North America
Alaska
Backpacking in Alaska
Canada
Hawaii
Honolulu city guide
USA phrasebook

South America
Argentina, Uruguay & Paraguay
Bolivia
Brazil
Brazilian phrasebook
Chile & Easter Island
Colombia
Ecuador & the Galápagos Islands
Latin American Spanish phrasebook
Peru
Quechua phrasebook
South America on a shoestring
Trekking in the Patagonian Andes
Venezuela

The Lonely Planet Story

Lonely Planet published its first book in 1973 in response to the numerous 'How did you do it?' questions Maureen and Tony Wheeler were asked after driving, bussing, hitching, sailing and railing their way from England to Australia.

Written at a kitchen table and hand collated, trimmed and stapled, *Across Asia on the Cheap* became an instant local bestseller, inspiring thoughts of another book.

Eighteen months in South-East Asia resulted in their second guide, *South-East Asia on a shoestring*, which they put together in a backstreet Chinese hotel in Singapore in 1975. The 'yellow bible' as it quickly became known to backpackers around the world, soon became *the* guide to the region. It has sold well over half a million copies and is now in its 8th edition, still retaining its familiar yellow cover.

Today there are over 140 Lonely Planet titles in print – books that have that same adventurous approach to travel as those early guides; books that 'assume you know how to get your luggage off the carousel' as one reviewer put it.

Although Lonely Planet initially specialised in guides to Asia, they now cover most regions of the world, including the Pacific, South America, Africa, the Middle East and Europe. The list of *walking guides* and *phrasebooks* (for 'unusual' languages such as Quechua, Swahili, Nepali and Egyptian Arabic) is also growing rapidly.

The emphasis continues to be on travel for independent travellers. Tony and Maureen still travel for several months of each year and play an active part in the writing, updating and quality control of Lonely Planet's guides.

They have been joined by over 50 authors, 110 staff – mainly editors, cartographers & designers – at our office in Melbourne, Australia, at our US office in Oakland, California and at our European office in Paris; another five at our office in London handle sales for Britain, Europe and Africa. Travellers themselves also make a valuable contribution to the guides through the feedback we receive in thousands of letters each year.

The people at Lonely Planet strongly believe that travellers can make a positive contribution to the countries they visit, both through their appreciation of the countries' culture, wildlife and natural features, and through the money they spend. In addition, the company makes a direct contribution to the countries and regions it covers. Since 1986 a percentage of the income from each book has been donated to ventures such as famine relief in Africa; aid projects in India; agricultural projects in Central America; Greenpeace's efforts to halt French nuclear testing in the Pacific; and Amnesty International.

Lonely Planet's basic travel philosophy is summed up in Tony Wheeler's comment, 'Don't worry about whether your trip will work out. Just go!'